THE UNITED STATES DEPARTMENT OF DEFENSE LAW OF WAR MANUAL

Commentary and Critique

The United States Department of Defense Law of War Manual: Commentary and Critique provides an irreplaceable resource for any politician, international expert, or military practitioner who wishes to understand the approach taken by the American military in the complex range of modern conflicts. Readers will understand the strengths and weaknesses of US legal and policy pronouncements and the reasons behind the modern American way of war, whether US forces deploy alone or in coalitions. This book provides unprecedented and precise analysis of the US approach to the most pressing problems in modern wars, including controversies surrounding use of human shields, fighting in urban areas, the use of cyberwar and modern weaponry, expanding understanding of human rights, and the rise of ISIS. This group of authors, including academics and military practitioners, provides a wealth of expertise that demystifies overlapping threads of law and policy amidst the world's seemingly intractable conflicts.

Michael A. Newton is a West Point graduate who serves as Professor of the Practice of Law at Vanderbilt University Law School. He has published over ninety articles, editorials, and book chapters including coauthored books *Proportionality in International Law* (2014), and *Enemy of the State: The Trial and Execution of Saddam Hussein* (2008), which received the Book of the Year Award from the International Association of Penal Law. Newton helped negotiate the International Criminal Court Elements of Crimes and served in the US Department of State during the Clinton and Bush Administrations.

The United States Department of Defense Law of War Manual: Commentary and Critique

Edited by

MICHAEL A. NEWTON

CAMBRIDGE
UNIVERSITY PRESS

CAMBRIDGE
UNIVERSITY PRESS

University Printing House, Cambridge CB2 8BS, United Kingdom

One Liberty Plaza, 20th Floor, New York, NY 10006, USA

477 Williamstown Road, Port Melbourne, VIC 3207, Australia

314–321, 3rd Floor, Plot 3, Splendor Forum, Jasola District Centre,
New Delhi – 110025, India

79 Anson Road, #06–04/06, Singapore 079906

Cambridge University Press is part of the University of Cambridge.

It furthers the University's mission by disseminating knowledge in the pursuit of
education, learning, and research at the highest international levels of excellence.

www.cambridge.org
Information on this title: www.cambridge.org/9781108427159
DOI: 10.1017/9781108659727

First published 2018

Printed and bound in Great Britain by Clays Ltd, Elcograf S.p.A.

A catalogue record for this publication is available from the British Library.

Library of Congress Cataloging-in-Publication Data
NAMES: Newton, Michael A., 1962– editor.
TITLE: The United States Department of Defense Law of War Manual : commentary
and critique / edited by Michael A. Newton.
DESCRIPTION: Cambridge, United Kingdom ; New York, NY, USA : Cambridge
University Press, 2018. | Includes bibliographical references.
IDENTIFIERS: LCCN 2018008149 | ISBN 9781108427159
SUBJECTS: LCSH: United States. Department of Defense. Office of General Counsel.
Department of Defense law of war manual. | War (International law) | Military law –
United States. | International and municipal law – United States. | Soldiers – United
States – Handbooks, manuals, etc.
CLASSIFICATION: LCC KZ6385 .U535 2018 | DDC 341.60973–dc23
LC record available at https://lccn.loc.gov/2018008149

ISBN 978-1-108-42715-9 Hardback
ISBN 978-1-108-44769-0 Paperback

Contents

Notes on Contributors

Laurie R. Blank is a Clinical Professor of Law, Director of the Center for International and Comparative Law and Director of the International Humanitarian Law Clinic at Emory University School of Law, where she teaches the law of armed conflict and works directly with students to provide assistance to international tribunals, non-governmental organizations and militaries around the world on cutting-edge issues in humanitarian law and human rights. Professor Blank is the coauthor of *International Law and Armed Conflict: Fundamental Principles and Contemporary Challenges in the Law of War*, a casebook on the law of war (with G. Noone, Aspen Publishing 2013; Concise Edition 2016). She is also the co-director of a multi-year project on military training programs in the law of war and the coauthor of *Law of War Training: Resources for Military and Civilian Leaders*. Professor Blank is a core expert on the *Woomera Manual on International Law Applicable to Conflict in Outer Space*, the Chair of the American Society of International Law Lieber Prize Committee, and the series editor of the ICRC's teaching supplements on IHL. She was a term member of the American Bar Association's Advisory Committee to the Standing Committee on Law and National Security (2011–14), a member of the Homeland Security Academic Advisory Council Subcommittee on Countering Violent Extremism, and a member of the Public Interest Law and Policy Group's High Level Working Group on Piracy. Before coming to Emory, Professor Blank was a program officer in the Rule of Law Program at the United States Institute of Peace. At USIP, she directed the Experts' Working Group on International Humanitarian Law, in particular a multi-year project focusing on New Actors in the Implementation and Enforcement of International Humanitarian Law. Her extensive publications focus on the law of targeting, defining the battlespace in modern law and practice, and the consequences of evolving interpretations of *jus in bello*. After graduating from Princeton *cum laude* with a degree in Politics, she earned an MA with distinction in International Relations from The Paul H. Nitze School of

Advanced International Studies at Johns Hopkins University and her law degree *cum laude* from New York University School of Law.

Air Commodore Bill Boothby (Ret'd.) served for thirty years in the Royal Air Force Legal Branch, retiring as Deputy Director of Legal Services in July 2011. In 2009 he took a Doctorate at the Europa Universität Viadrina, Frankfurt (Oder) in Germany and published *Weapons and the Law of Armed Conflict* (Oxford University Press) in the same year (2nd ed., 2016). His second book, *The Law of Targeting* (Oxford University Press), appeared in 2012. He has been a member of the Groups of Experts that addressed Direct Participation in Hostilities, that produced the HPCR Manual on the Law of Air and Missile Warfare, and that produced the Tallinn Manual on the Law of Cyber Warfare. His third book, *Conflict Law: The Influence of New Weapons Technology, Human Rights and Emerging Actors* (Asser Press) was published in 2014. He teaches at the Australian National University, at the University of Western Australia, at the University of Southern Denmark, and at the Geneva Centre for Security Policy. He lectures and speaks widely on international law issues.

Gary D. Brown is currently serving as a Cyber Policy and Strategy Analyst for the US Department of Defense Joint Staff. He was previously Professor of Cyber Security at Marine Corps University, Quantico, Virginia. He also served as Head of Communications and Congressional Affairs for the Washington Delegation, ICRC; he was with the ICRC from 2012 to 2015. Prior to joining the ICRC, he served twenty-four years as a judge advocate with the United States Air Force. Colonel Brown deployed twice to the Middle East during his Air Force career, the second time for a year at the Combined Air Operations Center, Southwest Asia as the senior legal advisor for combat air operations in Afghanistan and Iraq. In his final military assignment, he was the first senior legal counsel for US Cyber Command, Fort Meade, Maryland, where he served for three years. Colonel Brown speaks on cyber operations law and policy, and has authored several articles related to cyberwarfare, including "Spying and Fighting in Cyberspace," *Journal of National Security Law & Policy* (2016); "Easier Said than Done: Legal Reviews of Cyber Weapons," *Journal of National Security Law & Policy* (2014) (coauthor); "Why Iran Didn't Admit Stuxnet Was an Attack," *Joint Forces Quarterly* (2011); and "On the Spectrum of Cyberspace Operations," *Small Wars Journal* (2012) (coauthor). He was the official US observer to the drafting the Tallinn Manual on the International Law Applicable to Cyber Warfare (2013) and is a member of the International Group of Experts that authored the second edition of the Tallinn Manual. He has a law degree from the University of Nebraska and an LLM in international law from Cambridge University.

Andrew Clapham is Professor of Public International Law at the Graduate Institute of International and Development Studies, Geneva. His current research relates to the concept of war. Andrew Clapham was the Director of the Geneva Academy of International Humanitarian Law and Human Rights from 2006 until 2014. His publications include *The 1949 Geneva Conventions: A Commentary* (co-edited with P. Gaeta and M. Sassòli) (Oxford University Press, 2015); *The Oxford Handbook of International Law in Armed Conflict* (co-edited with Paola Gaeta) (Oxford University Press, 2014); *Human Rights: A Very Short Introduction*, 2nd ed. (Oxford University Press, 2015); *Human Rights Obligations of Non-State Actors* (2006); and *International Human Rights Lexicon* (Oxford University Press, 2005), with Susan Marks. He is an academic associate member of Matrix Chambers in London.

Karl Chang is an Associate General Counsel in the Department of Defense, Office of General Counsel (International Affairs). Since 2006, he has worked as a lawyer at the Department of Defense on a variety of national security and international law issues, including in the areas of international humanitarian law, international criminal law, *jus ad bellum*, and international law on the exercise of jurisdiction and immunities. He has worked on US policy on reducing civilian casualties, US policy towards the International Criminal Court, the drafting of DoD policies on the use of autonomy in weapon systems and detention operations, and litigation against DoD officials involving issues of international law. His primary practice area is the law of war. He was the principal drafter of the 2015 Department of Defense Law of War Manual and two updates to the manual promulgated in 2016. He has published in the *Texas International Law Journal* on applying standards from the law of neutrality as a legal framework for the military detention of enemy aliens in non-international armed conflict. He is a graduate of Yale College and Harvard Law School.

Geoffrey S. Corn is The Vinson & Elkins Professor of Law at South Texas College of Law Houston in Houston Texas. Prior to joining the South Texas faculty in 2005, Professor Corn served in the US Army for twenty-one years as an officer, and a final year as civilian legal advisor to the Army Judge Advocate General. Professor Corn's teaching and scholarship focuses on the law of armed conflict, national security law, criminal law and procedure, and prosecutorial ethics. He has appeared as an expert witness at the Military Commission in Guantánamo, the International Criminal Tribunal for the former Yugoslavia, and in the Federal Court. He is the lead author of *The Law of Armed Conflict: An Operational Perspective* (Aspen, 2012), and *The War on Terror and the Laws of War: A Military Approach*, 2nd ed. (Oxford University Press, 2015). He is also coauthor of *Principles of Counter-Terrorism Law* (West, 2011). His Army career included service as the Army's senior law of war expert advisor, tactical intelligence officer in Panama; supervisory defense counsel for the Western United States; Chief of International Law for US Army Europe; Professor of International and National Security Law at the US Army Judge Advocate General's School; and Chief Prosecutor for the 101st Airborne Division. He earned his BA from Hartwick College in Oneonta, NY; his JD with highest honors from George Washington University; and his LLM as the distinguished graduate from the US Army Judge Advocate General's School. He is also a distinguished military graduate of US Army Officer Candidate School, and a graduate of US Army Command and General Staff Course.

Charles J. Dunlap Jr., the former Deputy Judge Advocate General of the United States Air Force, joined the Duke Law faculty in July 2010 where he is Professor of the Practice of Law and Executive Director of the Center on Law, Ethics and National Security. His teaching and scholarly writing focus on national security, international law, civil–military relations, cyberwar, airpower, counterinsurgency, military justice, and ethical issues related to the practice of national security law. Professor Dunlap retired from the Air Force in June 2010, having attained the rank of major general during a thirty-four-year career in the Judge Advocate General Corps. In his capacity as Deputy Judge Advocate General from May 2006 to March 2010, he assisted the Judge Advocate General in the professional supervision of more than 2,200 judge advocates, 350 civilian lawyers, 1,400 enlisted paralegals, and 500 civilians around the world. In addition to overseeing an array of military justice, operational, international, and civil law functions, he provided legal advice to the Air Staff and commanders at all levels. Professor Dunlap's legal scholarship also has been published in the *Stanford Law Review*, the *Yale Journal of International Affairs*, the *Wake Forest Law Review*, the *Fletcher Forum of World Affairs*, the *University of Nebraska Law Review*, the *Texas Tech Law Review*, and the *Tennessee Law Review*, among others. He is the author of "The Origins of the Military Coup of 2012," originally published in 1992, which was selected for the 40th Anniversary Edition of Parameters (Winter 2010–11). He is also the author of "Airpower" in *Understanding Counterinsurgency* (Thomas Rid and Thomas Keaney, eds., Routledge, 2010), and his essay on "The Military Industrial Complex" appeared in the Summer 2011 issue of *Daedalus*.

Katharine Fortin is an Assistant Professor of Public International Law and Human Rights at Utrecht University's Netherlands Institute of Human Rights (SIM). The focus of her current research is the legal framework which applies to non-international armed conflicts. In October 2015, she defended her PhD on the accountability of armed groups under human rights law and was awarded a *cum laude*. In addition to her research at SIM, she teaches human rights law, public international law, and international humanitarian law, as well as regularly coaching students for the Jean Pictet and Frits Kalshoven competitions in international humanitarian law. She is the founder and co-editor of the Armed Groups and International Law blog and has published widely in the field.

David E. Graham is the Associate Director for Programs at the Center for National Security Law, the University of Virginia School of Law. He is the former Executive Director of the Army's Judge Advocate General's Legal Center and School (LCS), having served in that capacity for fourteen years. He earlier served as a professor and Department head of the School's International/Operational Law Department, as well as the Academic Director of the School and the Director of the Center for Law and Military Operations, now an integral part of the LCS. A retired Army Judge Advocate Colonel, with thirty-one years of experience, he was the Chief of the International/Operational Law Division, Office of the Judge Advocate General, Department of the Army, for the last eight years of his active duty, following a mix of assignments in the United States, Europe, Latin America, and the Middle East. During the course of his career, Mr. Graham played the seminal role in developing the field of Operational Law. He is a published author in multiple legal publications and has lectured extensively in both US and international fora. His education includes: Texas A&M University, BA in History, 1966; George Washington University, MA in International Affairs, 1968; University of Texas School of Law, JD, 1971; Certificate, the Hague Academy of International Law, 1977. Mr. Graham is a Distinguished Graduate of the National War College, a graduate of the Armed Forces Staff College, and is currently a member of the ABA's Standing Committee on Law and National Security. He is admitted to the Supreme Court of Texas, the Court of Military Appeals, and the Supreme Court of the United States.

Adil Ahmad Haque is Professor of Law and Judge Jon O. Newman Scholar at Rutgers Law School. His first book, *Law and Morality at War* (Oxford University Press) was published in 2017. Professor Haque received his JD in 2005 from Yale Law School, where he was executive editor of the *Yale Journal of International Law* and senior editor of the *Yale Law Journal*. From 2005 to 2006, he served as a law clerk to the Honorable Jon O. Newman of the US Court of Appeals for the Second Circuit. For two years prior to joining the Rutgers faculty, Professor Haque was an associate in the New York office of

Debevoise & Plimpton LLP, where he focused on white-collar criminal investigations and prisoners' rights litigation. Professor Haque is a member of the Associate Graduate Faculty of the Rutgers University Department of Philosophy and an advisor to the Rutgers Institute of Law and Philosophy. He is a member of the Board of Editors of *Just Security*.

Steven Hill is Legal Advisor and Director of the Office of Legal Affairs at NATO. As the senior lawyer in NATO, he advises the Secretary General and International Staff on all legal aspects of NATO operations and coordinates NATO activities in the legal field. Mr. Hill came to NATO after serving as Counselor for Legal Affairs at the US Mission to the United Nations. Prior to his work in New York, Mr. Hill led the legal unit at the International Civilian Office in Kosovo. In both roles, his responsibilities included a strong policy component focused on supporting the rule of law in conflict- and post-conflict situations. He previously worked in the Office of the Legal Advisor at the US Department of State, where he advised on the law of armed conflict, human rights law, economic sanctions, and the law governing diplomatic premises. He was responsible for negotiating a wide range of bilateral and multilateral instruments, including as chief US negotiator for the landmark UN Convention on the Rights of Persons with Disabilities. He was assigned to the US Embassy in Baghdad from 2004 to 2005. He also served as Counsel in proceedings before the International Court of Justice in 2003 and in several cases before the Inter-American Commission on Human Rights from 2006 to 2007. Mr. Hill also actively engages in teaching and research on international law, including as Visiting Professor of Law at the Hopkins-Nanjing Center in China during the 2010–11 academic year. Mr. Hill graduated from Yale Law School and Harvard College.

Chris Jenks teaches the law of armed conflict (LOAC), criminal law, evidence and directs the Criminal Clinic at the SMU Dedman School of Law in Dallas, Texas. He received a BS from the United States Military Academy at West Point, a JD from the University of Arizona, and LLMs from the US Army Judge Advocate Generals School and from Georgetown. During the 2017/18 academic year, Professor Jenks served in the Pentagon as the Special Counsel to the General Counsel of the Department of Defense. In 2015, he was awarded a Fulbright Senior Scholars Grant to research lethal autonomous weapons as part of a multidisciplinary research group based out of Melbourne Law School in Australia. In 2014, he served on a working group on the environment and armed conflict at the United Nations in New York organized by the Special Rapporteur for the International Law Commission. Prior to joining the SMU law faculty, Professor Jenks served for twenty years in the US

Army, first as an Infantry Officer in Germany, Kuwait, and as a NATO peacekeeper in Bosnia and later as a judge advocate near the demilitarized zone in the Republic of Korea and in Mosul, Iraq, where he provided LOAC advice during combat operations. In his last military assignment, Professor Jenks served as the chief of the international law branch for the US Army.

Peter Margulies teaches National Security Law and International Law at Roger Williams University School of Law. Professor Margulies, who received a BA from Colgate University and a JD from Columbia Law School, served as the 2014 Chair of the American Association of Law Schools' Section on National Security Law. He is a regular contributor to the influential *Lawfare* blog on a broad range of topics, including international humanitarian law and the legality of NSA surveillance. Professor Margulies has also been co-counsel for *amici curiae* in numerous cases, including *Humanitarian Law Project v. Holder*, 561 US 1 (2010) (upholding statute barring material support to foreign terrorist organizations) and *Bank Markazi v. Peterson*, 136 S. Ct. 1310 (2016) (upholding statute that designated Iranian assets for attachment by victims of Iran-sponsored terrorist attacks). Professor Margulies has published widely in the area of national security law. Along with Geoff Corn, Jimmy Gurule, and Eric Jensen, Professor Margulies is coauthor of the treatise, *National Security Law: Principles and Policy* (Aspen, 2015). Professor Margulies's recent book chapters include, "Valor's Vices: Against a State Duty to Risk Forces in Armed Conflict," in *Counterinsurgency Law: New Directions in Asymmetric Warfare* (William C. Banks ed., Oxford University Press, 2012); "Interpretations of IHL in Tribunals of the United States" (with Prof. Michael W. Lewis), in *Applying International Humanitarian Law in Judicial and Quasi Judicial Bodies* (Philip Van Tongeren ed., T.M.C. Asser Press, 2014); and "Making Autonomous Weapons Accountable: Command Responsibility for Computer-Guided Lethal Force in Armed Conflicts," in *Handbook on Remote Warfare* (Jens David Ohlin ed., Edward Elgar 2017).

Ray Murphy is an expert in the international legal regulation of emerging forms of warfare. He serves as a Professor at the Irish Centre for Human Rights, National University of Ireland Galway, Ireland. Having completed his BA in Political Science and Legal Science in 1979 he then took a Bachelor in Law (LLB) degree in 1981. He studied at Kings Inns in Dublin where he completed a BL degree and was called to the Irish bar in 1984. He completed his MLitt degree in International Law at Dublin University (Trinity College) in 1991. In 2001 he was awarded a PhD in International Law from the University of Nottingham, England. In addition to his position at the Irish Centre for Human Rights, Professor Murphy is on the faculty of the International Institute for

Criminal Investigations and Justice Rapid Response. He is a former captain in the Irish Defence Forces and he served as an infantry officer with the Irish contingent of UNIFIL in Lebanon in 1981/82 and again in 1989. He practiced as a barrister for a short period before taking up his current appointment at the National University of Ireland, Galway. He was Chairperson of the Broadcasting Complaints Commission from 1997 to 2000. He has field experience with the OSCE in Bosnia in 1996 and 1997. He has also worked on short assignments in West and Southern Africa and the Middle East for Amnesty International, the European Union, and the Irish Government.

Michael A. Newton is Professor of the Practice of Law and Professor of the Practice of Political Science at Vanderbilt University Law School, Nashville Tennessee. He previously taught in the Department of Law, United States Military Academy. Professor Newton helped negotiate the Elements of Crimes document for the International Criminal Court as part of the US delegation, and coordinated the interface between the FBI and the International Criminal Tribunal for the former Yugoslavia, while deploying into Kosovo to do the forensics fieldwork to support the Milosevic indictment. Professor Newton served in the Office of War Crimes Issues, US Department of State during both the Clinton and Bush Administrations. As the Senior Advisor to the United States Ambassador-at-Large for War Crimes Issues, he shaped a wide range of policies related to the law of armed conflict, including US support to accountability mechanisms worldwide. He was the US representative on the UN Planning Mission for the Sierra Leone Special Court and currently serves on the Advisory Board of the American Bar Association International Criminal Court Project. After helping establish the Iraqi High Tribunal, he served as International Law Advisor to the Judicial Chambers from 2006 to 2008. He has published over ninety articles, editorials, and book chapters in journals such as *The New York Times, International Review of the Red Cross, Stanford Journal of International Law, Military Law Review,* and *Virginia Journal of International Law.* His book *Proportionality in International Law* (Oxford University Press, 2014), coauthored with Larry May, is the most comprehensive treatment of this complex topic in the field. He also coauthored with Michael Scharf the definitive history of the Dujail trial, *Enemy of the State: The Trial and Execution of Saddam Hussein* (St. Martin's Press, 2008). He has worked on a trial team in the International Criminal Court and advised litigators in human rights cases around the world. In addition, he has coordinated legal support to many governments, international entities, and private organizations. Examples include UN organizations; the World Bank; the International Bar Association; US

Departments of State and Defense; and the governments of Uganda, Israel, Kosovo, Iraq, Afghanistan, Kenya, Ukraine, and Peru, among others. During his distinguished military career, Professor Newton served as an army officer after graduating from the US Military Academy at West Point and attended the University of Virginia School of Law. He served as the Chief of Operational Law with the United States Army Special Forces Command (Airborne) supporting Desert Storm and deployed on Operation Provide Comfort to assist Kurdish civilians in Northern Iraq. He was the Judge Advocate for the 7th Special Forces Group (Airborne) and led the human rights and rules of engagement education for all Multinational Forces and International Police deploying into Haiti.

Yaël Ronen is Professor of Law, Sha'arei Mishpat Academic Center. She earned her PhD in 2006 from the University of Cambridge, UK (Supervisor: Professor James Crawford) in addition to an LLM and LLB from Hebrew University of Jerusalem. She is an expert in international law, international human rights law, and private international law. In addition to participating on the International Law Association Working Groups on Non-State Actors and on Recognition and Non-Recognition she also serves on the Organizing Committee for the IHL conference series of the Minerva Center, Hebrew University. Her books include *Transition from Illegal Regimes under International Law* (Cambridge University Press, 2011); *The Iranian Nuclear Issue* (Hart, 2010); and *Law and Practice of the International Court* (4th ed., Brill, 2006), coauthored with Rosenne Shabtai. She has also written more than two-dozen book chapters and law review articles and is one of the field's most well-known names.

Aurel Sari is currently serving as Senior Lecturer in Law at the University of Exeter, specializing in public international law. His work focuses mainly on questions of operational law, including the law of armed conflict, the legal status of foreign armed forces, and the application of human rights law in deployed operations. He is one of Europe's most prominent young scholars on the interface of human rights norms and *jus in bello* principles. He has published widely in leading academic journals on status of forces agreements, peace support operations, and the legal aspects of European security and defense policy. He also maintains close working relationships with legal practitioners in the armed forces and lectures regularly on the subject of international law and military operations in the UK and abroad. He is also a Fellow of the Allied Rapid Reaction Corps.

Abbreviations

AP I	Additional Protocol I to the 1949 Geneva Conventions
AP II	Additional Protocol II to the 1949 Geneva Conventions
CCW	Convention on Prohibitions or Restrictions on the Use of Certain Conventional Weapons
CDE	collateral damage estimate
CIL	customary international law
DoD	US Department of Defense
DoJ	Department of Justice
DoS	Department of State
DPH	direct participation in hostilities
GC I	First Geneva Convention for the Amelioration of the Condition of the Wounded in Armies in the Field
GC II	Second Geneva Convention for the Amelioration of the Condition of Wounded, Sick and Shipwrecked Members of Armed Forces at Sea
GC III	Geneva Convention on Prisoners of War
GC IV	Geneva Convention on the Protection of Civilian Persons in Time of War
IAC	international armed conflict
ICC	International Criminal Court
ICCPR	International Covenant on Civil and Political Rights
ICJ	International Court of Justice
ICRC	International Committee of the Red Cross
ICTY	International Criminal Tribunal for Yugoslavia
IFOR	Implementation Force
IHL	international humanitarian law
IMT	International Military Tribunal
ISAF	International Security Assistance Force

ISIS   Islamic State in Iraq and Syria
JAG   judge advocate
LOAC   law of armed conflict
MSF   Médecins Sans Frontières
NATO   North Atlantic Treaty Organization
NGO   nongovernmental organizations
NIAC   non-international armed conflict
NSL   no-strike list
PID   personal identification
PGM   precision-guided munitions
PoW   prisoner of war
PUC   persons under control
ROE   rules of engagement
STANAG   Standardization Agreement

BACKGROUND AND BUREAUCRATIC FORMATION
OF THE MANUAL

PART I

BACKGROUND AND BUREAUCRATIC FORMATION
OF THE MANUAL

Framing Thoughts on the DoD Law of War Manual and this Commentary

Michael A. Newton[*]

1 INTRODUCTION

The US Department of Defense (DoD) Law of War Manual (the Manual) is a remarkable accomplishment. It is a watershed document that took form over nearly three decades culminating with the publication of the first edition in June 2015. DoD professed its willingness in the Preface to consider changes recommended from users in the field and provided a method for such submissions from experts and academics. It moved with rare (and refreshing) alacrity to ameliorate some of the most egregious flaws in the original text by issuing a Revised Manual less than a year later on May 31, 2016 followed by a second updated edition on December 13, 2016.[1] The stakes in this endeavor are high: debates over the applicability of the laws of war often carry profound policy consequences, including momentous implications for human dignity and the possibility of building sustainable peace following hostilities.

This Commentary and Critique points the way toward further needed improvements, even as it highlights many areas of international consensus that accord with US practice. The Manual is already a highly visible component of the international discourse in this field. It provides an important resource to international experts who continue to debate the contours of law and policy amidst the world's seemingly intractable conflicts. Thus, it provides a useful touchstone for assessing the common threads of legality that bind complex operations conducted in the modern world.

[*] The author is deeply appreciative to the friends and great professionals who have authored chapters in this work, and in particular to Dave Graham, Charles Garraway, Hays Parks, Brianne McGonigle Leyh, Paul Williams, Geoff Corn, Peter Margulies, Ian Henderson, Michael Scharf, Dru Brenner-Beck, Charlie Dunlap, and Chris Gracey whose assistance and insight has been invaluable. Errors and oversights are my sole responsibility.
[1] Unless otherwise noted, all references in this volume to the Manual refer to the Dec. 13, 2016 edition, which is the most current at the time of this writing.

The Manual is remarkable because for the first time in American history it represents the single most authoritative consolidation of US policy and legal positions regarding the lawful conduct of hostilities. Its 7,029 footnotes[2] contain a rich set of references to US law and practice, as well as ample offerings from US policy documents, current operational guidance, and selected academic commentary. It also has inherent value as a rich compilation of historical examples and precedent ranging, among many other sources, from General Petraeus's Rules of Engagement guidance, to policy speeches by key US officials, to details of US statutory guidance. The Manual exceeds the 1956 Army Law of War Manual by nearly 1,000 pages, yet shares the primary purpose of any military manual, which is to facilitate the lawful conduct of military operations across the spectrum of modern hostilities. As two distinguished American scholars have noted:

> Manuals are not an end in themselves. They are an instrument for achieving an end: the prescription and application of a law of armed conflict that tempers the harshness and cruelty of combat and confines human and material destruction to targets of military necessity and utility.[3]

In its opening paragraphs, the Manual acknowledges that it is "not a definitive explanation of all law of war issues."[4] It nonetheless "seeks to address the law of war that is applicable to the United States, including treaties to which the United States is a Party, and applicable customary international law. It provides legal rules, principles, and discussion, particularly with respect to DoD practice." The Manual significantly advances these important goals, notwithstanding the reality that its voluminous approach often obscures the precise take-away needed by tactical level war-fighters and lawyers.

Consistent with the nature of the Manual, this volume contains contributions from some of the world's most remarkable practitioners and scholars in the field. Every author in this Commentary and Critique shares a deep commitment to the rule of law and to the core purposes of the laws and customs of warfare or, as many North Atlantic Treaty Organization (NATO) manuals refer to the same field, the "law of armed conflict" (LOAC).[5] DoD

---

[2] See Table 1.1 for a breakdown of notes by source and by chapter.

[3] Michael Reisman and William Lietzau, "Moving International Law from Theory to Practice: The Role of Military Manuals in Effectuating the Law of Armed Conflict" (1991) 64 *International Law Studies* 12.

[4] DoD Law of War Manual, ¶ 1.1.2.

[5] The phrase "law of armed conflict" serves a sort of straddling function between "the laws of war" and "international humanitarian law." Many NATO militaries and other experts prefer usage of "the law of war," and manuals of, *inter alia*, Australia, Canada, UK, and Germany employ that term in addition to many US policy documents. Authors in this volume frequently use the shorthand annotation LOAC to refer to the phrase "the law of armed conflict."

accepts and occasionally uses the nearly synonymous phrase "international humanitarian law." These chapters do not form an unbalanced polemic taken together, but guide readers into probing inquiry of the Manual's place within the larger field of international humanitarian law. DoD construes the term "law of war" as having "the same substantive meaning" as the increasingly common phrase "international humanitarian law." The Manual is careful to note the DoD view that the latter phrase has narrower application due to the omission of the law of neutrality (which in itself is a bit curious as the entirety of Chapter XV addresses the law of neutrality).[6] The approach of these authors is deeply thoughtful but of necessity an incomplete summation of every detail of this ponderous document. They focus on the many laudable aspects of the Manual, yet do not shirk examination of its flaws.

In the memorable framing of Yoram Dinstein, "every single norm" within the laws and customs of armed conflict operates as "a parallelogram of forces; it confronts an inveterate tension between the demands of military necessity and humanitarian considerations, working out a compromise formula."[7] Since the end of World War II, the United States military has fought three conventional armed conflicts with other States for a cumulative period of less than five years. In the same span, it has conducted counterinsurgency operations in three major conflicts and numerous smaller operations lasting more than a cumulative thirty years. Previously promulgated American military manuals proved to be insufficient over the years because they failed to incorporate evolving treaty obligations and became less fitted to the changing character[8] of modern armed conflicts as the decades passed and World War II-era technologies became obsolete. The Manual is notable for its inclusion of chapters devoted to modern weaponry such as lasers,[9] as well as Air and Space Warfare[10] and Cyberwar.[11]

American commanders have frequently been faced by enemies seeking to use the constraints of humanitarian law as a force multiplier to facilitate asymmetric warfare that helps negate the technological superiority of US forces. The Manual accordingly addresses many modern operational realities. For example, the Manual speaks to an array of modern themes such as

---

[6]   DoD Law of War Manual, ¶ 1.3.1.2.

[7]   Yoram Dinstein, *The Conduct of Hostilities under the Law of International Armed Conflict*, 2nd ed. (Cambridge University Press, 2010), 5.

[8]   Many experts in the field and military practitioners argue persuasively that the nature of warfare has changed little; rather its character and contexts have undergone dramatic evolution. Hence, Pembroke College at Oxford maintains the Changing Character of War Centre, www.ccw.ox.ac.uk.

[9]   DoD Law of War Manual, ¶ 6.15.   [10]   *Ibid.*, Chapter XIV.

[11]   See Chapter 15 of this book for a thoughtful assessment of the limitations of Chapter XVI of the Manual.

the use of human shields, the modern meaning of the commander's duty to take "feasible measures" to eliminate human suffering and damage to protected property, and the evolving law of occupation in the aftermath of the occupation of Iraq. In recent decades, even as the corpus of the law of war developed, Article 3 Common to the 1949 Geneva Conventions and its progeny in the form of the welter of applicable human rights treaties have become load-bearing pillars of modern conflicts and flashpoints for disputes concerning the applicability of particular protections for civilians. When it was promulgated in 1956, the Army Field Manual that formed the impetus for beginning the effort to draft the Manual confined its entire discussion of that body of law to one paragraph. Though the text of Common Article 3 represented the sole aspect of the 1949 Conventions touching on armed conflicts not of an international character, such non-international armed conflicts (NIACs) merited a full chapter in the Manual some sixty-six years later.

In its broadest contours, the Manual is part hornbook, part pablum, part practical guidance, yet suffused throughout with an overlay of specific US policy imperatives. For many practitioners or lawyers, the hornbook function of the Manual will be helpful. For example, the text defines the commonly encountered concept *"hors de combat"* that is used without explanation in Common Article 3 of the 1949 Geneva Conventions and Article 41 of Additional Protocol I.[12] There are many other places where drafters defined key terms such as *"lex specialis"*[13] and *"tu quoque."*[14] Experts will note that DoD drafters in many instances have not selected the most pertinent sources supporting such definitions, but they are nevertheless substantively accurate. At the other extreme, there are hundreds of instances where the main text states a treaty rule using identical language drawn from international law, but the footnote merely cites the relevant article and restates precisely the same

---

[12] DoD Law of War Manual, ¶ 5.9.1 ("Notes on Terminology. Hors de combat is a French phrase that means 'out of the battle.' It is generally used as a term of art to mean persons who may not be made the object of attack because they are out of the fighting and who therefore must be treated humanely."). The accompanying footnote makes clear that persons who are hors de combat are legally entitled to be equated with a civilian who remains uninvolved in the conflict. To do so is to place at risk the respect, based on law, to be accorded to the civilian population.

[13] *Ibid.*, ¶ 1.3.2.1 (The maxim *lex specialis derogat legi generali* means that "[a]s a rule the special rule overrides the general law." The rule that is more specifically directed towards the action receives priority because it takes better account of the particular features of the context in which the law is to be applied, thus creating a more equitable result and better reflecting the intent of the authorities that have made the law.)

[14] *Ibid.*, ¶ 18.21.2 (The international law doctrine *tu quoque* may be understood as an argument that a State does not have standing to complain about a practice in which it itself engages.)

language in quotation marks.[15] Such redundancies add to the Manual's bulk and do not advance its objectives.

The Manual also contains numerous instances where drafters inserted bland phraseology as the predicate for more detailed legal and policy discussions. Such attempted aphorisms appear throughout the text. The reader may groan reading the obvious truism that the "trial and punishment of POWs must comport with the rules prescribed by the GPW [1949 Geneva Convention III Relative to the Treatment of Prisoners of War],"[16] but note that it serves a constructive purpose by directing the reader to the relevant provisions found in Chapter IX dealing with the subject in more detail. Other trite sentences such as the reminder that "[a]dversary use of human shields can present complex moral, ethical, legal, and policy considerations" provide the placeholder to support citation to other US policy documents, speeches, or US cases.[17]

In sum, readers must be diligent to decode the Manual with some precision and consider the totality of its many cross-references. The merits of particular propositions can be assessed only after reconstructing the baseline of support marshalled by DoD, which is seldom limited to one concise section, as well as the actual merit of supporting citations. It is not an intuitive document that can be rapidly referenced. The Manual's complexity, along with the interconnected crosscurrents of law and policy, create some uncertainty at the macro level regarding its most important function. Some national manuals, such as the 2006 Australian manual were written primarily for commanders; principles are plainly stated, and citations are almost uniformly to the applicable treaty provisions. The Manual accords with the 2001 Canadian Joint Service Manual, the German Manual, and the UK Manual in providing extensive citations to the relevant law, key policy documents, and other explanatory texts. Because modern armed conflicts are infrequently conducted by a single service acting alone, the trend toward consolidated joint service manuals that assist commanders and their lawyers is likely to continue.[18]

---

[15] *Ibid.*, ¶ 18.9.3 (replicating the Grave Breach provisions of the Geneva Conventions in verbatim text and in sequential footnotes), ¶ 4.12 (duplicating language from Art. 27 of the Second Geneva Convention), ¶ 9.17.3 ("Canteen profits shall be used for the benefit of the POWs, and a special fund shall be created for this purpose," citing Art. 28 of the Third Convention and including identical language).

[16] *Ibid.*, ¶ 18.21.4.1.

[17] *Ibid.*, ¶ 5.12.3.4 (directing the reader in turn to the Presidential Policy Directive issued on June 24, 2015 by President Obama entitled *U.S. Nationals Taken Hostage Abroad and Personnel Recovery Efforts*).

[18] Earle A. Partington, "Manuals on the Law of Armed Conflict," in Frauke Lachenmann and Rüdiger Wolfrum (eds.), *The Law of Armed Conflict and the Use of Force: The Max Planck Encyclopedia of Public International Law* (Oxford University Press, 2017), 673, 677.

As a result, the Manual seldom presents clear statements that are self-supporting and independent of the larger whole. The DoD decision to deviate from prior US practice in Field Manual 27–10 by eliminating the concise index magnifies the importance of careful reading and comparison of companion texts. Taking the time to consider the interdependent sections will enable readers to evaluate the relative merits of US policy promulgations as authoritative statements of law and practice. Likewise, the decision not to produce a published text and rely instead on purely digital forms makes the document more difficult for a casual user to decode successfully. Phrased another way, readers must carefully consider the Manual's many policy pronouncements as part of an interwoven totality. Of course, this very feature of the Manual erodes its utility as a ready reference in the midst of operational demands. The chapters in this Commentary and Critique endeavor to assess various policy and legal statements in the entirety of the holistic text.

2 THE NEED FOR A NEW AMERICAN MANUAL

Despite its internecine nature and overall complexity, The Manual is a notable bureaucratic achievement. The United States ratified the 1949 Geneva Conventions in 1955, and issued the classic Field Manual, entitled *The Law of Land Warfare*, only a year later as Department of the Army Field Manual 27–10, known in expert circles around the globe as FM 27–10. Efforts to update FM 27–10 began as a side project under the leadership of one of the most distinguished law of war experts in the world, who subsequently shared drafts with a coterie of highly influential international experts. Although reviewed by officials or scholars affiliated with close US allies, authorship of its early draft was limited to a small cadre of lawyers in the DoD General Counsel's Office. The Preface to the Manual merely notes that:

> The origin of this manual may be traced to work in the late 1980s to update Department of the Army Field Manual 27–10, The Law of Land Warfare. Then, in the mid-1990s, work began on an all-services law of war manual to reflect the views of all DoD components. It was envisioned that the manual would provide not only the black letter rules, but also discussion, examples of State practice, and references to past manuals, treatises, and other documents to provide explanation, clarification, and elaboration. The present manual has sought to realize that vision and thus it falls within the tradition of the 1914 War Department manual, as well as the 1989 and 1997 Commander's Handbook on the Law of Naval Operations, which also adopted this general approach of an annotated manual.

To those experts from around the world who know him and respect his work and decades of service to the American Republic, this bland reference in the Manual to the enduring value of Hays Parks's work is puzzling, and indeed off-putting. He was the architect of the Manual for some two decades while serving in the Office of the US Army Judge Advocate General, before he moved to the DoD Office of General Counsel prior to his retirement. While acknowledging his role only implicitly in a footnote,[19] the Manual does reference Mr. Parks's works as substantive authority for the US position in more than thirty instances. His vision of an apolitical document based on the integrity of the law, rather than political expedience or situational convenience, provided the driving force behind early drafting. The Manual achieved consensus from the US Armed Forces as early as 2010 grounded in the firm position that it should represent a definitive statement of the law rather than seeking to advance political formulations.

In this sense, it represented the culmination of the American articulation of key LOAC principles that began during the Civil War era. The first comprehensive effort to describe the law of war in a written code, the Lieber Code, began as a request from the General-in-Chief of the Union Armies, based on his confusion over the distinction between lawful and unlawful combatants.[20] General Henry Wager Halleck recognized that the LOAC never accorded combatant immunity to every person who conducted hostilities, but confronted the necessity for providing pragmatic guidance to Union forces adapting to the changing tactics of war.[21] On August 6, 1862, General Halleck wrote to Dr. Francis Lieber, a highly regarded law professor at the Columbia College in New York, to request his assistance in defining guerrilla warfare.[22] This request, appropriately described as the catalyst that precipitated more than 150 years of legal effort that produced the modern web of international agreements and the publication of the Manual's first edition in 2015, read as follows:

> My Dear Doctor: Having heard that you have given much attention to the usages and customs of war as practiced in the present age, and especially to the matter of guerrilla war, I hope you may find it convenient to give to the public your views on that subject. The rebel authorities claim the right to send men, in the garb of peaceful citizens, to waylay and attack our troops, to burn bridges and houses and to destroy property and persons within our lines.

---

[19] DoD Law of War Manual, v fn. 15.
[20] Letter from General Halleck to Dr. Francis Lieber, Aug. 6. 1862, reprinted in Richard Shelly Hartigan ed., *Francis Lieber, Lieber's Code and the Law of War* (Chicago: Precedent, 1983), 2.
[21] *Ibid.*   [22] *Ibid.*

They demand that such persons be treated as ordinary belligerents, and that when captured they have extended to them the same rights as other prisoners of war; they also threaten that if such persons be punished as marauders and spies they will retaliate by executing our prisoners of war in their possession. I particularly request your views on these questions.[23]

The Union Army issued a disciplinary code governing the conduct of hostilities, known worldwide as the Lieber Code, as "General Orders 100 Instructions for the Government of the Armies of the United States in the Field" in April 1863.[24] General Orders 100 was the first comprehensive military code of discipline that sought to define the precise parameters of permissible conduct during conflict; it in turn spawned military manuals in other nations. From this baseline, the principle endures in the law today that persons who do not enjoy lawful combatant status are not entitled to the benefits of combatant status derived from the laws of war, including prisoner of war (PoW) status,[25] and are subject to punishment for their warlike acts.[26] There are many other instances of text where the Manual neatly summarizes extant LOAC and illustrates the consistency of the US interpretation with that of key allies.[27]

The legal landscape changed dramatically in the six decades between the publication of FM 27–10 and the 2016 Revisions due to a welter of new treaty provisions. Chapter XIX of the Manual provides a summation of "DoD views and practice relating to those documents as of the date of publication of this manual." The Manual as issued in 2015 was an overdue compilation for three important reasons. As the Preface notes, early work grew out of a "concept plan for a new all-Services law of war manual that would be a resource for implementing the 1977 Additional Protocols to the 1949 Geneva Conventions." At the time, US experts expected ratification of the Protocols because the United States had been deeply engaged in their negotiation. Forty-one years after the adoption of the 1977 Additional Protocols, the United States

---

[23]   *Ibid.*

[24]   For a description of the process leading to General Orders 100 and the legal effect it had on subsequent efforts, see Grant R. Doty, "The United States and the Development of the Laws of Land Warfare" (1998) 156 *Military Law Review* 224; George B. Davis, "Doctor Francis Lieber's Instructions for the Government of Armies in the Field" (1907) 1 *American Journal of International Law* 13.

[25]   DoD Law of War Manual, ¶ 4.3 ("Unlawful combatants" or "unprivileged belligerents" are persons who, by engaging in hostilities, have incurred one or more of the corresponding liabilities of combatant status (e.g., being made the object of attack and subject to detention), but who are not entitled to any of the distinct privileges of combatant status (e.g., combatant immunity and PoW status)).

[26]   *Ibid.*, ¶ 18.19.3.7.

[27]   See *ibid.*, ¶ 18.3–18.4 (discussing the law of reprisals and describing its contours and practical considerations among nations).

has yet to ratify either treaty despite early aspirations to do so, yet operates in coalitions alongside States that are fully bound, subject to express national reservations, to the treaty texts. For much of that period, US legal and policy positions *vis-à-vis* the Protocol I articulations of law were scattered in academic literature, litigation materials and final opinions, treaty negotiation positions, and formal diplomatic responses to nongovernmental initiatives. Thus, the Manual purports to stake out definitive positions on many of the key issues arising from the 1977 Additional Protocols. Areas of Protocol I practice where allies would expect clear statements that the United States accepts a particular provision as binding law by virtue of custom, yet do not find such express admissions in the Manual, are among its persistent wrinkles.

The Manual does address US policy regarding an array of other treaties that post-date FM 27–10, *inter alia* the Convention on Prohibitions or Restrictions on the Use of Certain Conventional Weapons Which May Be Deemed to Be Excessively Injurious or to Have Indiscriminate Effects Certain Conventional Weapons Convention and its Protocols (the CCW provisions);[28] the Rome Statute of the International Criminal Court;[29] the Convention on the Prohibition of Development, Production and Stockpiling of Bacteriological (Biological) and Toxin Weapons and on Their Destruction of April 10, 1972 (Biological Weapons Convention);[30] the Convention on the Prohibition of Military or Any Other Hostile Use of Environmental Modification Techniques of May 18, 1977 (ENMOD Convention);[31] and the Convention on the Prohibition of the Development, Production, Stockpiling and Use of Chemical Weapons and on Their Destruction of January 13, 1993 (Chemical Weapons Convention);[32] the Ottawa Landmines Convention; and the Optional Protocol to the Convention on the Rights of the Child on the involvement of Children in Armed Conflict. In doing so, it addresses many of the key controversies of the post 9/11 era.[33]

Second, as noted above, technological developments have generated intense debates among practitioners, resulting in an entire chapter on information and cyberwar operations.[34] In contrast to the single page devoted to weapons in FM 27–10, the Manual contains a ninety-seven-page chapter on

---

[28] *Ibid.*, ¶ 19.21.
[29] See Chapter 16 of this book for assessment of the Manual's relationship to the provisions of the Rome Statute of the International Criminal Court.
[30] DoD Law of War Manual, ¶ 19.19.   [31] *Ibid.*, ¶ 6.10.   [32] *Ibid.*, ¶ 19.22.
[33] For a concise explanation of the Manual's approach to these important debates, see DoD Law of War Manual Workshop, The American Bar Association's Standing Committee on Law and National Security (Jan. 9, 2017), www.abanet.org/natsecurity.
[34] See Chapter 15 of this book for a thoughtful assessment of the limitations of Chapter XVI of the Manual.

weapons.[35] The extended period of revisions and interagency debate between 2010 and the Manual's first edition in June 2015 proved inconsequential, as that chapter changed little during interagency discussion.

Finally, the synergy of sources cannot be forgotten. FM 27–10 and other US service manuals preceded the generation of jurisprudential developments that have become widely cited as forming kernels of customary international law as the ad hoc and hybrid tribunals matured. The Manual cites the jurisprudence of international tribunals, but to my taste is far too hesitant in doing so. At the same time, the International Committee of the Red Cross (ICRC) has convened expert groups in recent years to publish guidance on such themes as the law of occupation and the meaning of "direct participation in hostilities." The massive ICRC Customary Law Study purports to prescribe definitive norms of State practice based in large part on military manuals around the world. By an odd quirk of history, the first revisions to the DoD Law of War Manual were released in May 2016 almost simultaneously with the newly Revised ICRC Commentary on the First Geneva Convention. The conjunction of the DoD Law of War Manual added an authoritative text that is highly relevant to the unresolved contestations among experts over *what* the Geneva Conventions, the 1977 Additional Protocols, and other relevant treaties mean, as well as *how* best to read and implement their tenets.

The Law of War remains in a transformative period in many areas, and the Manual provides concrete US perspectives to inform those debates. As only one of many possible examples, the Manual and the Revised ICRC Commentary reach diametrically opposite conclusions on the question of whether wounded and sick members of the armed forces participating in conflict may be categorically excluded from the scope of the proportionality assessment that commanders must undertake.[36] DoD revised the Manual to highlight the US perspective on this point. The Manual restates the truism that wounded and sick members of the armed forces may not be made the object of attack, but nonetheless excludes them from the scope of the prohibition on disproportionate attacks on the ground that they are deemed to have "assumed" such a risk. It also notes that those planning or conducting attacks may consider such military personnel as a matter of practice or policy when applying the proportionality principle.[37] The Revised ICRC Commentary, on the other hand, considers that "in view of the specific protections accorded to

---

[35]   DoD Law of War Manual, ¶¶ 6.1–6.20.   [36]   DoD Law of War Manual, ¶ 5.10.1.2.

[37]   *Ibid.*, ¶ 7.3.3.1 addressing the wounded, sick, and shipwrecked reiterates this position, noting that combatants who are wounded, sick, or shipwrecked on the battlefield are deemed to have accepted the risk of death or further injury due to their proximity to military operations.

the wounded and sick, namely the obligation to respect (and to protect) them in all circumstances, a fortiori they should also benefit from the protection accorded to civilians. In other words, if civilians are to be included in the proportionality assessment all the more so should the wounded and sick."[38] The ICRC view does not include concretized examples of State practice.

In this light, the Manual provides a badly needed predictor of actual practice by US forces in the field rather than continued reliance on ad hoc and often adaptive responses to the conundrums of modern operations. As the Manual states "analysis of State practice should include an analysis of actual operational practice by States during armed conflict. Although manuals or other official statements may provide important indications of State behavior, they cannot replace a meaningful assessment of operational State practice."[39] In this vein, the US perspective on the ICRC Customary International Humanitarian Law Study is worth recalling because, in the US view, the ICRC Customary Law collection:[40]

> places too much emphasis on written materials, such as military manuals and other guidelines published by States, as opposed to actual operational practice by States during armed conflict. Although manuals may provide important indications of State behavior and *opinio juris*, they cannot be a replacement for a meaningful assessment of operational State practice in connection with actual military operations. We also are troubled by the extent to which the Study relies on non-binding resolutions of the General Assembly, given that States may lend their support to a particular resolution, or determine not to break consensus in regard to such a resolution, for reasons having nothing to do with a belief that the propositions in it reflect customary international law.

In other words, American views over the scope and substance of the customary norms applicable to the conduct of hostilities remain highly relevant, and the Manual provides important new insights. The Manual's failure to provide a consolidated listing of the provisions of Protocols I and II that the US accepts as binding customary international law is one of its key shortcomings. Its text is nevertheless an important counterbalance to other perspectives over whether the silences and ambiguities of the modern treaties are bargains to be valued or voids to be filled.

---

[38] ICRC, *Commentary on the First Geneva Convention: Convention (I) for the Amelioration of the Condition of the Wounded and Sick in Armed Forces in the Field*, 2nd ed. (Cambridge University Press, 2016), para. 1357.

[39] DoD Law of War Manual, ¶ 1.8.2.2.

[40] *Ibid.*, fn. 139 (citing the US Response to the ICRC CIHL Study, 515).

3 THE TENOR OF THE MANUAL

The Manual represents an important benchmark, particularly insofar as experts juxtapose it against the new ICRC Commentary. FM 27–10 incorporated the 429 articles of the four 1949 Geneva Conventions into sparse text that omitted many relevant historical examples and salient instances of State practice. Both the US Navy and Air Force published service-specific military manuals in later years. The 1956 Field Manual was primarily drafted by Harvard Law Professor Richard Baxter, who later served on the International Court of Justice. Judge Baxter used the provisions of the Conventions as the centerpiece of FM 27–10 while compiling a comparative matrix of the interlocked treaty provisions between the Hague Regulations and the four 1949 Geneva Conventions; FM 27–10 contains no footnotes but an extensive index.

Beginning in the mid-1990s, the Manual took on important momentum as senior military lawyers and the Office of General Counsel launched efforts to craft a consolidated DoD product that could also inform all branches of the US armed forces. In May 2008, the Department of Defense General Counsel, Jeh Johnson (who later served as US Homeland Security Secretary under President Obama), hosted an international peer review of the near-final draft manual. Leading law of war scholars from the United Kingdom, Canada, Australia, New Zealand, and the United States, including senior State Department attorneys, participated in a five-day meeting at the Army Judge Advocate General's School, Charlottesville, Virginia, and provided their comments. Department of Justice lawyers declined the invitation to attend, as they did with every Law of War Working Group meeting. Assembled experts were extremely positive about the overall manual but offered many points requiring clarification.

In contrast to FM 27–10, the Manual as published contains 7,029 footnotes (see Table 1.1). For the first time in US practice, it helps cut through the cacophony of contexts to present an integrated and informed whole alongside key supporting citations.

The Manual's clear intent was to provide an authoritative voice for scholars and experts to assess the ongoing debates over the interpretation and application of the laws and customs of warfare. Expert authors in this present volume have frequently commented on the legal utility of the footnotes in support of textual positions. However, the very length and detail of the text undercuts its utility as a quick reference for practitioners. As noted by Geoffrey Corn,[41]

---

[41] See Chapter 6 of this book for a thoughtful assessment of the impact of the Manual from a subordinate service perspective.

TABLE 1.1 Comparative Chart of Manual authorities by Chapter and Source

Chapter	# of foot- notes	Inter- nal Refer- ences	Treat- ies	US Practi- ce	DoD Directi- ves & Instruct- ions	US Military Manua- ls	US Cases Pre 1900	US Cases 1901– 1950	US Cases Post 1951	US Const, USC, EO	Non- US Practice	Non-US Military Manuals	Non- US Cases	UN Doc- ume- nts	ICRC Doc- ume- nts	Schol- arship	R3d on Foreign Relatio- ns	News	Soft Law	Dicti- onary	Total Citati- ons
1	239	92	38	60	4	13	8	0	7	6	1	0	25	10	1	35	7	0	0	0	307
2	131	106	8	9	0	13	2	1	0	0	2	8	13	0	1	23	1	0	0	0	187
3	153	96	47	19	2	4	6	0	5	1	2	0	16	1	6	13	0	0	0	0	218
4	544	265	147	58	12	34	3	18	13	17	15	22	25	3	27	91	0	0	0	0	750
5	840	386	193	146	1	57	1	3	15	16	49	50	30	1	31	125	0	4	0	0	1108
6	488	156	181	140	16	15	0	0	0	4	16	2	6	2	7	46	0	1	0	0	592
7	467	186	267	15	1	8	0	0	6	0	7	5	3	1	58	22	0	1	0	0	574
8	132	68	75	16	19	4	1	1	6	7	7	5	1	1	18	0	0	1	10	1	229
9	942	293	541	28	5	19	0	4	3	6	8	15	14	1	71	34	0	0	0	0	1042
10	644	151	436	6	0	9	0	0	0	0	10	0	0	0	67	0	0	0	0	0	679
11	490	191	111	40	0	82	12	8	3	0	33	8	15	3	37	44	0	0	0	0	587
12	220	60	29	16	0	100	1	2	0	3	3	36	3	4	0	17	1	0	0	0	275
13	226	90	64	29	0	128	15	2	0	0	0	8	4	1	1	18	0	0	0	0	360
14	174	115	36	36	7	11	0	0	0	2	0	10	0	1	0	12	0	0	0	0	230
15	372	115	155	28	0	97	6	2	0	3	4	8	3	2	0	53	0	0	0	0	477
16	78	44	1	37	0	0	0	0	0	0	0	0	0	0	0	1	0	0	0	0	83
17	222	131	79	21	0	6	3	1	3	3	9	1	6	2	9	23	0	1	0	0	298
18	370	94	181	40	37	19	4	7	11	51	10	4	33	26	4	24	4	0	6	0	555
19	297	162	80	71	0	2	0	0	0	3	9	0	7	1	3	12	0	0	0	0	350
Total	7029	2801	2669	815	104	621	62	49	66	122	178	177	204	60	342	593	12	9	16	1	8901
Total %		31.47	29.99	9.16	1.17	6.98	0.70	0.55	0.74	1.37	2.00	1.99	2.29	0.67	3.84	6.66	0.13	0.10	0.18	0.01	100.00

generations of Army judge advocates and commanders found FM 27–10 to be a highly portable and efficient means for ascertaining the content of a particular provision of the law of war. In fact, upon its publication, the DoD decision not to include an index in the Manual became one of the most commonly voiced complaints among young officers and their lawyers.

By 2009, the draft was virtually ready for publication as a final draft and enjoyed the consensus of the DoD Law of War Working Group, including Department of State representatives. The lengthy process for producing the early drafts is best attributable to two key factors. The Manual was always a secondary effort relegated to the professional margins while its drafters coordinated major military operations in the Balkans, Iraq, and Afghanistan, as well as many other LOAC developments. Second, the early decision to field a sophisticated text relying on relevant treaty provisions, illustrated by abundant examples of State practice to explain the law and its proper employment, required extraordinary research efforts. The footnotes provide great value to the text.

Eyewitnesses confirm that the Department of Justice declined invitations to attend meetings of the Law of War Working Group, while State Department experts attended an estimated 98 percent of the meetings convened to work on the Manual. Nevertheless, the lengthy delay between the consensus final draft produced by the Law of War Working Group within DoD in early 2010 and publication of the final text is largely attributable to interagency arguments over its final public form. In particular, a schism that generated extended delays developed within the Department of Justice between litigators who sought Manual provisions to bolster ongoing federal litigation and the Office of Legal Counsel. One particularly memorable section that was added in the aftermath of the Law of War Working Group consensus text simply noted "in general, journalists are civilians,"[42] but added that "[r]eporting on military operations can be very similar to collecting intelligence or even spying . . . [T]o avoid being mistaken for spies, journalists should act openly and with the permission of relevant authorities."[43] These provisions seemed to undercut the press freedoms and implied that journalism and media reporting were not fully protected activities under existing *jus in bello* provisions. They were met with fierce and appropriate criticism from the moment of publication.

The first revision published in May 2016 noted with some understatement that the offending paragraphs received "substantial revisions." The May 2016 text amplified the bland statement that "in general, journalists are civilians" by adding:

---

[42]   US Department of Defense, *Law of War Manual*, 1st ed. (2015), ¶ 4.24.   [43]   *Ibid.*, ¶ 4.24.2.

and are protected as such under the law of war. Journalists play a vital role in free societies and the rule of law and in providing information about armed conflict. Moreover, the proactive release of accurate information to domestic and international audiences has been viewed as consistent with the objectives of U.S. military operations. DoD operates under the policy that open and independent reporting is the principal means of coverage of U.S. military operations. In addition to responding to press inquiries and providing briefings to members of the press on U.S. military operations, DoD practice has also been to embed journalists with units during military operations. Embedded journalists are assigned to a unit, and they eat, sleep, and move with the unit.[44]

There are other examples to demonstrate improvements in the text based on comments from external critiques, but the purpose of this book is not to provide a line-by-line exegesis of the Manual. Though States seek to retain the authoritative role in shaping State practice for the purposes of solidifying customary international norms, the ICRC and other nongovernmental groups also seek to expand their influence, particularly insofar as modern conflicts continue to raise vexing legal and political difficulties. The involvement of such groups in assessing DoD compliance with the Manual provisions and evaluating their technical accuracy under the law is undoubtedly of continuing importance.

Finally, and of particular note, there are many instances when the Manual's drafters used archaic case law to support a premise of modern US practice. Figure 1.1 illustrates the frequency with which outdated US cases are used to illustrate modern practice. Authors herein frequently note mismatches between cited sources of authority and the modern import of the *jus in bello* norm.

These areas in the Manual are troubling due to the reliance on outdated or inapposite US cases because there are often far more applicable cases or illustrations drawn from more recent jurisprudence. The reality that 2.29 percent of the citations in the Manual are drawn from foreign cases represents an enormous lost opportunity on the part of DoD. Many manual provisions are technically correct but read as if they are categorical truths pronounced with insufficient attention to the nuances of consistent allied positions and barely any recognition of alternative perspectives that warfighters are likely to encounter as they apply the Manual's tenets.

[44]   DoD Law of War Manual, ¶ 4.24.

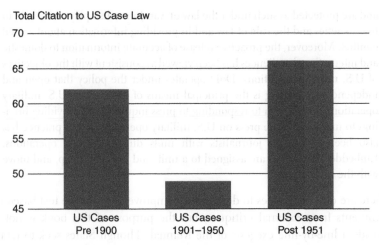

FIGURE 1.1 Temporal Comparison of US Federal Court cases cited in the Manual

4 AN OVERVIEW OF THE MANUAL'S CONTRIBUTIONS AND CONTROVERSIES

The authors herein discuss the Manual's formidable contributions at length and with considerable insight. It provides needed clarity on many positions of US understanding and *jus in bello* practice. In particular, many portions state US views with admirable frankness, albeit with an occasional caveat that a particular premise represents the "law of war, as applied by the United States."[45] Manual drafters also strove to provide lists of considerations and other criteria for actually applying *jus in bello* norms. Practitioners are well served by reference to those checklists, and DoD should consider publication of a separate appendix of such checklists as a standalone digital file.[46] In many other instances, long-held US positions are articulated with strikingly candid and logical force. For example, the discussion of military necessity acknowledges countervailing views, but plainly states the US position as follows:

[45] See *ibid.*, ¶ 5.8.4.2 ("The law of war, as applied by the United States, gives no 'revolving door' protection; that is, the off-and-on protection in a case where a civilian repeatedly forfeits and regains his or her protection from being made the object of attack depending on whether or not the person is taking a direct part in hostilities at that exact time. Thus, for example, persons who are assessed to be engaged in a pattern of taking a direct part in hostilities do not regain protection from being made the object of attack in the time period between instances of taking a direct part in hostilities.").

[46] See *ibid.*, ¶¶ 5.8.3–5.8.4 (giving examples of direct participation in hostilities).

Some commentators have argued that military necessity should be interpreted so as to permit only what is actually necessary in the prevailing
circumstances, such as by requiring commanders, if possible, to seek to
capture or wound enemy combatants rather than to make them the object
of attack. This interpretation, however, does not reflect customary international law or treaty law applicable to DoD personnel. For example, the law of
war does not require that enemy combatants be warned before being made
the object of attack, nor does the law of war require that enemy combatants be
given an opportunity to surrender before being made the object of attack.
Moreover, the law of war may justify the use of overwhelming force against
enemy military objectives.

This statement is absolutely correct as an articulation of *jus in bello*, but also
illustrates a recurring weakness of the Manual. Close analysis reveals that
DoD drafters missed many opportunities to engage the merits of opposing
viewpoints. For example, the Manual only implicitly confronts the tensions
between the applicability of the law of occupation and the larger field of
human rights law.[47] In truth, the US position *vis-à-vis* military necessity
noted above illustrates a recurring theme. The US position is often substantively identical to that of key allies, even if the legal pathway taken by various
nations to reach the same substantive destination occasionally varies.[48] DoD
admits that while "the views of other States may be referenced in this
manual, it is not a purpose of this manual to describe the views of other
States, which may differ from views expressed in this manual." In some
instances, such as the law related to reprisals, drafters noted consistency
with the positions of other nations.[49] Nevertheless, by relying on citations
to non-US military manuals in only 1.99 percent of the footnotes and to non-
US practice in only 2.00 percent of the notes, drafters missed many opportunities to demonstrate the alignment of US views with the practices of other
nations.

Compounding this error, the Manual cites the Elements of Crimes of the
International Criminal Court with reference to a single substantive issue (the

---

[47]   E.g., in noting that the Occupying Power may suspend laws permitting discrimination, the
Manual cites Coalition Provisional Authority Order 7, which echoed core principles of
human rights law by mandating the following: "In exercising their official functions, all
persons undertaking public duties or holding public office, including all police, prosecutors,
and judges, must apply the law impartially. No person will be discriminated against on the
basis of sex, race, color, language, religion, political opinion, national, ethnic or social origin,
or birth." DoD Law of War Manual, ¶ 11.9.2.1 fn. 163.

[48]   M. A. Newton, "Exceptional Engagement: Protocol I and a World United against Terror"
(2009) 42 *Texas International Law Journal* 323.

[49]   Law of War Manual, ¶ 11.9.2.1.

war crime of pillage)[50] and in one instance to illustrate the consistency
between the International Criminal Court (ICC) approach and US policy
with respect to expanding bullets.[51] In fact, the US delegation was one of the
leaders in the Elements discussions, and joined consensus on their final
adoption. The vast majority of US positions articulated in the Manual accord
with the Elements of Crimes document used by the ICC. As only one
example, the ICC Elements are not referenced despite their complete consistency with the stated US view that assessing the proportionality prong
"whether the expected incidental harm would be excessive" means that "the
totality of the circumstances must be considered. This holistic judgment
should consider any relevant moral, legal, and military factors."[52]

Lastly, granular analysis of the Manual's interrelated passages illustrate
some subtle, but striking, intellectual inconsistencies. For example, the
DoD position is clearly stated that geographic boundaries may not be an
essential aspect of a NIAC. David Graham responds to that view with precision in Chapter 9. Though it is wholly appropriate that the Manual included a
full chapter devoted to NIAC, its obvious intent to buttress US litigation
positions with respect to the geographical nexus for hostilities generates an
unintended variance with the substantive law described in the chapter. In fact,
the vast majority of the specific legal rules relied upon by DoD are citations to
1977 Additional Protocol II, which in itself embeds an explicit geographic
requirement.

As another example, while eschewing specific embrace of the law of transformative occupation, US practice in fact embarked upon precisely such an
endeavor in the early days of the invasion of Iraq in 2003. Similar to the UK
position, General Franks's "Freedom Message" oozed tenets of occupation
law via his language about "promoting law and order so that Iraqis can live in
security, free from fear."[53] The second proclamation by General Franks on the
same day (April 16, a month prior to both Coalition Provisional Authority
(CPA) Order # 1 and UNSC 1483) is of perhaps greater importance, though it
is far less well known and commented upon (except by the indubitable Adam

[50] *Ibid.*, ¶ 18.18.3.4 (noting consistency between the Manual language and the statements of
      Germany, Italy, UK, France, and Egypt).
[51] *Ibid.*, ¶ 6.5.4.5 (noting that the States Party reiterated that the ICC Elements of Crimes mean
      that during both international and non-international armed conflicts "the crime is committed
      only if the perpetrator employs the bullets to uselessly aggravate suffering or the wounding
      effect upon the target of such bullets, as reflected in customary international law").
[52] *Ibid.*, ¶ 5.12.3.
[53] S. Talmon, *The Occupation of Iraq, II: The Official Documents of the Coalition
      Provisional Authority and the Iraqi Governing Council* (Oxford: Hart Publishing, 2013), 169,
      www.psywar.org/product_2003IFIZCo148.php.

Roberts).[54] General Franks's second message, entitled *Instructions to the People of Iraq*, imposed a whole series of transformative measures onto the Iraqi people in order to "Ensure the safety, security, and public order of the people of Iraq and Coalition Forces."[55] Though this language echoes Article 43 of the 1907 Hague Regulations, its import was to implement a modern transformative occupation in Iraq from the moment US forces displaced domestic authorities. There are manifold instances in the Manual of similar lacunae, and the authors herein provide extensive analysis of the Manual's many wrinkles and oddities.

5 THE STRUCTURE OF THE BOOK

This book is a unique collection of essays. Part I is entitled the "Background and Bureaucratic Formation of the Manual," and focuses on the process of its production amidst competing political/legal perspectives. Karl Chang sets forth the DoD posture in Chapter 2 and provides his lessons learned to future manual drafters, while Chris Jenks describes the competing interagency pressures that affected the Manual's tone and timing in Chapter 3.

Part II presents a series "Prominent Perspectives on the DoD Manual" based on its actual utility. Major General (Ret'd.) Charles Dunlap provides a perfect transition from Part I by considering in Chapter 4 how the Manual as drafted meets the actual operational needs of the US military. The current NATO Legal Advisor, Stephen Hill, presents the NATO perspective in Chapter 5, while Geoff Corn conveys the perspective of the US Army as a subordinate service in Chapter 6.

Part III logically builds on that work to present detailed chapters focusing on specific "Substantive Contributions and Controversies." The goal of Part III is to assess the normative baseline and identify areas where the Manual adds to ongoing debates, or in the view of some experts where its influence is less certain and should be seen more as an outlier in State practice. Ray Murphy assesses the Manual's treatment of basic LOAC principles in Chapter 7, while David Graham dissects the DoD posture toward one of the most foundational aspects of the field in Chapter 8; to wit, the contours of a NIAC which demarcate the very applicability of *jus in bello* norms. Bill Boothby describes the details of the DoD approach to targeting and the principle of distinction in

---

[54] A. Roberts, "Transformative Military Occupation: Applying the Laws of War and Human Rights," in M. Schmitt and J. Pecjic (eds.), *International Law and Armed Conflicts: Exploring the Faultlines* (Leiden: Martinus Nijhoff, 2007), 439, 479 fn. 101.

[55] Talmon (above note 53), 170.

Chapter 9. Chapter 10 follows logically because it is an incisive exposition by Peter Margulies that describes the substantive flaws in the DoD approach to precautions in the attack based on the use of citations that fall short of providing the substantive support alleged by the Manual's text. In particular, the cases relied upon by the Manual drafters to buttress important aspects of the targeting analysis are inapposite when closely examined. Adil Haque's Chapter 11 provides a more lengthy exposition on the details of the Manual's approach to targeting. He argues that the Manual compounds the unavoidable factual complexity of warfare with entirely avoidable legal complexity. Chapter 12, by Laurie R. Blank, extends Haque's thoughts by describing the imprecision and inconsistency in the DoD terminology with respect to targeting determinations. Andrew Clapham's Chapter 13 provides an essential guide to the Manual's approach to detention issues, while Yaël Ronen provides a wonderful analysis of the flaws in the Manual's approach to the law of occupation in Chapter 14. Chapters 13 and 14 each illustrate the mismatch between the Manual's intentions and the specificity of its text.

Finally, Part IV focuses on "The Manual's Long-Term Prospects and Implications". Gary Brown describes the weaknesses of the Manual's approach to cyber operations in Chapter 15, while Chapter 16 addresses the impacts of the Manual's formulations as they relate to viable coalition operations. The Manual's consideration of the human rights dimension of modern military operations is perhaps its most fundamental flaw because the US approach is often demonstrably unsuited to the complexities of hybrid warfare conducted against non-State adversaries. Classic law of war concepts based on reciprocity and the formalized lines of command authority over military forces flowing from the power of the sovereign State are strained in modern NIACs. Chapters 17 and 18, by Katharine Fortin and Aurel Sari respectively, consider some of the difficult dimensions of the relationship between non-State actors and the established *jus in bello* regime.

This Commentary and Critique explains the Manual's key provisions, debates the normative impact of its innovations, and describes its likely future impact on the conduct of hostilities. Authors have deliberately highlighted recommendations for improvements that will help the Manual achieve its intended purpose. DoD is clear that the Manual is not a substitute for the careful practice of law and cautions legal advisors to "consider relevant legal and policy materials (e.g., treaty provisions, judicial decisions, past U.S. practice, regulations, and doctrine)" and "apply the law to the specific factual circumstances" posed by the difficult dilemmas confronted during modern operations. The Manual is important precisely because US military commanders and lawyers do not approach LOAC as an esoteric intellectual exercise.

The precepts of humanitarian law are the lifeblood of the military profession because they developed as a restraining and humanizing necessity that simultaneously facilitates commanders' ability to accomplish the military mission even in the midst of fear, moral ambiguity, and horrific scenes of violence.

The Manual seeks to aid lawful military operations, while hindering those who would co-opt the field and divorce it from State practice or adversaries who exploit legal ambiguities to advance their own military objectives. Illegitimate exploitation of *jus in bello* norms could permit the legal structure to be portrayed as a mass of indeterminate subjectivity that is nothing more than another weapon in the moral domain of conflict at the behest of the side with the best cameras, biggest microphones, and most compliant media accomplices. The Manual is an undeniably powerful effort to instill deeper awareness that the law of war cannot be permitted to atrophy. Misrepresentations of the law and manipulation of the media to mask genuine war crimes could lead to a cycle of cynicism and second-guessing that weakens the overall commitment of some military members to remain bound by the law. The DoD Law of War Manual is a bulwark that seeks to prevent that most undesirable future.

2

The DoD Law of War Manual: Why, What, and How

Karl Chang

1 INTRODUCTION

I thank Professor Newton for editing this volume, as well as the contributors, and look forward to reading this Commentary and Critique. For me, the effort to produce the manual meant many things, but chief among them, it was a kind of quest to gather, to the extent we could, everything that the Department of Defense knew about the law of war in one place. "Quest" probably sounds too grand and, although some might conjure up a picture of bringing stone tablets down from the mountaintop, a more humble effort comes to my mind – something more like herding animals into a crowded, smelly boat. As I noted in public remarks on the manual:

> I think humility was essential to the creation of the manual in so many ways. A humble attitude is necessary for editing: you will never be able to improve a draft, if you think it is already perfect. A humble attitude also greases the bureaucratic cogs: you will not convince colleagues to concur in your draft, if you act like a know-it-all.[1]

Striving to maintain a humble attitude was also fundamental to the creation of the manual as an epistemic endeavor. Searching for knowledge begins with understanding your own ignorance – as Socrates interpreting the oracle at Delphi put it – recognizing that you are "in truth of no account in respect to wisdom."[2]

I believe the Manual reflects sound and creditable interpretations of the law of war. It was approved by senior counsel of all the key legal offices within

---

[1] K. Chang, "U.S. and International Perspectives on the New U.S. Department of Defense Law of War Manual, Remarks" (2016) 110 *Proceedings of the American Society of International Law Annual Meeting* 115, 116.

[2] Plato, Apology, 23b, www.perseus.tufts.edu/hopper/text?doc=Perseus%3Atext%3A1999.01.0170 %3Atext%3DApol.%3Asection%3D23b.

DoD, and it reflects longstanding – and current – practice of the United States and the best of advice of scores of military and civilian law of war experts. Significantly, following its publication in June 2015, DoD has continued to demonstrate a Socratic spirit by inviting dialogue on the manual. The Department invites the submission of comments on the Manual in a variety of fora – starting with the Manual's Preface, which requests that comments are sent to an email address established for this express purpose.[3] I hope the Department continues to hear from academics, nongovernmental organizations (NGOs), and, especially from fellow practitioners in the law of war – including those associated with US military operations and defense activities as well as such practitioners from a wide range of countries whether or not allied or partnered with the United States. In this same spirit, my colleagues and I hope to learn from the fellow contributors to this book and welcome their comments on and critique of the Manual.

For this cornerstone chapter, Professor Newton asked me to describe what we did and why we did it. The "what" is fairly straightforward. The Manual stands as DoD's first Department-wide publication on the law of war, and the best way to understand the "what" is to read it.[4] In drafting, we always wanted the Manual to speak clearly for itself – *res ipsa loquitur* – and not be a set of gnomic utterances requiring expert interpretation.[5]

I also think the "why" is straightforward. The Manual's purpose is to help the Department comply with and implement the law of war. Complying with the law of war, as noted in the foreword of the Manual, is of fundamental importance to DoD. I have been honored to serve under senior civilian and military officials, including senior counsel, who have made adherence to the law of war in military operations a priority, and alongside many judge advocates and civil servants who have worked hard to make this a reality. Helping the Department's practice in the law of war was also our guiding principle for every choice about the Manual's format or content. Does this help the practitioner? How can we make this section more useful to the lawyers within the Department practicing this body of law?

---

[3] DoD Law of War Manual, Preface ("Comments and suggestions from users of the DoD Law of War Manual are invited. All such correspondence should be addressed by email to: osd. pentagon.ogc.mbx.ia-law-of-war-manual-comments@mail.mil.").

[4] Given the length, perhaps not all at once. I think the foreword is a good, brief introduction to the law of war for a lay reader. Chapter II, addressing law of war principles, and Chapter V, addressing conduct of hostilities, are probably the most interesting to the average international lawyer. Specialists in a particular area of the law of war will no doubt want to review those portions addressing their specialty.

[5] E.g., ¶ 1.2 of the Manual explains the Manual's usage of footnotes, sources, cross-references, and signals.

In this chapter, I elaborate on Professor Newton's questions of what and why, and also address how. First, I discuss *why* States issue law of war manuals by explaining some of the practical functions that manuals perform. Second, I explain *what* makes the DoD Law of War Manual distinctive as a State's perspective on the law of war. Lastly, I share lessons learned from *how* the Manual was produced.

Although my answers to why, what, and how are necessarily incomplete, and I must add, do not necessarily reflect the official views of DoD, I hope that readers will gain a better understanding of the Manual and DoD's practice in the law of war, as well as insights useful to government lawyers working on similar projects.

2 WHY DO STATES ISSUE LAW OF WAR MANUALS?

As a general matter, manuals help the armed forces comply with the law of war by providing information about the requirements of the law. Some treaties provide specific requirements to disseminate the text of a treaty or to train the armed forces,[6] and manuals can help fulfill those requirements. However, manuals also help implement the law of war in ways that are less obvious. I will discuss four mutually reinforcing functions that manuals can perform: (a) implementing inter-State obligations in the domestic system; (b) clarifying ambiguities in international law; (c) facilitating interoperability with coalition partners; and (d) facilitating a consistent interpretation throughout the armed forces.

2.1 *Implementing Inter-State Obligations in the Domestic System*

Law of war manuals can help States implement international obligations domestically into rules of conduct for military personnel. When a State accepts an obligation in a treaty, under traditional interpretations of international law, these obligations run from State to State.[7] Law of war rules,

---

[6] See DoD Law of War Manual, ¶ 18.6.

[7] See, e.g., *Head Money Cases*, 112 US 580, 598 (1884) ("A treaty is primarily a compact between independent nations. It depends for the enforcement of its provisions on the interest and the honor of the governments which are parties to it. If these fail, its infraction becomes the subject of international negotiations and reclamations, so far as the injured party chooses to seek redress, which may, in the end, be enforced by actual war."); *Johnson v. Eisentrager*, 339 US 763, 789 n. 14 (1950) ("The United States, by the Geneva Convention of July 27, 1929, 47 Stat. 2021, concluded with forty-six other countries, including the German Reich, an agreement upon the treatment to be accorded captives. These prisoners claim to be and are entitled to its protection. It is, however, the obvious scheme of the Agreement that responsibility for

however, must apply to individuals on the battlefield. So, a manual can perform a useful function by assisting in the State's effort to take an inter-State obligation and translate it into a rule of conduct for the State's personnel within the framework of the State's domestic law.

The translation of an inter-State obligation into a rule of conduct for the armed forces is in the strictest sense a procedural matter of promulgating international legal requirements within the domestic system. Under domestic law, treaties or customary international law might not automatically constitute binding sources of law.[8] The issuance of a manual, however, can help give the international obligation force at the domestic level. In US practice, the implementation of the law of war has historically occurred through the issuances of military orders and directives, rather than through comprehensive domestic legislation.[9] Currently, under Department procedures, DoD Directive 2311.01E, the DoD Law of War Program, prescribes a general requirement for Department personnel to comply with the law of war.[10] The DoD Law of War Manual, issued pursuant to DoD Directive 2311.01E, provides information for Department personnel on the law of war to help them meet this requirement.[11]

The translation of an inter-State obligation into a rule of conduct for personnel can also involve substantive elaboration on the rule. For example, international law might provide a general requirement that feasible

---

observance and enforcement of these rights is upon political and military authorities. Rights of alien enemies are vindicated under it only through protests and intervention of protecting powers as the rights of our citizens against foreign governments are vindicated only by Presidential intervention.").

[8] W. P. Barr, Assistant Attorney General, US Department of Justice, Office of Legal Counsel, "Authority of the Federal Bureau of Investigation to Override International Law in Extraterritorial Law Enforcement Activities," Memorandum Opinion for the Attorney General (June 21, 1989), 179 (explaining that under US domestic law "unexecuted treaties, like customary international law, are not legally binding on the political branches") www .justice.gov/sites/default/files/olc/opinions/1989/06/31/op-olc-v013-p0163_0.pdf.

[9] W. Winthrop, *Military Law and Precedents*, 2nd ed. (Washington: Gov't. Printing Office, 1920), 733 ("Unlike Military Law Proper, the Law of War *in this country* is not a formal written code but consists mainly of general rules derived from International Law, supplemented by acts and orders of the military power and a few legislative provisions.").

[10] US Department of Defense Directive 2311.01E, DoD Law of War Program (May 9, 2006, Incorporating Change 1, Nov. 15, 2010, Certified Current as of Feb. 22, 2011), 2 ("It is DoD policy that: 4.1. Members of the DoD Components comply with the law of war during all armed conflicts, however such conflicts are characterized, and in all other military operations.").

[11] *Ibid.*, 2–3 ("The General Counsel of the Department of Defense (GC, DoD) shall: . . . Develop and promulgate the DoD Law of War Manual. To ensure consistency in legal interpretation, the DoD Law of War Manual will serve as the authoritative statement on the law of war within the Department of Defense.").

precautions to reduce the risk of civilian casualties be taken. But, what is "feasible" and who within the State determines feasibility? A manual can help clarify issues such as the substantive meaning of requirements or who within the State is charged with implementing them.[12] Such clarification, however, can also be viewed as a separate function.

2.2 *Clarifying Ambiguities in International Law*

Law of war manuals can perform an important function by helping to clarify ambiguities in international law. Treaties can have ambiguities for a variety of reasons. For example, an ambiguity may reflect a choice by States to retain discretion for each to implement an international rule in light of its own domestic considerations. Ambiguity sometimes can reflect a lack of agreement between States; skilled treaty negotiators use ambiguity to cloak different views on an issue, so that parties can agree on a text even if they do not agree fully on its meaning. Ambiguity in treaty provisions can also be a drafting oversight; such mistakes are more probable when treaties are drafted and negotiated hastily, late into the night, or in multilateral contexts in which State delegations might prioritize negotiating issues that are more important to their national interests rather than correcting relatively minor mistakes on ancillary issues.

Customary international law, by its nature, seems to present even greater problems of ambiguity. Customary international law is a form of law that results from the general and consistent practice of States in respect of which they have a sense of legal obligation.[13] Because customary law does not result from a single written document, different lawyers can more readily produce different interpretations of the law. Manuals can allow States to offer treaty interpretations as well as their interpretations of customary international law.

The DoD Law of War Manual denotes law of war treaty provisions applicable to the United States as well as statements of treaty interpretation drawn from a variety of sources, such as treaty analyses given to the US Senate during the US domestic process of seeking Senate advice and consent to ratification, advice given by military lawyers during military operations, and commentaries commonly relied on by practicing government lawyers.

The Manual also provides interpretation of customary international law. Perhaps most significant in this regard, it provides the Department's views on the customary rules addressed by the 1977 Additional Protocol I to the 1949

---

[12]   E.g., DoD Law of War Manual, ¶ 5.2.3.
[13]   *Ibid.*, ¶ 1.8 (citing Third Restatement of Foreign Relations Law of the United States).

Geneva Conventions (AP I).[14] The United States is not a party to AP I, which articulates a number of provisions relating to the conduct of hostilities in international armed conflicts (IACs), such as the prohibitions on targeting civilians, the principle of proportionality, and the requirements to take precautions in planning and conducting attacks.

At one point the United States was planning to seek US ratification of the AP I, and DoD lawyers developed internal plans for a proposed "all-services" law of war manual to help implement the treaty. In the early 1980s, however, the Reagan administration conducted a thorough review of the treaty and decided not to ratify the AP I. The US Government identified many concerns with the treaty, including a military review that concluded that the treaty suffered from "numerous ambiguities and defects."[15]

The Reagan administration's decision not to ratify AP I has been accepted by every subsequent US administration. Instead of ratifying AP I, the United States noted that it would explain US views on AP I provisions in due course, including through the issuance of military manuals.[16] The Manual works to fulfill that vision; for example, explaining how the Department interprets some of the fundamental, customary protections for civilians on the battlefield, which are also addressed by the provisions of AP I. To the extent possible, our goal was for the Manual to provide an interpretation of the corresponding rule under customary international law that AP I parties could also adopt as an interpretation of AP I. We are hopeful that coalition partners that are parties to the 1977 AP I will find these provisions useful in working constructively with the United States in addressing some of the ambiguities in the 1977 AP I, at least in those instances when it is necessary to work together in coalition operations. This, of course, leads to another function of law of war manuals.

---

[14] *Ibid.*, ¶ 19.20.1.
[15] Appendix to John W. Vessey, Jr., Chairman, Joint Chiefs of Staff, Review of the 1977 First Additional Protocol to the Geneva Conventions of 1949 (May 3, 1985), 97.
[16] The Sixth Annual American Red Cross–Washington College of Law Conference on International Humanitarian Law: A Workshop on Customary International Law and the 1977 Protocols Additional to the 1949 Geneva Conventions, "Session One: The United States Position on the Relation of Customary International Law to the 1977 Protocols Additional to the 1949 Geneva Conventions, Remarks of Michael J. Matheson" (1987) 2 *American University Journal of International Law and Public Policy* 415, 421("We recognize that certain provisions of Protocol I reflect customary international law or are positive new developments, which should in time become part of that law. We therefore intend to consult with our allies to develop appropriate methods of incorporating these provisions into rules that govern our military operations, with the intention that they will in time win recognition as customary international law. One obvious possible way of doing this is to develop common principles that might be incorporated into or serve as the framework for individual national military manuals.").

2.3 Facilitating Interoperability with Allies and Coalition Partners

Law of war manuals can facilitate interoperability with allies and coalition partners. States often conduct military operations as part of coalitions, but States often have different law of war obligations depending on the treaties that they have accepted. Having a single document, such as the DoD Law of War Manual, helps other States understand more fully the US military's interpretations of the law of war and in turn helps facilitate coalition operations.

In this connection, I should also mention how helpful the manuals of allies and coalition partners were to the preparation of the DoD Law of War Manual. These manuals were useful to consult for examples of State practice or legal views, as well as on matters that, although mundane, are important, such as ensuring a logical organization of chapters and determining the range of topics to be addressed. In particular, I used the office copy of the 2004 UK Joint Services Manual on the Law of Armed Conflict so much that colleagues had to tape it together when the binding fell apart.

2.4 Facilitating Consistent Legal Interpretation across the Armed Forces

A final function performed by law of war manuals is promoting the consistent interpretation and application of the law of war across the armed forces. The problem of ensuring consistency is related to the problem of ambiguity. Ambiguity in rules means that reasonable people can interpret the same rule differently. However, it is important during military operations that a State interpret its obligations consistently throughout its armed forces. For example, it could raise concerns for one commander to interpret the law to say that some detainees are classified as PoWs, while another commander interprets the law differently and says that these detainees are classified as civilians. That could lead to confusion and what appears to be an arbitrary application of the law. A single reference work facilitates a common interpretation and application of the law.

Consistency also helps facilitate interoperability with allies and coalition partners in multinational operations; the US armed forces need to speak with one voice in providing their interpretations of the law of war to coalition partners. Within DoD, issues of consistency can also arise because different components of DoD are tasked with training their respective forces on the law of war and with implementing the law of war during military operations. The Military Departments (i.e., the Departments of the Army, Navy, and Air Force) have the responsibility for training and equipping the armed forces, including training on the law of war.[17] The conduct of hostilities and military operations is under the responsibility of the Combatant Commanders, who operate in a "joint" (i.e., multi-service) manner, receiving personnel and forces from each of the Military Departments.[18]

In theory, one can see how inconsistent interpretations of the law of war between DoD components could be problematic. In the joint environment in which military operations are conducted, a Navy judge advocate could supervise subordinate lawyers from the Air Force and advise an Army commander. It would prove unworkable if some personnel adhered to one set of legal interpretations while others adhered to another. In practice, counsel from the Military Departments and the operational DoD components have communicated and coordinated frequently to avoid inconsistencies in legal interpretation. Nonetheless, having a common DoD-wide issuance in the form of the Manual facilitates everyone's work and promotes a more consistent interpretation of the law of war throughout the Department.

3 WHAT IS THE STATE PERSPECTIVE ON THE LAW OF WAR?

I thought it would be useful in an academic commentary on the DoD Law of War Manual to seek to explain what I call the "State perspective" on the law of war as compared to the perspectives generally offered by academics or NGOs. Why was it important that the Department expend the effort necessary to issue the Manual, rather than commission an academic institution or NGO to write it? Academics and NGOs can develop expertise in the law, but often they may view the law of war differently from States – which by the very definition of "international" are chiefly responsible for implementing international law.[19]

[17] US Department of Defense Directive 2311.01E (above note 10), 4–5 ("The Secretaries of the Military Departments shall develop internal policies and procedures consistent with this Directive in support of the DoD Law of War Program to: 5.8.1. Provide directives, publications, instructions, and training so the principles and rules of the law of war will be known to members of their respective Departments.").

[18] See 10 USC § 162 (providing, *inter alia*, that "[a]s directed by the Secretary of Defense, the Secretaries of the military departments shall assign specified forces under their jurisdiction to unified and specified combatant commands or to the United States element of the North American Aerospace Defense Command to perform missions assigned to those commands" and that "[u]nless otherwise directed by the President, the chain of command to a unified or specified combatant command runs – (1) from the President to the Secretary of Defense; and (2) from the Secretary of Defense to the commander of the combatant command").

[19] Compare Foreword by the International Committee of the Red Cross, J. S. Pictet, *Commentary IV Geneva Convention Relative to the Protection of Civilian Persons in Time of War* (Geneva: ICRC, 1958), 1 ("Although published by the International Committee, the Commentary is the personal work of its authors. The Committee, moreover, whenever called

Of course, among States and among academics, there will be diverse viewpoints. Nonetheless, I believe it is possible to offer a few generalizations.

Ultimately, such differences emanate from the fact that States must interpret and apply the law of war in practice – they need to use the law of war as a functional instrument for the regulation of the armed forces in hostilities. I propose three affirmative propositions of the State perspective, contrast them with scholarly viewpoints, and seek to explain the State perspective.

First, the law of war both justifies and restrains military action. Second, the law of war reflects a convergence of military and humanitarian interests. Third, the law of war lives in the character of the armed forces and their daily work, preparing for and fighting wars.

3.1 *The Law of War both Justifies and Restrains Military Action*

The aspect of the law of war that is most apparent and discussed is its protective aspect; that is, how it restrains the armed forces in the conduct of hostilities. For example, the law of war protects civilians, combatants who have surrendered, the wounded and sick, and medical personnel. But just as the law functions as a restraint or shield to protect the defenseless, it also can serve as a sword – a justification for legitimate military action. For example, the law of war can be viewed as justifying a soldier's killing of enemy combatants in war, which is not murder, but instead is privileged belligerency.[20]

It is possible to conceive of the law of war as purely a restraining body of international law that in no way contains authorities.[21] This conception is

---

upon for an opinion on a provision of an international Convention, always takes care to emphasize that only the participant States are qualified, through consultation between themselves, to give an official and, as it were, authentic interpretation of an intergovernmental treaty.").

[20] See DoD Law of War Manual, ¶ 4.4.3.

[21] See, e.g., R. R. Baxter, "So-called 'Unprivileged Belligerency': Spies, Guerrillas, and Saboteurs" (1951) 28 *British Yearbook of International Law* 323, 323–24 ("The propriety of statements that international law confers a 'right' to resort to war and to exercise 'belligerent rights' is highly questionable, and it is probably more accurate to assert that international law has dealt with war as a state of fact which it has hitherto been powerless to prevent. Animated by considerations of humanity and by the desire to prevent unnecessary suffering, states have nevertheless recognized limits on the unfettered power which they would otherwise actually enjoy in time of war. The law of war is, in the descriptive words of a war crimes tribunal, 'prohibitive law', in the sense that it forbids rather than authorizes certain manifestations of force. During the formative period of codified international law, delegates to international conferences repeatedly declared that they would not accept proposed provisions which involved acquiescence in an enemy's exercise of jurisdiction over nationals of their state. The report of the committee which dealt with the laws and usages of war to the Hague Conference of 1899 emphasized that it was not intended by Convention No. II to sanction the

more probable if one sees the law primarily as the texts of treaties intended to reflect agreed upon prohibitions and restrictions. However, States have not tended to implement the law in this way, and instead have applied the law of war as a comprehensive body of law that both justifies and restrains military action in armed conflict.

First, if the law of war lacks any authorities to take military action, then significant aspects of military operations in armed conflict are necessarily beyond the law of war. The law of war then becomes an incomplete system of law that must rely on other bodies of law to function. The practical utility of having a *lex specialis* – a body of law specifically adapted to, and useful for, regulating armed conflict – is undermined if the law of war is incomplete and lacking in necessary authorities.

Second, the functional application of the law of war in military operations (even under the view that the law of war is purely restrictive) results in legal judgments that are practically indistinguishable from judgments that military actions are authorized by the law of war.

Lawyers advise on military operations and review proposed plans, policies, or decisions for legal sufficiency. In practice, government lawyers must almost always respond; returning an answer of *non-liquet* is generally not an option. More to the point, even if the lawyers advise that the law is unclear, in practice, this answer could have a legal effect as decisions are made following receipt of counsel's best legal advice. For example, it could be the decision-maker is advised that the action may not proceed without a clear legal basis or that the action may proceed because there is no legal objection to it.[22]

Whether lawyers advise that they concur in the action as justified under the law or with the more modest assertion there is no legal objection, the practical

employment of force and that the purpose of the Convention was rather to restrict the exercise of power which an enemy might in fact wield over another state.").

22   *Cf.* H. Lauterpacht, *The Function of Law in the International Community* (Oxford: Clarendon Press, 1933), 77 ("If consent is the essential condition for the existence of a rule of international law, then a revealed and deliberate absence of agreement should clearly point to the existence of a gap on the subject. In fact, this category of gaps is regarded by some as the main instance of *lacunae* in international law. It is submitted that this view can be adopted only subject to the qualification that the gap is virtually filled when the States recognize the authority of obligatory judicial settlement. The absence of agreement does not mean that the States in question desire the controversial subject to remain altogether outside the sphere of law, so as to render it impossible for the judge to decide the case. Such a desire could not in any case produce legal effects. The utmost that can be said is that its consequence would be to leave the controversial subject out of the sphere of express legal regulation; with the result that, in the absence of an agreed rule, the judge would have to reject the demand of the plaintiff State on the ground that no evidence of a rule of international law limiting the freedom of action of the defendant State has been produced.").

result of such review may be the same. The action has been reviewed and approved by lawyers, in the context of the State's broader policy and requirements to adhere to the law of war. When lawyers reviewing military operations apply the law of war and in doing so object to some activities but not others, the inference that the non-objected-to activities are authorized is legitimately drawn and functionally results in State practice.

Third, the incorporation of the law of war into domestic law also supports the interpretation of the law of war as including authorizations for military action. A series of US Supreme Court cases, in which the law of war was used as a justification for the exercise of emergency war powers under US domestic law, exemplify this approach. In my experience, these cases have been very influential in how lawyers within the Executive have given legal advice, and they reflect how the law of war is used in practice to justify actions under domestic law.

In the Civil War-era *Prize* cases, the US Supreme Court invoked the law of war to uphold the legality of President Lincoln's seizure of property by blockading Southern ports.[23] In the World War II case *Ex parte Quirin*, the Supreme Court found the trial by military commission of German saboteurs caught inside the United States to be in accordance with the law of war and upheld such trial.[24] In 2003 in *Hamdi v. Rumsfeld*, a plurality of the Supreme Court found that the capture and detention of enemy combatants on the battlefield was an accepted law of war principle, and upheld the detention of a Taliban fighter who happened to be a US citizen.[25]

In each of these cases, serious questions were raised as to whether a US domestic law rule would prohibit the government action. In each of these cases, the Supreme Court found domestic justification in the international law of war's acceptance of the government action.

One might argue that the Supreme Court is wrong in all of these cases, and cogent arguments to this effect could constitute thoughtful and interesting scholarship. However, a practicing lawyer in the United States would need to consider these Supreme Court precedents as authoritative in giving legal advice.

It is possible to reconcile these cases with the theoretical view that the international law of war is purely restrictive by regarding the application of authorities as a product of the incorporation of the international law of war into domestic law. Under this view, the incorporation of the international law of war into domestic law also necessarily includes the sovereign's war powers as

---

[23] *The Prize Cases*, 67 US 635, 671 (1862) (finding that "the President had a right, *jure belli*, to institute a blockade of ports in possession of the States in rebellion which neutrals are bound to regard").

[24] *Ex parte Quirin*, 317 US 1, 27–46 (1942).

[25] *Hamdi v. Rumsfeld*, 542 US 507, 518–21 (2004) (plurality).

a kind of domestic appurtenance to the international restrictions to ensure that the government can fully exercise the State's sovereign powers;[26] for instance, to punish unprivileged belligerents.[27]

The more simple explanation, of course, is that States have authorities under the international law of war.[28]

3.2 *The Law of War Reflects a Convergence of Military and Humanitarian Interests*

There is an often-taught view that the law of war reflects a "balance" between the principles of military necessity and humanity. Some academics and the

---

[26] *United States v. Curtiss-Wright Export Corp.*, 299 US 304, 318 (1936) ("It results that the investment of the federal government with the powers of external sovereignty did not depend upon the affirmative grants of the Constitution. The powers to declare and wage war, to conclude peace, to make treaties, to maintain diplomatic relations with other sovereignties, if they had never been mentioned in the Constitution, would have vested in the federal government as necessary concomitants of nationality. Neither the Constitution nor the laws passed in pursuance of it have any force in foreign territory unless in respect of our own citizens; and operations of the nation in such territory must be governed by treaties, international understandings and compacts, and the principles of international law. As a member of the family of nations, the right and power of the United States in that field are equal to the right and power of the other members of the international family. Otherwise, the United States is not completely sovereign. The power to acquire territory by discovery and occupation, the power to expel undesirable aliens, the power to make such international agreements as do not constitute treaties in the constitutional sense, none of which is expressly affirmed by the Constitution, nevertheless exist as inherently inseparable from the conception of nationality. This the court recognized, and in each of the cases cited found the warrant for its conclusions not in the provisions of the Constitution, but in the law of nations." [citations omitted]).

[27] *Cf.* Case No. 11-1324, DC Circuit, *Al Bahlul v. United States*, Brief for the United States on Petition for Review from the US Court of Military Commission Review (July 10, 2013), 61–62, https://lawfare.s3-us-west-2.amazonaws.com/staging/s3fs-public/uploads/2013/07/2013-07-10-Bahlul-En-Banc-Brief-FILED.pdf ("Thus, because Congress has authority under its war powers to provide military commission jurisdiction over offenses that have traditionally been triable by military commission regardless of whether they are prohibited by international law, there is no reason to construe Article 21, contrary to its text, legislative history, and the Supreme Court's Quirin decision, as limiting military commissions' jurisdiction to violations of international law. Instead, consistent with Article 21 and the 2006 MCA, military commission jurisdiction extends to offenses committed in the context of hostilities that international law permits States to punish, and that the United States has historically punished.").

[28] Thirty-Second International Conference of the Red Cross and Red Crescent, Resolution 1, Strengthening international humanitarian law protecting persons deprived of their liberty, Geneva, Switzerland (Dec. 8–10, 2015), http://rcrcconference.org/wp-content/uploads/2015/04/32IC-AR-Persons-deprived-of-liberty_EN.pdf ("*mindful* that deprivation of liberty is an ordinary and expected occurrence in armed conflict, and that under international humanitarian law (IHL) States have, in all forms of armed conflict, both the power to detain, and the obligation to provide protection and to respect applicable legal safeguards, including against unlawful detention for all persons deprived of their liberty").

International Committee of the Red Cross (ICRC) suggest that the law reflects a tension or compromise between doing the most militarily effective thing and doing the humane thing.[29] Taken to its extreme, this view is captured in the metaphor one hears on occasion that complying with the law of war is like fighting with one hand tied around your back.

States, especially those conducting military operations, often have a different perspective. States often interpret the principle of military necessity and the principle of humanity as consistent with one another rather than in tension with one another. The Manual articulates the principles of military necessity and humanity as follows: "Military necessity may be defined as the principle that justifies the use of all measures needed to defeat the enemy as quickly and efficiently as possible that are not prohibited by the law of war."[30] "Humanity may be defined as the principle that forbids the infliction of suffering, injury, or destruction unnecessary to accomplish a legitimate military purpose."[31]

The Manual explains that "[b]ecause humanity forbids those actions that are unnecessary, the principle of humanity is not in tension with military effectiveness, but instead reinforces military effectiveness."[32] This may seem like an abstract point, but I believe it is important for two reasons. First, interpreting necessity and humanity as consistent with one another, rather than as competing imperatives, reflects the realities of war. The directive on the law of war for US armed forces during the US Civil War, approved by President Lincoln and often known as the Lieber Code, explains: "The more vigorously wars are pursued, the better it is for humanity. Sharp wars are brief."[33] Recent US operations in Iraq during 2017 illustrate this point.

---

[29]   See, e.g., M. N. Schmitt, "Military Necessity and Humanity in International Humanitarian Law: Preserving the Delicate Balance" (2010) 50 *Virginia Journal of International Law* 795, 798 ("Rather, IHL represents a carefully thought out balance between the principles of military necessity and humanity. Every one of its rules constitutes a dialectical compromise between these two opposing forces.").

[30]   DoD Law of War Manual, ¶ 2.2.   [31]   *Ibid.*, ¶ 2.3.

[32]   *Ibid.*, ¶ 2.3.1.1; see also UK Ministry of Defence, The Joint Service Manual of the Law of Armed Conflict, JSP 383 (2004), 23 ("Humanity forbids the infliction of suffering, injury, or destruction not actually necessary for the accomplishment of legitimate military purposes. The principle of humanity is based on the notion that once a military purpose has been achieved, the further infliction of suffering is unnecessary. Thus, if an enemy combatant has been put out of action by being wounded or captured, there is no military purpose to be achieved by continuing to attack him. For the same reason, the principle of humanity confirms the basic immunity of civilian populations and civilian objects from attack because civilians and civilian objects make no contribution to military action.").

[33]   Instructions for the Government of Armies of the United States in the Field: Originally Issued as General Orders No. 100, Adjutant General's Office, 1863, 11, ¶ 29 (1898), www.loc.gov/rr/frd/Military_Law/Lieber_Collection/pdf/Instructions-gov-armies.pdf.

Lieutenant General Townsend, then serving as Commander of Operation Inherent Resolve, was asked about collateral damage while attacking Islamic State in Iraq and Syria (ISIS) targets inside Mosul. He replied:

> Yes. So, there's a significant amount of destruction on the west side. I think probably double the destruction from the east side. We had 100 days of combat on the east side. And towards the end of that 100 days, the FLOT [forward line of our own troops] advanced, the friendly forces advanced very rapidly. And what we've learned is that the faster the friendly troops advance, the less destruction of infrastructure there is and the fewer civilian lives are lost.
>
> When – when fronts become stationary, and you have two modern – relatively modern forces with high explosives slugging it out for a period of days on a stationary front, it – the destruction just skyrockets and so do civilian casualties, and casualties on both sides of the fight.[34]

General Townsend's observation should offer a note of caution to those who would seek to add as many restrictions as possible to the armed forces during military operations. Although their intentions may be humanitarian, the consequences of interpretations of the law of war that do not permit belligerents to win wars quickly and with less overall collateral damage may needlessly exacerbate overall damage and human suffering.

A second practical reason for interpreting military necessity and humanity as consistent with one another is that this is a more persuasive, and therefore more effective, way of formulating the law. US Supreme Court Justice, Robert Jackson, served as the Attorney General for President Roosevelt right before World War II and served as a Supreme Court Justice during World War II. Justice Jackson, reflecting on civil liberties and national security after the war, observed that "if the people come deeply to feel that civil rights are being successfully turned against their institutions by their enemies, they will react by becoming enemies of civil rights."[35] Justice Jackson's insight was that, despite the stirring passion of Patrick Henry's cry, most people will not pick civil rights over safety. I think a similar principle applies here. Telling members of the armed forces that they need to compromise their military effectiveness is not rhetorically the best approach for maximizing compliance with the law of war.

---

[34] Operation Inherent Resolve, "Remarks by General Townsend in a media availability in Baghdad, Iraq" (July 11, 2017), www.inherentresolve.mil/News/Article/1249025/remarks-by-general-townsend-in-a-media-availability-in-baghdad-iraq/.

[35] R. H. Jackson, "Wartime Security and Liberty Under Law" (1951) 1 *Buffalo Law Review* 103, 116.

Of course, it is important to emphasize that complying with the law is necessary because it is the right thing to do, regardless of immediate considerations of military effectiveness. However, we can support the broadest possible respect for and compliance with the law of war, not just through appeals to saints and heroes, but if we also explain why complying with the law is in the military interest.[36]

3.3 *The Law of War Lives in the Character of the Armed Forces and their Daily Work, Preparing for and Fighting War*

Most scholars will approach the law of war from the perspective of a treaty text. Often scholars interpret the law of war using opinions from war crimes trials. Although these are part of the law, I think that an undue focus on these instantiations of the law results in an inaccurate understanding of it. Most people who are subject to the law of war are not war criminals, and most people do not read the treaties.

For States, the law of war lives in the character of the armed forces, and their daily work, preparing for and fighting war. This is the dark matter of the law of war, the part of the universe, largely invisible to scholars, but exerting its gravitational influence to hold everything together.

The Manual emphasizes the principle of honor, and in the second update (December 2016), citations were added to help explain the importance of honor in the implementation of the law of war. The Manual cites the following discussion by the historian John Keegan to explain the importance of honor in implementing the law of war:

> There is no substitute for honour as a medium of enforcing decency on the battlefield, never has been and never will be. There are no judges, more to the point, no policemen at the place where death is done in combat; that may be, in fact, the intended and all too often true, meaning of "silent leges inter arma". All turns on the values of the junior leader present at the moment when the opponent's capacity or will to resist fails,

---

[36] See DoD Law of War Manual, ¶ 8.4.1 fn. 52 citing Department of the Army Field Manual 34–52, "Intelligence Interrogation" (Sept. 28, 1992), 1–8 ("Experience indicates that the use of prohibited techniques is not necessary to gain the cooperation of interrogation sources. Use of torture and other illegal methods is a poor technique that yields unreliable results, may damage subsequent collection efforts and can induce the source to say what he thinks the interrogator wants to hear. Revelation of use of torture by US personnel will bring discredit upon the US and its armed forces while undermining domestic and international support for the war effort. It also may place US and allied personnel in enemy hands at a greater risk of abuse by their captors.").

he ceases to be a combatant and he must hope for the mercy of the suddenly stronger.[37]

The second update also included a quote from Hugh Thompson, a US Army helicopter pilot who stopped a massacre of civilians during the Vietnam War. He put himself in harm's way immediately to save a number of civilians from being killed. He then reported the incident, which stopped a larger massacre. When Mr. Thompson was asked why he behaved differently from others that day, he replied:

> No, I don't believe it was any military training, because I had been through the training that everybody else had been. We had a 50-minute class of instruction on the Geneva Convention, a 50-minute class of instruction on the Code of Conduct, and a 50-minute class of instruction on the rules of engagement ... But [my parents] always taught me to help the underdog. Don't be a bully and live by the golden rule. That golden rule says so much, and it's so simple and so basic. You know, I can't say it was a leadership 405 or whatever. I just think it was my parents, and they taught me right from wrong.[38]

I hope that readers take away from these sources the understanding that, on the battlefield, people comply with the law of war because compliance reflects the standards of the military profession or because they have otherwise internalized its values; the law of war is part of who they are.[39] I also hope that readers recognize that law of war implementation for States is too important a task to be left to lawyers alone. Lawyers are advising commanders, who are responsible for implementing the law of war within their commands. Lawyers are training military members, who must respect the law's commands during military operations.

I urge scholars seeking to understand, and advocacy groups seeking to improve, the real-world implementation of the law of war to consider that the principle of honor, the professional ethics of the armed forces, and improving best practices and policies can be more effective in increasing compliance than other approaches, such as the promulgation of new instruments or more war crimes trials.

---

[37] DoD Law of War Manual, ¶ 2.6.1 fn. 109 citing J. Keegan, "If You Won't, We Won't: Honour and the Decencies of Battle," The Times Literary Supplement, Issue 4834 (Nov. 24, 1995), 11.

[38] DoD Law of War Manual, ¶ 2.6.1 fn. 109 citing "Moral Courage in Combat: The My Lai Story," Lecture by Hugh Thompson, US Naval Academy Center for Professional Military Ethics, 2003, 26.

[39] DoD Law of War Manual, foreword.

4 ADVICE ON DRAFTING, COORDINATING, AND ISSUING A LAW OF WAR MANUAL

I would like to conclude by offering some lessons learned from the process of producing the Manual. The effort to produce it was not only an effort to collect the knowledge of DoD on the law of war, but also a bureaucratic process to articulate and explain the Department's official views. Many will be familiar with bureaucratic coordination procedures in which one office that issues a statement or document will need the approval of other offices in the government before the document can be issued. A similar procedure was applied to all the more than 1,200 pages of the Manual before it was formally promulgated by the DoD General Counsel.[40]

The bureaucratic challenge of coordinating the drafts was probably much more difficult than the epistemic one of collecting treaty provisions, commentaries, and legal precedents. But, in my opinion, this bureaucratic difficulty resulted in a great strength of the Manual. As I've noted in other remarks:

> The military services each have different perspectives on the law of war, which are based in different cultures and operational domains. Lawyers also brought different perspectives from their different experiences and roles, *e.g.*, training military personnel or advising commanders during military operations. Trainers tend to want clear lines to teach their trainees; advisors often recognize that nuance and ambiguity in rules can mean more legally available options for their commander or policymaker. Similarly, war crimes prosecutors sometimes see the law of war differently from their colleagues defending the United States against allegations of war criminality.[41]

The different offices and the different experiences of the many lawyers who reviewed the manual strengthened the manual by ensuring it more accurately reflects the many ways the law of war is practiced within the Department.

---

[40] "US and International Perspectives on the New US Department of Defense Law of War Manual, Remarks by Karl Chang" (2016) 110 *Proceedings of the American Society of International Law Annual Meeting* 115 ("The general counsel is supported in the preparation of the manual by a working group, which includes representatives from key international and operational law offices in the Pentagon – Army, Navy, Air Force, and Marine Corps, and the Legal Counsel to the Chairman of the Joint Chiefs of Staff. Roughly the process worked like this. The DoD Office of General Counsel circulated drafts; other members of the working group gave comments. We incorporated the comments and circulated revised drafts for further comment. We repeated this process for approximately 1,200 pages, until staff lawyers could recommend to each's principal official (*e.g.*, The Judge Advocate General of the Army) that she concur in the manual. Lawyers from the Department of State and the Department of Justice also gave very helpful comments. After the principal-level lawyers reviewed, the General Counsel signed the promulgation memorandum.").

[41] *Ibid.*, 115–16.

Below are my lessons learned during the process of drafting and coordinating the DoD Law of War Manual (June 2015) and the two updates promulgated in 2016. I hope that others working on similar publications find these notes to be useful.

Goals and Assumptions:

1. The manual should facilitate the giving of accurate and timely legal advice to commanders, policy-makers, and other personnel.
2. The manual should reflect the government's official views.
3. The manual should help people who are not experts in the law of war.

    a. It should contain all the applicable rules.
    b. It should give examples of lawful and unlawful conduct.
    c. It should provide reasoning and explanation.

Key Challenges:

1. Coordinating the manual among the variety of offices with responsibilities relating to the law of war within the government. For example, practitioners in the Department of Justice or the Department of State may express views on the law of war in litigation or in diplomatic fora.
2. Presenting coherent and consistent legal views throughout the manual.
    a. It is difficult to be coherent and consistent over a broad range of subjects and an entire field of law, especially the law of war. The same legal rule might be worded differently in different legal instruments. Moreover, often the same legal issues may arise in different factual contexts (*e.g.*, naval or air operations).
    b. Consistency is a particularly difficult problem because there will be many persons commenting and contributing edits. Moreover, different authors or offices may have different legal positions that they will seek to advance in the process.
3. Devoting sufficient resources to accomplish this project, given the day-to-day requirements.

    a. Without senior leaders prioritizing the publication of the manual, it is unlikely that sufficient resources will be devoted to its completion. In any event, the manual should be in fact, and also be viewed as, authoritative legal guidance sound legal interpretation and not as a political or policy document.

b. Those preparing the manual need sufficient time solely devoted to that project to complete it. However, to make the manual most useful to practitioners, the staff preparing the manual should be those who are familiar with government's views and the challenges of day-to-day practice.

Recommendations:

1. Include discussion of the authorities to conduct military operations under the law of war (*e.g.*, giving examples of activities that have been commonly justified in past operations).
    a. Treaty provisions are generally framed in terms of restrictions on authorities, which can be viewed as part of customary law.
    b. Nonetheless, in practice, it can be very useful for practitioners to understand what the government considers the relevant authority to be.
2. Use the manual primarily to compile existing legal positions that have been developed and tested in past cases, rather than as a vehicle to issue new policy statements or new legal interpretations.
    a. As a matter of bureaucratic process, the more new statements the manual contains, the more difficult it will be to coordinate the draft among offices because such new policy or legal statements will have to be vetted.
    b. As a substantive matter, a common law approach that respects past precedents developed by the government is likely to be more accurate and serve the practitioner's need for clear guidance on existing legal interpretations as necessary to advise commanders, rather than aspirational language suggesting how the law should develop prospectively. If the manual is a vehicle for progressive development, it might burden the armed forces with impractical requirements that were developed in the abstract or remove time-tested restrictions that have worked in preventing poor application of and uneven compliance with the law of war.
    c. *Draft sentences about government views in the past tense.* This way, if there are developments or new views, those can be added, while the sentences describing past views remain accurate in stating what was previously done (which may remain relevant to a full understanding of a given principle).

d. When progressive legal development is warranted, use other processes that are tailored to include the relevant stakeholders to
address those developments, and incorporate the results of those
processes into the manual. Different issues implicate different institutional actors, so allowing development of new positions to occur
in different processes is more likely to be bureaucratically efficient.
3. Be comprehensive in providing all rules that the government will need
to apply.
   a. If applicable rules are omitted, then practitioners cannot rely on the
   manual as a sort-of checklist of all the potential issues that may need
   to be addressed.
   b. *Include even the rules that the drafters may find dull and unin-
   teresting.* It will be tempting to focus on the interesting issues of
   debate and discussion, but these are the types of issues for which
   the manual will be less necessary in the sense that many practitioners will be familiar with the complexities of those legal
   problems. Users are more likely to need to consult a reference
   work to find information about the more obscure and arcane
   subjects.
   c. *Include pertinent references to domestic law or policy, where such law
   or policy serves as the more pertinent constraint that practitioners
   must apply.*
4. Make the text intelligible to persons without expertise in the law of war.
   a. *Give the black letter rules at the beginning of sections.*
   b. *Have the text clearly indicate what the black letter legal rules are.*
      i. The 1956 Army Field Manual 27–10, the Law of Land Warfare,
      used bold type to indicate when treaty provisions were provided
      verbatim.
      ii. The DoD Law of War Manual tries to adhere exactly to the
      language of relevant treaties, with minor updates to make the
      language more clear or gender neutral, and we include the
      verbatim treaty language in footnotes.
   c. *Use examples, especially examples drawn from actual practice.*
   d. Explain differences of view or debates over issues.
   e. Explain different usages of terminology.
   f. Convey clear positions, or if the manual interprets the law to contain
   an ambiguity, then clearly convey that the law has such ambiguity.
   g. Have non-experts read drafts with a view toward understanding
   a difficult area of the law or using the draft to find more information
   about a practical issue or problem.

5. Organize the content of the manual according to the legal rules rather than according to the factual situations in which the rules may be presented.

   a. *Try to put each legal rule in only one place and provide all relevant information about it in that one place. When that legal rule is relevant in other places in the manual, cross-reference this discussion, rather than duplicate it.*

   b. Ideally, all of the related language about a legal rule would be linked in the text – either in one place in the text or through cross-references.

      i. This facilitates the reader understanding the rule and finding all relevant discussion.

      ii. This facilitates keeping the manual internally consistent.

      iii. This facilitates updating of the manual, as there are fewer places where the text will need to be updated, and the editors can use the links in the manual to issue any corrections or elaborations to all relevant sections.

   c. The problem to avoid is extensive discussion of the same legal rule in different places in the manual. If those discussions are different, then the reader is left wondering which section is controlling. If those discussions are not linked in the text, then some readers might only find one section, while other readers might only find the other.

6. Work on the specific discussion first and the general discussion later, or finalize the general discussion only after finalizing the specific discussion.

   a. This helps ensure consistency between the general discussion of the law and the more specific treatments.

   b. For example, our Chapter 2 discusses law of war principles and references other rules throughout the manual. Although we drafted Chapter 2 before the other chapters, we had to revise it again substantially after working through the remainder of the manual.

7. Use citations.

   a. Citations will facilitate coordination and allow for a better understanding of the document.

   b. The reviewers from different offices can see where language originated (*e.g.*, Pictet Commentary, U.S. Government statement of interpretation) and may be less likely to object to the language because they have that background.

c. Citations and explanatory notes can be helpful even if not ultimately included in the final publication because they allow for the preservation of a drafting history of the document. For example, we consulted an annotated draft of the 1956 Army Field Manual 27–10 on the Law of Land Warfare, which contains rationale for the changes from the previous edition as well as citations of relevant cases or other sources.

d. The law of war is sometimes taught or understood idiosyncratically. Making a practice of using citations reduces the risk that there will be debates over what academic characterization is correct without objective evidence to help resolve the debate.

e. Human memory is generally imprecise and unreliable. Using citations and sources will aid in the rigor of a large work, especially when the work reflects factual statements about past operations or past legal positions stated by the government.

8. Understand the difference between individual and institutional views.

a. Have staff working on the manual understand that the manual is to reflect the institutional views of the government. If the publication is at odds with the government's official views, then it is not useful to practitioners and could pose problems for the government (*e.g.*, it could be cited against the government in litigation).

b. Bureaucracies can operate inefficiently in terms of how offices represent their institutional views. Some of the comments that people will provide in coordination processes will be their own personal comments and be either independent of, or not fully aligned with, the interests of their organization. Understanding what issues offices will ultimately place great importance on (*e.g.*, because the issue relates to core institutional responsibilities of that office) is critical.

9. Have a team of reviewers who review and edit the entire publication to ensure consistency and coherency between chapters.

a. The only way to ensure that the document is internally consistent and coherent is to have a person (or ideally multiple persons) review the entire manual with that purpose in mind.

b. Widely circulate drafts and welcome edits and comments on drafts within the government.

i. Widely circulating drafts allows more people to spot issues and inconsistencies.

ii. Widely circulating drafts, especially at an early stage, prevents people from objecting on the basis that they have not had sufficient time to review the drafts.

10. Listen to comments and use them as opportunities to improve the text.
    a. Especially when one has drafted a text, there is a psychological reflex to reject criticisms and comments. That can be the easiest course of action and, when one is charged with facilitating the process, there is some capacity to reject comments because sometimes people will accept your rejection of their comment.
    b. However, it is generally time well spent to work to address and incorporate every comment or criticism. Even if one finds a comment not to be very good, there is probably some version of the comment that is insightful. Spin straw into gold. Try to find the most insightful and persuasive point that a comment would have made and to address that criticism, and the end result will be improved.
    c. Similarly, when divergent comments or perspectives are offered, think of creative ways to reflect underlying perspectives or divergences of views, as this will be useful to the reader, rather than adopting a "lowest common denominator" approach.

3

Specifically Vague: The Defensive Purpose of the DoD Law of War Manual

Chris Jenks[*]

The purpose of this manual is to provide information on the law of war to DoD personnel responsible for implementing the law of war and executing military operations.[1]

1 INTRODUCTION

The US Department of Defense (DoD) first published the 1,193-page Law of War Manual (the Manual) on June 12, 2015. The long-awaited Manual was the result of more than twenty years of writing, peer review, revisions and editing. Striking an appropriate balance between the pragmatic needs of commanders and lawyers and the larger purpose of consolidating US perspectives was an ambitious undertaking from the outset. The process was painstaking and often polarized to the point that at times it was unclear whether the Manual would be published at all despite the significant investment of time and expertise. To the amusement of some and the chagrin of others, the Manual seemed perpetually forthcoming.

The delays in publishing the Manual were problematic and increasingly embarrassing. They were problematic because at the same time the United States was seemingly unable to publish its own manual, it did not have difficulty in commenting unfavorably on publications of the International

---

[*] In the interests of full disclosure, while working as the Army's International Law Branch chief the author attended a small number of Law of War Working Group Meetings at which versions of the Manual were discussed. Other than a general memory of having attended, the author did not play any role in the development of any of the Manual's versions. This chapter focuses on the Manual as published. The author does not seek to distinguish or prioritize between Manual versions and has only relied on publicly available source material.

[1] DoD Law of War Manual, ¶ 1.1.1.

Committee of the Red Cross (ICRC). The delays later become embarrassing as the long-serving primary drafter of the Manual shifted from delivering public remarks that the Manual would be published in mere months to openly lamenting the Manual's demise and criticizing nearly every person and agency involved in its development.

More importantly, by the time the Manual was published, the US military had been engaged in armed conflict in Afghanistan since 2001, fought for over a decade in Iraq, and had begun fighting Islamic State in Iraq and Syria (ISIS) on several fronts. The international nature of those first two armed conflicts was short-lived: the United States and its coalition partners toppled Taliban-ruled Afghanistan in roughly twelve weeks and Saddam Hussein's Iraq in less than six. Armed conflict most certainly continued, but in a non-international, and thus much more complex, form. The US and other countries partnered with the new interim governments of Afghanistan and Iraq to fight insurgencies comprised of non-State actors. In terms of the fight against ISIS, that has been a non-international armed conflict (NIAC) from the start. Significantly, while there is a robust amount of the law of armed conflict (LOAC) that applies in international armed conflict (IAC), there is relatively little operable NIAC law. The changing character of armed conflict in the modern era was one of the driving factors at the outset of drafting yet delays diluted its usefulness.

The confluence of the US military's prolonged engagement in the type of armed conflicts for which there is correspondingly much less law amplified both the need for, and importance of, a contemporary Manual that applied across DoD. This chapter suggests that what US military commanders and their legal advisors needed (and wanted) was for the Manual to provide specific guidance as to the LOAC applicable to US armed forces during NIAC. This chapter assesses how effectively the Manual met its stated purpose to "provide information on the law of war to DoD personnel responsible for implementing the law of war and executing military operations"[2] as applied to two important issues in NIAC: customary international law (CIL) and detention.

Section 2 of this chapter highlights the gap the Manual needed to fill as the result of the limited LOAC that applies to NIACs. Sections 3 and 4 explain why the Manual's guidance on CIL and detention respectively is too general to meaningfully inform those executing military operations. Section 5 details internal and external factors that limited, or perhaps prevented, the Manual's ability to better meet its purpose.

[2] *Ibid.*

2 INVERSE RELATIONSHIP OF APPLICABLE LOAC TO FREQUENCY OF ARMED CONFLICT

International law is clear that armed conflict waged in any form between two or more nation-States is legally termed IAC.[3] The existence of an IAC triggers the largest amount of the LOAC applicable as a matter of law, generally expressed in a range of applicable treaty provisions.[4] The LOAC applicable to and during IAC, as a matter of law, includes all four of the 1949 Geneva Conventions[5] and a series of eighteen Hague Conventions from 1899 and 1907.[6]

As noted above, however, the armed conflicts in Afghanistan and Iraq quickly transitioned to NIACs. The conflict with ISIS (or Da'esh as it is termed in the region) was non-international from its outset. Regardless of how many States are on one side, if they are not opposed by another State the armed conflict is a NIAC.[7] There is very little LOAC that applies as a matter of law to all NIACs – but one article of the 1949 Geneva Conventions, which deals with armed conflict "not of an international character."[8] And while those

---

[3] See ICRC, "How Is the Term 'Armed Conflict' Defined in International Humanitarian Law?" Opinion Paper (Mar. 2008).

[4] See Geneva Convention Relative to the Treatment of Prisoners of War, Art. 2, Aug. 12, 1949, 6 UST 3316, 75 UNTS 135 (GC III) (stating that "the present convention shall apply to all cases of declared war or any other armed conflict which may arise between two or more high contracting parties, even if the state of war is not recognized by one of them"). The United States, Afghanistan, and Iraq, like other States, have either signed and ratified or acceded to the 1949 Geneva Conventions. Chapter XIX of the Manual describes in some detail the treaty provisions applicable to US forces as well as the range of reservations taken to those treaty provisions upon accession.

[5] The 1949 Geneva Conventions deal with the wounded and sick in armed forces in the field. See Geneva Convention for the Amelioration of the Condition of the Wounded and Sick in Armed Forces in the Field, Art. 3, Aug. 12, 1949, 6 UST 3114, 75 UNTS 31; Geneva Convention for the Amelioration of the Condition of Wounded, Sick and Shipwrecked Members of Armed Forces at Sea, Art. 3, Aug. 12, 1949, 6 UST. 3217, 75 UNTS 85 (wounded, sick and shipwrecked members of the armed forces at sea); see GC III (above note 4); Geneva Convention Relative to the Protection of Civilian Persons in Time of War, Art. 3, Aug. 12, 1949, 6 UST 3516, 75 UNTS 287 (protection of civilians). International armed conflict also triggers the application of Protocol Additional to the Geneva Conventions of Aug. 12, 1949, and Relating to the Protection of Victims of International Armed Conflicts, June 8, 1977, 1125 UNTS 3 (AP I) for those States which have agreed to be bound by it.

[6] Convention (II) with Respect to the Laws and Customs of War on Land, July 29, 1899, USTS 403, 32 Stat. 1803, 1 Bevans 247.

[7] See, generally, S. Sivakumaran, *The Law of Non-International Conflict* (Oxford University Press, 2012).

[8] GC III (above note 4). Additional Protocol II (AP II) to the 1949 Geneva Conventions applies to NIACs, but only binds States Party. The comparison between the size of AP I, which applies to IAC, and AP II, which applies to NIAC, is striking. AP I is some eighty-two pages long; AP II is ten pages.

provisions (known as Common Article 3) are significant in that they require humane treatment of vulnerable persons, as well as a baseline of other express protections, they comprise but one article.[9]

The paucity of law applicable to NIACs creates a profound regulatory gap. This problem is exacerbated because NIACs occur far more frequently than IACs.[10] For the US military engaged in NIACs, two areas in which detailed DoD guidance through the Manual would have been appreciated by practitioners and lawyers are CIL and detention.

3 CIL

3.1 The US Approach to CIL

There are a range of possible responses to the dearth of LOAC applicable in NIAC. One possible response is to apply CIL, but doing so requires a State to clarify what rules it considers binding as a matter of CIL in lieu of specifically applicable treaty provisions. The Manual recognizes the potential role of CIL, but never specifies what that CIL is. In particular, the gaps in specifically extending key provisions of AP I to NIAC as a matter of US acceptance is striking. This represents a missed opportunity to inform those in DoD who implement LOAC and execute military operations, as well as in providing clear signals to US allies.

The Statute of the International Court of Justice describes customary international law as "a general practice accepted as law."[11] The existence of CIL "requires the presence of two elements, namely State practice (usus) and a belief that such practice is required, prohibited or allowed, depending on the nature of the rule, as a matter of law (*opinio juris sive necessitates*)."[12]

---

9   See M. A. Newton, "Contorting Common Article 3: Reflections on the Revised ICRC Commentary" (2017) 45 *Georgia Journal of International and Comparative Law* 513. Article 3 of the 1949 Geneva Conventions is known as Common Art. 3 because its text and placement are identical in all four 1949 Conventions. "The Geneva Conventions of 1949 and their Additional Protocols," ICRC Overview (Nov. 29, 2010), www.icrc.org/eng/war-and-law/treaties-customary-law/geneva-conventions/overview-geneva-conventions.htm. Common Art. 3 requires that those no longer actively participating in hostilities, the wounded and the sick be humanely treated and cared for. *Ibid.* The article also prohibits cruel, inhumane and degrading treatment and torture. *Ibid.*

10 E. Melander, "Organized Violence in the World 2015: An Assessment by the Uppsala Conflict Data Program," UCDP Paper 9 (2015), 3. Indeed estimates are that over the past fifty years, over 90 percent of the armed conflicts have been NIACs.

11 Statute of the International Court of Justice, Art. 38, para. 1(b).

12 The International Law Commission began an exhaustive study of the field in 2012. See Resolution adopted by the General Assembly on 14 Dec. 2012 [on the report of the Sixth

Customary international law consists "of rules that come from a general practice accepted as law and exist independent of treaty law."[3] While all countries acknowledge CIL's existence, beyond a limited number of peremptory norms there are varied understandings of what rules are or are not considered CIL.[4] The United States, like other countries, generally does not feel the need to detail what rules are considered to be formally binding as a matter of CIL.[5] While understandable on some levels, the refusal to inform DoD practitioners of the precise scope of rules the United States considers as CIL is not helpful. Rather than inform, the Manual only expands an unfortunate practice of claiming that DoD complies with CIL, without ever clarifying what those rules are.

In 2006, DoD issued a directive to "update the policies and responsibilities ensuring DoD compliance with the law of war obligations of the United States."[6] The directive defined the law of war as:

> That part of international law that regulates the conduct of armed hostilities. It is often called the "law of armed conflict." The law of war encompasses all international law for the conduct of hostilities binding on the United States or its individual citizens, including treaties and international agreements to which the United States is a party, and applicable customary international law.[7]

The directive then announced that it is DoD policy that "[m]embers of the DoD Components comply with the law of war during all armed conflicts,

Committee (A/67/467)], 67/92. Report of the International Law Commission on the work of its sixty-third and sixty-fourth sessions, UN Doc. A/Res/67/93, Jan. 14, 2013. At the time of this writing, the Special Rapporteur, Sir Michael Wood of the UK has produced and submitted five interim reports to the Commission: http://legal.un.org/ilc/guide/1_13.shtml. As the ICRC notes, "[t]he exact meaning of the two elements [of CIL] has been the subject of much academic writing." ICRC Customary International Law Study.

[13] ICRC, "Customary International Humanitarian Law" (Oct. 29, 2010), www.icrc.org/en/docu ment/customary-international-humanitarian-law-0: Customary international law "is of crucial importance in today's armed conflicts because it fills gaps left by treaty law in both international and non-international conflicts and so strengthens the protection offered to victims."

[14] See E. de Wet, "*Jus Cogens* and Obligations *Erga Omnes*," in D. Shelton (ed.), *The Oxford Handbook on Human Rights* (Oxford University Press, 2013), 543 (*jus cogens* norms include genocide, slavery, crimes against humanity, torture, piracy, and racial discrimination).

[15] The United States is not just coy about what it considers CIL, it is contradictory. In 1987, the Deputy Legal Advisor at the Department of State claimed that the United States considered Art. 75 of AP I as CIL. See S. L. Hodgkinson, "Detention Operations: A Strategic View," in G. S. Corn, R. E. van Landingham, and S. R. Reeves (eds.), *U.S. Military Operations: Law, Policy & Practice* (Oxford University Press, 2016), 275, 281: "This position was refuted during the early years of the War on Terror but later reinstated in 2011."

[16] DoD Directive 2311.01E, DoD Law of War Program (2006) (DoD Directive).

[17] *Ibid.*, para. 1.1.

however such conflicts are characterized, and in all other military operations."[18] Given the definition of the law of war, the application of the policy means, among other things, that the United States military complies with CIL while engaged in military operations. But the directive never clarifies what rules are CIL.[19] While clarifying CIL in a relatively short directive is perhaps unrealistic, the Manual could have played an important role.

3.2 *The DoD Manual on CIL*

With respect to current views on CIL, the Manual accepts "many of the rules applicable to non-international armed conflict are found in customary international law."[20] However, rather than list what those rules might be, even as a matter of policy, it merely provides guidelines which "may be helpful in assessing" the CIL applicable to NIAC.[21]

The guidelines include:

1. Use of Law of War Principles to Discern Rules Applicable to NIAC
2. Considered Absence of a Restriction in NIAC
3. Application of IAC Rules by Analogy
4. Application of Law Enforcement Rules.[22]

Thus, far from providing answers, the Manual directs the reader to conduct four different inquiries. The answers to each guideline could reasonably vary depending on who is conducting the inquiry. The result would seem to be the very real and unhelpful potential for legal inconsistency within DoD.

As only one example of many possibilities to demonstrate the way that DoD could have set forth much clearer guidance, the position that Article 75 of AP I is accepted by the United States as being binding during IAC is explicit. The Manual states that:

---

[18]   *Ibid.*, para. 4.1.
[19]   The 2006 version revised and reissued the directive which had been previously published in 1998. DoD Directive 5100.77, DoD Law of War Program (1998) (1998 Directive). The 1998 version revised the 1979 version of DoD's Law of War Program Directive. *Ibid.*, 1. The 1998 and 2006 memos share an identical definition of the law of war. *Cf.* the 1998 Directive with the DoD Directive. However, the 1998 memo policy was much more limited in scope, announcing only that "the law of war obligations of the United States are observed and enforced by the DoD Components." *Ibid.* Such language is superfluous as what it means is the United States is bound by that law to which it has agreed to be bound. M. S. Paulsen, "The Constitutional Power to Interpret International Law" (2009) 118 *Yale Law Journal* 1762, 1813. This is, of course, the case regardless of a policy memo.
[20]   DoD Law of War Manual, ¶ 17.2.2.   [21]   *Ibid.*   [22]   *Ibid.*

Article 75 of AP I reflects fundamental guarantees for the treatment of persons detained during international armed conflict. Although not a Party to AP I, the United States has stated that the U.S. Government will choose out of a sense of legal obligation to treat the principles set forth in Article 75 as applicable to any individual it detains in an international armed conflict, and expects all other nations to adhere to these principles as well. This statement was intended to contribute to the crystallization of the principles contained in Article 75 as rules of customary international law applicable in international armed conflict.[23]

In another section, the Manual states that "the foundational principles of the law of war are common to both international and non-international armed conflict."[24] Andrew Clapham observes in Chapter 13 of this book that DoD missed an opportunity to provide consistency and credibility to its operations during NIAC by extending Article 75 into NIAC as a matter of CIL. This simple expedient, which the footnote admits would be "consistent" with US "policies and practice and is one that the United States has historically supported," would have aligned US practice plainly to that of all North Atlantic Treaty Organization (NATO) Allies. In other words, providing multiple interpretative guidelines and directing the reader to assess which CIL rule may apply is not particularly helpful to those executing military operations. Reasonable military legal advisors might well apply those guidelines differently, problematically yielding different answers as to applicable CIL.

4 MANUAL ON DETENTION

Within NIACs, one of the most challenging issues military commanders and their legal advisors face is detention. This may be the area where DoD guidance was most needed. In the Manual's NIAC chapter, detention nevertheless warrants one page and the important issue of nonpunitive detention one brief paragraph.

The Manual makes the significant claim that nonpunitive or security detention "may be conducted on a variety of legal theories under international

---

[23] *Ibid.*, ¶ 8.1.4.2 (Art. 75 of AP I and Relevant AP II Provisions).

[24] *Ibid.*, ¶ 17.1.2.2 (the footnote favorably cites the landmark *Tadić* case for the proposition that "Indeed, elementary considerations of humanity and common sense make it preposterous that the use by States of weapons prohibited in armed conflicts between themselves be allowed when States try to put down rebellion by their own nationals on their own territory. What is inhumane, and consequently proscribed, in international wars, cannot but be inhumane and inadmissible in civil strife." *Prosecutor v. Tadić*, Case No. IT-94-1-A, Decision on the Defense Motion for Interlocutory Appeal on Jurisdiction, ¶ 119 (ICTY, Appeal Chamber, Oct. 2, 1995)).

law" yet the support for that proposition is a single reference to British practice during the 1950s Mau Mau rebellion.[25] To be clear, the Manual does contain a standalone or separate detention chapter. This chapter provides useful information, but is only twenty-two pages out of an 1,176-page Manual, providing neither sufficient depth nor detail.[26] By contrast, the Prisoner of War chapter[27] addressing detention during IAC is 119 pages long and unhelpfully detailed, providing a breakdown of how many Swiss francs different-ranked PoWs should receive in advance pay (while acknowledging that no country has ever implemented such an advance-pay plan)[28] and listing the antiquated requirement of access to telegraph.[29]

The detention chapter states that "it may be appropriate to apply the principles of the [Geneva Conventions], even when the relevant provisions do not apply as a matter of law."[30] Yet the Manual doesn't clarify what those principles are. Finally, while the detention chapter also briefly discusses the process by which the United States reviews security detention, it does so in generalities and through references to the Copenhagen Process.[31] This is particularly perplexing as DoD has developed a Periodic Review Secretariat which "develops and administers the periodic review process for eligible Guantánamo Bay detainees."[32] The Periodic Review Secretariat is the result of an Executive Order President Obama signed on March 7, 2011, over four years before DoD published the Manual.[33] Indeed by the time of the Manual's publication, the Periodic Review Secretariat had conducted initial, file, and full reviews of eligible detainees. Not only does the Manual not include (or even mention) that information, it states in generalized language that there is no fixed requirement for the frequency of reviews and provides a list of factors for readers to answer detention review questions DoD has elsewhere already answered.[34]

Thus the Manual to some degree fails to achieve its stated purpose of providing information to those executing military operations, at least in terms of the operation CIL and detention in NIAC.[35] It's not that the

---

[25] DoD Law of War Manual, ¶ 17.17.1.1.   [26] *Ibid.*, Chapter VIII.   [27] *Ibid.*, Chapter IX.
[28] *Ibid.*, ¶ 9.18.3.1.   [29] *Ibid.*, ¶ 9.24.4.6.   [30] *Ibid.*, ¶ 8.1.4.4.
[31] *Ibid.*, ¶ 8.1.4.5. See B. "Ossie" Oswald and T. Winkler, "Guidelines on the Handling of Detainees in International Military Operations," *American Society of International Law Insights* (Dec. 26, 2012), www.asil.org/insights/volume/16/issue/39/copenhagen-process-principles-and-guidelines-handling-detainees (describing the background and significance of the guidelines).
[32] DoD, Periodic Review Secretariat, http://www.prs.mil/.
[33] Exec. Order No. 13567, 76 Fed. Reg. 13277 (Mar. 7, 2011).
[34] DoD Law of War Manual, ¶ 8.14.2.
[35] Without question the Manual makes a number of important, positive, contributions both substantively and process-wise. The substantive contributions include robust sections on the

Manual does not attempt to achieve its stated purpose but rather that it also sought to accommodate a variety of implacable factors which were, to varying degrees, incongruous with providing useful information to the DoD personnel implementing the law of war and executing military operations.

5 COMPETING FACTORS AND PURPOSES

5.1 Internal

5.1.1 Within DoD

The Manual's creation was itself a saga, spanning decades and with no shortage of drama. According to the Manual itself, the idea for the manual originated in the 1970s and "may be traced to work in the late 1980s."[36] On November 18, 2010, the original primary author, Hays Parks, speaking to the American Bar Association's Standing Committee on Law and National Security, referred to the Manual's production process as taking place between 1996 and 2010 but admitted that:

> [o]n the average, at best fifteen per cent of the period between 1996 and 2010 was devoted to the manual. Participants had their "day jobs", that is, their regular duties, to perform in addition to working on the manual. The operational tempo, including military operations in Somalia, Haiti, and the Balkans, and the two fullscale wars of the past decade, demanded much attention.[37]

In terms of publication timing, Parks predicted that:

> [a]ll chapters will be in the hands of members of the law of war working group by the end of this month for a final readthrough. Its members will have one month to identify any "red flag" points, reconcile them, brief their respective

conduct of hostilities and weapons, including the weapons review process. Additionally, the Manual provides information on relatively newer areas of LOAC including autonomous weapons and cyber operations. Process-wise, DoD has proven receptive to comments, questions, and critiques of the Manual. And while the June 2015 initial publication was a saga, in Dec. 2016 DoD published an updated version. That the Manual was published online makes updates easier as well as provides useful functionality in searching the text.

[36]   DoD Law of War Manual, Preface (stating that "[m]emoranda and meeting notes from the 1970s reflect that the international law offices of the Department of the Army's Office of the Judge Advocate General and the Department of the Navy's Office of the Judge Advocate General generally agreed on a concept plan for a new all-Services law of war manual").

[37]   W. Hays Parks, "National Security Law in Practice: The Department of Defense Law of War Manual," Remarks delivered to the American Bar Association's Standing Committee on Law and National Security (Nov. 18, 2010), www.americanbar.org/content/dam/aba/migrated/2011_build/law_national_security/hays_parks_speech_2010.authcheckdam.pdf.

superiors, and obtain their approval. Once that is accomplished, the manual will be forwarded to the DoD General Counsel, Mr. Jeh Johnson, for his review prior to his forwarding it to the Secretary of Defense for approval and release.[38]

On February 21, 2011, Parks spoke at Chatham House in London on what he labeled the "forthcoming" manual, which he said was then "proceeding through an informal interagency review."[39] Parks joked that "[k]nowing those present, you have heard about [the manual], but wonder if it really exists or is likely to see the light of day in your lifetime."[40] By December 2012, the Manual had still not been published and Parks returned to the ABA and delivered a seven-page statement describing what he labeled the Manual's "demise." Parks ended his remarks with this statement:

> Thus the original plan of reaching consensus with a manual containing an introductory letter signed by the Secretary of Defense or the DOD General Counsel to the effect that the manual is the statement of DOD interpretation of U.S. law of war obligations is unlikely, returning the situation to the potential legal Tower of Babel a DOD manual intended to avoid. It is a disappointment that a draft manual over which many experienced individuals toiled diligently for fourteen years, a manual praised by an international peer review, has not been published principally for political reasons. In the midst of an ongoing conflict, inside-the-beltway bureaucratic complacency ignores the vacuum that desperately required filling to ensure military commanders fulfill their obligation to conduct their operations in a manner consistent with the law stated therein.[41]

Parks complained that lawyers from the State and Justice Departments were taking too long in reviewing the Manual and despite a claimed agreement to only make substantive comments were instead submitting edits Parks likened to "changing 'puppy' to 'small dog.'"[42] Parks was also critical that "[e]diting responsibilities were assumed by a young DOD attorney lacking military or law of war training or experience" who, according to Parks, "deleted all the historical examples because they lacked law review-type citations. This action

[38] *Ibid.*

[39] Meeting Summary: The US and the Laws of War, Summary of the International Law Discussion Group Meeting held at Chatham House (Feb. 21, 2011), www.chathamhouse.org /sites/files/chathamhouse/field/field_document/il210211summary.pdf.

[40] *Ibid.*

[41] W. Hays Parks, "Update on the DOD Law of War Manual," Remarks delivered to the American Bar Association's Standing Committee on Law and National Security (Dec. 2012), https://law fare.s3-us-west-2.amazonaws.com/staging/s3fs-public/uploads/2012/12/Parks.Manual.pdf.

[42] *Ibid.*

destroyed material praised by the Peer Review – contents invaluable to judge advocate practitioners and the military commanders they advise." A week later, this very public incident was later the subject of a post on the prominent national security law blog *Lawfare*.[43]

Seven months later, Parks escalated his public disdain over the process by which the completed draft Manual had been derailed. On July 22, 2013, Parks and a former Department of State (DoS) Legal Advisor coauthored an article in the *Weekly Standard* magazine entitled "Where Is the Law of War Manual?"[44] The authors directed their ire in a number of directions, blaming "political appointees without law of war experience," "human rights activists on the National Security Council," DoS employees for proposing "egregious changes," Department of Justice (DoJ) employees for extreme and incorrect positions, and the judge advocate generals of the four services for their "disturbing" silence.[45] This escalation led to a unique, and awkward, response by the DoD General Counsel in the form of a letter to the editor. The response claimed that Park's description of the Manual production process was inaccurate and that DoD was "working towards publishing a DoD Manual in 2014."[46] And this public exchange was, of course, repeated in another *Lawfare* post.[47]

It remains unclear what effect Parks's actions had on the Manual's substance or the timing of publication. They almost certainly played a role in ensuring that the Manual was in fact published, though apparently not in a form of which Parks approves. His public criticisms also likely increased the scrutiny that the resulting Manual would receive.

5.1.2 Within the Executive Branch

While not seeking to espouse Parks's views (attacks) on the role of DoJ and DoS lawyers in the Manual's creation, there is an underlying element that

---

[43] R. Chesney, "Hays Parks on the Demise of the DOD Law of War Manual," *Lawfare* (Dec. 8, 2012), www.lawfareblog.com/hays-parks-demise-dod-law-war-manual.

[44] W. Hays Parks and E. Williamson, "Some Questions for State and DoD Legal Advisor Nominees," *Weekly Standard* (July 22, 2013), www.weeklystandard.com/where-law-war-manual/article/739267.

[45] *Ibid.*

[46] R. S. Taylor, Letter to the Editor of the *Weekly Standard* (Aug. 18, 2013), https://lawfare.s3-us-west-2.amazonaws.com/staging/s3fs-public/uploads/2013/07/Letter-to-The-Weekly-Standard_18Jul2013.pdf.

[47] B. Wittes, "Where Is the Law of War Manual? Here!," *Lawfare* (July 26, 2013), www.lawfareblog.com/where-law-war-manual-here

bears exploration. The Manual is "a Department of Defense (DoD)-wide resource for DoD personnel – including commanders, legal practitioners, and other military and civilian personnel – on the law of war."[48] It is not the DoS or DoJ or US Manual. That is not to say that other departments should not have been involved or that they shouldn't have been able to influence the contents. Instead it is a reflection of the obvious. DoD, DoJ, and DoS have different missions[49] and correspondingly view and apply the LOAC differently.

It should not be surprising that a lawyer with DoJ views the world through a litigation lens and may seek to ensure that the Manual's contents are consistent with legal terminology and arguments offered in litigation.[50] Similarly, a lawyer with DoS views the world through a foreign policy lens and may approach the Manual's contents with the goal of ensuring language creating the least risk of confusion or claims of inconsistency with US foreign policy statements at international fora and with consultations with allies.[51] So DoS or DoJ views on the LOAC may not be at odds with DoD at all, yet they have a different context and set of concerns. The greater the desire for interagency consensus, the more DoS and DoJ views on the LOAC need to be incorporated. The inevitable result of the process post-2010 was more generalized language and restatements of LOAC that are equal parts unobjectionable yet more unhelpful to the military. In addition, there were external factors that seemed to shape the Manual's contents, notably that the United States had criticized the work of the ICRC.

---

[48]   DoD Law of War Manual, Preface.
[49]   The mission of DoD is to "provide the military forces needed to deter war and to protect the security of our country." DoD, "About the Department of Defense (DoD)," www.defense.gov /About/. The mission of DoJ is to enforce the law and defend the interests of the United States according to the law; to ensure public safety against threats foreign and domestic; to provide federal leadership in preventing and controlling crime; to seek just punishment for those guilty of unlawful behavior; and to ensure fair and impartial administration of justice for all Americans. DoJ, "About DoJ," www.justice.gov/about. The mission of DoS is to "shape and sustain a peaceful, prosperous, just, and democratic world and foster conditions for stability and progress for the benefit of the American people and people everywhere." DoS, "Discover Diplomacy What is the Mission of the U.S. Department of State?," https://diplomacy.state.gov /discoverdiplomacy/diplomacy101/issues/170606.htm.
[50]   Stated another way, one would not want to be the DoJ lawyer who, in defending the United States in litigation and making argument "A," has an opposing party citing the Manual and claiming it says or means "B" or even simply "a."
[51]   Stated another way, one would not want to be the DoS lawyer who, in representing the United States in multilateral or bilateral talks or discussions, is discussing US practice "A" only to be questioned about why the Manual says either "B" or even "a."

5.2 *External*

5.2.1 CIL Study

In 2005, the ICRC published its multi-volume *Customary International Humanitarian Law* (CIL Study). In response the DoD General Counsel and DoS Legal Advisor wrote a letter to make clear to the ICRC and to the greater international community that, based upon the US review, the United States was

> concerned about the methodology used to ascertain rules and about whether the authors have proffered sufficient facts and evidence to support those rules. Accordingly, the United States is not in a position to accept without further analysis the Study's conclusions that particular rules related to the laws and customs of war in fact reflect customary international law.[52]

In 2010, Parks, in one of his presentations on the "forthcoming" Manual referred to the CIL Study as "the ICRC's careless use of any and all materials to bolster its arguments without weighing their authoritativeness."[53]

5.2.2 DPH

In 2008, the ICRC published the Interpretative Guidance on the Notion of Direct Participation in Hostilities (DPH Guidance).[54] The DPH Guidance was the product of a five-year process, involving, forty to fifty legal experts from, among other countries, the United States.[55] Yet, at the end of the process, the ICRC circulated a draft that was deemed so controversial that a "significant number of experts asked for their names to be deleted as participants."[56] Two of the US experts, along with an expert from the United Kingdom and another

---

[52] J. B. Bellinger III and W. J. Haynes II, "A US Government Response to the International Committee of the Red Cross Study Customary International Humanitarian Law" (2007) 89 *International Review of the Red Cross* 443, www.icrc.org/eng/assets/files/other/irrc_866_bellin ger.pdf.

[53] Meeting Summary, The US and the Laws of War Summary of the International Law Discussion Group Meeting Held at Chatham House on Monday Feb. 21, 2011, www .chathamhouse.org/sites/files/chathamhouse/field/field_document/il210211summary.pdf.

[54] "Interpretative Guidance on the Notion of Direct Participation in Hostilities under International Humanitarian Law" (2009) 90 *International Review of the Red Cross* 991, www .icrc.org/eng/assets/files/other/irrc-872-reports-documents.pdf.

[55] ICRC, "Overview of the ICRC's Expert Process (2003–2008)," www.icrc.org/eng/assets/files/ other/overview-of-the-icrcs-expert-process-icrc.pdf.

[56] M. N. Schmitt, "The Interpretative Guidance on the Notion of Direct Participation in Hostilities: A Critical Analysis" (2009) 1 *Harvard National Security Journal* 5.

from Canada, each authored articles documenting their dispute with the ICRC.[57]

While the Manual would receive considerable scrutiny under any circumstances, that the United States had criticized the work product and methodology of the ICRC placed an even larger "bullseye" on the Manual. That in turn provided an incentive for more generalized and thus defensible language. Viewed in this light, choices like regurgitating the PoW Convention and referring to the Copenhagen Process for detention as opposed to articulating actual US practice are more understandable.

6 CONCLUSION

While understandable from a bureaucratic perspective, drafting the Manual from a defensive perspective, and in some instances incorporating DoS and DoJ concerns, allowed the text to be watered down. Thus, the Manual's language as promulgated decreased its practical utility for its purported primary audience, those executing military operations. The Manual specifically states in one instance that the "importance of prevailing during armed conflict often justifies taking actions based upon limited information that would be considered unreasonable outside armed conflict."[58] However, this does not serve as a blank check. The US statement expressing the consent to be bound by Protocol III of the Certain Conventional Weapons Convention (Incendiary Weapons), accepts the reality that any "decision by any military commander, military personnel, or any other person responsible for planning, authorizing or executing military action shall only be judged on the basis of that person's assessment of the information reasonably available to the person at the time the person planned, authorized, or executed the action under review."

In many areas, the Manual falls short in its goal to usefully and specifically inform DoD personnel responsible for implementing the law of war and executing military operations. However, its formulations of law and policy must henceforth be regarded as information that is "reasonably available" to decision-makers, even if it is bulky and difficult to discern in its applicable details. There remain many areas where comments from the US perspective, while welcome, are too cautious in light of real-world operational dilemmas. At the same time, the mere publication of the Manual is an important

---

[57]   http://nyujilp.org/new-issue-forum-on-direct-participation-in-hostilities/. The two US experts who had participated in the years of discussions leading to the DPH Guidance were Hays Parks and Professor Mike Schmitt.

[58]   DoD Law of War Manual, ¶ 5.4.1.

benchmark because it affords many opportunities for dialogue with other nations and international organizations. That value is real regardless of the lack of precise details that practitioners might have sought. Nevertheless, the manual's lack of specificity on what LOAC applies as a matter of policy to US forces during NIACs may prove usefully defensible in that it preserves a kind of strategic flexibility.

PART II

PROMINENT PERSPECTIVES ON THE DOD MANUAL

4

Practitioners and the Law of War Manual

Charles J. Dunlap

1 INTRODUCTION

Law of war manuals matter not just to lawyers and diplomats, but also to the individual combatant who is responsible for adhering to the rules the manuals pronounce. Indeed, it is unconscionable for any nation to send its troops into harm's way without a clear statement of the law to which they will be held accountable. For too many years that was the case with the United States, which forced operational lawyers and commanders to maximize innovative legal solutions to fill doctrinal voids. While there were a variety of manuals issued by the individual services, there was no holistic, overarching guidance from the Department of Defense (DoD) as to the law applicable to war.[1] Thus, the issuance in 2015 of the DoD Law of War Manual (the Manual) was more than just a legal watershed, it can be properly seen as an overdue ethical obligation.

In addition, there was a very practical, warfighting need for the Manual – the growing centrality of law in twenty-first-century conflicts. As Professor Orde Kittrie observes:

> Law is becoming an increasingly powerful and prevalent weapon of war. The reasons for this development include the increased number and reach of international laws and tribunals, the rise of non-governmental organizations (NGOs) focused on law of armed conflict and related issues, the information

---

[1] "Promulgating a DoD-wide manual on the law of war has been a long-standing goal of DoD lawyers. Memoranda and meeting notes from the 1970s reflect that the international law offices of the Department of the Army's Office of the Judge Advocate General and the Department of the Navy's Office of the Judge Advocate General generally agreed on a concept plan for a new all-Services law of war manual ... the current manual may be traced to work in the late 1980s." Preface to DoD, Law of War Manual (2015; updated Dec. 2016), v, https://tinyurl.com/yal6c2q2.

technology revolution, and the advance of globalization and thus economic interdependence.[2]

Belligerents, especially those hostile to the United States, have become adept at waging what this writer has called "lawfare."[3] Lawfare is "the use of law as a means of accomplishing what might otherwise require the application of traditional military force."[4] In today's conflicts, lawfare often manifests itself in situations where a technologically inferior opponent attempts to use allegations of violations of the law of war to undermine the public support that democracies so often need to successfully wage war. The predicate to countering this strategy is a keen understanding of the pertinent law, and the Manual provides practitioners with ready access to DoD's position on it.

The purpose of this chapter is to briefly discuss the Manual's utility not just as a compendium of legal requirements to which a law-abiding military must adhere, but also comment on its potential as a practical tool to help shape military operations in an era of lawfare. It will also examine the Manual's promise as a "norm-setter" in the coming years as new weapons and warfighting methodologies emerge.

2 THE MANUAL'S AUDIENCE AND AUTHORITY

The Manual is not designed to be a quick reference for the unschooled. Weighing in at 1,193 pages, in its printed form it is not as physically accessible as, for example, the legendary US Army Law of Land Warfare Field Manual 27–10, which was less than 250 pages – which were themselves a mere six by nine inches in size.[5] Still, its availability in a digital format makes it readily downloadable to mobile electronic devices. Thus, it is both easily transportable and, perhaps even more importantly, searchable even in remote field settings.

However, legal practitioners cannot expect – and should not necessarily want – commanders and other clients to regularly be leafing through the Manual in an effort to find answers for themselves. It is rather, as Professors Jeremy Rabkin and John Yoo correctly point out, "in effect, a sourcebook for

---

[2]   O. F. Kittrie, *Lawfare: Law as a Weapon of War* (New York: Oxford University Press, 2016), 1.
[3]   See, e.g., Major General C. Dunlap, Jr., USAF (Ret'd.), "Lawfare 101: A Primer," *Military Review* (May–June 2017), 8, www.armyupress.army.mil/Portals/7/military-review/Archives/English/MilitaryReview_20170630_Lawfare-101.pdf.
[4]   *Ibid.*, 9.
[5]   FM 27–10.

detailed research efforts."[6] Typically, that is a task best assigned to trained attorneys. Thus, the Manual will increase the demand for military lawyers – called judge advocates or "JAGs" – as they will be needed to provide real-time advice and to help translate legal requirements into planning documents and, particularly, rules of engagement.

While some may yearn for the relative simplicity of an FM 27–10 approach, or decry the so-called "overlawyering" of war,[7] the reality is that armed conflict in the twenty-first century is an extraordinarily legally complex endeavor. This is especially so with respect to conflicts against non-State actors utilizing terrorism and other asymmetrical methodologies that have occupied the US military since the attacks of 9/11.[8] Journalist Charlie Savage's 2015 book *Power Wars* amply shows how legal issues permeated virtually every national security decision of the post-9/11 era.[9] Much the same could be said about the battlefield where adversaries make it a point not to comply with the law of war, and to immerse themselves among the civilian population in the hopes of deterring attacks upon themselves by law-respecting militaries.[10]

Indeed, the sheer breadth of the Manual's scope, addressing everything from the sources of the law of war, targeting, cyber operations, and rather arcane matters of occupation law, militates against attempts to master all of its constituent elements, even by a specialist. Moreover, it must be kept in mind that the law of armed conflict (LOAC) is only one feature of a

---

[6] J. Rabkin and J. Yoo, *Striking Power: How Cyber, Robots, and Space Weapons Change the Rules for War* (New York: Encounter Books, 2017), 125.

[7] M. Barone, "The Overlawyered War," American Enterprise Institute (Sept, 17, 2007), www.aei.org/publication/the-overlawyered-war/print/.

[8] 9/11 references the events of Sept. 11, 2001 when "19 militants associated with the Islamic extremist group al-Qaeda hijacked four airplanes and carried out suicide attacks against targets in the United States." See "9/11 Attacks," History.com (2010), www.history.com/topics/9-11-attacks.

[9] See, generally, C. Savage, *Power Wars* (New York: Little, Brown and Co. 2015).

[10] Maria Alejandra Martinovic points out:

> The specificities of asymmetrical hostilities nowadays responds, to a certain extent, to the development of NIACs as the predominant type of confrontation and the necessary involvement of OAGs that do not hesitate to violate the most sacred IHL norms when engaging enemy forces becomes difficult and their survival is at stake.
>
> As a consequence, it is easy to observe scenarios where State actors somehow become the disadvantaged parties, given that they are bound to comply with IHL (and correctly so) even when the enemy does not simply disobey it, but actually undertakes to violate it, for instance, through the use of human shields.

M. A. Martinovic, *The Challenges of Asymmetric Warfare: Enhancing Compliance with International Humanitarian Law by Organized Armed Groups* (Hamburg: Anchor Academic Publishing, 2016), 116.

larger corpus of law with which a warfighting lawyer must be familiar, called "operational law." Operational law is a discipline which covers a very wide variety of legal issues that can arise in a deployed or contingency setting.[11]

What authority does the Manual carry? On its face, it does not appear to comprise *opinio juris* of the United States.[12] As Eric Jensen has noted, the Manual "goes to great lengths to preclude" such use.[13] He points to this Manual paragraph:[14]

> This manual represents the legal views of the Department of Defense. This manual does not, however, preclude the Department from subsequently changing its interpretation of the law. Although the preparation of this manual has benefited from the participation of lawyers from the Department of State and the Department of Justice, this manual does not necessarily reflect the views of any other department or agency of the U.S. Government or the views of the U.S. Government as a whole.[15]

As other authors in this Commentary have noted, the 2006 US response to the study by the International Committee of the Red Cross (ICRC) on customary international humanitarian law documents the view that the United States was "troubled by the Study's heavy reliance on military manuals" and that it did not agree that *opinio juris* has been established when the evidence of a State's sense of legal obligation consists predominately of military manuals."[16] The US response then added:

> Rather than indicating a position expressed out of a sense of a customary legal obligation, in the sense pertinent to customary international law, a State's military manual often (properly) will recite requirements

---

11 See, generally, The Judge Advocate General's Legal Center & School, International & Operational Law Department, US Army, JA 422, "Operational Law Handbook" (2017), http://loc.gov/rr/frd/Military_Law/pdf/operational-law-handbook_2017.pdf.

12 According to the Legal Information Institute: "In customary international law, opinio juris is the second element (along with state practice) necessary to establish a legally binding custom. Opinio juris denotes a subjective obligation, a sense on behalf of a state that it is bound to the law in question." Legal Information Institute, Cornell University, www.law.cornell.edu/wex/opinio_juris_international_law.

13 E. Jensen, "Law of War Manual: Information or Authoritative Guidance?," *Just Security* (July 1, 2015, 10:37 AM), www.justsecurity.org/24332/law-war-Manual-information-authoritative-guidance/.

14 See Chapters 1, 2, 3, and 6 of this book.

15 DoD Law of War Manual, ¶ 1.1.1.

16 Letter from John Bellinger III, Legal Advisor, US Dept. of State, and William J. Haynes, General Counsel, US Dept. of Defense, to Dr. Jakob Kellenberger, President, International Committee of the Red Cross, Regarding Customary International Law Study (Nov. 3, 2006), www.state.gov/s/l/2006/98860.htm.

applicable to that State under treaties to which it is a party. Reliance on provisions of military manuals designed to implement treaty rules provides only weak evidence that those treaty rules apply as a matter of customary international law.[17]

Professors Yoo and Rabkin seem to think the Manual should be more of an affirmative, public diplomacy tool. They argue that while there is "much to admire" about the Manual, it does not adequately highlight the United States' deviations from Additional Protocol I,[18] adding that it "it is not always completely persuasive on why or how much the U.S. might pursue a different approach." They contend:

> It is the usual instinct of lawyers to downplay any novelty in their arguments. Diplomats often have the same instinct to nurture acquiescence by skirting provocation. But lulling the drowsy or disengaged is not the same as securing their agreement or even their patient respect when real-world events awaken their attention. The lawyering in the manual may be helpful for many purposes but it is not the stuff of public diplomacy or political advocacy.

They have a point, but it is not fully persuasive. The fact is that when combined with US State practice the Manual does – and will continue to – make a real contribution to norm development.

Indeed, clarification of existing norms is already occurring. For example, the Manual provided legal support for the adoption of an interpretation of the concept of military objective[19] that in the not too distant past was eschewed by most nations. Specifically, the Manual includes "economic objects associated with military operations or with war-supporting or war-sustaining industries" within the concept of legitimate military objectives subject to attack.[20] This broadened concept of lawful military objectives has long been a US position, but until recently one with little noticeable support in the international community.

---

[17] *Ibid.*

[18] Yoo and Rabkin are referencing Protocol Additional to the Geneva Conventions of Aug. 12, 1949, and Relating to the Protection of Victims of International Armed Conflicts, June 8, 1977, 1125 UNTS 3. The United States is not a party to the Protocol, and Yoo and Rabkin believe that the United States should be more aggressive in stating its differences as they believe the Protocol unnecessarily inhibits the use of force for proper purposes.

[19] The ICRC says "military objectives are limited to those objects which by their nature, location, purpose or use make an effective contribution to military action and whose partial or total destruction, capture or neutralization, in the circumstances ruling at the time, offers a definite military advantage." ICRC, Definition of Military Objectives, Customary Humanitarian Law, rule 108, https://ihl-databases.icrc.org/customary-ihl/eng/docs/vi_rul_rule8.

[20] DoD Law of War Manual, ¶ 5.6.8 (5).

When coalition forces battling the Islamic State in Iraq and Syria (ISIS) began attacking oil facilities and tanker trucks in an effort to disrupt ISIS finances, controversy – mostly academic – resulted.[21] Few nations openly complained because the tactic permitted the coalition to strike ISIS under circumstances where the risk to civilians was minimal. This was an especially important innovation given that ISIS was utilizing human shields on a massive scale.[22] It demonstrates how the law of war as represented in the Manual can be responsive to authentic battlefield conundrums.

The technique is now being utilized in Afghanistan to strike Taliban drug facilities. According to the US Central Command, the bombing is aimed to hit the Taliban "where it hurts, which is their finances."[23] The commander said that narcotics trafficking was one of the criminal enterprises the enemy was using to "fund their insurgency."[24] He added, however, that the campaign was not aimed at farmers who were sometimes forced to participate. Interestingly enough, this technique has not as yet garnered criticism, even among academics.

3 THE MANUAL AND RULES OF ENGAGEMENT

In contemporary conflicts the issue is not often compliance with the law of war, *per se*, but rather with the rules of engagement (ROE).[25] The Manual explains that:

> ROE reflect legal, *policy*, and *operational* considerations, and are consistent with the international law obligations of the United States, including the law of war. ROE may restrict actions that would be lawful

---

[21] See, e.g., J. E. Padeanu, "Accepting that War-Sustaining Objects are 'Legitimate Targets' under IHL is a Terrible Idea," *Yale Journal of International Law* (Mar. 2, 2017), www.yjil.yale.edu/accepting-that-war-sustaining-objects-are-legitimate-targets-under-ihl-is-a-terrible-idea/.

[22] See, generally, Major General C. J. Dunlap, Jr., "Understanding War-Sustaining Targeting: A Rejoinder to Iulia Padeanu," *Yale Journal of International Law* (Apr. 6, 2017), www.yjil.yale.edu/understanding-war-sustaining-targeting-a-rejoinder-to-iulia-padeanu/.

[23] See L. Ferdinando, "U.S., Afghan Force Target Taliban Drug Labs, Hit 'Where It Hurts,'" DoD News, Defense Media Activity (Nov. 20, 2017), www.centcom.mil/MEDIA/NEWS-AR TICLES/News-Article-View/Article/1377978/us-afghan-forces-target-taliban-drug-labs-hit-wh ere-it-hurts/ (quoting US Army General John W. Nicholson).

[24] *Ibid.*

[25] Rules of engagement are "[d]irectives issued by competent military authority that delineate the circumstances and limitations under which United States forces will initiate and/or continue combat engagement with other forces encountered." Joint Chiefs of Staff, Joint Pub. 1–04, Legal Support to Military Operations (Aug. 2, 2016), Gl-3, www.dtic.mil/doctrine/new_pubs/jp1_04.pdf.

under the law of war, but may not permit actions prohibited by the law of war.[26]

Generally speaking, warfighters are less concerned with complying with the law of war – a requirement which they take as a given – and more with policy-driven restrictions.[27] In current conflicts, policies that become ROE have imposed restrictions that are *far* greater than anything the law or the Manual might have required; for example, the policy established in 2013 for the use of force in counterterrorism operations outside the United States or areas of active hostilities.

Among other things, that policy mandated that before lethal action could be taken, there needed to be a "near certainty" that noncombatants would not be injured or killed.[28] The public announcement of the policy helped – in this writer's view – to instigate a significant increase in the use of human shields in contemporary conflicts.[29] Obviously, an enemy who knows that proximity to a civilian will foreclose an attack is incentivized to burrow into civilian areas, exactly what the law of warfare hopes to preclude.

A somewhat different issue was raised in a recent article by two retired JAG officers, Lieutenant Colonel David G. Bolgiano, USAF (Ret'd.), and LTC John Taylor, USA (Ret'd.).[30] Bolgiano and Taylor argue that former Chairman of the Chiefs of Staff Navy Admiral Michael Mullen was wrong when he said, "We can't kill our way to victory."[31] They say that "[t]hose given the awful task of combat must be able to act with the necessary savagery and purposefulness to destroy those acting as, or in direct support of, Islamic

---

[26] DoD Law of War Manual, ¶ 1.6.5.

[27] See, e.g., C. Dunlap, "Complying with the Geneva Conventions Doesn't Trouble Today's Warfighters, but Overly-Restrictive Rules of Engagement Are Another Matter," *Lawfire* (Apr. 1, 2016), https://sites.duke.edu/lawfire/2016/04/01/complying-with-the-gen eva-conventions-doesnt-trouble-todays-warfighters-but-overly-restrictive-rules-of-engage ment-are-another-matter/. See also H. McKay, "Trump, Mattis Turn Military Loose on ISIS, Leaving Terror Caliphate in Tatters," *Fox News* (Dec. 8, 2017), www.foxnews.com/ world/2017/12/08/trump-mattis-turn-military-loose-on-isis-leaving-terror-caliphate-in-tatters .html ("President Trump scrapped his predecessor's rules of engagement, which critics say hamstrung the military, and let battlefield decisions be made by the generals in the theater, and not bureaucrats in Washington.").

[28] FACT SHEET: U.S. Policies and Procedures for the Use of Force in Counterterrorism Operations (May 23, 2013), www.whitehouse.gov/the-pressoffice/2013/05/23/fact-sheet-us-pol icy-standards-and-procedures-use-forcecounterterrorism.

[29] C. Dunlap, "Sadly, We Have to Expect More Civilian Casualties if ISIS Is to Be Defeated," *Lawfire* (Mar. 26, 2017), https://sites.duke.edu/lawfire/2017/03/26/sadly-we-have-to-expect- more-civilian-casualties-if-isis-is-to-be-defeated/.

[30] Lieutenant Colonel D. G. Bolgiano, USAF (Ret'd.) and LTC J. Taylor, US Army (Ret'd.), "Can't Kill Enough to Win? Think Again" (Dec. 2017) 144 *Proceedings* 18, www.usni.org/ma gazines/proceedings/2017–12/cant-kill-enough-win-think-again.

[31] *Ibid.*, 20.

terrorists worldwide."[32] According to Bolgiano and Taylor, "too many commanders and their 'operational law' judge advocates have neutered U.S. military forces with far too restrictive rules of engagement and investigations."[33] Moreover, they indicate that what they call an "overabundance of ill-trained lawyers in the force" is hampering battlefield success.[34]

Unsurprisingly, their essay provoked fierce responses. Their contentions were almost immediately attacked by Adam Weinstein, a former Marine who is a lawyer now working as a policy analyst.[35] According to Weinstein, Bolgiano and Taylor are "sorely misguided." Weinstein insists:

> Long-term success in places like Afghanistan and Iraq requires a credible alternative to insurgency and sectarian conflict; it requires the building of central governments with legitimacy. This feat has so far eluded the United States and its allies in Iraq and Afghanistan. Killing many, and often, hasn't helped.[36]

In another critique, Lieutenant Colonel Daniel Sukman, a US Army strategist, correctly points out that "[r]ules of engagement are the responsibility of commanders, and the staff leads are the [operations and plans directorates]."[37] Staff judge advocates "merely assist." He has similar concerns to those of Weinstein, and adds that "we lose wars when we lose our moral compass." Sukman argues that the "instant we become a monster to slay a monster, war is lost."[38]

Interestingly, neither the original writers nor their critics have any complaint about the law, *per se*, but rather about the wisdom (or lack thereof) of policies that implement it. Plainly, aspects of the Bolgiano and Taylor essay are overheated, lacking in factual support, and even mistaken, but the critics are also wrong not to acknowledge the very real problems the restrictive ROE produces. Retired Air Force Lieutenant General Dave Deptula (and Joseph Raskas) pointed out the practical – and moral – perils of overly restrictive ROE:

---

[32] *Ibid.*

[33] *Ibid.*

[34] *Ibid.*, 22.

[35] A. M. Weinstein, "No, We Can't Kill Our Way to Victory Despite What 2 Misguided Lieutenant Colonels Might Think," *Task & Purpose* (Dec. 8, 2017), http://taskandpurpose.com/no-cant-kill-way-victory-despite-2-misguided-lieutenant-colonels-might-think/.

[36] *Ibid.*

[37] Lieutenant Colonel D. Sukman, US Army, "Moral Repugnance: A Response to 'Can't Kill Enough to Win? Think Again'," *Best Defense* (Dec. 11, 2017, 10:10 AM), http://foreignpolicy.com/2017/12/11/moral-repugnance-a-response-to-cant-kill-enough-to-win-think-again/.

[38] *Ibid.*

[C]urrent policies guiding the war on terror unreasonably restrict the use of airpower. Such policies limit civilian casualties that may result from attacking the terrorists, but allow the certainty of civilians being slaughtered at the hands of those same terrorists if they are not eliminated. That is self-defeating at best, and counterproductive at worst. To be sure, it is immoral.[39]

This writer calls the concept they discuss the "moral hazard of inaction in war."[40] Anecdotal evidence from Afghanistan supports the more robust strategy envisioned by Bolgiano and Taylor. General Stanley McChrystal's Tactical Directive, issued in his capacity as the International Security Assistance Force (ISAF) Commander (overall commander of all North Atlantic Treaty Organization (NATO) forces in Afghanistan), implemented restrictions on the use of artillery, helicopter gunships, and close air support. It noted that "carefully controlled and disciplined employment of force entails risk to our troops – and we must work to mitigate that risk wherever possible. But excessive use of force resulting in an alienated population will produce far greater risks."[41] McChrystal's order continued: "I expect leaders at all levels to scrutinize and limit the use of force like close air support (CAS) against residential compounds and other locations likely to produce civilian casualties in accordance with this guidance."[42]

However, when apologizing to Afghan officials for the September 2009 bombing that killed seventy-two civilians, General McChrystal's explanation was interrupted by a council chairman named Ahmadullah Wardak. According to the *Washington Post* account, General McChrystal was "caught off guard" as Wardak asserted that the allies had been "too nice to the thugs" and demanded a more aggressive policy to protect the Afghan people.[43] This might not have been an isolated sentiment. An anonymous Pakistani sounded a similar theme to the *Wall Street Journal* some years later, "I am a government official so I can't say it publicly, but I really want the drones to increase because they have eliminated all of the bad people."[44] Another American commander reported that Afghans in his

---

39 D. Deptula and J. Raska, "Just Warfare Entails Risk; Movie 'Eye in The Sky' Perverts Just War Laws," *Breaking Defense* (May 16, 2016 at 4:01 AM), https://breakingdefense.com/2016/05/just-warfare-entails-risk-movie-eye-in-the-sky-perverts-just-war-laws/.

40 C. Dunlap, "The Moral Hazard of Inaction in War," *War on the Rocks* (Aug. 19, 2016), https://warontherocks.com/2016/08/the-moral-hazard-of-inaction-in-war/.

41 S. McChrystal, COMISAF Tactical Directive, July 6, 2009.

42 *Ibid.*

43 R. Chandrasekaran, "Sole Informant Guided Decision on Afghan Strike," *Washington Post* (Sept. 6, 2009), A1.

44 D. Nissenbaum, "In Former Taliban Sanctuary, An Eerie Silence Takes Over," *Wall Street Journal* (Jan. 26–27, 2013), A1.

area of operations "only respect strength. The people expected us to swing a large baseball bat and make the insurgents go away. They praised us every time we and the Afghan National Army did just that. They chided us each and every time about the overall lack of security in all the areas [we patrolled]."

A little-noticed provision in the Manual provides some support for the view that the absence of the use of force can carry real consequences. In discussing whether the expected incidental harm to civilians in an attack is excessive in relation to the anticipated military advantage, the Manual makes clear that evaluating the "civilians at risk if the attack is not taken" is a proper factor in the attack decision.[45] General McChrystal might have focused on the willingness of local leaders to work with the NATO coalition and Afghan government as the operational center of gravity. If the military objective was conceptualized as providing tangible encouragement to law-abiding Afghans seeking to ally with the government against the depredations and human rights violations of the Taliban, one might imagine a radically different ISAF Tactical Directive. Overlooking this consideration can present, as Deptula and Raskas argue, a moral if not legal conundrum.

4 THE MANUAL AS A COUNTER-LAWFARE WEAPON

Because it is an authoritative statement of the DoD view of the LoW, the Manual provides an excellent basis for practitioners to build a counter-lawfare campaign.

Still, the challenge for practitioners will be ensuring commanders correctly understand the law and its nuances. Commendably, commanders and other senior officers are increasingly taking the lead to counter lawfare techniques used not only by battlefield opponents, but by other critics who, though not associated with the enemy in any way, nevertheless could undermine public support for combat operations should their criticisms be internalized by electorates and other political influencers.

US Army Lieutenant General Stephen Townsend recently penned a forceful counter to allegations of excessive civilian casualties in operations against the Islamic State.[46] As effective as that was, other public statements by senior

---

[45] DoD Law of War Manual, ¶ 5.12.3.
[46] S. J. Townsend, "Reports of Civilian Casualties in the War against ISIS Are Vastly Inflated," *Foreign Policy* (Sept. 15, 2017, 4:48 PM), https://foreignpolicy.com/2017/09/15/reports-of-civilian-casualties-from-coalition-strikes-on-isis-are-vastly-inflated-lt-gen-townsend-cjtf-oir/.

commanders are not always as accurate as they need to be.[47] While it is almost always more effective for commanders to take the lead, legal practitioners need to coordinate closely with them to ensure their pronouncements track with the Manual's interpretations.

Misunderstandings of the law of war still persist, even in leading media outlets.[48] Part of the problem is that restrictive ROE policies have become so pervasive that when they appear to have been breached in a given circumstance, such deviations from *policy* are too often conflated into allegations of illegality which they seldom are. It is often the case that the mere existence of any civilian casualties makes a particular attack seem to be, *ipso facto*, unlawful, which is certainly not the case under any informed application of *jus in bello* principles.

The Manual provides a more than sufficient resource for practitioners to build a formal counter-lawfare plan. Regrettably, however, as Professor Kittrie notes:

> Despite the term having been coined by a U.S. government official, the U.S. government has only sporadically engaged with the concept of lawfare. It has no lawfare strategy or doctrine, and no office or interagency mechanism that systematically develops or coordinates U.S. offensive lawfare or U.S. defenses against lawfare.[49]

Practitioners need to change this situation if they are to fully meet the needs of command, not to mention the challenges of twenty-first century lawfare-infused conflict. However, this challenge requires more than just expertise in the law and support from command for developing and implement a lawfare strategy. Practitioners need to thoroughly understand the client's "business." Although Bolgiano and Taylor may be overstating their case by claiming an "overabundance of ill-trained lawyers in the force,"[50] it is nevertheless true that what is vitally important is for practitioners to have a keen familiarity with the weapons, the strategies and – perhaps most importantly – the mindset of their warfighting clients.

---

[47] C. Dunlap, "Getting The Law Right on Carpet Bombing and Civilian Casualties," *War on the Rocks* (Mar. 16, 2016), https://warontherocks.com/2016/03/getting-the-law-right-on-carpet-bombing-and-civilian-casualties/.

[48] See, e.g., C. Dunlap, "How the New York Times Misconstrues the Law on Civilian Casualties," *Lawfire* (Oct. 13, 2017), https://sites.duke.edu/lawfire/2017/10/13/how-the-new-york-times-misconstrues-the-law-on-civilian-casualties/.

[49] Kittrie (above note 2), 3.

[50] Bolgiano and Taylor (above note 30).

5 CONCLUDING THOUGHTS

One of the most interesting aspects of the Manual is that it is a living document in the sense that it continues to evolve. It has already undergone two updates, and overtly invites recommendations. In this sense it reflects the Nuremberg Tribunal's observation, that the "law is not static, but by continual adaption follows the needs of a changing world."[51] The Manual has generated discussion and controversy,[52] but it will continue to provide a starting point for legal analysis as new issues arise.

And, of course, there are plenty of fresh legal challenges, mainly as a result of technological developments. It would be easy to criticize the Manual for not more extensively addressing cyber operations, a matter of great concern to US forces.[53] Yet it must be said that the inclusion of a chapter on that subject was something of legal inflection point for the United States as the topic had hardly been broached previously.[54] The extent to which the United States becomes the predominate influencer of norm development in the arena of cyber operations remains to be seen.[55]

Similarly, the Manual addresses autonomous weaponry in general terms,[56] and that is an area of the law that will surely develop further, particularly as science creates not only systems that can act autonomously within an established framework, but which also have the ability to learn. The Defense Advanced Research Projects Agency (DARPA) has established a research program called Assured Autonomy which aims to enhance the safety and trustworthiness of learning-enabled autonomous systems.[57] It is only a matter

---

[51] *Trial of Major War Criminals Before the International Military Tribunal* (Nuremburg: IMT, 1947), I, 221, www.loc.gov/rr/frd/Military_Law/pdf/NT_Vol-I.pdf.

[52] "Reader's Guide to our Mini-Forum on DoD's Law of War Manual," *Just Security* (Aug. 12, 2015), www.justsecurity.org/25371/readers-guide-mini-forum-dods-law-war-manual/.

[53] D. R. Coats, Director of National Intelligence, Worldwide Threat Assessment of the US Intelligence Community, statement for the Record, Senate Select Committee on Intelligence (May 11, 2017), www.dni.gov/files/documents/Newsroom/Testimonies/SSCI%20Unclassified %20SFR%20-%20Final.pdf.

[54] C. Dunlap, "Cyber Operations and the New Defense Department Law of War Manual: Initial Impressions," *Lawfare* (June 15, 2015), www.lawfareblog.com/cyber-operations-and-new-defe nse-department-law-war-manual-initial-impressions.

[55] The US has serious competition in this area in M. N. Schmitt and L. Vihul (eds.), *Tallinn Manual 2.0 on the International Law Applicable to Cyber Operations* (Cambridge University Press, 2017). This document, like its 1.0 predecessor, was prepared by global experts and was facilitated and led by the NATO Cooperative Cyber Defence Centre of Excellence. It differs in some important respects from the US position on certain issues.

[56] See DoD Law of War Manual, ¶ 6.5.9.

[57] "DARPA Assured Autonomy Seeks to Guarantee Safety of Learning-Enabled Autonomous Systems," DARPA Public Affairs (Aug, 16, 2017), www.darpa.mil/news-events/2017-08-16.

of time when a future update to the Manual addresses the many legal issues such developments occasion.

Challenges associated with the development of so-called "super soldiers" (human beings enhanced) are even more legally complex. An ethicist recently described the phenomena and its importance:

> Modern technologies that actively seek to combine bio, nano, info and neuro elements can give us the ability to "enhance" human beings in ways that we want. This ability – to make soldiers more capable of defeating their enemies and/or surviving the perils of conflict – is of great interest to militaries throughout the world.[58]

Experts are already identifying an extraordinary range of issues associated with this development. For example, since at least 2013, some have claimed that science can turn people into weapons that commit war crimes.[59] This area may well require a place in the Manual.

Some commentators, such as retired Brigadier General Ken Watkin argue that conflict in the twenty-first century is increasingly becoming dominated by conflicts involving non-State actors who are well-armed, determined, and quasi-organized as fighting organizations.[60] States are ever more frequently employing their militaries to confront these serious threats to their very stability. Watkin and others contend that the law of war is frequently inadequate for these situations and urge greater incorporation of human rights law into such operations as a gap-filler. There is real merit to this conceptually – and the Manual recognizes the "complex" application of *jus in bello* during non-international armed conflict (NIAC) situations.[61] Nevertheless, it has yet to be demonstrated that States and their publics prefer human rights law as being the overarching approach, at least insofar as the extraterritorial use of

---

[58] Dr. A. Henschschke, "'Supersoldier': Ethical Concerns in Human Enhancement Technologies," *Humanitarian Law & Policy* (July 3, 2017), http://blogs.icrc.org/law-and-pol icy/2017/07/03/supersoldiers-ethical-concerns-human-enhancement-technologies-2/.

[59] P. Lin, "Could Human Enhancement Turn Soldiers into Weapons that Violate International Law? Yes," *The Atlantic* (Jan. 4, 2013), www.theatlantic.com/technology/archive/2013/01/ could-human-enhancement-turn-soldiers-into-weapons-that-violate-international-law-yes/266 732/. See also C. E. Sawin, "Laws of War: The Legality of Creating an Army of Super Soldiers," *Journal of High Technology Law* (Nov. 3, 2015), https://sites.suffolk.edu/jhtl/2015/ 11/03/laws-of-war-the-legality-of-creating-an-army-of-super-soldiers/ ("[U]ntil there are some precautions, studies, and strict standard operating procedures for how super soldiers should be designed, manufactured, utilized, and eventually deployed, then it would be obtuse for any country to implement such an elite killing machine at this time.").

[60] See, generally, K. Watkin, *Fighting at the Legal Boundaries Controlling the Use of Force in Contemporary Conflict* (Oxford University Press, 2016).

[61] DoD Law of War Manual, ¶ 17.1.

force in NIACs is concerned, so long as the applicable the law of war principles are strictly enforced.

In the meantime, the legal (and, indeed, ethical) principles reflected in the Manual will be the common starting point for American legal practitioners. The Manual is not a cookbook with a set formula for every factual permutation that can arise in combat. Beyond having (as previously noted) a solid understanding of their client's weapons, organization, strategies, and other relevant factors of friendly forces, astute practitioners will also internalize the same elements about the enemy. Only then can properly nuanced legal advice address the vagaries of warfighting writ large.

Practitioners should be cautioned against the assumption that the Manual is a panacea for every law of war issue that might arise. The facts always matter, and as much as manuals and descriptions of precedents are helpful, in the chaos and extraordinary stress of war there will always be hard decisions to make based on imperfect information. It is at those times when thoughtful consideration of the Manual's basic principles of military necessity, humanity, proportionality, distinction and, especially, honor – may be the practitioner's best recourse. Once a decision is made as to what the law provides, the practitioner must have the moral courage to communicate that analysis as clearly and as forthrightly as the situation requires, irrespective of the personal consequences. Practitioners ought to keep in mind British General William Slim's[62] observation that "Moral courage is higher and a rarer virtue than physical courage."[63]

---

[62] "William Joseph 'Bill' Slim, 1st Viscount Slim," *New World Encyclopedia*, www.newworlden cyclopedia.org/entry/William_Slim,_1st_Viscount_Slim.

[63] *BrainyQuote.com*, www.brainyquote.com/quotes/william_slim_143518.

5

A NATO Perspective on the Manual

Steven Hill[*]

1 INTRODUCTION

The revised Department of Defense (DoD) Law of War Manual (the Manual) is a significant development not just for the United States but for all twenty-nine Allies within the North Atlantic Treaty Organization (NATO). Its publication comes at a crucial period of activity for the Alliance. In 2017 alone, the Alliance deployed four battle groups to Estonia, Latvia, Lithuania, and Poland as part of the Enhanced Forward Presence and increased its presence through the Tailored Forward Presence in Romania. NATO worked to combat hybrid and cyber-threats, including through the Warsaw Summit decision of Allied Heads of State and Government to declare "cyber" an operational domain.[1] In May 2017, these leaders tasked the Alliance to take on a greater role in counterterrorism, including by agreeing that NATO would become part of the Counter-ISIS coalition.[2] At the same time, NATO operations in Afghanistan and Kosovo continue, NATO's maritime operation in the Mediterranean has been reshaped, and NATO continues its Aegean Sea activity to help address Europe's migration challenges. Along with this increased operational tempo, NATO has developed a number of new policies on matters related to the law

* The views expressed in this article are mine alone and do not necessarily represent the views of NATO or its Allies. I gratefully acknowledge the support provided by Emanuele Marchi and Katrin Inan-Stahl of the NATO Office of Legal Affairs.

1 Warsaw Summit Communiqué issued by the Heads of State and Government participating in the meeting of the North Atlantic Council in Warsaw July 8–9, 2016, Press Release (2016) 100, ¶ 70, www.nato.int/cps/en/natohq/official_texts_133169.htm?selectedLocale=en.

2 NATO Summit of Heads of State and Government, held in Brussels on May 25, 2017; see "NATO Leaders Agree to Do More to Fight Terrorism and Ensure Fairer Burden Sharing," www.nato.int/cps/en/natohq/news_144154.htm?selectedLocale=en.

of armed conflict such as protection of civilians and children in armed conflict.[3]

Compliance with international law is a key component of NATO's success in all of these endeavors and everything else the Alliance does. The demand for legal advice from the some seventy legal offices that make up what we call the NATO legal community has never been higher.[4] NATO has also launched or reinvigorated a number of legal dialogues, including both with Allies and with partners. The scope of issues on which the typical NATO legal advisor is called to advise can be daunting and guidance on Allied views is not always available, especially in an easy-to-access consolidated format. National efforts like the Manual can be of great assistance in trying to understand the perspective of Allies on key legal issues facing the Alliance.

This chapter aims to present one view of the potential impact of the Manual on NATO's work in the legal field. The chapter begins by highlighting the importance of legal interoperability among NATO Allies with often diverging legal frameworks and explaining how national law of war manuals can contribute to the mission accomplishment in a multinational setting. It then examines the references to NATO in the Manual and offers views on how these references might contribute to our collective understanding of certain perennial legal issues that arise in NATO operations. Finally, the chapter examines the Manual's usefulness in promoting further dialogue among Allies and with NATO's partners on key legal issues as well as its potential role in NATO's training activities.

2 MULTINATIONAL MILITARY OPERATIONS AND THE CHALLENGE OF LEGAL INTEROPERABILITY

NATO is an Alliance of values, and these values include the rule of law. The commitment to respect the rule of law is enshrined in the preamble to the 1949 North Atlantic Treaty and is reaffirmed in declarations by NATO Heads

---

[3] Military Guidelines on Children and Armed Conflict (2012); NATO/EAPC Policy for the implementation of UNSCR 1325 on Women, Peace and Security and related resolutions (2014), www.nato.int/cps/en/natohq/official_texts_109830.htm?selectedLocale=en; The Protection of Children in Armed Conflict – Way Forward, AC/332(ISAF)N(2014)0062-REV5; NATO Policy for the Protection of Civilians endorsed by the Heads of State and Government participating in the meeting of the North Atlantic Council in Warsaw July 8–9, 2016, Press Release (2016) 135, www.nato.int/cps/en/natohq/official_texts_133945.htm?selectedLocale=en.

[4] S. Hill, "The Role of NATO's Legal Adviser," in A. Zidar and J. P. Gauci (eds.), *The Role of Legal Advisers in International Law* (Leiden: Brill; Boston: Nijhoff, 2016), 213–36.

of State and Government at their regular summit meetings.[5] It is a key element of NATO and/or NATO-led operations and is key to ensuring their legitimacy and securing public support. NATO is an alliance of twenty-nine Allies that makes its decisions by consensus of all members. These Allies have different domestic legal systems and different international legal obligations. They also often have their own understanding on what international law obligations are applicable to them and under what conditions. Part of the challenge in a multilateral environment like NATO is to enable nations to act together consistently with the individual legal obligations of each Nation and despite potentially different content of those obligations. A key technique that legal advisors use to help achieve consensus despite these legal differences is what is often referred to as legal interoperability.

There is no agreed definition of legal interoperability. The notion is modelled after the broader concept of force interoperability, which NATO doctrines define as "[t]he ability of the forces of two or more nations to train, exercise and operate effectively together in the execution of assigned missions and tasks."[6] In the Warsaw Summit Communiqué, Allied Heads of State and Government referred to the need for interoperability to accomplish NATO's goals:

> through training and exercises, the development of NATO standards and common technical solutions, the NATO Response Force, Assurance Measures, forward presence in the eastern part of the Alliance, and joint operations in Afghanistan, Kosovo and the Mediterranean ... This enables [our] armed forces to work together successfully, be it in NATO operations or in national, coalition, EU or UN formats.[7]

Applied to the legal context, interoperability refers to the need for nations to work together in a variety of contexts despite differing legal frameworks applicable to (or interpreted differently by) each nation.[8] As one close observer of NATO operations defined it, "'[l]egal interoperability' is understood here as the ability of the forces of two or more nations to operate effectively together in

---

[5] See, e.g., Warsaw Communiqué, para. 129: "NATO is an alliance of values, including individual liberty, human rights, democracy, and the rule of law. These shared values are essential to what NATO is and what it does. Further incorporating them into all areas of our work will make NATO stronger."

[6] NATO Standardization Office, NATO Glossary of Terms and Definitions, AAP-06(2014), http:// wcnjk.wp.mil.pl/plik/file/N_20130808_AAP6EN.pdf.

[7] *Ibid.*, para. 49.

[8] See ICRC, "International Humanitarian Law and the Challenges of Contemporary Armed Conflicts," Report 2011, 32, highlighting that "[a]n important practical challenge is to ensure that peace operations are conducted taking into consideration the different levels of ratification of IHL instruments and the different interpretations of those treaties and of customary IHL by troop contributing states."

the execution of assigned missions and tasks and with full respect for their legal obligations, notwithstanding the fact that nations concerned have varying legal obligations and varying interpretations of these obligations."[9] Another legal advisor with NATO legal experience echoed this definition and emphasized "the ability to have a generally shared single common body of law, as it allows for a critical analysis to focus, compare and identify potential areas of legal divergences and strains and, in turn, assess, for the operational commander, the impact these divergences may have on operational interoperability."[10] This "generally shared single common body of law" is arrived at in a pragmatic manner.[11]

The first step to promoting legal interoperability is to have a broad understanding of these areas of legal divergence. This task requires careful analysis of the legal positions expressed by NATO Allies. This may be a relatively straightforward exercise, or it may be difficult. As I put it when describing some of the challenges facing NATO legal advisors:

> [W]hen called upon to advise on the obligations of Allies, NATO legal advisers must seek evidence of how Allies interpret these obligations. In many cases, the Allies have not had occasion to opine on such matters. In some cases, they may be looking to international organizations of which they are members in order to consult on such matters. They may even be looking for guidance in this regard or, by contrast, they might not find the views of an international organization to be relevant. In the absence of evidence of State views, NATO legal advisers must make their best prediction of the state of affairs.

In this sense, the NATO legal community is only as strong as its links with Allied lawyers. These kinds of link are needed for NATO legal advisors to be effective in their mission of producing the kind of practical and workable legal advice based on actual State experience. From the perspective of a NATO lawyer, the DoD Law of War Manual will be a useful way of getting insight into DoD views.

---

9   M. Zwanenburg, "International Humanitarian Law Interoperability in Multinational Operations" (2013) 95 *International Review of the Red Cross* 681–84.

10   K. Abbott, "A Brief Overview of Legal Interoperability Challenges for NATO Arising from the Interrelationship between IHL and IHRL in Light of the European Convention on Human Rights" (2014) 96 *International Review of the Red Cross* 107.

11   See P. Olson, "Convergence and Conflicts of Human Rights and International Humanitarian Law in Military Operations: A NATO Perspective," in E. de Wet and J. Kleffner (eds.), *Convergence and Conflicts of Human Rights and International Humanitarian Law in Military Operations* (Pretoria: PULP, 2014), 254, noting that "NATO addresses legal questions ... pragmatically rather than doctrinally ... rather than requiring adherence to a single common body of law, the Alliance's expectation is that all States participating in a NATO or NATO-led operation will act lawfully within the legal framework applicable to them."

3 NATO PRACTICE IN THE DOD LAW OF WAR MANUAL

References to NATO practice are scattered throughout the Manual. Although citations to NATO practice are not as extensive as in other legal publications prepared under DoD auspices,[12] the Manual does rely on NATO practice in a number of ways.

The relatively focused use of NATO practice is on a par with the approach to citing NATO operations taken in other recent national law of war manuals. For example, the 2012 French manual uses a NATO definition of terrorism;[13] its 2013 German counterpart refers to the Alliance's work on cyber-defense and nuclear deterrence;[14] the United Kingdom manual of the same year refers to NATO practice on such matters as camouflage, prisoners of war standards, and interrogation procedures;[15] and the 2016 Danish manual includes a section dedicated to the Danish translation of the NATO Status of Forces of Agreement and its evolving interpretation.[16] What these national manuals have in common with DoD's effort is the willingness to draw on NATO practice as a useful example of State practice.

In other words, even if the Manual's use of NATO practice is relatively limited, it still helps illustrate the potential value of international organizations as repositories of State practice that might be relevant to broader understanding of international law. While processes such as the formation of customary international law are naturally largely State-driven, the Manual helps show how international organizations can play an important role in assisting in its identification.

3.1 Use of NATO Definitions

One way in which the Manual uses NATO practice is by making use of NATO definitions. In some places, definitions used in NATO are cited to illustrate a specific point. Some of these definitions are agreed by the Allies. For

---

[12] E.g., the Operational Law Handbook 2015 produced by the US Army's Judge Advocate General's Legal Center and School includes a full section on NATO operations, in particular NATO rules of engagement. See International and Operational Law Department, "Operational Law Handbook (2015)," 449–52 (outlining NATO's basic structure and principal decision-making processes as well as NATO ROE).

[13] French Ministry of Defence, "Manuel de Droit des Conflits Armés – Edition 2012" (2012), 89.

[14] German Federal Ministry of Defence, "Law of Armed Conflict – Manual" (2013), ¶ 131 and ¶ 465.

[15] UK Ministry of Defence, "The Joint Service Manual of the Law of Armed Conflict" (2013), ¶7.25.2 (NATO STANAG 2931), ¶ 8.25 (NATO STANAG 2044), ¶ 8.34.3 (NATO STANAG 2033).

[16] Danish Ministry of Defence, "Militærmanual om Folkeret for Danske Væbnede Styrker i Internationale Militære Operationer" (2016), Chapter 3, section 6.

example, the discussion of the principle of military necessity makes reference to a definition upon which consensus was reached by the Allies.[17]

Other definitions might not necessarily reflect an agreed position of the Allies, but may still be useful in identifying Allied practice. The section on non-lethal weapons, for instance, cites a report of the NATO Research and Technology Organization, a former NATO agency that was replaced in 2012 by the NATO Science and Technology Organization. That agency produced a variety of studies, including a 2006 report on the non-lethal technologies. In attempting to categorize such weapons, that report made reference to the practice of NATO Allies.[18] In other words, while the report itself was not necessarily agreed by Allies, it was based on their practice.

3.2 NATO Practice on Jus ad Bellum Issues

Aside from the use of definitions, NATO practice helps illustrate the Manual's treatment of several key issues of contemporary international law. For example, there are several references to NATO experience in the Manual's discussion of *jus ad bellum*, in particular in relation to what the Manual calls "Rationales for the Use of Forces."[19]

3.2.1 September 11, 2001 Invocation of Article 5

One such rationale relates to the use of force in self-defense against non-State actors. This section explains that "[t]he inherent right of self-defense, recognized in Article 51 of the Charter of the United Nations, applies in response to any 'armed attack,' not just attacks that originate with States."[20] One of the key

---

[17]   See DoD Law of War Manual, ¶ 2.2 fn. 13 (citing NATO Glossary of Terms and Definitions, AAP-6 at 2-M-6 (2009), which defines military necessity as "the principle whereby a belligerent has the right to apply any measures which are required to bring about the successful conclusion of a military operation and which are not forbidden by the laws of war").

[18]   See DoD Law of War Manual, ¶ 6.5.10.2, fn. 113, citing NATO Research and Technology Organisation Technical Report RTO-TR-HFM-073, "The Human Effects of Non-Lethal Technologies," §6-4 (August 2006) ("The military forces of the North Atlantic Treaty Organisation (NATO) use the descriptor 'non-lethal'. This term in the military context does not imply nil casualties or damage, but is a statement of intent to achieve the lowest achievable probability of casualties and physical damage. The term has often been challenged as being inappropriate, but an alternative descriptor that can provide a better interpretation has yet to be widely adopted within international circles.").

[19]   DoD Law of War Manual, ¶ 1.11.4.   [20]   DoD Law of War Manual, ¶ 1.11.5.4.

examples cited was the North Atlantic Council's decision to invoke Article 5 in response to the September 11 attacks.[21]

This was of course the first (and, so far, the only) time that the North Atlantic Council decided to invoke Article 5 of the North Atlantic Treaty. That Article provides in part that:

> The Parties agree that an armed attack against one or more of them in Europe or North America shall be considered an attack against them all and consequently they agree that, if such an armed attack occurs, each of them, in exercise of the right of individual or collective self-defence recognised by Article 51 of the Charter of the United Nations, will assist the Party or Parties so attacked by taking forthwith, individually and in concert with the other Parties, such action as it deems necessary, including the use of armed force, to restore and maintain the security of the North Atlantic area.

According to the Council's statement on the day following the attacks, "the North Atlantic Council met again in response to the appalling attacks perpetrated yesterday against the United States. The Council agreed that if it is determined that this attack was directed from abroad against the United States, it shall be regarded as an action covered by Article 5 of the Washington Treaty."[22] Adopted by consensus in the Council, this statement was a strong example of Allies' political support for and solidarity with the United States. It also formed the basis for NATO's direct support to the United States immediately following the attacks, including the deployment of Airborne Warning and Control System (AWACS) aircraft to assist with monitoring US airspace, as well as Operation Active Endeavour, NATO's counterterrorism operation in the Mediterranean Sea launched after the attacks.

Aside from its political and operational impact, the Council's decision remains of lasting legal significance as tangible evidence of State practice in support of the proposition that non-State actors can be the authors of an armed attack that could trigger the use of force in inherent right of individual or collective self-defense under international law. This has not always been a widely accepted idea and has attracted debate even in recent years where non-State actors have been at the forefront of conflict. In this sense, the Council's decision can be seen as a significant contribution by NATO to the development of international law.

The decision is also highly relevant to the current security environment. Non-State armed groups are part of the daily landscape surrounding NATO's

---

[21] *Ibid.*, see fn. 235 (citing Digest of United States Practice in International Law, US Department of State, Office of the Legal Advisor (2002), 1011–12).

[22] Statement by the North Atlantic Council, Press Release (2001), 124, www.nato.int/docu/pr/2001/p01-124e.htm.

operation in Afghanistan, its work on countering piracy off the coast of Somalia, operations in the Mediterranean, and contribution to the international community's fight against ISIS, to name just a few recent NATO activities. The potential role of non-State armed groups in cyberwarfare and the challenges associated with such groups also occupies significant time in Alliance discussions of cyber-doctrine and practice. Finally, non-State armed groups loom large since Russia's 2014 annexation of Crimea, especially in adopting a strategy to address the challenges posed by hybrid warfare.[23]

3.2.2 1999 KOSOVO INTERVENTION

In addition to self-defense, the Manual also deals with other frequently advanced justifications for the use of force. One of these is humanitarian intervention, a basis which the Manual ultimately rejects. In its discussion, the Manual makes reference to NATO's practice in the 1999 Kosovo intervention. In doing so, it provides an interesting example of the way in which NATO functions when Allies hold different legal views.

The Manual rejects humanitarian intervention as an independent basis for the use of force under international law: "Although the United Kingdom and certain other States have argued that intervention for humanitarian reasons may be a legal basis for the resort to force, the United States has not adopted this legal rationale."[24] It goes on to explain that humanitarian intervention was not among the legal justifications advanced by the US to support NATO's intervention to address the humanitarian catastrophe in Kosovo in 1999. The Manual notes that the US "rather expressed the view that such action was justified on the basis of a number of factors."[25] The footnote to this section expands on the "number of factors" that were relevant to US decision-making, citing in particular the public explanation made during May 1999 oral proceedings before the International Court of Justice (ICJ).[26]

---

[23] In the Warsaw Summit Communiqué in July 2016, our Heads of State and Government highlighted the role of non-State armed groups in hybrid warfare, which they described as a "broad, complex, and adaptive combination of conventional and non-conventional means, and overt and covert military, paramilitary, and civilian measures, are employed in a highly integrated design by state and non-state actors to achieve their objectives."

[24] DoD Law of War Manual, ¶ 1.11.4.4.   [25] Ibid.

[26] See fn. 221 (citing David Andrews, Legal Advisor, Department of State, Oral Proceedings, May 11, 1999, Legality of Use of Force (Yugoslavia v. United States) ICJ 10 (¶ 1.7) ("As you have already heard, the actions of the Members of the NATO Alliance find their justification in a number of factors. These include: – The humanitarian catastrophe that has engulfed the people of Kosovo as a brutal and unlawful campaign of ethnic cleansing has forced many hundreds of thousands to flee their homes and has severely endangered their lives and well-

Indeed, different NATO members took different views on the legal basis for the Kosovo operations. For example, while the United States relied on the multifactor approach explained to the ICJ, it is well known that other members took different positions.[27] In explaining the political and legal basis for the intervention, then NATO Secretary General Lord Robertson recounted that before the campaign began

> there was a major discussion in the North Atlantic Council, during which the Council took the following factors into consideration: the Yugoslav government's non-compliance with earlier UN Security Council resolutions; the warnings from the UN Secretary General about the dangers of a humanitarian disaster in Kosovo; the risk of such a catastrophe in the light of Yugoslavia's failure to seek a peaceful resolution of the crisis; the unlikelihood that a further UN Security Council resolution would be passed in the near future; and the threat to peace and security in the region.[28]

Faced with these factors, Robertson wrote, "the Council agreed that a sufficient legal basis existed for the Alliance to threaten and, if necessary, use force against the Federal Republic of Yugoslavia."[29] In other words, there was agreement among Allies that a legal basis for the use of force existed, although there was not an agreement on the specific grounds.[30] This is a fairly common technique in NATO, where different nations have different international legal obligations or positions but where there is a need to take consensus decisions that enable an operation to go forward in the spirit of legal interoperability discussed above. NATO's experience with differing legal justifications by different nations shows the way in which Alliance structures can accommodate such differences in a practical way.

---

being; – The acute threat of the actions of the Federal Republic of Yugoslavia to the security of neighbouring States, including the threat posed by extremely heavy flows of refugees and armed incursions into their territories; – The serious violation of international humanitarian law and human rights obligations by forces under the control of the Federal Republic of Yugoslavia, including widespread murder, disappearances, rape, theft and destruction of property; and, finally – The resolutions of the Security Council, which have determined that the actions of the Federal Republic of Yugoslavia constitute a threat to peace and security in the region and, pursuant to Chapter VII of the Charter, demanded a halt to such actions.").

[27] See, e.g., P. E. Gallis, "Kosovo: Lessons Learned from Operation *Allied Force*," Congressional Research Services Report for US Congress (Nov. 19, 1999).

[28] NATO Secretary General Lord Robertson of Port Ellen, "Kosovo: One Year On – Achievement and Challenge," Report of Mar. 21, 2000, p. 24.

[29] *Ibid.* [30] *Ibid.*

4 NATO'S ASSISTANCE TO ALLIES ON LAW OF WAR IMPLEMENTATION

In addition to helping provide definitions of law of war concepts or examples of practice to illustrate the approach of NATO Allies to key *jus in bello* questions, another area where NATO practice is used in the Manual is in its discussion of international or multinational actions to implement and enforce the law of war.[31] Serving as a forum for collective action to support the implementation of law of war obligations is in many ways at the core of NATO's everyday work. For example, while Article 5 of the North Atlantic Treaty is arguably the best-known provision in the treaty, the bulk of NATO's day-to-day work is captured in Article 3, which refers to the need for "continuous and effective self-help and mutual aid" among Allies to build their capacity to defend themselves.[32] An important part of this capacity is the ability to implement law of war obligations. NATO helps Allies do this in a number of ways that are highlighted in the Manual.

NATO's significant practice of assistance in carrying out obligations under the law of war might raise the question of whose obligations these really are. As explained above, NATO's approach is emphatically that the obligations belong to States. This conclusion is endorsed by the Manual for the straightforward reason that "[i]nternational organizations, such as the United Nations or NATO, are not Parties to law of war treaties, such as the 1949 Geneva Conventions. Thus, these organizations do not have obligations under those treaty instruments."[33] Although it has been asserted that such obligations could be binding on international organizations by virtue of customary international law, at least in the specific context of NATO, there are many reasons to doubt this conclusion. These include the fact that it would be difficult if not impossible for NATO as an international organization to comply with law of armed conflict obligations on its own without acting through a particular Ally or Allies.[34]

---

[31] DoD Law of War Manual, ¶ 18.1.3.

[32] Article 3 Washington Treaty: "In order more effectively to achieve the objectives of this Treaty, the Parties, separately and jointly, by means of continuous and effective self-help and mutual aid, will maintain and develop their individual and collective capacity to resist armed attack."

[33] DoD Law of War Manual, ¶ 18.1.4.

[34] See, e.g., P. M. Olson, "A NATO Perspective on Applicability and Application of IHL to Multinational Forces" (2013) 95 *International Review of the Red Cross* 653–57 (noting that "NATO is not a free-standing entity differentiated from its member states; rather, the Organisation was created as a mechanism for coordination of a group of sovereign states,

4.1 Agreed Common Procedures

In some cases, Allies may be able to agree upon common procedures to assist in the implementation of their obligations under the law of war. In other cases, this may not be possible, or it may not be desirable. Where Allies can find common procedures, this does not change the nature of the legal obligation as belonging to each Ally. The Manual notes this practice, when it explains that "States sometimes take actions on the international or multinational level to implement and enforce the law of war."[35]

As an example of this kind of collective action, the Manual cites NATO Standardization Agreements.[36] Standardization is an important part of NATO's work. It refers to "the development and implementation of concepts, doctrines and procedures to achieve and maintain the required levels of compatibility, interchangeability or commonality needed to achieve interoperability."[37] A Standardization Agreement, known by its acronym STANAG, is a NATO document that "specifies the agreement of member nations to implement a standard, in whole or in part, with or without reservation, in order to meet an interoperability requirement."[38] STANAGs go through a process called "ratification" whereby each Ally decides whether to adopt and implement the provisions of the STANAG.[39] Partner nations (that is, non-NATO States that cooperate with NATO) are also invited to adopt STANAGs.

and is better understood as a tool, or set of tools, available for use by the Allies when and if they wish to do so … [T]he actions taken by NATO in conducting military operations are, with only a few exceptions for assets owned by the Alliance collectively, carried out by contingents provided by, and under the command of, the participating individual Allies or NATO operational partners – and over which those states retain ultimate, and often substantial daily, control.").

35 DoD Law of War Manual, ¶ 18.1.3.   36 Ibid.

37 See NATO, "Standardization", www.nato.int/cps/en/natohq/topics_69269.htm.   38 Ibid.

39 For a thorough description of the procedure to adopt a STANAG, see S. L. Bumgardner, Z. Hegedus, and D. Palmer-DeGreve (eds.), NATO *Legal Deskbook*, 2nd ed. (Mons/Norfolk: NATO, 2010), 63–64. A NATO Standardization Agreement has been defined as "the *record of an agreement* among several or all member nations to adopt like, or similar, military equipment, ammunition, supplies and stores; and operational, logistic and administrative procedures" (italics added). STANAGs developed and adopted through a defined procedure. Although nations may choose to participate or not to participate in the development of standards, "[c]onsensus/unanimity is required for all STANAGs covering Key/Capstone documents derived from the MC and those pertaining to Policy documents," as set out in AAP-03 Ed. J Version 3, Production, maintenance and management of NATO standardization documents (2015). Finally, Nations are expected to respond to the ratification request by using a specific format (Annex E to AAP-03). In addition to deciding not to ratify or not to participate in a particular STANAG, options open to Allies include choosing to ratify and implement, ratify with reservations, or ratify with future implementation. AAP-03 itself recalls that the "ratifying and implementing" response "indicates that a Nation is in full agreement with the STANAG and intends to implement the covered Allied standards within a specified

There are a variety of STANAGs relevant to armed conflict. Recent STANAGs include two agreements that help illustrate a common view of how international obligations should be implemented. The first such example is a 2013 STANAG that provides guidelines for a multinational medical unit.[40] This agreement establishes certain baseline requirements for a multinational medical unit that could be seen as evidence of Allied views on the minimum requirements of international law.

The second example is a 2015 STANAG that sets forth Allied doctrine for the military contribution to stabilization and reconstruction.[41] This agreement covers a range of legal issues that might arise in a stabilization and reconstruction operation, including the potential applicability of the armed conflict legal framework.[42] The STANAG provides an overview of legal issues that arise in a non-international armed conflict (NIAC).[43] It also addresses the legal basis for detention in a NIAC[44] as well as detention standards[45] and the requirements for transfer of detainees to third parties.[46] Finally, the STANAG discusses the role of the International Committee of the Red Cross, stressing the fundamental contribution that it can make such as in accessing detention facilities to ensure the necessary relief and appraising detainee treatment and conditions.[47]

STANAG 2590 also includes an annex that details legal considerations that bear upon NATO-led military operations in support of stabilization and reconstruction. The annex points out that NATO-led forces conducting such activities are bound to comply with international law, including the law of war and international law regarding human rights, as applicable, as well as with their respective national laws and regulations. The annex notes that the fact that the law of war dealing with international armed conflicts (IACs) would not usually apply to these conflicts "might lead to a legal position that can be a source of confusion" for NATO forces. In this respect,

---

timescale" (para. 2.5.2.1.1). In the latter case, it is worth noticing that a "ratifying reference" is to be included in the Annex E form returned by the nation (para. 2.5.2.1.2).

[40] STANAG 2552, Guidelines for a Multinational Medical Unit, 2nd ed. (July 5, 2013).

[41] STANAG 2590, Allied Joint Doctrine for the Military Contribution to Stabilization and Reconstruction (1st ed.), Dec. 14, 2015.

[42] *Ibid.*, Annex C – "Legal Considerations," Section C002.   [43] *Ibid.*, Section C003.

[44] *Ibid.*, Section C004.   [45] *Ibid.*, ¶ c.   [46] *Ibid.*, ¶ d.

[47] *Ibid.*, ¶ e, noting that "the ICRC must be permitted to visit detainees and provide them certain types of relief" and that the "responsible national or multinational legal advisor should serve as the escort and liaison with the ICRC." Also, the annex emphasizes that "[b]oth the JFC and the legal advisor should recognize that the ICRC, as an impartial humanitarian organization … capable of providing assistance in a variety of ways." To conclude, "[i]nvolving the ICRC is a central issue when considering detainee issues."

the annex emphasizes that Common Article 3 to all four of the 1949 Geneva Conventions is specifically intended to apply to NIACs.

Another area of major consideration in the annex consists of detainee operations of civilians that, although occasionally involving NATO-led forces, generally remain a national responsibility. The legal basis for detention is regarded as one of the most significant aspects to be addressed. Common Article 3 of the 1949 Geneva Conventions is referred to in this respect too as the provision setting out the minimum standards for detention and internment (i.e., humane treatment until release), regardless of the precise legal status of those persons captured, detained, or otherwise held. The legal considerations also take into account "the international human rights commitments of the NATO nations," having particular regard to the "conditions under which NATO-led forces may not transfer the custody of detainees to the [host nations] or any other foreign government." The annex expressly refers to some of the Allies' obligations under the European Convention on Human Rights (ECHR), notably, the prohibitions on torture or inhuman or degrading treatment.

Finally, a particular interest in recent standardization work has been the area of law of war training. Although training is a national responsibility, given the prevalence of multinational operations, a certain degree of basic standards were deemed desirable in order to promote interoperability. In 2013, work was completed on STANAG 2449, entitled "Training in the Law of Armed Conflict." This STANAG sets out a minimum standard of necessary training for NATO forces, including a range of law of war topics.[48] Twenty-three Allies have ratified the STANAG, with only one nation with a specific reservation.[49]

4.2 Support for International Criminal Tribunal for the former Yugoslavia (ICTY)

In addition to agreed common procedures for the implementation of law of war obligations, the Manual devotes attention to the international community's mechanisms for collective enforcement. One of these is the ICTY, with

---

[48] See J. M. Prescott, "STANAG 2449 – Training in the Law of Armed Conflict" (2009) 19 NATO Legal Gazette 7. For a discussion of the STANAG situated within a broader discussion of the challenges of law of war training in multinational operations in Afghanistan, see J. M. Prescott, "Tactical Implementation of Rules of Engagement in a Multinational Force Reality," in G. S. Corn, R. E. van Landingham, and S. R. Reeves (eds.), U.S. Military Operations: Law, Policy, and Practice (Oxford University Press, 2016).

[49] Among NATO Allies, the United States, Turkey, Slovakia, Montenegro, Luxembourg, and Iceland have not ratified STANAG 2449 and its accompanying training standard, Allied Training Publication-2 on Law of Armed Conflict Training.

regard to which the Manual notes that NATO played a key role. For example, the Manual recalls that the "United States has, through its membership in the U.N. Security Council, supported both the efforts of the ICTR and (also acting through NATO) the efforts of the ICTY."[50] The Manual further notes that a key aspect of NATO's involvement was its facilitating of operations to apprehend, transfer, and support the prosecution of Persons Indicted for War Crimes (PIFWC) in the ICTY, including through NATO's support to the European Union.[51]

As agreed when the NATO-led Implementation Force (IFOR) operation was authorized on December 16, 1995,[52] the North Atlantic Council reaffirmed its full cooperation with the ICTY. There were two basic parts of the Council policy. First, IFOR would detain and transfer to the ICTY persons indicted for war crimes by the ICTY, when coming into contact with them and carrying out its duties as defined by the military annex of the Dayton Peace Agreement. On the other hand, IFOR would continue to support the Tribunal in the theatre by providing logistical support to the ICTY on a case-by-case request and to the extent that IFOR's primary duties and available resources so permitted.[53]

To support these efforts, in 1996, the Supreme Headquarters Allied Powers Europe (SHAPE) and the ICTY concluded a Memorandum of Understanding which codified practical arrangements or the detention and transfer of persons indicted for war crimes to the ICTY, and for support by IFOR to the ICTY.[54] NATO's support to the work of ICTY was reaffirmed in the mandate of Stabilization Force in Bosnia-Herzegovina (SFOR), the peace enforcement operation that took over from IFOR and operated under Chapter VII of the UN Charter.[55]

NATO forces have been instrumental in many arrests. For example, over the course of its deployment, SFOR was instrumental in bringing thirty-nine PIFWCs to the Tribunal in The Hague. SFOR also provided security and logistical support to ICTY investigative teams as well as surveillance of and

---

[50] DoD Law of War Manual, ¶ 18.20.2. [51] *Ibid.*

[52] Operation Implementation Force (IFOR – Joint Endeavour), Dec. 20, 1995 to Dec. 20, 1996.

[53] As an example of such a support, NATO assisted the ICTY in the secure transport of two persons detained as suspects and potential witnesses from Sarajevo to The Hague on February 12 for further investigation by the Tribunal. Likewise, another example consists of the assistance that IFOR gave to an ICTY team carrying out investigations in the Srebrenica area.

[54] See Press Statement on Signing of the Memorandum of Understanding between SHAPE and the International Criminal Tribunal for Former Yugoslavia, Press Release (1996) 074 (May 9, 2006), www.nato.int/cps/en/SID-49C0A60C-5CF4F0F6/natolive/news_24933.htm.

[55] UN Security Council Resolution 1088 (1996), adopted by the Security Council at its 3723rd meeting, Dec. 12, 1996.

ground patrolling around alleged mass graves. NATO's commitment has consistently been reiterated.[56] Alongside cooperating with ICTY through its deployed operation, NATO also exerted diplomatic pressure on the countries concerned, affirming that "co-operation with the ICTY is a key conditionality for further progress in NATO/BiH relations."[57]

5 CONCLUSION

From a NATO perspective, the drafters of the Manual can be commended for making use of multinational practice. It is heartening to see NATO practice recognized as a useful yardstick in areas such as definitions, agreed common frameworks to implement obligations, training programs, and support to international institutions. In the end, States remain central to the development and application of international law. For a NATO legal advisor, it is crucial to have a firm understanding of the legal position of nations in order to be able to help them come to consensus and operate together in an effective manner. The Manual will help in that process. It may motivate other States to make their views known as well or, for those States that have done so, it might spur increased discussion and interaction. Such interaction would be useful for a variety of reasons, including because it could help identify selected areas in which Manual views may be different than those held by other Allies. In that sense, like its recent counterparts in several nations across the Alliance, the Manual stands to make a lasting contribution to NATO's work in the legal field.

---

[56] See, e.g., Statement on Kosovo issued by the Heads of State and Government participating in the meeting of the North Atlantic Council in Washington, DC, Press Release S-1(99) 062, Apr. 23, 1999, para. 11. The Secretary General reaffirmed on several occasions that NATO's operational capabilities were devoted to investigate all those responsible for war crimes and crimes against humanity, secure relevant information on the ground, and that "[a]ll Allies believe strongly that all indicted war criminals should be placed in the custody of the ICTY in The Hague as rapidly as possible" (Statement by the Secretary General in reaction to Washington Post article on SFOR'S role with respect to Indicted War Criminals, Press Release (1998) 046, Apr. 23, 1998).

[57] Speech by NATO Secretary General, Jaap de Hoop Scheffer at the meeting of the United Nations Security Council, Nov. 11, 2004. See also Istanbul Summit Communiqué issued by the Heads of State and Government participating in the meeting of the North Atlantic Council, Press Release (2004) 096, June 28, 2004, para. 7: "While welcoming improvement in cooperation with the International Criminal Tribunal for the Former Yugoslavia (ICTY), where it has occurred, we stress that all countries concerned must cooperate fully with the ICTY, in particular bringing to justice all those who are indicted by the Tribunal", www.nato.int/cps/en/natohq/official_texts_21023.htm?selectedLocale=en.

6

What's in a Name, and What's Not: The DoD Law of War Manual and the Question of Operational Utility

Geoffrey S. Corn[*]

1 INTRODUCTION

According to Webster's Dictionary, a manual is, "a book that is conveniently handled; *especially*: [a] handbook[:] an instruction manual . . . "[1] Manuals are utilized extensively in US military practice to provide practical guides that instruct the user how to perform a given task, set of tasks, or function. This chapter asks whether the Department of Defense (DoD) Law of War Manual (the Manual) is actually aligned with Webster's definition.[2] This requires first asking what "task" or "function" the Manual is intended to facilitate. This chapter argues that the effort to be "all things for all consumers" compromised the effort to produce a genuine manual, resulting in a product that, albeit valuable for some purposes, failed to hit the most important target.

Exploring these questions need not be cast in negative terms. Indeed, it may be that while the Manual is not a manual *per se*, it nonetheless makes a valuable contribution to US military and government understanding and implementation of the law of armed conflict (LOAC). But understanding what the Manual truly is, and what it is not, is important for considering whether it left dangerous gaps in achieving the goal of maximizing US LOAC compliance, and how those gaps should be addressed. This indeed is the ultimate point of this chapter – to highlight why the Manual is fundamentally mischaracterized as such, and to suggest how DoD and the military Services should respond to this reality.

---

[*] Geoffrey S. Corn is The Vinson & Elkins Professor of Law at South Texas College of Law Houston in Houston Texas.
[1] "Manual," *Merriam-Webster Online Dictionary* (2017), www.merriam-webster.com/dictionary/manual.
[2] DoD Law of War Manual.

Section 2 of this chapter will highlight why a genuine LOAC "manual" is essential for compliance with LOAC obligations during all phases of military operations. Section 3 will explain how the Manual misses the mark in providing "the force" with the type of manual needed to accomplish this goal. Section 4 will consider what may account for the delta between the title "Manual" and the true nature of the document, which in turn accounts for the gap between the title and the reality of its impact. Section 5 will then explain why a more accurate characterization for this important document will contribute to both enhancing its actual impact and identifying how to fill the implementation gaps it created.

2 TACTICAL AND TECHNICAL PROFICIENCY AND THE VALUE OF MANUALS

Manuals are essential to developing tactically and technically proficient soldiers.[3] Therefore, it should be unsurprising that the US Army, like all US military Services, developed and maintains a large library of "field" manuals.[4] These field manuals cover virtually every tactical and operational function that soldiers should be prepared to perform. More importantly, they are essential for translating institutional doctrine – the vetted and institutionally endorsed statement of "what right looks like" – into implementation guidance that can be readily assessed and understood by the soldier. Need to construct a fighting position? Check the field manual. Need to breach an obstacle? Check the field manual. Need to set up a forward arming and refueling point? Check the field manual. And the list goes on and on.

Since the adoption of Francis Lieber's famous Code – a General Order applicable to all members of the Union armed forces in the American Civil War – a similar process of translating institutional "doctrine" into accessible and understandable implementation guidance has been relied on to maximize US LOAC compliance.[5] Indeed, perhaps the greatest innovation of the Lieber Code was the recognition by both Dr. Lieber and the senior US commanders who commissioned his work that meaningful compliance with and implementation of the principles of the *jus belli* necessitated a "field manual" type translation – a "code" of conduct for forces in the field.

---

[3] "Soldiers" used generically for all members of the armed forces.

[4] See http://usacac.army.mil/sites/default/files/misc/doctrine/CDG/fms.html.

[5] General Order No. 100, Instructions for the Government of Armies of the United States in the Field (Apr. 24, 1863), reprinted in *The War of the Rebellion: A Compilation of the Official Records of the Union and Confederate Armies*, Series III, Vol. 3 (GPO 1899) (the Lieber Code), www.loc.gov/rr/frd/Military_Law/Lieber_Collection/pdf/Instructions-gov-armies.pdf.

Of course, the Lieber Code was not technically a field manual. However, its simplicity along with the direct nature of its mandate provided just the type of translation to "implementable" guidance that characterizes the modern field manual.

This approach to providing necessary guidance for the implementation of obligations imposed by the laws and customs of war led to the publication of the 1940 Field Manual (FM) 27–10, Rules of Land Warfare.[6] This manual included treaty and customary based rules considered binding on all US armed forces engaged in land warfare. The content is functionally organized, focusing on rules of conduct with short explanations, and citation to corresponding treaty provisions. This manual style was replicated with the publication of a successor FM 27–10, The Law of Land Warfare.[7] Like the 1940 version of FM 27–10, the more detailed July 1956 version was functionally organized, providing an easily accessible source of rules considered binding on US armed forces engaged in land warfare. FM 27–10 received another update in 1976, which was organized in the same manner.[8]

FM 27–10 defines its purpose as "provid[ing] authoritative guidance to military personnel on the customary and treaty law applicable to the conduct of warfare on land and to relationships between belligerents and neutral States."[9] This purpose statement is instructive, for it indicates not only that the Manual provides authoritative guidance, but that this guidance is intended for military personnel engaged in operations. Like other field manuals, FM 27–10 translated the legal equivalent of "doctrine" – treaty and customary international law obligations derived from "customary and treaty law" regulating land warfare – into rules that could be understood and applied by forces in the field; a true "field" manual.

The US Navy adopted a similar approach to providing operational forces with a clear and accessible statement of rules applicable to naval warfare. In 1997 the Navy published its Annotated Supplement; and by 1999, the publication was further distributed through the International Law Studies "Blue Book" series:

---

6   Field Manual 27-10, Rules of Land Warfare (Washington: US Dep't. of Army, 1 Oct. 1940).
7   Field Manual 27-10, The Law of Land Warfare (Washington: US Dep't. of Army, July 18, 1956) (FM 27-10).
8   *Ibid.*
9   *Ibid.*, ¶ 1 (The same paragraph adds the following qualification: "Although certain of the legal principles set forth herein have application to warfare at sea and in the air as well as to hostilities on land, this Manual otherwise concerns itself with the rules peculiar to naval and aerial warfare only to the extent that such rules have some direct bearing on the activities of land forces.").

Originally prepared in soft cover in late 1997 for use by students at the Naval War College and by judge advocates and others responsible for advising operational commanders on the law, it has been so well received that we are pleased to be able to make it available to a wider audience through the "Blue Book" series . . .

. . . the *Annotated Supplement* will achieve a much wider distribution to academic institutions and military commands around the world. That distribution will facilitate research on the law of naval operations and will serve to promote the rule of law in the conduct of future operations.[10]

And although the Annotated Supplement enjoyed distribution to multiple audiences, the publication remained true to its intended use as a "manual." As the Preface to this document indicates:

This publication is intended for the use of operational commanders and supporting staff elements at all levels of command. It is designed to provide officers in command and their staff with an overview of the rules of law governing naval operations in peacetime and during armed conflict. The explanations and descriptions in this publication are intended to enable the naval commander and his staff to comprehend more fully the legal foundations upon which the orders issued to them by higher authority are premised and to understand better the commander's responsibilities under international and domestic law to execute his mission within that law. This publication sets forth general guidance. It is not a comprehensive treatment of the law nor is it a substitute for the definitive legal guidance provided by judge advocates and others responsible for advising commanders on the law.[11]

Accordingly, like FM 27–10, the Annotated Supplement is functionally organized and focused on operational issues to provide naval commanders and their staffs with essential information to facilitate LOAC implementation. Note specifically that this Naval "manual" explicitly disavows any attempt to be a comprehensive restatement of the LOAC.[12]

It should be noted, however, that a "field manual" approach to providing US armed forces essential guidance that enables them to implement the LOAC is inevitably more complicated than guidance necessary to implement other types of doctrine. Indeed, it may be naïve to compare any legal implementation process with the process of executing specific operational tasks.

---

[10] Center for Naval Warfare Studies, Oceans Law and Policy Department, *Annotated Supplement to the Commander's Handbook on the Law of Naval Operations* (Newport: US Naval War College, 1997) (excerpt from the Forward and Introduction of the 1999 publication of the Annotated Supplement in the 73rd Volume of the US Naval War College International Law Studies series).

[11] *Ibid.*, Preface.   [12] *Ibid.*

As the Naval Commander's Annotated Supplement notes, an overview or summary of applicable rules may assist commanders in understanding the legal frameworks in which they operate, but is not a substitute for "definitive legal guidance provided by judge advocates."[13] This reveals the challenge that drafters of the DoD Manual obviously confronted: was the ultimate product intended to be a true "manual," providing clear and relatively concise guidance to subordinate forces to assist them in understanding the relationship of law to their operations and the basic nature of those obligations? Or was it intended to provide a comprehensive treatment of the law that ostensibly might serve as a substitute for the type of legal advice provided by judge advocates?

Paragraph 1.1.1 articulates the purpose of the DoD Manual, which "is to provide information on the law of war to DoD personnel responsible for implementing the law of war and executing military operations."[14] The Manual undoubtedly provides a substantial amount of "information," but what is less clear is whether the nature of the information provided is really targeted at the members of the armed forces responsible for implementing the law of war and executing military operations. Unlike its relatively streamlined predecessors, the Manual is a massive publication, nearly 1,200 pages in length. And while it does follow FM 27-10's model of functional organization based on various types of operational situations and accordant issues, the very density of the document renders it much more like a legal treatise than a military manual.

Of course, this begs the question of who the Manual drafters envisioned as being responsible for implementing the law of war during military operations. But the answer to this question seems self-evident – military commanders. Indeed, one of the great challenges of contemporary LOAC implementation is to develop a leadership culture that not only embraces the logic of the law, but an understanding that the law truly "belongs" to commanders, and not legal advisors or judge advocates (JAGs). This "command ownership" is deeply embedded in the LOAC. For example, as I explained in my article entitled "Contemplating the Meaning of 'Responsibility' in Responsible Command," the very privilege granted by international law to directly participate in hostilities – the combatant's privilege – is contingent on operating under responsible command, not under a responsible military lawyer.[15]

---

[13]   *Ibid.*   [14]   DoD Law of War Manual, ¶ 1.1.1.
[15]   See G. S. Corn, "Contemplating the Meaning of 'Responsibility' in Responsible Command 9–11" (2015) (unpublished manuscript) (on file with author), https://papers.ssrn.com/sol3/papers.cfm?abstract_id=2546594.

This is not to suggest that the role of the legal advisor is insignificant, or that a comprehensive treatise-type statement of the DoD's approach to the LOAC would serve no useful purpose. To the contrary, legal advisors, or JAGs, have never been more significant and influential in the planning and execution of military operations. And the reality is that a unified statement of DoD positions on LOAC issues was long overdue. The long absence of a comprehensive document, like the Manual, required that each military Service adopt its own positions on when, where, and how the law applied to US military operations. This interpretation and dissemination process often occurred at the respective Service JAG Schools. For example, US Army JAGs relied extensively on the products produced by the International and Operational Law Department in Charlottesville, such as the Law of War Deskbook, as an authoritative statement on the law.[16] Some efforts were made to produce products that were more oriented towards "joint" or inter-Service interpretations, such as the venerable Operational Law Handbook, and products produced by the US Army Center for Law and Military Operations.[17] However, none of these publications – publications extensively relied on by JAGs in every aspect of operational law practice – carried DoD's official endorsement.

Because much of the information provided in these publications was based on FM 27–10, treaties binding on the United States, and associated commentaries, this decentralized process of defining relevant legal obligations seemed to work relatively well – that is, until September 11, 2001. The initiation of responsive military action against al-Qaeda produced an intersection of situational uncertainties related to the conflict and the participants, and doctrinal uncertainty resulting from various lacunae in Departmental guidance. In response, JAGs began to fill these voids by resorting to the instruction and materials they had been provided by their JAG schools. So, for example, when the US Marine Corps first began to process captives in Afghanistan, it applied the methodology outlined in the then-current 2000 Law of War Deskbook:

> 5. ... While the United States TREATS all persons initially detained
> consistent with the provisions of the GPW [Geneva Convention
> Relative to the Treatment of Prisoners of War], this is only a policy.

[16] International & Operational Law Department, The Judge Advocate General's Legal Center & School, US Army, Law of Armed Conflict Deskbook (2016). As stated in the Deskbook itself, "[the] Law of Armed Conflict Deskbook is intended to replace, in a single bound volume, similar individual outlines that had been distributed as part of the Judge Advocate Officer Graduate and Basic Courses and departmental short courses."

[17] International & Operational Law Department, The Judge Advocate General's Legal Center & School, US Army, JA 422, "Operational Law Handbook" (2016) ("The Operational Law Handbook is a 'how to' guide for Judge Advocates practicing operational law.").

6. The Phenomenon of Detainees. In operations other than war, the status of a person temporarily detained is frequently at issue. Therefore, our policy is to initially provide the greatest protections this person could receive until our government determines their legal status[:]

    a. We train our soldiers to always treat captured persons as EPWs [Enemy Prisoners of War] (Doctrine).[18]

But just identifying a term for these captives proved problematic. Were they to be designated as PoWs? Detainees? Unlawful combatants? After pleading for guidance, the answer from DoD was emphatic: they were *not* PoWs and nothing should be done to suggest they might ever even qualify for such status. Hence, the original designation as Persons Under Control, "PUCs."[19]

Nor was DoD pleased to learn that lawyers representing detainees at Guantánamo were citing the Army JAG School Law of War Deskbook and Operational Law Handbook to support their assertion that the human treatment obligation codified in Article 75 of Protocol Additional to the Geneva Conventions of August 12, 1949, and Relating to the Protection of Victims of International Armed Conflicts, June 8, 1977, 1125 UNTS 3 (AP I) was recognized by the US as binding customary international law. This statement did actually appear in these publications:

C. ... The U.S. has not ratified these treaties [the Additional Protocols to the Geneva Conventions of 1949]. Portions, however, do reflect state practice and legal obligations – the key ingredients to customary international law.

...

4. U.S. views these GP [Geneva Protocol, or AP] I articles as either customary international law or acceptable practice though not legally binding: ... 73–89 (treatment of persons in the power of a party to the conflict; women and children; and duties regarding implementation of GP [Geneva Protocol, or AP] I).[20]

---

[18] International & Operational Law Department, The Judge Advocate General's Legal Center & School, US Army, "Law of War Deskbook" (2000), 79–80.

[19] Center For Law & Military Operations, The Judge Advocate General's Legal Center & School, US Army, "Legal Lessons Learned from Afghanistan and Iraq, Vol. I: Major Combat Operations 11 Sept. 2001–1 May 2003" (Aug. 1, 2004), 54.

[20] 2000 LOW Deskbook (above note 18), 150 ("U.S. views these GP [Geneva Protocol, or AP] I articles as either customary international law or acceptable practice though not legally binding: ... 73–89 (treatment of persons in the power of a party to the conflict; women and children; and duties regarding implementation of GP [Geneva Protocol, or AP] I).").

However, at the instruction of the DoD General Counsel, this language was promptly removed. Furthermore, the General Counsel instructed the JAG School to include the following disclaimer in all its publications related to the LOAC and the law of military operations:

> This Deskbook is not a substitute for official publications. Similarly, it should not be considered to espouse an "official" position of the U.S. Army, Department of Defense, or U.S. Government. While every effort has been made to ensure that the material contained herein is current and correct, it should be remembered that these are merely a collection of teaching outlines, collected, bound, and distributed as a matter of instructional convenience, intended only to introduce students to the law and point them to primary sources of that law. Accordingly, the only proper citation to a substantive provision of this Deskbook should be for the limited proposition of how the Army JAG School teaches its judge advocate students.[21]

This disclaimer seems quite odd to be included in a publication relied on so substantially in operational law practice. However, it is a manifestation of the danger DoD perceived from allowing the Services to fill what they perceived as legal voids.[22]

All of the above is merely to highlight the immense value of a comprehensive statement of Departmental LOAC interpretations. The Manual provides both the JAG schoolhouse and the JAG practitioner with what had long been missing – a definitive source of authority to guide operational law practices. And, unlike its predecessor, the treatise-like approach to the Manual substantially mitigates the risk that the Service JAG schools will perceive a need to "gap fill." But if the Manual's stated objective is to be taken at face value, it was not intended to provide a treatise in support of JAGs and other legal advisors; it was intended to provide a "how to" guide to commanders, the decisive agents of LOAC implementation. Unfortunately, the Manual misses that mark.

3 WHAT COMMANDERS NEED, AND WHAT THEY DON'T NEED

LOAC implementation during military operations has never been more complicated, subjected to more scrutiny, or more important. Commanders

---

[21] 2016 LOAC Deskbook (above note 16), Preface.

[22] A 1999 publication of the Annotated Supplement includes the following disclaimer in a footnote of its Preface: "Although The Commander's Handbook on the Law of Naval Operations is a publication of the Department of the Navy, neither The Handbook nor its annotated supplement can be considered as legislative enactment binding upon courts and tribunals applying the rules of war. However, their contents can possess evidentiary value in matters relating to U.S. custom and practice." Annotated Supplement (above note 10), fn. 1.

who lead the armed forces of a democracy like the United States bear an immense responsibility to ensure a reality and perception of respect for law during armed conflict. This is essential not only because it mitigates the human suffering caused by war, but also because it contributes to the legitimacy of US military operations, and in so doing advances the nation's strategic objectives.

This importance is reflected in contemporary US joint operational doctrine, specifically Joint Publication (JP) 3–0, which includes legitimacy among principles of military operations.[23] These principles are intended to guide commanders in the planning and execution of all military operations and are in a very real sense the foundational building blocks of all operational doctrine. As JP 3–0 indicates:

> . . . Joint Publication 3–0, Joint Operations, reflects the current guidance for conducting joint activities across the range of military operations and is the basis for US participation in multinational operations where the US has not ratified specific doctrine or procedures. This keystone publication forms the core of joint warfighting doctrine and establishes the framework for our forces' ability to fight as a joint team.
>
> Often called the "linchpin" of the joint doctrine publication hierarchy, the overarching constructs and principles contained in this publication provide a common perspective from which to plan and execute joint operations independently or in cooperation with our multinational partners, other US Government departments and agencies, and international and nongovernmental organizations.[24]

JP 3–0 then generally explains these principles of joint operations:

> The principles of joint operations are formed around the traditional principles of war. Three additional principles – restraint, perseverance, and legitimacy – are relevant to how the Armed Forces of the United States use combat power across the range of military operations. These three, added to the original nine, comprise 12 principles of joint operations.[25]

JP 3–0 then defines each of these principles in detail. One of these principles, legitimacy, is described as follows:

>   1 The purpose of legitimacy is to maintain legal and moral authority in the conduct of operations.

---

[23] Joint Chiefs of Staff, "Joint Pub. 3-0, Joint Operations" (11 Aug. 2011) (JP 3-0), I-2, www.jcs.mil /Portals/36/Documents/Doctrine/pubs/jp3_0_20170117.pdf.
[24] *Ibid.*, Introductory Letter from Admiral M. G. Mullen.   [25]   *Ibid.*, A-1.

2 Legitimacy, which can be a decisive factor in operations, is based on the actual and perceived legality, morality, and rightness of the actions from the various perspectives of interested audiences. These audiences will include our national leadership and domestic population, governments, and civilian populations in the OA, and nations and organizations around the world.[26]

If, as joint doctrine now emphasizes, legitimacy can be a decisive factor in operations, it is critical that US military operations comply with the LOAC. Indeed, it is this compliance that will serve as the touchstone of legitimacy. This obviously means that commanders and the units they command understand applicable and relevant LOAC rules. But how is this understanding best effectuated?

There is no perfect answer to this question. It is, however, easier to answer what is unlikely to effectuate this outcome: an overly academic recitation of the law. Military personnel and the units they compose develop competence in a wide range of tasks and functions, not through the process of academic study, but through training: first learning, then practicing these tasks. Understanding the role of law requires integration of a legal dimension to the training and development process. The US military recognized this several decades ago, which led to the incorporation of both law and legal oversight into the battle-command training programs that are the culmination of the unit training process.

This does not mean that study of the law is unnecessary. To the contrary, an understanding of essential requirements of the law provides the foundation for incorporating the law into the training process. But no one can expect a commander or members of his or her unit to develop a level of expertise that should be demanded from the legal advisor. Nor would we want the commander or members of the unit focusing on LOAC rules that are not particularly relevant to the nature of the operations and missions they expect to engage in. Furthermore, whatever knowledge foundation they bring to the training process must be supplemented by the ability to quickly and efficiently access relevant LOAC rules during the training process.

What this indicates is that while the Manual in its current form is undoubtedly a useful resource for JAGs, it is not well-suited to contribute to the professional development of the commanders and units they advise. What these consumers need is something much more aligned with the manuals that contribute to their development and competence in the battle tasks they must be prepared to perform. This means a true "field manual" format that distills

---

[26]   *Ibid.*, A-4.

complex concepts down to a statement of rules; that organizes those rules in a functional manner that aligns with the progression of military operations; and that provides a readily accessible and functionally understandable restatement of essential legal obligations.

Unfortunately, the Manual fails to provide this type of tactically and operationally accessible and relevant guidance for commanders. Instead, it is likely that most commanders would view the Manual as a "JAG" or "legal" document, targeted not (as the Manual indicates) at them, but at the advisors who support them. And again, this is not an insignificant contribution. However, it is folly to assume that commanders and their subordinates will have ready access to JAG support and advice whenever a LOAC issue arises. Instead, these forces must be prepared to navigate complex battle spaces with a self-reliant ability to access and understand key legal rules and obligations. A true "rule" focused field manual – one derived from the more comprehensive DoD Manual – would substantially contribute to that goal.

There are a number of ways this gap between the stated goal of the Manual and the product that emerged could be narrowed. One would have been to include "appendices" in the Manual that digest the chapters into rule sets, with reference back to the more comprehensive treatment of the rules in the Manual text. These appendices could have also been tailored to specific battlefield operating functional areas to emphasize the most relevant rules. For example, the Manual could have included appendices on rules for maneuver forces, fire support, air and missile operations, military police operations, convoy operations, combat engineers, military intelligence, civil affairs, and the list goes on. Another approach would be to encourage subordinate Services to publish more Service-oriented field manuals better tailored to the operational force. In fact, the Army and Marine Corps are currently collaborating on such a field manual. The fact that such an initiative was undertaken indicates these Services perceive a need for more operationally tailored guidance for their respective forces.

4 WHAT MIGHT ACCOUNT FOR THE MANUAL THAT EVOLVED?

One of the most interesting aspects of the Manual's promulgation is that its backstory captured almost as much attention as its publication. For more than a decade, W. Hays Parks was the focal point and principal architect for the Manual. When he initiated the process of revising FM 27–10, Parks served as the Special Assistant to the US Army Judge Advocate General for Law of War Matters and the Chief of the Law of War Branch at The Judge Advocate General's Office of International and Operational Law. But as impressive as his titles were, Parks's reputation and influence in the field transcended his position as the Army's LOAC subject matter expert. For many years, although he technically worked for the Army, Parks was seen as DoD's principal LOAC expert, a particularly important role as there was no DoD counterpart for his position. The Navy, Marine Corps, and Air Force all had similar positions, but Parks was truly seen as the elder statesman of this small circle of LOAC experts and advisors.

Furthermore, Parks's influence extended well beyond DoD, as experts supporting allies and nongovernmental organizations maintained close ties with him for decades. When Parks initiated the process of revising FM 27–10, he sought a product that would combine 27-10's functional and "bare bones" approach with an inclusion of limited annotations to provide essential background to specific rules. Parks labored at this task for many years, and when he neared culmination in the late 1990s, he initiated several conferences with allied LOAC experts to solicit their contributions to the draft and to identify important areas of divergence that needed to be addressed to mitigate coalition interoperability challenges. However, the September 11 terrorist attacks on the United States presented challenges to the Manual's publication that no one could have anticipated.

The US military response to the September 11 attacks almost immediately exposed the complex LOAC issues that this "new" type of armed conflict against a transnational non-State enemy would create. Concerns quickly emerged over US policies related to detention, transfer, and treatment of captives, along with the projection of combat power beyond areas of "active" operations. DoD and other government agencies soon found themselves in the proverbial cross-hairs of legal criticisms and attacks. Indeed, the degree of interest in legal aspects of military operations was arguably unprecedented, and that interest only increased with time. What had been somewhat of a legal niche prior to September 11 suddenly attracted the attention of a veritable army of lawyers, scholars, journalists, and others engaged in public and intergovernmental dialogue.

This phenomenon had a profound impact on the Manual's evolution. First, Parks was elevated from his Army billet to a position in the DoD General Counsel's office. This new responsibility, coupled with the deluge of legal issues arising from this new conflict and the one that would soon occur in Iraq, inevitably slowed the process of completing the Manual's revision. Second, it soon became clear that the potential impact of the Manual transcended military operations. Other government agencies and highly significant policymakers began to turn to DoD doctrinal publications, including FM 27–10, as sources of authority for both the development and scrutiny of US policies.

And, once the courts began hearing cases related to US military operations and policies, the significance of these publications took on a new dimension. As a result, the revision's publication was no longer seen as just a DoD issue, but instead a process that would impact the efforts of other government agencies such as the Department of Justice and the Department of State. Because of this, these agencies sought, or perhaps demanded a proverbial seat at the revision table.

The impact of this new dimension to the Manual's revision was particularly challenging in relation to litigation concerns. For the first time in recent memory, federal courts were wading into the murky waters of military detention operations. The litigation related to the authority to detain, the adequacy of detainee status determination procedures, and treatment of detainees made it increasingly apparent that Departmental and Service publications could, and often did influence the litigation process. While this was not in itself all that concerning, the absence of any established government policy or doctrine addressing the unconventional "status" of transnational terrorist detainees – the "unlawful combatants" or "unprivileged belligerents" characterization – became monumentally problematic. Unfortunately for the government, neither of these characterizations were addressed in FM 27–10, any of the Geneva Conventions, or any other DoD or Service policies, regulations, or directives. This contributed to the legal uncertainty that permeated detainee litigation. Even the Supreme Court's seminal decision in *Hamdi v. Rumsfeld* exposed this uncertainty. The plurality opinion pointed out that existing Joint Service regulatory authority *seemed* to provide an established procedural framework for assessing detainee status, a process that DoD had never utilized.[27]

These cases indicated that any revision of FM 27–10 would almost inevitably have an impact on future litigation. This added a new dimension to the revision process: every provision had to be assessed for this potential impact. As W. Hays Parks noted in a speech criticizing the final version of the Manual: "[a]t the very least, the Justice Department sought to alter the manual to make it consistent with legal terminology and arguments it has offered in litigation rather than ensure its terminology and arguments are consistent with the law or war."[28]

---

[27] *Hamdi v. Rumsfeld*, 542 US 507, 538 (2004) ("There remains the possibility that the standards we have articulated could be met by an appropriately authorized and properly constituted military tribunal. Indeed, it is notable that military regulations already provide for such process in related instances, dictating that tribunals be made available to determine the status of enemy detainees who assert prisoner-of-war status under the Geneva Convention.").

[28] W. Hays Parks, "Update on the DoD Law of War Manual, Remarks at the ABA 22nd Annual Review of the Field of National Security Law" (Nov. 30, 2012), 5 (on file with author).

Nor was this the only added dimension to the revision process. As noted, Parks's original revision initiative incorporated concerns related to coalition interoperability. Furthermore, as the Manual's Preface indicates, the LOAC manuals published by many of these allies served as important reference points during the revision process:

> The preparation of this manual also has benefited greatly from consulting foreign experts and resources – for example, the 2004 edition of the Manual of the Law of Armed Conflict by United Kingdom Ministry of Defence. In this way, the preparation of this manual is no different from its predecessors. For example, the 1956 Army Field manual benefited from considering a draft of what ultimately became the 1958 United Kingdom law of war manual, and the preparation of the 1914 War Department manual benefited from the Rules of Land Warfare prepared by officers of the English Army and Professor Lassa Oppenheim. The law of war manuals of Germany, Australia, and Canada were also helpful resources in the preparation of this manual.[29]

These considerations of allied LOAC interpretations, however, focused primarily on *operational* interoperability. However, after September 11, diplomatic interoperability took on substantially increased importance. Just as DoJ's interest in the revision spiked with concerns over litigation impact, a significantly increased State Department interest arose as the result of the impact of operational policies and practices on coalition building, preservation, and strategic diplomatic dialogue.

None of these influences were *per se* negative; indeed, the increased emphasis on interagency collaboration probably enhanced the accuracy of the final product. However, it also may have influenced an increased emphasis on the political, diplomatic, and litigation-related consequences of the Manual, which in turn may have distracted the revision from its articulated purpose. One impact is without question: publication of the Manual was delayed to facilitate interagency review. This is somewhat ironic, as DoD emphasized upon publication that the Manual did not represent a coordinated and authoritative reflection of US LOAC interpretations, but instead only DoD interpretation of this law. Specifically, the Manual includes the following qualification:

> This manual represents the legal views of the Department of Defense. This manual does not, however, preclude the Department from subsequently changing its interpretation of the law. Although the preparation of this

---

[29] DoD Law of War Manual, iv–v.

manual has benefited from the participation of lawyers from the Department of State and the Department of Justice, this manual does not necessarily reflect the views of any other department or agency of the U.S. Government or the views of the U.S. Government as a whole.[30]

Whether this is an indication that consensus could not be reached between the different government agencies is unclear. However, whatever the reason, it does seem unfortunate that this qualification was necessary – a qualification that led to even more questions about the usefulness of the Manual.

Of course, that usefulness for US armed forces should not be significantly impacted, if at all, by a qualification that indicates the Manual reflects only DoD interpretation of relevant LOAC obligations. For these subordinate commands, a statement of departmental interpretation of the law is considered binding, even if the qualification might allow the government to disavow such an impact during litigation or diplomatic engagements. But for observers outside of DoD, it is understandable such qualification might be considered frustrating; after all, the long-awaited Manual was probably perceived as a valuable tool in the process of ensuring broader US government accountability for LOAC compliance. If the Manual is what it purports to be – a "how to" guide for the force – this qualification is not particularly significant. But is it truly a "manual" in the traditional field manual sense? Perhaps not and, in a sense, the criticism of the qualification was itself a reflection of the uncertain function the Manual was both intended and expected to fulfill.

Ultimately, the shift in the revision process that began after September 11 led to unfortunate public recriminations between the Manual's original architect, W. Hays Parks, and DoD General Counsel. In a public speech delivered at the annual meeting of the ABA Standing Committed on Law and National Security, Parks lamented how the revision process became politicized in direct contradiction of the course he and the DoD Law of War Working Group had charted years earlier. In a section of his speech titled, "The Demise of the Law of War Manual," Parks essentially attributed the failure to publish a "true" law of war manual to the hijacking of the revision process by a handful of General Counsel lawyers determined to bend to interagency demands. For example, lamenting the dilution of the discussion of the principle of military necessity in response to State Department criticism, Parks noted:

---

[30]   DoD Law of War Manual, ¶ 1.1.1.

Without consultation with the DOD Law of War Working Group, the new
DOD editor deleted the discussion of military necessity from the main body
of the manual, copying it and inserting it as a footnote, apparently to "reduce
its emphasis"; and placed the paragraphs on proportionality ahead of the
discussion of the principle of distinction until it was brought to his attention
that but for the centuries-old pedigree of the principle of distinction there
would be no principle of proportionality.[31]

In response to Parks's criticisms, the DoD General Counsel – or more
specifically the Chief of the International Affairs Division – mounted
a determined counterattack. But Parks's ultimate conclusion seems credible:
the final version of the Manual did not hit the mark originally intended.
Perhaps that was both deliberate and understandable. What is more troubling
about Parks's conclusion is that by trying to please too many masters, the
Manual will fail to provide the essential guidance so critically important for
commanders and their subordinates:

> The consensus the manual enjoyed at the end of 2010 no longer exists. JAG
> representatives have indicated the manual as amended by the Departments of
> State and Justice, or through other injudicious editing such as I have noted, is
> not likely to be accepted by the leadership of all the military services. In that
> regard it has been pointed out to me on more than one occasion that as
> a result of legislation enacted during the administration of President George
> W. Bush, senior military lawyers for the four military services by law have
> a right to provide "independent legal advice" to their respective Department
> Secretary and/or military service chief. Thus the original plan of reaching
> consensus with a manual containing an introductory letter signed by the
> Secretary of Defense or the DOD General Counsel to the effect that the
> manual is the statement of DOD interpretation of U.S. law of war obligations
> is unlikely, returning the situation to the potential legal Tower of Babel
> a DOD manual intended to avoid.[32]

Ultimately, the man who labored more than a decade to provide the force with
what was so sorely needed condemned the outcome of a process he saw as
fundamentally flawed: "[I]n the midst of an ongoing conflict, inside-the-
beltway bureaucratic complacency ignores the vacuum that desperately
required filling to ensure military commanders fulfill their obligation to
conduct their operations in a manner consistent with the law stated therein."[33]

Only time will tell if Parks's conclusion was accurate. And, while it is clear
he sought to distance himself from the final published product, there can be
little doubt that many of the positive aspects of the Manual reflect his years of

---

[31] Parks Speech (above note 28), 4 (emphasis removed).   [32] *Ibid.*, 6.   [33] *Ibid.*

effort to provide a useful product for the field. Many of us who know Parks and worked with him, especially those involved in the revision process, were disappointed that the final publication triggered this fallout. But personal loyalties aside, Parks raised legitimate concerns that the shifting focus for the Manual – or perhaps the broader interests the General Counsel sought to achieve with the Manual – diluted its intended effect. If there is merit to this concern, then the question arises, what now?

5 BUILDING ON THE POSITIVE

Whatever the weaknesses of the Manual may be, there is widespread consensus that it represents a major advancement by providing clarity in DoD's LOAC interpretations.[34] Even assuming the Manual may not be ideally suited as a "how to" guide for commanders and the units they lead, or that it may include provisions that are more focused on assuaging interagency concerns than providing useful operational guidance, no one can question its comprehensiveness and value. In this regard, there is little doubt that it will profoundly influence the development of other policies and doctrine, and will be relied on heavily in the development of JAGs and the operational practice they engage in.

Nonetheless, from a practical, operational perspective, the Manual is not well-suited to the needs of the field commander. And this is unfortunate, because it is the commander that should, and indeed must, be the focal point of LOAC compliance. The central role played by the commander in the implementation and compliance equation may have suffered a certain degree of distortion as the result of the nature of counterinsurgency operations. These operations frequently allow for substantial deliberation in relation to LOAC implementation, with equally frequent involvement of JAGs or other legal advisors in the decision-making process. The potential speed and lethality of future conflicts demands that commanders and their subordinates prepare for a high degree of LOAC implementation self-reliance. Even when legal advisors are accessible, their role will only be enhanced when the operational decision-makers they advise have ready access to authoritative restatements of the law better tailored to their needs.

Adding to the existing Manual with more operationally or functionally oriented supplements need not be controversial. Whether in the form of appendices, or Service manuals, so long as these supplements reflect the

---

[34] See C. J. Dunlap, Jr., "The DoD Law of War Manual and its Critics: Some Observations," (2016) 92 *International Legal Studies* 85, 115–18.

same substantive rules and interpretations published in the Manual, they can fill an important need. Developing and publishing such supplements would also be consistent with the one very positive aspect of the new Manual: DoD's demonstrated commitment to identify areas of beneficial improvement and move quickly to update the Manual in response. In fact, from the first day of publication, the General Counsel sought comment and criticism of the Manual as part of its commitment to constant improvement.[35] While it is apparent that DoD will not agree with all criticisms or recommended improvements, the two sets of 2016 revisions indicate that unlike its predecessor, this Manual will be far more responsive to changes in the law and identification of gaps that necessitate revision.

To date, the revision process has focused on substance. However, there is no reason why the rule sets in the Manual might not be digested into a format more aligned with the needs of operational forces. As noted above, the Army and Marine Corps have been collaborating to produce their own LOAC field manual, which is apparently very close to publication. Both the format of that manual and its alignment or divergence from the DoD Manual will provide interesting and important insight into internal departmental perceptions of the strengths and weaknesses of the Manual. Will the new Army/Marine Corps manual be as substantively comprehensive as the DoD Manual? Or will it be more of a streamlined "how to" source of authority focused more directly on the operational and tactical needs of commanders? If, as expected, the new Army/Marine Corps LOAC manual does reflect an effort to provide a more readily accessible source of guidance for commanders and subordinate units, it might lead DoD to consider adding supplemental appendices to the Manual to achieve the same objective.

6 CONCLUSION

The legal challenges confronting our armed forces today and for the indefinite future are substantial, and only likely to increase. Enemies understand the strategic value of creating a perception of legal indifference or noncompliance by US forces, and will accordingly seek to exploit every opportunity to paint this picture. Even when US forces fully comply with the LOAC, misunderstandings of what the law requires contribute to these enemy efforts.

---

[35] *Cf.* DoD Law of War Manual, ¶ 1.1.1 ("This manual does not, however, preclude the Department from subsequently changing its interpretation of the law."); DoD Dir. 2311.01E, *DoD Law of War Program* (May 9, 2006, current Feb. 22, 2011).

Accordingly, when the law is in fact violated, the impact is exponentially more problematic.

So much is recognized by the inclusion of legitimacy as a principle of military operations in US joint doctrine. It is therefore beyond dispute that US commanders and the forces they lead into combat must not only understand key LOAC obligations but must also embrace the wisdom of constantly striving for compliance with these obligations. To that end, these "consumers" need a product that is tailored to the realities of their professional development – a true LOAC field manual. The DoD Law of War Manual is a major advancement in providing these forces with necessary information and direction to develop such competence, filling a void of authority that existed for far too long. However, perhaps in the effort to "be all things for all people," the Manual's density and, at times, scholarly flavor may dilute its effectiveness as a true field manual.

This does not mean the Manual is without value. To the contrary, by providing a comprehensive statement of DoD LOAC interpretation, the Manual will guide JAGs and other legal advisors as they engage in their complex operational law tasks. The Manual also provides a critical reference point for the development of other policies, directives, and doctrine that will increase the probability that the LOAC will be more effectively integrated into these sources of authority. Finally, the Manual has generated substantial discourse between the DoD General Counsel's office and external experts, primarily in academia, that will ideally contribute to enhanced understanding of the LOAC within DoD, and an enhanced understanding among this external audience on how the law functions during operations.

But it is essential that the warfighter not get lost in this equation. It is critical that DoD consider the benefit of distilling the LOAC rules explained in depth in the Manual into appendices or subordinate Service manuals tailored to the needs of the operational force. Ultimately, a "manual" must enable the consumer to better understand more of the "how" of a given task than necessarily the "why." Rule-oriented supplements will advance this objective, leaving the more complicated aspect of professional development – understanding why the rules matter and why they must be embraced – to the training and development process built on a rule-based manual and the more comprehensive DoD "treatise."

PART III

SUBSTANTIVE CONTRIBUTIONS AND CONTROVERSIES

7

Back to the Basics: Core Law of War Principles through the Lens of the DoD Manual

Ray Murphy

1 INTRODUCTION TO CHAPTER II: PRINCIPLES

Chapter II is simply entitled "Principles." It begins with a statement reiterating the interdependent nature of the basic principles – military necessity, humanity, and honor. These provide the foundation for other law of war principles, namely proportionality and distinction and most of the treaty and customary rules of international humanitarian law (IHL). It is then that the principles of proportionality and distinction come into play. Taken in their totality, these general principles provide an overarching and reinforcing set of rules that form part of a coherent system. Acknowledging the priority attached to military necessity and the interdependence of this principle with that of humanity and honor at the outset is significant.

By their very nature such principles are not specific but must underpin all military action taken during all aspects of armed conflict. They are not based on a separate source of international law, but on treaties, custom, and general principles of law.[1] In this way they can and must often be derived from the existing rules, expressing their substance and meaning. At the same time they inspire, reinforce, and render understandable existing rules and must be taken into account when interpreting them.[2]

These general principles are reflected in most military manuals[3] and not to have included them would have constituted a serious omission. It appears that each State remains at liberty to decide the status of such manuals.

---

[1] M. Sassòli, A. Bouvier, and A. Quentin (eds.), *How Does Law Protect in War*, 3 vols. (Geneva: ICRC, 2011), I, 158.

[2] *Ibid.*

[3] E.g., Swiss Military Manual on Behaviour during Deployment, Rechtliche Grundlagen für das Verhalten inm Einsatz, Reglement 51.007/IV, ¶ 158. See also ICRC Customary Law Study, Vol. II.

In particular, it is for each State to decide whether its manual constitutes a binding authority. The German and Swiss manuals, unlike the US or British versions, are issued as binding "regulations" within their respective domestic systems. This probably reflects different legal systems and traditions.

2 MILITARY NECESSITY

Military necessity may seem like a straightforward concept to grasp and apply in armed conflict. In reality it is anything but simple.[4] This is reflected in the fact that there is more than one definition of military necessity depending on whether the source derives from military publications, judicial decisions, or scholarly works.[5] The US Department of Defense (DoD) Law of War Manual (the Manual) provides a concise working definition: "*Military necessity* may be defined as the principle that justifies the use of all measures needed to defeat the enemy as quickly and efficiently as possible that are not prohibited by the law of war."[6]

2.1 *The Lieber Code*

Military necessity was fundamental in the first modern attempt to draft a binding set of rules or code of conduct for armed forces during armed conflict. The Lieber Code was promulgated by President Lincoln during the American Civil War. Although only binding on US forces, it was based on what Lieber considered the generally accepted law of the day.

The Lieber Code prescribed that:

> Military necessity ... consists in the necessity of those measures which are indispensable for securing the ends of the war, and which are lawful according to the modern law and usages of war.[7]
> ...
> Military necessity does not admit of cruelty – that is the infliction of suffering for the sake of suffering or for revenge ... [8]

It is important to stress that military necessity cannot be invoked to avoid compliance with IHL. Otherwise the principle could be used to justify a range

---

[4] N. Hayashi, "Requirements of Military Necessity in International Humanitarian Law and International Criminal Law" (2010) 28 *Boston University International Law Journal* 39.

[5] DoD Law of War Manual, ¶ 2.2.   [6]   *Ibid.*

[7] General Order No. 100, Instructions for the Government of Armies of the United States in the Field (Apr. 24, 1863), reprinted in *The War of the Rebellion: A Compilation of the Official Records of the Union and Confederate Armies*, Series III, Vol. 3 (GPO 1899) (the Lieber Code), www.loc.gov/rr/frd/Military_Law/Lieber_Collection/pdf/Instructions-gov-armies.pdf, Art. 14.

[8] *Ibid.*, Art. 16.

of actions that could constitute a violation of the laws of war. This is clear when the Manual states that it "justifies the use of all measures needed to defeat the enemy as quickly and efficiently as possible *that are not prohibited by the law of war*" (emphasis added).[9] Though there are valid criticisms that the Manual often couches legal and policy pronouncements in broad and imprecise terms, the text is explicit that "*Military necessity* does not justify actions that are prohibited by the law of war."[10]

In this way, military necessity is a requirement or justification for any military action proposed or carried out. This includes destroying and seizing persons and property, or the capture of enemy persons.[11] A good example in practice is in relation to children engaged in hostilities, a common occurrence in many contemporary conflicts. They are legitimate targets while participating in hostilities and showing hostile intent but military necessity as a restriction to violence should require that they be arrested rather than killed whenever possible.[12] However, IHL principles are unclear on an affirmative duty to arrest in lieu of applying normal *jus in bello* principles. Thus, it is noteworthy that the Manual talks about alternative ways of fighting an enemy other than violence and destruction (e.g., capture enemy persons, propaganda, intelligence-gathering).[13]

Military necessity can seldom be assessed without reference to the other principles. For example, attacks against persons other than combatants would violate both the principles of necessity and distinction.[14] Military victory can only be achieved by defeating enemy combatants. This does not preclude military objectives such as armaments factories from being attacked. However, any such attack must satisfy the military necessity test and is not unlawful because of the risk to a civilian in the same location who may be harmed, provided the principle of proportionality is applied.[15] The importance of what constitutes military objectives in this context is discussed later in this chapter under "Distinction."

---

[9] DoD Law of War Manual, ¶ 2.2.   [10] *Ibid.*, ¶ 2.2.2.1.   [11] *Ibid.*

[12] Sassòli, Bouvier, and Quentin (above note 1), 218. The Manual makes this linkage in the context of military necessity as follows: "*Military necessity* also justifies certain incidental harms that inevitably result from the actions it justifies. The extent to which *military necessity* justifies such harms is addressed by the principle of proportionality." DoD Law of War Manual, ¶ 2.2.1.

[13] DoD Law of War Manual, ¶ 2.2.1. This is discussed further under "Humanity" later in this chapter.

[14] Sassòli, Bouvier, and Quentin (above note 1), 255. DoD Law of War Manual, ¶ 2.2.1.

[15] The Manual makes this linkage in the context of military necessity as follows: "*Military necessity* also justifies certain incidental harms that inevitably result from the actions it justifies. The extent to which *military necessity* justifies such harms is addressed by the principle of proportionality." DoD Law of War Manual, ¶ 2.2.1. See also Sassòli, Bouvier, and Quentin (above note 1), 256.

The Manual acknowledges that military necessity is a difficult concept to define and apply. According to the Manual, the laws of war seeks to ameliorate the difficulties in applying the principle by:

(1) "Permitting consideration of the broader imperatives of winning the war as quickly and efficiently as possible (and not only the demands of the immediate situation)";

(2) "Recognizing that certain types of actions are, as a general matter, inherently militarily necessary"; and

(3) "Recognizing that persons must assess the military necessity of an action in good faith based on the information available to them at the relevant time and that they cannot be judged based on information that subsequently comes to light."[16]

In this way the Manual provides a coherent interpretation of how military necessity may be implemented in practice. It also reflects the jurisprudence of the United States Military Tribunal in the *High Command Trial* which offered a concise interpretation of the principle when it declared:

> It has been the viewpoint of many German writers and to a certain extent has been contended in this case that military necessity includes the right to do anything that contributes to the winning of a war. We content ourselves on this subject with stating that such a view would eliminate all humanity and decency and all law from the conduct of war and it is a contention which this Tribunal repudiates as contrary to the accepted usages of civilized nations.[17]

Other complexities surrounding this principle were evident in the *Hostages* case before the Nuremberg Military Tribunals.[18] The German General Lothar Rendulic was acquitted of the charge of wanton devastation on the grounds that although he may have erred in believing that there was military necessity for the widespread environmental destruction entailed by his use of a "scorched earth" policy in Norway, he was not guilty of a criminal act. This demonstrates how actual or constructive knowledge of the grave environmental consequences of an attack may be difficult to prove. In the same case, however, cited in the Manual to support the proposition that military necessity cannot be perverted into an all-consuming norm, the military tribunal rejected the right of commanders to ignore the law *vis-à-vis* civilian rights:

---

[16]   DoD Law of War Manual, ¶ 2.2.3.

[17]   *United States v. von Leeb et al.* ("*The High Command Trial*") (1948) 11 LRTWC 1, 9 TWC 462 (United States Military Tribunal), 541.

[18]   11 *Trials of War Criminals* (1950), 1296.

It is apparent from the evidence of these defendants that they considered military necessity, a matter to be determined by them, a complete justification of their acts. We do not concur in the view that the rules of warfare are anything less than they purport to be. Military necessity or expediency do not justify a violation of positive rules.[19]

2.2 The International Criminal Tribunal for the former Yugoslavia

At the outset it is important to state that findings in the international tribunal and court judgments are not binding on States.[20] They are, however, of abiding importance in the interpretation and application of IHL as practiced.[21]

There is authority for invoking military necessity as a defense in the post-World War II trials.[22] Although the principle of military necessity does not imply that the rules of IHL can be disregarded, some rules of war offer a possibility to invoke military necessity. "Military necessity" is explicitly mentioned in the Statute of the International Criminal Tribunal for the former Yugoslavia:

- Under Article 2(d) it is possible to prosecute someone for: "extensive destruction and appropriation of property, not justified by military necessity and carried out unlawfully and wantonly."
- Under Article 3(b), a person may be prosecuted for "wanton destruction of cities, towns or villages, or devastation not justified by military necessity."[23]

---

[19]   DoD Law of War Manual, ¶ 2.2.2.1 fn. 26 (citing *United States v. List et al. (The Hostage Case)*, Trials of War Criminals Before the IMT XI, 1255–56. The citation neglected to include the pertinent conclusion that "International Law is prohibitive law. Articles 46, 47, and 50 of the Hague Regulations of 1907 make no such exceptions to its enforcement. The rights of innocent population therein set forth must be respected even if military necessity or expediency decree otherwise.").

[20]   The Manual recognizes this principle but cites former Legal Advisor Harold Koh for the proposition that "Although these decisions cannot, as a strictly legal matter 'bind' other courts, there is no doubt that the jurisprudence of the ICTY and ICTR has been influential in the broader development of international criminal law." DoD Law of War Manual, ¶ 1.9.1 fn. 155.

[21]   Y. Sandoz, "The Dynamic but Complex Relationship between International Penal Law and International Humanitarian Law," in J. Doria, H.-P. Gasser, and M. C. Bassiouni (eds.), *The Legal Regime of the ICC: Essay in Honour of Professor Igor Pavlovich Blishchenko* (Leiden: Martinus Nijhoff, 2009), 1049, 1061.

[22]   W. Schabas, *The International Criminal Court: A Commentary on the Rome Statute* (Oxford University Press, 2010), 495.

[23]   Statute of the International Criminal Tribunal for the former Yugoslavia, UN Doc. S/RES/827 (1993), annex, Arts. 2(d) and 3(b).

The International Criminal Tribunal for the former Yugoslavia (ICTY) Statute does not define military necessity. It depends on the context and it needs to be decided on a case-by-case basis. There are two categories of crime in which the ICTY has issued judgments on the question of military justification:

1. large-scale destruction of property
2. forced displacements of persons.

It is also important to differentiate between combat and noncombat circumstances. The general rule is that in noncombat situations there can be no military necessity.

It is noteworthy that in the *Orić* case (2006), the Trial Chamber stated that it could be legitimate to invoke military necessity as a justification for carrying out "preventive destruction" in limited circumstances.[24] However, "except for the rare occasions in which such preventive destruction could arguably fall within the scope of 'military necessity', the principle must be upheld that the destruction of civil settlements, as a rule, is punishable as a war crime."[25]

In 2003, the Trial Chamber issued the judgment in the *Galić* case and reverted to the findings of the *Hostage* case from the World War II era; the Chamber stated that civilians and the civilian population as such should not be the object of attack.[26] Such action can never be justified by invoking military necessity. The case involved, among other incidents, the shelling of a football match when there were both civilians and off-duty soldiers present in the stadium. The Chamber found that the attack did not discriminate between civilians and soldiers.[27] It should have been possible to foresee the outcome in terms of casualties and loss of lives. The damages were excessive in relation to the anticipated military advantage and were thus not militarily necessary.

---

[24] *Prosecutor v. Orić*, Case No. IT-03-68-T, Trial Judgment, ¶ 588 (ICTY, June 30, 2006) ("The Trial Chamber finds that 'collateral damage' may occur in the course of combat, when, as a result of the destruction of objects which make an effective contribution to military action, other objects, such as adjacent buildings, are destroyed that do not fulfil this criterion. However, after the fighting has ceased, destruction can in principle no longer be justified by claiming 'military necessity'. A different situation arises if a military attack is launched against a settlement from which previously, due to its location and its armed inhabitants, a serious danger emanated for the inhabitants of a neighbouring village who are now seeking to remove this danger through military action. It may be the case that, after such a settlement has been taken, destruction of houses occurs in order to prevent the inhabitants, including combatants, to return and resume the attacks. A submission that such destruction is covered by 'military necessity' will be entertained on a case-by-case basis.").

[25] *Ibid.*

[26] *Prosecutor v. Galić*, Case No. IT-98-29-T, Judgment, ¶¶ 44–45 (ICTY, Dec. 5, 2003).

[27] *Ibid.*, ¶¶ 372–76.

When the court assesses a situation, it looks to the information that was available at the time when a decision was taken and what the "commander" reasonably knew. A court cannot judge someone based on information that became known at a later stage.

In the appeal judgments in respect of the *Blaškić* and the *Kordić and Čerkez* cases, which came after the *Galić* decision in the Trial Chamber, the Appeals Chamber reversed the decisions of the first instance which suggested that military necessity might be a defense to a charge of targeting civilians.[28] The Appeals Chamber followed the reasoning in *Galić* stating that there is an "absolute prohibition on targeting civilians and referred to the principle of distinction as a 'cardinal principle' of IHL."[29]

Other ICTY Trial Chambers accepted that attacks on civilian property could be justifiable under certain circumstances and supported findings by referring to the recognition of military necessity as a defense to the war crime of destruction of civilian property.[30] It is noteworthy that cultural objects are considered civilian objects under special protection. They may not be attacked or used for military purposes. Their immunity may only be waived in the case of "imperative military necessity."[31]

2.3 The International Criminal Court

The International Criminal Court (ICC) is bound to apply established principles of the law of armed conflict by virtue of Article 21(1)(b) of the Rome Statute.[32] According to the Manual, "although military necessity cannot justify actions that have been prohibited by the law of war, some law of war rules expressly incorporate military necessity."[33] Similarly, under the Rome Statute

---

[28] *Prosecutor v. Blaškić*, Case No. IT-95-14-A, Appeal Judgment, ¶¶ 109, 145 (ICTY, July 29, 2004); *Prosecutor v. Kordić and Cerkez*, Case No. IT-95-14/2, Appeal Judgment, ¶ 54 (ICTY, Dec. 17, 2004).

[29] *Prosecutor v. Kordić and Cerkez* (above note 28), quoting *Legality of the Threat or Use of Nuclear Weapons* (ICJ Advisory Opinion) [1996] ICJ Rep 226, [78].

[30] *Prosecutor v. Blagojević and Jokic*, Case No. IT-02-60-T, Trial Judgment, ¶¶ 593, 615 (ICTY, Jan. 17, 2005). It also noted that forcible transfer or displacement of a civilian population could be justified on the grounds of "overriding, i.e. imperative, military reasons" (¶ 598). See also *Prosecutor v. Gotovina, Markač and Čermak*, Case No. IT-060-90-T, Trial Chamber Judgment, ¶ 1770 (ICTY, Apr. 15, 2011) (re destruction of civilian objects).

[31] Sassòli, Bouvier, and Quentin (above note 1), 269. *Prosecutor v. Strugar*, Case No. IT-01-42-T, Trial Chamber Judgment, ¶¶ 229-33, 298-329 (ICTY, Jan. 31, 2005).

[32] Article 31(1)(c) of the Statute also provides a controversial provision for the exclusion of criminal responsibility for certain acts, including those reasonably taken in defense of property essential to accomplishing a military mission. Schabas (above note 22), 390-93 and 487-89.

[33] DoD Law of War Manual, ¶ 2.2.2.2.

the absence of military necessity is an element of each of the crimes listed below:

1. "Extensive destruction and appropriation of property, not justified by military necessity." (A Grave Breach of the Geneva Conventions (Article 8(2)(a)(iv).)
2. Destruction or seizure of the enemy's property, "unless . . . imperatively demanded by the necessities of war." (A serious violation of the laws and customs of war in international armed conflict (Article 8(2)(b)(xiii).)
3. Ordering the displacement of the civilian population for reasons related to the conflict, "unless the security of the civilians involved or imperative military reasons so demand." (A serious violation of the laws and customs of war in a non-international armed conflict (NIAC) (Article 8(2)(e)(viii).)
4. Destruction or seizure of the property of an adversary, "unless . . . imperatively demanded by the necessities of the conflict." (A serious violation of the laws and customs of war in a NIAC (Article 8(2)(e)(xii).)

In this way military necessity is an exception, rendering "unless" a key word in Article 8 of the Rome Statute. This concept is also reflected in the ICC Elements of Crimes (which it must be noted included the US delegation in its consensus adoption) in the sense that the general chapeau provides that the element of unlawfulness is not replicated in each and every set of elements, but is implicit in every *actus reus*. Pleading military necessity does not constitute a defense. Rather, it challenges the notion that a crime was committed in the first place. This principle is reflected in the provisions of the Manual dealing with incorporation of military necessity into IHL.[34]

The *Katanga* case before the ICC provides a good example of how military necessity may be invoked under the Rome Statute. The Trial Chamber stated that it is important to assess the "military advantage" from the attacker's perspective for each targeted object, and such an advantage must be definite and cannot in any way be indeterminate or potential.[35] The Trial Chamber went on to state that:

---

[34] *Ibid.*
[35] *Prosecutor v. Katanga and Mathieu Chui,* Case No. ICC-01/04-01/07, Pre-Trial Chamber I, Decision on the Confirmation of Charges, ¶¶ 477–518 (Sept. 30, 2008); ICRC, *Commentary on the Additional Protocols of 8 June 1977 to the Geneva Conventions of 12 August 1949* (Geneva: ICRC, Martinus Nijhoff, 1987), ¶¶ 2024, 2028. See also *Galić* (above note 26), ¶ 51: "Whether a military advantage can be achieved must be decided . . . from the perspective of the 'person contemplating the attack, including the information available to the latter, that the object is being used to make an effective contribution to military action'."

The destruction of property therefore does not constitute a crime under article 8(2)(e)(xii) of the Statute where such destruction is justified by military necessity. As did the Appeals Chamber of the ICTY in *Kordić and Čerkez*, the Chamber will adopt the definition of "military necessity" in article 14 of the Lieber Code of 24 April 1863, which lays down: "Military necessity ... consists in the necessity of those measures which are indispensable for securing the ends of the war, and which are lawful according to the modern law and usages of war". With respect to this exception, article 8(2)(e)(xii) refers explicitly to cases where the destruction "[is] imperatively demanded by the necessities of the conflict". The Chamber observes that only "imperative" reasons of military necessity, where the perpetrator has no other option in this regard, could justify acts of destruction which would otherwise be proscribed by this provision. To determine whether the destruction of property fell within military necessity, the Chamber will conduct a case-by-case assessment by considering, for example, whether the destroyed property was defended or whether specific property was destroyed.[36]

There are several offences in the ICC Statute that implicitly admit exceptions on account of military necessity; for example, the crime of unlawful deportation or transfer, a Grave Breach of the Geneva Conventions and listed as a war crime in Article 8(2)(a)(vii) of the Rome Statute. This Grave Breach is based on Articles 45 and 49 of the Fourth Convention. Article 49 exceptionally permits temporary evacuation of an area in occupied territory if "imperative military reasons so demand," among other things. As such, temporary evacuations demanded for similar reasons are not "unlawful" within the meaning of Article 8(2)(a)(vii) of the Rome Statute.

The offence of deportation or forcible transfer of a population, a crime against humanity under Article 7(1)(d) of the Rome Statute, contains as one of its elements the requirement that the victim was forcibly displaced "without grounds permitted under international law," hence allowing for the possibility for military necessity, as prescribed in Article 7(2)(d).

Article 31(1) of the Rome Statute allows for the exclusion of criminal liability for acts essential for a military mission, extending the focus from self-defense to encompass the principle of military necessity. The potential use of military necessity as a justification or excuse affects those war crimes that do not provide for military necessity exceptions and, accordingly, of which the absence of military necessity is not an element.

---

[36] *Prosecutor v. Katanga* (above note 35), ¶ 894.

Bemba Case

In the case of *Bemba*,[37] the defendant was charged with the war crime of pillaging.[38] The defense argued that the property allegedly seized was not in fact "pillaged," but rather "required for military necessity" and the prosecution failed to establish beyond a reasonable doubt that it was not appropriated on the grounds of military necessity.[39]

The Trial Chamber held that:

> The concept of military necessity is mentioned in footnote 62 of the Elements of Crimes, which specifies, with reference to the requirement that the perpetrator intended to appropriate the items for "private or personal use", that "[a]s indicated by the use of the term 'private or personal use', appropriations justified by military necessity cannot constitute the crime of pillaging."[40]

The Chamber found that if the Prosecution proves that property was appropriated for private or personal use, it is not obliged to disprove military necessity for the purpose of a charge.[41] Furthermore, in the context of the war crime of destroying or seizing the enemy's property, military necessity "can only be invoked 'if the laws of armed conflict provide for it and only to the extent that these laws provide for it'."[42]

2.4 The DoD Manual

Although the cases before the ICTY primarily deal with the narrow issue of property destruction and to a lesser degree enforced disappearances, they provide insights into how military necessity may be interpreted by international tribunals. The Manual provides somewhat of a general definition of military necessity. It is difficult to compare them since the focus of the ICTY judgments and the Manual is quite different. However, while the Manual is quite broad in its approach, it emphasizes that fundamental rules such as military necessity cannot justify departures from IHL because States have crafted the law specifically with exigencies of war in mind.[43] They are similar in their treatment of incidental harms. Such harm may be justified by military

---

[37] *Prosecutor v. Jean-Pierre Bemba Gombo*, Case No. ICC-01/05-01/08, Judgment pursuant to Art. 74 of the Statute (21 Mar. 2016).

[38] Rome Statute of the International Criminal Court, Art. 8(2)(e)(v).

[39] *Prosecutor v. Bemba Gombo* (above note 37), ¶ 122.   [40]   *Ibid.*, ¶ 123.

[41] *Ibid.* (under Art. 8(2)(e)(v) of the Statute).   [42]   *Ibid.*, ¶ 123.

[43] DoD Law of War Manual, ¶ 2.2.2.1.

necessity and this requires that the principle of proportionality be taken into account.[44]

In outlining the challenges in applying military necessity, the Manual reflects the jurisprudence of the ICTY, even if this is not the intention.[45] Necessity is something that must be assessed from the perspective of the "person contemplating the attack, including the information available to the latter, that the object is being used to make an effective contribution to military action."[46]

3 HUMANITY

The principle of humanity and the prohibition on causing unnecessary suffering are long established. The Manual defines humanity "as the principle that forbids the infliction of suffering, injury, or destruction unnecessary to accomplish a legitimate military purpose."[47] It should be recalled that the broader purpose of IHL is to protect the victims of armed conflicts and regulate hostilities based on a balance between military necessity and humanity.[48] This is reflected in the manner in which the Manual stresses the relationship between both humanity and military necessity.[49] Its centrality as a principle within the framework of IHL is captured in the following definition offered by the International Committee of the Red Cross (ICRC):

> IHL is a compromise between two underlying principles, of humanity and of military necessity. These two principles shape all its rules. The principle of military necessity permits only that degree and kind of force required to achieve the legitimate purpose of a conflict, i.e. the complete or partial submission of the enemy at the earliest possible moment with the minimum expenditure of life and resources. It does not, however, permit the taking of measures that would otherwise be prohibited under IHL. The principle of humanity forbids the infliction of all suffering, injury or destruction not necessary for achieving the legitimate purpose of a conflict.[50]

The United Kingdom Manual of the Law of Armed Conflict describes the principle as forbidding "the infliction of suffering, injury, or destruction not actually necessary for the accomplishment of legitimate military

---

[44] *Ibid.*, ¶ 2.2.1. [45] *Ibid.*, ¶ 2.2.3.
[46] *Prosecutor v. Galić* (above note 26), ¶ 51; *Prosecutor v. Katanga* (above note 35), ¶ 894.
[47] DoD Law of War Manual, ¶ 2.3 Humanity.
[48] N. Melzer, *International Humanitarian Law: A Comprehensive Introduction* (Geneva: ICRC, 2016), 16.
[49] DoD Law of War Manual, ¶ 2.3.1.1.
[50] ICRC, "International Humanitarian Law: Answers to Your Questions" (Jan. 22, 2015), 6.

purposes."[51] This is a view that is widely shared and not dissimilar to that expressed in the Manual and outlined in a range of relevant treaties going back to the 1863 Lieber Code (and indeed predating that code in American conscience).[52] In this way the position outlined in the Manual is consistent with the generally accepted view of the principle of humanity. Linked to this is the prohibition on causing unnecessary suffering which is especially relevant to the nature and type of weapons used in combat. It is a general principle by which all means and methods of warfare have to be measured.[53] According to the International Court of Justice (ICJ), "[i]t is prohibited to cause unnecessary suffering to combatants: it is accordingly prohibited to use weapons causing them such harm or uselessly aggravating their suffering ... States do not have unlimited freedom of choice of means in the weapons they use."[54]

Later in the seminal *Tadić* decision before the ICTY it was held that regardless of whether the armed conflict is international or internal:

> Elementary considerations of humanity and common sense make it preposterous that the use by States of weapons prohibited in armed conflicts between themselves be allowed when States try to put down rebellion by their own nationals on their own territory. What is inhumane, and consequently proscribed, in international wars, cannot but be inhumane and inadmissible in civil strife.[55]

The ICTY invoked the principle when considering reprisals and declared that due "to the pressure exerted by the requirements of humanity and the dictates of public conscience," a customary rule of international law has emerged with regard to reprisals.[56] Furthermore, the principle of humanity can be found in the Martens Clause,[57] which "enjoins, as a minimum, reference to those principles [humanity] and dictates [of public conscience] any time a rule of

---

51 UK Ministry of Defence, *Law of Armed Conflict Manual* (Oxford University Press, 2005), ¶ 2.1.

52 J. F. Witt, *Lincoln's Code: The Laws of War in American History* (New York: Free Press, 2012), 31.

53 Melzer (above note 48), 110.

54 *Legality of the Threat or Use of Nuclear Weapons*, Advisory Opinion, 1996 ICJ 226, ¶ 78 (July 8).

55 *Prosecutor v. Tadić*, Case No. IT-94-1-A, Decision on the Defense Motion for Interlocutory Appeal on Jurisdiction, ¶¶ 119, 129 (ICTY, Appeal Chamber, 2 Oct. 1995).

56 *Prosecutor v. Kupreškić*, Case No. IT-95-16-T, Trial Judgment, ¶ 531 (ICTY, Jan. 14, 2000).

57 The Martens Clause was first set forth in the preambular provisions of the 1899 Hague Convention concerning the Laws or customs of War on Land which reads as follows: "Until a more complete code of the laws of war is issued, the High Contracting Parties think it right to declare that in cases not included in the Regulations adopted by them, populations and belligerents remain under the protection and empire of the principles of international law, as they result from the usages established between civilised nations, from the laws of humanity, and the requirements of the public conscience."

   A modern version of the clause may be found in Art. 1(2) of Additional Protocol I of 1977, which refers, instead, to "the principles of humanity and ... the dictates of public conscience."

international humanitarian law is not sufficiently rigorous or precise."[58] The ICTY Trial Chamber also invoked the principle of humanity in defining what constitutes inhuman treatment and described this as "intentional treatment which does not conform with the fundamental principle of humanity."[59]

In recent years there has been controversy regarding the implications of this principle.[60] Should enemy soldiers be captured rather than be killed or wounded whenever this is possible? This is an example of the expansion of human rights principles into IHL. There are valid arguments on both sides, but it is submitted that the appropriate response to this and other related questions can only be judged when all of the principles, especially military necessity, are taken into account. This is how balance between military necessity and humanity is ascertained and is expressed in the other core principles discussed below. The final word is given to the ICRC Manual:

> Accordingly, the principle would restrict the permissibility of inflicting injury and suffering on combatants to that which is not otherwise prohibited under IHL and which, additionally, is reasonably necessary to achieve a lawful military purpose in the prevailing circumstances. For example, where the same military advantage can be achieved through less harmful means, considerations of humanity would require the use of such means. While this interpretation of military necessity as a restrictive factor in the use of means and methods of warfare against combatants and other military objectives is not generally accepted, it corresponds best to the original spirit of the St Petersburg Declaration and reflects the official position of the ICRC.[61]

There are a number of IHL provisions that limit the means of warfare and certain weapons during an international armed conflict (IAC).[62] The Manual refers to "prohibitions on weapons that are inherently indiscriminate."[63] Any weapons used must not be calculated to cause unnecessary suffering or superfluous injury. In reality, the implementation of this basic rule is a compromise between military necessity and humanity. The principle of avoiding unnecessary suffering refers to the harmful consequences that would not be justified by

---

[58] *Prosecutor v. Kupreškić* (above note 56), ¶ 525.

[59] *Prosecutor v. Delalić*, Case No. IT-96-21-T, Trial Judgment, ¶ 543 (ICTY, Nov. 16, 1998).

[60] N. Melzer, *Interpretive Guidance on the Notion of Direct Participation in Hostilities under International Humanitarian Law* (Geneva: ICRC, 2009), 78; and G. Solis, *The Law of Armed Conflict*, 2nd ed. (Cambridge University Press, 2016), 269.

[61] Melzer (above note 48), 110.

[62] 1907 Hague Regulations, Arts. 22 and 23; Protocol Additional to the Geneva Conventions of Aug. 12, 1949, and Relating to the Protection of Victims of International Armed Conflicts, 1977, 1125 UNTS 3 (AP I), Art. 35.

[63] DoD Law of War Manual, ¶ 2.3.2.

military necessity, either because of the lack of military advantage or because any advantage is outweighed by the suffering caused.[64]

According to Melzer, despite the absence of distinct treaty criteria as to what suffering is "unnecessary" and what injury "superfluous," the rule requires that a balance be struck between considerations of military necessity and of humanity.[65] The ICRC study on Customary Rules indicates that this is the approach taken by many States.[66] Furthermore, the ICJ in its Advisory Opinion on nuclear weapons, argues that "it is prohibited to cause unnecessary suffering to combatants."[67] Accordingly, it is "prohibited to use weapons causing them such harm or uselessly aggravating their suffering" and "states do not have unlimited freedom of choice of means in the weapons they use."[68] The prohibition on causing unnecessary suffering makes it unlawful to cause combatants "harm greater than that unavoidable to achieve legitimate military objectives."[69]

In this way, the principle would restrict the permissibility of inflicting injury and suffering on combatants to that which is not otherwise prohibited under IHL and which, additionally, is reasonably necessary to achieve a lawful military purpose in the prevailing circumstances. According to the ICRC, where the same military advantage can be achieved through less harmful means, considerations of humanity would require the use of such means. This is a controversial interpretation of military necessity that seeks to restrict the right to resort to means and methods of warfare against combatants and other military objectives during armed conflict. As such, it is an interpretation that is not generally accepted.[70]

4 PROPORTIONALITY

The principle of proportionality is one of the more challenging and imprecise concepts to apply in practice. The Manual states in unambiguous terms "that even where one is justified in acting, one must not act in a way that is unreasonable or excessive."[71] It would be difficult to find a clearer statement

---

[64] Sassòli, Bouvier, and Quentin (above note 1), 284.   [65] Melzer (above note 48), 110.
[66] J.-M. Henckaerts and L. Doswald-Beck (eds.), *Customary International Humanitarian Law*, I: *Rules* (Cambridge University Press, 2005), rule 70, 237–44.
[67] *Legality of the Threat or Use of Nuclear Weapons* (above note 54), ¶ 78.   [68] *Ibid.*
[69] *Ibid.*
[70] Melzer (above note 60), Section IX. For a critique of this approach and the ICRC's official response, see "Forum on 'Direct Participation in Hostilities'" (2010) 42 *New York University Journal of International Law and Politics* 769–916.
[71] DoD Law of War Manual, ¶ 2.4 Proportionality.

of the principle so readily comprehensible to military personnel of all ranks and services.

The death of civilians and collateral damage does not automatically imply there has been a war crime. However, there remains a broader duty to minimize civilian casualties, even if they cannot be eliminated entirely.[72] This duty finds expression in the principle of proportionality. One useful definition can be found in AP I which proscribes "an attack which may be expected to cause incidental loss of civilian life, injury to civilians, damage to civilian objects, or a combination thereof, which would be excessive in relation to the concrete and direct military advantage anticipated."[73]

The imprecise nature of the principle means it is more easily stated than applied in practice.[74] However, in "applying this principle, it is necessary to assess the importance of the target in relation to the incidental damage expected: if the target is sufficiently important, a greater degree of risk may be justified."[75] However, this test is only relevant if the principle of distinction is applied and the target is a legitimate military objective. Furthermore, the military necessity test must also be met before proportionality comes into play and this is reflected in the Manual.[76] This is important, as meeting the military necessity test at the outset is fundamental to IHL. The restatement of this rule in the Manual is a welcome confirmation of this principle. It is then that the requirement outlined in the Manual to take all reasonable precautions in planning and conducting attacks to reduce the risk comes into play.[77]

Unfortunately, the customary rule of proportionality does not include any concrete guidelines on the critical question of what kind of damage can be considered to be excessive.[78] Balancing military advantage and anticipated incidental damage is critical to respecting this principle. Any effort to assess this in hindsight is also problematic. Each case and set of individual factors must be considered on its merit.

A practical application of this principal would occur where a commander has a choice of different means or methods of attack; in such instances the attacker should choose the option that would avoid or minimize incidental

---

[72] Y. Dinstein, "Discussion: Reasonable Military Commanders and Reasonable Civilians," in A. E. Wall (ed.), *Legal and Ethical Lessons of NATO's Kosovo Campaign*, International Law Studies 78 (Newport: Naval War College, 2002), 173, 219.

[73] AP I, Art. 51(5)(b).

[74] UN International Criminal Tribunal for the former Yugoslavia, "Final Report to the Prosecutor by the Committee Established to Review the NATO Bombing Campaign Against the Federal Republic of Yugoslavia" (1999), ¶ 19.

[75] *Ibid.* [76] DoD Law of War Manual, ¶ 2.4.1.1, Justification in Acting.

[77] DoD Law of War Manual, ¶ 2.4.1.2.

[78] Final Report NATO Bombing (above note 74), ¶ 20.

damage. The principle was discussed in the Prosecutors Report on the NATO Bombing in 1999:

> Taken together, this suggests that in order to satisfy the requirement of proportionality, attacks against military targets which are known or can reasonably be assumed to cause grave environmental harm may need to confer a very substantial military advantage in order to be considered legitimate. At a minimum, actions resulting in massive environmental destruction, especially where they do not serve a clear and important military purpose, would be questionable.[79]

4.1 ICTY

The ICTY considered proportionality on a number of occasions and first addressed the principle in the *Kupreškić* case when the Trial Chamber held that "any incidental (and unintentional) damage to civilians must not be out of proportion to the direct military advantage gained by the military attack."[80]

> [I]t is nevertheless beyond dispute that at a minimum, large numbers of civilian casualties would have been interspersed among the combatants ... Even if it can be proved that the Muslim population of Ahmici was not entirely civilian but comprised some armed elements, still no justification would exist for widespread and indiscriminate attacks against civilians. Indeed, even in a situation of full-scale armed conflict, certain fundamental norms still serve to unambiguously outlaw such conduct, such as rules pertaining to proportionality.[81]

Subsequently in the *Galić* judgment, the Trial Chamber held that when assessing the responsibility for crimes committed during the siege of Sarajevo:

> [o]nce the military character of a target has been ascertained, commanders must consider whether striking this target is "expected to cause incidental loss of life, injury to civilians, damage to civilian objectives or a combination thereof, which would be excessive in relation to the concrete and direct military advantage anticipated." If such casualties are expected to result, the attack should not be pursued. The basic obligation to spare civilians and civilian objects as much as possible must guide the attacking party when considering the proportionality of an attack.[82]

---

[79]   *Ibid.*, ¶ 22.   [80]   *Prosecutor v. Kupreškić* (above note 56), ¶ 524.   [81]   *Ibid.*, ¶ 513.

[82]   *Prosecutor v. Galić* (above note 26), ¶ 58. The Appeals Chamber affirmed the Trial Chamber's legal findings in respect of the principle of proportionality: *Prosecutor v. Galić*, Case No. IT-98-29-A, Judgment, Appeals Chamber, Nov. 30, 2006 (*Galić* Appeals Judgment), ¶¶ 190–92.

In determining whether an attack was proportionate it is necessary to examine whether a reasonably well-informed person in the circumstances of the actual perpetrator, making reasonable use of the information available to him or her, could have expected excessive civilian casualties to result from the attack.[83]

4.2 ICC

The ICC Statute[84] provides that in an IAC "intentionally launching an attack in the knowledge that such attack will cause incidental loss of life or injury to civilians or damage to civilian objects ... which would be clearly excessive in relation to the concrete and direct overall military advantage anticipated" constitutes a war crime.[85] The Manual reflects this provision in its outline of what is unreasonable or excessive.[86] In that sense the Manual is consistent with established international practice which affords some appropriate degree of deference to the warfighter subject to the good faith application of the underlying principles of distinction and proportionality.[87]

An obvious weakness in this provision is its applicability to situations of IAC only. The ICC has also reaffirmed the basic principle of proportionality and made it clear that collateral damage *per se* is not a violation of the principle and therefore not unlawful.[88] Under "customary law, attacks directed at military objectives may cause 'collateral civilian damage' which is not unlawful *per se*, provided that the rules of custom prescribing proportionality in the conduct of hostilities were respected."[89]

The Manual does not elaborate on the degree of care required to be taken to respect the principle of proportionality. It is noteworthy, however, that the edits between its first edition published in June 2015 and its second iteration published on May 31, 2016 clarified that the principle of proportionality in its

---

[83] *Prosecutor v. Galić* (above note 26), ¶ 58. Since "in the circumstances of the actual perpetrator" includes the position of the accused as a commander, this finding is similar to what is suggested in the Final Report to the Prosecutor, namely to use the standard of the "reasonable military commander": Final Report NATO Bombing (above note 74), ¶ 50.

[84] Schabas (above note 22), 213.

[85] Rome Statute of the International Criminal Court, Art. 8(2)(b)(iv). See R. Bartels, "Dealing with the Principle of Proportionality in Armed Conflict in Retrospect: The Application of the Principle in International Criminal Trials" (2013) 46 *Israel Law Review* 271–315.

[86] DoD Law of War Manual, ¶ 2.4.1.2 Unreasonable or Excessive.

[87] M. A. Newton and L. May, *Proportionality in International Law* (Oxford University Press, 2014), 157–64.

[88] *Prosecutor v. Katanga* (above note 35), ¶ 895.

[89] *Ibid.* See also Decision on the Confirmation of Charges, ¶ 313. See also *Prosecutor v. Kordić and Cerkez* (above note 28), ¶ 52; Henckaerts and Doswald-Beck (above note 66), rule 14, 46–50.

broadest sense embodies the underlying obligation to take feasible precautions when conducting attacks. That said, how is proportionality to be responsibly measured? Sometimes a commander will have to accept a high level of risk to his or her own forces to avoid collateral damage. In this regard the overall military purpose of the operation is crucial. These are fundamental issues for any military commander and a law of war manual can only offer general guidance. Although the section dealing with proportionality in the Manual is relatively short, it is consistent with international jurisprudence. In the end, each situation must be assessed on its own merit. Here reliance will also be placed on the professionalism and training of US military personnel.

5 DISTINCTION

The principle of distinction requires military commanders to distinguish between military objectives and civilian persons or objects. It has been described as the most significant battlefield concept a combatant must observe.[90] According to Pilloud and Pictet, "[a]lthough it was never officially contained in an international treaty, the principle of *protection* and of *distinction* forms the basis of the entire regulation of war, established in Brussels in 1874 in the form of a draft, and later in the Hague Conventions of 1899 and 1907."[91]

5.1 *Current Jurisprudential Approaches*

According to the ICTY, the principle of distinction is a fundamental principle of IHL, which "obliges warring parties to distinguish *at all times* between the civilian population and combatants and between civilian objects and military objectives and accordingly to direct their operations only against military objectives."[92] The Trial Chamber considered that direct attacks on a hospital constituted examples of the campaign of attacks on civilians.[93] The Manual is consistent with this principle and highlights the need for all parties, whether in attack or defense, to ensure they distinguish themselves and all enemy forces and military objectives from the civilian population and civilian objects.[94] The Manual emphasizes the practical implications of the duty to distinguish and this is appropriate in such a publication. However, distinction raises some complex issues.

---

[90]   Solis (above note 60), 269.   [91]   ICRC (above note 35), ¶ 1826. Emphasis in original.
[92]   *Prosecutor v. Galić* (above note 26), ¶ 45.   [93]   *Ibid.,* ¶ 509.
[94]   DoD Law of War Manual, ¶¶ 2.5.2 to 2.5.3.1.

The practical application of this principle today is reflected in Article 57 of AP I which, in part, requires those who plan or decide upon an attack to "do everything feasible to verify that the objectives to be attacked are neither civilians nor civilian objects."[95] The obligation to do everything feasible is high, but not absolute. Nevertheless, reckless disregard for the possibility that persons being attacked are civilians may be enough to violate this principle.[96]

How would this work in practice? A military commander must establish effective intelligence-gathering systems to collect and evaluate relevant information concerning potential targets. In addition, the commander must direct the use of available technical means to properly identify targets during operations. Commanders at all levels engaged in operations must be permitted some degree of discretion to determine which resources are available and in what manner they shall be used. Furthermore, when assessing whether adequate efforts have been made to distinguish between military objectives and civilians or civilian objects, account should be taken of the operations as a whole and not focused exclusively on a specific incident.[97] If precautionary measures adopted have proved adequate in a very high percentage of cases in the past, then the fact they have not worked well in a small number of incidences does not necessarily mean they are generally inadequate.[98]

The Manual emphasizes the need to discriminate in conducting attacks against the enemy.[99] According to the ICTY, "Attacks, even when they are directed against legitimate military targets, are unlawful if conducted using indiscriminate means or methods of warfare, or in such a way as to cause indiscriminate damage to civilians."[100]

The principle of distinction is linked to other broad principles and definitions. For example, there is a divergence of opinion on what constitutes a military objective and this has significant implications for commanders seeking to respect the need to distinguish between military objectives and civilian objects and in so doing abide by the principle of distinction and laws of war. The definition of military objective contained in Protocol I has been subject to criticism by Hays Parks, the Special Assistant for Law of War Matters

---

95 Protocol Additional to the Geneva Conventions of Aug. 12, 1949, and relating to the Protection of Victims of International Armed Conflicts, June 8, 1977 (AP I).

96 *Prosecutor v. Kupreškić* (above note 56), ¶ 523.

97 Final Report NATO Bombing (above note 74), ¶ 29.   98 *Ibid.*

99 DoD Law of War Manual, ¶ 2.5.2.

100 *Prosecutor v. Kupreškić* (above note 56), ¶ 524. The Trial Chamber considered these principles have to some extent been spelled out in Arts. 57 and 58 of the First Additional Protocol of 1977.

to the US Army Judge Advocate General. He considers it too narrowly focused on definite military advantage with too little attention paid to war-sustaining capability.[101] In this context, it has been suggested that war-sustaining capabilities should include economic targets such as export industries. This is a controversial subject over which opinions differ. For example, there was criticism of the Coalition conduct in the Gulf War which suggested that the air campaign, despite being directed against legitimate military objectives within the scope of the Protocol I, caused excessive long-term damage to the Iraqi economic infrastructure with a consequential adverse effect on the civilian population.[102]

It has been suggested that it may be necessary to establish exactly what the effect has been of the damage to the civilian infrastructure brought about by the hostilities, including the likely cumulative effect on the civilian population.[103] A similar view was expressed by the ICTY which offers a glimpse of how these fundamental principles are interlocked:

> [R]egard might be had to considerations such as the cumulative effect of attacks on military objectives causing incidental damage to civilians. In other words, it may happen that single attacks on military objectives causing incidental damage to civilians, although they may raise doubts as to their lawfulness, nevertheless do not appear on their face to fall foul *per se* of the loose prescriptions of Articles 57 and 58 (or of the corresponding customary rules). However, in case of repeated attacks, all or most of them falling within

---

[101] W. Hays Parks, "Air War and the Law of War" (1990) 32 *Air Force Law Review*, 135–45.

[102] Human Rights Watch, *Needless Deaths in the Gulf War: Civilian Casualties during the Air Campaign and Violations of the Laws of War* (New York: HRW, 1991), Introduction and Summary of Conclusions: "Despite this exceptional opportunity to conduct the allied bombing campaign in strict compliance with the legal duty to take all feasible precautions to avoid civilian harm, we find that the actual conduct of the war fell short of this obligation in several significant respects. This divergence between legal duty and actual practice emerged both in the choice of the means and methods to prosecute the air war and in the selection of targets for attack. All of these shortcomings appear to have involved deliberate decisions by allied commanders to take less than the maximum feasible precautions necessary to avoid harm to civilians.In noting these discrepancies between duty and conduct, we do not suggest that the allies in general violated the requirements of the laws of war. To the contrary, in many if not most respects the allies' conduct was consistent with their stated intent to take all feasible precautions to avoid civilian casualties. At the same time, the existence of these shortcomings in allied conduct reveals that the effort of U.S. and allied commanders to portray the bombing campaign as a near-perfect attempt to avoid civilian harm was not entirely accurate, and that in some instances coalition forces appear to have violated the laws of war." We believe these findings are important both for understanding the extent to which the suffering of Iraqi civilians might have been lessened and for avoiding similar deficiencies in any future air war. See also J. G. Gardam, "Proportionality and Force in International Law" (1993) 87 *American Journal of International Law* 391, 404–10.

[103] F. Hampson, "Means and Methods of Warfare in the Conflict in the Gulf," in P. Rowe (ed.), *The Gulf War 1990–91 in International and English Law* (London: Sweet & Maxwell, 1993), 78–96. Final Report NATO Bombing (above note 74), ¶ 41.

the grey area between indisputable legality and unlawfulness, it might be warranted to conclude that the cumulative effect of such acts entails that they may not be in keeping with international law. Indeed, this pattern of military conduct may turn out to jeopardise excessively the lives and assets of civilians, contrary to the demands of humanity.[104]

With regard to attacks on civilians based on military necessity, the ICTY Appeals Chamber did not accept the contention that attacks against civilians and civilian objects would not be a crime when justified by military necessity. It declared:

> [The] prohibition against attacking civilians stems from a fundamental principle of international humanitarian law, the principle of distinction, which obliges warring parties to distinguish at all times between the civilian population and combatants, between civilian objects and military objectives and accordingly to direct military operations only against military objectives. Article 48 of Additional Protocol I enunciates the principle of distinction as a basic rule.[105]

The Appeals Chamber went on to cite the ICJ *Legality of the Threat or Use of Nuclear Weapons* Advisory Opinion where distinction was described as a cardinal principle "aimed at the protection of the civilian population and civilian objects and establishes the distinction between combatants and non-combatants; States must never make civilians the object of attack."[106] These fundamental rules are to be observed by all States whether or not they have ratified the relevant conventions "because they constitute intransgressible principles of international customary law."[107]

5.2 Military Objective and Distinction

The concept of a military objective is central to the principle of distinction insofar as "[a]ttacks shall be limited strictly to military objectives" as set out in AP I.[108] Although this rule is not found in AP II, it is included in other treaty provisions that refer to NIACs.[109] It is important to note that the ICRC Customary Law Study

---

[104]   *Prosecutor v. Kupreškić* (above note 56), ¶ 526.
[105]   *Prosecutor v. Kordić and Čerkez* (above note 28), ¶ 54.
[106]   *Legality of the Threat or Use of Nuclear Weapons* (above note 54), ¶ 78.   [107]   *Ibid.*
[108]   1977 Additional Protocol I, Art. 52(2). E.g., Protocol on Prohibitions or Restrictions on the Use of Mines, Booby-Traps and Other Devices (Protocol II), Geneva, Oct. 10, 1980, EIF Dec. 2, 1983, 2(6); Second Protocol to the Hague Convention of 1954 for the Protection of Cultural Property, Art. 1(f); Protocol on Prohibitions or Restrictions on the Use of Incendiary Weapons (Protocol III), Geneva, Oct. 10, 1980, EIF Dec. 2, 1983, 2(6).
[109]   E.g., Protocol on Prohibitions or Restrictions on the Use of Mines, Booby-Traps and Other Devices (Protocol II), Geneva, Oct. 10, 1980, EIF Dec. 2, 1983, 2(6); Second Protocol to the Hague Convention of 1954 for the Protection of Cultural Property, Art. 1(f); Protocol on

states that "[S]tate practice establishes this rule as a norm of customary international law applicable in both international and non-international armed conflicts."[110]Likewise, the San Remo Manual concludes that this definition represents customary law and points out that while the United States has not ratified AP I, it has accepted the Protocol on Prohibitions or Restrictions on the Use of Mines, Booby-Traps and Other Devices, as amended,[111] which includes, at Article 2(6), essentially the same definition (as AP I).[112]

In examining the targeting policies adopted in Kosovo and Iraq, Sassòli posits that the term "effective" [contribution] and "definite" [advantage] "exclude" the possibility of "indirect contributions and possible advantages."[113] He concludes that "the separate requirement that the attack must offer a definite military advantage means that even an attack on an objective of a military nature would not be lawful if its main purpose is to affect the morale of the civilian population and not to reduce the military strength of the enemy."[114] In this way he is critical of the US position that a target which supports the "war-sustaining capability" (the DoD instruction includes this in a definition of a military objective[115]) being legitimate in effect means the abandonment of the limitation on military targets and admits "political, financial ... and psychological targets, as long as they influence the possibility or the decision ... of the enemy to continue the war."[116] Dinstein is also of the opinion that the US concept of "war-sustaining" (as opposed to military advantage) "goes too far" and says that "[f]or an object to qualify as a military objective, there must exist a proximate nexus to military action (or 'war-fighting')."[117]

The Manual also includes the statement that: "[a]lthough terms such as 'war-fighting', 'war-supporting', and 'war-sustaining' are not explicitly reflected

---

Prohibitions or Restrictions on the Use of Incendiary Weapons (Protocol III), Geneva, Oct. 10, 1980, EIF Dec. 2, 1983, 2(6).

[110] Henckaerts and Doswald-Beck (above note 66), rule 8, 29.

[111] The Protocol on Prohibitions or Restrictions on the Use of Mines, Booby-Traps and Other Devices as amended on May 3, 1996 (Amended Protocol II).

[112] M. Schmitt, C. Garraway, and Y. Dinstein, *The Manual on the Law of Non-International Armed Conflict* (Leiden/Boston: Martinus Nijhoff, 2006), 6.

[113] M. Sassòli, "Targeting: The Scope and Utility of the Concept of Military Objectives for the Protection of Civilians in Contemporary Armed Conflict," in D. Wippman and M. Evangelista (eds.), *New Wars, New Laws? Applying the Laws of War in 21st Century Conflicts* (New York: Transnational Publishers, 2005), 181–210, 186. Emphasis in original.

[114] *Ibid.*, 186. Emphasis added.

[115] DoD, Military Commission Instruction No. 2, Apr. 30, 2003 (2003), section 5 (D).

[116] Sassòli (above note 113), 196.

[117] Y. Dinstein, "Legitimate Military Objectives Under the Current Jus in Bello," in A. E. Wall (ed.), *Legal and Ethical Issues of NATO's Kosovo Campaign*, International Law Studies 78 (Newport: Naval War College, 2002), 139, 146.

in the treaty definitions of military objective, the United States has interpreted the military objective definition to include these concepts."[118]
In November 2016 DoD General Counsel Jennifer O'Connor referred to
a "specific set of targets that have generated a lot of discussion lately." She
said that "these targets include such things as oil production or oil transpor-
tation assets and bulk cash storage sites" and considered that such targets
meet "[t]he definition of military objective" which she says "is generally
broken down into two prongs: (1) 'effective contribution to military action'
and (2) 'definite military advantage'."[119] The reference to "two prongs" dates
to the 1982 commentary on the Additional Protocols which includes the
following definition of military objective:

> The objects classified as military objectives under this definition include
> much more than strictly military objects such as military vehicles, weapons,
> munitions, stores of fuel and fortifications. Provided the objects meet the
> two-pronged test, *under the circumstances ruling at the time* (not at some
> hypothetical future time), military objectives include activities providing
> administrative and logistical support to military operations such as trans-
> portation and communications systems, railroads, airfields and port facil-
> ities and industries of *fundamental importance for the conduct of the armed
> conflict*.[120]

State practice would suggest that the United States is in a minority, if
not alone, in adopting such a broad view.[121] Parks considers that "[t]he
debate regarding the distinction between 'war-sustaining', 'war-fighting' and
'military action' is not clear, and perhaps primarily academic"[122] but adds that
"[h]owever disagreeable the term may be to some, 'war-sustaining' is accurately descriptive of the actual practice of States in armed conflict."[123] Meyer
refers to Clausewitz's much-quoted view that "war is not merely an act of
policy but a true political instrument, a continuation of political intercourse,

---

[118] DoD Law of War Manual, ¶ 5.7.6.2.

[119] DoD General Counsel Jennifer O'Connor, "Applying the Law of Targeting to the Modern
Battlefield," NYU School of Law (Nov. 28, 2016), www.defense.gov/Portals/1/Documents/pu
bs/Applying-the-Law-of-Targeting-to-the-Modern-Battlefield.pdf.

[120] M. Bothe, K. Josef Partsch, and W. Solf, *New Rules for Victims of Armed Conflicts:
Commentary on the Two Protocols Additional to the Geneva Conventions of 1949*, 1st ed.
(Leiden/Boston: Martinus Nijhoff, 1982), 322–23. Emphasis in original. Footnote omitted.

[121] E. Crawford, "The Principle of Distinction and Remote Warfare," in J. D. Ohlin (ed.),
Research Handbook on Remote Warfare (Cheltenham: Edward Elgar, 2017), fn. 49.

[122] W. Hays Parks, "Asymmetries and the Identification of Legitimate Military Objectives," in
W. H. von Heinegg and V. Epping (eds.), *International Humanitarian Law Facing New
Challenges* (New York: Springer, 2007), 65–116, 99.

[123] *Ibid.*, 99.

carried on with other means"[124] in support of her view on the benefits of "directly attack[ing] the enemy's capability and will to fight" and the conclusion that "[r]estrictive interpretations of Article 52(2), however, limit this capability unnecessarily."[125]

6 HONOR

Honor has a long tradition in IHL and may be traced back to the now old-fashioned concept of chivalry that created a duty to act honorably, even in war. Chivalry required soldiers to behave in a civilized manner and it remains one of its most enduring legacies.[126] While honor was mentioned in the Lieber Code,[127] it barely rates any mention in the Manual.[128]

The importance of honor stems from the fact that it is part of the untested foundation of all IHL principles. Relying on such an undefined concept alone would be naïve but inculcating a sense of honor into all aspects of behavior might well ensure greater observance of the law. The Manual suggests that honor "may be understood to provide a foundation for obligations that help enforce and implement the law" and explains that it forbids certain conduct that may undermine the protections of the law and prospects for restoring peace.[129]

In this context, the Manual reference to Hugh Thompson, the man who intervened at My Lai in Vietnam to prevent further killings of innocent civilians, is noteworthy.[130] Interestingly, Thompson attributed his sense of values to his parents, and not military training or regulations. The official US Army inquiry into My Lai (known as the Peers Inquiry) noted that

---

[124]   C. von Clausewitz, *On War*, ed. and trans. M. Howard and P. Paret, 2 vols. (Princeton University Press, 1976), I, 87.
[125]   J. M. Meyer, "Tearing Down the Facade: A Critical Look at the Current Law on Targeting the Will of the Enemy and Air Force Doctrine" (2001) 51 *The Air Force Law Review* 143, 181–2.
[126]   T. Meron, *Bloody Constraint: War and Chivalry in Shakespeare* (New York: Oxford University Press, 1998), 4–5, 49.
[127]   Lieber Code (above note 7), Art. 4.
[128]   UK Manual (above note 51), ¶¶ 10.29.1 at 268 and 1.16 at 6.
[129]   DoD Law of War Manual, ¶¶ 2.6.2.1 and 2.6.2.2.
[130]   Ibid., ¶ 2.6.1 fn. 109:

   Question Do you attribute your ability to see through the moral fog that day, better than those who made the massacre at My Lai happen, to any prior military training or experience? *Mr. Thompson* No, I don't believe it was any military training, because I had been through the training that everybody else had been. We had a 50-minute class of instruction on the Geneva Convention, a 50-minute class of instruction on the Code of Conduct, and a 50-minute class of instruction on the rules of engagement … But [my parents] always taught me to help the underdog. Don't be a bully and live by the golden rule. That golden rule says so much, and it's so simple and so basic. You know, I can't say it was a leadership 405 or whatever. I just think it was my parents, and they taught me right from wrong.

Thompson was among a group of helicopter pilots that "were of an extremely high caliber" in part because they had "been put through an intensive course of instruction to qualify as helicopter pilots and then sent off to South Vietnam."[131] Acknowledging his actions and the importance of his sense of right and wrong should remind all military personnel of the centrality of honor in ensuring observance of the basic principles. The main purpose of IHL is to minimize the horrors of armed conflict to the extent possible taking into account the need for efficient use of force to achieve victory and minimize casualties on all sides. While the law is set out in various treaties and rules, the demands of military necessity are limited by legal and moral considerations. It is in this context that ethical and humanitarian principles, often embodied in treaty provisions, play an important role. It is the realm where honor among all those engaged in armed conflict has the potential to play a positive influential role.

The Nuremberg Tribunal stated that crimes against international law are committed by men, not by abstract entities.[132] It was referring to the need to punish individuals. However, it is also important to emphasize the importance of honor among individual soldiers in ensuring the foundational values of IHL are respected. Invoking such a concept in a contemporary military manual is likely to be dismissed by some commentators and for this reason its inclusion in the US Manual is to be welcomed.

7 CONCLUSION

The principles outlined are applicable regardless of the legality or justness of the armed conflict. In practice it is important to express the basic principles of IHL in concise and simple language readily comprehensible to military personnel in the field. The Manual succeeds in doing so while indicating there are many issues that remain to be resolved on a case-by-case basis. It does not complicate the issues for a military commander. There are a number of challenges to implementation, in particular the "civilianization of armed conflicts," that compound the principle of distinction. Direct participation in hostilities by noncombatants and concepts such as "continuous combat function" add further to the complexity of contemporary armed conflicts. Furthermore, the role played by private military and security companies

---

[131]   Lieutenant General W. R. Peers, *The My Lai Inquiry* (New York: Norton, 1979), 76.
[132]   *France et. al. v. Goering et. al.*, 22 IMT 411, 466 (IMT 1946).

may be critical to their status and difficult to determine in theaters where different companies play multiple roles.

The Manual seeks to find a balance between military necessity and humanity and this finds more specific expression in the core principles outlined. However, it is in the interpretation and application of other IHL rules that the principle of humanity can be most beneficial. The principle of distinction raises complex issues that are not addressed in this chapter and reference must be made to Chapter V of the Manual, "The Conduct of Hostilities." However, the fundamental obligations enshrined in these principles are outlined with clarity and easy to follow. While the rules outlined in the Manual governing proportionality reflect customary law, they do not incorporate the express provisions of AP I and should be read in conjunction with Chapter V of the Manual. It is significant that the Manual reiterates that where there is no justification for military action, a proportionality analysis would not be necessary to reach the conclusion that the attack would be unlawful.[133] On the other hand, the reference to proportionality and reprisals seems out of place in a contemporary law of war manual.[134]

Some of the ICTY decisions outlined refer to relatively narrow issues, such as military necessity and property destruction, and to a lesser extent, enforced disappearances. Nevertheless, they provide examples of how issues in IHL were addressed before international tribunals and courts. The chapter deals with the fundamental principles and values. These are presented in a style that is practical and comprehensible for all members of the armed services to follow. In the long run this is critical as it is they who will be charged with its implementation in situations of armed conflict. The inclusion of honor as a key principle is important. Emphasis on maintaining values which support IHL and similar rules may do more to encourage compliance by a professional military than the prospect of sanctions.

---

[133]   DoD Law of War Manual, ¶ 2.4.1.1.   [134]   *Ibid.*, ¶ 2.4.1.2.

8

The Manual's Redefined Concept of Non-International Armed Conflict: Applying Faux LOAC to a Fictional NIAC

David E. Graham

1 INTRODUCTION

Chapter XVII of the Department of Defense (DoD) Law of War Manual (the Manual) is dedicated exclusively to Law of Armed Conflict (LOAC) issues arising in the context of non-international armed conflicts (NIACs). And, in an unintended, but wholly accurate, foreshadowing of the exceptionally problematic content of this chapter, its opening paragraph states that "the application of the law of war to non-international armed conflicts may be complex."[1]

On the surface, the promulgation of an entire chapter of the Manual dedicated to the most commonly encountered legal dilemmas in post-9/11 conflicts is a positive, if long overdue, development. Indeed, this form of conflict received only cursory guidance in the classic 1956 Army Field Manual 27–10, "The Law of Land Warfare," which was superseded by the Manual's publication, as noted throughout this volume. FM 27–10 essentially dealt with NIAC by reproducing the text of Common Article 3 of the 1949 Geneva Conventions.[2] With the exception of Protocol II to the 1949 Conventions concluded in 1977[3] and one provision of the Hague Cultural

---

[1] DoD Law of War Manual, ¶ 17.1.
[2] Geneva Convention for the Amelioration of the Conditions of the Wounded and Sick in Armed Forces in the Field, Aug. 12, 1949, 6 UST 3114, 75 UNTS 31; Geneva Convention for the Amelioration of the Condition of the Wounded and Sick and Shipwrecked Members of Armed Forces at Sea, Aug. 12, 1949, 6 UST 3217, 75 UNTS 85; Geneva Convention Relative to the Treatment of Prisoners of War, Aug. 12, 1949, 6 UST 3316, 75 UNTS 135; Geneva Convention Relative to the Protection of Civilian Persons in Time of War, Aug. 12, 1949, 6 UST 3516, 75 UNTS 287.
[3] 1977 Additional Protocol II to the 1949 Geneva Conventions (AP II).

Property Convention of 1954,[4] little treaty law has been effected that expressly applies to NIAC.[5]

Given this setting, the publication of the Manual afforded the United States the opportunity to effectively capture and summarize the contemporary view of the international community concerning the LOAC applicable to NIAC. Moreover, the Manual provided a highly visible platform through which the United States might have addressed the oft-expressed concerns of its allies associated with this subject, given the need to conduct NIAC in conjunction with these allies based on a common understanding of the difficult legal issues arising in such operations.[6] Unfortunately, DoD chose, instead, to use the Manual's treatment of NIAC as a means by which to justify – and defend – many of the questionable legal positions taken by the United States, post-9/11, with respect to al-Qaeda, its members, and its associated forces. Essential to this approach was a need for the Manual to substantively redefine the customary and universally accepted concept of NIAC itself. Why? Because the veracity of the greater portion of Chapter XVII, as well as that of significant aspects of several other chapters of the Manual, is premised entirely upon the assumed validity of this revised definition.

And, while the Manual attempts to validate this assumption by framing its redefined concept of NIAC, and all of the Manual's resultant LOAC corollaries, as *lex lata*, this is – and should not be – unquestionably accepted as an accurate statement of existing international law. There is scant support for the concept of global, or transnational, NIAC defined solely by a reference to the status of the non-State participant, absent any geographical element. In practice, the DoD approach toward NIAC remains largely divorced from the practice of other States. This chapter thus concludes with the recommen-

---

[4]   1954 Hague Cultural Property Convention, Art. 19, ¶ 1 provides the formulation that is common to the key treaty texts that extend to NIAC. It provides that "In the event of an armed conflict not of an international character occurring within the territory of one of the High Contracting Parties, each party to the conflict shall be bound to apply, as, a minimum, the provisions of the present Convention which relate to respect for cultural property." Moreover, in keeping with the primary concerns of the drafters of the Geneva Conventions, the key Convention provisions also provide that the application of legal protections and principles based on treaty provisions applicable to NIAC have no effect in changing the legal status of persons or territory. DoD Law of War Manual, ¶ 17.2.3.

[5]   DoD Law of War Manual, ¶ 17.2.1.1 (for a listing of the treaties that explicitly apply to NIAC).

[6]   Chapters 4, 5, 7, 9, 12, 13, 16, 17, and 18 of this volume address differing aspects of this precise problem.

dation that the current US view of NIAC be reconsidered and the Manual accordingly revised.

2 THE UNIVERSALLY RECOGNIZED NATURE OF NON-INTERNATIONAL ARMED CONFLICTS

To derive the recognized – and practiced – understanding of the nature of NIACs, one must look to Common Article 3 of the 1949 Geneva Conventions, Article 1 of Protocol II Additional to these Conventions (AP II), and, more recently, to the 1995 International Criminal Tribunal for the former Yugoslavia (ICTY) *Tadić* interlocutory appeal on the jurisdiction of the ICTY. These important texts will be considered, *in seriatum.*

Common Article 3 represents, by all accounts, one of the "most important Articles" of the 1949 Geneva Conventions.[7] As such, it figures prominently in the modern jurisprudence.[8] More importantly, for purposes of evaluating the Manual definition of NIAC, it is noted that the official International Committee of the Red Cross (ICRC) Commentary explaining the intent of those who drafted Common Article 3 was based "primarily on the negotiating history of the respective treaties, as observed firsthand by the authors, and on prior practice, especially that of World War II."[9]

Article 3 reads in full as follows:

> In the case of armed conflict not of an international character occurring in the territory of one of the High Contracting Parties, each Party to the conflict shall be bound to apply, as a minimum, the following provisions;
>   (1) Persons taking no active part in the hostilities, including members of armed forces who have laid down their arms and those placed hors de combat by sickness, wounds, detention, or any other cause, shall in all circumstances be treated humanely, without any adverse distinction

---

[7] J. S. Pictet (ed.), *The Geneva Conventions of 1949: Commentary*, 4 vols. (Geneva: ICRC, 1952), III, 27–44 (Pictet Commentary on Common Art. 3).

[8] See, e.g., *Prosecutor v. Blaškić*, Case No. IT-95-14-T, Trial Judgment, ¶ 166 (ICTY, Mar. 3, 2000), http://icty.org/x/cases/blaskic/tjug/en/bla-tj00 0303e.pdf ("Common Article 3 must be considered as a rule of customary international law."); *Prosecutor v. Kunarac, Kovač, and Vuković*, Case Nos. IT-96-23, IT-96-23/1-A, Appeals Judgment, ¶¶ 49–70 (ICTY, June 12, 2002) (extending the coverage of Common Art. 3 to include rapes committed during armed conflict not of an international character and rejecting arguments that Common Art. 3 is limited to the protection of property and the proper use of permitted weapons).

[9] L. Cameron, B. Demeyere, J.-M. Henckaerts, E. La Haye, and H. Niebergall-Lackner, "The Updated Commentary on the First Geneva Convention – a New Tool for Generating Respect for International Humanitarian Law" (2015) 97 *International Review of the Red Cross* 1209, 1214.

founded on race, colour, religion or faith, sex, birth or wealth, or any other similar criteria.

To this end, the following acts are and shall remain prohibited at any time and in any place whatsoever with respect to the above mentioned persons;

  (a) violence to life and person, in particular murder of all kinds, mutilation, cruel treatment and torture;
  (b) taking of hostages;
  (c) outrages upon personal dignity, in particular, humiliating and degrading treatment;
  (d) the passing of sentences and the carrying out of executions without previous judgment pronounced by a regularly constituted court affording all the judicial guarantees which are recognized as indispensable by civilized peoples.

  (2) The wounded and sick shall be collected and cared for. An impartial humanitarian body, such as the International Committee of the Red Cross, may offer its services to the Parties to the conflict. The Parties to the conflict should further endeavour to bring into force, by means of special agreements, all or part of the other provisions of the present Convention. The application of the preceding provisions shall not affect the legal status of the Parties to the conflict.

The key Article 3 language at issue, here, is, of course, its first sentence: "In the case of armed conflict not of an international character occurring in the territory of one of the High Contracting Parties . . ." Since 1949, this phrase has carried with it a consistent and universally accepted meaning – owing to the authoritative interpretation provided by the ICRC Commentary to the Geneva Conventions (Pictet's Commentary). Pictet noted that certain "convenient criteria" might be used in determining the existence of a NIAC:

  (1) That the Party in revolt against the de jure Government possesses an organized military force, an authority responsible for its acts, acting within a determinate territory and having the means of respecting and ensuring respect for the Convention.
  (2) That the legal Government is obliged to have recourse to the regular military forces against insurgents organized as military and in possession of a part of the national territory.
  (3)
    (a) That the de jure Government has recognized the insurgents as belligerents; or
    (b) That it has claimed for itself the rights of a belligerent; or
    (c) That it has accorded the insurgents recognition as belligerents for the purposes only of the present Convention; or

    (d) That the dispute has been admitted to the agenda of the Security Council or the General Assembly of the United Nations as being a threat to international peace, a breach of the peace, or an act of aggression.

(4)

    (a) That the insurgents have an organization purporting to have the characteristics of a State.

    (b) That the insurgent civil authority exercises de facto authority over the population within a determinate portion of the national territory.

    (c) That the armed forces act under the direction of an organized authority and are prepared to observe the ordinary laws of war.

    (d) That the insurgent civil authority agrees to be bound by the provisions of the Convention.[10]

Pictet then offers further commentary as to whether these criteria are to be deemed dispositive in assessing the existence of a NIAC, commentary that, as later discussed, has been selectively referenced in the Manual in support of its redefinition of NIAC:

> Does this mean that Article 3 is not applicable in cases where armed strife breaks out in a country, but does not fulfil any of the above conditions? We do not subscribe to this view. We think, on the contrary, that the scope of application of the Article must be as wide as possible. There can be no drawbacks in this, since the Article in its reduced form, contrary to what might be thought, does not in any way limit the right of a State to put down rebellion, nor does it increase in the slightest the authority of the rebel party. It merely demands respect for certain rules, which were already recognized as essential in all civilized countries, and embodied in the national legislation of the States in question, long before the Convention was signed.[11]

Concluding his commentary directed at Article 3's field of application, Pictet states: "[I]t must be recognized that the conflicts referred to in Article 3 are armed conflicts, with 'armed forces' on either side engaged in 'hostilities' – conflicts, in short, which are in many respects similar to an international war, *'but take place within the confines of a single country'*."[12]

Notwithstanding the fact that the US Senate has failed to give its advice and consent to AP II, the constitutional predicate for the United States to be *de jure* bound by a treaty text, the Manual liberally cites its substantive provisions in

---

[10] Pictet Commentary on Common Art. 3, 36. [11] *Ibid.*
[12] Pictet Commentary on Common Art. 3, 37. Emphasis added.

Chapter XVII. Of particular note, Article 1 of AP II (entitled Material Field of Application) reads as follows:

1. This Protocol, which develops and supplements Article 3 common to the Geneva Conventions of 12 August 1949 without modifying its existing conditions of application, shall apply to all armed conflicts which are not covered by Article 1 of the Protocol relating to the Protection of Victims of International Armed Conflicts (Protocol I) and which take place in the territory of a High Contracting Party between its armed forces and dissident armed forces or other organized armed groups which, under responsible command, exercise control over a part of its territory as to enable them to carry out sustained and concerted military operations and to implement this Protocol.
2. This Protocol shall not apply to situations of internal disturbances and tensions, such as riots, isolated and sporadic acts of violence and other acts of a similar nature, as not being armed conflicts.[13]

Furthermore, Article 3 of AP II (Non-Intervention) states:

1. Nothing in this Protocol shall be invoked for the purpose of affecting the sovereignty of a State or the responsibility of the government, by all legitimate means, to maintain or re-establish law and order in the State or to defend the national unity and territorial integrity of the State.
2. Nothing in this Protocol shall be invoked as justification for intervening, directly or indirectly, for any reason whatever, in the armed conflict or in the internal or external affairs of the High Contracting Party in the territory of which that conflict occurs.[14]

Finally, in October 1995, the ICTY issued a landmark ruling that has become known as the Tadić Jurisdiction Decision.[15] In considering the issue of when a conflict – that is, a "non-international armed conflict" – exists for the purpose of applying the provisions of Common Article 3 to the Geneva Conventions, the ICTY Appeals bench concluded that "[a]n armed conflict exists whenever there is a resort to armed force between States or protracted armed violence between governmental authorities and organized groups or between such groups within a State." While there is "certainly no unanimity" among lawyers concerning the existence of a "definitive standard regarding the categorization of conflict,"[16] the Manual's approach to this issue, as described in the next

---

[13] AP II, Art. 1. See also DoD Law of War Manual, ¶ 17.2.1.1 fn. 38.   [14] AP II, Art. 3.

[15] *Prosecutor v. Tadić*, Case No. IT-94-1-A, Decision on the Defense Motion for Interlocutory Appeal on Jurisdiction, ¶ 70 (ICTY, Appeal Chamber, Oct. 2, 1995).

[16] K. Watkin, *Fighting at the Legal Boundaries: Controlling the Use of Force in Contemporary Conflict* (New York: Oxford University Press, 2016), 292.

section, is divorced from the larger contextual debates that have divided experts since 9/11.

Common to each of these three authoritative sources dealing with NIAC is the definitive reference to the fact that this form of conflict occurs "within" the confines of a State – waged either between governmental authorities and an armed group attempting to displace the constituted government of that State, or between two or more armed groups themselves. That is, all of the customary and codified LOAC related to the nature and scope of NIAC has systematically centered on hostilities that occur within the boundaries of a State – hence the colloquial term "internal armed conflict" (used within Chapter XVII as well).[17] Thus, the geographical context in which NIACs have historically – and legally – been defined is supported by both longstanding State practice and *opinio juris*.

3 THE DOD LAW OF WAR MANUAL'S REDEFINITION OF NON-INTERNATIONAL ARMED CONFLICT

The Introduction to Chapter XVII begins with the statement that the chapter "addresses the Law of War rules applicable to armed conflicts not of an international character, or non-international armed conflict."[18] So far so good. However, it next proceeds to define NIAC as simply "those armed conflicts that are not between States,"[19] citing as the exclusive support for this newly derived definition of NIAC (as is often the case in this Manual) but another section of the Manual that conveniently sets forth this same definition.[20] Similarly, the Manual provides only internal cross-references for the proposition that "[c]ertain non-international armed conflicts, however, are not internal armed conflicts."[21] It then goes on to note that "[a]lthough there has been a range of views on what constitutes a non-international armed conflict, the intensity of the conflict and the organization of the parties are criteria that have been assessed to distinguish between non-international armed conflict and internal disturbances, such as riots ... and other acts of a similar nature."[22]

The Manual offers no evidence to support its contention that a "range of views" exists within the international community regarding the nature of NIAC. Too, while referencing only those criteria used in the *Tadić* decision to determine the existence of a NIAC, the Manual pointedly fails to make any

---

[17] DoD Law of War Manual, ¶ 17.1.3.1 (arguing that Common Art. 3 applies to internal armed conflicts, even though other aspects of the Geneva Conventions would not, based on a strict textual reading).

[18] *Ibid.*, ¶ 17.1.   [19] *Ibid.*, ¶ 17.1.   [20] *Ibid.*, ¶ 3.3.1.   [21] *Ibid.*, ¶ 17.1.3.1.

[22] *Ibid.*, ¶ 17.1.1; see also Rome Statute of the International Criminal Court, Art. 8(2)(d).

mention of Pictet's extensive commentary regarding the nature of the conflicts to which the provisions of Common Article 3 apply in either Chapter XVII or Chapter III (Application of the Law of War). Moreover, the same is true of the provisions of Article 1, Protocol II, which speak specifically to the type of conflicts dealt with by that Protocol; that is, conflicts which occur "within" the territory of a State against an armed group attempting to displace the *de jure* government of that State. And, even with respect to the *Tadić* criteria, the ICTY Appeals Chamber made it clear that these criteria are to be applied, once again, in the context of "protracted armed violence between governmental authorities and organized armed groups or between such groups 'within' a State,"[23] a statement that the Manual drafters selectively chose to omit.

Those drafting the Manual clearly recognized that the international community's long-established and well-documented consensus regarding NIACs as "internal" armed conflicts would pose a substantial obstacle to the possibility of the publication's newly minted definition of such hostilities achieving any degree of legitimacy. Accordingly, this issue is addressed, early on, in the Manual's paragraph 17.1.1.2.[24]

> *NIAC and Internal Armed Conflict.* In some cases, the term internal armed conflict is used as a synonym for non-international armed conflict. Such usage may reflect a traditional definition of non-international armed conflict as only those armed conflicts occurring within the borders of a single State. Non-international armed conflicts, however, are classified as such simply based on the status of the Parties to the conflict, and sometimes occur in more than one State. The mere fact that an armed conflict occurs in more than one State and thus may be characterized as international "in scope" does not render it "international in character."

The assertions contained in the last two sentences of paragraph 17.1.1.2 are simply not supported by international law or State practice. Instead, there is an attempt, at least ostensibly, to exclusively couch the authority for both these statements in US domestic case law; namely, the Supreme Court language in *Hamdan v. Rumsfeld*.[25] Authority for the statement that "Non-international armed conflicts ... are classified as such simply based on the status of the parties to the conflict, and sometimes occur in more than one State" is footnoted to the Manual's paragraph 3.3.1 (International Armed Conflict and Non-International Armed Conflict), which quotes Hamdan as opining that "an armed conflict described in Common Article 3 of the 1949 Geneva

---

[23] *Prosecutor v. Tadić*, Case No. IT-94-1-A, Decision on the Defense Motion for Interlocutory Appeal on Jurisdiction, ¶ 70 (ICTY, Appeal Chamber, Oct. 2, 1995).

[24] DoD Law of War Manual, ¶ 17.1.1.2.   [25] *Hamdan v. Rumsfeld*, 548 US 557 (2006).

Conventions 'does not involve a clash between nations'." Well, yes, this is a valid observation. The *Hamdan* opinion then notes that "A non-international armed conflict is distinct from an international armed conflict because of the legal status of the entities opposing each other."[26] Again, a valid point, but certainly not language that supports the Manual's contention that NIACs are classified as such "simply" based on the status of the parties involved.

Next, the Manual states that "when States are not on opposite sides of a conflict . . . [t]hese other types of conflicts are described as 'not of an international character' or a 'non-international armed conflict'," linking what, again, is a valid observation to language contained in the *Hamdan* lower court decision at the DC Circuit Court of Appeals.[27] The language footnoted in this instance is that contained in the concurring opinion of Justice J. Williams:

> [T]he words "not of an international character" are sensibly understood to refer to a conflict between a signatory nation and a non-state actor. The most obvious form of such a conflict is a civil war. But given the Convention's structure, the logical reading of "international character" is one that matches the basic derivation of the word "international", i.e., between nations. Thus, I think the context compels the view that a conflict between a signatory and a non-state actor is a conflict "not of an international character".[28]

A reasonable finding by Justice Williams, to be sure. However, once again, despite the apparent conclusions drawn by the authors of the Manual, resulting, apparently, from their reading of the cited language of the *Hamdan* opinions, nothing in the text of either of these opinions, even that penned by Justice Williams, supports the Manual's contention that NIACs are classified as such simply based on the status of the parties to the conflict or that they sometimes occur in more than one State at the same time.

Section 3.3.1 then ends with the statement that: "[T]wo non-State armed groups warring against one another or States warring against non-State armed groups may be described as 'non-international armed conflict,' even if international borders are crossed in the fighting."[29] And, the sole authority provided for this statement? It is the Manual's paragraph 17.1.1.2 (NIAC and Internal Armed Conflict), which, as previously noted, cites, in turn, paragraph 3.3.1 as the exclusive authority for the contention that NIACs sometimes occur in more than one State. In other words, the validity of the content of both these paragraphs of the Manual is said to be supported by the fact that both say the same thing.

---

[26] *Ibid.*, 565–68.   [27] DoD Law of War Manual, ¶ 3.3.1.
[28] *Hamdan v. Rumsfeld*, 415 F.3d 33, 44 (DC Cir. 2005).
[29] DoD Law of War Manual, ¶ 3.3.1.

And then, there is the somewhat head-scratching statement that, "The mere fact that an armed conflict occurs in more than one State, and thus may be characterized as 'international in scope', does not render it 'international in character'." This assertion is also derived from an assessment regarding the nature of NIAC made by the Supreme Court in *Hamdan*. However, leaving aside the fact that the Court does not, and cannot, speak for the international community on matters of multilateral treaty interpretation, its reading of Pictet's Commentary to Common Article 3, on which the Manual's statement is based, is itself transparently faulty.

In *Hamdan*, the Court opined that, in view of the facts before it, Common Article 3 was, in fact, applicable to a "a conflict not of an international character," ostensibly sanctioning the idea that the United States was engaged in such a conflict, globally, with al-Qaeda. Its reasoning: The phrase "conflict not of an international character" was said to appear in Article 3 simply to evidence a contradistinction to a conflict between nations. While acknowledging that "the official commentaries (Pictet's Commentary) accompanying Common Article 3 indicate that an important purpose of the provision was to furnish minimal protection to rebels involved in one kind of 'conflict not of an international character'; i.e., a civil war," the Court noted that "the commentaries also make clear 'that the scope of the article must be as wide as possible'."[30] That is, the Court found that this particular Commentary language supported the view that "a conflict might be international in scope, yet non-international in character." In referencing this portion of the Commentary, however, the Court, significantly, chose to ignore its complete text. The Commentary, following the listing of several criteria that might be used in determining the existence of a NIAC, reads as follows:

> Does this mean that Article 3 is not applicable in cases where armed strife breaks out "in a country", but does not fulfil any of the above conditions? We do not subscribe to this view. We think, on the contrary, that the scope of the application must be as wide as possible. There can be no drawbacks in this, since the article, ... contrary to what might be thought, does not in any way limit the right of a State "to put down rebellion", nor does it increase in the slightest the authority of "the rebel party".[31]

Clearly, the Commentary language referenced by the Court in grounding its view that a conflict might be "international in scope, yet non-international in character," when viewed in its full context, fails to support the Court's

---

[30] *Hamdan v. Rumsfeld* (above note 25), 568.
[31] Pictet Commentary on Common Art. 3, 36. (Emphasis added.)

reasoning. Furthermore, the negotiating record for what became Common Article 3 supports the view that its text was designed to apply to protect insurgents, while fully respecting the rights of the territorial State. At the beginning of the discussion of Common Article 3 in the Joint Committee, France expressed concerns that civilians on the opposing side in a civil war would be entitled to receive overly generous protection from the proposed article.[32] The French delegation argued that including insurgents within the scope of Common Article 3 would undermine the sovereignty of the State and that the text should make it impossible for insurgents to "claim the protection of the Convention under a mask of politics or any other pretext."[33] Greece echoed the concern for protecting State sovereignty by stating that there was a danger that rebels would be entitled to the protections of prisoners of war and could not be charged for their crimes.[34]

While some delegations (*inter alia* Romania) argued that Article 3 should have the broadest possible application, this view was not shared by the majority of the delegates.[35] Most of the delegates believed that the Article should be applied only to those opposing forces that were organized and professional, rather than bandits or anarchists, in order to preserve the sovereign flexibility of the territorial State.[36] The Swiss delegation argued that Article 3 strikes the perfect balance between a State's sovereignty and humanitarian protections, as it preserved the ability of the "legitimate government whose duty it is, in a non-international war, to compel rebels and insurgents to respect the national law of the country."[37] The drafters of Common Article 3 were focused on preserving State sovereign prerogatives, hence the notion that they sought to protect persons who were beyond the sovereign authority of the territorial State is illogical in light of their overarching goal. In short, there is nothing in the negotiating record to suggest that the concept of wide coverage was intended to create an extensive scope of NIAC, untethered from geographic (read law enforcement) authority.

In truth, the Court engaged in a transparent cherry picking of the Commentary to achieve its desired policy result. In considering this fact, the question has to be posed: Did the Court fail to appreciate, or deliberately choose to ignore, the historic and consistent interpretation of Common Article 3's application to, exclusively, internal armed conflicts? Perhaps it was a little of both, but it would appear to be more of the latter. Unwilling to overtly

---

[32] Final Record of the Diplomatic Conference of 1949, Vol. II, Section B10 (Federal Political Department Berne 1949), www.loc. gov/rr/frd/Military_Law/pdf/Dipl-Conf-1949-Final_Vol-2-B.pdf.
[33] *Ibid.* [34] *Ibid.*, 10–11. [35] *Ibid.*, 11. [36] *Ibid.* [37] *Ibid.*, 334.

confront the contention by the Bush Administration that the United States was engaged in a "Global War on Terrorism," the Court chose, instead, by using its selective interpretation of the Commentary, to levy certain requirements on the government. In essence, the Court was conveying this message: "If you seek to invoke the LOAC to indefinitely incarcerate individuals seized in this 'war', you must, at the very least, afford these individuals the minimal safeguards provided by this body of law; i.e., those of Common Article 3." And, rather than framing such safeguards as customary LOAC provisions (given both the Administration's and the Court's disdain for the legitimacy of customary international law), the Court postured these requirements as Geneva Convention, Article 3, "treaty" obligations, legally applicable to the judicially determined "conflict not of an international character" deemed to be underway with al-Qaeda.

Thus came into being the Supreme Court-originated concept that, "while a conflict might be international in scope, it need not be international in character." And, although the US Government had actually argued before the Court that Common Article 3 could not apply to *Hamdan*, as the ongoing "conflict" with al-Qaeda did not, in fact, qualify as a "conflict not of an international character,"[38] immediately upon the Court's "correction" of the government's interpretation of the relevant Article 3 treaty language, the latter quickly moved to embrace the Court's interpretation of the nature of the ongoing US–al-Qaeda "conflict," as evidenced by the Manual's paragraph 17.1.1.2 text.

Finally, it is noted that, as another aspect of the Manual's attempted redefinition of NIAC, reference is made in paragraph 17.1.1.3 to the concept of "transnational NIACs," a term said to be used "to indicate that a noninternational armed conflict may take place in more than one State."[39] And, while the Manual offers no citatory support for its statement that this term is used to describe multi-State NIACs, it is one that has been employed, but in different ways, by a number of academics. One commentator makes use of the term to describe a hybrid form of conflict that is neither international nor noninternational in character, but hostilities that fall somewhere in between and which represent an extraterritorial application of combat power by the regular armed forces of a State against a transnational non-State entity.[40] Others have identified "transnational" armed conflicts in the same manner as that conveyed by the Manual; that is, those that occur between a State and a non-State

---

[38]   *Hamdan v. Rumsfeld* (above note 25), 567.   [39]   DoD Law of War Manual, ¶ 1.1.3.
[40]   G. S. Corn, "Hamdan, Lebanon, and the Regulation of Armed Conflict: The Need to Recognize a Hybrid Category of Armed Conflict" (2007) 40 *Vanderbilt Journal of Transnational Law* 295.

armed group (or between non-State armed groups) on the territory of more than one State. In their view, "Internal conflicts are distinguished from international armed conflicts [IAC] by the parties involved, rather than by the territorial scope of the conflict."[41] Neither of these attempts to assign a definition to this term has gained traction within the international community.

4 THE MANUAL'S DEPARTURE FROM THE DEFINITIONAL NORM OF NIAC: "WHY?"

The definition of NIAC set forth in Chapter XVII of the Manual represents a distinct departure from the definitional norm of this form of hostilities long formulated and practiced by the international community. Nevertheless, it accurately reflects a substantially altered US Government view on this subject. The pivotal question thus becomes, "Why?" "Why has the United States chosen to engage in a wholesale revision of the definitional scope of NIAC?"

The answer to this question is easily discerned. In order to provide an international legal basis for both the US use of force against al-Qaeda, on a global scale, and, very significantly, the manner in which the United States has dealt with captured al-Qaeda personnel, it was necessary that these actions be viewed as occurring within the context of some form of armed conflict. Thus, with an eye on the *Hamdan* decision, both the Obama Administration, and now, apparently, that of President Trump, have taken the position that the United States has been – and continues to be – engaged in a "global, yet non-international armed conflict with Al Qaeda and its associated forces."[42]

[41] A. Paulus and M. Vashakmadze, "Asymmetric War and the Notion of Armed Conflict-A Tentative Conceptualization" (Mar. 2009) 91 *International Review of the Red Cross* 112.

[42] President Barack Obama, Address at the National Defense University, Washington, DC, May 23, 2013, www.whitehouse.gov/the-press-office/2013/05/23/remarks-president-barrack-obama. In this speech, the President asserted that: "Under domestic and international law, the United States is at war with al-Qaeida, the Taliban, and their associated forces." See also E. Holder, US Attorney General, Address at Northwestern University School of Law, Mar. 5, 2012, www.justice .gov/opa/speech/attorney-general-eric-holder-speaks-northwestern-university-school-law ("Because the United States is in an armed conflict, we are authorized to take action against enemy belligerents under international law . . . None of this is changed by the fact that we are not in a conventional war."); J. O. Brennan, Assistant to the President for Homeland Security and Counterterrorism, "Strengthening Our Security by Adhering to Our Values and Laws," Address at Harvard Law School, Sept. 16, 2011, www.whitehouse.gov/the-press-office/2011/09/16/ remarks-john-o-brennan-strengthening-our-security-adhering-our-values-an. ("We are at war with al Qa'ida. In an indisputable act of aggression, al Qa'ida attacked our nation . . . "; H. H. Koh, Legal Advisor to the Department of State, "The Obama Administration and International Law," Address to the American Society of International Law, Mar. 25, 2010, www.state.gov/s/l/ releases/remarks/139119.htm. ("As a matter of international law, the United States is in an armed

In essence, then, the US-crafted definition of NIAC serves as a basis upon which the post-9/11 US decisions regarding the manner in which it has dealt with al-Qaeda as a whole, as well as its individual members, might be justified and defended. This expansion of previous State practice significantly serves to establish the legal basis for the uniquely crafted LOAC principles and practices, set forth in various chapters of the Manual, that are to be applied in all future US "conflicts" with non-State armed groups.[43] In sum, it is clear that the definition and its supporting LOAC provisions have been conceived with one purpose in mind: to deal specifically with the unique legal issues generated exclusively by the United States solely as the result of its post-9/11 decision-making process. Accordingly, as previously submitted, given the purposes this definition is intended to serve, it is evident that the validity of essentially all of the content of the Manual's Chapter XVII, as well as that of many of the LOAC norms set forth in the Manual's other chapters, is directly dependent upon the perceived validity of the Manual's redefinition of NIAC itself. And this validity can best be assessed by examining the international community's reaction to the US contention that, based upon its substantially expanded concept of NIAC, it is now permissible for any State to engage a non-State armed group, globally, applying, it is assumed, those relevant LOAC "norms" contained within the Manual.

5 THE INTERNATIONAL COMMUNITY'S REACTION TO THE US REDEFINITION OF NON-INTERNATIONAL ARMED CONFLICT

In considering the issue of the global community's reaction to the US redefinition of NIAC, it must be noted, initially, that, despite the Bush Administration's post-9/11 declaration of a "Global War on Terrorism," the UN demonstrated no support for the proposition that the 9/11 attacks triggered the initiation of an "armed conflict" between the United States and al-Qaeda. The UN Security Council unanimously adopted a resolution condemning "the terrorist attacks" of 9/11, which the Council regarded, "like any act of

conflict with al-Qaeda, as well as the Taliban and associated forces, in response to the horrific 9/11 attacks.").

[43] LOAC "norms" substantially dependent upon the legitimacy of the Manual's Chapter XVII definition – and general approach toward the nature – of NIAC are set forth in several chapters of the Manual: Chapter III, "Application of the Law of War"; Chapter IV, "Classes of Persons"; Chapter V, "The Conduct of Hostilities"; and Chapter VIII, "Detention: Overview and Baseline Rules." For a more extensive discussion of this matter, as well as that of the Manual's problematic treatment of NIAC in general, see DoD Law of War Manual Workshop, The American Bar Association's Standing Committee on Law and National Security (Jan. 9, 2017), www.abanet.org/natsecurity.

international terrorism, as a threat to international peace and security."[44] The Council also unanimously adopted, under Chapter VII of the UN Charter, a US-sponsored resolution obligating all member States to deny financing, support, and safe haven to terrorists.[45] Additionally, each of these resolutions affirmed, in the context of the events of 9/11, the inherent right of both individual and collective self-defense, as well as the need "to combat by all means" the "threats to international peace and security caused by 'terrorist' acts."[46] However, while these resolutions made repeated references to "terrorist attacks" and "international terrorism," conspicuously absent was any UN reference to, or recognition of, the existence of any form of armed conflict between al-Qaeda and the United States. Nevertheless, despite this lack of UN recognition of any ongoing US–al-Qaeda "global armed conflict," the US Government doggedly and consistently maintained in the ensuing years that it was, indeed, engaged in "some" type of conflict with the al-Qaeda organization and its associated forces. As it turned out, as indicated previously, it simply had to await the Supreme Court's instructive *Hamdan* decision to enable it to fully grasp and define the "true" nature of these ongoing "hostilities" – a conflict international in scope, but not in character; that is, a "global, yet non-international armed conflict."

As the United States has moved over the past decade to redefine NIAC and the LOAC norms associated with it (culminating in the "codification" of this effort in the Manual), how has the international community reacted to this initiative? Has there been any indication that other States have demonstrated a willingness to accept this significant US revamping of the NIAC landscape, to include what the Manual now submits are the applicable LOAC principles? In answering these questions, reference is made, first, to comments regarding this subject made by the eminent international law scholar, Yoram Dinstein, that, in this instance, serve to accurately reflect the view of the vast majority of both US and international commentators. "The first vital ingredient of NIAC relates to its internal nature, i.e., that it is waged within a State . . . Virtually all commonly used definitions of a NIAC are restrictive in that the armed conflict is circumscribed to a single State . . . [T]he idea that a NIAC can be global in nature is oxymoronic: an armed conflict can be a NIAC and it can be global, but it cannot be both."[47]

---

[44] SC Res. 1368, para. 4, UN SCOR, 4370th Meeting, UN Document S/RES/1368 (Sept. 12, 2001).

[45] SC Res. 1373, UN SCOR, 4385th Meeting, UN Doc. S/RES/1373 (Sept. 28, 2001).

[46] *Ibid.* and SC Res. 1368 (above note 44).

[47] Y. Dinstein, "Concluding Remarks on Non-International Armed Conflicts," in K. Watkin and A. J. Norris (eds.), *Non-International Conflict in the Twenty-First Century*, International Law Studies 88 (Newport: US Naval War College, 2012), 399.

In further assessing international reaction to the US effort to redefine NIAC and its relevant LOAC principles, it is also instructive to note the ICRC's Revised 2016 Commentary on Common Article 3 of the Geneva Conventions. For, while the ICRC has, on occasion, tended to overreach in purporting to represent the views of the global community at large on LOAC issues, its 2016 Commentary dealing with the nature of NIAC appears to encapsulate an international consensus. Reflecting the impact of the *Tadić* decision, the ICRC defined the concept of NIAC as follows:

> Non-international armed conflicts are "protracted armed confrontations" occurring between governmental armed forces and the forces of one or more armed groups or between such groups arising on the territory of a State [party to the Geneva Conventions]. The armed confrontation must reach a "minimum level of intensity", and the parties involved in the conflict must show a "minimum of organization."[48]

Having proffered this definition of NIAC, the ICRC then proceeds to an extensive discussion of the nature of such conflicts. It notes the existence of some evidence of State practice that does support the view that NIAC may occur across State borders, albeit "in certain limited circumstances."[49] It also observes that NIACs with an extraterritorial aspect have been described, variously, as "cross-border" conflicts, "spillover" conflicts, "transnational" armed conflicts, and "extraterritorial" NIACs.[50] As an example of the use of such terms, reference is made to the possibility of an existing NIAC "spilling over" from the territory of the State in which it began into that of a neighboring State not party to the conflict. In such cases, it is submitted that State practice appears to indicate that such a "spillover" does not alter the NIAC character of the conflict. However, very importantly, it is also noted that all examples of such State practice relate to situations in which the conflict has "spilled" over from one State's territory into only that of a neighboring State or States.[51] Given this empirical evidence, the ICRC concludes that a fundamentally important question arises as to whether, depending upon geographical circumstances or technical abilities (read unmanned aerial vehicles), the "spilling over" of an existing NIAC is, in fact, limited to a neighboring country or countries. Or, stated differently: Is it possible for a

---

[48] L. Cameron, B. Demeyere, J.-M. Henckaerts, E. La Haye, and I. Müller, "Common Article 3: Conflicts Not of an International Character," in ICRC, *Commentary on the First Geneva Convention (I) for the Amelioration of the Condition of the Wounded and Sick in Armed Forces in the Field*, 2nd ed. (Cambridge University Press, 2016) (ICRC Commentary).

[49] ICRC Commentary, ¶ 471. [50] *Ibid.*, ¶ 472. [51] *Ibid.*, ¶ 474.

NIAC between a State and a non-State armed group to exist, absent an anchor in a particular State as the primary theater of operations?[52]

In addressing this question, the ICRC states that such a scenario raises the possibility of a NIAC arising solely on the basis of actions taken by a non-State armed group, but where hostilities occur and the members of the armed group are present in geographically disparate locations. In such a situation, it is said, the principal question is that of whether it is possible to assess far-flung hostilities as a whole in order to conclude that there exists but one NIAC between a State and a non-State armed group. That is, while the criteria of the degree of organization of the non-State armed group and the intensity of the hostilities required for the existence of a NIAC would not be abandoned, "this approach would accept the fact that acts that may seem sporadic or isolated within the confines of each State in which they occur may be considered cumulatively as amounting to a NIAC."[53]

In considering this potential approach toward significantly reconfiguring the parameters of NIAC, the ICRC correctly observes that "the assumption of such a 'global' or 'transnational' non-international armed conflict could make humanitarian law [LOAC] applicable in the territory of a State not involved in the confrontation between the Parties to such a conflict."[54] The logical conclusion would then be that when a party to an armed conflict, whether a State or non-State armed group during such a global or transnational NIAC, engaged in an attack on personnel of the opposing party in the territory of another State not party to the conflict, the LOAC principles and rules set forth in the Manual, to include those governing targeting considerations, would apply. This, in turn, would inevitably place the population of such a State at risk. Why? Because, depending upon the circumstances, under the applicable LOAC targeting principles contained in the Manual, a certain amount of "collateral damage" among the State's civilian population resulting from such attacks might not be deemed unlawful. Given this fact, the ICRC has determined that a sanctioning of the concept of a global or transnational NIAC "would considerably diminish the protection of this [civilian] population under international law."[55] The ICRC's bottom line: "[T]he practice of States Party to the Geneva Conventions in support of a 'global' or 'transnational' non-international armed conflict is 'isolated'."[56]

---

[52] *Ibid.*, ¶ 478. [53] *Ibid.*, ¶ 478. [54] *Ibid.*, ¶ 479. [55] *Ibid.*, ¶ 480. [56] *Ibid.*, ¶ 482.

6 STRATEGIC IMPLICATIONS OF THE MANUAL'S REDEFINITION OF NIAC

One can perhaps understand the perceived need on the part of the current US leadership to both defend and justify demonstrably flawed legal and policy decisions made post-9/11. And, yes, the idea of a "global" NIAC conveniently serves as a "legal" basis for both past and current US practices undertaken with respect to al-Qaeda and its associated forces. For example, what legal justification exists, other than the US claim that it remains engaged in an ongoing "global NIAC" with al-Qaeda, for the continued US incarceration of the small number of "legacy" detainees at Guantánamo Bay? However, have US policymakers carefully thought through not only the legal, but, importantly, the strategic implications of the US contention, captured in the Manual's redefinition of NIAC, that it is now permissible, under international law, for a State – any State – to engage in a "global" NIAC with a non-State armed group? That is, are US decision-makers truly comfortable with the fact that the US has provided, in the form of its treatment of NIAC in the Manual, the proverbial legal green light for any State to cite the US legal reasoning contained in the Manual as the legal basis for its ability to strike members of a non-State armed group worldwide? Listen up Russia, China, Syria, and other States of the global community. The United States has determined that NIAC is "boundary-less." Feel free to pursue – and attack – your non-State opponents wherever you might find them. The only requirement, apparently, is that States abide by the Manual's LOAC provisions applicable to this newly defined NIAC when they do so. In brief, why has the United States not seriously taken into consideration the potential adverse strategic impact of the Manual's expanded concept of NIAC?

7 CONCLUSION

The current US approach toward redefining the nature of NIAC – and, concomitantly, creating new LOAC principles applicable to such conflict – is the direct result of legally deficient US post-9/11 decisions. Having made these decisions, and putting into place implementing policies, the United States has since seized upon the Manual as an instrument through which it might codify these actions by constructing the fig-leaf of a "legal" basis and supporting LOAC "principles" designed to afford them a certain degree of "legitimacy." In doing so, the Manual sets forth these newly formulated LOAC principles as, essentially, *lex lata*. They are not. Nor should they be.

As noted, the validity of essentially all of the Manual's chapter dealing with NIAC, as well as that of many of the NIAC-related LOAC provisions contained in other chapters of the Manual, is directly premised upon an assumed legitimacy of the Manual's definition of – and general approach toward – the nature of NIAC itself. This is, as has been evidenced, a baseless and unsupported assumption. The US concept of a "global, yet non-international armed conflict" has garnered, at best, very minimal support among international law commentators and, most importantly, no discernible support from the international community. As referenced, the ICRC has determined that the practice of States in support of a "global" non-international armed conflict is "isolated."

Given the demonstrated lack of legitimacy of those portions of the Manual dealing with NIAC – a shortcoming that affects the credibility of the Manual as a whole – the time has come for the United States to reconsider and revise its current approach toward defining the nature of such conflict. Such an approach has forced the United States to unilaterally "create" a hybrid form of law that is to be applied to a "global NIAC." This approach is based on an unprecedented combination of partially context-dependent factors, self-serving-LOAC principles, and selectively applied US domestic law. Additionally, as frequently noted in the Manual, the United States submits that, in certain global NIAC scenarios, these LOAC principles are to be applied simply as a matter of "policy," rather than as "law." This ambiguity, this lack of clarity, understandably generates confusion in the minds of practitioners. Significantly, such an approach also diminishes the validity of this specific aspect of the LOAC as a whole, adversely impacting its effective regulation of legitimate internal armed conflicts.

Finally, one must wonder whether it would be realistic to believe that, in the future, the United States will choose to continue contending that it is engaged in "global NIACs" with various non-State armed groups, when the legal and political pitfalls that this approach has produced over the past sixteen years show no signs of abating? Is it really in the interest of global stability for such an approach to become the international norm? In brief, continued US adherence to its "isolated" approach toward the nature of NIAC serves neither its legal, nor strategic, interests. It is time for a break from the policy-driven legal decisions of the 9/11 past and a return to the pre-9/11 world of the Law of Armed Conflict – when an IAC was an IAC, a NIAC was a NIAC, insurgents were insurgents, and terrorists were, well, just terrorists.

Section 1.1.1 of the Manual states: "This manual represents the views of the Department of Defense. This manual does not, however, preclude the

Department from subsequently changing its interpretation of the law."[57] It will best serve the collective interests of the United States if DoD soon seizes the opportunity to engage in such an interpretive change regarding the manner in which the Manual approaches the legal nature and nomenclature of NIAC – and convinces the US Government, as a whole, to do the same.

[57] DoD Law of War Manual, ¶ 1.1.1.

9

Aspects of the Distinction Principle under the US DoD Law of War Manual

Bill Boothby

1 INTRODUCTION

Before embarking on an assessment of how the US Department of Defense (DoD) Law of War Manual (the Manual)[1] addresses aspects of the principle of distinction, a few preliminary remarks are in order. The first is to congratulate the United States on the decision to publish a Manual on the law of war. It is well known that draft texts for the Manual have been in gestation for a significant number of years and that the decision finally to publish cannot have been easy. There is always the fear that by publishing an authoritative statement of the national position on such a subject, the State may be tying itself to legal interpretations that may prove inconvenient or damaging in light of future, unpredictable circumstances. The operational flexibility that silence may appear to afford could be an attractive argument to sway some officials against publication. That a country like the United States is prepared to set forth its appreciation of what the law requires, and its basis for reaching those conclusions, advances the law itself, gives the United States a departmentally approved benchmark against which personnel can be trained in this most important body of law and should incentivize other States to consider and express their own explanations of the applicable law.

In preparing this chapter, an attempt has been made to comment on apparently noteworthy aspects of the first sections of Chapter V of the Manual, entitled "Conduct of Hostilities." That is a substantial component in the Manual (indeed the longest single chapter), and the present text therefore limits itself to considering those sections and paragraphs of the chapter that deal with the principles of distinction and discrimination, with attacks and with the precautions and proportionality rules, namely paragraphs 5.1 to 5.12 inclusive.

---

[1] DoD Law of War Manual, ¶ 17.1.

Comment has been made below for any one of a number of reasons, including that the relevant passage is of particular legal value, that it raises issues of legal interest, because it contains assertions that can be questioned. It should not be assumed that the present author necessarily agrees with all of the statements to which no reference is made in the present text. Indeed, the challenge in preparing a chapter of this nature is to limit sufficiently the scope of the matters that are considered and of the comments that are made with a view to achieving a text that is manageable in length, that discusses the issues with the required clarity, and that, it is hoped, adds value. That is what is being attempted here. When considering any words of criticism, however, the reader should bear in mind, as the present author has done, the difficult task that the writing of a Manual of this sort represents and should appreciate the scholarship and hard work that it represents.

For ease of reference, the text of the elements of the chapter under review will be followed sequentially, with reference being made to the relevant section and paragraph numbers of the Manual's text. Topics will accordingly be addressed as and when they arise.

2 PROTECTION OF CIVILIANS

After setting the scene with what are clear and satisfactory explanations of the terms "means of warfare" and "method of warfare," section 5.3 gives an overview of the rules as to the protection of civilians. Footnote 20 is an interesting example of something that one observes in numerous parts of the Manual, namely the use of previous correspondence[2] or statements from US officials[3] in support of stated legal rules. Some such correspondence or statements will be evidence of single national – namely US – State practice[4] or of the US interpretation of the meaning of a rule, and are therefore of considerable utility in a military manual the purpose of which, after all, is to set out the relevant State's understanding of the law that binds it. Such correspondence and statements are, however, not conclusive evidence of the existence of a rule of international law as such. The reader is left with the impression that sometimes the cited single national statements and correspondence are being used

---

[2] DoD Law of War Manual, ¶ 5.2.1, fn. 20 (citing a letter from the DoD General Counsel to Senator Ted Kennedy written in Sept. 1972.

[3] See for DoD Law of War Manual, ¶ 5.1.2.1 fn. 9 (citing the Department of State Legal Advisor comments to the American Society of International Law).

[4] This will frequently be the case where, e.g., the reference is to the Final Report on the Persian Gulf War, which is a reference to "Conduct of the Persian Gulf War, Final Report to Congress," issued by the US Department of Defense in 1992.

as the basis for the existence of the particular rule of law, which would not therefore be a correct approach.

Footnote 20 is referring to the prime responsibility of the party to the conflict that controls civilians and civilian objects for their protection. It is curious that, rather than refer to Article 58 of Additional Protocol I (AP I)[5] to which at the time of writing 174 States are bound,[6] reference instead is being made to internal US correspondence dating from 1972. Article 58, the general propositions of which are widely accepted as having customary law status,[7] would seem to be a more persuasive indicator of the protection requirement at law than internal, single national correspondence.

The text accompanying footnotes 17 to 33 addresses a somewhat tricky issue, namely the distinction between the law of targeting rules as to "attacks" and those rules, reflected in Articles 48, 51, and 57 of AP I, that relate to "military operations." More will be said on the general way in which the Manual addresses that distinction in later paragraphs of this chapter. At this stage, it is worthy of note that footnote 30 is lengthy and cites, in the main, US practice. To establish the status in international law of the specific proposition advanced in the text[8] – namely that it is legitimate temporarily to detain civilians for reasons of mission accomplishment, self-defense or for their own safety, a proposition which the present author is not seeking to dispute – it would have been preferable to cite authorities of a more international nature.

Taking paragraphs 5.2.2 and 5.2.2.1 together, one can deduce a US position as to which military operations against civilians are prohibited during international armed conflict (IAC). Paragraph 5.2.2 makes it clear that civilians must not be made the object of attack. The first sentence of paragraph 5.2.2.1 asserts that the "principle that military operations must not be directed against civilians does not prohibit military operations short of violence that are militarily necessary." So, it is being made clear here that the prohibited military operations against civilians are characterized by violence. Given

---

[5] AP I, when used here and hereafter, will refer to the Protocol Additional to the Geneva Conventions of Aug. 12 1949 and Relating to the Protection of Victims of International Armed Conflicts, Geneva, June 8, 1977.

[6] www.icrc.org.

[7] See, e.g., HPCR Manual on the International Law Applicable to Air and Missile Warfare, 2010 (AMW Manual), Section H; Tallinn Manual on the International Law Applicable to Cyber Warfare (2013) (Tallinn Manual), rule 59; J.-M. Henckaerts and L. Doswald-Beck (eds.), *Customary International Humanitarian Law*, I: *Rules* (Cambridge University Press, 2005), rules 22–24.

[8] DoD Law of War Manual, ¶ 5.2.2.1 fn. 30.

that the use of violence against the enemy, whether in offence or defense is the customary law definition of an attack,[9] it would seem that the effect of this US position is to limit the protection of civilians to protection from attack. Certainly, the Manual does not give a list of operations other than attack that may not be directed at civilians. The problem here lies in the subtle distinction referred to in the previous paragraph. If the military operations that those customary rules in Articles 48,[10] 51,[11] and 57[12] regulate are limited to attacks, why was the word "attack" not used in those provisions, given that the "attack" word is specifically employed in relation to other detailed rules in Articles 49 to 58 of the Additional Protocol? In an era of new military technologies when increased options are being developed for offensive operations that lie at the boundaries of what might be seen as "violence" one might legitimately question whether limiting prohibited military operations to attacks remains acceptable.

3 FEASIBLE PRECAUTIONS

Paragraph 5.2.3.2 discusses what precautions to protect civilians are to be regarded as "feasible" and thus obligatory. The paragraph states: "The standard for what precautions must be taken is one of due regard or diligence, not an absolute requirement to do everything possible." UK Prime Minister Neville Chamberlain's statement of June 21, 1938 is cited in a footnote in support of this formulation. Interestingly, in footnote 40 Michael J. Matheson's 1987 article in the *American University Journal of International Law and Policy* is cited as follows: "[w]e support the principle that all practicable precautions, taking into account military and humanitarian considerations, be taken in the conduct of military operations to minimize incidental death, injury, and damage to civilians and civilian objects, and that effective advance warning be given of attacks which may affect the civilian population unless circumstances do not permit."[13] This is the formulation that

---

9 AP I, Art. 49(1); San Remo Manual on International Law Applicable to Armed Conflicts at Sea 1994 (San Remo Manual), rule 13(b); AMW Manual, rule 1(e).
10 AP I, Art. 48 (requiring that Parties "shall at all times distinguish between the civilian population and combatants and between civilian objects and military objectives and accordingly shall direct their operations only against military objectives."
11 So far as relevant to the point that is being made here, Art. 51 of AP I provides that the "civilian population and individual civilians shall enjoy general protection against dangers arising from military operations."
12 Article 57(1) of AP I provides that "[i]n the conduct of military operations, constant care shall be taken to spare the civilian population, civilians and civilian objects."
13 DoD Law of War Manual, ¶ 5.2.3.1 fn. 40.

seems to approximate closely to a requirement to "do everything possible"; after all, that which is practicable is also that which is possible and if something is not possible it is also not practicable. The Matheson position was being put forward in 1987 as being the US position as to the relationship between customary law and the Additional Protocols of 1977, and one wonders therefore whether the US interpretation has in the intervening years become more restrictive. If it has not, revision of this paragraph of the Manual text would seem to be necessary.

If the US interpretation has indeed become more restrictive, one would also expect to see a clear explanation as to why this is the case. Such an explanation ought, it is suggested, to note and explain the revised interpretation by reference to the novel technologies associated with offensive operations referred to above.

The position becomes potentially opaque if one reads further in paragraph 5.2.3.2. Having in the first sentence said that the standard is not an absolute one to do everything possible, the Manual then asserts: "[f]easible precautions are those that are practicable or practically possible, taking into account all circumstances ruling at the time, including humanitarian and military considerations." There would at first glance seem to be something of an inherent conflict between this statement and the earlier statement mentioned above. However, it is a completely correct statement of the law to say that the obligation is not indeed one to do everything that is theoretically possible. Rather, the duty is to do that which is contextually possible, and the context for these purposes consists of the surrounding military and humanitarian considerations.

As an example, the Manual asserts that "if a commander determines that taking a precaution would result in operational risk (i.e. a risk of failing to accomplish the mission) or an increased risk of harm to their own forces, then the precaution would not be feasible and would not be required." As noted in the previous paragraph, the decision as to whether a precaution is practicable is reached by "taking into account" military and humanitarian considerations. This suggests that both such classes of consideration must be taken into account and does not suggest that one trumps the other. One cannot therefore help wondering whether the example has been expressed in rather absolute terms when a somewhat more nuanced explanation might have been in order. If, for example, the humanitarian consequences of failing to take a precaution were to be dire, and the increase in operational risk or increase in the chance of harm to own forces were to be relatively small, it would seem inappropriate to conclude that just because there is some such increase, however trivial, the precaution is thereby automatically rendered impracticable and thus is not required. That would seem to play into the hands of those who suggest that some interpretations of the law of targeting devalue civilian life.[14] The citation to support the example is drawn from a US official statement from 1991 commenting on an International Committee of the Red Cross (ICRC) Legal Memorandum.[15]

Such citations are of course entirely legitimate as a way of clarifying the stated US position. However, in a Manual of this sort and in the context of this part of the discussion, one might have expected a disclosure of the basis in international law of the proffered interpretation. One cannot therefore but agree with the statement in the final sentence of the paragraph that "military commanders must make reasonable efforts to reduce the risk of harm to civilians and civilian objects" and with the view expressed immediately before-hand that what is reasonable will, of necessity, be a contextual issue.

Paragraph 5.3.3.5 draws attention to the AP I, Article 57(1) obligation to take "constant care to spare the civilian population, civilians and civilian objects." This is a rule that is widely recognized as having customary law status.[16] It is therefore disappointing that it is described merely as a rule that States Party to AP I have accepted, and that no indication is given as to whether the United States considers itself to be bound by the rule. While acknowledging, as the paragraph observes, that States may interpret the rule differently, it would have been useful to learn here how the United States interprets it.

4 ASSESSING INFORMATION

Section 5.3 of the Manual makes the important point that decisions in war must be made on the basis of all available information interpreted in good faith. Some of the factors that are liable to arise in war and that may limit the availability of information or the ability to process it accurately are properly referred to. The section deals with the matter in an admirably practical way,

---

[14]   Note, e.g., UK Ministry of Defence, *Law of Armed Conflict Manual* (Oxford University Press, 2005), ¶ 5.32.2.e, where it is noted that any commander selecting a target will have to pay regard to a number of factors which may include "the risks to his own forces necessitated by target verification." In the associated footnote in the UK Manual, it is observed that "[t]raditionally commanders have accepted some risk in identifying targets by using, for example, artillery spotters, forward air controllers, and intelligence gatherers operating in enemy-held territory"; at 82 fn. 202.

[15]   DoD Law of War Manual, ¶ 5.2.3.2 fn. 50.

[16]   See, e.g., the effect of San Remo Manual, para. 46; AMW Manual, rule 30; Tallinn Manual, rule 52; ICRC Customary Law Study, rule 15. References in military manuals of States that are party to AP I are not relevant, of course, to the customary status of the rule because they will reflect the treaty obligations of the relevant State.

noting for example that the circumstances of armed conflict may make an accurate determination of facts difficult, that the enemy may be actively seeking to deceive, and that some uncertainty is inevitable. When the section notes that it may be difficult to determine whether a person is a combatant, civilian, or directly participating civilian, whether an object is making an effective contribution to military action or the direct military advantage to be derived from an attack, those observations are correct as far as they go. To deduce from them, however, that it would be lawful to attack a target in ignorance of whether it is a lawful target would not, however, be right.[17] In that regard, perhaps some clarification would have been helpful of what the notion, emphasized in the text, of good faith actually requires.

It would not, of course, be right to imply, nor for the Manual's reader to deduce, that in a situation where there is little or no information on which to conclude that a person or object is a lawful target, the obligations of the law are in any sense dispensed with. It is noted that the only jurisprudence cited in support is from 1921 and 1944 decisions of US domestic judges.[18] It would have been interesting to see international court decisions being referenced in these assessments of international law obligations. However, the point is properly made that it is the decision-maker's "good faith" assessment of the "information available to them at the time" of the situation that is to be considered in evaluating the legality of the action rather than information that may only have become available later. Here it is noteworthy that the equivalent positions of eight other States are cited in support. Perhaps that approach could profitably have been adopted in relation to some of the propositions discussed earlier in this chapter.

5 THE CONDUCT OF ATTACKS

Section 5.4 of the Manual starts with a useful clarification of the applicable terminology, in which the important distinction is made between persons and objects being made the object or purpose of an attack and injury or damage being caused to such persons or objects as an incidental consequence of an attack directed at some other person or object. Having cleared up this point, the Manual notes that "[p]arties to a conflict must conduct attacks in accordance with the principles of distinction and proportionality"[19] and then lists in

---

[17] Consider, e.g., the obligation in AP I, Art. 57(2)(a)(i) to "do everything feasible to verify that the objectives to be attacked are neither civilians nor civilian objects and are not subject to special protection." This would seem to follow logically from the widely accepted and customary constant care obligation.

[18] DoD Law of War Manual, ¶ 5.3.2 fnn. 62 and 66.   [19] DoD Law of War Manual, ¶ 5.4.2.

summary form rules that must be observed. At the risk of being pedantic, it could be argued that the proportionality *principle* is one of the core principles underlying the law of armed conflict and requires that "the expected losses resulting from a military action should not be excessive in relation to the anticipated military advantage,"[20] an altogether more general notion than the proportionality *rule* as reflected in AP I, Articles 51(5)(b) and 57.[21]

Having, as we have seen, already addressed the requirement of commanders to make decisions on the basis of the information available at the time, the Manual returns to that matter in paragraph 5.4.3. In the second sentence of the latter provision, the point is made that "the commander must, on the basis of available information, determine in good faith, that a target is a military objective before authorizing an attack." Clearly, the ambiguity we noted earlier in relation to section 5.3 must be interpreted in the light of this later, legally accurate statement. Indeed, it would have been appropriate and perhaps helpful if the sentence under review had made it clear that the obligation to make this determination applies not just to commanders but to all persons who decide upon attacks.[22]

In the second part of paragraph 5.4.3, it is stated that in making judgments required by the law in relation to attacks "persons may rely on information obtained from other sources, including human intelligence or other sources of information" and that "in a long distance attack, a commander may rely on information obtained from aerial reconnaissance and intelligence units in determining whether to conduct an attack." The use here of the word "may" has the potential to mislead the reader. The obligation at law is quite simple. Commanders, planners, and other decision-makers are obliged to consider all reasonably available information.[23] They will then act on the basis of their interpretation of that information. Thus, while it is strictly correct to say that they "may" rely on particular classes of information, it would perhaps be preferable to explain to commanders and decision-makers the twin aspects of considering all available information and of acting on their interpretation of it.

---

[20]   UK Manual (above note 14), ¶ 2.6 as amended.

[21]   Article 51(5)(b) of AP I gives as an example of an indiscriminate, and thus unlawful, attack "an attack which may be expected to cause incidental loss of civilian life, injury to civilians, damage to civilian objects, or a combination thereof, which would be excessive in relation to the concrete and direct military advantage anticipated."

[22]   This aspect of Art. 57(2) of AP I would seem to be customary and thus binding on all States.

[23]   This proposition is reflected in the statement "c" made by the UK on ratification of AP I on Jan. 28, 1998 but is essentially a widely accepted reflection of the obligation of an attacker to take constant care to spare civilians and civilian objects, as noted in Art. 57(1).

Paragraph 5.4.3.1 should be considered with some care. It argues that "[a]lthough doing so would exceed the requirements of the law of war, applying heightened standards of identification may be a policy choice to reduce the risk of incidental harm in conducting an attack." As a general proposition, it would be correct to point out that commanders may always require, as a matter of policy, that action above that required by the law be taken to enhance the protection to be afforded to protected persons and objects. The problem is that the wording chosen in paragraph 5.4.3.1 might be understood as asserting that heightened standards are not required by the law of war. Widely accepted law requires, as we have noted, that all available information be considered in making attack decisions. It also requires that constant care be taken, and that all feasible – that is, practically possible – steps be taken to verify that the object of attack is a lawful target and that the planned attack, if undertaken, will not breach targeting law, such as the proportionality rule. Perhaps the paragraph is simply in the wrong place, in that if it were to appear after the points mentioned here have been explained, any ambiguity as to its intended meaning would cease to exist.

Footnote 87 cites as a supporting authority a White House Fact Sheet of 2013 about US Policy Standards on the use of force in counterterrorism operations outside areas of active hostilities. The strict relevance of such a source is debatable given that the use of force outside armed conflict will be governed not by the law of war but by applicable domestic and human rights law. Later in the same footnote, an extract from the Report on the Persian Gulf War is cited. In that extract instructions were noted to the effect that, if a pilot could not positively identify the target (in American rules of engagement (ROE) parlance termed "PID") or could not be confident that the weapon would guide properly, he could not deliver that weapon. Again, it is to be doubted that this is indicative of the application of rules above what the law of war requires in terms of constant care, the taking of all practically possible precautions, and the consideration of all available information. After all, a pilot who cannot be confident that a weapon is going to guide properly but who nevertheless fires that weapon is taking an obvious risk that the attack he is about to launch will be indiscriminate and thus unlawful. It is difficult to accept that such conduct could be seen as consistent with any sensible interpretation of the principle of distinction.

The final authority cited in footnote 87 is an extract from the ROE issued in 1971 during the Vietnam War. The textual extract has been duplicated for reasons which are unclear. The comment made in the above paragraph would also apply to this cited passage in the footnote, unless it is being suggested that the stated requirement went beyond the requirements of the law as it stood in

1971, but such a point has not been argued in the footnote entry. Perhaps the intended point here would emerge more clearly if the respects in which positive identification exceeds the feasibility requirements of applicable law were to be explained, so that the reader can understand how the cited ROE impose more exacting obligations.

On a point of minor detail, the extract from Article 52(3) of AP I set forth in the first part of paragraph 5.4.3.2 of the Manual should refer to "military action," not "military actions." Subject to that minor comment, the paragraph, which addresses the doubt rules in Articles 52(3) and 50(1) of the same treaty, explains the basis for the known US objections to these rules persuasively and well. Paragraph 5.4.4 correctly notes that the failure by the enemy to separate or distinguish does not relieve the attacker of the obligation to discriminate in attack. In particular, the second part of the paragraph helpfully notes that while, confronted by such enemy failure, the attacker must continue to seek to discriminate, his practical ability to do so will inevitably be affected by that enemy failure, or by the enemy's illegal activity.[24]

The second part of paragraph 5.4.5 talks about the legitimacy of conducting attacks outside the immediate area of hostilities. The broad way in which the paragraph is drafted might, however, lead to misinterpretation. The discussion in this part of the Manual, it must be remembered, is centered on *jus in bello* as it applies in IACs. There is indeed no rule of law that specifically requires that attacks be limited to the location where fighting has previously been taking place. Provided that the object of attack is a lawful target, and that other aspects of targeting law are complied with, the attack is likely to be unobjectionable. During a non-international armed conflict (NIAC), the use of lethal force outside the territory where that conflict is occurring and without the consent of the relevant sovereign authorities is of course a highly controversial legal issue.

Paragraph 5.4.6 correctly asserts the lawfulness of the use of overwhelming force. Section IX of the ICRC's Interpretive Guidance famously argued, incorrectly, that "the kind and degree of force which is permissible against persons not entitled to protection against direct attack must not exceed what is actually necessary to accomplish a legitimate military purpose in the prevail-

---

[24] Consider in this regard the AP I, Art. 51(8) requirement that "[a]ny violation of these prohibitions shall not release the Parties to the conflict from their legal obligations with respect to the civilian population and civilians, including the obligation to take the precautionary measures provided for in article 57." The prohibitions referred to here include the prohibition of making the civilian population or individual civilians the object of attack and the prohibition of indiscriminate attacks.

ing circumstances."[25] It is therefore useful to see specific State practice to the contrary effect recorded in the paragraph under review. The only matter for regret is that internal US correspondence, training course materials and single service US manuals are exclusively cited as the relevant authorities as opposed to the recognized sources of international law, but then this is a criticism that applies to diverse parts of the Manual. It is indeed difficult to see how so many elements of an authoritative treatise on international law can be properly based on so relatively few references to its recognized sources.[26]

After correctly reporting the lawfulness of surprise attacks, attacks on retreating forces, and harassing fires in legally unobjectionable terms,[27] the Manual turns to what some might regard as the controversial topic of "attacks on specific individuals." It is good that this descriptor is used and that the term assassination is avoided, no doubt on the basis that it would have involved inappropriate and irrelevant overtones. The main Manual text is commendably brief and accurate in asserting that military operations may be undertaken against specific enemy combatants and that the United States has often conducted such operations. It specifically lists examples of precisely such US practice to rebut arguments that such targeted operations during armed conflict are not lawful are reported and correctly rejected.[28]

Paragraph 5.4.7 repeats the well-established rules on the denial of quarter and explains them accurately. Curiously, a sentence is added at the end of the paragraph asserting that this rule also applies in NIACs. That is a sentence that has not appeared in relation to the previous rules, and it would not be right to imagine that none of those previous rules applies in NIACs. The sudden appearance of the sentence in this paragraph might therefore cause misunderstanding, and all the more so because it is inserted without reference to human rights norms that might otherwise be deemed dispositive.

The Manual addresses the wearing of uniform by combatants in paragraphs 5.4.8 and 5.4.8.1. The Manual correctly states that the customary law position as to the obligation of combatants to distinguish themselves goes somewhat wider than the corresponding obligation in Article 44(3) of AP I as it is not

---

[25] N. Melzer, *Interpretive Guidance on the Notion of Direct Participation in Hostilities under International Humanitarian Law* (Geneva: ICRC, 2009), 82.

[26] The recognized sources of international law comprise "international conventions, whether general or particular, establishing rules expressly recognized by the contesting states"; "international custom, as evidence of a general practice accepted as law"; and "the general principles of law recognized by civilized nations"; Statute of the International Court of Justice, 1945, Art. 38(1)(a)–(c). It should be noted, however, that it can be argued persuasively that contemporary international law is also increasingly being developed by non-State activities, such as the decisions of judicial bodies.

[27] DoD Law of War Manual, ¶¶ 5.4.6.1 to 5.5.6.4.   [28] *Ibid.*, ¶ 5.4.6.4 fnn. 115 and 116.

limited to when they are conducting attacks or in military operations preparatory to an attack. It also briefly refers to the prohibition of treacherous killing
and to certain other matters. An example taken from the writings of
J. M. Spaight of an airman fighting without uniform is cited in support.[29]
Of course, if the airman was at the time flying a properly marked military
aircraft, as is assumed to have been the case, it is the required nationality
markings and military markings of the aircraft that will have satisfied the
requirements of the principle of distinction, and the presence or absence of
the airman's uniform would only become relevant in the exceptional circumstance that for some reason the airman continues the fight outside and separate
from his military aircraft.

In the second part of paragraph 5.4.8.1, it is stated that "[m]ilitary personnel
not in uniform may resist an attack, so long as they are not wearing the enemy's
uniform and do not kill or wound treacherously." The example is then given of
military personnel not in uniform who resist an attack and who do not
purposefully seek to conceal their status as combatants, noting that they
commit no violation of the law of war and remain entitled to combatant
privileges. This would at face value seem to be a most remarkable part of the
Manual. The present author has always understood that the second sentence
in Article 44(3) of AP I is a provision to which the United States is vehemently
opposed and constitutes one of the core reasons why it will not ratify that
treaty.[30] Unless, as is entirely possible, the present author is completely mis-
interpreting the paragraph in the Manual, it would rather seem that the
Manual is according customary law status to a rule that bears a remarkable
resemblance to that sentence in AP I. In that connection, for example, the idea
of "not purposefully seeking to conceal their [combatant] status" would seem
to have its parallel in the idea of carrying arms openly. As a side issue, it is
assumed that the term "attack" is being used here, as elsewhere, in the sense of

---

[29] *Ibid.*, ¶ 5.4.8.1 fn. 127, citing J. M. Spaight, *Air Power and War Rights*, 3rd ed. (Aberdeen:
      Longmans, 1947), 101.

[30] Article 44(3) of AP I provides:
      In order to promote the protection of the civilian population from the effects of hostilities,
      combatants are obliged to distinguish themselves from the civilian population while they are
      engaged in an attack or in a military operation preparatory to an attack. Recognizing, however,
      that there are situations in armed conflicts where, owing to the nature of the hostilities an
      armed combatant cannot so distinguish himself, he shall retain his status as a combatant
      provided that, in such situations, he carries his arms openly:
      (a) during each military engagement; and
      (b) during such time as he is visible to the adversary while he is engaged in a military
      deployment preceding the launching of an attack in which he is to participate.
      Acts which comply with the requirements of this paragraph shall not be considered as
      perfidious . . .

an act of violence against the adversary, whether in offence or defense.[31] The proposition discussed in the previous paragraph would therefore apply irrespective of whether the violent force is being used in an offensive or defensive posture.

6 LAWFUL OBJECTS OF ATTACK AND THE DEFINITION OF MILITARY OBJECTIVES

Section 5.6 differentiates between the persons and objects that, respectively, may and may not be made the object of attack. After introducing that idea and indicating the kinds of person and object that come into each category, the focus narrows to the idea of military objectives, which, for the purposes of the Manual, are quite properly interpreted as comprising persons and objects. It is made clear that dual-use objects will be military objectives by virtue of their military use. However, there is a degree of repetitiveness or redundancy in the section and it might have been more helpful for the reader if the definition of military objectives, as that notion applies to objects, had been given within this section before, for instance, the dual-use notion is discussed. This would have enabled the reader to appreciate more readily the significance of the military use aspect of such dual-use objects.

The definition of military objectives, insofar as objects are concerned, is given at paragraph 5.6.3. The paragraph reads as follows: "Military objectives, in so far as objects are concerned, include 'any object which by its nature, location, purpose or use makes an effective contribution to military action and whose total or partial destruction, capture or neutralization, in the circumstances ruling at the time, offers a definite military advantage.'" It is somewhat intriguing that in the associated footnote, no reference is made to the primary international law source for this formulation, namely Article 52(2) of AP I (reproduced verbatim in the Manual text) and that the prime reference is instead drawn from the Amended CCW Mines Protocol, the States Party to which number only 102.[32]

In a later section, the Manual goes on to state that:

> Military action has a broad meaning and is understood to mean the general prosecution of the war. It is not necessary that the object provide immediate tactical or operational gains or that the object make an effective contribution to a specific military operation. Rather, the object's effective contribution to the war-fighting or war-sustaining capability of an opposing force is sufficient. Although terms such as "war-fighting," "war-supporting," and "war-sustaining"

---

[31] AP I, Art. 49(1). [32] DoD Law of War Manual, ¶ 5.6.3 fn. 157.

are not explicitly reflected in the treaty definitions of military objective, the United States has interpreted the military objective definition to include these concepts.[33]

This broadening of the military objectives notion may place the cardinal, intransgressible principle of distinction in some peril. As the early part of this section of the Manual makes clear, that principle has at its core the idea that there are certain kinds of person and object that it is lawful to attack and certain others that must be protected. If distinguishing between those respective kinds of object is made more difficult, maintaining respect for the underlying principle becomes potentially problematic. While objects that are making a direct contribution to military action can often be differentiated fairly readily from those which are not, the scope of objects that sustain the war effort is very much wider and the notion of sustainment is itself less precise, thus reducing the sharpness of the distinction between objects that can and respectively cannot be made the object of lawful attack.

The Manual observes in an earlier section that the "definition of military objective may be viewed as a way of evaluating whether military necessity exists to attack an object."[34] While there might be an element of circularity in that observation, given that the notion of military utility if not necessity is inherent in the cited definition, nevertheless the implicit point is both correct and useful.

In the next paragraph,[35] the Manual argues that two types of object are categorically recognized as military objectives, that is "the definition of military objective is always considered to be met as a matter of law with regard to these objects." If the definition of military objective given in the first part of paragraph 5.6.3 is regarded as binding, then the twin tests[36] must apply irrespective of the type of object concerned and irrespective whether it is nature, location, purpose or use that causes the object to become a military objective. It would be accurate to say that the objects listed in paragraphs 5.7.4.1 and 5.7.4.2, such as military bases, vehicles, ships, weapons and supplies, military headquarters, ministries of defense and intelligence facilities, will almost always in the prevailing circumstances satisfy the two tests in the definition and therefore will almost always be military objectives. Indeed, the circumstances may well be such that very little thought is required before

---

[33] *Ibid.,* ¶ 5.6.6.2.   [34] *Ibid.,* ¶ 5.6.3.   [35] *Ibid.,* ¶ 5.6.4.
[36] *Ibid.,* ¶ 5.6.3. Insofar as objects are concerned, include "any object which by its nature, location, purpose or use makes an effective contribution to military action *and* whose total or partial destruction, capture or neutralization, in the circumstances ruling at the time, offers a definite military advantage." (Emphasis added.)

concluding that such objects are indeed military objectives and thus liable to be attacked. It is however only by making that determination that the requirements of the widely accepted definition in AP I, Article 52(2) can be satisfied and a proper interpretation of that article, and thus of the rule that is widely accepted as having customary law status,[37] demands that the twin tests set forth in that article must be applied to all objects being considered for attack. In footnote 160, the UK Manual, paragraph 5.4.1, is cited in support of the stated US position. It would have been more accurate, however, if the Manual had also cited the third sentence of the paragraph of the UK Manual in which the point is explicitly made that "[o]bjects are only military objectives if they come within the [AP I] definition." This latter extract from the UK Manual reflects what is understood to be the widely accepted interpretation of the law.

So it is in this context that the next paragraphs develop the notion of military objective in more detail. Paragraph 5.6.5 correctly points out that there are twin tests implicit in the recognized definition, and refers to objects that "somehow" make an effective contribution to military action as satisfying the first of these. The lengthy paragraph 5.6.6 proceeds to break down the definition of military objective into its constituent parts. In the discussion of objects that by nature are military objectives, it is suggested that "'nature' can also be understood to refer to objects that may be used for military purposes." This would not seem to be a correct statement. Many ordinarily civilian objects, such as civilian buildings, the tower of a church, civilian cybernetworks or a civilian automobile *may* be used for military purposes. If that occurs, they become military objectives by virtue of that use, not by their "nature."

The Manual then contends that an object becomes a military objective by virtue of "purpose" as a result of "its intended or possible use in the future."[38] In the supporting footnote,[39] extracts from the Australian and UK Military Manuals are cited, both of which actually describe "purpose" in terms of the intended future use of an object, which, in the view of the present author, is the widely accepted and correct interpretation of the "purpose" language. No supporting justification is given for the reference in the Manual's text to *possible* future use. Moreover, if one recognizes that almost any object or location is capable of being used for military purposes, to say that possible future use renders an object a lawful target clearly has the potential,

---

[37] Consider San Remo Manual, para. 40; AMW Manual, rule 1y; Tallinn Manual, rule 38. It will be appreciated that the military manuals of States Party to AP I will reflect the treaty obligations of those States and will not therefore assist in determining the customary law status of the definition.

[38] DoD Law of War Manual, ¶ 5.6.6.1.   [39] *Ibid.*, fn. 170.

depending on how the idea is understood, to expand the notion of military objective to such a degree that the principle of distinction risks being deprived of meaning. It would seem more accurate to refer to "purpose" as intended future use, including future uses that can properly be inferred from an understanding of the developing tactical situation and from the information from all sources that is reasonably available to the decision-maker at the relevant time.

At paragraph 5.6.6.2, the correct point is made that "[m]ilitary action has a broad meaning and is understood to mean the general prosecution of the war." Tony Rogers is cited in support of this proposition.[40] The legal problem, as the present author sees it, with the US position arises in the next sentence when the object's "effective contribution to war-fighting or war-sustaining capability" is considered to suffice for these purposes. An indirect contribution to war-sustaining capabilities is liable to be afforded by a wide selection of objects and, as has been noted, the wider the selection of objects that are capable of being lawfully regarded as military objectives, the less constraining, and thus the less effective in protective terms, the associated principle of distinction becomes. Effective protection of civilians in war presupposes reasonable restrictiveness in this regard. War-sustaining, as Yoram Dinstein has opined, goes too far.[41]

However, as reflected in footnote 175, Hays Parks draws attention to State practice that supports the war-sustaining interpretation. There can be no doubt that during World War II, during Gulf War One and during recent air operations in Iraq and Syria, war-sustaining targets have been attacked not just by the United States but also by other coalition members.[42] Some observers may choose to speculate that the definition of military objective in Article 52(2) of AP I was something of an aberration and that the customary definition goes, and always went, wider to encompass war-sustaining objects.[43] Such

---

[40] DoD Law of War Manual, ¶ 5.6.6.2 fn. 173.

[41] Y. Dinstein, *The Conduct of Hostilities under the Law of International Armed Conflict*, 2nd ed. (Cambridge University Press, 2010), 95.

[42] For recent such events, see, e.g., Operation United Resolve website at www.defense.gov/News/Special-Reports/0814_Inherent-Resolve; M. R. Gordon and E. Schmitt, "US Steps Up Its Attacks against ISIS Controlled Oil Fields in Syria," *New York Times* (Nov. 12, 2015), www.nytimes.com/2015/11/13/us/politics/us-steps-up-its-attacks-on-isis-controlled-oil-fields-in-syria.html?_r=0. The UK has also conducted attack missions against such targets: F. Perraudin, H. Siddique, and M. Safi, "Syria Airstrikes: Britain Launches 'offensive operation' after Vote to Bomb ISIS Targets: As it Happened," *The Guardian* (Dec. 3, 2015), www.theguardian.com/world/live/2015/dec/03/syria-air strikes-britain-launches-bombing-against-isis-targets-rolling-report; and "French Airstrike Hits IS Group Oil Facility in Syria," *France 24* (Nov. 9, 2015), www.france24.com/en/20151109-france-syria-strike-islamic-state-oil-facility-military.

[43] Consider W. Hays Parks, "Air War and the Law of War" (1990) 32 *The Air Force Law Review* 1,141 et seq.

a view might imply that States Party to the Protocol are accepting a more restrictive interpretation of the military objective notion that would not, according to that view, be binding on all States. Of course, States that are party to AP I, and thus bound by the article treaty-based definition, but nevertheless attacking war-sustaining targets in Syria, must of necessity have an explanation for their adoption of such a position. Perhaps the approach in this part of the Manual will help them to develop such a narrative.

The terms "capture" and "neutralization" are discussed in paragraph 5.6.7.1. In relation to "capture" the Manual suggests that "the seizure of a city may be a military objective because of its strategic location." This statement seems to mix up two rather distinct, and different, meanings of "objective." In the context of the relevant discussion, objective is being used to describe objects that it would be permissible, *inter alia*, to attack. It is assumed for the purposes of this discussion that the authors of the Manual are not seeking to argue for differing interpretations of military objective depending on whether attack, capture, or neutralization are contemplated. The inference that some may draw from the cited part of the text that the whole of a city may be a military objective and might therefore lawfully be made the object of attack is, it is assumed and hoped, not an inference intended by the Manual's authors. However, the idea that seizure is a military objective as that term is used in Article 52(2) or its customary equivalent is also clearly wrong, because seizure is not a physical or other object but, rather, an aim, intent, or purpose.

The Manual then gives helpful and legally accurate explanations of three concepts, namely neutralization, the vital contextual aspect to the definition and the idea of "definite military advantage."[44]

In the succeeding paragraphs examples are given of objects that may, or that have often been, regarded as military objectives. This would seem to be a better way of expressing such a point, because it properly reflects the contextual nature of the determination that an object is or has become a military objective. However, economic objects associated with war-sustaining industries are included and this again would seem to be stretching the definition too much. Even those who advocate a war-sustaining approach in the recent literature[45] limit targets justifiable on this basis to "staples," as opposed to objects whose contribution may be less vital to the continuation of the enemy's war effort.[46] It has been long accepted in the literature that the

---

[44]   As to the last of these, see DoD Law of War Manual, ¶ 5.7.7.3.
[45]   R. Goodman, "Targeting 'War-Sustaining' Objects in Non-International Armed Conflicts" (2016) 110 *American Journal of International Law* 663.
[46]   *Ibid.*

only method of economic warfare that is permissible in accordance with the law of armed conflict constitutes blockade.[47] To attack targets on the basis of the economic value they have for the opposing party is highly controversial.[48]

7 COMBATANTS AND MEMBERS OF ARMED GROUPS

Section 5.7 of the Manual addresses the law of war idea of "combatants." Immediately, the difference of approach between the United States and States that are party to AP I becomes evident as the Manual refers to ideas of privileged and unprivileged combatants. Under Article 43 of the AP I, members of the armed forces of a party to an IAC, other than medical and religious personnel, are defined as combatants, "that is to say, they have the right to participate directly in hostilities."[49] It is therefore clear that combatant status under AP I confers the combatant's privilege. With such an approach there can be no such thing as an unprivileged combatant. In the US approach, the term combatant does not afford status under the law but, rather, describes what the individual is doing; namely, engaging in combat. It is therefore entirely logical, given that understanding of the meaning of the term, that US practitioners should wish to qualify the notion by the descriptors "privileged" and "unprivileged" to reflect that not all persons taking a direct part in the fight have the legally conferred right to do so.

It is noteworthy that the expression that has also frequently been used in the past, namely "unlawful combatant,"[50] is not the expression of choice in the Manual. It might be argued that the Manual's use of the term "unprivileged combatant" brings the US and AP I positions a step closer together, but the fundamental difference in view remains.

Paragraph 5.7.1 looks at the liability of members of armed forces and of armed groups to be made the object of attack and concludes that all members of both are liable to be attacked irrespective of whether the person concerned is taking a direct part in hostilities at the relevant time. The view that members of the armed forces are liable to be attacked at all times during an armed conflict is, of course, uncontroversial. However, the Manual's stated position in respect of members of armed groups puts the US approach into clear conflict with the ICRC's interpretation that it is only members of organized armed groups that have a continuous combat function who are liable to be

---

[47] Dinstein (above note 41), 95. [48] *Ibid.* [49] AP I, Art. 43(2).
[50] The US Commanders' Handbook on the Law of Naval Operations, NWP 1-14M dated July 2007 (NWP 1-14M), para. 5.4.1.2 provides as follows: "Unlawful enemy combatants are persons not entitled to combatant immunity who engage in acts against the United States or its coalition partners in violation of the laws and customs of war during armed conflict."

attacked at all times.[51] Absent that continuous combat function, the ICRC would limit the liability of such members to attack to the occasions when they are directly participating in the hostilities.[52] The ICRC's interpretation creates an inherent imbalance between the vulnerability to attack, respectively, of members of the armed forces and members of armed groups. The US approach does not imply such imbalance and would accordingly seem to be the preferable understanding of the position.

In the second part of paragraph 5.7.1, it is accordingly stated that "combatants may be made the object of attack at all times, regardless of the activities in which they are engaged at the time of attack." The reader from an AP I State looking at this and other provisions of the Manual relating to combatants in general must recall that the AP I definition of combatants is not necessarily, indeed is necessarily not, being referred to here, and will look to the definition in paragraph 5.7.2, which is entitled "Categories of Persons who are Combatants for the Purpose of Assessing their Liability to Attack." This is a curious title. It suggests that a person may be a combatant for the stated purpose but not a combatant for other purposes. In the present discussion, that proposition, and the arguable risk that it may confuse, will not be pursued.

More to the present point, paragraph 5.7.2 answers the pressing question of who are liable to be lawfully attacked at any time by virtue of being, in the US view, combatants. They are listed as "members of the armed forces of a state; members of militia and volunteer corps; participants in a *levee en masse* persons belonging to non-State armed groups; and leaders whose responsibilities include the operational command and control of the armed forces or of a non-State armed group."

This definition therefore defines the combatant notion by reference to membership of an armed force of some kind, whether State or non-State. It excludes persons who take a direct part in hostilities without being a member of an armed group, but the Manual addresses the position of those individuals a little later in the text. One observation should be made, namely that the inclusion of all those who are members of non-State armed groups might be slightly over-inclusive. Thus, some such members may have functions that are limited to diplomatic or other activities that do not constitute participation in the armed conflict. It could be argued that such individuals should not be included in the combatant classification. Paragraph 5.7.3 certainly suggests that such individuals would be liable to be lawfully attacked, although it could perhaps be argued that they lack the intention of personally taking part in the group's "hostile intent."

[51]   See Melzer (above note 25), 33–34.   [52]   *Ibid.*, 35.

In paragraph 5.7.1.1, the US practice in declaring a force hostile is mentioned. For an AP I State, once a situation of IAC has arisen, the lawful human targets for attack will comprise combatants as defined in Article 43, and directly participating civilians. No declaration is required in that regard.

The first part of paragraph 5.7.3.1 most helpfully lists some direct information that would indicate the formal membership of an individual of an armed group.[53] Recognizing that in many instances direct information may not be available, the Manual lists other information that "might indicate that a person is a member of a non-State armed group." The listed indicators would all seem to be both relevant and useful. It may, however, be that in particular cases more than one such indicator may need to be present for a reliable determination of membership to be made, and it might be helpful for the Manual to make that point.

The Manual then develops a notion of functional membership in an armed group, a concept that is applied to persons who are integrated into the group without necessarily having formal membership but to whom the hostile intent of the group can be imputed. Paragraph 5.7.3.2 stipulates that such individuals may also be made the object of attack by virtue of this functional membership. There would likely need to be clear information demonstrating the required integration and shared hostile intent, because this really constitutes the line of distinction between combatants, as that term is employed by the Manual, and civilians. Clearly, this distinction is of utmost importance. It differentiates between persons who are liable to be attacked at any time and irrespective of what they are actually doing at the time of attack, and persons whom all involved in the armed conflict have a legal responsibility to spare. Any determination that an individual who is not a formal member of a group is nevertheless constantly liable to be lawfully attacked must be based on clear information not just that the individual shares the general objectives and perspectives of the group, but that he or she is sufficiently involved in its hostile activities.

---

53   DoD Law of War Manual, ¶ 5.7.3.1:
      In some cases, there might be formal or direct information indicating membership in the group. This might include:
      • using a rank, title, or style of communication;
      • taking an oath of loyalty to the group or the group's leader;
      • wearing a uniform or other clothing, adornments, or body markings that identify members of the group; or
      • documents issued or belonging to the group that identify the person as a member, such as membership lists, identity cards, or membership applications.

After dealing in appropriate terms with how an individual might achieve dissociation from, or renunciation of membership of, a group,[54] the Manual at paragraph 5.7.4 considers when leaders are liable to be made the object of attack. It is of course correct that leaders who are members of the armed forces are liable to be attacked on the basis of their combatant status. Equally, it is right that leaders who take a direct part in the hostilities, whether by virtue of their functional responsibilities or because they become involved (e.g. in target approval), are liable to be attacked while so participating. Having noted that the President of the United States, as Commander in Chief of the US armed forces, would be liable to be attacked, the Manual then makes a rather broad assertion that the Prime Minister of a constitutional monarchy would be similarly liable. If a Prime Minister of a constitutional monarchy is not a member of the armed forces and has no role in relation to the conduct of the hostilities, for example on the basis that all such responsibilities have been passed to the Minister of Defense, that Prime Minister would not be liable to lawful attack merely by virtue of his or her position as Prime Minister. It is the status as a combatant (in the AP I sense) or the participation of the individual in the hostilities that renders him or her liable to be targeted, and this aspect could be more clearly articulated in this part of the Manual's text.

8 DIRECT PARTICIPATION IN HOSTILITIES

Section 5.8 addresses the customary yet controversial topic of direct participation in hostilities. This section contains one of the most pointed areas of vocal US disagreement with many commentators in other nations. While it is recognized in the general practice of States that a civilian who directly participates in hostilities loses his or her protection as a civilian while doing so,[55] the States that negotiated these treaty provisions did not adopt commonly agreed language to explain the notion, and an important attempt by international experts to reach agreement on such meaning was not successful.[56]

---

[54] *Ibid.*, ¶ 5.7.3.3.

[55] Contrast Geneva Conventions 1949, Common Art. 3 which refers to active participation and AP I, Art. 51(3) using "direct participation." These concepts are generally regarded as being synonymous. Note also the statement in the Manual that, while the US does not accept that AP I, Art. 51(3) has customary status, it does accept the customary provision on which that paragraph of AP I is based; DoD Manual, ¶ 5.9.1.2 and fn. 218. Quite what the difference is between recognition of the underlying customary principle and acceptance of customary status of the treaty rule is not made clear.

[56] The ICRC and the Asser Institute co-sponsored a series of annual meetings of experts from 2003 to 2008. The failure of that initiative to achieve consensus among the experts as to a general interpretation of the direct participation notion is within the personal knowledge of

Moreover, while some elements of the Interpretive Guidance published by the ICRC are accepted as reflecting customary law, substantial parts of it are not so accepted, *inter alia*, by the US[57] and indeed the Interpretive Guidance has been the subject of controversy in the academic literature.[58] Section 5.8 therefore articulates the US interpretation of a concept that international law has conspicuously failed to explain. Of course, the interpretation offered in the Manual is also not necessarily customary in status, recognizing as one must that there is unlikely to yet be a sufficient generality of practice or indeed of interpretation to justify any particular understanding as having achieved customary status.

Paragraph 5.8.2 makes the important and accurate point that the rule specifically applies to civilians. It also correctly notes that civilians are persons who are not combatants (ignoring for the time being the question of non-combatants). An issue arises because as we have seen the US definition of combatants in paragraph 5.8.2 includes members of non-State armed groups whereas, as has been noted above, the AP I, Article 43 definition of combatants does not include such persons. This has the effect that for an AP I State, civilians would include members of such non-State armed groups that do not satisfy the definition of "armed forces" whereas for the United States they are counted as combatants and are therefore persons to whom the direct partici-pation notion does not apply. Of course, the reason why the United States treats the act of belonging to a hostile, non-State armed group as a basis on which a person is liable to attack is that the United States classifies such persons as combatants. The Manual correctly states that "members of hostile, non-State armed groups may be made the object of attack unless they are placed *hors de combat*" but cautions US practitioners that coalition partners will often reach the same legal conclusion via different methodologies.[59] All combatants are liable to be attacked at all times and the relevant persons are classed by the United States as combatants.

Paragraph 5.8.3 tackles the difficult task of explaining direct participation in hostilities as such. It does so by making the proper distinction between, on the one hand, taking part in the combat or substantially contributing to a party's ability to conduct or sustain combat operations, both of which would in the US view amount to direct participation, and, on the other hand, providing

---

the author who participated as one of the experts. At the end of the process, the ICRC on its own initiative published the Interpretive Guidance to which reference is made in n. 25 above.

[57] DoD Law of War Manual, ¶ 5.8.1.2.

[58] See, e.g., the Forum in (2010) 42 *New York University Journal of International Law and Politics* 3.

[59] DoD Law of War Manual, ¶ 5.8.2.1.

general support to the war effort, such as by purchasing war bonds. The Manual does well to emphasize the importance of the context in which an act is performed in determining whether it does or does not amount to direct participation, and it is most helpful that later in the paragraph some considerations that may be relevant in making that determination are suggested, it being implicitly recognized that the offered considerations are illustrative, not an exclusive list. In paragraph 5.8.3.1 examples are given, again on a non-exhaustive basis, of actions that would be regarded as direct participation. The examples that are chosen would all seem to be noncontroversial. In the next paragraph, 5.8.3.2, examples are given, again on a noncontroversial basis, of activities that would not amount to direct participation.

In paragraph 5.8.4, the Manual appropriately rejects the notion of the revolving door of protection,[60] a concept that is explained and discussed in more detail in paragraph 5.8.4.2 where the position is adopted that civilians who repeatedly perform acts of direct participation do not regain protection during the time intervals between such direct participation acts.[61] As paragraph 5.8.4.1 suggests, it must also be right to hold that a person who has permanently renounced direct participation ceases as a consequence to be liable to be attacked and the assessment of whether a person has indeed permanently ceased directly to participate must be based on a good faith evaluation which, one would suggest, must be informed by all the information from all sources that is reasonably available to the decision-maker at the relevant time.

9 PERSONS WHO ARE *HORS DE COMBAT*

Section 5.9 explains the legal arrangements concerning persons who are placed *hors de combat*. The provisions of Article 41 of AP I are cited, and the Manual text starts by summarizing those who are to be regarded as *hors de*

60　The idea of the revolving door of protection has its roots in a strict interpretation of the treaty provision that civilians retain protection from attack "unless and for such time as" they directly participate. If the idea of direct participation is interpreted, in accordance with the Interpretive Guidance approach, as limited to specific acts, it logically follows that during the intervals between these specific acts, an individual regains protected status, hence the revolving door of protection. So far as the ICRC is concerned, the revolving door is not a malfunction of the law; Melzer (above note 25), 70.

61　The rejection of the revolving door concept is based in part on the imbalance it would imply between the position of combatants and directly participating civilians and on the view that such an interpretation would actually erode the protection of civilians; DoD Manual, ¶ 5.8.4.2, final sentence.

combat. Much of the discussion in this section is not controversial. An ongoing point of some difficulty, however, concerns surrender. Article 41 of AP I provides that a "person is *hors de combat* if … [h]e clearly expresses an intention to surrender." The Manual takes the position that, in addition to being a "genuine offer to surrender" expressed in a "clear and unconditional" manner,[62] "[f]or an offer to surrender to render a person *hors de combat*, it must be feasible for the opposing party to accept the offer."[63] The Final Report on the Persian Gulf War, a DoD document, is cited as the authority for this interpretation. Article 41 of AP I, however, makes no specific mention of such a feasibility requirement as a condition for *hors de combat* status. According to that text, it is the act of manifesting an intention to surrender that produces that status.

The discussion of these issues at paragraph 5.9.3.3 may at first glance seem to provide ample justification for the feasibility aspect of the Manual position.[64] Certainly, a soldier who indicates a willingness to surrender in circumstances, such as those discussed in that paragraph, where it is manifestly impractical to accept that surrender, cannot reasonably expect to be taken into custody. However, the observations in the AMW Manual are relevant here. That manual comments:

> Enemy personnel who surrender will normally be taken into the custody – and placed under the protection – of the detaining Belligerent Party. However, this is not always feasible. If the military unit, in whose custody the surrendering personnel are, is incapable … to escort them to a POW-camp, they must be released without harm. Thus the obligation on the part of the Belligerent Party is not necessarily to detain surrendering enemy personnel, but to desist from further attack on persons complying with the conditions set out in rule 127.[65]

It is suggested that it would have been better if the Manual had expressed the legal position in these or similar terms, thereby emphasizing that the practical ability to accept surrender and thereafter take the individuals into custody are not the determinants of *hors de combat* status. Rather, surrender is contingent on three cumulative conditions: clearly communicating the intent to surrender; desisting from further hostile acts; and not attempting to evade capture.

---

[62] *Ibid.*, ¶ 5.9.3.   [63] *Ibid.*, ¶ 5.9.3.3.
[64] It is emphasized that what is being discussed here is the US position on the matter, not the correct interpretation of the requirements of AP I, Art. 41, which applies to treaty parties.
[65] AMW Manual, Commentary accompanying rule 125, para. 5. The conditions in rule 127 are to communicate the intention to surrender in a clear manner to the enemy; not to engage in any further hostile acts; and to make no attempt to evade capture.

Persons complying with these conditions are *hors de combat* and must not be made the object of attack, whether capturing them is practicable or not.

Paragraph 5.9.4 correctly outlines the protected status of persons who are rendered unconscious or who are otherwise incapacitated by wounds, sickness, or shipwreck while paragraph 5.9.5 addresses the status of persons parachuting from an aircraft in distress. It is accurately stated that this protected status is analogous to that accorded to combatants who are *hors de combat*. However, in the final element of the paragraph it is argued that paratroopers parachuting from an aircraft in distress outside the context of an airborne assault would be protected from attack as being *hors de combat*. A number of potential difficulties arise with this formulation, despite its consistency with Article 42 of AP I.[66] It may be impossible for defending forces to determine from which of a group of aircraft paratroopers are emerging, particularly if only one such aircraft is stricken. Similarly, it may be difficult for defenders to determine whether the descending paratroopers are genuinely out of the fight, or are intent on continuing the hostilities, and delaying an attack on them until they have landed and manifested their intent may be to forego the only opportunity for successful engagement of them.

While it may be correct as a matter of strict interpretation of the applicable law that such persons are capable of being *hors de combat*, therefore, it would seem that only if the persons concerned clearly come within the provisions of Article 41 should they be entitled to protection, it being acknowledged, as appears to be the US position, that Article 41 does not necessarily contain an all-embracing definition of the persons who may be classed as *hors de combat*.

10 ATTACKERS' PRECAUTIONS

Paragraph 5.11 is an important provision in that it addresses the precautions that an attacker is obliged to undertake. There is a clear link, as the Manual acknowledges, between these precautionary obligations and the practical implementation of the discrimination principle.[67] The corresponding provisions in AP I are to be found in Article 57, so while recognizing here as elsewhere that the United States is not a party to that treaty, the widely accepted provisions of the article will provide a useful baseline for considering the stated US position.

---

[66] AP I, Art. 42(1): "1. No person parachuting from an aircraft in distress shall be made the object of attack during his descent."

[67] DoD Law of War Manual, ¶ 5.11 fn. 336 (citing an extract from a letter from Harold Koh, Legal Advisor, Dept. of State dated Dec. 30, 2009).

The section starts with a reference to the duty to give an effective advance warning of an attack that may affect the civilian population unless the circumstances do not permit.[68] It is unfortunate that in the paragraph discussing warnings reference is also made to the entirely different warning obligations that arise before any attack of certain medical units, vessels, or facilities is permissible. Including reference to those warning requirements in paragraph 5.11.5.1 may cause confusion, for example, when it is suggested in paragraph 5.11.5.2 that there is no set form for warnings, that they may be general, and that they may be communicated in a variety of ways. While such remarks are correct insofar as they refer to warnings of attacks that may affect civilians, they do not reflect the specific requirements as to warning of attacks on, for example, medical facilities.[69]

Paragraph 5.11.5.3 makes the correct point that there is no obligation under Article 57 to give warnings of, for example, attacks that will not affect the civilian population. Interestingly, this paragraph gives no guidance as to the interpretation of the word "affect." Specifically, it does not suggest that the notion is limited to attacks that are intended or that may be expected to cause death or injury to civilians.

Paragraphs 5.11.2 to 5.11.4 address some of the general precautionary measures that can be taken with a view to minimizing civilian casualties and include the proper point that international law does not, as such, specify any requirement to use precision-guided munitions on any particular occasion.

Paragraph 5.11.7.1 then expresses the US view that the rule in AP I, Article 57(3) is not a rule of customary law.[70] This would lead one to conclude that, so far as the United States is concerned, where a choice is possible between a number of military objectives for achieving a similar military advantage, there is no legal obligation to choose the target the attack of which offers the least danger to civilians. The associated footnote[71] cites the US reply to the

---

[68]   *Ibid.,* ¶ 5.11.

[69]   Note, e.g., Art. 13 of AP I which is concerned with the discontinuance of protection of civilian medical units and which specifies that protection of such units may cease "only after a warning has been given setting, whenever appropriate, a reasonable time limit, and after such warning has remained unheeded" (Art. 13(1)). The nature of the warning will involve pointing out the respects in which the unit is being used outside its humanitarian function to commit acts harmful to the adversary and will require the cessation of such activities. Thus, the nature, purpose, and intended effect of this kind of warning are fundamentally different to that prescribed by Art. 57(2)(c) of AP I.

[70]   AP I, Art. 57(3): "[w]hen a choice is possible between several military objectives for obtaining a similar military advantage, the objective to be selected shall be that the attack on which may be expected to cause the least danger to civilian lives and to civilian objects."

[71]   DoD Law of War Manual, ¶ 5.11.7.1 fn. 379.

ICRC following the Gulf War of 1990 from which it appears that the rejection of customary status of this rule derives from notions of mission accomplishment, allowable risk and the possibility that the decision-maker may conclude that making such a determination is not possible. Arguably, if mission accomplishment is going to be rendered impossible, if taking the precaution would involve unacceptable own forces risk or if making such a determination is simply not possible, then either the choice referred to in the rule is impossible or the military advantage anticipated from the attack is no longer similar. In either such circumstance, the rule would not be engaged, so it is difficult to agree that the stated arguments provide a sound basis for the rejection of the rule as it is expressed in AP I.

So what do these paragraphs tell us about the rules as to protection in attack that the United States accepts? Footnote 336 cites, seemingly with approval, Article 27 of the Hague Regulations, 1907 and, in relation to naval forces, Article 5 of Hague Convention IX of the same year. Correspondence from Harold Koh, Legal Advisor at the Department of State and dated December 30, 2009, is quoted to the effect that the United States accepts Article 57(2)(ii) and (4) as "an accurate statement of the fundamental law of war principle of discrimination."[72] Paragraphs 5.11.1 to 5.11.4 of the Manual stipulate that combatants must take feasible precautions in conducting attacks to reduce the risk of harm to civilians and other protected persons and objects, noting that such feasible precautions may include warnings, adjusting the timing of an attack to reduce the risk of incidental harm,[73] selecting certain weapons with a view to reducing the risk of incidental harm while achieving a given or superior military advantage,[74] and identifying zones in which military objectives are more likely to be present or civilians are more likely to be absent. However, it should be noted that these are described in terms of possible feasible precautions, it being pointed out that what it is in fact feasible to do by way of precautions will depend on the prevailing circumstances.[75]

---

[72] Article 52(2)(a)(ii) of AP I, which is the provision to which the erroneous reference to Art. 57(2)(ii) is intended to refer, provides that with respect to attacks, the following precautions shall be taken: "those who plan or decide upon an attack shall ... (ii) take all feasible precautions in the choice of means and methods of attack with a view to avoiding, and in any event to minimizing, incidental loss of civilian life, injury to civilians and damage to civilian objects." Article 57(4) provides that in the conduct of military operations at sea or in the air "each Party to the conflict shall, in conformity with its rights and duties under the rules of international law applicable in armed conflict, take all reasonable precautions to avoid losses of civilian lives and damage to civilian objects."

[73] DoD Law of War Manual, ¶ 5.11.3.   [74] *Ibid.*, ¶ 5.11.6.

[75] *Ibid.*, ¶ 5.11 (second sentence).

It is therefore instructive to note which explicit precautionary duties stipulated by AP I, Article 57 are not specifically reflected in this section of the Manual text[76] as being accepted by the United States as mandatory obligations.[77] They are:

   a. the requirement that those who plan or decide upon an attack shall "do everything feasible to verify that the objectives to be attacked are neither civilians nor civilian objects and are not subject to special protection but are military objectives within the meaning of paragraph 2 of Article 52 and that it is not prohibited by the provisions of th[e] Protocol to attack them"[78]
   b. the requirement that those who plan or decide upon an attack shall "refrain from deciding to launch any attack which may be expected to cause incidental loss of civilian life, injury to civilians, damage to civilian objects, or a combination thereof, which would be excessive in relation to the concrete and direct military advantage anticipated"[79]
   c. the obligation that "an attack shall be cancelled or suspended if it becomes apparent that the objective is not a military one or is subject to special protection or that the attack may be expected to cause incidental loss of civilian life, injury to civilians, damage to civilian objects, or a combination thereof, which would be excessive in relation to the concrete and direct military advantage anticipated"[80]
   d. the requirement that, "[w]hen a choice is possible between several military objectives for obtaining a similar military advantage, the objective to be selected shall be that the attack on which may be expected to cause the least danger to civilian lives and to civilian objects."[81]

Undoubtedly, US forces will in practice frequently undertake the precautions listed in elements (a) to (d) of the previous paragraph. In operational terms, there will often be little or no difference in the precautionary steps therefore

---

[76]   Note, however, fn. 380 which relates to the next section on proportionality. An extract from Field Manual 27-10, The Law of Land Warfare (Washington: US Dep't. of Army, July 18, 1956) (FM 27-10) addresses some relevant concepts but in terms which are somewhat different from the corresponding AP I provisions. The Manual's reader is invited to consider Arts. 51(5)(b) and 57(2)(a)(iii) but there is no indication as to whether these rules are considered binding on the United States in the stated terms.

[77]   The point being made here is that these AP I obligations are not explicitly reflected in terms in these paragraphs of the Manual. It is a matter of interpretation whether some or all of these explicit obligations of AP I are regarded as being subsumed within the somewhat more generally expressed rules that the Manual expresses.

[78]   AP I, Art. 57(2)(a)(i).   [79]   *Ibid.*, Art. 57(2)(a)(iii).   [80]   *Ibid.*, Art. 57(2)(b).

[81]   *Ibid.*, Art. 57(3).

that US and AP I States Party respectively take. The significance from the perspective of the Manual lies in the arguably limited and general nature of the precautions that the currently discussed paragraphs of the Manual regard as being legally required. Such a divergence of legal interpretation may have implications for interoperability, for example during coalition operations.

11 THE RULE OF PROPORTIONALITY

Section 5.12 is where the Manual addresses the proportionality rule as it applies to targeting law. It does this in the following terms: "Combatants must refrain from attacks in which the expected loss of civilian life, injury to civilians, and damage to civilian objects incidental to the attack, would be excessive in relation to the concrete and direct military advantage expected to be gained."[82] Interestingly, here again there are evident departures from the language that binds the numerous States that are party to the Additional Protocols. Thus, the Manual does not explicitly link the proportionality rule to the prohibition of indiscriminate attacks; it only addresses combatants, impliedly omitting application of the rule to civilians who are taking a direct part in the hostilities. It is also noteworthy that the military advantage to be considered must be expected, it being an interesting question worthy of consideration whether the requirement for expectation is, arguably, more exacting than the AP I reference in Article 52(5)(b) to anticipation.

One really wonders why the AP I definition, which has always been understood as having generally accepted customary status, has not been precisely replicated here. From a grammatical perspective, it offers a text that is noticeably clearer and thus preferable to the formulation put forward in the Manual.

Paragraph 5.12.1 makes the valid point that the rule only applies where civilians or civilian objects are at risk of harm from an attack while the next paragraph, 5.12.1.2, notes that forms of harm that are less than death, injury, or damage need not be considered; that is, mere inconvenience to civilians is acceptable. While that comment may well be correct, more contentious is the observation that temporary losses would be an example of such lesser forms of harm that do not need to be considered. Whether this is accurate as a statement of law will depend on the meaning to be given to "temporary losses." A temporary loss of functionality in a computer network that can be

---

82   The corresponding provision of AP I, namely Art. 51(5)(b), provides that "the following types of attack are to be considered as indiscriminate: . . . (b) an attack which may be expected to cause incidental loss of civilian life, injury to civilians, damage to civilian objects, or a combination thereof, which would be excessive in relation to the concrete and direct military advantage anticipated."

expected, in turn, to cause death, injury or damage to civilians or civilian objects would indeed need to be considered in a proportionality evaluation of a proposed cyberattack. If, however, the intended point here is that temporary loss of service or use that does not in turn occasion death, injury, or damage does not have to be considered in the proportionality evaluation, perhaps this might usefully be spelt out, it being in the present author's view a less controversial position. Paragraph 5.12.1.3 makes the generally correct point that consequences of an attack that are too remote should not be considered, it being understood that we are talking here about remoteness in causal terms. Ultimately, the proportionality rule requires attackers to consider expected collateral damage, and whether particular damage would be too remote to be expected will depend on the relevant facts.

Paragraph 5.12.1.4 contends that "harm caused by the attacking forces' actions in conducting the attack must be considered. Harm caused by enemy action, or beyond the control of either party, need not be considered." As is well understood, the AP I proportionality rule uses expectation as the criterion for distinguishing between collateral consequences that either must, or that do not have to, be considered. One can visualize circumstances in which it is known that, if a particular kind of attack is undertaken, the enemy will employ a particular capability or technique in response which can be expected to have a particular effect. To fail to consider that expected effect on the basis that it is attributable to enemy action would appear to be to fail to apply the proportionality rule as that rule is widely articulated and understood. Similarly, circumstances may be beyond the control of either party, such as weather conditions, yet their effect on the expected consequences of an attack may be evident. In such circumstances also, it is surely the case that the expected consequences must be considered in the proportionality evaluation, irrespective of the inability of either party to control the particular circumstance. These interpretation difficulties would be avoided if the Manual were to focus on the relevant issue of expectation and to analyze hypothetical scenarios accordingly.

Paragraph 5.12.2 makes the point that harm to military objectives, combatants, and directly participating civilians that is incidental to the intended target of the attack is understood not to prohibit an attack under the proportionality rule. This is correct.[83] The Manual also suggests that harm to certain persons who may be employed in or on military objectives would also be understood not to prohibit an attack on grounds of proportionality. The examples cited are persons authorized to accompany the armed forces,

---

[83]   DoD Law of War Manual, ¶ 5.12.2.

parlementaires, and civilian workers who place themselves in or on the military objective knowing that it is susceptible to attack, such as ammunition factory workers. For a State that is party to AP I, there is no blanket exclusion from the collateral damage calculus of persons in the stated categories. Rather, Article 51(4) and (5)(b) obliges the attacker to take these and any other classes of persons protected from attack into account in considering whether the expected collateral damage is indeed excessive.

Accordingly, in the case of ammunition factory workers for example, the expected casualties among the civilian workers in the factory should be considered along with casualties among civilians living in the vicinity of the factory and all other categories of collateral damage,[84] it being appreciated that only in relatively rare cases will the expected casualties among the workers be excessive in relation to what is likely to be the considerable military advantage accruing directly from the planned attack on the ammunition factory.[85] There will be those who would argue that such workers should be reckoned with reduced value in the proportionality assessment because of their, it is assumed voluntary, assumption of risk. Be that as it may, it is generally recognized that they should be considered, whatever the value accorded to them, and that their expected deaths and injuries should not be simply ignored. So, while it is right that such individuals are unlikely to prohibit the proposed attack on proportionality grounds, it would probably be more legally accurate to say that the proportionality rule should be applied, that the relevant persons should be considered when doing so and that in normal circumstances the attack is likely to be found not to breach the rule.

12 HUMAN SHIELDS

Paragraph 5.12.3.4 turns to the legally vexed question of human shields and starts by correctly noting that the use of civilians to shield military objectives from attack is unlawful. The paragraph goes on to observe, again correctly, that the party using human shields takes responsibility for injury to them provided that the attacking party takes feasible precautions in attack. This formulation of the position does not, however, fully reflect the position binding on AP I States Party by virtue of Article 51(7) and (8), in that the treaty provisions, having asserted the illegality of human shielding, then require that attackers comply with their legal obligations with respect to the civilian population and civilians, including the obligation to take precautionary measures, notwithstanding the violations by the opposing party. Regrettably, the Manual does

---

84   Dinstein (above note 41), 131.   85   DoD Law of War Manual, ¶ 5.12.3.3 fn. 412.

not analyze the US position with regard to human shields against the language of the Additional Protocol.

Paragraph 5.12.2 addresses what it describes as "concrete and direct military advantage expected to be gained." The thought that by requiring the military advantage to be expected rather than anticipated, the Manual is raising the bar for allowable military advantage was discussed earlier. In the ensuing discussion, the idea of definite military advantage in the military objective definition is linked to the proportionality rule's concept of concrete and direct military advantage, and the interpretation is offered that while the military advantage does not have to be immediate it cannot be merely speculative or hypothetical. This is a widely accepted and correct interpretation. The military advantage is not limited to tactical gains, may indeed – as the Manual proposes – be interpreted in the context of the war strategy, and should refer to the attack as a whole, not to isolated or particular parts of it. Here, interestingly, statements by a number of States on ratification of AP I are referred to in the associated footnote.[86]

Paragraph 5.12.3 properly draws attention to the "excessiveness" aspect of the proportionality rule. Later in the same paragraph, the open-ended, subjective, and imprecise nature of the inquiry that the rule requires in cases other than those that are clear-cut is appropriately noted. A rich selection of sources including well-known and authoritative extracts from the Final Report to the ICTY Prosecutor by the Committee Established to Review the NATO Bombing Campaign against the Federal Republic of Yugoslavia, from the writings of Tony Rogers, and of W. Hays Parks is cited.

13 AMENDMENTS TO THE MANUAL'S TREATMENT OF PROPORTIONALITY

At the time when the first draft of this chapter was written, the text of Chapter V was that originally published by DoD in June 2015. In December 2016 some extensive revisions of Chapter V, particularly in its treatment of proportionality, were published by the Department. In this final substantive section of the present chapter, the amended texts of sections 5.10, 5.11, and 5.12 will be briefly considered.

The opening paragraphs of section 5.10 refer to an obligation to reduce the risk of harm to civilians and other protected persons and objects. It would be more accurate to refer to an obligation to avoid and in any event to minimize such risks, as reflected in AP I, Article 57(2)(a)(ii), a provision that is widely

---

[86]   DoD Law of War Manual, ¶ 5.12.2.1 fnn. 394–99.

accepted and probably customary. The immediately following paragraph restates the proportionality rule correctly, except that it talks of "expected" military advantage when the reference should be to the military advantage that is anticipated. Expectation is arguably a more limiting criterion than anticipation. It is good that paragraph 5.10.1 notes that feasible precautions must also be taken to reduce the harm to protected military personnel (e.g. those who are *hors de combat*).

Curiously, paragraph 5.10.1.2 then suggests that the prohibition on attacks expected to cause excessive incidental harm does not require consideration of military medical personnel, military wounded and sick, and military medical facilities. This seems to be an illogical conclusion. Given that each of these categories of personnel and facility must be respected and protected and indeed that they are entitled to protection (e.g. in the form of warnings) that goes beyond that to which civilians are entitled, it cannot be right that expected injury or as the case may be damage to them is simply ignored in applying the proportionality rule. The better view must be that such persons and objects must be considered when an attack is being planned or decided upon. It is of course right that the expected damage to a sick bay on a warship would not serve to prohibit an attack on the warship. The mere fact that the expected collateral damage would not be likely to outweigh the anticipated military advantage is not, however, justification for the suggestion that it is not necessary to consider injury or damage that ought, in the present author's view, to feature in the proportionality evaluation. The paragraph concludes by observing that feasible precautions must be taken to reduce the risk of harm to such persons and objects. Again, it would be more accurate to state that all feasible precautions must be taken to avoid, and at any event to minimize, that risk.[87]

The important role of commanders in the implementation of the proportionality rule is properly emphasized in paragraph 5.10.2. Paragraph 5.10.2.1 develops the point by noting that those "who are responsible for making the decisions and judgments required by the principle of proportionality are those who have the authority" to make them. It might be more appropriate to observe that those with the authority to make such decisions have the responsibility to do so with appropriate care. That said, the paragraph makes the correct point that aspects of the proportionality judgment, such as anticipated military advantage, and determining the feasibility of taking particular precautions are matters that are likely to require decisions by those with suitable authority over military operations. The paragraph discusses whether what it

[87]   AP I, Art. 57(2).

describes as the principle of proportionality requires military personnel to take actions such as providing warnings.

   This is not really the right approach in the view of the present author. The proportionality rule, not principle, describes a kind of attack that is considered indiscriminate. If proportionality is breached, the attack is indiscriminate and therefore unlawful. It may be possible by taking certain precautions to render a planned attack compliant with the proportionality rule. If however it is determined that the relevant precautions cannot feasibly be undertaken, that does not give the attacking force the right to undertake an indiscriminate attack. The correct approach in such a circumstance would be to refrain from undertaking the planned attack and to find some other lawful way to achieve the desired military purpose.

   Paragraphs 5.10.2.2 and 5.10.2.3 correctly note that the commander's decisions on proportionality must be reasonable, necessarily involve subjective aspects, and must be based on common sense and good faith, with reasonable commanders not necessarily making the same decisions. Paragraph 5.10.2.4 recognizes that the duty not to comply with clearly unlawful orders also applies to proportionality violations, explaining correctly that subordinates may not be competent to assess whether proportionality would be breached. Paragraph 5.10.2.5 rightly points out the circumstances in which subordinates have discretion as to the conduct of attacks and paragraph 5.10.3 points to the military procedures through which the proportionality rule is in practice applied, including rules of engagement, doctrine, standard operating procedures, and special instructions.

   Paragraph 5.10.4 again makes the fundamental error of treating the rules as to precautions in attack as an element of the proportionality rule. The two are related but distinct. As noted earlier, attacks that breach the proportionality rule are examples of attacks that are indiscriminate and thus prohibited. When the paragraph suggests that "the available time is a constraint in assessing whether an attack is expected to cause excessive incidental harm" the inference is that when time is pressing the proportionality rule, and by extension the indiscriminate attacks prohibition, do not apply; such an inference is legally incorrect. It would however be right to say that the pressure of time may affect the precautions that it is feasible for the attacker to take. This issue is addressed explicitly in paragraph 5.10.5 where the Manual's approach is justified on the basis that the proportionality and precautions rules are "fundamentally connected and mutually reinforcing obligations." They may well be both of those things, but they are also distinct legal obligations and seeking to wrap them together in the way the Manual seeks to do may lead to misunderstanding. Nevertheless, the final sentence of the paragraph notes that feasible precautions must be taken even where excessive incidental harm is not expected and that even when feasible precautions have been taken an attack could be prohibited as one expected to cause excessive incidental harm. Of course, if feasible precautions are properly taken, an attack expected to cause excessive incidental harm will not be undertaken, which rather reinforces the point being made here as to the distinctness of the rules.

14 PROPORTIONALITY – FEASIBLE PRECAUTIONS

In section 5.11 the Manual discusses, on a non-exclusive basis, different kinds of precaution that can be taken to reduce the risk of harm to protected persons and objects and each precaution is discussed in turn in the ensuing paragraphs. Paragraph 5.11.1 addresses the assessment of risks to civilians, noting that this may involve general assessments not necessarily linked to a particular attack, pre-strike assessments, battle-damage assessments, and other after-action reviews and investigations. The need to learn from such processes and to apply the lessons learned is sensibly mentioned. The important point is then made that the responsibility of commanders should not be assessed on the basis of information that only becomes available after the event.

Paragraph 5.11.2 suggests that identifying and designating zones in which military objectives are more likely to be present, or civilians and protected persons or objects are more likely to be absent, may reduce incidental risks. Similarly, paragraph 5.11.3 refers to the possible adjustment of the timing of attacks. These matters are discussed on the basis that such action "may be appropriate." Really the discussion in the Manual should go further and explicitly note that in certain circumstances, an attack can only be conducted in compliance with the proportionality rule and thus will only be lawful if the timing of the attack is adjusted so that the expected civilian injuries and/or damage are no longer excessive. The reader must not be left with the impression that if the timing cannot be adjusted, the proportionality rule somehow no longer applies. This is again a risk associated with the failure to acknowledge and operationalize the discreteness of the proportionality and precautions rules.

Paragraph 5.11.4 notes that commanders may decide to cancel or suspend attacks when new information raises concerns as to expected civilian casualties. Acknowledging rightly that subordinates will not have the authority to cancel or suspend simply because they disagree with the commander's proportionality assessment, the paragraph properly explains the need to refer up the command chain new information of that sort that comes to light. The Manual also correctly notes that subordinates should be understood to have the authority to make decisions required by the law of war. Unhelpfully, however, the Manual restricts this authority by adding the words "in order to effectuate the commander's intent." Those words should be deleted as the precautionary obligations apply to all persons who decide upon attacks, and these individuals must of necessity include those who actually undertake them. Moreover, the rule applies irrespective of the commander's intent.

Paragraph 5.11.5 and its subparagraphs describe the obligation to give warnings, adopting the language of Article 57(2)(c) of AP I and explaining that language in uncontroversial terms. Paragraph 5.11.6 is a revised section to the December 2016 edition and addresses "weaponeering, *i.e.* the selection of appropriate weapons, sizes of weapons, aim points etc to achieve the desired military purpose while minimising civilian risks." An interesting example is given, namely the use of an incendiary weapon to attack biological weapons thus preventing the biological agents from adversely affecting the civilian population. As is discussed in Chapter VI of the Manual, the United States made a declaration on ratification of Protocol III to the Conventional Weapons Convention that would cover such circumstances. States Party to the Protocol that made no such statement would only be permitted to use such weapons against such targets in circumstances that comply with Article 2 of the Protocol. Usefully the paragraph notes that commanders may legitimately decide not to use precision weapons in order to preserve the capability for use on other occasions. This would not, of course, justify an indiscriminate attack on the occasion in question, a point that might usefully be added at the end of the paragraph.

Paragraph 5.11.7 starts with an odd sentence: "In planning or conducting an attack, the selection of a military objective may reduce the risk of incidental harm." This sentence again gets matters the wrong way around. An attack that is not directed at a specific military objective is indiscriminate and thus unlawful. The implication that attacks may be planned or undertaken with no particular military objective in mind is therefore wrong and the sentence needs to be changed to remove any such implication; for example, by referring to the requirement to select. The paragraph then discusses the situation where a choice exists between different military objectives to yield a military advantage, acknowledging that where "all other factors are equal" the object to be selected for attack shall be that the attack on which may be expected to cause the least danger to civilian lives and civilian objects. The Manual spells out the US view that the rule does not prevent the commander from attacking multiple military objectives; does not prevent the commander from pursuing every military advantage believed to warrant pursuit; does not apply when the choice of targets involves differing risks and benefits potentially yielding differing military advantage; and does not prevent the commander undertaking an attack of a military objective involving higher risk of incidental harm if the attack on that military objective involves a greater likelihood of achieving the military purpose.

Paragraph 5.11.7.1 takes the view that, if Article 57(3) of AP I is interpreted consistently with the foregoing, it can be regarded as reflecting customary law. The present author takes the view that States Party to AP I would indeed interpret Article 57(3) in that way, and that the US stipulations are essentially wrapped up in the Article 57(3) notion of similarity of military advantage; that is, that military advantage in that provision is to be interpreted broadly.

15 PROPORTIONALITY – PROHIBITION ON ATTACKS EXPECTED TO CAUSE EXCESSIVE INCIDENTAL HARM

Section 5.12 describes the proportionality rule in language that differs from Article 51(5)(b) of AP I, which is difficult to understand given that the latter provision is widely accepted as representing customary law. The failure to refer in the definition explicitly to the possibility that a combination of civilian injury and civilian damage might be excessive is unfortunate but, given the chosen wording and the reference to this aspect in paragraph 5.12.1, is not critical. As noted earlier, the reference to "expected" military advantage would seem to require a greater probability associated with the military advantage than the AP I use of the word "anticipated" implies. Paragraph 5.12.1.1 probably correctly suggests that injury and death of civilians should be given greater consideration than damage to civilian objects and that damage to cultural property should receive greater consideration than damage to what is described as "ordinary property," meaning presumably civilian property in general. The Manual correctly states that mere inconvenience or disruption to civilian life need not be considered in the proportionality assessment.[88]

Paragraph 5.12.1.3 discusses respectively foreseeable and remote harms suggesting that expected harms "mean such immediate or direct harms foreseeably resulting from the attack." The correct qualifier of the collateral damage to be considered in the proportionality assessment is "expected." Many outcomes may be foreseeable but not expected. It is therefore noteworthy that the Manual chooses a formulation that would arguably render the proportionality test more restrictive by requiring that outcomes that do not necessarily meet the AP I criterion of "expected" must nevertheless be taken

---

[88] DoD Manual, ¶ 5.12.1.2.

into account. The paragraph then refers to the exclusion of what it describes as "remote harms" from the test. This part of the discussion unnecessarily complicates matters in the view of the present author. The word "expected" as used in the widely accepted formulation of the rule should be interpreted by reference to its normal meaning in the English language. Either an outcome is to be expected or it is not and, it is suggested, no more need be said. As to the examples discussed in the paragraph, economic loss does not fall to be considered simply because it does not amount to death, injury, or damage, so its remoteness or otherwise is irrelevant. The Manual is right however in noting that the consequences of a possible but unexpected munition malfunction do not generally need to be considered.

Paragraph 5.12.2 correctly explains that the military advantage to be gained must be more than hypothetical or speculative but need not be immediate. Based on statements made by a number of States when ratifying AP I, paragraph 5.12.2.1 rightly asserts that "[t]he military advantage expected from an attack is intended to refer to the advantage gained from the attack considered as a whole, rather than only from isolated or particular parts of an attack" while military advantage is not limited to tactical gains but may be referable to the overall war strategy. The point is then appropriately illustrated using the example of an attack on a communications relay facility.

As paragraph 5.12.3 correctly observes, the notion of excessiveness at the core of the proportionality test involves comparing unlike quantities and values. Reference is properly made both to the requirement for professional military judgment and to the moral and ethical judgments involved in comparing civilians at risk from the attack with civilians or friendly forces at risk if the attack is not undertaken. The paragraph properly refers to the potentially open-ended nature of the enquiry in other than clear-cut cases, pointing to the possibly subjective and imprecise nature of the answer. As to paragraph 5.12.3.1, the present author has some difficulty in seeing the proportionality rule as an expression of the notion of "economy of force" (which language was added in the December 2016 amendments). The former is a core rule of the law of targeting while the latter concept is essentially grounded in military doctrine and probably has a more tangible link with the principle of military necessity.

Paragraph 5.12.13.2 argues that "incidental harm expected to result from strikes in which additional precautions are feasible, but have not been taken, would be more likely to be considered excessive." This is rather a doubtful proposition. The better view is that either the expected civilian death, injury and/or damage is excessive or it is not. A failure to take feasible precautions renders it more likely that a case in which it is excessive will not be identified before the attack, but it will not retrospectively affect whether an attack was in fact in breach of the proportionality rule. This is another respect in which this blending together of proportionality and precautions is leading to potentially misleading interpretations.

Paragraph 5.12.3.3 deals generally correctly with the situation of civilians who work on military facilities noting that by doing so they assume certain risks. However, the reference in the paragraph to "those determining whether a planned attack would be excessive" should be replaced with language along the lines of "those determining whether a planned attack would breach the proportionality rule." At the end of the first part of the paragraph, the suggestion is made that those making such determinations "may consider all relevant facts and circumstances." The verb used is wrong. They *must* consider all relevant facts and circumstances.

Paragraph 5.12.3.4 deals with the enemy use of human shields. The paragraph properly draws attention to the obligation of the attacking party, notwithstanding the enemy's use of human shields, to undertake feasible precautions. Reference might usefully have been made to AP I, Article 51(7) and (8). The paragraph correctly states that civilians not taking a direct part in hostilities and that are being used as human shields must be evaluated by the attacking party as civilians but again refers to the planned attack being excessive when the issue is whether the proportionality rule would be breached. The possibility is offered in the paragraph that voluntary human shields may be regarded by a commander as taking a direct part in the hostilities. It would have been helpful if the paragraph had offered guidance as to the factors that would justify a commander in coming to such a conclusion.

16 CONCLUSION

The author maintains that the decision of the United States to publish its Manual is to be applauded. That there are passages in the text with which issue can legitimately be taken should not detract from the value of the document as a whole, nor should it blind commentators to the importance of the text in setting forth the US position on these matters and in driving forward the debate on many pressing issues of controversy in contemporary international law.

If the text of the Manual is to be the subject of periodic revision, it is hoped that these comments may be of some, if limited, use to those charged with taking that process forward. If in making comments, the author has misunderstood the Manual authors' intent, may he be forgiven. The point remains, however, that the law of war is a body of law of the utmost importance, and central to it is the law on the conduct of hostilities. It is vital that the relevant rules be correctly stated, thoroughly understood by those whose task it is to comply with them, and that they be universally and consistently implemented in good faith. Writing a Manual of this magnitude and depth on the topic can only further that process and is therefore a monumental, and commendable, undertaking.

10

At War with Itself: The DoD Law of War Manual's Tension between Doctrine and Practice on Target Verification and Precautions in Attack

Peter Margulies[*]

1 INTRODUCTION

The rule on precautions in attack helps maintain the balance between humanity and military necessity in the law of armed conflict (LOAC).[1] Under this rule, a commander should take "feasible" precautions to minimize expected harm to civilians resulting from a military attack. The duty to take feasible precautions in turn reflects the customary obligation to employ "constant care" in reducing harm to civilian persons or objects.[2] The treatment of precautions in the revised US Department of Defense (DoD) Law of War Manual (the Manual) is flawed in two respects. First, the Manual's rich examples from practice clash with its narrow doctrinal[3] analysis of

[*] The author thanks Bill Boothby, Chris Harland, and Charlie Trumbull for comments on a previous draft, and reference librarians Stephanie Edwards and Lucinda Harrison-Cox for their expert assistance.

[1] For a historical analysis of the evolution of this balance, see M. N. Schmitt, "Military Necessity and Humanity in International Humanitarian Law: Preserving the Delicate Balance" (2010) 50 *Virginia Journal of International Law* 795–839, 796.

[2] Article 57(1), Protocol Additional to the Geneva Conventions of Aug. 12, 1949, and Relating to the Protection of Victims of International Armed Conflicts, June 8, 1977, 1125 UNTS 3 (AP I). The United States is not a signatory to AP I. It has accepted many of its provisions as indicative of customary international law. M. J. Matheson, "The United States Position on the Relation of Customary International Law to the 1977 Protocols Additional to the 1949 Geneva Conventions" (1987) 2 *American University Journal of International Law and Policy* 419; Air Force Pamphlet, II state prac., 339, para. 28; DoD Law of War Manual, ¶ 5.2.3.5. For further support for the "constant care" duty, see J.-M. Henckaerts and L. Doswald-Beck (eds.), *Customary International Humanitarian Law*, I: *Rules* (Cambridge University Press, 2005), 51, rule 15 (ICRC Customary IHL Study); ICRC Customary IHL Study, II: *Practice*, 337–39, paras. 6–29 (discussing State practice and articulation of binding principles that is expressly or substantively consistent with "constant care" phrase in AP I); ICRC, *Commentary on the Additional Protocols of 8 June 1977 to the Geneva Conventions of 12 August 1949* (Geneva: ICRC, 1987) (affirming "constant care" standard).

[3] This chapter uses the term, "doctrinal," in its legal sense, as referring to the interpretation of core principles relevant to law. Unless otherwise noted, this chapter does not use the term to

precautions' role in the targeting process. That narrow role includes the Manual's subsuming of precautions under the principle of proportionality, which bars attacks that a commander expects will cause "excessive" collateral civilian harm.[4] As a corollary, the Manual fails to acknowledge that precautions also play a role in the identification and verification of appropriate military targets. Moreover, the Manual denies that reasonableness governs target identification and verification. This chapter addresses each of these concerns.

Under the analysis offered in this chapter, LOAC's constant care requirement entails what this chapter calls "dynamic diligence."[5] The tenets of dynamic diligence track customary international law. Most importantly, a State that practices dynamic diligence must take reasonable care in target identification and verification, as well as assessment of collateral harm to civilians. The standard of reasonableness governs the two principles that, together with precautions, comprise LOAC's overarching triumvirate: distinction, which requires that fighters refrain from targeting civilians not directly participating in hostilities,[6] and proportionality, which bars attacks in which the harm to civilians anticipated by a commander is excessive in light of the military advantage that the commander expects to achieve.[7] Reasonable care includes measures routinely taken by the United States, such as the involvement of lawyers in the targeting process and the methodical estimate of collateral damage (CDE) expected from a prospective attack.[8] Under dynamic diligence, the duty to take feasible precautions to reduce civilian harm applies to *both* target identification *and* CDE.[9]

---

refer to principles of military tactics or strategy. J. Dill, "The 21st-Century Belligerent's Trilemma" (2015) 26 *European Journal of International Law* 83–108, 93.

[4] AP I, Arts. 51(5)(b) and 57(2)(a)(iii). AP I, along with customary international law, defines excessive harm by weighing that harm against the military advantage that a commander anticipates. Article 57(2)(a)(iii), AP I; M. N. Schmitt and L. Vihul (eds.), *Tallinn Manual 2.0 on the International Law Applicable to Cyber Operations* (Cambridge University Press, 2017) (hereinafter Tallinn Manual 2.0), rule 113, 471, para. 1.

[5] P. Margulies, "Making Autonomous Weapons Accountable: Command Responsibility for Computer-Guided Lethal Force in Armed Conflicts," in Jens David Ohlin (ed.), *Handbook on Remote Warfare* (Northampton: Edward Elgar, 2017).

[6] Articles 48 and 51(2), AP I; M. Bothe, K. J. Partsch, W. Solf, and M. Eaton, *New Rules for Victims of Armed Conflicts*, 2nd ed. (Leiden: Martinus Nijhoff, 2013), 320 (noting that commanders act on "information reasonably available to them at the time of decision").

[7] Article 57(2)(a)(iii), AP I.

[8] J. O'Connor (DoD General Counsel), "Applying the Law of Targeting to the Modern Battlefield," New York University School of Law (November 28, 2016), www.defense.gov/Port als/1/Documents/pubs/Applying-the-Law-of-Targeting-to-the-Modern-Battlefield.pdf.

[9] G. S. Corn, "War, Law, and the Oft Overlooked Value of Process as a Precautionary Measure" (2015) 42 *Pepperdine Law Review* 419–66, 459; G. S. Corn and J. A. Schoettler, Jr., "Targeting and Civilian Risk Mitigation: The Essential Role of Precautionary Measures" (2015) 223

Diligence is "dynamic," by virtue of its adjustment to both changing battle-space conditions and past experience. For example, in target selection, as information becomes reasonably available suggesting that an apparent military objective is actually civilian in character, a commander needs to address that information. Those efforts could include seeking further information to clarify the possible objective's true nature and seeking additional advice from lawyers or more senior commanders.[10] Moreover, dynamic diligence requires a *systemic* look backward and forward in tactics, techniques, and procedures (TTP) governing the targeting process. A State has a duty to both investigate possible past violations of LOAC and *apply* the knowledge gained in that investigation to adjustments of TTP. Similarly, a State should be proactive, and assess when both target selection and CDE require *additional* measures, such as the no-strike lists (NSLs) specifying protected archaeological, historical, and cultural objectives that the United States pioneered in the First Gulf War.[11]

The DoD Manual is ambivalent on the binding nature of dynamic diligence. Its rich examples embody a robust commitment to the approach. Reflecting the Manual's commitment to diligence, it cites the US use of NSLs. However, the Manual's narrow account of legal doctrine clashes with the examples it deploys.[12]

Consider the Manual's treatment of the relationship between precautions and the LOAC principles of distinction and proportionality. The principle of distinction governs target identification: a State may lawfully target only military objectives.[13] The principle of proportionality governs permissible collateral damage to civilians: it prohibits attacks that a reasonable

---

Military Law Review 785–842, 837; J.-F. Queguiner, "Precautions under the Law Governing the Conduct of Hostilities" (2006) 88 *International Review of the Red Cross* 793–821, 797.

[10] Corn (above note 9).

[11] DoD Law of War Manual, ¶ 5.18.4 fn. 606 (citing comments by US Deputy Secretary of State Strobe Talbott regarding US practice that designated certain sites as "off limits from attack," and also cordoned off certain "otherwise legitimate targets" that were deemed too close to protected sites to be attacked safely).

[12] The Manual's Dec. 2016 iteration added many examples that detailed US practice on proportionality and precautions. DoD Law of War Manual, Introductory Notes on Changes Promulgated on May 31 and Dec. 13, 2016. For an informed defense of the first publicly circulated version of the Manual, see C. J. Dunlap, Jr., "The DoD Law of War Manual and its Critics: Some Observations" (2016) 92 *International Law Studies* 85–118, 101–3 (arguing that the United States was correct in discerning a measure of flexibility in the rule stated in Art. 57(3), AP I that, "[w]hen a choice is possible" between attacks on different military objectives with a "similar" military advantage, the commander should select the option that causes the "least danger" to civilians).

[13] See AP I, Art. 48; Tallinn Manual 2.0, rule 93, 420–21, para. 2; Y. Dinstein, *The Conduct of Hostilities Under the Law of International Armed Conflict*, 2nd ed. (Cambridge University

commander would expect to cause excessive harm to civilians in light of the military advantage anticipated.[14] International law, embodied in most State practice, views the duty to take feasible precautions to minimize harm to civilians as applying to *both* target identification *and* collateral damage assessments.[15] In contrast, the Manual states that the rule of precautions in attack only applies to estimates of collateral harm, not to the accuracy of target identification. However, the Manual's examples from practice complicate its narrow view of precautions' scope. Those examples, including the use of NSLs, apply to both target identification and collateral harm assessment, just as international law requires.

International sources also state that a reasonableness standard governs both identification of targets *and* assessment of collateral harm.[16] In contrast, the Manual imposes a less demanding *good faith* standard on target identification.[17] Here, too, however, the Manual's examples suggest that a more robust standard applies in US practice.

This tension between articulation of LOAC rules and examples from US practice detracts from the guidance that the Manual seeks to impart. Commanders in the field may rely on the Manual's narrow reading of LOAC rules. The result might be target identification that skirts the mandate of "constant care" arising from customary international law. On the other hand, commanders might fully internalize the Manual's examples, which often exhibit the dynamic diligence invoked in this chapter. The Manual would appear to permit either choice. More concrete and consistent guidance is necessary.

Unfortunately, the Manual's idiosyncratic methodology on citation of legal authority compounds this guidance deficit. On key issues, the Manual takes a haphazard approach to citation of authority for its doctrinal assertions.[18] For example, on the vital question of whether a reasonableness standard applies to

---

Press, 2010), 8 (writing that International Court of Justice has supported distinction between combatants and noncombatants to protect civilian population).

[14] Tallinn Manual 2.0, rule 113, 470–71, paras. 1–2.

[15] *Ibid.*, 479, rule 115, para. 4 (noting that duty to take feasible precautions applies to verification of military *nature* of targets; *ibid.*, 479–80, rule 116, para. 2 ("feasible precautions must be taken to minimize collateral damage").

[16] *Ibid.*, 450, para. 10 (target selection turns on information "reasonably available to the attacker at the time of attack"); M. C. Waxman, "Detention as Targeting: Standards of Certainty and Detention of Suspected Terrorists" (2008) 108 *Columbia Law Review* 1365–429, 1387 (citing "reasonable effort" standard for accuracy of target selection).

[17] DoD Law of War Manual, ¶ 5.2.3.3. The Manual concedes that the more robust reasonableness standard governs proportionality. *Ibid.*, ¶ 5.10.2.2.

[18] D. Glazier, "Failing our Troops: A Critical Assessment of the New Department of Defense Law of War Manual" (2017) 42 *Yale Journal of International Law* 216.

target identification and verification, the Manual cites US Supreme Court Justice Robert Jackson's dissent in *Korematsu v. United States*[19] and Justice Oliver Wendell Holmes's opinion for the Court in *Brown v. United States*.[20] Even if US practitioners overlook the fact that both decisions far predate the development of modern LOAC principles, neither opinion supports the Manual's position. This methodological flaw further undermines the Manual's usefulness.

The present chapter will proceed in three sections. Section 2 discusses dynamic diligence and the right relationship under international humanitarian law (IHL) between the principles of distinction, proportionality, and precautions in attack. Section 3 discusses the acute tension between the Manual's doctrinal statements and its examples from practice. Section 4 discusses the methodological flaws with the Manual's effort to support its doctrinal assertions.

2 CUSTOMARY LAW ON PRECAUTIONS IN ATTACK AND TARGET VERIFICATION: THE DYNAMIC DILIGENCE MODEL

The twin touchstones of IHL are humanity and military necessity.[21] From this balance, international law derives the principle of distinction, and the rules of proportionality, and precautions in attack. The concept of reasonableness is the correct standard for integrating these principles.

The principle of distinction provides that a State may only target combatants or military objectives.[22] Permissible targets include not only uniformed forces, but nominal civilians who directly participate in hostilities (DPH). The rule of proportionality prohibits attacks that would, based on the standpoint of the commander considering whether to engage in the attack, cause harm to civilian persons or objects that would be "excessive" when compared with the military advantage anticipated.[23] The rule of precautions in attack requires a warfighter planning or engaging in an attack to take all "feasible" precautions to reduce harm to civilian persons and objects.[24]

Strong authority supports the proposition that the duty to take feasible precautions supplements both distinction *and* proportionality.[25] According to Article 57 of AP I, which sets out duties regarding "precautions in attack,"

---

[19] 323 US 214, 244 (1944) (Jackson, J., dissenting).   [20] 256 US 335, 343 (1921).
[21] Schmitt (above note 1).
[22] See AP I, Art. 48 (noting obligation to distinguish between civilians and combatants).
[23] *Ibid.*, Art. 57(2)(a)(iii); M. A. Newton and L. May, *Proportionality in International Law* (New York: Oxford University Press, 2014), 4.
[24] AP I, Art. 57(2)(a)(i).   [25] Corn and Schoettler (above note 9).

"constant care" is required in efforts to reduce harm to civilians.[26] To be constant in the sense that Article 57 requires, a commander must do "everything feasible to verify that the objectives to be attacked are neither civilians nor civilian objects."[27] The duty to take feasible precautions thus must apply to *both* the selection of targets and the assessment of possible incidental harm to civilians. Precautions cannot merely be *possible*; they must also be feasible, meaning practicable under the circumstances.[28] For example, the risk of enemy fire will typically prevent a US commander planning an aerial attack on an apparent ISIS compound from sending ground troops to map each square foot of the targeted area and precisely determine the number of civilians in each location. Similarly, militaries adopt technological advancements gradually.[29] New technology is initially experimental and unproven in battle. Even once the technology is effective, it may be quite expensive to deploy.[30] However, when a decrease in effort, time, and expense makes it practicable to employ a given precaution, IHL requires that step. As the International Committee of the Red Cross (ICRC) 1987 Commentary observed, assessment of "feasible" precautions entails both "good faith" and "common sense."[31]

As noted above, taking feasible precautions is necessary for the selection and verification of targets, as well as avoidance of collateral damage. With respect to target selection, the influential 1987 Commentary of the ICRC noted that the principle of precautions in attack "appropriately supplements the basic

---

[26] AP I, Art. 57(1).

[27] *Ibid.*, Art. 57(2)(a)(i); Bothe et al. (above note 6), 405, para. 2.5 (citing the "obligation to do everything feasible to verify" that a prospective target constitutes a "military objective"); ICRC Customary IHL Study, I, 55, rule 16 ("Each party to the conflict must do everything feasible to verify that targets are military objectives"); ICRC Customary IHL Study, II, 370, para. 237 (UK requires that target verification include "everything feasible"); *ibid.*, para. 238 (US Rules of Engagement for Vietnam stated that "target must be clearly identified as hostile"); *ibid.*, 370, para. 239 (US Air Force pamphlet required "everything feasible" for target verification).

[28] Tallinn Manual 2.0, 479, para. 4 (noting that feasibility requires precautions that are "practicable or practically possible, taking into account all circumstances ruling at the time") (citations omitted).

[29] E. T. Jensen, "The Future of the Law of Armed Conflict: Ostriches, Butterflies, and Nanobots" (2015) 35 *Michigan Journal of International Law* 253–317, 257–58; S. Watts, "Regulation-Tolerant Weapons, Regulation-Resistant Weapons and the Law of War" (2015) 91 *International Law Studies* 540.

[30] M. N. Schmitt, "Precision Attack and International Humanitarian Law" (2005) 87 *International Review of the Red Cross*, 445–66, 460–61.

[31] 1987 ICRC Commentary, 682, para. 2198. E.g., even when a commander has precision-guided munitions (PGMs) available, the commander may decide to use less precise munitions for a given attack, in order to preserve the PGMs for a subsequent engagement where their attributes will be even more valuable. Schmitt (above note 30), 460–61.

rule" of distinction.[32] The tragic history of total war has cemented the relationship between the principles of distinction and precautions in attack. As the 1987 Commentary observed, armed conflicts such as World War II included numerous attacks which mistakenly targeted nonmilitary objectives, causing substantial harm to civilians and civilian objects.[33] To remedy these problems, the Commentary states that LOAC requires "precise identification of [military] objectives" to be attacked.[34] Target identification requires "great care."[35]

The need to obtain accurate formation mandates a model that this chapter calls "dynamic diligence."[36] Diligence requires that State forces take affirmative steps to gather information before definitively selecting a target. State practice reinforces this requirement. For example, the ICRC Customary Law Study quoted a 1993 DoD report to Congress on the First Gulf War as observing that the need to "properly identify" natural and cultural resources in Iraq that were off-limits for military targeting required "utilization of scarce resources" to ensure accurate intelligence collection.[37]

Diligence is dynamic because affirmative measures taken prior to an attack, such as the gathering of intelligence, will vary with prior experience and the situation on the ground. Attention to those shifting demands is a key element of what Article 57 means by the duty to take "constant care" to minimize harm to civilians. Information-gathering for targeting purposes is not merely a snapshot, frozen in time. Instead, the acquisition of information is an iterative *process*[38] that intensifies or slackens as a battlespace evolves and an armed force acquires experience from previous attacks. Consider the US conflict with the Islamic State in Iraq and Syria (ISIS). Suppose a previous attack on a particular set of structures that initially appeared to be an ISIS compound led to either mistaken targeting of civilians or excessive collateral damage. These mishaps could demonstrate that the information commanders relied on in planning and executing the ill-fated attack was inadequate, and that procedures followed in the attack were flawed. In future engagements under comparable circumstances, State forces would have a duty to revise their procedures and obtain *more* information before commencing an attack.

Customary IHL's candid acknowledgment of the effect of "doubt" in target identification and verification harmonizes with the dynamic diligence model. Article 50 of AP I states that in case of doubt, individuals are to be

---

[32] 1987 ICRC Commentary, 682, para. 2191.   [33] *Ibid.*, para. 2193.

[34] *Ibid.*, 680, para. 2194. Geoffrey Corn describes this duty as an "obligation to gather and assess all reasonably available information prior to target engagement." Corn (above note 9), 454.

[35] 1987 ICRC Commentary, 680, para. 2195.   [36] Margulies (above note 5).

[37] ICRC Customary IHL Study, I, 352, para. 123.   [38] Corn (above note 9), 456.

"considered" civilians. Article 52 suggests that in case of doubt, objects are to be "presumed" to be nonmilitary in character.[39] The doubt involved cannot be evanescent or ethereal. If even a whisper of doubt sufficed to suspend an attack, defenders who violated IHL by purposely commingling civilians and military objectives would gain an unfair advantage.[40] Rather, doubt should be "substantial" or "significant."[41] Thus crafted, the *dubio* rule effectively models an iterative process that is consistent with IHL. Suppose that a commander initially determined that a given person or object was not civilian in nature. Prior to execution of the planned attack, no information that gave rise to a significant doubt about target identification was reasonably available. In that situation, a commander could authorize execution of the planned attack. When no information that gives rise to a significant doubt about target identification is reasonably available, a commander can authorize a planned attack. However, when significant doubt arises, a commander cannot blithely ignore this countervailing evidence. Indeed, when such evidence is reasonably available, a commander must *seek it out.* At the very least, reasonably available evidence triggering doubt about target identification obliges the commander to take additional time to verify a target's status. The time needed to resolve significant doubts about a target's status can involve consultation with lawyers and with senior commanders.

The duty to investigate possible war crimes is also consistent with the norm of dynamic diligence.[42] Recent instances of such investigations include the Turkel Commission Report on actions by the Israeli Defense Force in 2010 to interdict a flotilla heading to Gaza from Turkey in violation of Israel's

---

[39] Tallinn Manual 2.0, rule 95, 424, para. 1.

[40] *Ibid.*, para. 2; S. Estreicher, "Privileging Asymmetric Warfare? Defender Duties under International Humanitarian Law" (2011) 11 *Chicago Journal of International Law* 425–37, 432–36; E. T. Jensen, "Precautions against the Effects of Attacks in Urban Areas" (2016) 98(1) *International Review of the Red Cross* 147–75, 156–57 (noting importance of defender's duty to take feasible precautions to reduce risk of harm to civilians, based in part on defender's access to and control over sites containing military objectives).

[41] Tallinn Manual 2.0, 424, para. 3 (citing UK, while noting that "[t]he precise threshold at which the doubt is sufficient . . . is unsettled"); ICRC Customary IHL Study, I, 244, para. 749 (citing Israel as observing that, "in cases of significant doubt as to whether a target is legitimate or civilian, the decision would be to refrain from attack"); A. A. Haque, *Law and Morality at War* (Oxford University Press, 2017), 108–09 (discussing customary law and State practice on standard for target identification and verification).

[42] Article 146, Convention (IV) Relative to the Protection of Civilian Persons in Time of War, Aug. 12, 1949, 75 UNTS 287 (GC IV). All of the other Geneva Conventions contain similar language. M. N. Schmitt, "Investigating Violations of International Law in Armed Conflict" (2011) 2 *Harvard National Security Journal* 31–84, 36.

blockade[43] and US Central Command's report on the 2015 attack in Kunduz, Afghanistan, in which US forces mistakenly targeted a Médecins Sans Frontières (MSF) hospital.[44] The US report is typical. It looked backward to determine whether the attack involved a war crime or instead resulted from errors that were noncriminal in nature. In addition, the US investigation identified flaws in the procedures underlying the planning and execution of the operation. The report, along with a subsequent memorandum from then Secretary of Defense Ash Carter,[45] looked *forward* by articulating "lessons learned" from this tragedy. The memorandum mandated implementation of those lessons through concrete changes to tactics, techniques, and procedures. The feedback loop illustrated by the Kunduz investigation and its aftermath is a crucial component of LOAC's "constant care" in reducing civilian harm.

The military can also use experience *proactively*, to avoid mishaps in the first place. In one of the compelling examples that make the DoD Manual essential reading, the Manual observes that in the First Gulf War the United States methodically compiled an NSL of "historical, archaeological, economic and politically sensitive installations."[46] Preparing an NSL for a particular area is a prudent and feasible precaution. It is prudent to be proactive about designating protected sites, to reduce the risk of targeting objectives that are in fact not military in character. That risk would be unreasonably high if commanders had to make ad hoc judgments about whether a particular objective had an archaeological, historical, or independent medical pedigree that precluded lawful targeting. Moreover, compiling an NSL is usually feasible, since such structures typically have locations that are known well in advance. Archaeological sites, for example, by definition have been in place for hundreds or even thousands of years. Organizations such as MSF that provide medical care routinely announce the location of their facilities, include identifying markings on such structures, and maintain

---

43 Second Report, the Turkel Commission, The Public Commission to Examine the Maritime Incident of 31 May 2010, "Israel's Mechanisms for Examining and Investigating Complaints and Claims of Violations of the Laws of Armed Conflict According to International Law," Feb. 2013, www.turkel-committee.gov.il/files/newDoc3/The%20Turkel%20Report%20for%20website.pdf.

44 United States Central Command, "Summary of the Airstrike on the MSF Trauma Center in Kunduz, Afghanistan on October 3, 2015: Investigation and Follow-on Actions," Nov. 21, 2015, info.publicintelligence.net/CENTCOM-KunduzHospitalAttack.pdf.

45 A. Carter, United States Secretary of Defense, "Memorandum Re: Investigation Review – Secretary of Defense Guidance," Apr. 28, 2016.

46 DoD Law of War Manual, ¶ 5.10.3 fn. 325; N. A. Canestaro, "Legal and Policy Constraints on the Conduct of Aerial Precision Warfare" (2004) 37 *Vanderbilt Journal of Transnational Law* 431–84, 472–73.

constant communications with relevant military forces in the area. The utility and feasibility of compiling an NSL make it a necessary precaution.

Advanced militaries also use proactive measures to comply with the principle of proportionality, which bars "excessive" collateral damage. States agree that a reasonableness standard governs the assessment of possible civilian harm.[47] To comply with the reasonableness requirement, the US uses CDE methodology.[48] CDE uses human and signals intelligence, maps, computers, lawyers, and myriad other resources to assess the likely collateral damage from a planned attack and weigh that risk against the military advantage that a commander anticipates. For example, then DoD General Counsel Jennifer O'Connor observed in a 2016 speech that US forces would use CDE to assess possible collateral damage from an attack on a bridge used by ISIS.[49] Assume that US forces have already acted consistently with dynamic diligence in determining that the bridge is a legitimate military target.[50] The commander's staff still has "a lot of homework" left to do.[51] The staff must gather intelligence on the risk of harm to civilians. That task would include information on the number of civilians who use the bridge at various points throughout the day. In addition, the staff will gather information on other bridges nearby that civilians can use if US forces destroy or damage the proposed target.[52]

The CDE or an analogous process promotes reasonable decisions on the planning and execution of attacks. While there is typically some uncertainty in estimating collateral damage, CDE provides guideposts to mark the path. Those guideposts prevent the mistakes that would result from an ad hoc attempt to assess the risk of civilian harm. Moreover, the knowledge that a CDE is required also serves as an *ex ante* constraint on careless targeting. To the extent that either a military's practice in interpreting proportionality or

---

47 DoD Law of War Manual, ¶ 5.10.2.2.
48 G. S. McNeal, "Targeted Killing and Accountability" (2014) 102 *Georgetown Law Journal* 681 (discussing CDM); L. A. Whittemore, "Proportionality Decision Making in Targeting: Heuristics, Cognitive Biases, and the Law" (2016) 7 *Harvard National Security Journal* 577. Israel also uses an extensive process. M. N. Schmitt and J. J. Merriam, "The Tyranny of Context: Israeli Targeting Practices in Legal Perspective" (2015) 37 *University of Pennsylvania Journal of International Law* 53, 73–75.
49 O'Connor (above note 8), 5.
50 At least one commentator with operational experience has argued that US targeting procedures should be more extensive, particularly in gathering information necessary for accurate target selection and verification. J. J. Merriam, "Affirmative Target Identification: Operationalizing the Principle of Distinction for U.S. Warfighters" (2016) 56 *Virginia Journal of International Law* 83–146, 132–37 (discussing flaws in the US military's "Positive Identification" targeting protocol).
51 O'Connor (above note 8).   52 *Ibid.*

the military's rules of engagement (ROE)[53] stipulate a maximum level of collateral damage, the requirement of a CDE takes off the table military actions in which it is obvious that the level of collateral damage will exceed the permissible range.

In sum, State practice regarding the principles of distinction, proportionality, and precautions in attack supports the dynamic diligence approach advanced above. A reasonable effort to acquire and assess information is the touchstone for both distinction and proportionality. The *dubio* rule operationalizes that reasonableness standard: when reasonably available evidence gives rise to significant doubt about the status of a target, a commander must take a second look at the law and/or facts before ordering an attack. The duty to take feasible precautions supplements both target selection and collateral damage assessment. As a feasible remedy for information deficits that plague warfighting, a State force may adopt a proactive approach, as the United States did in the First Gulf War in compiling NSLs that supplant ad hoc judgments about the protected status of a proposed target. Viewed in this light, dynamic diligence is an uncontroversial account of IHL's underlying principles. Unfortunately, as the next section demonstrates, the Manual introduces ambiguity about the application of those principles.

3 THE MANUAL'S MIXED SIGNALS ON THE ROLE OF PRECAUTIONS IN ATTACK AND THE STANDARD GOVERNING THE PRINCIPLE OF DISTINCTION

The Manual's treatment of precautions in attack and the standard for target identification is a case study in ambivalence. The Manual's doctrinal statements regarding the role of precautions in attacks and the standard governing target identification and verification impose narrower duties than AP I and other authoritative statements of customary law. In contrast, the Manual's rich examples are generally *consistent* with customary guidance. In other words, the Manual is at war with itself.

At the doctrinal level, the Manual and international sources part company on the relationship between distinction and proportionality and the role of precautions in attack. As explained above, international sources state that a reasonableness standard applies to both the identification of targets and

---

53   G. P. Corn, "Should the Best Offense Ever Be a Good Defense? The Public Authority to Use Force in Military Operations: Recalibrating the Use of Force Rules in the Standing Rules of Engagement" (2016) 49 *Vanderbilt Journal of Transnational Law* 1–57.

the assessment of incidental harm to civilians.[54] In contrast, the Manual asserts that a *good faith* standard governs target identification and verification,[55] while conceding that a reasonableness standard applies to proportionality. Relatedly, the Manual rejects the formulation of the *dubio* rule in AP I and in many States' account of their practice.[56] Finally, international sources, in keeping with the obligation to use "constant care" to minimize civilian harm, state that the duty to take feasible precautions supplements both target identification and collateral damage assessments.[57] However, the Manual's doctrinal analysis holds that the precautions principle only covers collateral damage assessments.[58]

When read together with the Manual's examples from US practice, these doctrinal differences with international accounts of IHL are less serious than they appear to be. The clear disconnect at the doctrinal level nonetheless blurs the guidance that the Manual aims to provide. To highlight the scope of the ambiguity that the Manual introduces, I address each doctrinal difference in turn.

First, consider the Manual's view that a commander has a duty to act in "good faith" in selecting a target. To explain its preference for good faith over reasonableness, the Manual cites the inevitability of imperfect information in the fog of war. In light of that inherent imperfection, the Manual suggests, commanders may approach target selection in a fashion that would be "unreasonable" in a civilian context.[59] The Manual also expresses concern about second-guessing commanders through hindsight bias – the after-the-fact view from the luxury of a spectator's armchair that untoward events could have turned out differently, despite the difficulties of making decisions on the spur of the moment.[60]

These concerns are legitimate. However, adopting a reasonableness standard for target selection is entirely consistent with acknowledging the inherent imperfection of information in an armed conflict and shielding commanders from undue second-guessing. Indeed, both the authorities the Manual relies on for its good faith formulation and the examples it cites actually point the way toward a reasonableness standard.

A number of the sources of State practice that the Manual cites observe that a commander's decision must be judged on the decision-maker's "assessment

---

54 Tallinn Manual 2.0, 450, para. 10. 55 DoD Law of War Manual, ¶ 5.2.3.3.
56 *Ibid.*, ¶ 5.4.3.2 ("no legal presumption of civilian status exists for persons or objects, nor is there any rule inhibiting commanders or other military personnel from acting based on the information available to him or her in doubtful cases").
57 Tallinn Manual 2.0, 479, rule 115, para. 4. 58 DoD Law of War Manual, ¶ 5.10.5.
59 *Ibid.*, ¶ 5.3.1 fn. 65. 60 *Ibid.*, ¶ 5.3.2.

of the information *reasonably available* to the person at the time."[61] Perhaps the Manual's drafters believed that the use of the adverb, "reasonably," by States in this context served only to impose a *limit* on the commander's duty. In other words, a commander need only assess information that is reasonably available. A commander need not aspire to an impossible degree of certainty, or exceed all reason in a quixotic quest for *all* data that could conceivably be relevant, no matter how elusive or obscure.[62] However, that reading of State opinion and practice does not relieve the commander of the duty to acquire and assess pertinent information about targeting selection, when such information is *reasonably* available. The best reading of reasonableness here is that it imposes both a ceiling *and* a *floor* on the commander's duty. The commander need not do *more* than is reasonable, but must not do less.

Moreover, the Manual's own examples tell the same tale. Two of the examples that the Manual cites from US practice are mentioned in the Manual's section on precautions in attack, which the Manual folds into its analysis of the principle of proportionality. However, both of these examples – the use of NSLs and consultation with senior commanders – inherently also apply to target selection.

Consider the Manual's discussion of NSLs. As noted above, the United States took a lead role in compiling NSLs to aid in target selection. Through adherence to NSLs, the United States was often able to avoid the mistaken targeting of sites of archaeological, cultural, or historic significance, or of protected sites such as hospitals.[63] Of course, an NSL will also aid feasible precautions to avoid excessive harm to civilian objects, when a commander initially targets a legitimate military objective that is located near a protected site. However, it is both artificial and inconsistent with US practice to hermetically seal off an NSL's benefits for target selection from its benefits for

---

[61] *Ibid.*, ¶ 5.3.2 fn. 66, citing United States, "Statement on Consent to Be Bound by CCW Protocol III on Incendiary Weapons" (Jan. 21, 2009); *ibid.*, fn. 67, citing, *inter alia*, Canada, "Statement on Ratification of AP I" (Nov. 20, 1990), 1591 UNTS 462, 464.

[62] W. H. Boothby, *The Law of Targeting* (Oxford University Press, 2012), 120 (recognizing that in targeting "there will always be uncertainty" which must be resolved by "the decision-makers' 'assessment of the information from all sources which is reasonably available to them at the relevant time'").

[63] DoD Law of War Manual, ¶ 5.18.4 fn. 606 (describing US practice during First Gulf War); *ibid.*, fn. 605 (citing General Dwight D. Eisenhower's directive to US commanders in World War II to "determine ... the locations of historical monuments" at or near the front lines or areas occupied by US forces); L. R. Blank, "Extending Positive Identification from Persons to Places: Terrorism, Armed Conflict, and the Identification of Military Objectives" (2013) *Utah Law Review* 1227, 1245–56 (discussing challenges of identifying and verifying military objectives in non-international armed conflicts).

incidental harm avoidance. Rather, a diligently compiled NSL promotes *both* sound target identification *and* accurate collateral damage assessment.

This functional connection between target identification and collateral damage assessment also counters the Manual's assertion that the US may make a "policy choice" to use "heightened standards of [target] identification."[64] The US may indeed make such policy choices from time to time.[65] However, the organic relationship between accurate target identification and verification on the one hand, and accurate collateral damage assessment on the other, is *not* the product of a mere "policy choice." Instead, that organic relationship reflects customary law and the dynamics of the targeting *process*. It is unpersuasive to herald a benefit for collateral damage assessment as complying with IHL, while discounting as a mere policy preference a similar benefit to target identification.

Similarly, in a lucid and insightful passage, the Manual notes that avoidance of needless incidental harm may involve "procedures for requesting higher-level approval of targets that involve high risks of incidental harm."[66] The Manual wisely notes that procedures for approval by more senior commanders "allow for a better evaluation of the expected military advantage from the attack (as it is likely that more senior commanders have a more comprehensive understanding of the strategic and operational context)."[67] Moreover, more senior commanders have a greater capacity to act on serious concerns about needless harm to civilians, since they have "greater resources under their control."[68] This safeguard unquestionably tends to reduce the risk of needless collateral damage, because a more senior commander may have a broader perspective on the interaction of civilian harm and overall strategic advantage.[69] For example, a senior commander in a counterinsurgency effort may view a given number of civilian casualties as prompting wider alienation among the civilian population, complicating State efforts to isolate insurgents. Moreover, a senior commander may have greater access to resources that can expand the range of weapons or ammunition available, including weapons that are precision-guided and thus may minimize civilian casualties.

Consultation with senior commanders will also often facilitate accurate target selection. Such consultation counteracts the effects of a cognitive flaw that can take hold in the fog of war: confirmation bias.[70] Confirmation bias

---

[64]   DoD Law of War Manual, ¶ 5.4.3.1.   [65]   Corn (above note 53).
[66]   DoD Law of War Manual, ¶ 5.10.3. The Manual's valuable discussion here and at fn. 327 relies on Corn (above note 9), 463–64.
[67]   DoD Law of War Manual, ¶ 5.10.3.   [68]   *Ibid.*   [69]   *Ibid.*, fn. 327.
[70]   D. Kahneman, *Thinking, Fast and Slow* (New York: Farrar, Straus, and Giroux, 2011), 80–81; A. Deeks, "Cognitive Biases and Proportionality Decisions: A First Look," University of

causes individuals assessing evidence to "exaggerate correlation and see it where it is not when they have a preconceived theory" of what the evidence shows.[71] Under the influence of confirmation bias, a junior commander in the heat of battle may fix on a given objective as military, even though evidence tilts against that assessment. For example, a large structure with vehicles repeatedly parking and departing in the vicinity could be an enemy stronghold or could be a hospital with an active emergency ambulance service.[72] A senior commander could point out that the evidence favored the latter interpretation, or ask for more information to confirm the junior commander's assessment. While this kind of feedback on target selection might not characterize every consultation with senior commanders, it might well occur in some subset of battlefield decisions. Here, too, it is artificially rigid to demarcate the collateral damage assessment benefits of senior command consultation and the benefits of the same safeguard for target identification and verification.

The same could be said of a technological element discussed in the Manual: the course-correction capability of precision-guided munitions (PGMs). Military personnel can change the path and direction of PGMs subsequent to launching. As the Manual acknowledges, this capability facilitates compliance with one element of the principle of precautions in attack, which requires that operators "have authority to make ... the decision to cancel or suspend an attack in light of new information" such as the unexpected proximity of civilians exceeding the CDE.[73] In that situation, an operator can modify the path of the weapon to avoid a site where the weapon would cause the threatened harm.

While the Manual focuses on the utility of course-correction for avoiding incidental civilian harm, the ability to alter a weapon's course also promotes *effective* target verification. In a given attack, evolving circumstances may

Virginia School of Law (2012), 5–7 (copy on file with the author); S. O. Lilienfeld, R. Ammirati, and K. Landfield, "Giving Debiasing Away: Can Psychological Research on Correcting Cognitive Errors Promote Human Welfare?" (2009) 4 *Perspectives on Psychological Science* 390, 391; C. Martin, "The Means–Methods Paradox and the Legality of Drone Strikes in Armed Conflict" (2015) 19 *International Journal of Human Rights* 142, 162–63; Whittemore (above note 48), 620–21.

[71] M. Rabin, "Psychology and Economics" (1998) 36 *Journal of Economic Literature* 11, 29.

[72] Similar competing interpretations helped produce the confusion about targeting that led to the tragic 2015 US attack on the MSF facility in Kunduz, Afghanistan. US Central Command (above note 44).

[73] DoD Law of War Manual, ¶ 5.11.4. While the course-correction capability of PGMs enhances the ability to cancel or suspend an attack, a State need not acquire PGMs if the State's lack of resources preclude this course. Schmitt (above note 30), 460. Similarly, a commander may determine that use of PGMs is not militarily advantageous in a particular situation. The touchstone is feasibility, informed by common sense and good faith. *Ibid.*, 461–62.

indicate that initial target identification was inaccurate. Suppose an operator launched a weapon with course-correction capability. Between the launch and the weapon's projected time of impact, suppose further that "reasonably available" information yielded significant doubt about the accuracy of target identification. In a variant of the Kunduz MSF hospital scenario, such information might include a video feed of clearly marked ambulances entering or exiting a structure suspected of being an enemy stronghold. That video evidence, coupled with the absence of fires emanating from the structure, would provide persuasive evidence that the structure was actually a hospital. To comply with the principle of distinction, the operator would then use the weapon's course-correction capability to divert the weapon from its intended target.[74] Viewed in this light, the valuable course-correction technology in PGMs can both enable effective target verification *and* reduce collateral damage. Here, too, the Manual's separation of the two goals is strained.

These examples also highlight the shaky support for the Manual's rejection of a "legal presumption of civilian status ... for persons or objects."[75] In rejecting the *dubio* rule that accompanies the presumption, the Manual rightly notes that information in war is inherently imperfect. Debunking the idea of a presumption of civilian status would be appropriate if the only alternative were the notion that *any doubt* whatsoever about an individual's status or role precludes targeting. However, these polar opposites are not the only available choices. Instead of going to extremes, a commander could agree that only "substantial"[76] or "significant"[77] doubt would trigger further inquiry. These criteria are entirely compatible with the examples that the Manual cites, such as consultation with senior commanders in appropriate instances. A "substantial" or "significant" doubt test also tracks a reasonableness standard for target identification and verification, without subjecting commanders to the paralyzing hindsight bias that the Manual rightly critiques.[78] Here, again, the Manual's examples from practice highlight the strained nature of its

---

[74]   The operator's duty would be clear under a reasonableness standard for target identification. As noted above, the Manual rejects this standard, opting instead for a good faith test. However, the Manual fails to note that the practical difference between the two standards may often be small. In our hospital attack scenario, e.g., a factfinder could infer bad faith from an operator's ignoring of video evidence that manifestly depicted the operation of a medical facility. The Manual would have provided more complete guidance if it had alerted its readers to this risk.

[75]   DoD Law of War Manual, ¶ 5.4.3.2.   [76]   Tallinn Manual 2.0, 424, para. 3.

[77]   ICRC Customary IHL Study, I, 244, para. 749 (citing Israel's statement regarding its practice).

[78]   Bothe et al. (above note 6), 320 (noting that "command decisions have to be made in the fog of battle under circumstances when clinical certainty is impossible and when the adversary is striving to conceal the true facts, to deceive and to confuse").

doctrinal divide between the respective standards for target verification and collateral damage assessment.

One benefit of the Manual's approach is its highlighting of the rule of proportionality. Impressing both commanders and their legal advisors with the importance of proportionality is a worthy goal. The Manual will enhance the values underlying LOAC if commanders internalize the complex calculus of proportionality. That salutary effect will presumably increase compliance with the rule of precautions in attack. Indeed, the drafters of the Manual may well have intended this consequence. Nevertheless, a clearer separation of the respective roles of proportionality and precautions would have been closer to the practice of other States and to customary law.

4 METHODOLOGICAL ISSUES WITH THE MANUAL'S CITATIONS TO LEGAL AUTHORITY ON THE TARGETING PROCESS

In addition to failing to justify the separation between the respective standards governing target identification and collateral damage assessment, the Manual cites inapposite case law for limiting the target selection standard to good faith. The Manual cites US Supreme Court Justice Robert Jackson's dissent in *Korematsu v. United States*[79] and Justice Oliver Wendell Holmes' opinion for the Court in *Brown v. United States.*[80] The Manual's reliance on these two opinions illustrates a problem that commentators have already noted: the poor fit between the Manual's cited authority and the assertions supposedly warranted by that authority.[81]

Reinforcing that concern about poor fit, *neither* opinion cited by the Manual as rejecting a reasonableness standard supports that proposition. Read in context, both opinions actually *affirm* the centrality of reasonableness, although they adjust the analysis of reasonableness to address exigent situations. Because the Manual's inapposite citation to Justice Jackson's dissent in *Korematsu* provides a window into the flawed methodology used by the Manual to support propositions that clash with customary law, it is helpful to unpack that citation in depth. A shorter explication of the poor fit between the Manual's doctrinal assertions and Justice Holmes's *Brown* opinion confirms the methodological problems with the Manual's approach.

---

[79] 323 US 214, 244 (1944) (Jackson, J., dissenting), cited in DoD Law of War Manual, ¶ 5.3.1 fn. 65.
[80] 256 US 335, 343 (1921), cited in DoD Law of War Manual, ¶ 5.3.1 fn. 62.
[81] Glazier (above note 18).

In *Korematsu*, the Supreme Court upheld the conviction of a US citizen for violating a military order mandating the relocation of Japanese-Americans during World War II. Invidious prejudice, combined with deliberate false-hoods promoted by US officials,[82] led the United States to take this step, despite the marked absence of evidence linking Japanese-Americans to colla-boration with hostile forces. Justice Jackson *dissented* from the Court's hold-ing. Jackson's dissent was hardly an endorsement of the government's tragically mistaken policy. It is true, as the Manual notes, that Jackson's dissent contains language that appears to impute sweeping discretion to military commanders. However, viewed in context, both Justice Jackson's language and the overall logic of his dissent clash with the Manual's conclusion. Moreover, on the broader matter of the legality of internment of civilians in an international armed conflict (IAC), the Manual itself acknowledges that IHL grants commanders far less discretion than Jackson's language appears to suggest. Experts readily recognize that the key provisions of the Geneva Conventions and the Additional Protocols, as well as modern human rights norms, all post-date Justice Jackson's opinion.

Jackson's core point is that military exigencies on occasion require measures that exceed the "limits that bind civil authority in peace."[83] Parsing the distinctions between peacetime and war, Justice Jackson acknowledged that the existence of an armed conflict required some adjustment of the "reason-able man" standard familiar to students of tort law.[84] According to Justice Jackson, the heedless importation of that civilian standard into the exigencies of armed conflict would clash with legitimate military interests. Reinforcing this point, Justice Jackson asserted, in language cited by the Manual, that the "very essence of the military job is to marshal physical force, to remove every obstacle to its effectiveness, to give it every strategic advantage."[85] However, the overall substance and tone of Justice Jackson's dissent reveal that the Justice's primary target was not those who would question unbridled military discretion, but instead the *Korematsu* majority, which voted to uphold Korematsu's forced evacuation.

To appreciate the clash between Justice Jackson's perspective and the Manual's position, consider that the disposition Jackson urged would have *substantially altered* the force of the military order at issue. Justice Jackson would have voided Korematsu's conviction for disobeying the evacuation order.[86] That proposed disposition would have made the order a dead letter.

---

[82] *Korematsu v. United States*, 584 F. Supp. 1406, 1416–19 (ND Ca. 1984).
[83] *Korematsu*, 323 US, 244 (Jackson, J., dissenting).   [84] *Ibid.*   [85] *Ibid.*   [86] *Ibid.*, 248.

Justice Jackson stopped short of stating that the military's evacuation order was illegal when issued.[87] However, if Justice Jackson's view had carried the day, any sensible military lawyer would have informed his or her commander that a future evacuation order of similar breadth would not pass muster with the courts. A wise commander would then have tailored any such order to the lawyer's advice. That tailoring would have substantially reduced the military discretion that Justice Jackson described in his dissent. Justice Jackson, who had served as Attorney General of the United States, surely understood this. The logical implications of Justice Jackson's dissent thus make his broad language on military discretion a shaky base for the Manual's claim that reasonableness does not govern target identification.

Justice Jackson's main concern in his dissent was that the *Korematsu* majority lent the arbitrary evacuation order an imprimatur under the Constitution. In his opinion for the Court, the usually libertarian-minded Justice Hugo Black scrambled to justify the forced evacuation of Japanese-Americans as a reasonable measure, asserting that the US Government had "ground for believing" in the need for evacuation.[88] In his dissent, Justice Jackson pushed back vigorously against this move. Justice Jackson sharply questioned whether the evacuation order had a "reasonable basis in necessity."[89] He remarked that "[n]o evidence whatever on that subject has been taken by this or any other court" and expressed skepticism about the "unsworn, self-serving statement" of the general responsible for the order.[90] According to Justice Jackson, the explanation for the order was not military necessity, but invidious animus: Korematsu's "crime" resulted "not from anything he did, said, or thought," but only from his national origin and ethnicity.[91]

The Manual fails in its attempt to transform Justice Jackson's critique into an endorsement of a lesser standard for military decisions. Jackson feared that the *Korematsu* majority's rush to endorse the evacuation order under a "reasonable man" standard would normalize the intrusion of arbitrary military decisions on civil constitutional authority. Of course, not *every* military order posed this risk. However, the majority's failure to push back against the arbitrary order in *Korematsu* exacerbated the hazard. In the most famous passage of his dissent, Justice Jackson predicted darkly that the *Korematsu* Court's constitutional endorsement of the evacuation order would not fade with the advent of peacetime, but would instead linger like a "loaded weapon" threatening civil liberties.[92] Justice Jackson did not choose his metaphors idly.

---

[87] However, Justice Jackson expressed serious doubts about the order's justification. *Ibid.*, 245 (noting the absence of any "real evidence" supporting the order).
[88] *Ibid.*, 218 (citation omitted). [89] *Ibid.*, 245. [90] *Ibid.* [91] *Ibid.*, 243. [92] *Ibid.*, 246.

He intended the resonance generated by the military connotations of the phrase, "loaded weapon." The language cited by the Manual on the military's wartime need to "remove every obstacle to its effectiveness ... [and] give it every strategic advantage" was meant to highlight the tension between unchecked military discretion and constitutional governance.[93] Justice Jackson's withering assessment of the military order at issue in *Korematsu* was a warning about the *dangers* of unlimited military discretion, not a celebration of such discretion's virtues.[94]

Moreover, Justice Jackson's stark characterization of military judgment probably did not accurately describe military decisions then, and certainly does not accurately describe such decisions today. To highlight the threat to constitutionalism posed by unchecked military power, Justice Jackson asserted

[93] Justice Jackson's draft dissent in *Korematsu* makes this abundantly clear. The draft dissent, which he ultimately replaced with the opinion published in US Reports, framed unchecked military discretion as a threat to constitutional values. Jackson was forthright in his condemnation of the evacuation order drafted by General John DeWitt, describing it as a "military order so unconventional in character as to raise doubts about its constitutionality." *Korematsu v. United States*, No. 22 (1944) (draft opinion) (Library of Congress, Washington, DC), 13 (*Korematsu* Draft Opinion); P. Irons, *Justice at War* (New York: Oxford University Press, 1983), 331; D. J. Hutchinson, "'The Achilles Heel' of the Constitution: Justice Jackson and the Japanese Exclusion Cases" (2002) *Supreme Court Review* 455. Moreover, Jackson described the evacuation order as wasteful and counterproductive even in military terms. Illustrating his grave doubts about the military rationale behind the evacuation order, Jackson quoted at length in his draft dissent from an *amicus curiae* brief supporting the petitioner Korematsu. General DeWitt had written a report in which he cited certain episodes involving Japanese military forces operating near the West Coast and speculated that those episodes included Japanese military communication with Japanese-Americans. As quoted by Jackson, the *amicus* brief pointed out that two of the three instances cited by General DeWitt clearly occurred *after* the internment, when the US Government closely monitored and controlled internees' external communications. *Korematsu* Draft Opinion, 10–11 n. 9. To explain this incongruity, General DeWitt would have needed explanations of how the internees managed to circumvent government monitoring and why information they learned during internment hundreds of miles inland would have had operational value to Japanese forces near the coast. The general offered no such account. Thus, General DeWitt's own justifications for the order were highly suspect. Passages such as this suggest that the sweeping view of military discretion in Jackson's published opinion was a mere rhetorical device, not a serious treatment of military judgment in practice. By deriding the evacuation order as "unconventional" in military terms, Justice Jackson appeared to affirm that *conventional* exercises of military judgment are more restrained. These more typical exercises of military authority would not assume the unchecked character of the order at issue in *Korematsu*. Therefore, they would not fit the ominous description of runaway military authority that the Manual quotes approvingly from Justice Jackson's published dissent.

[94] Justice Jackson subsequently developed this theme in the separation of powers context. *Youngstown Sheet & Tube Co. v. Sawyer*, 343 US 579, 637 (1952) (Jackson, J., concurring) (finding that President Truman had acted unconstitutionally in seizing steel mills during Korean War when federal statute appeared to preclude that remedy).

that the "very essence of the military job is to ... give it every strategic advantage."[95] However, his description of the evacuation order as "unconventional"[96] suggests that he did not view its arbitrary and invidious nature as representative of typical military orders. That clash between the evacuation order and lawful orders is even more salient today. Far from seeking *every* advantage, the US military will temper its pursuit of military advantage with compliance with the principles of distinction, proportionality, and precautions in attack, as well as other rules governing IHL.[97]

A good example of this tempered discretion is the Manual's own analysis of the limits on military authority to intern another State's civilian nationals during an armed conflict. The Manual acknowledges that such internment is permitted only when security concerns make it "absolutely necessary."[98] In addition, internees may seek periodic review of their detention by a court or administrative agency.[99] This robust regime of safeguards contrasts markedly with the blanket classification based on national origin that the *Korematsu* majority endorsed, or with the unbounded military discretion that Justice Jackson invoked as a rhetorical construct in his *Korematsu* dissent.

That is not to say that targeting, which often is driven by exigency, should contain procedural safeguards that track precisely the legal protections in an internment regime. The crucial point here is that the language on military discretion in Justice Jackson's dissent is not a reliable description of legally permissible internment in armed conflict. The precedential value of that language is minimal, given its lack of current relevance to the subject of internment that the Supreme Court confronted in *Korematsu*. The language in Justice Jackson's dissent has even less relevance to the use of lethal force in wartime targeting. Here, "Exhibit A" is Justice Jackson's own career. It is unimaginable that Justice Jackson, who after World War II served as the United States' Chief Prosecutor at the International Military Tribunals at Nuremberg, would have endorsed the lethal targeting of civilians based solely on their national origin. Indeed, imposing accountability for such targeting as a war crime was a key project of the Nuremberg tribunals in which Justice Jackson played such a prominent role.

In sum, the stark picture of unchecked military discretion that Justice Jackson sketched in the passage quoted in the Manual does not support the Manual's rejection of a reasonableness standard for target identification. Justice Jackson's dissent argued for vacating Korematsu's conviction. This

---

[95] *Korematsu v. United States*, 323 US 214, 244 (1944) (Jackson, J., dissenting).
[96] Irons (above note 93), 331.   [97] McNeal (above note 48).
[98] DoD Law of War Manual, ¶ 10.9.2.1.   [99] *Ibid.*, ¶ 10.9.2.3.

would have had the practical effect of sharply reducing the ambit of discretion that Justice Jackson described. Moreover, read in light of the fierce disagreement between Justice Jackson and the *Korematsu* majority, Jackson's invocation of sweeping military discretion was primarily a rhetorical device that highlighted the folly of the majority's effort to normalize the invidious evacuation order. Indeed, Jackson's draft dissent shows that he viewed the order as manifestly failing the test of military necessity. Finally, to the extent that Jackson actually intended his description as an accurate portrait of military judgment, that stark portrayal did not faithfully depict military judgment then or now, as the Manual's own analysis of internment criteria demonstrates.

Perhaps the Manual's citation to Jackson's dissent in *Korematsu* merely critiques mechanically importing a reasonableness standard from peacetime serenity to wartime exigencies. That critique is well-aimed. However, the Manual's failure to clearly endorse *any* kind of reasonableness standard – even one tailored to the challenges of armed conflict – suggests that the Manual's drafters intended to reject reasonableness as a guide to targeting.

The same weaknesses attend the Manual's citation to Justice Holmes's opinion for the Court in *Brown v. United States*,[100] a self-defense case in which the defendant had killed an individual while protecting himself against a knife attack. Holmes, perhaps even more than Jackson, was a vivid writer. His stirring prose at first blush supports the Manual's rejection of a reasonableness standard. Displaying his gift for aphorisms, Justice Holmes opined that, "Detached reflection cannot be demanded in the presence of an uplifted knife."[101] Rejecting a trial court's narrow instruction on the law of self-defense, Justice Holmes noted the absurdity of instructing the jury that a claim of self-defense should fail if an individual confronting deadly force could "pause to consider whether a reasonable man might not think it possible to fly with safety or to disable his assailant rather than to kill him."[102]

However, Justice Holmes's rejection of this particular instruction did not mean that Holmes rejected a reasonableness standard for self-defense. Rather, Justice Holmes stressed that the defendant could "stand his ground" only if he *"reasonably believes* that he is in immediate danger of death or grievous bodily harm from his assailant."[103] Reinforcing his recasting of reasonableness, Justice Holmes explained in commonsense fashion that, "Rationally the failure to retreat is a circumstance to be considered with all the others in order to determine whether the defendant went farther than he was justified in doing ... "[104] In considering the totality of the circumstances and rejecting

---

[100]   256 US 335, 343 (1921).   [101]   *Ibid.*   [102]   *Ibid.*   [103]   *Ibid.*, 342 (emphasis added).
[104]   *Ibid.*, 343.

a rigid focus on the possibility of retreat, Justice Holmes was actually *affirming* the appropriateness of a reasonableness standard. Justice Holmes's opinion in *Brown* therefore does not support the Manual's rejection of a reasonableness test for targeting.

Shorn of its citations to *Korematsu* and *Brown*, the Manual offers slender authority for its embrace of a targeting standard lower than reasonableness. This methodological void is a poor exemplar for the legal reasoning that the Manual expects of military lawyers. Fortunately, many of the examples from US practice that the Manual cites provide compelling evidence of US adherence to IHL. However, US military lawyers should not have to comb through the Manual's examples (often relegated to lengthy footnotes) for guidance. The Manual's examples should drive the doctrinal assertions in the Manual. Too often in the current Manual the doctrinal assertions undercut the examples' force.

5 CONCLUSION

"[C]onstant care" is not supposed to be easy. In applying the principle of precautions in attack to both target identification and assessments of collateral damage, LOAC lives out this central duty. Subjecting target identification to a reasonableness standard achieves the same vital goal. So does requiring further information-gathering or consultation when a commander has significant doubts about the status of a proposed target. The dynamic diligence model outlined in this chapter affirms these pillars of customary practice.

While the Manual's compelling examples send the same salutary signal, its doctrinal positions mask the guidance it seeks to provide. In asserting that the principle of precautions only modifies collateral damage assessment, not target identification, the Manual's doctrine clashes with customary law. The same clash occurs regarding the Manual's assertion that good faith, rather than reasonableness, governs target identification and verification.

The Manual's doctrine is inconsistent with its examples from practice, such as the United States' pioneering of NSLs or the lessons learned by the United States after the tragic, mistaken attack on the Kunduz MSF facility. The United States and other State practice cited by the Manual should be a beacon for LOAC compliance. Unfortunately, the Manual's doctrinal positions blur that guidance. The Manual's inapposite citations to legal authority compound this problem.

To sort out its mixed signals, the Manual's drafters should use its examples as a guide on the proper role of precautions and the appropriate standard for target identification and verification. Armed with those examples, the Manual's drafters can generate guidance that sends a clear message to commanders in the field. That clear message would fulfill the Manual's promise.

11

Misdirected: Targeting and Attack under the DoD Manual

Adil Ahmad Haque

1 INTRODUCTION

The stated purpose of the US Department of Defense (DoD) Law of War Manual (the Manual) "is to provide information on the law of war to DoD personnel responsible for implementing the law of war and executing military operations."[1] Unfortunately, with respect to the rules governing the conduct of hostilities, the Manual fails to achieve its stated purpose. With respect to some rules, the Manual provides insufficient information to help US forces understand and fulfill their legal obligations. With respect to other rules, the Manual provides *mis*information that, if followed, will lead US forces to violate their legal obligations.

In a previous article, I critically examined the Manual's original provisions regarding target selection, precautions in attack, and proportionality with respect to human shields.[2] Fortunately, the December 2016 updates to the Manual partially correct some of the most alarming errors of the original. Unfortunately, significant problems remain. I will briefly revisit these topics at the end of this chapter. However, my primary concerns lay elsewhere. As I wrote in my previous article, "[l]awful targeting begins with lawful targets. Problems with the Manual begin there as well."[3] It is these problems that I wish to discuss here.

When do civilians lose their protection from attack? What steps must combatants take to confirm that particular civilians are liable to attack? When must combatants refrain from attack in case of doubt? In my view, the Manual's substantive standard for the loss of civilian protection is broad

---

[1] DoD Law of War Manual, ¶ 1.1.1.
[2] A. A. Haque, "Off Target: Selection, Precaution, and Proportionality in the DoD Manual," (2016) 92 *International Law Studies* 31.
[3] *Ibid.*, 32.

and vague; its evidentiary standard for determining that specific civilians have lost their protection is weak and subjective; and its license to attack civilians in cases of doubt is unreasonable and dangerous. On each point, the Manual reflects neither the *lex lata* nor the *lex ferenda*, neither the law as it is nor the law as it should be. Moreover, the combination of these positions multiplies the risk that US forces who follow the Manual will erroneously target civilians or erroneously discount expected incidental harm to civilians. For the sake of our troops and the civilians affected by our military operations, the relevant provisions of the Manual must be revised immediately.

2 DIRECT PART IN HOSTILITIES

The Manual states that "[c]ivilians who take a direct part in hostilities forfeit protection from being made the object of attack."[4] This statement is correct, but incomplete. Under international law, civilians enjoy *general* protection against dangers arising from military operations.[5] The specific protections of the law of war merely *give effect* to this general protection.[6] Accordingly, civilians who take a direct part in hostilities not only forfeit their protection from being made the object of attack, but also forfeit their protection under the precautions rule, the proportionality rule, the prohibition on the use of human shields, and so on.

Strangely, in over 1,200 pages, the Manual never endorses the axiom that civilians enjoy general protection from which all their specific protections derive.[7] Instead, the Manual discusses direct participation in hostilities solely in the context of making civilians the object of attack. Only later does the Manual explain that the proportionality principle – which encompasses both the proportionality rule and the precautions rule – does not protect persons that may be made the object of attack.[8] Accordingly, an excessively broad and vague legal standard for direct participation in hostilities will expose civilians

---

[4] DoD Law of War Manual, ¶ 5.8.

[5] Protocol Additional to the Geneva Conventions of Aug. 12, 1949, and Relating to the Protection of Victims of International Armed Conflicts, June 8, 1977, 1125 UNTS 3 (AP I), Art. 51(1).

[6] *Ibid.*

[7] When the Manual cites AP I, Art. 51(3), in a footnote, it materially alters the text from its treaty form: "Civilians shall enjoy the protection afforded by this Section, unless and for such time as they take a direct part in hostilities," to "Civilians shall enjoy the protection [from being made the object of attack], unless and for such time as they take a direct part in hostilities." DoD Law of War Manual, ¶ 5.8.1.1 fn. 226. Importantly, the relevant section of AP I includes not only the prohibition on making civilians the object of attack but also the precautions rule, the proportionality rule, and the prohibition on using human shields.

[8] DoD Law of War Manual, ¶ 5.10.1.

not only to direct attack but also to unrestricted collateral harm, to use as human shields, to reprisal attacks, and so forth.

2.1 Direct Participation in Hostilities or "Direct Participation in Hostilities"?

The Manual states that:

> [t]his manual uses the phrase "direct part in hostilities" to indicate what activities cause a civilian to forfeit his or her protection from being made the object of attack. This usage does not mean that the United States has adopted the direct participation in hostilities rule that is expressed in Article 51 of AP I.[9]

This provision suggests that some activities will cause a civilian to forfeit his or her protection from being made the object of attack under customary law but not under AP I. Yet the Manual provides no information regarding what those activities might be. Nor does the Manual offer any evidence of State practice or opinion reflecting such a discrepancy. For example, the Manual provides no evidence that States Party to AP I and AP II apply different legal standards to conflicts to which neither treaty applies (for example, UK operations against Islamic State in Iraq and Syria (ISIS) in Syria). Conversely, this section of the Manual cites the practice of only one State that is not a party to either Protocol, in the form of an important decision of the Israeli Supreme Court.[10] As it happens, that decision states unequivocally that "all of the parts of article 51(3) of The First Protocol express customary international law."[11]

Later, the Manual states that, "[a]lthough, as drafted, Article 51(3) of AP I does not reflect customary international law, the United States supports the customary principle on which Article 51(3) is based."[12] Strangely, the Manual provides no information regarding how, as drafted, Article 51(3) of AP I diverges from customary international law. This omission seems particularly unfortunate, since the ICRC and the Israeli Supreme Court have concluded that Article 51(3) of AP I *does* reflect customary international law.[13] Ideally, the Manual would give DoD personnel reasons to rely on its contested views on such consequential matters.

---

[9] DoD Law of War Manual, ¶ 5.8.1.
[10] *Public Committee against Torture in Israel et al. v. Government of Israel et al.*, HCJ 769/02, Israel Supreme Court Sitting as the High Court of Justice (Dec. 11, 2005), cited in DoD Law of War Manual, ¶ 5.8.3.1 fn. 249.
[11] *Ibid.*, ¶ 30.   [12]   DoD Law of War Manual, ¶ 5.8.1.2.
[13] J.-M. Henckaerts and L. Doswald-Beck (eds.), *Customary International Humanitarian Law*, I: *Rules* (Cambridge University Press, 2005), 19.

Finally, the Manual states that "the terms 'active' and 'direct'... are understood to be terms of art addressing a particular legal standard, and there are a range of views as to what that legal standard means."[14] Importantly, describing "direct" as a term of art suggests that we ought not give "direct" its ordinary meaning, but instead should give it some special or technical meaning.[15] Accordingly, a civilian's participation in hostilities might not be "direct" in the ordinary meaning of the term but nevertheless "direct" in the special meaning of the term. Unfortunately, the Manual never tells us what the special or technical meaning of "direct" might be, or how it differs from the ordinary meaning of "direct."

Now, if the Manual were to explain that the meaning of "direct" should reflect its context, as well as the object and purpose of the rule in which it appears, then there might be no cause for serious concern.[16] However, it is possible that the Manual reflects a stronger position, namely that the term of art "direct" has *no* meaning of its own, but simply states a legal conclusion reached on other grounds. On the traditional view, legal reasoning proceeds as follows:

> Factual Premise: This civilian has taken a direct part in hostilities.
> Legal Conclusion: This civilian has forfeited her protection from attack.

The Manual suggests an alternative view, according to which legal reasoning should instead proceed in the opposite direction:

> Factual Premise: This civilian has engaged in certain conduct.
> Legal Conclusion 1: This civilian has forfeited her protection from attack.
> Legal Conclusion 2: This civilian has "taken a direct part in hostilities," in the special meaning of those terms.

To see why this possibility cannot be dismissed, recall the provision quoted above, which states that the Manual uses the phrase "direct part in hostilities" to *indicate* what activities cause a civilian to forfeit his or her protection. This provision suggests that the Manual does not use the phrase "direct part in hostilities," however understood, to *determine* what activities cause a civilian to forfeit his or her protection. Put another way, the phrase "direct part in hostilities," however understood, does not *describe* but merely *names* those activities which cause a civilian to forfeit his or her protection.[17] On this view,

---

[14]   DoD Law of War Manual, ¶ 5.8.1.1.
[15]   *Cf.* Vienna Convention on the Law of Treaties, Art. 31(1) with Art. 31(4).
[16]   *Cf.* Vienna Convention on the Law of Treaties, Art. 31(1).
[17]   By way of analogy, in context, "Tiny" both described and named Nate Archibald, who was indeed smaller than most of his fellow basketball players. However, even in context, "Tiny"

DoD personnel learn nothing about a civilian's legal status by asking whether she "takes a direct part in hostilities." Indeed, they would be advised to mentally insert "scare quotes" around this term of art wherever it appears. For *information* on when civilians lose their protection from attack, they must look elsewhere in the Manual.

2.2 Direct Participation in Hostilities or "Effective and Substantial Contribution to the Ability to Conduct or Sustain Military Operations"?

What conduct constitutes taking a direct part in hostilities and results in liability to attack? In addition to the ordinary meaning of its terms, as well as its object and purpose, the context of the AP I rule provides two important clues. First, the term "hostilities" refers to a narrower category of conduct than distinct terms such as "military action," "military operations," and "the military effort."[18] Second, AP I defines a mercenary, in part, as any person who "is specially recruited locally or abroad in order to fight in an armed conflict" and who "does, in fact, take a direct part in the hostilities."[19] The words "in fact" indicate that a person recruited to fight in an armed conflict who takes a direct part in the hostilities does exactly what she was recruited to do. Accordingly, taking a direct part in hostilities means fighting in an armed conflict; that is, individually or jointly carrying out acts of violence regulated by the law governing the conduct of hostilities.

This view was elegantly expressed by the US Air Force in 1976, which stated that:

> taking a direct part in hostilities covers acts of war intended by their nature and purpose to strike at enemy personnel and material. Thus a civilian taking part in fighting, whether singly or as a member of a group, loses the immunity given civilians.[20]

Since AP I had not yet been adopted, the Air Force presumably took itself to be describing customary international law as it existed in 1976 and as it applied to US service members. The same view was later adopted by the International Committee of the Red Cross (ICRC), the International Criminal Tribunal for Rwanda (ICTR), the International Criminal

---

named but did not describe Tommy Lister, who was in fact larger than many of his fellow professional wrestlers.

[18] See, e.g., AP I, Arts. 52(2), 56(2), and 53(b).   [19] *Ibid.*, Art. 47.

[20] Department of the Air Force, AFP 110–31, "International Law – The Conduct of Armed Conflict and Air Operations" (1976), 5–8 (italics omitted).

Tribunal for the former Yugoslavia (ICTY), and the Special Court for Sierra Leone (SCSL).[21]

For its part, the Manual begins by stating that, "[a]t a minimum, taking a direct part in hostilities includes actions that are, by their nature and purpose, intended to cause actual harm to the enemy."[22] However, the Manual goes on to assert that "[t]aking a direct part in hostilities extends beyond merely engaging in combat and also includes certain acts that are an integral part of combat operations or that effectively and substantially contribute to an adversary's ability to conduct or sustain combat operations."[23] This passage implies that "engaging in combat" does not include "acts that are an integral part of combat operations." The better view seems to be that taking a direct part in hostilities does not extend beyond merely engaging in combat, but that engaging in combat includes acts that are an integral part of combat operations. As the US Air Force recognized in 1976, taking a direct part in hostilities means taking part in *fighting*, whether singly or *as a member of a group*.

Analytical issues aside, the substantive problem with this passage lies in its startling claim that taking a direct part in hostilities includes "certain acts that effectively and substantially contribute to an adversary's ability to conduct or sustain combat operations." I have been unable to locate a single occurrence of this purported legal standard prior to 2015. As far as I can tell, this formulation is simply an invention of the Manual.

This novel legal standard departs sharply from the ordinary meaning of "taking a direct part in hostilities," understood contextually and purposively. We can see the contrast in Table 11.1.

Under AP I, civilians may only lose protection through *direct* involvement; under the Manual, civilians may lose protection through *indirect* involvement that is *effective and substantial*.

Under AP I, civilians may only lose protection through one mode of involvement, namely *participation*. Under the Manual, civilians may also lose protection through an entirely different mode of involvement, namely *contribution*.

---

[21] ICRC, *Commentary on the Additional Protocols of 8 June 1977 to the Geneva Conventions of 12 August 1949* (Geneva: ICRC, 1987), para. 1944; N. Melzer, *Interpretive Guidance on the Notion of Direct Participation in Hostilities under International Humanitarian Law* (Geneva: ICRC, 2009), 46; *Prosecutor v. Rutaganda*, ICTR-96-3-T, Judgment (ICTR, Dec. 6, 1999), para. 100; *Prosecutor v. Galić*, Case No. IT-98-29-T, Judgment (ICTY, Dec. 5, 2003), para. 48; *Sesay*, Judgment (SCSL, Mar. 2, 2009), para. 85, 102–4; *Mbarushimana*, Decision on the Confirmation of Charges (ICC, Dec. 16, 2011), para. 148.
[22] DoD Law of War Manual, ¶ 5.8.3.   [23] *Ibid.*

TABLE 11.1 *Direct Participation in Hostilities or the Manual's Effective and Substantial Contribution*

	Quality	Mode	Object
AP I	*direct*	*part in*	*hostilities*
Manual	*effective and substantial*	*contribution to*	*ability to conduct or sustain combat operations*

Finally, under AP I, civilians may only lose protection by involving themselves *in hostilities*. Under the Manual, civilians may also lose protection by involving themselves in *the ability to conduct or sustain combat operations*.

The Manual departs substantially from the ordinary meaning of "taking a direct part in hostilities," understood in context and in light of the object and purpose of the rule, namely to carve out a specific exception to the general prohibition on attacking civilians. Instead, the Manual appears to treat "taking a direct part in hostilities" as a term of art that bears only an attenuated relationship with the legal standard that it names but apparently does not describe.

With respect to the substantive legal standard, the Manual departs from the 1976 US Air Force Manual, AP I, the ICRC, ICTY, ICTR, ICC, and SCSL. Why? On what legal basis? And to what end? When does a civilian make an effective and substantial contribution to an adversary's ability to conduct or sustain combat operations, and thereby lose her legal protection? In support of its novel standard, the Manual provides only one citation (quoted in full):

> See Guenter Lewy, America in Vietnam 232 (1978) ("We know that on occasion in Vietnam women and children placed mines and booby traps, and that villagers of all ages and sexes, willingly or under duress, served as porters, built fortifications, or engaged in other acts helping the communist forces. It is well established that once civilians act as support personnel they cease to be noncombatants and are subject to attack.").

This rather chilling passage indicates that children forced to serve as porters are subject to attack. As we have seen, it follows that attackers are not required to take feasible precautions to avoid or minimize incidental harm to such children. In addition, the proportionality rule will not prohibit an attack expected to cause incidental harm to such children, no matter how great the expected harm or how small the anticipated military advantage. The Manual's quotation of this passage, in full, suggests that DoD agrees.

To be clear, placing mines and booby traps are, by their nature and purpose, acts intended to cause actual harm to the enemy. In contrast, since neither serving as porters nor building fortifications are themselves an integral part of combat operations, these must be examples of acts that effectively and substantially contribute to an adversary's ability to conduct or sustain combat operations. For the Manual to use such inflammatory examples to illustrate its legal position, one would expect that the source at least provides strong support for the position. However, this is simply not the case.

According to the Manual, the introductory signal "see" indicates that the cited source "[c]learly supports the proposition but does not directly state it."[24] It is hardly surprising that this source does not directly state the proposition in question, which appears to be an invention of the Manual. Moreover, this source does not clearly support the proposition for which it is cited. First, according to the Manual, a source "may have been selected because its author was a particularly influential and respected international lawyer."[25] However, Guenter Lewy was not an international lawyer at all, but instead a political scientist with no legal training. As for the specific work in question, *America in Vietnam* was not a legal text, but instead a work of revisionist history.[26] The book was published almost forty years ago, and therefore does not reflect subsequent developments in State practice and opinion. The quoted passage seems to conflict with the Air Force Manual issued two years earlier, according to which civilians lose their immunity by taking part in fighting, not by contributing to the ability of others to fight. Most conspicuously, the quoted passage states a legal conclusion without providing any supporting legal argument.

Most importantly, the assertion that "once civilians act as support personnel they cease to be noncombatants and are subject to attack" is hardly "well established." Indeed, the United Kingdom seems to reject this view:

> Whether civilians are taking a direct part in hostilities is a question of fact. Civilians manning an anti-aircraft gun or engaging in sabotage of military installations are doing so. Civilians working in military vehicle maintenance depots or munitions factories or driving military transport vehicles are not,

---

[24] *Ibid.*, ¶ 1.2.4. [25] *Ibid.*, ¶ 1.2.2.1.

[26] L. Morrow, "Viet Nam Comes Home," *Time Magazine* (Apr. 23, 1979) ("Guenter Lewy, a University of Massachusetts political scientist, fired what may be the opening shot of a revisionist view of the war in his 1978 book, America in Viet Nam."); Dr. I. Horwood, review of *Triumph Forsaken: The Vietnam War, 1954–1965* (review no. 584), www.history.ac.uk/revi ews/review/584 ("There have, however, been serious revisionist histories of the Vietnam War: Guenter Lewy's America in Vietnam (1978) was an excellent early example").

but they are at risk from attacks on those objectives since military objectives may be attacked whether or not civilians are present.[27]

Presumably, civilians working in military vehicle maintenance depots or driving military transport vehicles act as support personnel, and effectively and substantially contribute to an adversary's ability to conduct or sustain combat operations. Yet, according to the UK, such civilians are not taking a direct part in hostilities and may not be the object of attack. Presumably, the UK approach would not license the deliberate targeting of children forced to serve as porters. The Manual provides no reason to rely on its novel standard and deliberately attack civilians who are not taking part in fighting, whether singly or as a member of a group.

2.3 Rules or "Considerations that May Be Relevant"?

The Manual states that "[w]hether an act by a civilian constitutes taking a direct part in hostilities is likely to depend highly on the context."[28] Indeed, the factual complexity of armed conflict cannot be overstated. Unfortunately, the Manual compounds such unavoidable factual complexity with entirely avoidable legal complexity. Rather than articulating clear legal criteria for loss of civilian protection, the Manual offers a list of *fifteen* "considerations [that] may be relevant" to making a civilian liable to attack and collateral harm:

- the degree to which the act causes harm to the opposing party's persons or objects, such as
  - whether the act is the proximate or "but for" cause of death, injury, or damage to persons or objects belonging to the opposing party; or
  - the degree to which the act is likely to affect adversely the military operations or military capacity of the opposing party;
- the degree to which the act is connected to the hostilities, such as
  - the degree to which the act is temporally or geographically near the fighting; or
  - the degree to which the act is connected to military operations;
- the specific purpose underlying the act, such as
  - whether the activity is intended to advance the war aims of one party to the conflict to the detriment of the opposing party;

---

[27] UK Ministry of Defence, *Law of Armed Conflict Manual* (Oxford University Press, 2005), ¶ 5.3.3.
[28] DoD Law of War Manual, ¶ 5.8.3.

- the military significance of the activity to the party's war effort, such as
  - the degree to which the act contributes to a party's military action against the opposing party;
  - whether the act is of comparable or greater value to a party's war effort than acts that are commonly regarded as taking a direct part in hostilities;
  - whether the act poses a significant threat to the opposing party;
- the degree to which the activity is viewed inherently or traditionally as a military one, such as
  - whether the act is traditionally performed by military forces in conducting military operations against the enemy (including combat, combat support, and combat service support functions); or
  - whether the activity involves making decisions on the conduct of hostilities, such as determining the use or application of combat power.[29]

As we shall see, this list of "considerations that may be relevant" fails to provide clear and sound legal guidance to US forces. The better approach would have been to identify the necessary and sufficient conditions for loss of civilian protection. No doubt, the application of legal criteria to specific factual contexts will require reasoned judgment. However, leaving the loss of civilian protection entirely to a multifactor "totality of the circumstances" approach seems to invite error, arbitrariness, and abuse. Such an approach does not provide combatants with clear guidance on whom they may lawfully target and does not provide civilians with clear guidance on how they may avoid becoming lawful targets.

Three features of this list make it particularly uninformative to its readers and users. First, the Manual does not identify any of the listed considerations as necessary or sufficient conditions for direct participation in hostilities. For example, could a civilian directly participate in hostilities without intending to support one party to the detriment of the other? On most views, such a "belligerent nexus" is a necessary condition for loss of protection, as it distinguishes participation in collective hostilities from perpetration of individual criminal violence.[30] Conversely, could a civilian fail to directly participate in hostilities despite making decisions on the conduct of hostilities, such as determining the use or application of combat power? On most views, planning, preparing, or commanding combat operations is a sufficient condition for direct participation in hostilities.

---

[29] *Ibid.*   [30] See, e.g., Melzer (above note 21), 58.

Second, the Manual does not explain how the listed considerations interact with one another. For example, if the degree to which the act is connected to military operations is very low, then it is hard to see how that act could constitute direct participation in hostilities even if the degree to which the act is temporally or geographically near the fighting is very high. Conversely, if an act is both the proximate and the "but for" cause of death to persons belonging to the opposing party then it is hard to see how it could fail to constitute direct participation in hostilities, even if it is both temporally and geographically far from the fighting. In addition, if an act is intended to support one party to the detriment of the other but is unlikely to cause physical harm or adversely affect military operations then it seems that the actor may be *trying* to directly participate in hostilities but is apparently failing to do so.[31]

Finally, several items on the list seem redundant. For example, what is the difference between the degree to which the act is connected to the hostilities, the degree to which the act is connected to military operations, and the degree to which the act contributes to a party's military action against the opposing party? Perhaps "military action" is meant to be broader than "military operations," which is in turn meant to be broader than "hostilities." But then why include three provisions when one – the broadest – would suffice? Similarly, what is the difference between the degree to which the act causes harm to the opposing party's persons or objects and whether the act poses a significant threat to the opposing party? The Manual should explain the distinctions that make a legal difference and eliminate those that do not.

Most importantly, several of the listed considerations are simply not relevant to civilian protection or its loss. As we have seen, temporal and geographical proximity to fighting is not, as such, relevant to whether an act constitutes direct participation in hostilities. If temporal or geographic proximity cannot outweigh competing considerations, then it is unclear how such proximity may be relevant to loss of civilian protection. Similarly, as the UK Manual makes clear, isolated acts of combat service support do not qualify as direct participation in hostilities.

The most striking of these irrelevant considerations is "whether the act is of comparable or greater value to a party's war effort than acts that are commonly regarded as taking a direct part in hostilities." Since the Manual never defines "war effort," or distinguishes it from "military action," "military operations," or "hostilities," the scope of this provision is unclear. According to the ICRC:

---

[31] Such failed attempts may express "mere sympathy or moral support for a party's cause," which the Manual acknowledges is "generally not considered taking a direct part in hostilities." DoD Law of War Manual, ¶ 5.8.3.2.

[g]enerally speaking, beyond the actual conduct of hostilities, the general war effort could be said to include all activities objectively contributing to the military defeat of the adversary (e.g. design, production and shipment of weapons and military equipment, construction or repair of roads, ports, airports, bridges, railways and other infrastructure outside the context of concrete military operations).[32]

It seems to follow that, according to the Manual, civilians who build or repair infrastructure may lose their protection from attack. After all, these activities may very well prove to be of comparable or greater value to a party's war effort than acts that are commonly regarded as taking a direct part in hostilities. For example, a road repair crew may contribute as much to a party's war effort as a truck driver who uses that road to deliver ammunition to the front lines, which the Manual states is commonly regarded as taking a direct part in hostilities.

It is axiomatic that "[t]aking a direct part in hostilities is more narrowly construed than simply making a contribution to the war effort."[33] Yet, the Manual broadly construes taking a direct part in hostilities to include making a *particularly valuable* contribution to the war effort. On this view, the difference between taking a direct part in hostilities and contributing to the war effort is not a difference in kind, but merely a difference in degree.

The Manual seems to draw this 'valuable contribution' standard from a 1989 memo written by Hays Parks, which states that:

one rule of thumb with regard to the likelihood that an individual may be subject to lawful attack is his (or her) immunity from military service if continued service in his (or her) civilian position is of greater value to a nation's war effort than that person's service in the military.[34]

This "rule of thumb" seems to entail that every civilian whose continued service in his or her civilian position is of *any* value to a nation's war effort, but who is too old, sick, or infirm to serve in the military, may be subject to lawful attack. Parks's "prime example would be civilian scientists occupying key positions in a weapons program regarded as vital to a nation's national security or war aims."[35] Evidently, such civilian scientists do not "take a direct part in hostilities" in the ordinary meaning of those terms. Moreover, Parks's rule of thumb sweeps far more broadly, and would cover any civilians better suited to civilian positions than to military service.

---

[32] Melzer (above note 21), 51. [33] UK Manual (above note 27), ¶ 2.5.2.
[34] DoD Law of War Manual, ¶ 5.8.3 fn. 245. [35] *Ibid.*

Finally, we must ask *why* the Manual insists on its novel "substantial contribution" standard and "valuable contribution" rule of thumb. After all, the Manual's illustrative examples of acts that are generally considered taking a direct part in hostilities would all satisfy the mainstream approach.[36] Conversely, the Manual's illustrative examples of activities that are generally not considered taking direct part in hostilities would all fail the mainstream approach.[37] Moreover, the Manual specifically exempts several acts that would seem to make a substantial and effective contribution to the enemy's ability to conduct or sustain military operations, including working in a munitions factory, paying taxes, and writing editorials supporting a war effort. Indeed, a wealthy individual's paying taxes may be far more valuable to the war effort than most acts that are commonly regarded as taking a direct part in hostilities – and far more valuable than that individual's own military service. Yet the Manual stipulates that such an individual retains her protection from attack.

What, then, is the point of introducing these novel standards and rules of thumb? At the end of the day, the Manual seems to depart from the mainstream approach on only two issues: targeting civilians who perform acts of combat service and combat service support; and targeting civilian scientists occupying key positions in vital weapons programs. In my view, this particular game is simply not worth the candle. As a practical matter, such civilians are regularly located in or near military objectives; those military objectives are themselves lawful targets; and incidental harm to such civilians will seldom prove excessive in relation to the concrete and direct military advantage of totally or partially destroying those military objectives. Accordingly, there is little military advantage to be gained from directly targeting such civilians rather than targeting the military objectives in, near, or with which they work. As a result, there is no pressing reason to distort the basic architecture of the law of war, according to which persons may not be targeted unless they join the armed forces of a party to an armed conflict or fight alongside them.

2.4 Conduct, Status, and Liability to Attack

Under AP I, and under the prevailing view of customary law, civilians lose their protection from attack only *for such time* as they take a direct part in hostilities.[38] This temporal limitation on liability to attack tracks the relevant

---

[36] See *ibid.*, ¶ 5.8.3.1.   [37] See *ibid.*, ¶ 5.8.3.2.
[38] J.-M. Henckaerts and L. Doswald-Beck (eds.), *Customary International Humanitarian Law*, I: *Rules* (Cambridge University Press, 2005), 19; *Public Committee against Torture in Israel et al.*

grounds for liability to attack. While combatants may be targeted at any time based on their ongoing *status, function,* or *membership* in an armed collective, civilians may only be targeted based on their current *conduct.* This fundamental distinction between status-based targeting and conduct-based targeting represents a basic structural principle at the heart of the law of war. At its core, armed conflict involves collective hostilities. Accordingly, there are two distinct ways of becoming liable to attack. One is by joining the collective; the other is by participating in the hostilities. So long as you are part of the collective, you are liable to attack even if you never participate in hostilities. So long as you participate in hostilities, you are liable to attack even if you never join the collective. The Manual effectively collapses this fundamental distinction. Or so I shall argue.

Strangely, the roughly 1,200-page Manual *never specifically discusses* the limitation that civilians lose their protection only *for such time as* they take a direct part in hostilities. The Manual does not endorse this limitation as reflecting customary law, reject it as deviating from customary law, or offer an interpretation of it that reconciles it with customary law. The Manual therefore gives no information to DoD personnel who must reconcile the Manual's view of loss of civilian protection with the treaty obligations of our coalition partners.

Instead, the Manual simply states that:

> [t]here has been a range of views about the duration for which civilians who have taken a direct part in hostilities forfeit protection from being made the object of attack.
>
> In the US approach, civilians who have taken a direct part in hostilities must not be made the object of attack after they have permanently ceased their participation because there would be no military necessity for attacking them.[39]

On this view, US forces may attack civilians who *are not taking* direct part in hostilities, if they determine that the civilians *have taken* direct part in hostilities in the past and *will take* direct part in hostilities in the future. These civilians are liable to attack not on the basis of their current conduct, but instead on the basis of their past conduct and (anticipated) future conduct.

In support of its position, the Manual cites a single example of State practice, namely the Israeli Supreme Court decision mentioned above. The Manual quotes one passage from that decision, which states that "the

---

(above note 10), para. 38 (holding that "all of the parts of article 51(3) of The First Protocol reflect customary international law, including the time requirement").

[39] DoD Law of War Manual, ¶ 5.8.34.

'revolving door' phenomenon, by which each terrorist has 'horns of the altar' (1 Kings 1:50) to grasp or a 'city of refuge' (Numbers 35:11) to flee to, to which he turns in order to rest and prepare while they grant him immunity from attack, is to be avoided."[40]

The key term in this passage is *terrorist*, the meaning of which is made clear by the immediately preceding paragraph – which the Manual does not quote – which states that:

> a civilian who has joined a terrorist organization which has become his "home", and in the framework of his role in that organization he commits a chain of hostilities, with short periods of rest between them, loses his immunity from attack "for such time" as he is committing the chain of acts. Indeed, regarding such a civilian, the rest between hostilities is nothing other than preparation for the next hostility.[41]

In other words, civilians may be liable to attack *between hostilities* only if they *join* an organized armed group and their *role* within that group is to commit a chain of hostilities. Accordingly, this decision provides no support for the view that civilians who are *not* members of armed groups may be liable to attack when they are not taking direct part in hostilities.[42]

Putting aside its dubious legal basis, how exactly is the Manual's approach supposed to work in practice? Let us distinguish between facts that *make* a civilian liable to attack and facts that *provide evidence* that a civilian is liable to attack. According to the Manual, a civilian is made liable to attack by the fact that she has participated in hostilities in the past and *will* participate again in the future. What would such a fact involve? One possibility refers to the civilian's *present intention*: if the civilian intends to participate in the future, then she remains liable to attack; if she intends not to participate in the future, then she regains her protection from attack. As we have seen, the present intention to participate in hostilities may be *necessary* for liability to attack, since such an intention creates a belligerent nexus. However, there is no obvious legal basis for the view that the present intention to participate in hostilities may be *sufficient* for liability to attack.

Another possibility refers to the civilian's *future intention*, or to the external circumstances that would trigger such a future intention: if the civilian will

---

[40] *Public Committee against Torture in Israel et al.* (above note 10), para. 40.

[41] *Ibid.*, para. 39.

[42] We need not settle the debate over whether membership within an organized armed group is a form of direct participation in hostilities, or an alternative basis for liability to attack. The important point here is that civilians who are *neither* members of armed groups *nor* currently taking direct part in hostilities are *not* liable to attack.

form the intention to participate in the future, then she remains liable to attack; if she will not form the intention to participate in the future, then she regains her protection from attack. For example, suppose that an armed group pays or forces a civilian to participate in hostilities on one occasion. On this view, if the armed group will pay or force that civilian to participate in hostilities on a future occasion then the civilian remains liable to attack, even if she has no present intention to do so. On this view, civilians may be liable to attack based on no present fact about her – neither her current conduct nor her present intention.[43] Again, there is no obvious legal basis for this view.

Turning to *evidence* of liability, how can an attacker *know* that a civilian who is not participating in hostilities will repeat her past participation in the future? The Manual says that "[t]he assessment of whether a person has permanently ceased participation in hostilities must be based on a good faith assessment of the available information."[44] We will examine this approach in greater depth later. For now, notice that the Manual elsewhere suggests the opposite conclusion by providing that "[a]ttacks ... may not be directed against civilians or civilian objects based on merely hypothetical or speculative considerations regarding their possible current status as a military objective."

Yet, the assessment that a civilian will participate in hostilities in the future will almost always be based on merely hypothetical or speculative considerations: assessment of her present or future intentions is almost always speculative and assessment of how she will respond to external circumstances that have not yet arisen is necessarily hypothetical.

In my view, the Manual's position effectively collapses the distinction between status-based targeting and conduct-based targeting, narrowing the distinction between combatants and civilians to a vanishing point. After all, combatants also make themselves liable to attack by performing one act – joining the armed forces – and remain liable until they permanently cease participation in hostilities – by leaving the armed forces or by becoming *hors de combat*. Moreover, according to the Manual, the basis for their ongoing liability to attack is their (imputed) present intention and ability to participate in the future:

> Membership in the armed forces or belonging to an armed group makes a person liable to being made the object of attack regardless of whether he or she is taking a direct part in hostilities. This is because the organization's

---

[43]　Another view would be that a civilian remains liable to attack if she has the present conditional intention to participate in the future if certain circumstances arise. Since most intentions are conditional, we need not consider this view separately.

[44]　DoD Law of War Manual, ¶ 5.8.4.1.

hostile intent may be imputed to an individual through his or her association with the organization. Moreover, the individual, as an agent of the group, can be assigned a combat role at any time, even if the individual normally performs other functions for the group.[45]

It seems that, according to the Manual, both combatants and civilians are liable to attack when they are not participating in hostilities if they have the intention – actual or imputed, conditional or unconditional, present or future – and capacity to participate in hostilities in the future.

On this view, civilians who participate in hostilities become civilians in name only. For targeting purposes, such civilians are just like combatants: liable to attack at any time, based not on their conduct but on their intentions and abilities. As I have argued, this view distorts the basic distinction between civilians and combatants at the heart of the modern law of war.

2.5 The Myth of the "Revolving Door"

The Manual claims that civilians who are not currently taking direct part in hostilities may be liable to attack. Apparently, the Manual adopts this view in order to deny such civilians so-called "revolving door" protection,

> that is, the off-and-on protection in a case where a civilian repeatedly forfeits and regains his or her protection from being made the object of attack depending on whether or not the person is taking a direct part in hostilities at that exact time. Thus, for example, persons who are assessed to be engaged in a pattern of taking a direct part in hostilities do not regain protection from being made the object of attack in the time period between instances of taking a direct part in hostilities.[46]

As a practical matter, the "farmer by day, guerilla by night" is a semi-fictional character, and "revolving door" protection is mostly theoretical. If the information available to an attacker indicates that an individual is engaged in a pattern of taking a direct part in hostilities, then the attacker may determine in good faith (and reasonably) that the individual is functionally integrated into the armed forces or armed group alongside whom she has repeatedly fought. Simply put, a civilian who is in fact a "farmer by day, guerilla by night" will look like a guerilla and be treated as such. In those exceptional cases in which an attacker has such detailed information about an individual that she determines that the individual is repeatedly fighting for an armed group but is *not* a functional member of that group, the attacker likely has effective control

---

[45] *Ibid.,* ¶ 5.7.1.   [46] *Ibid.,* ¶ 5.8.4.2

over the area or is monitoring the individual using a remotely piloted vehicle. If the attacker has effective control over the area, then typically she can arrest, detain, or intern the individual, and kill her if she forcibly resists. If the attacker is monitoring the individual using a remotely piloted vehicle, then typically she can continue to monitor the individual and kill her if and only if she again takes a direct part in hostilities.

Accordingly, in practice, a civilian who is in fact a "farmer by day, guerilla by night" will reap the benefits of "revolving door" protection only if the attacker:

(a) knows that the civilian *is* engaged in a pattern of taking a direct part in hostilities

(b) knows that the civilian *is not* a functional member of the opposing armed group

(c) cannot arrest, detain, or intern the civilian, or kill her if she forcibly resists and

(d) cannot monitor the civilian and kill her if and only if she again takes a direct part in hostilities.

Such scenarios seem more imaginary than real. Certainly, such scenarios will occur so rarely that the desire to resolve these rare cases in favor of attackers does not warrant collapsing the fundamental distinction between conduct-based targeting of civilians and status-based targeting of combatants. We should not allow such exceptional cases to undermine the general protection of civilians.

The Manual offers two arguments in favor of its position. First, the Manual claims that "[a] 'revolving door' of protection would place these civilians who take a direct part in hostilities on a better footing than lawful combatants, who may be made the object of attack even when not taking a direct part in hostilities."[47]

Of course, in many respects, the law of war places lawful combatants on a better footing than civilians who take a direct part in hostilities. Most notably, lawful combatants are entitled to combatant immunity and prisoner of war status upon capture. In contrast, civilians may be criminally prosecuted under national law for taking a direct part in hostilities, even if they do not otherwise violate the law of war. In any event, the purpose of the law of war is not to place combatants and civilians on an equal footing, but to protect civilians to the greatest extent practically possible. As we have seen, "revolving door" protection creates little practical obstacle to effective military operations.

[47]   Ibid.

Second, the Manual claims that "[a]doption of such a rule would risk diminishing the protection of the civilian population."[48] This claim simultaneously begs the question and fails on its own terms. After all, the question in dispute is whether certain persons are protected members of the civilian population. By claiming that adoption of such a rule would risk diminishing the protection of the civilian population, the Manual simply assumes its own conclusion, namely that such persons *are not* protected members of the civilian population. Evidently, if these persons *are* protected members of the civilian population, then adoption of a rule prohibiting attacks upon them would be *required* for the protection of the civilian population.

The Manual also fails on its own terms. Presumably, civilians who have *never* taken a direct part in hostilities are protected members of the civilian population. Now, is a civilian who has never taken a direct part in hostilities more likely to be mistaken for:

(a) a civilian currently taking direct part in hostilities or
(b) a civilian currently taking direct part in hostilities *or* who has taken direct part in hostilities in the past and will again in the future?

The correct answer is (b), not only because (b) encompasses (a) but also because (b) introduces a greater risk of mistaken identity. Typically, attackers will conclude that a person is currently taking direct part in hostilities by directly observing a person's current conduct and immediately attacking the person whom they are observing. In contrast, to conclude that a person has taken direct part in hostilities in the past and will again in the future, attackers must *first* conclude that some civilian A has taken direct part in hostilities in the past and will again in the future and *then* conclude that the person in their sights, who is not currently taking direct part in hostilities, is civilian A. This additional "matching" step introduces additional risk of mistakenly targeting a civilian who has never taken direct part in hostilities.

Accordingly, which of the following two rules would most risk diminishing the protection of the civilian population?

(1) It is *never* lawful to attack a civilian who is not currently directly participating in hostilities.

or

(2) It is *sometimes* lawful to attack a civilian who is not currently directly participating in hostilities.

[48]   *Ibid.*

Clearly, the first rule is less susceptible to error, arbitrariness, and abuse. Accordingly, it is adoption of the second rule – the rule of the Manual – that would most risk diminishing the protection of the civilian population.

True, the risk of erroneously targeting civilians who have never taken direct part in hostilities could be reduced by other legal rules. Attackers could *do everything feasible to verify* that a civilian has taken direct part in hostilities in the past, and will again in the future, prior to attack. Attackers could *presume* that a civilian has not taken direct part in hostilities in the past and will not do so in the future, and refrain from attack *in case of doubt* regarding a civilian's past or future conduct. Unfortunately, as we shall see, the Manual requires no such thing. Instead, the Manual combines its broad and vague standards for loss of civilian protection with subjective and permissive rules for determining that a particular civilian satisfies those broad and vague standards. Taken together, these mistakes compound the risk that US forces who follow the Manual will erroneously attack civilians in violation of international law.

3 TARGET VERIFICATION AND THE RULE OF DOUBT

Under AP I, attackers must "do everything feasible to verify that the objectives to be attacked are neither civilians nor civilian objects and are not subject to special protection but are military objectives ... and that it is not prohibited ... to attack them."[49] AP I also provides that "[i]n case of doubt whether a person is a civilian, that person shall be considered to be a civilian."[50] On this approach, attackers must take active steps to gather evidence that confirms that a person is not protected but is instead liable to attack. If confirmation fails, and sufficient doubts remain, then the person may not be attacked.

In sharp contrast, the DoD Manual states that, "[u]nder customary international law, no legal presumption of civilian status exists for persons or objects, nor is there any rule inhibiting commanders or other military personnel from acting based on the information available to him or her in doubtful cases."[51]

On this view, attackers need not *consider* or *presume* that persons are protected civilians, and may attack persons whose liability to attack remains *in doubt* or *doubtful*. The Manual then states that "[a]ttacks, however, may not be directed against civilians or civilian objects based on merely hypothetical or speculative considerations regarding their possible current status as a military objective."[52] On this view, attackers need not *verify* or *confirm* that a person is

---

[49] AP I, Art. 57(2)(a)(1).   [50] *Ibid.*, Art. 50(1).   [51] DoD Law of War Manual, ¶ 5.4.3.2.
[52] *Ibid.*

liable to attack, so long as the decision to attack is not based on *merely hypothetical or speculative considerations.*

Finally, the Manual states that, "[i]n assessing whether a person or object that normally does not have any military purpose or use is a military objective, commanders and other decision-makers must make the decision in good faith based on the information available to them in light of the circumstances ruling at the time."[53] On this view, commanders are not required to *do everything feasible* to gather relevant information, so long as they decide to attack based on *the information available to them.* Moreover, a commander's decision to attack a person who is normally protected from attack need not be *reasonable* so long as it is made in *good faith.* Let us discuss each of these issues in turn.

3.1 Target Verification

According to the ICRC, the target verification rule – that is, the requirement to do everything feasible to verify that a target is not protected but is instead liable to attack – is now a rule of customary international law, applicable in both international armed conflicts (IACs) and non-international armed conflicts (NIACs).[54] For example, the Israeli Supreme Court decision discussed above states that:

> [i]nformation which has been most thoroughly verified is needed regarding the identity and activity of the civilian who is allegedly taking part in the hostilities ... In the case of doubt, careful verification is needed before an attack is made.[55]

Strangely, in over 1,200 pages, the DoD Manual does not discuss the target verification rule even once. The Manual does not accept, reject, modify, or amend the rule. As a result, the Manual provides DoD personnel with no information regarding the rule's application to US military operations or to coalition operations with parties to AP I.

As we have seen, while AP I clearly requires attackers to do everything feasible to *actively gather* information regarding a person's legal status prior to attack, the Manual requires only that attackers make the decision to attack based on the information *available.* The Manual does not explain whether these are two substantively different legal standards, or merely two formulations of the same legal standard. Of course, the information *available* to a commander might include both the information she *already has* and the information she *could feasibly acquire.* However, the Manual's passive voice

---

[53] *Ibid.*   [54] ICRC (above note 38), 55.
[55] *Public Committee against Torture in Israel et al.* (above note 10), para. 40.

suggests that commanders need only consider the information already in hand. In any case, this is an ambiguity too consequential to tolerate.

Interestingly, in 1976, even before AP I was adopted or entered into force, the US Army took the view that under customary international law:

> [t]hose who plan or decide upon an attack, therefore, must take all reasonable steps to ensure not only that the objectives are identified as military objectives or defended places ... but also that these objectives may be attacked without probable losses in lives and damage to property disproportionate to the military advantage anticipated.[56]

In one respect, the Army's view goes beyond AP I, anticipating the ICRC's view that, under customary international law, attackers must also "do everything feasible to assess whether the attack may be expected to cause incidental loss of civilian life, injury to civilians, damage to civilian objects, or a combination thereof, which would be excessive in relation to the concrete and direct military advantage anticipated."[57]

The Manual's neglect of the target verification rule is particularly surprising considering that it adopts its first cousin, the precautions rule, which provides that:

> [c]ombatants must take feasible precautions in planning and conducting attacks to reduce the risk of harm to civilians and other persons and objects protected from being made the object of attack.[58]

Strangely, the Manual does not say that combatants must take feasible precautions to reduce the risk of *attacking* civilians and other protected persons and objects. While the precautions rule seeks to reduce incidental or collateral harm to civilians, the target verification rule seeks to avoid misdirected attacks on civilians. It seems illogical to accept the former but neglect the latter.

More broadly, the Manual identifies seven precautions in planning and conducting attacks that may be feasible and therefore legally required.[59] Conspicuously, verifying that the target is not civilian but military is not one of them. It is hard to imagine that such an omission was not deliberate.

---

[56] Department of the Army Field Manual 27-10, The Law of Land Warfare (Washington: US Dep't. of Army, July 18, 1956, Change 1, July 15, 1976), 5.

[57] ICRC (above note 38), 58.   [58] DoD Law of War Manual, ¶ 5.8.11.

[59] *Ibid.*, ¶ 5.11. Interestingly, the Manual recognizes that assessing the risks to civilians of incidental harm from a planned attack is legally required wherever feasible.

3.2 The Rule of Doubt

As we have seen, the Manual asserts that, "[u]nder customary international law, no legal presumption of civilian status exists for persons or objects, nor is there any rule inhibiting commanders or other military personnel from acting based on the information available to him or her in doubtful cases."[60] In direct support of this claim, the Manual cites no State practice or legal opinion. Instead, the Manual cites only two sources. In a 1993 book chapter, Christopher Greenwood wrote that "it is very doubtful that Article 52(3) [of AP I] represents customary international law."[61] Similarly, in their 1982 treatise on AP I, Michael Bothe, K. J. Partsch, and Waldemar A. Solf quote a Rapporteur's observation at the Diplomatic Conference that the rule of doubt "will be a significant new addition to the law."[62] With all due respect to these distinguished authors, the Manual purports to provide "a description of the law as of the date of the manual's promulgation," not a description of the law as it existed decades ago.[63] As we shall see, even if the rule of doubt was not part of customary international law in 1977, 1982, or 1993, it is now widely accepted as part of customary international law.

Importantly, the Manual provides no evidence that States Party to AP I apply the rule of doubt in international armed conflicts but do not apply the rule of doubt in NIACs. The Manual also ignores evidence that States that are *not* party to AP I *accept* the rule of doubt as a rule of customary international law. For example, the very Israeli Supreme Court decision that the Manual cites endorses the view that:

> if a belligerent were allowed to fire at enemy civilians simply suspected of somehow planning or conspiring to plan military attacks, or of having planned or directed hostile actions, the basic foundations of international humanitarian law would be seriously undermined. The basic distinction between civilians and combatants would be called into question and the whole body of law relating to armed conflict would eventually be eroded.[64]

The Court rightly concludes that "[t]he burden of proof on the attacking army is heavy."[65]

---

[60] *Ibid.*, ¶ 5.8.4.3.2.

[61] C. Greenwood, "Customary international law and the First Geneva Protocol of 1977 in the Gulf conflict," in P. Rowe (ed.), *The Gulf War 1990–91 in International and English Law* (London: Routledge, 1993), 63, 75.

[62] M. Bothe, K. J. Partsch, W. A. Solf, *New Rules for Victims of Armed Conflicts* (The Hague/Boston/London: Martinus Nijhoff, 1982), 327.

[63] DoD Law of War Manual, ¶ 1.1.2.

[64] *Public Committee against Torture in Israel et al.* (above note 10), para. 40, quoting A. Cassese, *International Law*, 2nd ed. (Oxford University Press, 2005), 421.

[65] *Ibid.*, para 40.

As we have seen, the Manual claims that *no* legal presumption of civilian status exists for persons or objects. At the same, the Manual accepts that "[a]ttacks ... may not be directed against civilians or civilian objects based on merely hypothetical or speculative considerations regarding their possible current status as a military objective."[66] Strictly speaking, these two claims contradict one another. A legal presumption of civilian status means that attackers must treat persons as protected civilians absent evidence that they are lawful targets. Yet *evidence* is simply the converse of *merely hypothetical or speculative considerations*. Accordingly, to prohibit attacking persons based on merely hypothetical or speculative considerations regarding their possible current status is simply to prohibit attacking persons without evidence that they are lawful targets. So, the Manual, in its own way, entails that a legal presumption of civilian status exists for both persons and objects.

Unfortunately, the Manual suggests that this legal presumption of civilian status is so weak that it may be rebutted by *any amount* of evidence. Put another way, the Manual seems to *accept* a rule inhibiting commanders from acting in doubtful cases. However, that rule is apparently satisfied whenever the commander acts on information rather than mere hypothesis or speculation. Similarly, the Manual states that:

> [i]n assessing whether a person or object that normally does not have any military purpose or use is a military objective, commanders and other decision-makers must make the decision in good faith based on the information available to them in light of the circumstances ruling at the time.[67]

The Manual does not say that the assessment that a person or object is a military objective must be *supported* or *warranted* by the information available, only that this assessment must be *based* on the information available. More importantly, the Manual does not say that the decision to attack must be *reasonable* in light of the circumstances ruling at the time, only that it must be made *in good faith*. This suggests that a commander may lawfully attack a person if there is *any* evidence that she is a lawful target, provided that she does so in good faith and based on available information rather than hypothesis or speculation. Attackers must have *some* evidence that a person is a lawful target, but that evidence need not be sufficient to ground a reasonable belief or to exclude serious doubts so long as it can support a good faith decision.

Tellingly, the Manual states that, "[a]lthough doing so would impose greater restrictions than the requirements of the law of war, applying heightened standards of identification may be a policy choice to reduce the risk of

---

[66] DoD Law of War Manual, ¶ 5.8.4.3.2.   [67] *Ibid.*

incidental harm in conducting an attack."[68] By way of illustration, the Manual cites the US rule of engagement providing that "Positive Identification (PID) is required prior to engagement. PID is a reasonable certainty that the proposed target is a legitimate military target."[69] By negative implication, the Manual indicates that US forces may lawfully attack a person or object even if they are *not* reasonably certain that the proposed target is a legitimate military target.

By way of contrast, the ICRC explains that, under customary international law, "when there is a situation of doubt, a careful assessment has to be made under the conditions and restraints governing a particular situation as to whether there are sufficient indications to warrant an attack."[70]

On this view, customary international law requires a *careful assessment* of the available information, not merely a decision made *in good faith*. This formulation implies an objective standard of reasonable care that would be violated by negligence as well as by bad faith. In addition, there must be *sufficient indications to warrant an attack*, implying an objective standard of sufficient evidence that reflects the gravity of the decision to attack persons whose legal status is in doubt. On this view, an attacker's determination that a person is a lawful target must be objectively reasonable and not merely made in subjective good faith.

3.2.1 The Realities of War and the Reasonable Military Commander

As we have seen, the Manual does not support its rejection of the rule of doubt with evidence of contemporary State practice and legal opinion. Instead, the Manual offers two policy arguments. According to the Manual, "[a] legal presumption of civilian status in cases of doubt may demand a degree of certainty that would not account for the realities of war."[71] Similarly, the Manual elsewhere claims that "the importance of prevailing during armed conflict often justifies taking actions based upon limited information that would be considered unreasonable *outside armed conflict*."[72] Notably, the

---

[68] *Ibid.*, ¶ 5.4.3.1.   [69] *Ibid.*   [70] ICRC (above note 38), 24.

[71] DoD Law of War Manual, ¶ 5.4.3.2.

[72] *Ibid.*, ¶ 5.3.1. In support of this proposition, the Manual cites the following source, which neither states nor clearly supports the proposition: *Korematsu v. United States*, 323 US 214, 244 (1944) (Jackson, J., dissenting) ("The very essence of the military job is to marshal physical force, to remove every obstacle to its effectiveness, to give it every strategic advantage. Defense measures will not, and often should not, be held within the limits that bind civil authority in peace. No court can require such a commander in such circumstances to act as a reasonable man; he may be unreasonably cautious and exacting. Perhaps he should be."). Evidently, to say that a commander may or should be unreasonably cautious or exacting is not to say that a commander may or should be unreasonably careless or lax.

Manual cites no examples of State parties to AP I complaining of the adverse effects of the rule of doubt on military operations, or rejecting the application of the rule of doubt to NIAC.

In fact, the prevailing interpretation of the rule of doubt fully accounts for the realities of war and considers the reasonableness of an action within the context of armed conflict, giving full weight to the circumstances ruling at the time. This standard does not apply peacetime rules to wartime actions, but instead reflects the realities of armed conflict.

For example, the expert authors of the HPCR Manual on International Law Applicable to Air and Missile Warfare concluded, without recorded objection, that the rule of doubt *is* a rule of customary international law that applies in both IACs and NIACs.[73] Importantly, the Commentary to the HPCR Manual explains that "[t]he degree of doubt necessary to preclude an attack is that which would cause a reasonable attacker in the same or similar circumstances to abstain from ordering or executing an attack."[74] According to this *reasonable attacker* standard, the decision to attack a person whose liability to attack is in doubt must be made reasonably and not merely in good faith. Importantly, the standard is that of a reasonable attacker *in the same or similar circumstances*, not that of a reasonable civilian in ordinary life or that of a reasonable police officer in a peacetime law enforcement context. Accordingly, the reasonable attacker standard fully accounts for the realities of war and the context of armed conflict.

Importantly, the Manual itself accepts a functionally equivalent legal standard for proportionality decisions and judgments, namely the standard of *the reasonable military commander*.[75] Accordingly, the Manual demands that "[t]he commander's decisions on proportionality must be reasonable."[76] Yet it seems illogical to require *reasonable* decisions regarding proportionality but only *good faith* decisions regarding liability to attack. The Manual should resolve this inconsistency by requiring reasonable decisions in both contexts.

The Manual muddies the waters somewhat by stating that "[t]he decisions and judgments required by the principle of proportionality in conducting attacks have subjective aspects."[77] Strictly speaking, a *subjective* judgment is one that is made true *by the beliefs* of the person making the judgment. Proportionality judgments are not subjective in this sense, since these judgments may be unreasonable even if made in good faith. While "there ... might

---

[73] *Commentary on the HPCR Manual on International Law Applicable to Air and Missile Warfare* (Cambridge University Press, 2013), 87 ("[i]n case of doubt as to whether a person is a civilian, that person shall be considered a civilian").

[74] *Ibid.* [75] DoD Law of War Manual, ¶ 5.10.2.2. [76] *Ibid.* [77] *Ibid.*, ¶ 5.10.2.3.

be variation in how reasonable persons would apply the principle of proportionality in a given circumstance," the space for reasonable disagreement is
not unlimited.[78] The reasonable military commander standard is therefore
objective, even though comparisons of civilian harm and military advantage
can never be *precise*.[79]

Importantly, the Manual cites a respected Committee Report to the ICTY
for the proposition that:

> [a]lthough there will be room for argument in close cases, there will be many
> cases where reasonable military commanders will agree that the injury to
> noncombatants or the damage to civilian objects was clearly disproportionate
> to the military advantage gained.[80]

Similarly, while there will be room for argument in close cases, there will be
many cases where reasonable military commanders will agree that an attack
should not have been carried out given substantial doubts regarding a person
or object's liability to attack.

In what circumstances would a reasonable attacker abstain from attack?
According to the ICRC:

> [o]bviously, the standard of doubt applicable to targeting decisions cannot be
> compared to the strict standard of doubt applicable in criminal proceedings
> but rather must reflect the level of certainty that can reasonably be achieved
> in the circumstances. In practice, this determination will have to take into
> account, *inter alia*, the intelligence available to the decision maker, the
> urgency of the situation, and the harm likely to result to the operating forces
> or to persons and objects protected against direct attack from an erroneous
> decision.[81]

On this view, the degree of doubt sufficient to preclude lawful attack varies
depending upon the relative costs of error, which naturally vary with the
circumstances. Reasonable attackers will compare the harm that an erroneous
decision to attack would inflict on protected civilians with the harm that an
erroneous decision not to attack would allow opposing forces to inflict upon
operating forces, protected persons, and protected objects. When the former
clearly outweighs the latter, substantial doubts regarding a target's liability to
attack would render an attack unreasonable. When the latter clearly outweighs

---

[78] *Ibid.*
[79] For my own views on proportionality, see A. A. Haque, *Law and Morality at War* (Oxford
University Press, 2017), Chapter 8.
[80] ICTY, Final Report to the Prosecutor by the Committee Established to Review the NATO
Bombing Campaign Against the Federal Republic of Yugoslavia (June 13, 2000), ¶ 50.
[81] Melzer (above note 21), 76.

the former, an attack may be reasonable despite substantial doubts. In close cases, reasonable attackers may disagree.

For example, if there is some reason to suspect that a group of ten young men are members of an armed group, but they pose no immediate threat and they can be effectively monitored, then in most cases it would be unreasonable to attack them. If you attack and they are in fact protected civilians, then you will kill ten protected civilians. If you refrain from attack and they turn out to be members of the armed group, then they may be effectively engaged when new information emerges or new circumstances arise. Conversely, if a van speeds toward a checkpoint despite symbolic, written, and verbal warnings to stop, and the circumstances include a pattern of suicide bombings in the area, then it may be reasonable to attack the van and, if necessary, the driver.[82] There remains a risk that the driver is a protected civilian who does not understand the warnings or who has urgent reasons to ignore them. However, the risk to operating forces, and in some cases to nearby civilians, may be sufficient to warrant an attack in the circumstances.

Several experts have endorsed such a balancing approach. A. P. V. Rogers, the General Editor of the United Kingdom's *Law of Armed Conflict Manual*, takes the view that

> If [an aircrew's] assessment is that (a) the risk to them of getting close enough to the target to identify it properly is too high, (b) that there is a real danger of incidental death, injury or damage to civilians or civilian objects because of lack of verification of the target, and (c) they or friendly forces are not in immediate danger if the attack is not carried out, there is no need for them to put themselves at risk to verify the target. Quite simply, the attack should not be carried out.[83]

Michael Schmitt takes a similar view that "[j]ust as advantage offsets collateral damage and incidental injury to some degree, so it also acts as an offset to doubt (which risks collateral damage). The greater the military advantage, the more doubt will be justified."[84] Finally, the balancing approach may capture the intent behind the stated view of the United Kingdom, among others, that "the rule of doubt does not override the commander's duty to protect the safety of troops under his command or

---

[82] Obviously, there are other feasible precautions that should be taken to further reduce risks to civilians and operating forces at checkpoints.

[83] A. P. V. Rogers, "Zero-Casualty Warfare" (2000) 82 *International Review of the Red Cross* 165, 179.

[84] M. N. Schmitt, "Fault Lines in the Law of Attack," in S. Breau and A. Jachec- Neale (eds.), *Testing the Boundaries of International Humanitarian Law* (London: British Institute of International and Comparative Law, 2006), 277, 304.

to preserve the military situation."[85] Presumably, the United Kingdom does not take the view that its forces may attack *any* person if there is *any* evidence that he or she poses *any* threat to its troops or its military situation. Instead, following Rogers, the better view is that, in certain exigent circumstances, the risk of erroneously attacking a protected civilian might be outweighed by the risk of erroneously refraining from attack.

Since reasonable military commanders will presumably take into account the relative costs of an erroneous decision, the reasonable military commander standard and the balancing approach complement one another. In close cases, reasonable military commanders may disagree about whether the risks of attack outweigh the risks of restraint or vice versa. Nevertheless, an attacker's subjective good faith cannot redeem an unreasonable decision to attack, when attacking carries a grave risk of erroneously targeting protected civilians while refraining from attack carries little risk for operating forces or the civilians they seek to protect.[86]

3.2.2 Incentives and Consequences

The Manual provides a second argument for rejecting the rule of doubt, namely that:

> [a]ffording such a presumption [of civilian status] could also encourage a defender to ignore its obligation to separate military objectives from civilians and civilian objects. For example, unprivileged belligerents may seek to take advantage of a legal presumption of civilian status. Thus, there is concern that affording such a presumption likely would increase the risk of harm to the civilian population and tend to undermine respect for the law of war.[87]

According to this argument, some unprivileged belligerents will blend with the civilian population if US forces apply the rule of doubt but distinguish themselves from the civilian population if US forces apply the Manual's good faith standard.

This argument is simply implausible. Blending with the civilian population costs unprivileged belligerents nothing – they are not entitled to lawful combatant immunity in any case – and benefits them *whichever standard US forces apply.* Even if US forces adopt the Manual's good faith standard,

---

[85] UK Manual (above note 27), ¶ 5.3.4.
[86] For my own view of how the rule of doubt should be understood and put into practice, see Haque (above note 79), Chapter 5.
[87] DoD Law of War Manual, ¶ 5.8.4.3.2.

unprivileged belligerents will *sometimes* avoid attack by blending with civilians. This expected benefit is incentive enough to blend with civilians, since doing so is costless.

Crucially, unprivileged belligerents will blend with the civilian population so long as the benefits *outweigh* the costs. Perhaps unprivileged belligerents would benefit *more* from blending with civilians if US forces apply the rule of doubt than they would benefit if US forces apply the Manual's good faith standard. However, so long as the benefits *outweigh* the costs, unprivileged belligerents will continue to blend with the civilian population.

Accordingly, it is not the rule of doubt but the Manual's rejection of it "that likely would increase the risk of harm to the civilian population." If US forces follow the Manual, unprivileged belligerents will still blend with the civilian population, while US forces will mistakenly attack more civilians in doubtful cases. Rejection of the rule of doubt brings with it serious humanitarian costs and promises no humanitarian benefit. Since both the reasonable military commander standard and the balancing approach give full weight to the military considerations ruling at the time, the rule of doubt must be recognized.

4 SELECTION, PRECAUTION, AND PROPORTIONALITY: OLD AND NEW PROBLEMS

Before concluding this chapter, let us briefly touch on three topics, discussed at greater length elsewhere.[88] On two points, the position of the Manual has changed in important respects, resolving some problems while creating new ones. On one point, the mistaken position of the Manual remains unchanged.

4.1 Target Selection

With respect to target selection, the original Manual stated that:

> AP I provides that "[w]hen a choice is possible between several military objectives for obtaining a similar military advantage, the objective to be selected shall be that the attack on which may be expected to cause the least danger to civilian lives and to civilian objects." The United States has expressed the view that this rule is not a requirement of customary international law.[89]

Indeed, the United States expressed that view in 1991. As I have argued, that view was probably mistaken in 1991, and it was certainly mistaken in 2015. The updated Manual repeats the quoted passage, but helpfully adds that:

---

[88]   Haque (above note 2).   [89]   DoD Law of War Manual (2015), 5.11.5 (the 2015 Manual).

Whether this AP I provision is consistent with customary international law would depend on how AP I Parties interpret it. If this AP I provision is interpreted as described in § 5.11.7 (Selecting Military Objectives), then this provision could be understood to be consistent with customary international law.[90]

In turn, the newly added § 5.11.7 provides that:

> when attempting to achieve a particular military advantage through an attack, a commander may confront a choice among several military objectives for achieving that advantage. When facing such a choice, provided that all other factors are equal, the object to be selected for attack shall be the object the attack on which may be expected to cause the least danger to civilian lives and to civilian objects.[91]

This provision closes most of the gap between DoD's legal views and the customary law of war, and its addition is most welcome.

Nevertheless, the updated Manual is still not quite correct. Wisely, the AP I rule applies *when a choice is possible* between targets and not only when *all other factors are equal*. The target selection rule is one of several precautions in attack and should be interpreted accordingly. On this consistent approach, a choice is *possible* if it is *feasible*, that is, if it is "practicable or practically possible, taking into account all circumstances ruling at the time, including humanitarian and military considerations."[92] Importantly, taking into account humanitarian and military considerations means *weighing* them when they conflict. There is no part of the contemporary law of war in which military advantage automatically trumps avoidable civilian harm.

Accordingly, the updated Manual is incorrect when it says that "a commander could decide to attack a military objective involving higher risks of civilian casualties because the attack on that objective affords a greater likelihood of achieving the military advantage."[93] This is too quick. In such cases, the commander must *weigh* the higher risks of civilian casualties against the greater likelihood of achieving the military advantage. If the former outweighs the latter then the target carrying greater operational risk must be selected. If the latter outweighs the former then the target carrying higher risks of civilian casualties may be selected.

Tellingly, the Manual presents the target selection rule, along with other precautions in attack, as instantiations of the proportionality principle.[94] The proportionality principle, in turn, "generally weighs the justification for acting

---

[90] DoD Law of War Manual, ¶ 5.11.7.1.   [91] *Ibid.*, ¶ 5.8.7.   [92] *Ibid.*, ¶ 5.2.3.2.
[93] *Ibid.*, ¶ 5.11.7.
[94] See, e.g., *ibid.*, ¶ 2.4.2 ("the principle of proportionality described in a more general sense in this section also underlies the affirmative duties to take feasible precautions for the protection

against the expected harms to determine whether the latter are disproportionate in comparison to the former."[95] It follows that the target selection rule, properly understood, requires weighing the justification for attacking one target rather than another against the greater expected harms of doing so.

Simply put, attackers must ask "*how much* more advantageous would it be to strike Target A rather than Target B?" and "*how much* more harm would we cause civilians by striking Target A rather than Target B?" If the answers are "slightly more advantageous" and "far more harmful" then the selection of Target A would be unlawful. In contrast, if the answers are "much more advantageous" and "somewhat more harmful" then the selection of Target A would be lawful. The Manual should inform DoD personnel of this important dimension of their precautionary obligations.

4.2 *Precautions in Attack*

Unfortunately, the same unbalanced approach infects the Manual's general treatment of precautions in attack, of which target selection is but one.[96] The Manual accepts that combatants must take feasible precautions in planning and conducting attacks to reduce the risk of harm to civilians. Moreover, the Manual accords with well-established international law by stating that "[f]easible precautions are those that are practicable or practically possible, taking into account all circumstances ruling at the time, including humanitarian and military considerations."[97] So far, so good.

Both the 2015 Manual and the 2016 Manual state that "a commander may determine that a precaution would not be feasible because it would result in increased operational risk (i.e., a risk of failing to accomplish the mission) or an increased risk of harm to his or her forces."[98] This passage suggests that *any* increased operational risk or *any* increased risk of harm to attacking forces would render a precaution infeasible. Again, this is not correct. The military considerations against taking a precaution must be weighed against the humanitarian considerations in favor of taking a precaution. If taking a precaution would slightly increase operational risk but greatly reduce risk to nearby civilians, then it is legally required. Conversely, if taking a precaution would

---

of civilians and other protected persons and objects"). In addition, Section 5.11 is entitled "Proportionality – Feasible Precautions in Conducting Attacks to Reduce the Risk of Harm to Protected Persons and Objects," and Section 5.10 identifies the precautions rule as a derivation of the proportionality principle.

95 *Ibid.*, ¶ 2.4.1.2.   96 *Ibid.*, ¶ 5.11. See also AP I, Art. 57.

97 DoD Law of War Manual, ¶ 5.2.3.2. See also ¶¶ 5.2.3 fn. 35, 5.2.3.1.

98 2015 Manual, ¶ 5.3.3.2; DoD Law of War Manual, ¶ 5.2.3.2.

greatly increase operational risk and only slightly reduce risk to nearby civilians, then it is legally optional.

As we have seen, the logic of the Manual compels such a balanced approach. According to the Manual, "the requirement to take feasible precautions should be applied as part of the principle of proportionality in conducting attacks."[99] Importantly, the proportionality principle "generally weighs the justification for acting against the expected harms to determine whether the latter are disproportionate in comparison to the former."[100] Logically, it follows that the precautions rule requires weighing the justification for acting *without taking a precaution* against the expected harms of acting *without taking that precaution*.

Put another way, the proportionality *principle* grounds both the precautions *rule* and the proportionality *rule*.[101] It follows that both the precautions *rule* and the proportionality *rule* require weighing the justification for acting against the expected harms. It would be illogical to give military considerations absolute priority over humanitarian considerations under the precautions rule – which governs how an attack may be carried out – while weighing the former against the latter under the proportionality rule – which governs whether an attack may be carried out at all. Hopefully, future editions of the Manual will resolve this self-inflicted paradox.

4.3 Human Shields

The law of war categorically prohibits defending forces from using civilians as human shields, that is, from intentionally co-locating with civilians for the purpose of obstructing or discouraging attacks on military objectives.[102] Importantly, such unlawful conduct by defending forces does not relieve attacking forces of their legal obligations, including their legal obligations under the proportionality rule.[103] Put another way, such unlawful use of civilians cannot deprive the civilians used of their general legal protection – including their protection under the proportionality rule – which they retain unless they choose to directly participate in hostilities.

Unfortunately, the original Manual took the alarming position that:

Harm to the following categories of persons and objects would be understood not to prohibit attacks under the proportionality rule: (1) military objectives;

---

[99] DoD Law of War Manual, ¶ 5.11. [100] *Ibid.*, ¶ 2.4.1.2.
[101] That is, the prohibition on attacks expected to cause civilian harm that would be excessive in relation to the concrete and direct military advantage anticipated.
[102] *Ibid.*, ¶ 5.16. [103] AP I, Art. 51(8); ICRC (above note 38), 71.

(2) certain categories of individuals who may be employed in or on military objectives; and (3) human shields.[104]

On this view, an attack that incidentally harms civilians used as human shields – voluntarily or involuntarily – would be deemed proportionate no matter how great the expected harm to those civilians or how small the anticipated military advantage. The arguments offered in the original Manual for this extreme view were, in my view, extremely unpersuasive.[105]

Fortunately, the updated Manual accepts that:

> [i]f civilians are being used as human shields, provided they are not taking a direct part in hostilities, they must be considered as civilians in determining whether a planned attack would be excessive, and feasible precautions must be taken to reduce the risk of harm to them.[106]

On this balanced view, harm to human shields would be understood to prohibit attacks under the proportionality rule if and only if the expected harm is excessive in relation to the anticipated military advantage. Expected harm to human shields will not automatically render a military objective legally immune from attack. At the same time, civilians will not lose their protection under the proportionality rule due to the unlawful conduct of the defending force.

Curiously, the updated Manual goes on to assert that "the enemy use of *voluntary* human shields may be considered as a factor in assessing the legality of an attack."[107] By negative implication, the enemy use of *in*voluntary human shields may *not* be considered as a factor in assessing the legality of an attack. On this view, an attack that would be excessive if the civilians in or near the target were there by chance or by force may be excessive if the same number of civilians are there by choice. No legal argument is provided for this assertion, and its legal basis is not obvious. The proportionality rule compares two variables: civilian harm and military advantage. The fact that the civilians who will be killed or maimed in an attack are voluntary human shields does not reduce the former or increase the latter.

By way of support, the Manual refers the reader to another subsection which asserts that "[t]he party that employs human shields in an attempt to shield military objectives from attack assumes responsibility for their injury, although the attacker may share this responsibility if it fails to take feasible

---

[104]   2015 Manual, ¶ 5.12.3.   [105]   See Haque (above note 2), 58–83.
[106]   DoD Law of War Manual, ¶ 5.12.3.4.   [107]   *Ibid.* (emphasis added). See also, ¶ 5.16.4.

precautions."[108] Apparently, the enemy use of voluntary human shields may be considered as a factor in assessing the legality of an attack *because* the enemy thereby assumes responsibility for their injury. A different section of the Manual states this explicitly:

> When the attacking force causes harms that are the responsibility of the defending force due to its use of voluntary human shields or due to the employment of civilian personnel in or on military objectives, the responsibility of the defending force is a factor that may be considered in determining whether such harm is excessive.[109]

This assertion leaves us where we began. Since the responsibility of the defending force does not reduce the expected harm to civilians or increase the military advantage anticipated from attack, it is unclear how such responsibility bears on the excessiveness of the former in relation to the latter. Importantly, the responsibility of the defending force for occasioning harm to human shields does not preclude the responsibility of the attacking force for inflicting harm to human shields out of proportion to anticipated military advantage.[110]

Finally, the updated Manual provides that, "[b]ased on the facts and circumstances of a particular case, the commander may determine that persons characterized as voluntary human shields are taking a direct part in hostilities."[111] If this provision means that, in some cases, civilians serving as voluntary human shields may perform *other* acts that constitute direct participation in hostilities, then it states the obvious. However, if this provision means that, in some cases, voluntary human shielding *itself* constitutes direct participation in hostilities, then it raises many questions.

Do civilians directly participate in hostilities by voluntarily creating *physical* obstacles to military operations, as the ICRC holds?[112] Or, as others argue, do civilians also directly participate in hostilities by voluntarily creating *legal* obstacles to military operations?[113] Alternatively, do civilians directly participate in hostilities only by voluntarily creating physical obstacles as an integral part of a coordinated military operation likely to directly cause harm, as I argue

---

[108] *Ibid.*, ¶ 5.16.5. Since an earlier sentence in ¶ 5.12.3.4 says the same thing as ¶ 5.16.5, readers may wonder whether the support to the former provided by the latter is more apparent than real.

[109] *Ibid.*, ¶ 5.12.1.4.   [110] See Haque (above note 2), 47.

[111] DoD Law of War Manual, ¶ 5.12.3.4.   [112] Melzer (above note 21), 56–57.

[113] M. N. Schmitt, "Human Shields in International Humanitarian Law" (2008) 38 *Israel Yearbook on Human Rights* 17, 50–51.

elsewhere?"[114] The Manual provides no information on the law of war to DoD personnel who may confront these questions on the battlefield.

5 CONCLUSION

Contrary to its stated purpose, the Manual provides misinformation to US forces and spreads dangerous ideas to the world beyond our shores. The Manual combines an overly broad substantive standard for loss of civilian protection with an unreasonably low evidentiary standard for determining whether specific persons satisfy that broad substantive standard. This deadly combination of mistaken views multiplies the risk that US forces following the Manual will unlawfully target civilians.

The Manual has already been revised twice at the time of this writing. For the sake of our troops and the civilians affected by our military operations, the Manual must be revised again.

---

[114]   Haque (above note 79), Chapter 9.

12

Muddying the Waters: The Need for Precision-Guided Terminology in the DoD Law of War Manual

Laurie R. Blank

The law of armed conflict's delicate balance between military necessity and humanitarian protections lies at the heart of efforts to protect persons and minimize suffering during armed conflict. Essential to these efforts is the differentiation between individuals and objects that can lawfully be attacked and those that cannot – the principle of distinction, one of the "intrangressible principles" of the law.[1] As recent and current conflicts demonstrate all too well, actually distinguishing between fighters and civilians in order to assess who is a legitimate target of attack and who is not is an extraordinarily challenging task, compounded by the deliberate efforts of insurgent groups to hide among the civilian population.

In the midst of the chaos of war, the law of armed conflict's principles, definitions and rules seek both to inject and to rely upon a measure of clarity and predictability. The principles of distinction, proportionality and precautions set forth obligations for parties to a conflict to take carefully delineated steps to maximize protection for and minimize harm to civilians during conflict. At the same time, the implementation of each of these principles relies heavily on the ability of those fighting to distinguish between those who are fighting and those who are not. In order to prevent deliberate attacks on civilians, one must be able to determine who is a civilian. In order to refrain from attacks that will cause incidental harm to civilians that is excessive relative to the military advantage gained, one must be able to determine who is a civilian and what is a civilian object. Finally, in order to take constant care and other precautions to protect civilians, one must, again, be able to determine who is a civilian. Similarly, implementing legal obligations during detention operations rests, at least in part, on knowing how to classify detainees

---

[1] *Legality of the Threat or Use of Nuclear Weapons*, Advisory Opinion, 1996 ICJ, ¶ 79 (July 8) (Nuclear Weapons Opinion).

with regard to the relevant detention authority and treatment standards. Accountability mechanisms, whether courts-martial, military commissions, national courts, or international tribunals, equally rely on legal definitions and categories to ensure that those accused of violations are prosecuted in the correct forum and that the elements of any given crime are met – for example, one cannot be convicted of the war crime of unlawful attacks on civilians if the individuals attacked were not civilians.

Treaty law, most notably the Geneva Conventions of 1949 and their Additional Protocols of 1977, therefore provides definitions of, among other categories, civilian, combatant, prisoner of war, civilian object, and military objective.[2] These definitions guide military personnel, civilian leaders, judges, and others in determining how to apply the law, how to determine obligations and protections, and how to assess responsibility for incidents during conflict. Naturally, such definitions and categories also appear in national military manuals, which form the foundation for military training and operational decision-making and serve as comprehensive resources for military and civilian personnel on the applicable law during times of armed conflict.[3] The US Department of Defense (DoD) Law of War Manual (the Manual) is no exception, with countless sections and discussions devoted to presenting these definitions and categories and the relevant application of rules based on such definitions and categories. Unfortunately, rather than ensure clarity in doing so, the Manual muddies the conceptual waters, unnecessarily introducing uncertainty, confusing terminology and inconsistent definitions for the categories of persons in armed conflict.

This chapter highlights the problematic use of terminology for persons throughout the Manual, which diminishes protections for civilians, endangering the animating force and core purpose of the law of armed conflict (LOAC). This recurring terminological imprecision undermines both the Manual's effectiveness and, potentially, the law's effectiveness in fulfilling its central purposes. The first section of this chapter provides the necessary

---

[2] 1907 Hague Regulations, Art. 3; 1949 Geneva Convention III (GC III), Art. 4; Protocol Additional to the Geneva Conventions of Aug. 12, 1949, and Relating to the Protection of Victims of International Armed Conflicts, June 8, 1977, 1125 UNTS 3 (AP I), Arts. 43, 44, 50, 52.

[3] See, e.g., DoD Law of War Manual, ¶ 1.3.4 (specifying that the cornerstone purposes of the law of war include "protecting combatants, noncombatants, and civilians from unnecessary suffering" and providing "fundamental protections for persons who fall into the hands of the enemy, particularly prisoners of war, civilians, and military wounded, sick, and shipwrecked"; UK Ministry of Defence, *Law of Armed Conflict Manual* (Oxford University Press, 2005), ¶ 1.8 ("By preventing the degeneration of conflicts into brutality and savagery, the law of armed conflict aids the restoration of peace and the resumption of friendly relations between the belligerents.").

foundation for understanding the inaccuracies and counterproductive terminology in the Manual with a discussion of LOAC's core principles and their
reliance on the key categories of individuals in times of conflict, and the
essential role for clarity in the presentation, interpretation, and implementation of the law of armed conflict. Section 2 examines three critical methodological problems the Manual evinces in its murky and inconsistent
presentation of the categories of civilian and combatant, and the rules that
rest on those definitions and categories: the creation of a third class of
individuals, the conflation of conduct and status in the characterization of
individuals, and the determination of status by the privileges an individual
enjoys or does not enjoy – the reverse of the appropriate methodology. Finally,
section 3 analyzes the dangers these uncertainties and interpretative problems
create for the protection of persons during armed conflict and the effective and
consistent application of the law, most importantly the way in which the
Manual's presentation of the legal definitions, categories and rules will undermine the protection of civilians during armed conflict.

1 CORE PRINCIPLES, DEFINITIONS AND THE IMPORTANCE OF CLARITY

LOAC – otherwise known as the law of war or international humanitarian
law – governs the conduct of both States and individuals during armed conflict
and seeks to minimize suffering in war by protecting persons not participating
in hostilities and by restricting the means and methods of warfare.[4] LOAC
applies during all situations of armed conflict, with the full panoply of the
Geneva Conventions and customary law applicable in international armed
conflict (IAC) and a more limited body of conventional and customary law
applicable during non-international armed conflict (NIAC). Identifying the
status of persons in the zone of combat and their rights, obligations, and
privileges is a critical first step in order to fulfill LOAC's core goals of regulating the conduct of hostilities and protecting persons and objects during
conflict. Individual status, whether on the battlefield or off, determines
whether a person can lawfully engage in hostilities, is immune from attack,
enjoys the privileges of prisoner of war (PoW) status upon capture, and a host
of other issues.

---

[4] See International Committee of the Red Cross (ICRC), "What Is International Humanitarian
Law? "(2004), www.icrc.org/eng/assets/files/other/what_is_ihl.pdf; 1949 Geneva Convention
I (GC I); 1949 Geneva Convention II (GC II); GC III; 1949 Geneva Convention IV (GC IV);
AP I; 1977 Additional Protocol II (AP II).

One of the most fundamental issues during conflict is identifying who or what can be targeted. Indeed, LOAC's central principles governing targeting and the use of force – distinction, proportionality and precautions – can only be understood and implemented based on a firm understanding of individual status categories. The principle of distinction, one of the "cardinal principles of international humanitarian law,"[5] requires that any party to a conflict distinguish between those who are fighting and those who are not, and direct attacks solely at the former. Similarly, parties must distinguish between civilian objects and military objects and target only the latter.[6] Distinction lies at the core of LOAC's seminal goal of protecting innocent civilians and persons who are *hors de combat*. Indeed, as the Commentary to AP I emphasizes, the basic rule of distinction "is the foundation on which the codification of the laws and customs of war rests: the civilian population and civilian objects must be respected and protected in armed conflict, and for this purpose they must be distinguished from combatants and military objectives."[7] The purpose of distinction, to protect civilians, is emphasized in Article 51 of AP I, which states that "[t]he civilian population as such, as well as individual civilians, shall not be the object of attack."[8]

The principle of proportionality builds on the protection that distinction mandates for civilians and seeks to minimize incidental harm to civilians. Thus, proportionality requires that parties refrain from attacks in which the expected civilian casualties will be excessive in relation to the anticipated military advantage gained. AP I contains three separate statements of the principle of proportionality. The first appears in Article 51, which sets forth the basic parameters of the obligation to protect civilians and the civilian population, and

---

5 Nuclear Weapons Opinion (above note 1), ¶ 78 (Higgins, J., dissenting) (declaring that distinction and the prohibition on unnecessary suffering are the two cardinal principles of the law of armed conflict).

6 Article 48 of AP I sets forth the basic rule: "In order to ensure respect for and protection of the civilian population and civilian objects, the Parties to the conflict shall at all times distinguish between the civilian population and combatants and between civilian objects and military objectives and accordingly shall direct their operations only against military objectives." The principle of distinction is customary international law in both international and non-international armed conflicts. See J.-M. Henckaerts and L. Doswald-Beck (eds.), *Customary International Humanitarian Law*, I: *Rules* (Cambridge University Press, 2005), 3–8; *Prosecutor v. Tadić*, Case No. IT-94-T, Decision on Defence Motion for Interlocutory Appeal on Jurisdiction, ¶¶ 111, 127 (ICTY, Oct. 2, 1995); see *Abella v. Argentina*, Case 11.137, Inter-Am. Comm'n HR, Report No. 55/97, OEA/Ser.L/V/II.98, doc. 6 rev. ¶ 178 (1997); Nuclear Weapons Opinion (above note 1), ¶ 79; DoD Law of War Manual, ¶ 2.5; UK Manual (above note 3), ¶ 2.5.

7 ICRC, *Commentary on the Additional Protocols of 8 June 1977 to the Geneva Conventions of 12 August 1949* (Geneva: ICRC, Martinus Nijhoff, 1987), ¶ 1863.

8 AP I, Art. 51(2).

prohibits any "attack which may be expected to cause incidental loss of civilian life, injury to civilians, damage to civilian objects, or a combination thereof, which would be excessive in relation to the concrete and direct military advantage anticipated."[9] Proportionality is not a mathematical concept, but rather a guideline to help ensure that military commanders weigh the consequences of a particular attack and refrain from launching attacks that will cause excessive civilian deaths.[10] The principle of proportionality is well-accepted as an element of customary international law applicable in all armed conflicts.[11]

Finally, the principle of precautions requires that parties to a conflict take certain precautionary measures to protect civilians. At the broadest level, Article 57(1) of AP I states: "[i]n the conduct of military operations, constant care shall be taken to spare the civilian population, civilians and civilian objects."[12] Next, parties must take all feasible precautions in launching attacks that may affect the civilian population. First, parties must do everything feasible to ensure that targets are military objectives.[13] Second, they must choose the means and methods of attack with the aim of minimizing incidental civilian losses and damage.[14] In addition, when choosing between two possible attacks offering similar military advantage, AP I specifies that parties must choose the objective that offers the least likely harm to civilians and civilian objects.[15] Proportionality considerations are also a major component

---

[9] *Ibid.*, Art. 51(5)(b).

[10] M. A. Newton and L. May, *Proportionality in International Law* (Oxford University Press, 2014), 3 ("proportionality as applied within moral and legal discussions is inherently complex because it is not simply a matter of mathematical expectancy or extrapolation of a known premise").

[11] Nuclear Weapons Opinion (above note 1), 226, 587; Henckaerts and Doswald-Beck (above note 6), 46; M. N. Schmitt, "Fault Lines in the Law of Attack," in S. Breau and A. Jachec-Neale (eds.), *Testing the Boundaries of International Humanitarian Law* (BIICL, 2006), 277, 292; Y. Dinstein, "The Laws of Air, Missile and Nuclear Warfare" (1997) 27 *Israel Yearbook on Human Rights* 1, 7 (citing C. Greenwood, "Customary International Law and the First Geneva Protocol of 1977 in the Gulf Conflict," in P. Rowe (ed.), *The Gulf War 1990–91 in International and English Law* (London: Sweet & Maxwell, 1993), 63, 77).

[12] AP I, Art. 57(1).   [13] *Ibid.*, Art. 57(2)(a)(i).

[14] *Ibid.*, Art. 57(2)(a)(ii). E.g., during the 1991 Persian Gulf War, "pilots were advised to attack bridges in urban areas along a longitudinal axis. This measure was taken so that bombs that missed their targets – because they were dropped either too early or too late – would hopefully fall in the river and not on civilian housing." J.-F. Quéguiner, "Precautions Under the Law Governing the Conduct of Hostilities" (2006) 88 *International Review of the Red Cross* 793, 801 (citing M. W. Lewis, "The Law of Aerial Bombardment in the 1991 Gulf War" (2003) 97 *American Journal of International Law* 481, noting that this angle of attack "also means that damage would tend to be in the middle of the bridge and thus easier to repair"). Another common method of taking precautions is to launch attacks on particular targets at night when the civilian population is not on the streets or at work, thus minimizing potential casualties.

[15] AP I, Art. 57(3).

of the precautions framework (as evidenced in part by the Manual's amended text from its original June 2015 language to the first revision on May 31, 2016).[16] Parties are required to refrain from any attacks that would be disproportionate and to cancel any attacks where it becomes evident that the expected civilian losses would be excessive in light of the anticipated military advantage.[17] Finally, Article 57(2)(c) of AP I requires attacking parties to issue an effective advance warning "of attacks which may affect the civilian population, unless circumstances do not permit."[18]

In the detention arena as well, status of persons is the essential prerequisite for determining the authority to detain, the treatment of persons, and potential accountability mechanisms. Individuals who qualify for PoW status must be detained in accordance with the rules and obligations set forth in the Third Geneva Convention.[19] In addition, PoWs are not liable to prosecution for their lawful wartime acts, in accordance with the privilege of combatant immunity.[20] For civilians in an IAC, the Fourth Geneva Convention explicitly contemplates the detention of civilians during an IAC "only if the security of the Detaining Power makes it absolutely necessary,"[21] or during belligerent occupation for "imperative reasons of security."[22] In situations of NIAC, LOAC does not specify categories of persons for detention or other purposes, but both Common Article 3 and AP I clearly contemplate detention of one or more forms, referencing persons who have been detained and individuals who are *hors de combat* because of detention, among other reasons.[23] Although treaty law does not

---

[16] DoD Law of War Manual, ¶ 2.4.2 (proportionality "underlies the affirmative duties to take feasible precautions for the protection of civilians and other protected persons and objects").

[17] AP I, Art. 57(2)(a)(iii), 57(2)(b). [18] AP I, Art. 57(2)(c).

[19] See GC III, Art. 4 for the categories of persons eligible for PoW status.

[20] Y. Dinstein, *The Conduct of Hostilities Under the Law of International Armed Conflict*, 2nd ed. (Cambridge University Press, 2010), 35 (citing A. Rosas, *The Legal Status of Prisoners of War: A Study of International Humanitarian Law Applicable in Armed Conflicts* (Helsinki: Suomalainen Tiedeakatemia, 1976), 82) (detention of PoWs "has only one purpose: to preclude the further participation of the prisoner of war in the ongoing hostilities. The detention is not due to any criminal act committed by the prisoner of war, and he cannot be prosecuted and punished 'simply for having taken part in hostilities"). See also GC III, Arts. 87, 99; *United States v. Lindh*, 212 F. Supp. 2d 541, 553 (ED Va. 2002) ("Lawful combatant immunity, a doctrine rooted in the customary international law of war, forbids prosecution of soldiers for their lawful belligerent acts committed during the course of armed conflicts against legitimate military targets. Belligerent acts committed in armed conflict by enemy members of the armed forces may be punished as crimes under a belligerent's municipal law only to the extent that they violate international humanitarian law or are unrelated to the armed conflict. This doctrine has a long history, which is reflected in part in various early international conventions, statutes and documents.") (footnotes omitted).

[21] GC IV, Art. 42. [22] *Ibid.*, Art. 78.

[23] Common Art. 3 to the four 1949 Geneva Conventions ("Persons taking no active part in hostilities, including members of armed forces who have laid down their arms and those

provide definitions of specific categories of persons in a NIAC such as those, discussed below, for an IAC, it is well-recognized that NIAC includes categories of civilians and members of armed forces or armed groups, at a minimum.[24]

It is evident from this brief background discussion that the categorization and status of persons during armed conflict is the essential ingredient for determining what an individual's rights, obligations and privileges are in any given situation. Although countless books and articles explore the meaning and consequences of the terms combatant and civilian, along with several other key LOAC terms, a brief statement of the treaty law definitions will suffice for the purposes of the instant analysis. First, "civilian" is defined in Article 50 of AP I – a "civilian is any person who does not belong to one of the categories of persons referred to in Article 4 A (1), (2), (3) and (6) of the Third Convention and in Article 43 of this Protocol."[25] This article further explains that the "civilian population comprises all persons who are civilians."[26] There are no competing or alternative definitions of civilian in this or other LOAC treaties or customary law.

Second, the term combatant is referenced at least as far back as the 1899 and 1907 Hague Regulations, and is defined in Article 43 of AP I and with reference to Article 4 of the Third Geneva Convention. Article 43 states that "[m]embers of the armed forces of a Party to a conflict (other than medical personnel and chaplains . . .) are combatants" and then explains that the "armed forces of a Party to a conflict consist of all organized armed forces, groups and units which are under a command responsible to that Party for the conduct of its subordinates . . ."[27] When read together with Article 4 of the Third Geneva Convention and the definition of civilian above, it is thus well-established that combatants are those categories of individuals set forth in Article 4(A)(1)–(3) and (6) of the Third Geneva Convention: members of the regular armed forces of a State party to an IAC; members of volunteer militia belonging to a party to an IAC who meet the four conditions mandated in Article 4(A)(2); members of regular armed forces of a party not recognized by the detaining power; and persons fighting as a *levée en masse*.[28] As discussed in greater detail

---

placed *hors de combat* by sickness, wounds, detention, or any other cause, shall in all circumstances be treated humanely . . ."); AP II, Art. 5.

[24] N. Melzer, *Interpretive Guidance on the Notion of Direct Participation in Hostilities under International Humanitarian Law* (Geneva: ICRC, 2009), 27–28 ("all persons who are not members of State armed forces or organized armed groups of a party to the conflict are civilians" and therefore noting that "[a]s the wording and logic of Article 3 GC I–IV and 1977 Additional Protocol II (AP II) reveals, civilians, armed forces and organized armed groups of the parties to the conflict are mutually exclusive categories also in non-international armed conflict").

[25] AP I, Art. 50(1).   [26] *Ibid.*, Art. 50(2).   [27] *Ibid.*, Art. 43.
[28] GC III, Art. 4; AP I, Arts. 43, 50.

in section 2 of this chapter, LOAC identifies only two categories of persons in armed conflict: civilians and combatants in IAC and civilians and members of armed forces or organized armed groups in NIAC.

Finally, a note about the importance of clarity in the definitions – both the actual meaning of the definitions and their implementation. LOAC, and particularly the presumption-based rules regarding use-of-force authority, serves the interests of all armed forces by providing a modicum of clarity in the midst of the chaos of armed hostilities. The consequences of each definition operationally are quite stark: combatants and members of organized armed groups are legitimate targets of attack at all times, except when *hors de combat* due to sickness, wounds, or detention;[29] civilians are protected from attack at all times unless and for such time as they directly participate in hostilities.[30] Similarly, combatants and members of organized armed groups may be detained without charge until the end of hostilities, while civilians may only be detained based upon imperative needs of security and only based on an individualized determination of the threat posed and until that security threat no longer exists. The failure to provide a clear definition would effectively handicap LOAC immeasurably in its fundamental goal of regulating the conduct of hostilities and protecting persons during armed conflict.

For these reasons and many more, a former president of the International Committee of the Red Cross (ICRC) emphasized that "there is no branch of law in which complete clarity is more essential than in that of the laws of war."[31] Effective implementation of LOAC depends on the clarity of the legal principles, definitions, and categories; their application during the heat of battle; and their credible application post-hoc in investigations and prosecutions. Commanders and their forces can best adhere to the law and carry out its central tenets when the law and the obligations it imposes are predictable and operationally logical. Clarity and predictability in the form of bright-line rules also bolster the law's equally important role with regard to soldiers' moral – not

---

[29]   See, e.g., ICRC (above note 7), ¶ 1677 ("all members of the armed forces (with the ... exceptions [of medical and religious personnel]) can participate directly in hostilities, i.e., attack and be attacked"); J. Gurulé and G. S. Corn, *Principles of Counter-Terrorism Law* (St. Paul: West Academic Publishing, 2011), 70–76 (discussing the rules governing targeting of enemy forces in international and non-international armed conflict and noting that (1) "a member of an enemy force ... is presumed hostile and therefore presumptively subject to attack" in IAC and (2) "subjecting members of organized belligerent groups to status based targeting pursuant to the LOAC as opposed to civilians who periodically lose their protection from attack seems both logical and consistent with the practice of states engaged in non-international armed conflicts"); Melzer (above note 24), 28 (stating that organized armed groups are targetable based on status in NIAC).

[30]   AP I, Art. 51.   [31]   ICRC (above note 7), ¶ 1390.

just physical – well-being. Bright-line definitions provide the necessary framework for soldiers to act decisively against the enemy and, at the same time, to minimize harm to persons and objects the law seeks to protect. Such clarity also helps give soldiers a sense of confidence that the suffering they themselves have inflicted when executing an order to attack enemy forces was not only tactically necessary, but also morally justified.[32]

2 THE MANUAL'S CATEGORIES AND PROBLEMS OF METHODOLOGY

In accordance with LOAC's fundamental framework, the Manual defines the categories of persons in armed conflict and relies on these definitions and categories to delineate and elaborate on the privileges, rights, and obligations such various categories enjoy and must uphold. Unfortunately, rather than build on and reinforce the clarity for which LOAC strives in the face of the complexities of conflict, the Manual introduces additional complexities and produces the opposite effect, using multiple definitions for the terms "combatant" and "civilian" that undermine efforts to provide effective guidance for operators and decision-makers – military and civilian alike – during armed conflict. More specifically, the Manual's undisciplined use of terminology reveals three highly problematic methodological approaches that pose significant challenges for effective implementation of the law based on the Manual's guidance and risk subverting the law's core purposes.

Before addressing three key methodological problems in the Manual's presentation of the categories of persons, it is useful to note that the Manual includes multiple definitions of "civilian" and "combatant," which runs directly counter to the object and purpose of LOAC. In order for the principle of distinction to effectively fulfill its function of protecting civilians and the civilian population, "it is essential to have a clear definition of [the] categories" of "military and civilian persons."[33] The Manual offers at least three different

---

[32] For a more comprehensive discussion of the importance of clarity in LOAC's rules and presumptions regarding status of enemy forces, see G. S. Corn, L. R. Blank, C. Jenks, and E. T. Jensen, "Belligerent Targeting and the Invalidity of a Least Harmful Means Rule" (2013) 89 *International Legal Studies* 586, 613–18, 620–26.

[33] ICRC (above note 7), ¶ 1911. The Manual highlights this reason for a clear framework as well, noting that "the law of war has created a framework of classes of persons to help confine the fighting between opposing military forces and thereby to help protect the civilian population from the effects of war." DoD Law of War Manual, ¶ 4.1; J. Dill, "The DoD Law of War Manual and the False Appeal of Differentiating Different Types of Civilians," *JustSecurity.org* (Dec. 1, 2016), www.justsecurity.org/35068/dod-law-war-manual-false-appeal-differentiating-types-civilians/ ("[t]he dichotomy between civilians and combatants as exhaustive and

definitions of the term civilian. First, the Manual explains that it "generally uses 'civilian' to mean a member of the civilian population; *i.e.*, a person who is neither part of nor associated with an armed force or group, nor otherwise engaging in hostilities."[34] The very fact of "generally" using a term rather than having a firm and uncompromised definition is itself troubling, particularly in light of the need for clarity in the definition of a category that determines whether an individual is protected from attack or not. A second definition the Manual offers is in explaining that it references "persons who are 'civilians' in the sense of not being members of the military . . ."[35] Third, in the section on direct participation in hostilities, the Manual defines civilians – for the purposes of the direct participation rule – as "persons who do not fall within the categories of combatants listed in § 5.7.2 [of the Manual] (Categories of Persons Who Are Combatants for the Purpose of Assessing Their Liability to Attack)."[36] These three definitions do not share the same precise boundaries, leading to uncertainty as to the contours of the category of civilians. The drafters of AP I, where the definition of civilian appears in Article 50, specifically sought to resolve the lack of precision from multiple definitions of civilian used historically by imposing a "more rigorous definition" and imposing clarity on the definition of civilian as a negative definition conceived in opposition to a clearly defined category of combatants.[37]

In the same manner, the Manual includes at least three definitions of "combatant," creating significant confusion not only with regard to who is a combatant, but also with regard to who is a civilian, because civilians are all persons who are not combatants. First, the Manual explains that the term "combatant" in the text "generally describe[s] individuals who are not 'civilians.'"[38] In a similarly non-rigorous manner, the Manual then states that it "generally uses 'combatant' to refer implicitly to lawful or privileged combatants,"[39] meaning combatants who retain the privileges of PoW status and combatant immunity. As with the first iteration of the term "civilian" above, the use of the qualifier "generally" is highly problematic in any manual or document that seeks to set forth the law and its appropriate application. Finally, in the third definition of "combatant," the Manual introduces confusion as to just who the term "combatant" refers to, stating that "in some cases, 'combatant' . . . has been used to refer to all persons who engage in hostilities, without taking a position as to whether they are entitled to receive the

mutually exclusive categories is the core structuring principle of contemporary [international humanitarian law]").

34   DoD Law of War Manual, ¶ 4.8.1.5.   35   *Ibid.*, ¶ 10.1.1.1.   36   *Ibid.*, ¶ 5.8.2.
37   ICRC (above note 7), ¶¶ 1912–13.   38   DoD Law of War Manual, ¶ 4.3.2.
39   *Ibid.*, ¶ 4.3.2.4.

privileges of combatant status."[40] In the space of a single page, the Manual sows substantial doubt about who falls into the category of combatant and how the parameters of the category are determined.

2.1 Creating a Third Category

It is axiomatic that LOAC contains only two categories of individuals based on status: civilians and combatants (or fighters as the equivalent in NIAC).[41] The definition of civilian in treaty and customary law is the clearest reminder of this basic structure – the use of a negative definition of civilian ensures that there can be no intermediate category of persons. An individual becomes a combatant by joining the military; that is, the determination is one of membership, not one based on the individual's conduct during the conflict. Indeed, the drafters of AP I specifically sought to reinforce this framework by eliminating any space for an intermediate or third category that leaves those falling within at risk of minimized or even no protections. The Commentary explains that "[t]his should therefore dispense with the concept of 'quasi-combatants', which has sometimes been used on the basis of activities related more or less directly with the war effort. Similarly, any concept of a part-time status, a semi-civilian, semi-military status, a soldier by night and peaceful citizen by day, also disappears."[42]

In contrast, the Manual both implicitly creates and explicitly suggests a third category, although the contours of that intermediate or third category are far from clear. In discussing unprivileged belligerents, a descriptive term used to reference an individual who participates in hostilities but does not

[40] *Ibid.*, ¶ 4.3.2.3.

[41] See A. P. V. Rogers, *Law on the Battlefield* (Manchester University Press, 1996), 8; *Public Committee Against Torture in Israel et al. v. Gov't of Israel*, HCJ 769/02 (2005), ¶¶ 27–28; *Anonymous v. State of Israel*, CrimA (TA) 6659/06 (2008), ¶ 12 ("the category of 'civilians' includes everyone who is not a 'combatant'"); M. Sassòli, "Targeting: The Scope and Utility of the Concept of 'Military Objectives' for the Protection of Civilians in Contemporary Armed Conflicts," in D. Wippman and M. Evangelista (eds.), *New Wars, New Laws?: Applying the Laws of War in 21st Century Conflicts* (Chicago: Transnational, 2005), 201–2; A. Cassese, Expert Opinion on Whether Israel's Targeted Killings of Palestinian Terrorists is Consonant with International Humanitarian Law, *Public Committee Against Torture in Israel et al.*, p. 14, www.stoptorture.org/il/eng/images/uploaded/publications/64.pdf.

[42] ICRC (above note 7), ¶ 1677. See also N. Melzer, *Targeted Killing in International Law* (London: Oxford University Press, 2008), 332 ("in view of the mutually exclusive conception of the terms 'civilian' and 'combatant', the term 'unprivileged combatant' should be used exclusively for persons who are not civilians, but who, for whatever reason, have forfeited or never attained combatant privilege").

enjoy the combatant's privilege,[43] the Manual includes an entire section entitled "Rights, Duties, and Liabilities of Unprivileged Belligerents," strongly suggesting that it is a standalone category of persons in LOAC that has a separate set of protections, rights, and obligations.[44] It further explains that, although not recognized in LOAC treaties, "the category of unprivileged belligerent may be understood as an implicit consequence of creating the classes of lawful combatants and peaceful civilians."[45] One might perhaps dismiss this explicit suggestion as unfortunate drafting. However, the implicit creation of a third category bereft of protections is significantly more troubling, as a careful read of the various uses of civilian and combatant demonstrates.

To start, the Manual's most direct definition of civilian is the first referenced above: "a member of the civilian population, *i.e.*, a person who is neither part of nor associated with an armed force or group, nor otherwise engaging in hostilities."[46] Here the Manual defines civilian not solely by reference to a person's membership status – or lack thereof – as mandated by LOAC, but includes both the undefined notion of "associated with" an armed group and a conduct component to the definition of civilian. As a result, the category of "civilian" in the Manual is narrower than the category of "civilian" in LOAC treaty and customary law – the latter includes all persons who are not members of the military or an organized armed group as civilians, while the Manual includes only persons who are not members of the military or an organized armed group, persons who are not "associated with" a military or armed group, and persons who are not engaging in hostilities. A second definition of civilians, used in clarifying the reach of the direct participation in hostilities rule, includes "members of the civilian population; persons authorized to accompany the armed forces; and members of the merchant marine and civil aircraft of parties to a conflict."[47] The term "engaging in hostilities" is

---

[43] K. Dörmann, "The Legal Situation of 'Unlawful/Unprivileged Combatants'" (2003) 85 *International Review of the Red Cross* 45, 46 ("the term 'unlawful/unprivileged combatant/belligerent' is understood as describing all persons taking a direct part in hostilities without being entitled to do so and who therefore cannot be classified as prisoners of war on falling into the power of the enemy"); G. Aldrich, "The Taliban, Al Qaeda and the Determination of Illegal Combatants"(2002) 96 *American Journal of International Law* 892.

[44] DoD Law of War Manual, ¶ 4.19. In ¶ 4.3.4, the Manual explains that unprivileged belligerents includes "persons who have initially qualified as combatants . . . but who have acted so as to forfeit the privileges of combatant status by engaging in spying or sabotage" and "persons who never meet the qualifications to be entitled to the privileges of combatant status, but who have, by engaging in hostilities, incurred the corresponding liabilities of combatant status (*i.e.*, forfeited one or more of the protections of civilian status)." *Ibid.*, ¶ 4.3.4.

[45] *Ibid.*, ¶ 4.3.1.   [46] *Ibid.*, ¶ 4.8.1.5.

[47] *Ibid.*, ¶ 5.8.2. The latter two groups are drawn directly from Art. 4(A)(4) and (5) of GC III as civilians entitled to PoW status if captured.

therefore essential to understanding the contours of the category of "civilian" in the Manual's orbit, because a person who is engaging in hostilities is deemed not a member of the civilian population – and thus not a civilian.[48] According to the Manual, "engaging in hostilities" includes (1) being part of a non-State armed group by "formally joining the group or simply participating sufficiently in its activities to be deemed part of it";[49] and (2) engaging in "other hostile acts" such as bearing arms against enemy personnel or attempting to kill or injure enemy personnel.[50]

Most important, based on this second prong of "engaging in hostilities," the Manual's definitions make clear that, for the Manual, a civilian who directly participates in hostilities is not included within the category of "civilian," a remarkable departure from universally accepted treaty and customary LOAC. The very concept of direct participation in hostilities is limited to civilians – by the express terms of Article 51(3) of AP I,[51] as well as jurisprudence, military manuals, and scholarly discourse.[52] Direct participation in hostilities is not a determination of status, but rather is conduct that causes a civilian to lose immunity from attack for the time that he so participates in hostilities.[53] The Manual's framework operates in direct contravention of this established rule, suggesting that a civilian who picks up a weapon to fight is, as a result, no longer a civilian, regardless of the fact that she has not joined the military or an organized armed group. The result: diminished protection for persons during armed conflict.

Furthermore, an examination of these definitions of civilians in light of the Manual's definitions of combatant highlight two critical gaps in protection. First, if one relies on the Manual's reference to possible definitions of combatant as "individuals who are not 'civilians,'"[54] or "all persons who engage in hostilities,"[55] then persons engaging in hostilities as described immediately above could instead be defined as combatants. However, they would not

---

[48] *Ibid.*, ¶ 4.8.1.5. [49] *Ibid.*, ¶ 4.18.4.1. [50] *Ibid.*, ¶ 4.18.4.2.

[51] "Civilians shall enjoy the protection afforded by this Section, unless and for such time as they take a direct part in hostilities." AP I, Art. 51(3).

[52] *Abella v. Argentina* (above note 6), ¶ 178; *Public Committee Against Torture in Israel et al.* (above note 41), ¶¶ 31–32 ("terrorists participating in hostilities do not cease to be civilians"); Melzer (above note 24), 12, 20.

[53] See K. Watkin, *Warriors Without Rights? Combatants, Unprivileged Belligerents, and the Struggle Over Legitimacy*, Program on Humanitarian Policy and Conflict Research, Occasional Paper Series (Winter 2005), 11 ("civilians taking a direct part in hostilities lose the protection of 'civilian' status but not the status itself"); Melzer (above note 42), 310 ("civilians taking a direct part in the hostilities without becoming members of the armed forces of a party to the conflict must remain civilians, even though they temporarily lose their protection against direct attack").

[54] DoD Law of War Manual, ¶ 4.3.2. [55] *Ibid.*, ¶ 4.3.2.3.

qualify as combatants under the treaty definition in LOAC and therefore would be left in a twilight zone between LOAC's two categories. However, a more problematic and more likely result stems from the Manual's juxtaposition of civilians for the purposes of the direct participation rule and combatants for the purpose of targeting. As noted above, the former consists of members of the civilian population (for which the Manual excludes persons engaging in hostilities), persons authorized to accompany the armed forces, and merchant marine and civil aircraft crews. The latter, categorized as "Persons Who Are Combatants for the Purpose of Assessing Their Liability to Attack," include: members of armed forces, members of militia and volunteer corps, participants in a *levée en masse*, persons belonging to non-State armed groups, and "leaders whose responsibilities include the operational command and control of the armed forces or of a non-State armed group."[56] When the two provisions are read together, a person who is not a member of any armed force or non-State armed group, and is not a leader[57] but is engaging in hostilities will be neither a civilian nor a combatant. Again, such a result directly contravenes the letter and spirit of LOAC and leaves such individuals without any legal framework for protection.

2.2 *Conflating Conduct and Status*

A second methodological shortcoming in the Manual with significant consequences for the application of LOAC and the protection of persons is the steady conflation of status and conduct throughout the discussions of categories of individuals. In both treaty and customary law, an individual's status is determined solely by his or her membership – in a military or armed group – or lack of membership in such a group. Combatants or fighters are members, that is, incorporated into such groups; civilians are not. An individual's conduct on the battlefield does not change this status; rather, one's conduct can change whether one continues to be entitled to the privileges or protections normally accorded with such status. Thus, civilians who directly participate in hostilities lose their immunity to attack, but do not become combatants simply by dint of such participation. Combatants who fight in civilian clothes lose their entitlement to PoW status and combatant immunity,[58] but do not become civilians simply because they stripped off their uniforms and tried to blend in with the

---

[56] Ibid., ¶ 5.7.2.   [57] Ibid., ¶ 5.7.4.
[58] *Ex parte Quirin*, 317 US 1 (1942); *Krofan v. Public Prosecutor* (1966) (Sing.), reprinted in 1 *Malayan Law Journal* 133 (1967); 52 ILR 497 (1979).

local civilian population. This clear line between status and conduct is essential to ensuring the protection of civilians in particular.

In contrast, the Manual regularly uses conduct as the measure to categorize individuals into status categories. The Manual's exclusion of persons engaging in hostilities, when not members of the military or an armed group, from the category of civilian is merely the most egregious example of this conflation. The same flawed methodology appears in the discussion of combatants throughout the Manual, foreshadowed by the preliminary statement that "in some cases, 'combatant' . . . has been used to refer to all persons who engage in hostilities, without taking a position as to whether they are entitled to receive the privileges of combatant status."[59] In contrast to LOAC's firm delineation that only persons who affirmatively join or incorporate into an armed force, thereby subordinating themselves to the command of that force, are combatants (or fighters), the Manual's conflation of status and conduct allows for the use of conduct – whether someone is engaging in hostilities, itself an ill-defined concept in the Manual – to determine whether someone merits the status of combatant, with its attendant privileges and liabilities. Indeed, the Manual is explicit in this respect, referring more than once to "persons who are subject to one or more of the liabilities of combatant status, but are not entitled to receive its distinct privileges."[60] There is little doubt that LOAC contemplates combatants who lose the privileges of combatant status, but those individuals must be combatants first, based on membership in a military force, before they can become unprivileged combatants of any sort. But by defining combatants effectively as "those who fight," the Manual diminishes protections for civilians.

In the same manner, the Manual's repeated reference to combatants in presenting the fundamental rules of targeting has the same effect. Presenting targeting rules and obligations as "combatants must take feasible precautions,"[61] "combatants must refrain from attacks"[62] that violate the

---

[59]   DoD Law of War Manual, ¶ 4.3.2.3.

[60]   Ibid., ¶ 4.3.2.4. In a highly problematic example of using conduct to determine or alter status, the Manual quotes from and relies on an incorrect and now-revised statement from the 2002 version of Joint Publication 3-60, Joint Targeting, A-2 (Jan. 17, 2002): "Civilians engaging in fighting or otherwise participating in combat operations, singularly or as a group, become unlawful combatants and lose their protected civilian status." Interestingly, the Joint Publication was revised to correct this mistake in 2007 ("Civilians engaging in combat or otherwise taking a direct part in combat operations, singularly or as a group, lose their protection against direct attack"), but the Manual specifically relies on the incorrect 2002 statement that wrongly conflates conduct and status by stating that civilians who are engaging in hostilities lose their civilian status.

[61]   DoD Law of War Manual, ¶ 5.10.   [62]   Ibid.

principle of proportionality, or "combatants must conduct their operations in accordance with the law of war"[63] leaves the reader with the impression that anyone engaging in attacks or military operations is a combatant – the alternative would be to argue that persons who are not combatants do not have to follow LOAC's basic principles, which is wholly untenable. Again, this methodology uses conduct to determine status. The danger is that the civilian who participates in hostilities once is then presumed to be a combatant or fighter because that is what the Manual creates as the framework. The discussion of targeting rules in NIAC offers the clearest example of this methodological flaw Although the status category of "combatant" does not exist in NIAC, the section on "Rules on Conducting Attacks in NIAC" explains each primary rule as "combatants may not" or "combatants must". The section then ends by noting that "these rules apply to all parties to a non-international armed conflict, including persons belonging to non-State armed groups, and persons who decide to participate in hostilities of their own initiative."[64] It is true that the rules on conducting attacks apply to all persons in an armed conflict, regardless of status. However, by framing the rules in terms of combatants and then explaining that the rules apply to members of armed groups and persons participating in hostilities of their own accord, the Manual unequivocally creates the impression that the act of participating in hostilities is the measure by which an individual is determined to be a combatant.

2.3 *Determining Status Based on the Purpose of the Inquiry*

On occasion, the Manual relies on another problematic technique for defining status categories, by characterizing the status inquiry based on the protections at issue. For example, ¶ 5.8.2 of the Manual defines civilians "for the purpose of applying the [direct participation] rule discussed in [that] section."[65] Similarly, ¶ 5.7.2 is entitled "Categories of Persons Who Are Combatants for the Purpose of Assessing Their Liability to Attack."[66] This framing begs the question of whether "civilian" or "combatant" are defined differently for different purposes; that is, for applying or determining different protections or obligations. Nothing in LOAC suggests that a person's status can be determined by starting with the purpose of the status inquiry. A combatant is a combatant based solely on his or her membership in the armed forces of a party to an IAC – LOAC does not countenance or foresee a category of combatants for targeting purposes and a different category of combatants for detention purposes. Given that the universe of individuals who

---

[63] Ibid., ¶ 4.4.1.   [64] Ibid., ¶ 17.7.   [65] Ibid., ¶ 5.8.2.   [66] Ibid., ¶ 5.7.2.

can be targeted is not the same as the universe of individuals who can be detained, creating status categories based on purpose would obscure the very clarity required for effective compliance with and implementation of the law.[67] The risks for the protection of persons are all too evident: defining "combatant" by identification of persons who are liable to attack opens the door to categorizing any person directly participating in hostilities as a combatant, thus changing civilians into combatants by dint of their conduct. Although a civilian who directly participates in hostilities is indeed liable to attack during the time of such participation, she remains protected from attack at all other times. If she is suddenly categorized as a combatant, she is not protected from attack at all in any location – a stark difference to be sure. The Manual offers a detailed example of this quixotic use of terminology:

> Since "combatant" is often used in different ways, "civilian," correspondingly, is also used in different ways. For example, sometimes "civilians" is used to refer to persons who lack the right to participate in hostilities. Other times "civilian" is used to refer to persons who neither have the right to participate in hostilities nor have in fact participated in hostilities. [As another] example, "civilian" casualty reports generally exclude insurgents or terrorists, even though some might call such persons "civilians" because they are not entitled to participate in hostilities.[68]

The problem with this approach is that the Manual is determining how to categorize or label an individual based on that individual's rights or privileges, the reverse of the correct methodology under LOAC. LOAC's treaty and customary law definitions of combatant and civilian are straightforward in relying solely on membership – or lack thereof – to determine status. That status determination then drives the individual's rights and privileges. The Manual's backwards approach poses substantial challenges for operators, who are left with little, if any, guiding framework for determining what is allowed or not allowed with respect to a given individual. The consequence, unfortunately, is far too likely to result in any person who appears to be participating or has participated in hostilities being labelled a combatant and therefore a legitimate target for attack at all times. Each civilian who is mistakenly categorized in this manner is a civilian who has lost the fundamental protection LOAC mandates for all civilians.

---

[67] Watkin (above note 53), 9 ("The traditional dual privileged status approach of dividing a population into combatants and civilians is only as effective as the accuracy with which the definition of 'combatant' is established and to the extent there is a clear understanding of when civilians lose the protection of their status by participating in hostilities").

[68] DoD Law of War Manual, ¶ 4.8.1.2.

3 SIMPLIFYING THE DISCOURSE: ENSURING PROTECTIONS FOR CIVILIANS

The Manual's publication sparked extensive discourse regarding the application of the law and several key areas of dispute regarding the Manual's presentation of the law, particularly with regard to legal principles designed to protect civilians during armed conflict. Questions about the application of the principle of proportionality, the protection for human shields, the obligations to take precautions, and the presumption of civilian status have all been the focus of extensive discourse and critique. Each of these questions is critically important for the protection of civilians in armed conflict and the debates and critiques regarding these issues sparked salutary revisions to the language in the original 2015 version of the Manual.

However, the risks to LOAC's core goal of protecting civilians during armed conflict run far deeper than the particular framing of proportionality or precautions or the interpretation of the protections for human shields. The Manual's imprecise – and at times seemingly deliberately murky – terminology and categorization of individuals renders these issues moot if the very basic obligation of distinction cannot be appropriately implemented because of an inability to determine who is a civilian and who is a combatant or fighter, or because of a shift in the line between civilian and combatant such that more civilians end up in the category of individuals susceptible to attack at all times. Effective implementation of the law requires that the law – especially the basic principles and frameworks – "are understood at all levels, and most of all, by those who will be responsible for putting them into practice."[69] If an individual is a civilian in one situation but not another, there is no process or methodology by which soldiers and commanders can prepare and train for effective adherence to the law during military operations. Furthermore, the importance of the presumption of civilian status diminishes precipitously if it is too difficult to identify the line between civilian and combatant as a starting point.[70] The debates over human shields, proportionality and precautions in the Manual, all of which are designed to enhance protections for civilians, become moot if it is simply too easy to categorize individuals in the area of an attack as combatants or fighters, eliminating the need for the precautionary measures required when civilians are in the area.

---

[69] ICRC (above note 7), xxxv.

[70] AP I, Art. 50(1). The customary law nature of the presumption of civilian status is unclear; the Manual does not accept it as customary law. DoD Law of War Manual, ¶ 5.4.3.2. See also M. Lederman, "Thoughts on Distinction and Proportionality in the December 2016 Revision to the Law of War Manual," *JustSecurity.org* (Dec. 19, 2016), www.justsecurity.org /35617/thoughts-distinction-proportionality-december-2016-revision-law-war-manual/.

Beyond those foundational concerns, however, the Manual's imprecise terminology opens the door to countless possibilities for minimizing civilian protections rather than maximizing civilian protections, with loopholes and terms that enable the exclusion of certain groups or individuals from LOAC's protections. Two examples are the terms "engaging in hostilities" and "peaceful civilians," which appear repeatedly throughout the Manual. Each term exposes persons who are civilians and entitled to the protections and privileges of that status under LOAC, to a more amorphous categorization with no specific protections, rights, or privileges.

First, "engaging in hostilities" is not a term of art in LOAC and does not have any particular meaning in treaty or customary law. In LOAC, the key issue with respect to civilians who participate or engage in some way in the conflict is whether such persons are "directly participating in hostilities." As noted above, in accordance with Article 51(3) of AP I, civilians who directly participate in hostilities lose their immunity from attack during and for such time as they so participate. The Manual's term "engaging in hostilities" appears to have a broader use, raising several questions with respect to protections for individuals who can be described as "engaging in hostilities." To begin, the term covers a cross-section of persons who otherwise would not be categorized together in LOAC: persons who are part of a hostile non-State armed group and persons who engage in other hostile acts, such as bearing arms against enemy personnel. The former are not civilians, but are members of an organized armed group and liable to attack at any time and to detention until the end of hostilities. The latter are civilians who may, at the time of the specific acts, be directly participating in hostilities. One significant problem, discussed above in section 2, is that the Manual's definition of civilian excludes all persons who are "engaging in hostilities," thus incorrectly narrowing the category of civilians.

Even if one were to adhere to LOAC's clear delineation of civilian vs. combatant, however, the term "engaging in hostilities" poses substantial risks for civilians. The Manual explains that this term is used "to refer to any of those actions that could cause a person to forfeit one or more protections under the law of war."[71] If this is understood differently than direct participation in hostilities and the loss of protection from attack at the time – as one can reasonably assume it is, given the different terminology – that difference raises a major concern: if an individual who is engaging in hostilities loses certain protections, does that mean that such person is no longer protected by proportionality and precautions, or by the constant care obligation, for

---

[71] DoD Law of War Manual, ¶ 4.18.1.

example? The logic of the direct participation notion is that a civilian who
fights should not be immune from attack at that time, but remains a civilian
and regains immunity from attack once he is not directly participating in
hostilities. Because "engaging in hostilities" has no temporal component,
there is a grave danger that it will be understood to mean that a person who
at any point in time has "engaged in hostilities" has then permanently lost her
protection under LOAC's fundamental rules of targeting – an extraordinarily
damaging result. The Manual fails to tackle or even recognize the stark
consequences of this terminological imprecision for civilians and equally
provides no guidance for warfighters or other decision-makers for assessing
obligations and protections.

   Second, the terms "peaceful civilians," "private persons," "persons who
would otherwise be civilians,"[72] and other similar phraseology introduce
the idea that there is a group of civilians who do not merit the protections of civilian status or even the status of civilian. It is unfortunately all
too easy to envision a party to a conflict rejecting any obligation to take
precautions, adhere to the rule of proportionality, ensure respect for
women and children, or any of the countless other LOAC obligations,
because they view relevant persons as "private persons who engage in
hostilities"[73] or as not "peaceful civilians" and therefore not deserving of
the mandatory protections for civilians. Examples from too many conflicts, both past and current, demonstrate that any loophole will be
exploited and manipulated to the detriment of those most vulnerable
during war. For this reason, the drafters of the Geneva Conventions were
adamant that *"There is no* intermediate status; nobody in enemy hands
can be outside the law."[74]

4 CONCLUSION

Below the surface of the sophisticated debates on how the rule of proportionality in the Manual applies in given circumstances, whether civilians at certain
military installations can be understood to have assumed the risk of harm from
military operations and many other questions, the Manual's lack of precision
with respect to terminology is a much deeper affliction that permeates across
its component parts. Perhaps in a quest to cover all imaginable permutations
and possible activities or perhaps through an effort to parse the law too closely,

---

[72] See, e.g., *ibid.*, ¶ 5.16.1.   [73] *Ibid.*, ¶ 4.18.1.
[74] O. M. Uhler and H. Coursier (eds.), *Geneva Convention: Relative to the Protection of Civilian Persons in Time of War: Commentary*, 4 vols. (Geneva: ICRC, 1958), IV, 51.

the Manual muddies the waters of the definitions of civilian and combatant and any number of spin-off terms. Both the purposes of the law and the dignity of those it seeks to protect demand that the same precision applied to military targets must be applied to the legal terms and terminology that guide the operational analysis.

13

Detention and Prosecution as Described in the DoD Manual

Andrew Clapham

1 INTRODUCTION

The possibility that detainees are abused in violation of the laws of war, and/or in violation of the law of the United States, has multiple implications. Not only can this be catastrophic for the well-being and dignity of the detainee but, as has been pointed out by those who have been closely involved at a senior level, mistaken policies can drain away valuable time and energy. This drain on resources comes in two guises: first as an issue of fighting litigation in the federal courts, and second in dealing with the concerns of allied governments as well as with the wider nongovernmental and humanitarian community.[1] Furthermore, those with on the ground experience make the compelling point that "overzealous detention practices risk alienating the local population, which represents significant risk in most contemporary military operations."[2]

In the critique that follows, this chapter considers not only whether the Department of Defense (DoD) Law of War Manual (the Manual) conforms to international law, but also whether it meets the expectations of a wider community which extends beyond the official understandings of the US Government as to what is binding on the United States as a matter of law. If one aim of a detention policy is that it be seen as legitimate and

---

[1] See S. L. Hodgkinson, "Detention Operations: A Strategic Overview," in G. S. Corn, R. E. van Landingham, and S. R. Reeves (eds.), *U.S. Military Operations: Law, Policy, and Practice* (Oxford University Press, 2016), 275–305, especially at 301 considering the "negative lessons" of Guantánamo; W. K. Lietzau, "U.S. Detention of Terrorists in the 21st Century," in G. Rose and B. Oswald (eds.), *Detention of Non-State Actors Engaged in Hostilities* (Leiden: Brill, 2016), 268–95.

[2] J. Bovarnick and J. Vrett, "Detention Operations at the Tactical and Operational Levels," in G. S. Corn, R. E. van Landingham, and S. R. Reeves (eds.), *U.S. Military Operations: Law, Policy, and Practice* (Oxford University Press, 2016), 307–40, 310.

acceptable, then we need to cast our eyes beyond the confines of what is generally accepted by the United States as a matter of legal obligation. It may be particularly relevant to know what others think international law demands in the context of detention. It almost goes without saying that, in contemporary conflicts, it is more likely than not that the United States will be operating on the ground in coalition with other States. While it might be impracticable to build a highest common denominator (as coalition partners enter and leave the field with different obligations), understanding how others see the international law on detention is vital to any sort of functioning interoperability.

In the same way, preparing war crimes for prosecution by the United States or others will fail at the judicial cooperation, extradition, or trial stage if there is mutual incomprehension over what constitutes an extraditable war crime, or an offence prosecutable under a form of universal jurisdiction, or a justiciable crime before an international court. This problem will be particularly marked if the legal basis for jurisdiction, extradition, or prosecution is premised on the fact that international law creates the offence and accompanying rights and duties to prosecute. Again, the implications of applying or interpreting the international law one way or another will not only affect the right to be treated with fairness and justice of the individual accused, but also in a way help to shape the emerging international criminal law framework. Any application of international criminal law to those the United States wishes to see prosecuted will almost certainly come to influence how international law develops, and how it could be used to prosecute US citizens and service personnel abroad or in international courts.

2 DETENTION

2.1 *Generating an Authority to Detain by Moving from Prohibitions to Permissions*

Chapter VIII of the Manual starts with a crucial point. It clearly states that "[t]here are no 'law-free zones' in which detainees are outside the protection of the law."[3] The chapter distinguishes the regime for prisoners of war (dealt with in Chapter IX) and internment of protected persons under the Fourth Geneva Convention (GC IV) in the home territory of a belligerent or in occupied territory (dealt with in Chapter X). The rules in Chapter VIII apply what the Manual terms "baseline" rules where no more specific rules apply. To the extent that this opening is addressed to the *protection* of detainees it

---

[3] DoD Law of War Manual, ¶ 8.1.1.

represents a welcome assertion that there are no legal black holes and that the laws of war protect all the victims of war. But the chapter then slides from protection issues into a discussion of permissions and suggests an inherent authority to detain found in the very nature of a sovereign State.

Apart from these established contexts, the detainees who do not fall into the established categories dealt with in the other chapters that are precisely of most concern and therefore those who give rise to the greatest confusion and controversy. Where someone does not fit in these well-established categories, the manual points out that "Detention may occur outside these contexts" and that the rules in this chapter cover those who have "participated in hostilities" or "belong to an armed group."[4]

Coming as it does in the very first paragraph, this statement deserves careful attention. This situation is so complex, and the quest for simplicity so great, that one might need to be a bit more careful about moving from the clear permission to intern prisoners of war – to the idea that permission exists for others to be similarly detained, particularly during non-international armed conflicts (NIACs). Of course, all detainees have the *protection* of the law, and of course detention *may* occur outside the contexts of international armed conflicts (IACs), but the reader needs to know that in situations of NIAC the State will need to be able to point to a specific authorization for detention. Furthermore, arguments based on sovereignty and self-defense are not considered satisfactory in other jurisdictions, nor can one necessarily argue by analogy with the situation in IACs. The issue has been recently litigated in the United Kingdom and before the European Court of Human Rights with particular reference to the detention policies of the multinational forces in Afghanistan and Iraq.

The Manual correctly identifies early on that the laws of war may grant States the authority to do things. Under the heading "Law of War as Permissive Law," the Manual states "[a]lthough the law of war is generally viewed as 'prohibitive law,' in some respects, especially in the context of domestic law, the law of war may be viewed as permissive or even as a source of authority."[5] The same section then gives as an example of law of war treaties also sometimes recognizing States' authorities in war Article 21 of the Third Geneva Convention (GC III) which recognizes that the "Detaining Power may subject prisoners of war to internment." In a separate instance, the Manual notes that "military necessity may justify the capture of enemy persons."[6] But when the chapter on detention starts to address the "legal authority to detain" the argument rests on what the Manual refers to as the "Detaining Power's

---

[4] *Ibid.*   [5] *Ibid.*, ¶ 1.3.3.2.   [6] *Ibid.*, ¶ 2.1.1.

sovereign rights under international law, and the footnote is an internal cross reference to the Manual's paragraph, not on "Permissive Law" but the "Law of War as Prohibitive Law."[7]

How does the Manual generate a legal authority to detain from the Law of War as Prohibition? Again we need to refer back to Chapter I and the idea that "the rules binding upon States in treaties and customary law reflect restrictions that they have accepted, and that States are otherwise independent entities with freedom to act." This idea that States have a residual freedom to do what they want is referenced back to the *SS Lotus Case* from 1927. The Manual continues by noting that the authority to take actions under the law of war can be seen as "emanating from the State's rights as a sovereign entity rather than from any particular instrument of international law."[8] The Manual's chapter on Detention applies this idea to provide the authority to detain as follows: "In many cases, the legal authority to detain would be understood as an exercise of the Detaining Power's sovereign rights under international law rather than, or in addition to, authorities arising from an international legal instrument."[9] This reasoning is problematic as it suggests that a State is authorized to detain someone just because it is a sovereign State and that no further authority is needed. Such reasoning does not sit comfortably with the latest human rights judgments from the UK courts or from the General Comment on Detention recently issued by the UN Human Rights Committee.

The idea that a State has some inherent right to detain individuals in a NIAC, or that there is international authority to detain outside the specific authorizations provided for in IACs, has come under sustained criticism.[10] The debate is rich and complex and the reader is referred to the growing literature on this topic.[11] For our purposes we will simply show how the

---

[7]   *Ibid.*, ¶ 8.1.3.1 fn. 6.   [8]   *Ibid.*, ¶ 1.3.3.1 ("Law of War as Prohibitive Law").

[9]   *Ibid.*, ¶ 8.1.3.1 ("Detention Authority").

[10] L. Hill-Cawthorne, *Detention in Non-International Armed Conflict* (Oxford University Press, 2016); M. Lippold, "Between Humanization and Humanitarization? Detention in Armed Conflicts and the European Convention on Human Rights" (2016) 76 *Heidelberg Journal of International Law, Zeitschrift für ausländisches öffentliches Recht und Völkerrecht* 53–95, 76.

[11] ICRC, Harvard Law School Program on International Law and Armed Conflict, and Stockton Center for the Study of International Law at US Naval War College, "The Future of U.S. Detention under International Law: Workshop Report" (2017) 93 *International Law Studies* 272–98. S. McCosker, "The Limitations of Legal Reasoning: Negotiating the Relationships between International Humanitarian Law and Human Rights Law in Detention Situations," in G. Rose and B. Oswald (eds.), *Detention of Non-State Actors Engaged in Hostilities* (Leiden: Brill, 2016), 23–64; S. Aughey and A. Sari, "Targeting and Detention in Non-International Armed Conflict: Serdar Mohammed and the Limits of Human Rights Convergence" (2015) 91 *International Legal Studies* 60–118; C. Landais and L. Bass, "Reconciling the Rules of

Manual's assertion that international law automatically provides the authority to detain outside the explicit provisions found for prisoners of war and civilians in times of IAC is not shared in other jurisdictions, or by the international bodies that have examined this question.

The reasons that have been given for not simply extending the authority to detain from international to non-international armed conflict are that States have been unwilling to authorize detention through the laws of war as this would suggest that armed groups (insurgents, rebels, etc.) would also enjoy an authority to detain. We see this in the reasoning of the Court of Appeal in their judgment in the *Serdar Mohammed* case brought against the UK Ministry of Defence relating to detention in Afghanistan:

> One of the reasons why the States subscribing to what became Common Article 3 and AP II did not make provision for a power to detain in a non-international armed conflict was that to do so would have enabled insurgents to claim that the principles of equality, equivalence and reciprocity (which would be usual in international humanitarian law) meant that they would also be entitled to detain captured members of the government's army.[12]

There has been considerable scholarly attention related to this pressing operational issue and serious studies have found that the international law of armed conflict does not provide a legal basis (or authority) to detain or intern in a NIAC.[13]

International Humanitarian Law with the Rules of European Human Rights Law" (2015) 97 *International Review of the Red Cross* 900, esp. 1309 which refers to Art. 21 Geneva Convention Relative to the Treatment of Prisoners of War as being the only explicit grounds providing for a right for States to detain and considers "Articles 43 and 78 of the Fourth Geneva Convention . . . merely regulate the exercise of this power and make no reference to an explicit right to detain. In fact, only Article 21 of the Third Geneva Convention explicitly recognizes the right of States to detain in relation to prisoners of war." A. Conte, "The Legality of Detention in Armed Conflict," in A. Bellal (ed.), *The War Report: Armed Conflict in 2014* (Oxford University Press, 2015), 476–510; G. Rona, "Is There a Way Out of the Non-International Armed Conflict Detention Dilemma?" (2015) 91 *International Law Studies* 32–59; R. Goodman, "Authorization versus Regulation of Detention in Non-International Armed Conflicts" (2015) 91 *International Law Studies* 155–70; B. R. Farrell, *Habeas Corpus in International Law* (Cambridge University Press, 2017), 116–38.

12 *Serdar Mohammed v. Secretary of State for Defence* [2015] EWCA (Civ) 843 (Eng.) at para. 178 and in the Supreme Court [2017] UKSC 2 paras. 10, 127, 158, and 263, the Supreme Court did not conclude on this issue as it found that the requisite authority to detain could be found in the relevant Security Council Resolutions (see below), see also in the detailed discussion by Lord Reed at paras. 243–76 and the comments by Lord Sumption at paras. 12 and 14.

13 See, e.g., E. Debuf, *Captured in War: Lawful Internment in Armed Conflict* (Paris: Pedone, 2013); Hill-Cawthorne (above note 10); L. M. Olson, "Practical Challenges of Implementing the Complementarity between International Humanitarian and Human Rights Law –

The International Committee of the Red Cross (ICRC) position on this issue with regard to Common Article 3 to the Four Geneva Conventions, as explained in its 2016 Commentary starts with the idea that "both customary and international humanitarian treaty law contain an inherent power to detain in non-international armed conflict."[14] The Commentary then continues, "However, additional authority related to the grounds and procedure for deprivation of liberty in non-international armed conflict must in all cases be provided, in keeping with the principle of legality."[15] We have then an apparent distinction between the inherent *power* to detain and the need for "additional authority" for the "grounds" for detention. In any event the idea that the sovereign rights of a State include a right to detain in a NIAC, so-called "law of war detainees," has been explicitly rejected in judicial decisions. In the most recent 2017 judgment of the UK Supreme Court, the issue was alternatively decided on the basis that detention had been authorized by a Security Council Resolution. We now turn to this topic.

2.2 *Security Council Resolutions as the Basis for the Authority to Detain*

At paragraph 8.1.3.1 the Manual states: "a U.N. Security Council Resolution may provide a basis for detention operations."[16] The footnote references are to Resolution 1546 and the annexed letter from Colin Powell. As already explained this issue has recently been litigated and the UK Supreme Court found that a Chapter VII Resolution of the Security Council, such as those adopted for Iraq and Afghanistan (Resolutions 1456 and 1386), which authorize troop-contributing countries to use "all necessary measures," constitute "authority in international law for the detention of members of the opposing armed forces whenever it was required for imperative measures of security."[17] The "implicit limitation" to occasions where "detention is necessary for imperative reasons of security" is taken from Articles 42 and 78 of GC IV.[18] The judgment considers that the Articles also suggest the minimum level of protection to ensure that detention is not imposed arbitrarily.[19] We now turn to the question of challenging arbitrary detention.

Demonstrated by the Procedural Regulation of Internment in Non-International Armed Conflict" (2009) 40 *Case Western Reserve Journal of International Law* 437–61.

[14] ICRC, *Commentary on the First Geneva Convention (I) for the Amelioration of the Condition of the Wounded and Sick in Armed Forces in the Field*, 2nd ed. (Cambridge University Press, 2016), para. 728.

[15] *Ibid.*   [16] DoD Law of War Manual, ¶ 8.1.3.1 ("Detention Authority").

[17] *Serdar Mohammed* [2017] (above note 12), paras. 28 and 30.   [18] *Ibid.*, para. 65.

[19] *Ibid.*, para. 68 subpara. 3.

2.3 *Challenging the Basis for Detention (Habeas Corpus)*

The Manual has separate paragraphs on the review of continued detention for "security reasons," for "participants in hostilities" or "persons belonging to armed groups."[20] Guidance on what it means to inform detainees "promptly for the reasons of their detention in a language they understand," is linked to references to a "reasonable time" referring in turn to "other essential tasks" and "resource limitations."[21] For a Manual seeking to provide guidance to forces in the field this seems overly flexible and it would seem that more guidance could be given both with regard to the timing of providing the reasons for detention and the modalities of any review proceedings.

The UN's Human Rights bodies have recently addressed the issue of detention in armed conflict. The UN Human Rights Committee, charged with monitoring compliance with the International Covenant on Civil and Political Rights, explained in its General Comment on Deprivation of Liberty that "If, under the most exceptional circumstances, a present, direct and imperative threat is invoked to justify the detention of persons considered to present such a threat, the burden of proof lies on States Party to show that the individual poses such a threat and that it cannot be addressed by alternative measures, and that burden increases with the length of the detention."[22]

Other human rights bodies have gone into more detail as what would be entailed by the right to challenge the arbitrariness or lawfulness of any detention. The UN Working Group on Arbitrary Detention does not see limits to the application of human rights even with regard to situations of armed conflict. Its Guiding Principle 4 (finalized in 2015) states that "[t]he right to bring proceedings before a court to challenge the arbitrariness and lawfulness of detention and to obtain without delay appropriate and accessible remedies is not derogable under international law." And it demands that this right not be restricted "even in times of war, armed conflict or public emergency."[23] Furthermore, according to the Working Group, "Prisoners of war should be entitled to bring proceedings before a court to challenge the arbitrariness and lawfulness of the deprivation of liberty and to receive without delay

---

[20] DoD Law of War Manual, ¶¶ 8.14.2 and 8.14.3.1.   [21] *Ibid.*, ¶ 8.14.1 fn. 95.

[22] HRC, General Comment 35, 16 December 2014, para. 15; see also paras. 45 and 64–66 for particular references to detention in armed conflict; see further Y. Shany (who participated in the elaboration of this general Comment), "A Human Rights Perspective to Global Battlefield Detention: Time to Reconsider Indefinite Detention" (2017) 93 *International Law Studies* 102–31, esp. 118–24 and 130–31.

[23] "United Nations Basic Principles and Guidelines on the right of anyone deprived of their liberty to bring proceedings before a court," WGAD/CRP.1/2015, May 4, 2015, paras. 22 and 23.

appropriate and accessible remedies where the detainee [*inter alia*]: (a) challenges his or her status as a prisoner of war."[24]

Whether or not the United States considers that these texts reflect the international law obligations of the United States,[25] the work of these UN bodies points towards a developing sense that in a NIAC detainees have *rights* to challenge the basis for their detention, and that review is not something left to the discretion of the detaining State. Moreover, whether or not the United States comes to consider that human rights treaty law may apply extraterritorially, the broad rules on arbitrary detention would be considered part of customary international human rights law, at least some of which one US Operational Law Handbook suggested applies to the acts of US forces operating in contact with the population abroad.[26] In the light of the habeas corpus challenges that continue to be brought in the US Courts under US law one might expect that the Manual would provide some detail as to what sort of action should be taken in designing the procedures for detainees to be able to challenge their detention to ensure that detention is not open to successful challenge through habeas corpus proceedings based on US Constitutional law and practice.[27]

Although the detainees in Guantánamo succeeded in convincing the US Supreme Court that the writ of habeas corpus (the right to challenge the legality of their detention) should apply to those detained there, when it came to challenges with regard to detainees in Afghanistan in Bagram the lower courts declined jurisdiction referring first to the idea of the Supreme Court that the reasoning would be different where the detainees are "located in an

---

[24]   *Ibid.*, para. 48.
[25]   See the Comments of the US Government at: www.ohchr.org/Documents/Issues/Detention/DraftBasicPrinciples/March2015/USA.pdf and www.ohchr.org/Documents/Issues/Detention/DraftBasicPrinciples/March2015/USA_Observations.pdf.
[26]   A. Clapham, "The Complex Relationship between the 1949 Geneva Conventions and International Human Rights Law," in A. Clapham, P. Gaeta, and M. Sassòli (eds.), *The 1949 Geneva Conventions: A Commentary* (Oxford University Press, 2015), 701–35, 704 referencing the "Operational Law Handbook" (2012) of the International and Operational Law Department of the Judge Advocate General's Legal Center and School of the US Army at 45; R. Goodman, "The United States' Long (and Proud) Tradition in Support of the Extraterritorial Application of International Human Rights Law," *Just Security* (Mar. 10, 2014), www.justsecurity.org/8035/united-states-long-and-proud-tradition-supporting-extraterritorial-application-international-human-rights-law/.
[27]   The manual states in a separate chapter, "In some cases, U.S. practice has, as a matter of domestic law or policy, afforded unprivileged belligerents more favorable treatment than they would be entitled to receive under international law." DoD Law of War Manual, ¶ 4.19.1 and see *Boumediene v. Bush*, 553 US 723 (2008). For some of the issues see Farrell (above note 11), 168–76.

active theater of war," and second to the idea that "Detention decisions made at Bagram are inextricably a part of the war in Afghanistan. Reviewing those decisions would intrude upon the President's war powers in a way that reviewing Guantanamo detentions does not."[28]

For completeness we might here list the three factors that the Supreme Court considered relevant for determining whether the writ of habeas corpus applies: "(1) the citizenship and status of the detainee and the adequacy of the process through which that status determination was made; (2) the nature of the sites where apprehension and then detention took place; and (3) the practical obstacles inherent in resolving the prisoner's entitlement to the writ."[29] But all this simply explains whether the US federal courts consider they have jurisdiction over a habeas corpus complaint; they do not really reflect whether the international law of human rights or indeed the constitutional law of other States would recognize that detainees have the right to challenge their detention and that some minimal procedural guarantees should accompany that right.[30]

Moreover, in *Boumediene v. Bush* the US Supreme Court stated, "To the extent barriers arise, habeas corpus procedures likely can be modified to address them."[31] The thrust of the Supreme Court's reasoning bears repeating as it specifically addresses detention by the Armed Forces in times of serious threats to security:

> Security depends upon a sophisticated intelligence apparatus and the ability of our Armed Forces to act and to interdict. There are further considerations, however. Security subsists, too, in fidelity to freedom's first principles. Chief among these are freedom from arbitrary and unlawful restraint and the personal liberty that is secured by adherence to the separation of powers. It is from these principles that the judicial authority to consider petitions for *habeas corpus* relief derives.[32]

As already explained the question of a habeas corpus-style right to challenge the lawfulness of detention, in situations such as detention by the Armed

---

[28] *Al Maqaleh v. Hagel*, DC Circuit Court of Appeals, 738 F.3d 312 (2013), 28, 38.

[29] *Boumediene v. Bush*, 553 US 723 (2008), 766; and see 767 for some of the procedural guarantees that would have to be put in place before the Court would consider that the Military had provided a suitable alternative; for suggestions from Lord Sumption see *Serdar Mohammed* (above note 12) regarding minimal procedural guarantees under the European Convention on Human Rights for detention in Afghanistan.

[30] In *Munaf v. Geren*, a unanimous US Supreme Court held that habeas rights may extend overseas, but do not bar all government decisions in the conflict zone. *Munaf v. Geren*, 553 US 674 (2008).

[31] *Boumediene* (above note 29), 770.   [32] *Ibid.*, 797.

Forces in Afghanistan, has now reached the UK's Supreme Court in the *Serdar Mohammed* case. In applying the terms of the European Convention of Human Rights (incorporated as the Human Rights Act 1998) Lord Sumption set out what he considered could constitute the adapted minimum guarantees:

> There is no treaty and no consensus specifying what fairness involves as a matter of international humanitarian law. But some basic principles must be regarded as essential to any fair process of adjudication. In the present context, the minimum conditions for fairness were
>   (i) that the internee should be told, so far as possible without compromising secret material, the gist of the facts which are said to make his detention necessary for imperative reasons of security;
>   (ii) that the review procedure should be explained to him;
>   (iii) that he should be allowed sufficient contact with the outside world to be able to obtain evidence of his own; and
>   (iv) that he should be entitled to make representations, preferably in person but if that is impractical then in some other effective manner.[33]

In short, there is an expectation that in a NIAC anyone detained, including those labelled "law of war detainees" or those detained for "security reasons," will enjoy a right (whether this is seen though a constitutional law lens or from the perspective of international law) to challenge the reasons for their detention. The history and pedigree of the writ of habeas corpus continues to exert considerable sway on both sides of the Atlantic.

2.4 Hunger Strikes

At paragraph 8.8.1 the Manual states that "it is not prohibited to order detainees to be fed, if they undertake a hunger strike."[34] There are references to the 1958 UK Military Manual,[35] suggesting that force-feeding would not be a violation of English law. However the 2004 edition of the UK Manual on the Law of Armed Conflict makes no such reference to the need to engage in force-feeding.[36] A more contemporary reference would be the conclusions of the UN Committee Against Torture with regard to the report of the United States. With particular reference to events in Guantánamo the Committee concluded: "In that connection, the Committee considers that force-feeding

---

[33] *Serdar Mohammed* [2017] (above note 12), para. 107.
[34] DoD Law of War Manual, ¶ 8.8.1.   [35] See p. 449 fn. 104.
[36] UK Ministry of Defence, *The Manual of the Law of Armed Conflict* (Oxford University Press, 2004).

of prisoners on hunger strike constitutes ill-treatment in violation of the Convention. Furthermore, it notes that lawyers of detainees have argued in court that force-feedings are allegedly administered in an unnecessarily brutal and painful manner (arts. 2, 11, 12, 13, 14, 15 and 16)."[37] The Committee calls for the United States to "Put an end to the force-feeding of detainees on hunger strike as long as they are able to take informed decisions."[38]

2.5 *Contacts with the Outside World*

At paragraph 8.10.2 the Manual states that "[d]etainees shall be allowed to send and receive letters and cards, the number of which may be limited by a competent authority if it deems necessary." One of the issues which has caught the attention of the UN monitoring bodies and human rights advocates is the denial of communication to those in Guantánamo wishing to complain about torture. The international obligations of the Unites States would seem to require revising the policy of denying contact with the outside world in the context of complaints about torture. This relates not only to contacts with the UN monitoring bodies but also with other governments where legal proceedings relating to torture and inhuman or degrading treatment may be being prepared. The Concluding Observations of the UN Committee Against Torture are clear:

> The Committee calls for the declassification of torture evidence, in particular accounts of torture by Guantanamo Bay detainees. The State party should ensure that all victims of torture are able to access a remedy and obtain redress, wherever acts of torture have occurred, and regardless of the nationality of the perpetrator or the victim.
>
> The State party should take effective steps to ensure the provision of mutual judicial assistance in all matters of criminal procedure regarding the offence of torture and the related crimes of attempting to commit, complicity and participation in torture. The Committee recalls that article 9 of the Convention obligates States Party to "afford one another the greatest measure of assistance in connection with criminal proceedings" related to violations of the Convention.[39]

Of course, the Manual suggests that it is only the number of letters that can be limited, but in practice it would be preferable to make it clear that communication with the UN is a right and that the United States has international obligations in this regard. The parameters of any restrictions and the possibilities for challenging these should be spelled out. The paragraphs

---

[37] CAT/C/USA/CO/3–5 (Dec. 19), para. 14.   [38] *Ibid.*   [39] *Ibid.*, para. 15.

which explain the prohibitions on torture and inhuman and degrading treatment ring hollow if the detainee is denied in practice the right to communicate with the outside world allegations about such treatment.

3 PROSECUTION

There are three elements to the prosecution question that we can usefully separate out: first, the rights of those suspected perpetrators of crimes, including international crimes, that are subject to prosecution by the United States; second, the scope of the concept of international crimes which would allow for prosecution where national law is not adequate or appropriate; third, the prospect that violations of the detention rules set out in the Geneva Conventions, and referenced as binding in the Manual could lead to prosecutions of US personnel in other jurisdictions or before the International Criminal Court.

3.1 *The Due Process Rights of Suspected Perpetrators*

Some of the major principles are set out in paragraph 8.16 and the footnotes suggest to the reader that they should "consider" the detailed provisions of Article 75 of AP I as well as a few references to Article 6(2)(a) of AP II. Taken together with paragraph 8.1.4.2, the reader could be forgiven for thinking that the detailed protections only apply to those detained in the context of an IAC. The paragraph states that the US "will choose out of a sense of legal obligation to treat the principles set forth in Article 75 as applicable to any individual it detains in an international armed conflict, and expects all other nations to adhere to these principles as well." But, of course, the bulk of those detained or likely to be detained by the United States and prosecuted will be those detained in an internal or non-international armed conflict. Without further explanation the reader would gloss over the details of Article 75 of AP I as cited in the footnotes and alight only on the minimal guarantees suggested by Article 6 of AP II. As the United States is a party to neither treaty these separate references to the treaty articles seem rather unfortunate as a good case can be made that the guarantees found in Article 75 of AP I are to be afforded to detainees facing prosecution in the case of a NIAC.[40] Indeed Article 75 has

---

[40] See J. Bellinger, "Obama's Announcements on International Law," *Lawfare* (Mar. 8, 2011), www.lawfareblog.com/obamas-announcements-international-law ("My assumption is that the Administration does plan to apply Article 75 to al Qaida and the Taliban and that it does not agree with (or overlooked) the Supreme Court's conclusion that the conflict is a non-international armed conflict.").

even been applied as a matter of obligation for a non-State party in a NIAC and so it would seem strange that the United States would not apply these guarantees as the expectation develops that armed groups with a certain capacity should respect these norms.[41]

Even where a detainee is detained for prosecution in an IAC they would be more likely to fall under the detailed provisions of the Third or Fourth Geneva Conventions as prisoners of war covered by Article 105 of GC III or Articles 117–126 of GC IV.[42] The reader looking for guarantees for a trial of a detainee would be unlikely to think of looking in Chapter XVIII "Implementation and Enforcement of the Law of War" and there are few cross references to this chapter and none to the specific paragraph 18.21.3 on "Fundamental Fairness Requirements."

In short, the Manual could in the future set out a single set of fair trial principles for those not covered by the more favorable regimes set out in relevant Geneva Conventions. The suggestion that certain provisions of Article 75 should be considered, without a clear statement that these principles should be applied to all detainees and not just those detained in an IAC, leaves the reader with very little guidance and the detainees with the possibility of enjoying very little protection for their due process rights.

3.2 *The Prosecution of International Crimes*

The Manual states in paragraph 8.16.1.2 the well-known rule that an individual cannot be punished for an act which was not a crime under either national or international law at the time it was committed. The Manual however gives little guidance on what sort of crimes can be prosecuted in Military Commissions in situations of armed conflict where individuals may be detained outside the United States and for acts committed outside the United States. The current controversies surrounding the prosecutions of those held in Guantánamo and prosecuted before the Military Commissions created by the US Military Commissions Act would suggest that care should be taken in preparing prosecutions. There is some uncertainty over whether the jurisdiction of the Military Commissions is limited by the need to determine that the crime charged exists under international law.

In the words of one expert:

---

[41] A. Clapham, "Detention by Armed Groups under International Law" (2017) 93 *International Law Studies*, 1–44 referencing the 1992 agreement by the parties in Bosnia and Herzegovina at fn. 35.

[42] Referenced with more detail in DoD Law of War Manual, ¶ 18.21.3.

Despite being one of the critical problems of the post-9/11 national security legal world, it remains an open question whether the military commissions at Guantanamo, ostensibly established under the law of war, can try individuals for federal law crimes that are not violations of the law of war. Two of the most significant charges in the US prosecutorial arsenal in terrorism-related cases – material support for terrorism and conspiracy to commit terrorism – fall into this category.[43]

The reader of the Manual is given no hint that such prosecutions risk being perhaps struck down in the Appeal Courts and eventually in the Supreme Court.

The Manual further boldly states that "Punishment on the basis of conspiracy, joint criminal enterprise, and other theories of secondary liability are not prohibited by this rule." It would seem appropriate to explain that building a case solely on the basis of conspiracy or joint criminal enterprise in a war crime could not only be later seen as a violation of the rights of the detainee but also lead to the conviction being overturned.[44] Of course this topic represents a moving target, as it is not yet decided whether such Military Commissions can prosecute war crimes which are defined by Congress but not considered war crimes under international law.[45] Nevertheless more detail on the uncertainties in this area would help decision-makers to see a fuller picture and avoid pursuing prosecutions that, at best, remain subject to complicated and resource intensive appeals and, at worst, constitute violations of international law as the individual is being prosecuted for something which was not actually a crime under law at the time of its commission.

As has been pointed out in the scholarly literature, untethering "Congress's discretion from the international law of war would, however, raise considerable questions about the legitimacy of trials by military commissions under international law, and could have the perverse effect of subjecting

---

[43] A. Blane, "How the Trump Administration Deals with Detainees Can Provide Insight into its Counterterrorism Priorities," *Just Security* (Nov. 14, 2017), www.justsecurity.org/47090/trump-administration-deals-detainees-provide-insight-counterterrorism-priorities/.

[44] The Manual references para. 18.23 on individual criminal responsibility which itself includes an expansive approach to joint criminal enterprise based on the case law of the International Criminal Tribunal for the former Yugoslavia and the International Military Tribunal. However, there are modern tendencies which may be narrowing the scope of criminal enterprise. See in this respect *R v. Jogee* [2016] UKSC 8 and *Ruddock v. The Queen* [2016] UKPC 7.

[45] D. Brenner-Beck, "Trial and Punishment for Battlefield Misconduct," in G. S. Corn, J. A. Schoettler, D. Brenner-Beck, V. M. Hansen, R. Jackson, E. T. Jensen, and M. W. Lewis, *The War on Terror and the Laws of War: A Military Perspective*, 2nd ed. (New York: Oxford University Press, 2015), 193–236, esp. 219–24.

U.S. military personnel to similarly subjective interpretations of criminal liability for military operations."[46] It is to the subject of the international prosecution of US personnel for war crimes that we now turn.

3.3 The Prospect of US Personnel being Prosecuted outside the United States

Under the heading 18.20.3.1 "Attempt to Assert Jurisdiction With Respect to Nationals of Non-Party States," the Manual explains that "[t]he Rome Statute also provides that the ICC may exercise its jurisdiction if [a State party is] . . . the State on the territory of which the conduct in question occurred." The paragraph heading's reference to attempted assertion of jurisdiction is explained in the following way: "The United States has a longstanding and continuing objection to any assertion of jurisdiction by the ICC with respect to nationals of States not Party to the Rome Statute in the absence of consent from such States or a referral by the Security Council." Arguments that the immunity enjoyed by US personnel under status of forces agreements, or other agreements that protect personnel from being surrendered to the Court, do not necessarily mean that personnel will not be investigated or indicted or subjected to arrest warrants in this context.[47] In a Law of War Manual designed to ensure respect for the laws of war it does seem remiss not to remind military forces that there could be international accountability for violations of the laws of war that amount to war crimes. While the United States may choose to maintain its opposition to such an assertion of jurisdiction by the Court, the prospect of investigation with regard to action in Afghanistan and on the territory of other States Party in this connection is a very real one.[48]

Moreover the prospect of US personnel being prosecuted in another State under some sort of universal jurisdiction is downplayed as unlikely on the grounds that universal jurisdiction is "controversial" and rarely undertaken without the consent of the accused's State.[49] The US Ambassador-at-Large for

---

[46] Ibid., 224.
[47] See M. A. Newton, "How the International Criminal Court Threatens Treaty Norms" (2016) 49 *Vanderbilt Journal of Transnational Law* 371–431 (but NB fn. 48 which criticizes the Manual); R. O'Keefe, "Response: 'Quid,' Not 'Quantum': A Comment on 'How the International Court Threatens Treaty Norms'" (2016) 49 *Vanderbilt Journal of Transnational Law* 433–41; C. Stahn, "Response: The ICC, Pre-Existing Jurisdictional Treaty Regimes, and the Limits of the Nemo Dat Quod Non Habet Doctrine – A Reply to Michael Newton" (2016) 49 *Vanderbilt Journal of Transnational Law* 443–54.
[48] www.icc-cpi.int/Pages/item.aspx?name=171103_OTP_Statement (Nov. 3, 2017); A. Whiting, "An ICC Investigation of the U.S. in Afghanistan: What does it Mean?," *Just Security* (Nov. 3, 2017), www.justsecurity.org/46687/icc-investigation-u-s-afghanistan-mean/.
[49] DoD Law of War Manual, ¶ 18.21.1.

War Crimes, Stephen Rapp, had stressed already in 2010 that the United States approved of universal jurisdiction in "cases [where] countries investigate based upon people that are really within their borders."[50] More recently, since leaving the post, Rapp is continuing to work with the Commission on Justice and Accountability on multiple dossiers of Syrian-regime officials for prosecution in Germany and Spain.[51] The idea that such prosecutions cannot take place seems misleading and opens up the United States to charges of double standards undermining its work on accountability for atrocity crimes more generally.[52]

Furthermore, because the reports being investigated by the International Criminal Court relate to torture, it bears mentioning that not only do dozens of State parties to the UN Torture Convention recognize universal jurisdiction over non-nationals who commit their crimes abroad and are found on their territory, but that the United States itself has legislation in place which allows for such prosecutions.[53] The reader of the Manual could be forgiven for getting the impression that no US national would ever be prosecuted abroad for any of the crimes mentioned in the Manual. In practice, it may well be that the political cost of such a prosecution might be too big to bear, but the Manual should seek to be dissuasive when it comes to torture and other crimes, rather than giving the impression that there is little chance of accountability.

---

[50]   Interview with Ambassador Rapp, US Ambassador-at-Large for War Crimes, www.ibanet.org/Article/NewDetail.aspx?ArticleUid=559B38A8-7FA0-4EA7-9943-E983782CAB89.

[51]   www.baladi-news.com/en/news/details/21964/Former_US_Ambassador_Seeks_New_Avenues_for_War_Crimes_Justice.

[52]   J. Stromseth, "The ICC's Afghanistan Investigation: What's at Stake for the U.S.?" (Dec. 5, 2017), www.justsecurity.org/47672/iccs-afghanistan-investigation-whats-stake-u-s/.

[53]   18 US Code § 2340A – Torture (The Extraterritorial Torture Statute).

14

The DoD Conception of the Law of Occupation

Yaël Ronen[*]

1 INTRODUCTION

The two most hotly debated issues with respect to the law of occupation are also the fundamental ones: the very applicability of the legal regime as *lex specialis*, and the limitations that it imposes on the authority of the Occupying Power to introduce long-term changes in the territory under its control. The two questions are related. States have repeatedly sought to avoid the applicability of the law of occupation and, when that law applied, to interpret their powers under it expansively.

These two foundational questions have attracted the attention of the international legal community in the context of the involvement of the United States (with the UK and associated States) in Iraq, which began in April 2003. This involvement refocused worldwide attention on the question of the legality under the law of occupation of transformative projects. Debates revolve first over the extent to which the law of occupation constrains the authorities of a State operating in territory beyond its sovereign authority when they seek to introduce fundamental changes in the constitutional, social, economic, and legal order within that territory in order to create the conditions for a more democratic and peaceful State.[1] If the law of occupation does apply, a further question is how such societal or institutional transformation can be reconciled with the cornerstone concept known as the conservationist principle, which traditionally has been understood as prohibiting wholesale changes in the legal and political institutions of the occupied territory. Under the conservationist principle, an Occupying Power should respect the existing

---

[*] The author is grateful to Yutaka Arai, Gregory Fox, and Jeremy Telman for their helpful comments on earlier drafts, but any errors or oversights remain her responsibility.
[1] A. Roberts, "Transformative Military Occupation: Applying the Laws of War and Human Rights" (2006) 100 *American Journal of International Law* 580.

laws and economic arrangements within the occupied territory and should therefore make as few changes as possible.[2]

This chapter examines the stance of the US Department of Defense (DoD) 2016 Law of War Manual (the Manual) on these two questions. Moving from the particular to the general, section 2 examines what the Manual says explicitly of transformative occupation. Section 3 proceeds to examine the Manual's interpretation of the Occupying Power's authority as a general matter and the extent to which this interpretation leaves room for engagement in transformative enterprises. Finally, section 4 considers the Manual's approach to the applicability of the law of occupation, by analyzing the circumstances in which the Manual purports to exclude that law. Both issues are considered through the doctrinal stipulations of the Manual, and through the practice to which it refers. This chapter demonstrates the Manual's preference for a strict interpretation of circumstances in which the law of occupation applies; and for an expansive interpretation of the Occupying Power's authority when that law does apply. The chapter demonstrates these propositions with particular reference to their implications for transformative occupation.

The occupation chapter in the 2016 Manual is not an original publication. It expands the corresponding language drawn from the 1956 US Army Field Manual (as amended in 1976) and its antecedents. In fact, there are some seventy different references to the text of the earlier Army Field Manual within the occupation chapter of the DoD Manual. Thus, the present analysis pertains to longstanding views of the United States as they are articulated and refined in Chapter XII of the 2016 Manual. Nevertheless, the recent update informs the analysis through a number of innovative features. First, it contains a much more elaborate doctrinal exposition with regard to the two questions, reflecting the engagement of practitioners and scholars with these issues through the years. This engagement stems from developments in international relations, such as military interventions that are not motivated by territorial aspirations and a growing participation of non-State actors who wield territorial control, as well as extensive emergence of international law principles related to the law of non-international armed conflict (NIAC), international human rights law, and self-determination. Furthermore, its treatment of issues is not entirely identical to that in the 1956 Army Field

---

[2] G. H. Fox, "The Occupation of Iraq" (2004) 36 *Georgetown Journal of International Law* 195. The conservationist principle draws its moral and legal authority from the underlying notion that occupation is intended to be of only temporary duration and insufficient in its own right to represent a transfer of full sovereign authority to the Occupying Power. DoD Law of War Manual, ¶ 11.4.2 ("Occupation is essentially provisional.").

Manual, indicating evolving views at least on the part of DoD on those matters. In addition, the 2016 Manual, unlike its antecedent, makes extensive use of references, especially in the sections on the framework of the law of occupation, citing judicial rulings, government action. and military manuals as well as academic writing (albeit drawing almost exclusively from US sources as discussed below).

The Manual's preference for a strict interpretation of circumstances in which the law of occupation applies and for an expansive interpretation of the Occupying Power's authority is hardly surprising or, generally speaking, an objectionable position for a State to adopt. Nor is it a novel policy on the part of the United States. This preference is manifest in the Manual's doctrinal interpretation of the international instruments with respect to the conservationist principle, in its reliance on practice that challenges this principle, and in its stance with regard to the very applicability of the law of occupation in the first place. Considered in totality, the Manual does not explicitly endorse the transformative view of occupation law, but implicitly goes a significant way towards accommodating it, in ways that could erode the conservationist principle.

2 READING THE LINES: REJECTION OF TRANSFORMATIVE OCCUPATION?

As a predicate matter, the Manual's wording follows closely the traditional approach of the 1956 Army Field Manual that merely quoted existing treaty law. When stating the source of the Occupying Power's authority over inhabitants, the 2016 Manual invokes not a general reformist imperative or even specific areas of policy such as human rights or democratic governance, but grounds the power in the Occupying Power's "war powers and from its duty to ensure public order and safety in occupied territory."[3] As for the duty of the Occupying Power to ensure public order and safety,[4] the Manual correctly states that "The duty of the Occupying Power to respect, unless absolutely prevented, the laws in force in the country prohibits it from arbitrarily exercising its authority to suspend, repeal, or change the municipal law applicable to occupied territory."[5] By repeating language drawn from Article 43 of the 1907 Hague

---

[3] DoD Law of War Manual, ¶ 11.7.

[4] In the authoritative French text of the 1907 Hague Regulations, the occupier must preserve "l'ordre et la vie publics" (i.e., "public order and life"), 1907 Hague Regulations, Art. 43. The Occupying Power's duties are subject to the caveat that they apply only "autant qu'il est possible."

[5] DoD Law of War Manual, ¶ 11.5.2.

Regulations almost verbatim, the Manual reiterates the conservationist principle in its stricter version. Furthermore, the Manual's description of the permissible grounds for changing local law[6] are virtually identical to the 1956 version.[7]

Professor Gregory Fox concludes that the Manual essentially adheres to the traditionally restrictive view of the conservationist principle. From his perspective, this policy preference is rooted in an understanding that transformative measures are available based on other developed bodies of international law rather than derived directly from a restrictive interpretation of occupation law. In this vein, the authors of the Manual may have assumed that the legitimacy of future transformative projects would likely be governed by Security Council authorization, which would simply override the conservationist principle by virtue of the overarching authority drawn from Chapter VII of the UN Charter. At the same time, the Manual avoids explicit reference to a broader conception of transformative occupation so as not to give credence to the common justification for such occupation, namely that Occupying Powers are bound by international human rights treaty obligations when operating in occupied territory.[8]

Fox's analysis of the terseness of the Manual's express wording is compelling and his explanations persuasive. However, in addition to what the Manual says (or refrains from saying) on the specific theme of transformative occupation, it is also useful to consider what the text of Chapter XI insinuates, as well as its overall attitude towards the underlying issues, namely the permissible parameters of the Occupying Power's authority, and even more fundamentally, to the applicability of the law of occupation. Those bear on the legitimacy of transformative measures directly, albeit not explicitly.

3 READING BETWEEN THE LINES: IMPLICIT ENDORSEMENT OF THE TRANSFORMATIVE MODEL?

This section holds that the principles guiding the Occupying Power's exercise of authority, as described in Chapter XI of the 2016 Manual, provide leeway for transformative measures, even without authorizing them expressly.

---

[6] *Ibid.*, ¶ 11.9.2.

[7] Field Manual 27-10, The Law of Land Warfare (Washington: US Dep't. of Army, Jul. 18, 1956) (FM 27-10), ¶ 369. Noting the addition that the Occupying Power is prohibited from "arbitrarily" changing the law (DoD Law of War Manual, ¶ 11.9.2), Fox concludes that the change has no substantive significance because it essentially reverts to the list of permissible purposes of change. G. H. Fox, "Guest Post: The Law of Occupation in the New DOD Law of War Manual," *Opinio Juris* (July 2, 2015), http://opiniojuris.org/2015/07/02/guest-post-the-law-of-occupation-in-the-new-dod-law-of-war-manual/.

[8] *Ibid.*

3.1 Doctrine on the Conservationist Principle

3.1.1 Evading the Conservationist Principle

The engagement in the Manual with the principles that directly concern the permissibility of transformative measures is minimal and limited to only two sections of its voluminous text relating to the position of the Occupying Power and its duties.[9] Paragraph 11.4.2, entitled "Limitations on the Power of the Occupying Power Stemming from Its Lack of Sovereignty over Occupied Territory," first states that "[b]ecause sovereignty is not vested in the Occupying Power, the fact of military occupation does not authorize the Occupying Power to take certain actions. For example, the Occupying Power is not authorized by the fact of belligerent occupation to annex occupied territory or to create a new State." Following these unequivocal almost-truisms, the Manual continues to discuss transformative measures explicitly: "Similarly, in view of the provisional nature of belligerent occupation, the authority of the Occupying Power under occupation law has been interpreted as being subject to limitations on the ability of the Occupying Power to alter institutions of government permanently or change the constitution of a country."

This, the only direct statement on transformative measures, is equivocal. It suggests that there are significant exceptions to the prohibition, or that the prohibition is so vague as to be a matter for the discretion of the Occupying Power. First, by qualifying the conservationist view and distancing themselves from it, the authors of the Manual indicate both that the assertion is controversial and that they do not subscribe to it. Moreover, the long supporting footnote only reinforces the ambiguity. The first source cited, the 2005 speech of John Bellinger, then Legal Advisor to the Department of State, does not address occupation law as such, but rather the Security Council's ability to remove any ambiguity that the law might contain.[10] The footnote also contains a quote from the UK 2004 Manual as an example of a permissible change, albeit a narrow one, that aims to fulfill the Occupying Power's duty to look after the welfare of the inhabitants.[11] The example in the footnote (fixing prices and securing the equitable distribution of food and other commodities) is irrelevant to the proposition at issue. If anything, its limited scope reinforces,

---

9   *Ibid.*, ¶¶ 11.4 and 11.5.
10   *Ibid.*, ¶ 11.4.2.1 fn. 100 citing John B. Bellinger III, Legal Advisor Address to International Institute of Humanitarian Law in San Remo (Sept. 9, 2005), www.state.gov/s/l/2005/87240.htm.
11   "fixing prices and securing the equitable distribution of food and other commodities," UK Ministry of Defence, The Manual of the Law of Armed Conflict (2004), ¶ 11.25.1.

a contrario, the impermissibility of truly transformative measures (although as Professor Fox notes, the UK Manual maintains that such measures are lawful under other bodies of law[12]).

A subsequent reference to the conservationist principle is Canadian Manual section 1205(1) which states that "[g]enerally speaking, the occupant is not entitled to alter the existing form of government, to upset the constitution and domestic laws of the occupied territory." The words "generally speaking" imply that such changes are not absolutely prohibited, although this does not mean that the exceptions are themselves unlimited. The footnote concludes by citing Julius Stone who stated in 1954 that "the limits on the legislative and regulatory power are as vague as the authority is general"; and while acknowledging that "the Occupant . . . cannot make permanent changes in regards to fundamental institutions," Stone added that it becomes "increasingly difficult to say with confidence what is a fundamental institution."[13] Although presented as authorities for the interpretation of the authority being limited, none of the references actually supports the text. They all qualify the impermissibility of fundamental constitutional changes, implicitly or explicitly. In brief, the footnote serves to reinforce the skepticism of the Manual's authors and undermines the conservationist proposition further.

3.1.2 Relaxing the conservationist principle

In stipulating the Occupying Power's authority to change the municipal law in the occupied territory, both the 1956 Manual and the 2016 Manual essentially quote Article 64 of the Fourth Geneva convention (GC IV).[14] Professor Fox remarks that the Manuals nonetheless differ in their elaboration on what would constitute permissible changes. Article 64 recognizes the duty of the Occupying Power to modify existing law to fulfill its obligations, and correspondingly, its power to do so.[15] In other words, it goes a long way towards the relaxation of the conservationist principle. Indeed, Article 64 was adopted to reflect the interests of States that in 1949 were engaged in reconstruction of post war economies.[16]

---

[12]   Ibid., ¶ 11.11.

[13]   J. Stone, *Legal Controls of International Conflict* (Sydney: Maitland Publications, 1954, repr. with supplement 1959), 698 cited in DoD Law of War Manual (2015) (the 2015 Manual), fn. 100.

[14]   DoD Law of War Manual, ¶¶ 11.9.2; Field Manual 27-10, The Law of Land Warfare (Washington: US Dep't. of Army, July 18, 1956) (FM 27-10), ¶ 369.

[15]   E. Benvenisti, *The International Law of Occupation*, 2nd ed. (Oxford University Press, 2012), 74.

[16]   M. A. Newton, "The Iraqi High Criminal Court: Controversy and Contributions" (2006) 88 *International Review of the Red Cross* 399. Although Art. 64 expressly concerns penal law, it is

Paragraph 371 of the 1956 Army Field Manual did not reflect the empowering aspect of Article 64. It merely quoted it and provided an exhaustive list of three types of laws that the Occupying Power may alter, repeal, or suspend.[17] With respect to the welfare of the population the text permits changes to "[l]egislation the enforcement of which would be inconsistent with the duties of the occupant, such as laws establishing racial discrimination." This provision imposes no obligation to engage proactively in providing for the welfare of the population, and assumes only negative duties, such as not to discriminate. By contrast, the 2016 Manual leaves a wide berth for legislative change by the Occupying Power.[18] First, it provides examples of permissible changes rather than an exhaustive list. Most of the examples overlap with the three types mentioned in the 1956 Manual and derive from the powers under both Hague Regulations, Article 43 and GC IV, Article 64 to protect the Occupying Power's security and the duty to restore and ensure public order.

But two examples merit particular mention. One is the power to change legislation "relating to the Occupying Power's obligations under the GC, such as legislation to help provide for child welfare, labor, food, hygiene, and public health of the occupied territory." This is the first time that the Manual expressly acknowledges the Occupying Power's obligation under Article 64 to be a proactive regulator and to ensure the social and economic welfare of the population in the occupied territory. This obligation correspondingly entails a more expansive reading of the Occupying Power's lawmaking authority under the Convention.[19] Another example of permissible change is legislation "relating to the administration of the law, such as repealing laws establishing racial discrimination or promulgating laws requiring the impartial application of the law by local officials." The American-led Coalition Provisional Authority relied upon this authority in order to suspend the application of capital punishment by Iraqi judicial authorities due to the defects of due process in the criminal code as applied under Saddam

---

widely regarded as extending also to other law. Benvenisti (above note 15), 101; Y. Dinstein, *The International Law of Belligerent Occupation* (Cambridge University Press, 2009), 111.

[17] "The occupant may alter, repeal, or suspend laws of the following types:

    a. Legislation constituting a threat to its security, such as laws relating to recruitment and the bearing of arms.

    b. Legislation dealing with political process, such as laws regarding the rights of suffrage and of assembly.

    c. Legislation the enforcement of which would be inconsistent with the duties of the occupant, such as laws establishing racial discrimination."

[18] DoD Law of War Manual, ¶ 11.9.2.2.   [19] Benvenisti (above note 15), 101.

Hussein.[20] The particular examples of racial discrimination and impartial application of the law are, as noted above, almost trivial. But the basic assertion that legislation on "the administration of the law" may be changed, is far-reaching given its open-endedness.

Even more permissive is another new stipulation in the Manual, which gives license to legislative change on the basis of a formalistic criterion, namely that "the duty to respect, unless absolutely prevented, the laws in force in the country has been interpreted not to apply to local administrative laws, such as regulations, executive orders, ordinances, and decrees."[21] This is supported by reference to von Glahn that "the occupant is generally conceded *very extensive powers to change, alter, or suspend the ordinances and decrees (as distinct from laws)* of the legitimate sovereign of an occupied territory. It is held that administrative regulations and executive orders are quite sharply distinct from the constitutional and statute law of a country and that they do not constitute as important or vital a part of the latter's legal structure."[22] Together with the Manual's minimalist (and tentative) prohibition on "alter[ing] institutions of government permanently or chang[ing] the constitution of a country,"[23] this leaves almost unlimited scope for changes to the law, so long as those are couched as secondary legislation. This wide latitude is even more significant today, given the growth of the regulatory State. Changes to secondary legislation which the Manual seems to permit without limitation are capable of having a tremendous impact on the social and economic makeup of the State, even if not on its formal constitution.

The expansive understanding of the powers of the Occupying Power is evident also in provisions on discrete issues. For example, the Manual notes that the prohibition in GC IV, Article 52 on measures aiming to create unemployment does not prohibit measures intended to reduce unemployment.[24] While this is logically correct, it is legally irrelevant. The absolute prohibition in Article 52 does not operate *a contrario* to grant any license, as the Manual implies; the authority of the Occupying Power remains regulated by Hague Regulations, Article 43 and GC IV, Article 64. Those may well permit measures to reduce unemployment. This would depend on the content of the measures. For this reason it is particularly odd

---

[20] Fox (above note 2). Coalition Provisional Authority Order No. 7 (June 9, 2003) Doc. No. CPA/ MEM/9 (June 3, 2003).

[21] DoD Law of War Manual, ¶ 11.5.2.

[22] *Ibid.*, ¶ 11.5.2 fn. 106 quoting G. Von Glahn, *The Occupation of Enemy Territory: A Commentary on the Law and Practice of Belligerent Occupation* (University of Minnesota Press, 1957), 99 (emphasis added). This distinction by von Glahn is unique in the literature.

[23] DoD Law of War Manual, ¶ 11.4.2.   [24] *Ibid.*, ¶ 11.20.5.2.

that the text is supported by a reference to Coalition Provisional Authority (CPA) Regulation 39 on foreign investment. Although this Regulation was guided, *inter alia*, by the intention to reduce unemployment, it was expressly adopted to "bring about significant change to the Iraqi economic system"[25] – one of the many far-reaching structural changes that underlay the question of the permissibility of transformative occupation. Whether Regulation 39 was lawful under international law or not, it does not substantiate it.

Another example of a new stipulation on a discrete issue that relaxes the conservationist principle is the provision on the permissibility of introducing customs duties. The Manual states (as did the 1956 Army Field Manual) that "[u]nless required to do so by considerations of public order and safety, the Occupying Power must not create new taxes."[26] Nonetheless, it postulates that a reconstruction levy imposed on Iraqi imports was permissible as a "customs duty," to which the rules on contributions applied.[27] There is no explanation why a customs duty constitutes a contribution rather than a tax, nor how a duty imposed "to assist the Iraqi people and support the reconstruction of Iraq" fulfills the parameters for levying contributions, namely "the needs of the occupying forces and the administration of the occupied Territory."[28] Only a very expansive interpretation of "administration" could encompass the reconstruction of the State. Again the Manual cites a CPA regulation, which in turns cites Security Council Resolution 1483 as a source of authority.[29] Reliance on Security Council authorization takes the matter outside the boundaries of the law of occupation, and the Manual clearly maintains that the Council may expand on an occupier's legislative authority.[30] Thus, the CPA regulation may be valid under international law, but it is not clear that it would have been so without Security Council authorization.

In both instances, the Manual addresses and confirms the permissibility of relatively minor aspects of legislative changes, which are not in themselves necessarily violations of the law of occupation. However, it mentions these changes in complete isolation from the wider context in which these changes have been adopted. That context presents a serious challenge to the conservationist principle. The Manual thus does not openly confirm the permissibility

---

[25] Coalition Provisional Authority Order No. 39, CPA/ORD/Sept. 19, 2003/39, preambular para. 3.

[26] DoD Law of War Manual, ¶ 11.22.1.2.   [27] *Ibid.*, ¶ 11.22.3.   [28] *Ibid.*, ¶ 11.22.2.1.

[29] *Ibid.*, ¶ 11.22.3 fn. 448, citing Coalition Provisional Authority Order No. 38, Reconstruction Levy, §1 (Sept. 9, 2003).

[30] *Ibid.*, ¶ 11.1.2.5, see discussion below.

of the larger measures at issue, but by affirming their components, it insinuates the validity of the overall project.

3.2 Practice Rejecting the Conservationist Principle

Generally speaking, reliance on early sources is useful in international legal writing for establishing the time element necessary for a norm to have crystallized into customary international law (or, if the norm had been codified, to establish that it has become customary). However, the value of early resources diminishes significantly when they contain laws which have since evolved in light of changes in the social and political phenomena which they regulate.[31] The law of occupation is a case in point. The examples of State practice referred to in the Manual derive almost exclusively from that of the United States. The Manual highlights three main eras and events: nineteenth-century case law including post-Civil War jurisprudence, post-World War II practice in Germany, and the administration of Iraq in 2003–4.[32] By evoking these sources, the Manual creates a universe of practice, purportedly under the law of occupation, which erodes the impermissibility of transformative measures, even if it does not directly authorize or condone them. This section demonstrates that each of these three sets of sources referenced by the Manual has, in its own way, the effect of undermining the conservationist principle.

3.2.1 Nineteenth-Century Sources: Outdated Doctrine

Early conceptions of occupation did not neatly distinguish it from conquest. Even when this distinction began to crystallize, its consequences were not always clear.[33] Thus, early occupation law consisted of the rejection of annexation, but did not impose limitations on the powers of the Occupying Power during occupation. The United States, in particular, subscribed to the view that while the authority of the Occupying Power was temporary, it was unlimited.[34] This doctrine was definitively put to rest in favor of the conservationist principle in the Hague Conventions of 1899

---

[31] Y. Arai-Takahashi, "Preoccupied with Occupation: Critical Examinations of the Historical Development of the Law of Occupation" (2012) 94 *International Review of the Red Cross* 51.

[32] This limited universe of practice is not only a consequence of the focus on American practice, since such practice could have included the occupation of Haiti (1914–34), Korea (1945–49), the Dominican Republic (1965), and more.

[33] R. Giladi, "A Different Sense of Humanity: Occupation in Francis Lieber's Code" (2012) 94 *International Review of the Red Cross* 81, 114.

[34] For a review of US doctrine and practice until 1907 see E. Benvenisti, "The Origins of the Concept of Belligerent Occupation" (2008) 26 *Law and History Review* 621, 635–40.

and 1907 and the Regulations annexed to them, and later in the 1949 GC IV. These instruments are without doubt binding on the United States. Not only has it ratified them, but the Hague Regulations have also been recognized as reflecting customary international law, both generally and specifically with respect to occupation.[35] The Manual itself acknowledges that "many of the provisions in Articles 42 through 56 of the Hague IV Regulations reflect customary international law."[36] In light of this, the heavy reliance in the Manual on legal sources from the nineteenth century is surprising, since those reflect an understanding of both the constitutional position of the Occupying Power and its legislative power that are very different from contemporary ones, and which the United States effectively abandoned when it ratified the Hague Regulations of 1907.

One example is the reference to an 1815 Supreme Court ruling which speaks of "occupation," to demonstrate that "[t]he practice of conducting military occupation is very old, and the law of military occupation has long been part of the law of war."[37] The case cited (and quoted in the footnote) recognized occupation as transferring sovereign power, even if temporarily.[38] In other words, the case used the term "occupation" in a different sense from its contemporary one. Similarly, the Manual correctly asserts that "[t]he fact of occupation is the basis for the Occupying Power to exercise authority over the occupied territory," but disturbingly cites an 1819 ruling that "[b]y the conquest and military occupation of Castine, the enemy acquired that firm possession which enabled him to exercise the *fullest rights of sovereignty* over

---

[35] *Legal Consequences of the Construction of a Wall in the Occupied Palestinian Territory*, Advisory Opinion, [2004] ICJ Rep. 136, paras. 78, 89. *Armed Activities on the Territory of the Congo (Democratic Republic of the Congo v. Uganda)*, Judgment [2005] ICJ Rep. 168, para. 219. For State practice see D. Kretzmer, "The Law of Belligerent Occupation in the Supreme Court of Israel" (2012) 94 *International Review of the Red Cross* 207, 212. GC IV is also widely regarded as reflecting customary international law.

[36] DoD Law of War Manual, ¶ 11.2.1.1. But see Yoo's claim that the Hague Regulations are not binding because Iraq was not party to them, and that subsequent practice overrides customary international law. J. Yoo, "Iraqi Reconstruction and the Law of Occupation" (2004) 11 *UC Davis Journal of International Law and Policy* 7, 16.

[37] DoD Law of War Manual, ¶ 11.1.1.

[38] *Ibid.*, fn. 4; *Thirty Hogsheads of Sugar v. Boyle* (1815) 13 US 191, 195 (US Supreme Court) (The Danish territory of Santa Cruz had been occupied by the UK. The property of a Danish national on the island was deemed to be enemy property. The Court held: "Although acquisitions made during war are not considered as permanent until confirmed by treaty, yet to every commercial and belligerent purpose, they are considered as a part of the domain of the conqueror, so long as he retains the possession and government of them. The Island of Santa Cruz, after its capitulation, remained a British island until it was restored to Denmark.").

that place" (emphasis added).[39] This jurisprudence is at odds with the contemporary law of occupation as found in the Hague Regulations and GC IV. The Manual errs in relying on it when only the terms "occupation," "fact of occupation," or "authority" have endured but their significance as legal terms has shifted.

A different source of concern is the recourse to Civil War legal doctrine and jurisprudence. The Manual rightly states that occupation involves "a complicated, trilateral set of legal relations between the Occupying Power, the temporarily ousted sovereign authority, and the inhabitants of occupied territory."[40] It supports this by a reference to a US Supreme Court case from 1879 regarding the Civil War.[41] It is well known that the Union Government recognized the Confederacy as a belligerent and therefore regarded the relations with it as akin to the relations with a foreign State, including with respect to occupation.[42] However, the assimilation of an internal conflict with an international one has its limitations. The Union Government did not recognize the sovereignty of the Confederacy. Consequently, in framing the Occupying Power's authority, the Lieber Code (and subsequent case law) paid no heed to preservation of the Confederacy's interests as those of an ousted sovereign, as it would have done under the law at the time had the occupation occurred within the

---

[39] DoD Law of War Manual, ¶ 11.2.1 fn. 49, citing *United States v. Rice*, 17 US 246 (1819). This case is discussed in M. G. Shanker, "The Law of Belligerent Occupation in the American Courts" (1952) 50 *Michigan Law Review* 1066, 1069–70. While this case is not cited as basis for the notion that occupation transfers sovereignty, it is an authority to an unlimited power of the occupant, at least during the occupation. E. Colby, "Occupation under the Laws of War" (1925) 25 *Columbia Law Review* 904, 914. The outcome of that case (that no customs were due to the United States with respect to goods imported into Castine, Maine, while it was under British Occupation) is not contrary to contemporary law of occupation; but this is largely because the matter is not one of the law of occupation but of domestic law (A. D. McNair, "Municipal Effects of Belligerent Occupation" (1941) 57 *Law Quarterly Review* 33, 50–51). It has nothing to do with obedience of the inhabitants of the occupied territory to the Occupying Power, as the ruling held.

[40] DoD Law of War Manual, ¶¶ 11.1, 11.4, 11.5.

[41] Ibid., ¶ 11.4.1 fn. 93; *Coleman v. Tennessee*, 97 US 509, 517 (1878): "The right to govern the territory of the enemy during its military occupation is one of the incidents of war, being a consequence of its acquisition; and *the character and form of the government to be established depend entirely upon the laws of the conquering State or the orders of its military commander*" (emphasis added).

[42] *Thorington v. Smith*, 75 US 1 (1868) 11 ("It seems to follow as a necessary consequence from this actual supremacy of the insurgent government as a belligerent within the territory where it circulated, and from the necessity of civil obedience on the part of all who remained in it, that this currency must be considered in courts of law in the same light as if it had been issued by a foreign government, temporarily occupying a part of the territory of the United States.").

territory of a foreign State.[43] Reliance on a domestic conflict where preservation of sovereignty is not an issue to delineate the powers of an
Occupying Power in an international conflict dilutes the strict confines of
the conservationist principle.

To be fair, the nineteenth-century sources are not expressly used by the
Manual to substantiate law that has since been abandoned. But such implicit
substantiation is avoidable only because the main text of the Manual that is
supported by the old dicta is so generally worded that it can be interpreted as
correct with respect to both old and new doctrine. If the sources are to be taken
seriously, the main text acquires an entirely different – and objectionable –
meaning.

3.2.2 Germany, Japan, and Iraq: Rewriting Legal History

In a fair number of instances, the Manual references the practice of the
US administrations of Germany and Japan in the aftermath of World War II
to demonstrate its propositions related to the law of occupation.[44] These
references could serve as powerful authorities for the legality or legitimacy of
transformative occupation, since social, economic, and political transformation were the very *raison d'être* of these administrations. However, to the extent
that their invocation is intended to substantiate any claim of legality specifically under the law of occupation, that invocation involves a revision of legal

---

[43] Benvenisti (above note 15), 36. The Civil War-era Lieber Code did not formally acknowledge
the interest of the population as a relevant factor. General Order No. 100, Instructions for the
Government of Armies of the United States in the Field (Apr. 24, 1863), reprinted in *The War
of the Rebellion: A Compilation of the Official Records of the Union and Confederate Armies*,
Series III, Vol. 3 (GPO 1899) (the Lieber Code), www.loc.gov/rr/frd/Military_Law/Lieber_
Collection/pdf/Instructions-gov-armies.pdf, Art. 3: "Martial Law in a hostile country consists
in the suspension, by the occupying military authority, of the criminal and civil law, and of the
domestic administration and government in the occupied place or territory, and in the
substitution of military rule and force for the same, as well as in the dictation of general
laws, *as far as military necessity requires* this suspension, substitution, or dictation" (emphasis
added).

[44] E.g., ¶ 11.1.2.6 on the applicability of the International Covenant on Civil and Political Rights
(ICCPR) ("This limit to the scope of the ICCPR's obligations was proposed by the United
States to preclude the creation of obligations for States with respect to territories that they
occupied, such as post-World War II Germany and Japan."); ¶ 11.8.2 on administration of
occupied territory through continued performance by local government ("It may, for example,
call upon the local authorities to administer designated rear areas, subject to the guidance and
direction of the Occupying Power."); ¶ 11.23.5 on the power of the Occupying Power to
institute Exchange and Asset Controls). Some of the obfuscation of status stems from the use
in the fact that these administrations consisted of military government which the Manual
identifies with "belligerent occupation" (¶ 11.1.1.1). While in some cases the two coincide, here
is one when they do not.

history. In 1945 the applicability of the law of occupation to those administrations was highly controversial, precisely because the situation was regarded as incompatible with the fundamentals of that law as seen through the conservationist premise. Many scholars espoused the view that the administrations did constitute occupation, with some of them contending that the law of occupation actually accommodated transformative occupation.[45] But the United States government rejected this view.[46] It relied on the defeated States' "unconditional surrender" to claim that the law of occupation was inapplicable once hostilities had ended.[47]

Incredibly, however, the Manual now proposes to rely on US practice in Germany and Japan as instances of implementation of the law of occupation. Even if one regards this as a late admission by the US that the law of occupation was applicable in those situations,[48] that is beside the point. Belated admission might render earlier practice subject to the law of occupation; but it offers no guarantee that the practice was actually compatible with the law of occupation in a manner which justifies referencing that practice as a reflection of the law. The problem is not merely the refusal by the US to acknowledge the applicability *de jure* of the law of occupation. Indeed, had the United States committed itself to apply the law of occupation *de facto* in Germany, for example, its practice could have been pertinent to identifying the law.[49] But the United States only declared that it would voluntarily apply in Germany "principles of international law" which are "pertinent" and expressed in the Hague Regulations.[50] This is a far cry from a commitment to apply the law of occupation *de facto*. The same caution that prompted the

---

[45] A. Roberts, "What Is a Military Occupation?" (1984) 55 *British Yearbook of International Law* 249, 269–70.

[46] Benvenisti (above note 15), 161. *United States v. Altstoetter et al.*, Trials of War Criminals Before the NMT III, 960. The case law of the US Supreme Court suggests that it was not averse to the application of the law of occupation, at least in some respects. *Madsen v. Kinsella*, 343 US 341 (1952) 357 ("Although the local government was no longer a 'Military Government,' it was a government prescribed by an Occupying Power, and it depended upon the continuing military occupancy of the territory.").

[47] The substantive shortcomings of this argument are considered below.

[48] Although in light of ¶¶ 11.1.3.2 and 11.1.3.4 this is difficult to maintain. Discussion below.

[49] As is the case of Israel, where the government denies the *de jure* applicability of GC IV but has committed to apply its humanitarian provisions. This renders Israeli practice to be considered as pertinent for identifying that law.

[50] Forrest Hannaman, Chief Legal Advice Division, Memorandum to Office of Economic Affairs – Finance Division on Revenues from Laender-Owned Property (Mar. 30, 1951), repr. in XX Selected Opinions, Jan. 1, 1951–Apr. 30, 1951 of Office of the United States High Commissioner for Germany, Office of General Counsel, Frankfurt, Germany, 57–58, cited in ¶ 11.1.3.4 fn. 44: "The Hague Regulations were designed to define the powers of a belligerent occupant of enemy territory during, or shortly after, hostilities. As such, they cannot be

US Government to avoid being fully constrained by the law of occupation in 1945 should now guide any attempt to present US practice at the time as a reflection of that law.

A similar quandary surrounds the Manual's reference to the administration of Iraq by the US-established and US-governed CPA[51] to demonstrate the implementation of the law of occupation. Again, controversy exists among those who consider that the goals of the administration have made the law of occupation inadequate and anachronistic[52] and advocated its replacement either through Security Council action or by modification of international law;[53] those who opine that the law of occupation can accommodate transformative projects at least in some circumstances;[54] and those who hold that the law of occupation can neither be stretched so far as to encompass transformative projects nor simply be set aside on that ground.[55] As the Manual notes, UNSC Resolution 1483 partially resolved the dispute over the status of Iraq when it recognized the fact of occupation in Iraq in 2003.[56]

considered literally applicable to the situation in Germany today, and we cannot consider without reflection that the Occupying Powers may ... the Hague Regulations may be considered as expressing principles of international law which are pertinent to our situation, those principles should be observed by us."); Major G. B. Crook and Major W. G. Downey, Memorandum for the Judge Advocate General, "Present Applicability of Hague and Geneva Conventions in Germany," repr. in E. H. Feilchenfeld and Members of the Institute of World Polity, *Status of Germany*, 1 World Polity 182, 196 (1958) cited in ¶ 11.1.3.4 fn. 44 ("We conclude, therefore, that: a. The authority of the Allied Control Council and of the United States zone commander in occupied Germany is not limited by the provisions of Section III of the Regulations annexed to the Hague Convention IV (1907) and such Regulations have not been applicable to the occupation of Germany since 5 June 1945 ... The general rules expressed in the Hague Regulations will be considered as guiding principles unless and until specific U.S. or Allied occupation policies require deviation.").

51   J. Dobbins et al., "Occupying Iraq: A History of the Coalition Provisional Authority," 13, www .rand.org/content/dam/rand/pubs/monographs/2009/RAND_MG847.pdf.

52   See K. Boon, "Obligations of the New Occupier: The Contours of *Jus Post Bellum*" (2008) 31 *Loyola LA International and Comparative Law Review* 101, 107.

53   D. J. Scheffer, "Beyond Occupation Law" (2003) 97 *American Journal of International Law* 842 (e.g., 849, "occupation law will continue to apply, albeit with qualified interpretations if necessary, even to the benevolent occupier unless either (1) the UN Security Council has acted in a manner that requires modification of occupation law obligations consistent with a Council mandate governing the deployment of military forces in another country or (2) international law evolves to accommodate modern transformational occupation").

54   Benvenisti (above note 15), 268–75; Y. Arai-Takahashi, *The Law of Occupation: Continuity and Change of International Humanitarian Law, and Its Interaction With International Human Rights Law* (Leiden: Brill, 2009), 115–36; J. Yoo, "Iraqi Reconstruction and the Law of Occupation" (2004) 11 *UC Davis Journal of International Law and Policy* 7, 10–21.

55   G. H. Fox, "Transformative Occupation and the Unilateralist Impulse – ICRC" (2012) 94 *International Review of the Red Cross* 237.

56   Security Council Resolution 1483(2003) (May 22, 2003) preambular para. 13 ("recognizing the specific authorities, responsibilities, and obligations under applicable international law of [the

The CPA's practice is nonetheless a poor authority for the implementation of the law of occupation (even if the two happened to coincide). First, according to the Manual itself, Security Council authorization can grant the Occupying Power authority beyond the limits of the law of occupation.[57] If that is the case, then the practice of the CPA subsequent to the adoption of Resolution 1483 cannot be regarded as necessarily grounded in, or compatible with, the law of occupation. For example, the Manual states, in the context of measures to remedy corruption or unfairness in the judicial system as a measure to ensure public order and safety, that "a facility may be established to help resolve conflicting property claims on a voluntary basis."[58] The only authority for this is CPA Regulation No. 4, which established such a facility. In other words, the Manual relies on conduct under authority which is not limited by the law of occupation to demonstrate the implementation of the law of occupation. This regulation changes local law, creates a new legal institution, and modifies the legal system. One might submit that the CPA acted within the confines of the law of occupation even if the Security Council had authorized it to go beyond that law; but the US Government has not made any such submission, and there is no reason to assume that it attempted to restrain itself in that respect.

Practice prior to the adoption of Resolution 1483 also cannot be used to demonstrate the implementation of the law of occupation, because at that time the United States had not explicitly acknowledged its status as an Occupying Power. In one instance, the Manual assumes that the legal status of occupation originated on April 16, 2003 with the promulgation by General Franks of his "Freedom Message to the Iraqi People," which established the CPA. That message implicitly adopted the rights and duties of an Occupying Power under modern international law, but did not reference the Geneva Conventions or proclaim an official Occupying Power status.[59] The eventual recognition by the United States of its status as an Occupying Power[60] does not retroactively render its earlier practice an example of compliance with the law

United States of America and the United Kingdom of Great Britain and Northern Ireland] as Occupying Powers under unified command").

[57] DoD Law of War Manual, ¶ 11.1.2.5 ("In cases of conflict with obligations in other treaties or under customary international law, such obligations provided by the U.N. Security Council may prevail. Thus, such authority may be used to take action that would not otherwise be permissible under the law of belligerent occupation.").

[58] *Ibid.*, ¶ 11.10.1.2.   [59] *Ibid.*, ¶ 11.2.4 fn. 75.

[60] Supplemental Brief of the United States, Apr. 22, 2005, *United States of America ex rel. DR, Inc. v. Custer Battles, LLC*, 376 F. Supp. 2d 617 (ED Va. 2005), 2005 Digest of United States Practice in International Law 228, 232, cited in the DoD Law of War Manual, ¶ 11.1.1.2 fn. 7 ("The United States and the United Kingdom, and other member states of the Coalition were

of occupation. The Manual, however, obfuscates this point. For example, it references the CPA's first regulation of May 16, 2003 (a week before the adoption of Resolution 1483) as an example of proclamation of occupation.[61] Since until the adoption of Resolution 1483 the CPA did not unambiguously regard itself as an organ of an Occupying Power, nor used the terminology of the law of occupation in practice, there appears to be no reason to regard its practice as reflective of the law of occupation.

3.2.3 Conclusion

There is nothing reproachable in a State's preference for a permissive inter-pretation of the law, and in its reliance on practice and other sources that corresponds with that view. Difficulties nonetheless arise when the sources are of dubious value as legal authorities for the propositions which they purport to support. There is much to criticize in the Manual's source selection, in particular that it is limited almost exclusively to unilateral US practice and therefore claims authority on the basis of prior conduct that it is questionable as a reflection of widespread State practice; and that it is devoid of any reference to the voluminous and influential scholarly writing on the law of occupation since the publication of the previous Manual.[62] With regard to the use of old sources, Professor David Glazier boldly suggests those were cited so as to avoid acknowledging subsequent developments constraining US conduct in ways that the drafters of the Manual wished to avoid.[63] One might venture to go further and suggest that the sources were selected not only for what they

the Occupying Powers in Iraq under the laws and usages of war. The CPA was the adminis-trative device that the Coalition created under the laws and usages of war to perform civil government functions in liberated Iraq during the brief period of occupation. As an active member of the Coalition, the United States played an important role in, and had certain responsibilities for, the occupation, which it chose to fulfill through creation of and participa-tion in the CPA.").

[61]   Coalition Provisional Authority Regulation No. 1, § 1(1) (May 16, 2003) ("The CPA shall exercise powers of government temporarily in order to provide for the effective administration of Iraq during the period of transitional administration . . . "). CPA Regulation 1 refers to Security Council Resolution 1483 (and to the "laws of war") but the resolution was not adopted until a week later. Accordingly, the Regulation cannot be regarded as referring to "occupation."

[62]   E.g., Dinstein (above note 16); R. Kolb and S. Vité, *Le Droit de l'occupation militaire: perspectives historiques et enjeux juridiques actuels* (Brussels: Bruylant, 2009); Arai-Takahashi (above note 54); E. Benvenisti, *The International Law of Occupation* (Princeton University Press, 1993); and Benvenisti (above note 15), to mention only the monographs. D. W. Glazier et al., "A Critical Assessment of the New Department of Defense Law of War Manual" (2017) 42 *Yale Journal of International Law* 215.

[63]   Glazier et al. (above note 62).

exclude from the Manual, but also for what they include in it. The Manual's consistent reliance on authorities that predate contemporary law, and on sources that reject the applicability of the law of occupation altogether, casts a heavy shadow on the credibility of the Manual's assertions. This section argues that the sources were selected because they give credence to a restrictive reading of the conservationist principle and to an expansive reading of the Occupying Power's scope of authority.

4 APPLICABILITY OF THE LAW OF OCCUPATION: EVADING THE LAW

Two propositions have been put forward to resolve the tension between transformative measures and the law of occupation. One, that other bodies of law need to be found that authorize transformative measures and take precedence over the law of occupation; the other, that the law of occupation does not apply in situations in which transformative measures are taken, and therefore its constraints are irrelevant to the legality of such measures. As noted above, the latter was the US argument with respect to post-World War II Germany. The view that situations involving transformative measures are inherently outside the scope of the law of occupation raises a broader question regarding the conditions for the applicability of this law.

It is not controversial that occupation exists (and the law of occupation applies) when territory is effectively placed under the authority of a hostile army.[64] Nonetheless, the precise meaning of these concepts has been a matter of dispute. The 2016 Manual's elaboration on this meaning is therefore a welcome addition. This section explores the interpretation of these concepts in the Manual and their implications for various situations. It does so by focusing on situations that the new Manual excludes from the scope of the law. As will be shown, the Manual adopts a very narrow definition of occupation, excluding, *inter alia*, situations in which transformative measures characteristically arise (such as liberation of friendly territory, or post-war).

4.1 *"Under the Authority": Distinguishing Invasion from Occupation*

The manual states that for occupation to exist "the Occupying Power must have taken measures to establish its authority"[65] and "the Occupying Power

---

[64] Hague Regulations Art. 42; see DoD Law of War Manual, ¶¶ 11.2.2.1, 11.2.2.2, 11.2.2.3.
[65] DoD Law of War Manual, ¶ 11.2.2.1 (citing Lieber Code, Art. 3).

must substitute its authority for that of the territorial State."[66] This wording reflects the view that occupation depends not on only territorial control, which gives rise to obligations towards the population, but requires also the direct assertion of control over the population through the establishment of an administration.[67]

This narrow interpretation of occupation finds support in the wording of Hague Regulations Article 42 that the territory must be "*actually* placed *under the authority* of the hostile army" (emphasis added).[68] The International Court of Justice appears also to subscribe to this understanding in the *Congo v. Uganda* ruling which states that for the law of occupation to be held applicable, the Court "will need to satisfy itself that the Ugandan armed forces in the DRC were not only stationed in particular locations but also that they had substituted their own authority for that of the Congolese Government."[69] Nonetheless, most prominent scholars[70] and the International Committee of the Red Cross (ICRC),[71] as well as judicial bodies such as the International Military Tribunal (IMT),[72] the International Criminal Tribunal for Yugoslavia (ICTY)[73] and the Israeli

---

[66] *Ibid.*, ¶ 11.2.2.2 (reiterating FM 27-10, ¶ 355).

[67] The 2016 Manual is nonetheless less explicit than the 1956 Army Field Manual which asserts the "necessity for military government" (although the necessity described may be factual rather than normative) (FM 27-10, ¶ 362).

[68] 1958 British Manual cited in HCJ 102/82 *Zemel and others v. The Minister of Defence and another*, PD 37(3) 365, 372.

[69] *Congo v. Uganda* (above note 35), para. 173. But see another interpretation of that ruling in Benvenisti (above note 15), 50.

[70] Benvenisti (above note 15), 46–47. See also M. Sassòli, "The Concept and the Beginning of Occupation," in A. Clapham, P. Gaeta, and M. Sassòli (eds.), *The 1949 Geneva Conventions: A Commentary* (Oxford University Press, 2015), 1389. Note that von Glahn and Stone, which the Manual cites profusely, are not mentioned in this section at all, perhaps because they make no mention of the requirement of setting up an administration.

[71] ICRC, *Commentary on the First Geneva Convention (I) for the Amelioration of the Condition of the Wounded and Sick in Armed Forces in the Field*, 2nd ed. (Cambridge University Press, 2016), para. 302: "effective control does not require the exercise of full authority over the territory; instead, the mere capacity to exercise such authority would suffice"; and para. 304: "the following three cumulative conditions need to be met in order to establish a state of occupation . . . foreign forces are in a position to exercise authority over the territory concerned (or parts thereof) in lieu of the local government," citing *Zemel* (above note 68).

[72] *Hostage Case, United States v. List (Wilhelm) and others*, Trial Judgment, Case No. 7, (1948) 11 TWC 757 ("To the extent that the occupant's control is maintained and that of the civil government eliminated, the area will be said to be occupied.").

[73] *Prosecutor v. Naletilić and Martinović*, Case No IT-98-34-T, Judgment, ¶ 217 (ICTY, Mar. 31, 2003) notes that guidelines for whether the authority has actually been established include that "the Occupying Power must be in a position to substitute its own authority for that of the occupied authorities" or that "a temporary administration has been established over the territory."

Supreme Court,[74] have rejected this narrow interpretation, which allows the invading force to determine unilaterally whether the law of occupation would be applicable to it or not, and to intentionally evade its obligations under that law by inaction,[75] or by installing a proxy government to exercise functions on its behalf.[76] A broader approach, which has been adopted in the ICRC's 2016 Commentary on the First Geneva Convention, is that authority is established not by the *exercise* of authority over the territory, but by the *capacity* to exercise such authority.[77] In other words, the invading force need only be *in a position* to substitute its authority for that of the territorial State's for the law of occupation to be applicable.[78] No formal administration is required.

The Manual's approach sets prerequisites for the applicability of the law of occupation that are actually even more demanding than the actual establishment of an administration. When distinguishing invasion from occupation, it states that mere presence might not constitute occupation, because it "might not constitute an effective and firm possession of enemy territory, or the belligerent State might lack *the intention to displace and substitute the enemy State's authority with its own*" (emphasis added).[79] This introduction of intent merits some comments. First, the notion that occupation depends on a particular intent or goal intent has no support in international law.[80] It might even appear inconsistent with the Manual's earlier assertion that occupation is a question of fact,[81] although the earlier wording emphasized only that intent was insufficient (and must be accompanied by actual control), rather than that it was not required (alongside that control).[82]

---

[74] *Zemel* (above note 68), 373 ("the applicability of the third section of the Hague regulations and the applicability of parallel provisions of the Fourth Convention are not dependent on there having been set up a special administrative system, which takes the form of military government. The obligations and powers of the military force, which derive from the effective possession of a particular territory, arise and are created by virtue of the military control over the territory, namely, even if the military force maintains its control only through its ordinary combat units, without setting up and dedicating a special military framework for governing purposes.").

[75] Benvenisti (above note 15), 46.

[76] T. Ferraro, "Determining the Beginning and End of an Occupation under International Humanitarian Law" (2012) 94 *International Review of the Red Cross* 133, 151.

[77] ICRC Commentary (above note 71), para. 302; *Zemel* (above note 68), 373.

[78] UK Manual (above note 11), ¶ 11.3.   [79] DoD Law of War Manual, ¶ 11.1.3.1.

[80] But see Ferraro (above note 76), 135.   [81] DoD Law of War Manual, ¶ 11.2.1.

[82] "The fact of occupation, as a requirement for the exercise of authority over the occupied territory, prevents a State from simply claiming the authorities of military government over an enemy territory without actually controlling such territory" (¶ 11.2.1). It is ironic that this assertion is supported by the *Rice* case, criticized above, which stated that "By the conquest

It is also interesting to note the change of wording from the 1956 Army Field Manual, which referred to the "intention of holding [the area]" as a requisite for occupation.[83] The previous requirement was almost redundant, since without intent to hold, there is unlikely to be "effective and firm possession." The new requirement of intent – to displace and substitute the enemy State's authority with its own – has new and far-reaching implications. For example, an invading force may deny its status as an Occupying Power on the ground that it does not intend to substitute the local government with its own authority but promotes and supports a transfer of power between local actors. Examples of such instances are the US interventions in the Dominican Republic in 1965, in Grenada in 1983–84, and in Panama in 1989; and perhaps also in Afghanistan in late 2001, when less than a month had passed between the time that the US-led coalition secured effective control over parts of Afghanistan, and the time that a local government was formed.[84]

What distinguishes occupation from sovereignty is not its purpose but its temporariness and lack of accountability *vis-à-vis* the local population.[85] Nonetheless, the argument that the law of occupation is ill-suited for the realization of projects with certain goals and therefore such projects do not fall within its ambit (rather than simply violate it) is at the heart of the debate on the law of occupation and transformative measures. By introducing intent as a relevant factor, the 2016 Manual limits the scope of the law of occupation and expands the foreign force's freedom of action, thereby implicating the law related to transformative measures.

---

and military occupation of Castine, the enemy acquired that firm possession *which enabled him to exercise the fullest rights of sovereignty over that place*" (emphasis added). This contradicts the Manual's view discussed above that occupation requires the actual exercise of powers rather than merely the ability to do so. *Cf.* the Canadian Manual which clarifies that intent is not a substitute for effective control (and does not require it in addition to effective control, either): "Occupation must be actual and effective, that is, there must be more than a mere declaration or proclamation that possession has been taken, or that there is the intention to take possession." Office of the Judge Advocate General, Law of Armed Conflict at the Operational and Tactical Levels, Joint Doctrine Manual (2001) section 1203(2), www.fichl .org/fileadmin/_migrated/content_uploads/Canadian_LOAC_Manual_2001_English.pdf.

[83] FM 27-10, ¶ 352. "intent to hold" appears in *MacLeod v. United States*, 229 US 416, 425 (1913), cited – ironically – in the 2016 Manual, noting "There has been considerable discussion in the cases and in works of authoritative writers upon the subject of what constitutes an occupation which will give the right to exercise governmental authority. Such occupation is not merely invasion, but is invasion plus possession of the enemy's country for the purpose of holding it temporarily at least." DoD Law of War Manual, ¶ 11.2.1 fn. 49.

[84] Benvenisti (above note 15), 187.

[85] P. Stirk, *The Politics of Military Occupation* (Edinburgh University Press, 2009), 43.

4.2 *"of a Hostile Army"*

According to the Manual, this term means that belligerent occupation "applies to enemy territory" and that "the existence of an occupation presupposes a hostile relationship between the invading force's State and the State of the occupied territory."[86] The Manual presupposes that occupation concerns the relationship only between State governments, and not, as contemporary conceptions hold, between the governing force and the population, which may not always be represented by an effective and constitutionally valid government. Consequently, the Manual excludes from the scope of occupation various situations in which, for whatever reason, there is no effective government, or it is not representative. As will be elaborated here, this narrow interpretation deprives a population from much necessary protection.

4.2.1 Liberation of Friendly Territory: No Hostility

The Manual excludes "liberation of friendly territory"[87] from the scope of belligerent occupation, on the ground that the requirement of "hostility" is not satisfied between the foreign State and the territorial State. This calls to mind the distinction between belligerent and pacific occupation. However, this distinction has little justification given the rationale of the law of occupation.[88] The Manual equates "hostility" with "unfriendliness." However, interpreting "hostile" as "unfriendly," as the Manual does, rather than as "unconsenting,"[89] is erroneous: consent is an objective criterion. Its existence is a factual question, capable of objective assessment (even if making this assessment in a given instance might be difficult).

In contrast, friendliness is a subjective criterion, dependent on how the foreign State perceives its relationship with the territorial one, and how it views its mission.[90] By excluding "liberation of friendly territory" from the law of occupation the Manual therefore allows an invading State to determine its legal obligations unilaterally. This is particularly problematic when two local governments, one friendly and the other not so, are vying for control, as was the

---

[86] DoD Law of War Manual, ¶ 11.2.2.3.   [87] *Ibid.*, ¶¶ 11.1.3.2, 11.2.2.3.
[88] Roberts (above note 45), 300–1.
[89] ICRC Commentary (above note 71), para. 304 ("the armed forces of a State are physically present in a foreign territory without the consent of the effective local government in place at the time of the invasion"); Sassòli (above note 70), 1402 MN 28.
[90] The Manual also mentions "co-belligerent" States, implying that friendliness stems from being engaged in a conflict with a common enemy, whether in alliance or not. J. P. Grant and J. C. Barker, "Co-belligerent(s)," in *Parry and Grant Encyclopaedic Dictionary of International Law* (Oxford University Press, 2009), 102.

case in Afghanistan in 2001. The ICRC has addressed this problem when it noted that restricting the applicability of the law of occupation to relations between States which declared mutual hostility leads to an "unreasonable" result, whereby the foreign State's subjective considerations determine the applicability of the law of occupation.[91] It would be equally unreasonable for a State to preempt a claim of occupation by declaring itself "friendly" to the territorial State.[92]

The Manual's avoidance of the requirement of consent to negate occupation is particularly conspicuous in comparison with the 1956 Army Field Manual, which distinguished occupation from "friendly territory subject to civil affairs administration" established "pursuant to an agreement, express or implied."[93] According to the 1956 Army Field Manual, the law of occupation is excluded when the substitution of authority is agreed upon. In the absence of such an agreement, the situation remains governed by the law of occupation (and therefore "military government may be established in the area"[94]). In other words, the 1956 Army Field Manual uses the term "friendly" but does not forego the requirement of consent to preclude the law of occupation. One might relax the notion of consent to include formal alliances in armed conflict, such as those of World War II,[95] or calls for assistance in exercising self-defense. Even this is not self-evident, since consent of a government to the presence of foreign forces on its territory in order to liberate it, while negating a violation of *jus ad bellum*, does not necessarily imply consent to be governed by the same forces. But in whichever manner consent may be expressed, the 2016 Manual does not require it at all.

Although the 2016 Manual no longer requires an agreement on civil affairs administration to preclude the law of occupation, it does recommend that such an agreement be concluded with the government of the territorial State, as was the case of the administration of France,[96] Belgium, the Netherlands, and Greece at the end of World War II.[97] This raises the question of whose consent can preclude the law of occupation. According to the Manual, it is the consent of the *de jure* government, hence the mention of agreements concluded with governments-in-exile, despite their lack of effective control over

[91] ICRC Commentary (above note 71), para. 327.   [92] See also GC IV, Art. 47.
[93] FM 27-10, ¶ 354. The UK Manual also refers to the presence in the territory of an allied State "in pursuance of a treaty or agreement between allies." UK Manual (above note 11), ¶ 11.1.2.
[94] FM 27-10, ¶ 354. Military government is "the form of administration which may be established and maintained for the government of areas of the following types *that have been subjected to military occupation*" (1956 Manual, section 12, emphasis added).
[95] Declaration by United Nations (Jan. 1, 1942), www.ibiblio.org/pha/policy/1942/420101a.html.
[96] DoD Law of War Manual, ¶ 11.1.3.2 fn. 30.   [97] Dinstein (above note 16), 37.

the territory. This position contradicts the principle that classification of a situation for the purposes of occupation law should be made only on the basis of the prevailing facts; it also leads to often endless controversies about the legitimacy of the authority concerned.[98] Therefore, the ICRC holds that consent is required "of the effective local government in place at the time of the invasion."[99] However, if the rationale of the law of occupation in this context is to protect the civilian population from a conflict of interests in the relationship between itself and the governing forces,[100] then any governing force which does not have the consent of an accountable authority should be regarded as an Occupying Power.[101] Accordingly, there is no reason to attach significance to consent by a *de facto* government if it is not itself accountable for giving that consent. Sassòli considers that the consent of both *de facto* and *de jure* governments is required.[102]

Arguably, however, it is not consent as such that should be a criterion in the first place, but the existence of a conflict of interests.[103] A *de jure* government is deemed to represent the interests of the population. Its consent to the governance by foreign forces creates a presumption that there is no conflict of interests between those forces and the population. If it is also a *de facto* government, it can ensure that no conflict arises in practice. But if either effective control or legitimacy are lacking, there is no one to ensure protection of the interests of the population. Consent should therefore obviate occupation only if it emanates from an authority which has both *de jure* and *de facto* power. Otherwise, a conflict of interests is inherent to the exercise of control by a foreign force, also in "friendly" and "liberated" territory.[104] A liberating force that is not

---

[98] Ferraro (above note 58), 153.

[99] ICRC Commentary (above note 71), para. 304 ("the armed forces of a State are physically present in a foreign territory without the consent of the *effective* local government in place at the time of the invasion" (emphasis added)). Arai-Takahashi (above note 54), 9; and in a slightly different context: ICRC Commentary (above note 71), para. 233: "The only possible way the nature of the armed conflict could change as a result of the defeat of the former government is to ascertain that the new government *is effective* and consents to the presence or military operations of foreign forces in its territory ... " (emphasis added).

[100] Benvenisti (above note 15), 59 citing Kolb and Vité (above note 62), 114.

[101] Benvenisti (above note 15), 59–60; Michael Bothe in expert meeting 37, cited by Sassòli (above note 70), 1404 MN 32 and surrounding text; Roberts (above note 45), 300.

[102] See also Sassòli (above note 70), 1402 MN 28. If both *de facto* and *de jure* governments give their consent, it is likely that the *de facto* government is itself governing with the *de jure* government's consent (e.g., when a first liberator acting with the consent of a government-in-exile voluntarily passes the baton to a subsequent government acting with similar consent). If the *de facto* government is not governing with the consent with the *de jure* government, it is unlikely to give its consent to a third party.

[103] Kyo Arai, Minerva/ICRC IHL conference presentation, May 22, 2017 (draft with the author).

[104] Dinstein (above note 16), 35; Benvenisti (above note 15), 59.

accountable to the population cannot benefit from any presumption of non-hostility. In 1925 Colby assumed convergence of consent and effective control, writing that occupation could not exist "in allied territory, for in such a case the friendly ally would conduct its own government and the troops would be assisting by invitation not exercising any belligerent power against the sovereign people in the lands they occupied."[105] Regrettably, the interpretation in the 2016 Manual of "liberation of friendly territory" is very different from Colby's formulation. The requisites of consent and effective control have been attenuated to such an extent that they have become meaningless.

Finally, like "friendly," the term "liberation" is open to subjective interpretation and therefore should not be a criterion for the applicability of the law. The authors of the 1956 Army Field Manual, writing in the aftermath of World War II and at the onset of the Cold War, perhaps assumed that an enemy's enemy was necessarily an ally. Accordingly, "friendly territory that was previously occupied by the enemy" (11.2.2) was easy enough to identify. But in contemporary armed conflicts this dichotomy is no longer tenable.

Moreover, while the Manual gives liberation of "friendly territory that was previously occupied by the enemy" as an *example* for the absence of a hostile relationship, it stipulates the rule more widely: "The law of belligerent occupation does not apply to the liberation of friendly territory."[106] There need not be an "enemy" as such. In fact, the Manual says nothing as to what constitutes "liberation." This omission might permit denial of the applicability of the law of occupation in a wider set of circumstances. To give the obvious example, in early 2003, some US policymakers asserted that US action in Iraq was not an occupation at all because it constituted "liberation."[107] This was said with respect to a State that was not involved in an armed conflict immediately prior to the US invasion, let alone occupied, by an "enemy" other than the one purporting to be liberating it.

In conclusion, the exclusion of "liberating friendly territory" from the ambit of the law of occupation permits an invading force to determine the applicability of the law of occupation by using subjective criteria, in disregard of the interests of the local population.

4.2.2 NIAC: No Inter-State Relations

The 2016 Manual considers, for the first time, the notion of occupation in NIAC.[108] It stipulates that the law of occupation does not apply when State

---

[105]   E. Colby, "Occupation under the Laws of War" (1925) 25 *Columbia Law Review* 904, 907.
[106]   DoD Law of War Manual, ¶ 11.1.3.2.   [107]   Roberts (above note 1), 608.
[108]   DoD Law of War Manual, ¶ 11.1.3.3.

forces liberate the State's own territory from rebel forces, or when foreign forces conduct operations (against non-State parties) with the consent of the territorial State (a transnational NIAC). In another section, the Manual rejects the possibility of occupation in a NIAC more comprehensively, including when effective control is exercised by a non-State actor.[109]

With respect to a purely internal conflict, the Manual relies on Baxter's reasoning that:

> [i]n internal conflict, the lawful government and the insurgents will both maintain that there is only "territory of a party to the conflict." Territory cannot be belligerently occupied by the lawful government or the rebels. There is no starting point which divides territory into friendly and enemy areas, so that, when the latter type of area is occupied, it will be belligerently occupied. It surely cannot be maintained that the insurgents should be required to treat all territory over which they exercise control as being belligerently occupied or that the lawful government should be forced to treat territory liberated from the control of rebels as belligerently occupied. It is of the essence of belligerent occupation that it should be exercised over foreign, enemy territory. Such requirements as that of Article 43 of the Hague Regulations that the occupant must respect, "unless absolutely prevented, the laws in force in the country" are simply unworkable in domestic conflict.[110]

The argument on the non-foreignness of the territory appears compelling, but it only applies if that sovereignty is undisputed.[111] That may not always be the case. The difficulty in leaving the applicability of the law of occupation dependent on the determination of territorial claims,[112] which, like legitimacy of government (and related to it) are often intractable, has been acknowledged by the Eritrea-Ethiopia Claims Commission, which stated that the law of occupation applies not only to uncontested

---

[109] *Ibid.*, ¶ 17.1.3.1 ("Similarly, it is the essence of belligerent occupation that it should be exercised over foreign, enemy territory; thus, occupation law rules would not apply to internal armed conflict.").

[110] R. A. Baxter, "Ius in Bello Interno: The Present and Future Law," in J. Moore (ed.), *Law and Civil War in the Modern World* (Baltimore: Johns Hopkins University Press, 1974), 518, 531, cited at DoD Law of War Manual, ¶ 17.1.3.1.

[111] See Sassòli who takes a similar stance as the Manual but restricts it to a situation in which sovereignty is uncontested. Sassòli (above note 70), 1406 MN 36. Similarly Kolb maintains that there is no occupation over territory which is internationally recognized as the State's sovereignty territory. R. Kolb, "Etude sur l'occupation et sur l'Article 47 de la IVème Convention de Genève du 12 Août 1949 relative à la protection des personnes civiles en temps de guerre: le degré d'intangibilité des droits en territoire occupé" (2002) 10 *African Yearbook of International Law* 267, 281.

[112] Arai-Takahashi (above note 54), 8.

territory.[113] The Claims Commission's view, which has been endorsed by the ICRC, was enunciated in the context of a regular international armed conflict (IAC). But it may be pertinent in other situations. Take a secessionist conflict in which the secessionist entity's assertion of independence is recognized by some States, for whom the conflict is an IAC (in which occupation may occur), but not by others, including the mother State, for which it is a NIAC (in which, according to the Manual, occupation cannot occur). For example, if Serbia regained control over Kosovo or part thereof, would its control constitute occupation? Serbia would regard itself as liberating sovereign territory from the control of rebels. In the view of Kosovo and many States, Serbia would be occupying foreign territory. Arguably, the obligations of Serbia should hinge in such a situation not on its territorial claim but on the relations between itself and the population. According to the Claims Commission's view, at the first stage, at least, Serbian forces would be considered hostile[114] and therefore an Occupying Power. Not so according to the Manual, according to which the matter first depends on whether the conflict is an IAC or not. This, however, is a matter of view, leaving the protection of the population dependent on political acts of recognition by other States.

Moreover, the difficulty raised by Baxter that "[t]here is no starting point which divides territory into friendly and enemy areas"[115] turns on the character of the territory. But the applicability of the law of occupation should turn on the relationship between the forces controlling the territory and the population in it.[116] Therefore, if at issue is control over territory by a non-State actor, then arguably it is sufficient that this control is hostile to the State and does not derive from the will of the inhabitants. The interests of the non-State actor, which is sovereign under neither international nor domestic law, are at odds with those of the population. It is therefore not clear why "it surely cannot be"

[113]   Eritrea-Ethiopia Claims Commission, Partial Award, Central Front, Ethiopia's Claim 2 (28 Apr. 2004), para. 29. See also Sassòli (above note 70), 1406 NM 36. This does not imply that contested territory is necessarily occupied. Kolb maintains that any presence outside the internationally recognized borders of the State would fall within the scope of occupation, on the ground that regardless of its status, it is not within the sovereignty of the invading force. Kolb (above note 111), 281. But this begs the question whether the territory is within or outside the internationally recognized borders.

[114]   The situation might change if Serbia declared that it was reestablishing its sovereignty over Kosovo. Its government would then be accountable to the residents of Kosovo as in the rest of Serbia. On the other hand, for those that today regard Kosovo as a State, this would be an unlawful annexation.

[115]   As Baxter's explanation states at the outset.

[116]   The focus on the territory rather than on the forces underlie the exclusion of "liberation of friendly territory" as well as "post-war."

that this conflict of interests be reflected in the law. Application of the law of occupation to an internal occupation and to a non-State actor might require some adjustments,[117] but there is no reason to dismiss it *a priori* in its entirety as "unworkable" according to the state of the modern law.

One might even query whether the matter is entirely one of *lex ferenda*. After all, the Lieber Code on which the Manual leans so heavily did envisage a situation of occupation in an internal conflict by analogizing the rebels to a State in some respects.[118] The notion of occupation by a non-State actor in an internal conflict can even find some (questionable) support in contemporary practice of international tribunals, for example the ICTY's recognition of acts in territory held by Serb Krajina as serious violations of the law of occupation,[119] and the reference by the ICC to Timbuktu as "occupied" by the Ansar Dine and al-Qaeda in the Islamic Magreb armed groups.[120]

The Manual seems to acknowledge the workability of the law of occupation in an internal conflict when it notes, in a novel stipulation, that "the law of belligerent occupation may be applicable to a non-international armed conflict when a non-State party to the conflict has been recognized as a belligerent."[121] The reference to belligerency raises a number of questions. First, how does recognition of belligerency vitiate the inherent problems that the Manual relates? After all, recognition of belligerency does not imply

[117] S. Sivakumaran, *The Law of Non-International Armed Conflict* (Oxford University Press, 2012), 529–32.

[118] It was important for Lieber to clarify that the Code concerned IAC but he did include the matter of internal conflicts at the end of the Code, in section X.

[119] *Prosecutor v. Martić*, Case No. IT-95-11, Trial Judgment, ¶¶ 100–04 (ICTY, June 12, 2007), www.icty.org/x/cases/martic/tjug/en/070612.pdf. Note, however, that although the Trial Chamber used the term "belligerent occupation" and referred to the Hague Regulations, the prohibition of plunder of public or private property, though derived from the Hague Regulations, is considered to have obtained both customary law status *and* applicability to NIAC. Thus, it may be that the Trial Chamber's usage of the term "occupation" should be regarded as a factual rather than a legal one.

[120] *Prosecutor v. Ahmad Al Faqi Al Mahdi*, Case No. ICC-01/12-01/15, Judgment and Sentence, ¶¶ 33, 36, 53 (Sept. 27, 2016), www.icc-cpi.int/CourtRecords/CR2016_07244.PDF. One might hold, however, that the ICC used the term "occupation" in these three paragraphs merely as a *factual or descriptive* sense. This is supported by its assertion that the area concerned "had fallen under the control of an armed group" (¶ 15).

[121] DoD Law of War Manual, ¶ 11.1.3.3. The text is unclear as to whether the occupant is the non-State actor or a third State occupying the territory previously controlled by a non-State actor. The better view seems to be that the text refers to the former, because the latter situation (1) is not clearly one of NIAC; (2) is either a regular instance of international armed conflict or, if the territorial State allowed the intervention, is covered by the first part of this section of the manual, i.e. foreign forces acting with the consent of the government; and (3) is self-contradictory: if a third party recognizes the non-State actor as belligerent, it is mandated to remain neutral and not become involved in the conflict.

recognition in a manner which enables Baxter's distinction of "friendly and enemy areas." For example, In the US Civil War, which was the paradigmatic recognition of belligerency, the Confederacy was recognized as belligerent, but that diplomatic act by no means conveyed recognition of its title to territory. So the "unworkability" of characterizing the territory which existed, still persists. Second, making occupation dependent on recognition of belligerency[122] leaves the protection of the population dependent on the discretion of the territorial or other States, rather than on relations on the ground. Third, the Manual is silent with regard to whose recognition is required for a state of belligerency to exist.[123]

Finally, belligerency and occupation address different relationships within a conflict. Historically, recognition of belligerency usually emanated from third States.[124] Even in the US Civil War, the Union Government recognized the Confederacy as a belligerent only because of the involvement of third parties, and, as the Manual notes, this was done in order to apply the laws of war to those third parties.[125] The matter is further complicated by the fact that recognition of belligerency triggers the applicability of the laws of armed conflict only between the recognizing State and the recognized belligerent, while occupation is an objective status based on the prevailing facts.[126] It cannot apply on a dispositive basis. If a territorial State recognizes a non-State actor as a belligerent, then the territory under its effective control becomes occupied not only in the relations between that State and the NSA, but also *vis-à-vis* third States, irrespective of whether they had recognized the belligerency.

In conclusion, to hinge the applicability of the law of occupation on belligerency is problematic. These problems and others have resulted in the concept of belligerency having been largely abandoned,[127] and contemporary

---

[122] For the controversy over whether belligerency depends on recognition see L. Moir, *The Law of Internal Armed Conflict* (Cambridge University Press, 2002), 11–14; V. Azarova and I. Blum, "Belligerency," *Max Planck Encyclopedia of International Law* 249 (September 2015), para. 20.

[123] For a view that recognition should be forthcoming from the territorial State's government see Dinstein (above note 16), 34.

[124] DoD Law of War Manual, ¶ 3.3.3.1, citing H. Lauterpacht, *Recognition in International Law* (Cambridge University Press, 1947), 175–76.

[125] DoD Law of War Manual, ¶ 3.3.3.2.

[126] It operates also between the Occupying Power and other States in secondary issues, such as the provision of humanitarian assistance. D. Akande and E.-C. Gillard, "Oxford Guidance on the Law Relating to Humanitarian Relief Operations in Situations of Armed Conflict," para. 33, https://docs.unocha.org/sites/dms/Documents/Oxford%20Guidance%20pdf.pdf.

[127] As the Manual acknowledges (¶ 3.3.3.1), in modern history there seems to have been only a single case of recognition of belligerency, cited by S. Talmon, *Recognition of Governments*

international law has repackaged it in Additional Protocol II to the Geneva Conventions (AP II). While the Manual's willingness to consider the applicability of the law of occupation in an internal conflict is innovative in comparison with existing law, it is based on an outdated and questionable foundation.

4.2.3 Post War: No State which Can Be Hostile

The Manual holds that before GC IV entered into force and specifically provided otherwise, the law of belligerent occupation was not applicable when hostilities had ceased completely. It explains that this law presupposes a hostile relationship between the foreign forces and the territorial State, but such hostility ceases to exist following an unconditional surrender or subjugation. As an example the Manual cites the American position on post-capitulation Germany in 1945, namely that unconditional surrender excluded the applicability of the law of occupation.[128] The legal argument with respect to unconditional surrender draws on the concept of *debellatio*, in which a party to a conflict ceases to exist altogether and thus there is no State in a position to consent or otherwise.[129] However, unconditional surrender and *debellatio* are not identical. Unconditional surrender may lead to *debellatio*, as in the case of Germany; but it might not, as demonstrated by the case of Japan. Indeed, the judicial authority cited by the Manual, the *Alstoetter* case, attributed the inapplicability of the law of occupation in post-World War II Germany not only to the unconditional surrender and consequent absence of hostilities, but also to the absence of a State with which a hostile relationship could exist.[130] In the case of Japan, sovereignty was retained in the terms of

---

    in *International Law* (Oxford: Clarendon Press, 1998), 309, citing the recognition by the members of the Andean Group (Bolivia, Colombia, Ecuador, Peru, and Venezuela) on June 17, 1979 of both sides in the Nicaraguan conflict as 'belligerents'" (¶ 3.3.3.1). S. Sivakumaran, *The Law of Non-International Armed Conflict* (Oxford University Press, 2012), 20 maintained that belligerency has not been abandoned entirely (desuetude) but has simply not been used.

[128] DoD Law of War Manual, ¶ 11.1.3.4. As noted earlier, this denial by the United States of the law of occupation to post-World War II Germany undermines the Manual's present reliance on it as implementation of that law.

[129] For an analysis and critique see Benvenisti (above note 15), 161.

[130] *United States v. Altstoetter et al.*, Trials of War Criminals Before the NMT III, 960 ("It is this fact of the *complete disintegration of the government in Germany*, followed by unconditional surrender and by occupation of the territory, which explains and justifies the assumption and exercise of supreme governmental power by the Allies. The same fact distinguishes the present occupation of Germany from the type of occupation which occurs when, in the

surrender, but those were sufficiently broad to enable the Occupying Power to introduce fundamental changes to Japanese law and institutions.[131]

In any case, under the contemporary emphasis in the law of occupation on protection of the population, the existence of an ousted government or the stage of hostilities seems to be immaterial. The conflict of interests between the foreign forces and the population exists regardless of those. To exclude the law of occupation on these grounds is simply to deprive the population of protection, by exempting the foreign force from any constraints. Needless to say, the complete absence of a government is the optimal ground for far-reaching changes which the law of occupation seeks to prevent. The 2016 Manual appears to mitigate the conclusion that occupation does not apply once hostilities have ended, when it acknowledges that under GC IV, Article 6, the Convention as a whole continues to apply in occupied territory until one year after the general close of military operations, and some of its provisions continue to apply for the full duration of the occupation.

However, reliance on GC IV, Article 6 to determine the applicability of the law of occupation is erroneous on a number of grounds. First, this Article regulates the applicability of the Convention and not of the law of occupation as a whole. Second, in light of the contemporary understanding of the law of occupation as applicable in a situation of hostility in the sense of a conflict of interests between the foreign force and the population, the effect of GC IV, Article 6 is actually to *terminate* in part the Convention's application at the end of a year (due to the absence of hostilities, and *despite* the continuing hostility). In other words, had it not been for Article 6, the Convention would have been fully applicable far beyond the termination of hostilities.[132] The reference in Article 6 to the continued applicability of certain provisions of the Convention until the end of the occupation only reinforces the fact that

---

course of actual warfare, an invading army enters and occupies the territory of another state, *whose government is still in existence and is in receipt of international recognition*, and whose armies, with those of its allies, are still in the field . . . By reason of the complete breakdown of government, industry, agriculture, and supply, they were under an imperative humanitarian duty of far wider scope to reorganize government and industry and to foster local democratic governmental agencies throughout the territory" (emphasis added).

[131] Benvenisti (above note 15), 160–61.

[132] The question arises whether GC IV, Art. 6 is still relevant following the adoption of Protocol Additional to the Geneva Conventions of Aug. 12, 1949, and Relating to the Protection of Victims of International Armed Conflicts, June 8, 1977, 1125 UNTS 3 (AP I), which provides that "the application of the Conventions and of this Protocol shall cease, in the territory of Parties to the conflict, on the general close of military operations and, in the case of occupied territories, on the termination of the occupation." The United States is not party to AP I, and the Manual is silent regarding the possibility that some of its provisions reflect customary international law.

the occupation is not defined by the Convention. Thus – contrary to the Manual's insinuation – GC IV, Article 6 does not trigger the law of occupation despite the absence of hostilities, but indicates that the Manual's claim as to the exclusion of this law because of the absence of hostilities (even prior to 1949) is misplaced to begin with.[133]

Finally, the doctrine of *debellatio* has been criticized, indeed abandoned, for its anachronistic vesting of sovereignty in the government of a State rather than in its people.[134] It is noteworthy that the 1956 Army Field Manual does not mention either *debellatio* or unconditional surrender. Their invocation in 2016, even if only by implication, is therefore rather surprising. Again, the occupation of Iraq appears particularly pertinent, since it fulfilled the factual requirements of *debellatio*,[135] although the United States did not claim that this was the case.[136] This may have been due to the absence of a formal surrender, or to the fact that resistance to Coalition forces, albeit by forces not of a State, had not ended.[137]

4.3 Application of the Law of Occupation by Analogy

The Manual's restrictive interpretation of what constitutes occupation cannot be divorced from the question of the alternative body of law that would apply, if not the law of occupation. With respect to invasion, liberation of friendly territory, and post-war, the Manual proposes that the law of occupation be applied by analogy, as a matter of policy. For those who advocate a broad interpretation of the law of occupation this proposal might at first sight appear to mitigate the consequences of the strict interpretation, and therefore attractive from a humanitarian perspective. However, it is not without flaws. The law of occupation consists not only of humanitarian protections, but a framework which balances humanitarian protections with the conflicting interests of the Occupying Power. Thus, it also includes the power to impose

---

[133] Third, unless GC IV, Art. 6 constitutes customary international law, a State not party to the Convention would not be affected by it, and the law of occupation would apply without a cut-off date.

[134] Benvenisti (above note 15), 163; E. Benvenisti, "Water Conflicts during the Occupation of Iraq" (2003) 97 *American Journal of International Law* 860, 862 ("Resolution 1483 confirms the demise of *debellatio*, the doctrine that would have passed sovereign title to the occupant in case of total defeat and disintegration of the governing regime.").

[135] Stirk (above note 85), 42.   [136] Benvenisti (above note 15), 56–57.

[137] K. H. Kaikobad, "Problems of Belligerent Occupation: The Scope of Powers Exercised by the Coalition Provisional Authority in Iraq, April/May 2003–June 2004 Current Developments: Public International Law: Part I" (2005) 54 *International & Comparative Law Quarterly* 253, 261.

restrictions on the civilian population, such as on the rights to property and to personal liberty. The Manual makes no distinction between the restraints applicable to Occupying Powers and their powers. It therefore appears to allow the application by analogy also of the permissive rules of the law of occupation.

If the law of occupation does not apply as a matter of law, one cannot reproach a State for imposing on itself, as a matter of policy, the *restrictions* or obligations under that law. However, the notion that a State may arrogate *powers* over individuals without authorization by law is more difficult to sustain. Its evaluation depends on the regime that would apply otherwise.

There is a growing international consensus that whenever a State maintains effective control of territory outside its sovereign territory, international human rights law applies.[138] However, the Manual reiterates the well-known US position to the contrary, namely that international human rights law does not apply extraterritorially.[139] This is stated in a section entitled "Occupation and the ICCPR and Other Human Rights Treaties."[140] Interestingly, the text does not refer to any treaties other than the ICCPR, perhaps in acknowledgment that the US objection to extraterritorial applicability is gradually eroding.[141] If legal void is the default "regime," then the applicability of the law of occupation, even "by analogy," might offer some consolation, since that law constrains the State in addition to empowering it.[142]

As for why the Manual proposes to apply the law by analogy where it regards it as inapplicable by law, the answer may follow lines similar to Fox's

---

[138] See discussion in Arai-Takahashi (above note 31), 551–82.

[139] The Manual also contends that in situations of occupation, the law of occupation takes priority as *lex specialis* over law that is not intended to address such a situation, if the two conflict. This means that international human rights law does not apply in occupation. However, the issue at present is situations where the law of occupation does not apply.

[140] DoD Law of War Manual, ¶ 11.1.2.6.

[141] With respect to the Convention against Torture (Convention against Torture and Other Cruel, Inhuman or Degrading Treatment or Punishment (entered into force June 26, 1987) 1465 UNTS 85) the United States has exceptionally taken the position that "US obligations under Article 16 (as well as under other provisions of the Convention with the same jurisdictional language) apply in places outside the United States that the US government controls as a governmental authority" (Statement by NSC Spokesperson Bernadette Meehan on the US Presentation to the Committee Against Torture (Nov. 12, 2014), https://obamawhitehouse .archives.gov/the-press-office/2014/11/12/statement-nsc-spokesperson-bernadette-meehan-us-pr esentation-committee-a). Another explanation may be the fact that the United States has not ratified most human rights treaties or has rendered them toothless with reservations, understandings, and declarations, including declarations that human rights treaties are non-self-executing.

[142] The UK Manual also suggests the application of the law of occupation by analogy, noting expressly that it contains both powers and limitations.

explanation of why the Manual adheres specifically to the conservationist principle: If the law of occupation offers a framework of law, even if only *de facto*, it deflects domestic or international pressure to acknowledge the applicability of IHRL.

4.4 Summary

The Manual adopts a very narrow interpretation of occupation, which emphasizes inter-State relations. Accordingly, any situation that is not a straightforward instance of effective control by one State over only part of the territory of another State whose government continues to function, is excluded from the category based on the language of the text. This leaves the Occupying Power with significant freedom of action which is arguably exempt from the constraints of the law of occupation.

Since transformative measures do not easily reconcile with the conservationist principle under the law of occupation, this narrow interpretation is convenient for those who advocate the permissibility of such measures. The general tenor of the Manual is permissive in this respect, *inter alia* by *a priori* evading the tension between the conservationist principle and transformative measures. This may be altogether too convenient, or it may well reflect the failure of the Manual's occupation chapter to articulate a comprehensive approach guided by modern law and practice.

5 CONCLUSION

The 2016 Manual focuses on issues that have historically been pertinent to US military interventions. These include occupation of friendly territory, postwar, belligerency, and more recently, the matter of Security Council authorization. Regrettably, the Manual does not address other topics, despite the fact that they have come to the fore of political and legal debate, such as occupation of disputed territory,[143] occupation by proxy,[144] and occupation by multinational forces that is not regulated directly by UN Security Council resolutions.[145] Relatedly (although not for lack of alternatives), the Manual is based almost entirely on US practice. This limited scope weakens the force of the Manual's claim to reflect the law rather than merely US practice.

---

[143]   ICRC Commentary (above note 71), ¶¶ 323–27; Sassòli (above note 70).

[144]   ICRC Commentary (above note 71), ¶¶ 328–32; Benvenisti (above note 15), 61–62; Sassòli (above note 70).

[145]   ICRC Commentary (above note 71), ¶¶ 333–41.

In essence the Manual's logic is to assert that a unilateral US assertion of authority is sufficient to justify conduct based on that assertion.[146]

In light of these foci, it is only natural to put the spotlight on scrutinizing the Manual on its implications for other US experience which is not explicitly mentioned, and especially on the transformative project in which the United States has been involved in Iraq since 2003, which has generated heated controversy on the parameters of occupation and its limitations, even if the law of occupation formally applied only to its inception. It is noteworthy that despite the fact that the last decade of the drafting of the Manual was carried out in the shadow of this project, the Manual is essentially silent on the matter, leaving the permissibility of transformative measures to interpretation and inference.

This chapter sheds light on the implications of the Manual for transformative projects, in light of the few statements pertaining to it directly, and of the general tenor of the Manual. First, the Manual's reading of the Occupying Power's authority is ambiguous. On the one hand its explicit provisions do not stray far from the traditional iterations of the conservationist principle; on the other hand, it utilizes various techniques to suggest that the discretion of the Occupying Power may be very wide. Second, this chapter demonstrates that the Manual adopts a very narrow view of what constitutes occupation, leaving great leeway for foreign forces acting in non-sovereign territory. Moreover, while the Manual restricts the scope of instances in which the constraints of the law of occupation apply, it does not specify what law would apply instead of the law of occupation. It denies the extraterritorial applicability of international human rights law (which does not explicitly regulate transformative measures but might justify them[147]), but offers no alternative.

The picture that emerges from the analysis is nuanced. The Manual does not explicitly endorse the legality of transformative measures under the law of occupation. Nonetheless, it goes a significant way towards accommodating such measures both by undermining the conservationist principle underlying

---

146   D. Glazier, "A Critical Assessment of the New Department of Defense Law of War Manual" (2017) 42 *Yale Journal of International Law* 2015. For an example, *cf.* the Manual's assertion of law that commercial relations between the occupied territory and the remaining territory of the enemy are normally suspended (¶ 11.23.4), with the reference it provides, ¶ 376 of the 1956 Manual, which clearly considers the matter one of policy: "The commander . . . will usually find it advisable to forbid intercourse between the occupied territory and the territory still in possession of the enemy."

147   Roberts (above note 1).

the law of occupation, and by denying the applicability of the law of occupation to various situations in which transformative measures may be prominent.

With respect to both the content of the law of occupation and its applicability, the reasoning and precedents on which the Manual's propositions rest are fraught with flaws and difficulties, casting heavy doubt on the tenability of some of those propositions.

PART IV

THE MANUAL'S LONG-TERM PROSPECTS AND IMPLICATIONS

15

Commentary on the Law of Cyber Operations and the DoD Law of War Manual

Gary D. Brown

1 INTRODUCTION

One of the challenges in addressing the law applicable to cyberwarfare is apparent from a statement in the introduction to the Department of Defense (DoD) Law of War Manual (the Manual). Stephen Preston, who was at the time serving as DoD General Counsel, wrote that the manual "reflects the experience of this Department in applying the law of war in actual military operations, and it will help us remember the hard learned lessons from the past."[1] Indeed, one indisputable advantage DoD brings to law of war discussions is concrete operational experience. No other organization is as practiced in actually applying the law of war in combat as well as a whole range of other operations. DoD has been involved in combat operations during most of its existence since its founding in 1947. There is no organization more experienced in kinetic warfare, and none better positioned to capture lessons learned.

That is not the case with regard to cyberwarfare, however, and the lack of lessons learned from operations is evident in the Manual's treatment of cyberwarfare. Chapter XVI of the Manual, "Cyber Operations," provides little in the way of useful guidance for cyber operations lawyers. Although they will be required to provide real-time legal advice on cyber operations, operations lawyers have no definitive sources and few references with sufficient depth to guide their endeavors. In that sense, the cyber operations chapter represents the most substantial shortfall between the Manual's aspiration in support of US forces and its actuality. In any event, Chapter XVI is by far the shortest chapter of the Manual at only sixteen pages (one of which has only two words of text along with a footnote).

---

[1] DoD Law of War Manual, ii.

Before discussing the text, a reflection on the underpinnings of Chapter XVI is in order. As noted above, acknowledged State-sponsored cyber operations are rare to non-existent, so there are few legal lessons to be gleaned from practice between contesting States. That leaves only government policy and academic study as starting points for the construction of a specific body of cyber operations law. In a choice starkly contrasting with the rest of the DoD Manual, the cyber operations chapter relies almost exclusively on two sources: a 1999 DoD Office of General Counsel legal assessment of "information operations" and a 2012 speech at the US Cyber Command Legal Conference delivered by the State Department Legal Advisor.[2] Chapter XVI of the Manual has only 44 percent as many footnotes when compared to the next most lightly footnoted chapter. Even more striking, 98.8 percent of the footnotes cite either to the Manual itself or to internal US policy documents and speeches.

Of particular note, the Manual avoids any mention of the Tallinn Manual on the International Law Applicable to Cyber Warfare, which has been well-received by academics and governments since its original publication in 2013.[3] As the Manual's footnotes are meant "to help practitioners research particular topics discussed in the main text," references to at least some of the literature in the field would have been appropriate.[4] That one of two foundational references dates from the last century and the other is a State Department speech considerably undermines the credibility of the chapter.

2 OVERVIEW

The broad scope of the DoD Manual is reflected in the statement of purpose, which is "to provide information on the law of war to DoD personnel responsible for implementing the law of war and executing military operations."[5] With that in mind, this commentary on the chapter "Cyber Operations" is organized according to the four most pressing issues that legal practitioners must address to provide proper legal advice to decision-makers:

---

[2] DoD, Office of the General Counsel, "An Assessment of International Legal Issues in Information Operations" (2nd ed., Nov. 1999), repr. in 76 US Naval War College International Law Studies (2002); and H. H. Koh, Legal Advisor, Department of State, International Law in Cyberspace, "Remarks as Prepared for Delivery to the USCYBERCOM Inter-Agency Legal Conference" (Sept. 18, 2012), repr. in 54 *Harvard International Law Journal Online* (Dec. 2012), 3, www.harvardilj.org/wp-content/uploads/2012/12/Koh-Speech-to-Publish1 .pdf. About half of the footnotes are to other portions of the DoD Manual.

[3] Since the publication of the DoD Manual, the Tallinn Manual has been updated to version 2.0, published in 2017. The references in the remainder of this chapter as to the 2017 edition.

[4] DoD Law of War Manual, ¶ 1.2.2.   [5] *Ibid.*, ¶ 1.2.1.

1. What is cyberwar?
2. What is cyberspying?
3. What is a cyberattack?
4. What is a cyberweapon?

Set out below is a discussion of why these questions are critical, and how well the Manual does as a reference for those who will be providing legal advice on military and other government cyber operations.

2.1 What Is Cyberwar?

One of the key answers legal advisors must provide is whether proposed cyber operations would cross the threshold from peace to war. Although it may be outside the normal area of expertise of an operations legal advisor, they still must be prepared to grapple with the thorny issues of how cyber operations might contribute to, or even drive, a transition from peace to war. Because cyberspace by its nature is global, even those operations meant to be collecting tactical information or focused on a specific region can have far-reaching consequences. The intent of cyberspace operators is often difficult to discern, and internet-based operations cross many jurisdictions in making their way to the intended target. That means information-gathering might appear to be something more aggressive. In addition, States might feel compelled to defend their "cyber-sovereignty" even from incursions falling short of aggression. Either of these could motivate hostile actions in response, so discerning the distinction between normal cyber operations and those that might be interpreted as aggressive (or transgressive) is of critical importance.

In examining that decision space, national decision-makers often ask the question, "Is this an act of war?"[6] This is a consideration of both States considering the wisdom of cyberspace activities, and States who are the victims of unfriendly cyber-acts. The term "act of war" is generally meant to be "any act by a State that would effectively terminate the normal international law of peacetime and activate the international law

---

[6] Although the phrase "act of war" is not a legal term, given the difficulties in determining what cyber-events cross the threshold of armed attack, it may be appropriate for States to note the importance of political considerations in their assessments of whether aggressive cyber-activities trigger the right of self-defense. As one cyber-expert puts it, "calling something an act of war is not a conclusion; it is a decision." M. Libicki, "An Act of War, Even Cyberwar, Is a Decision," *New York Times* (Feb. 28, 2013), www.nytimes.com/roomfordebate/2013/02/28/what-is-an-act-of-cyberwar/an-act-of-war-even-cyberwar-is-a-decision.

of war."[7] In modern usage, an act of war may be considered the equivalent of armed attack or, for the United States, a use of force.[8] For cyber
operations lawyers advising decision-makers it is appropriate to ask, as the
DoD Manual does, whether a certain cyber-act is an unlawful use of force
or an international armed attack.

The ultimate goal is determining which activity rises to a level that would
justify a State's use of force in self-defense.[9] For most States, that would mean
the cyber-activity would have to be an armed attack, which would trigger
Article 51 of the UN Charter. The United States, however, has consistently
asserted that the right of self-defense may be exercised based on a lower
threshold: that of a use of force.[10] Whichever standard is used, sorting out
which cyber-activities would push States to armed conflict is difficult to
describe in an abstract *ex ante* manner.

The Manual concludes that if a cyber-activity has kinetic results, it may
lawfully be treated the same as if it were caused by non-cyber means. Thus,
"if cyber operations cause effects that, if caused by traditional physical
means, would be regarded as a use of force ... then such cyber operations
would likely also be regarded as a use of force."[11] The caveat of "likely" in
the statement is critical. Cyber-means of warfare are not exempt from the
application of international law, but the Manual suggests the application of
the law is unsettled. In the kinetic realm, decades of history and precedent
are available to study what States consider adequate to support armed self-
defense. If the aggressor uses cyber-means, however, the US position is that
the legal question cannot be answered merely based on the effects of the
attack. States "must evaluate factors including the context of the event, the
actor perpetrating the action ..., the target and location, effects and intent,
among other possible issues" before determining whether the action constitutes a use of force.[12]

---

7   D. Turns, "Act of War," in R. Gutman and D. Rieff (eds.), *Crimes of War: What the Public Should
    Know* (New York: W. W. Norton, 1999), 24, www.crimesofwar.org/a-z-guide/act-of-war-2/.
8   A proposed bill, H.R.5220 – 114th Congress (2015–2016), was titled The Cyber Act of War Act,
    yet it would have tasked the President to "develop a policy for determining when an action
    carried out in cyberspace constitutes a *use of force* against the United States." (emphasis
    added). www.congress.gov/bill/114th-congress/house-bill/5220/text?q=%7B%22search%22%3A
    %5B%22Cyber+Act+of+War+Act+of+2016%22%5D%7D&resultIndex=1. Some provisions of
    the Act were included in the Fiscal Year 2017 (National Defense Authorization Act).
9   The DoD Manual asserts that self-defense is available against non-State actors as well as other
    States (¶ 16.3.3.4), a position supported by a majority of the Tallinn experts, as well. See
    Tallinn Manual 2.0, rule 71(19).
10 See DoD Law of War Manual, Chapter I fn. 230.   11 *Ibid.*, ¶ 16.3.1.
12 *Ibid.*, ¶ 16.3.1 fn. 22, citing Harold Hongju Koh (above note 2).

Perhaps because the Manual's authors were unable to glean much in the way of helpful operations law guidance from existing international law, they also provided examples to illustrate the principles. For examples of cyber-events that would trigger a resort to war, the Manual lists: using cyber-capabilities to trigger a nuclear plant meltdown, open a dam above a populated area, or disable air traffic control services resulting in airplane crashes. According to the Manual, these instances would "likely" be regarded as cyberattacks.[13] These clear examples are very similar to the ones used in the extensively referenced 1999 paper, but there are subtle differences that may reflect a new understanding of the law in the area. The 1999 paper did not mention the possibility of a nuclear plant meltdown; that may be an understandable sensitivity that creates a clear red-line in the opinion of US legal experts. Somewhat more curiously, the Manual dropped the references to cyber operations that shut down banking systems, financial systems, and public utilities. All of these systems have been the target of cyber operations and, although they were not shut down on a large scale, the exclusion of them from the list of operations that could drive States to war may be a reflection of modern State practice.

States have not engaged in armed conflict premised only on cyber-aggression against financial institutions.[14] Similarly, they will not, it seems, wage war over foreign actors establishing a persistent presence on industrial control systems controlling public utilities.[15] State practice seems to be tilting in favor of negotiated agreements between States to refrain from such actions rather than recognizing the resort of armed retaliation. It is possible the non-response from States is because they lack good evidence connecting the actors to States, or even non-State armed groups.[16] State norms and practice regarding cyberspace operations are rapidly forming and being refined. If the US position is that these activities would engender armed self-defense given

---

[13] *Ibid.*, ¶ 16.3.1.

[14] D. Volz and J. Finkle, "U.S. Indicts Iranians for Hacking Dozens of Banks, New York Dam," *Reuters* (Mar. 25, 2016), www.reuters.com/article/us-usa-iran-cyber-idUSKCN0WQ1JF. M. Riley, "How Russian Hackers Stole the Nasdaq," *Bloomberg* (July 21, 2014), www .bloomberg.com/news/articles/2014-07-17/how-russian-hackers-stole-the-nasdaq.

[15] C. Strohm, "Foreign Governments Have Hacked U.S. Grid, NSA Head Says," *Bloomberg* (Nov. 20, 2014), www.bloomberg.com/news/articles/2014-11-20/foreign-governments-have-hacked-u-s-power-system-nsa-head-says; M. Riley and J. Robertson, "UglyGorilla Hack of U.S. Utility Exposes Cyberwar Threat," *Bloomberg* (June 13, 2014), www.bloomberg.com/ne ws/articles/2014-06-13/uglygorilla-hack-of-u-s-utility-exposes-cyberwar-threat; B. Makuch, "Canada Discovers Its Under Attack by Dozens of State-Sponsored Hackers," *Vice News* (Jan. 25, 2016), https://news.vice.com/article/canada-discovers-its-under-attack-by-dozens-of-state-sponsored-hackers.

[16] See section 3.1 of this chapter.

sufficient evidence of the actor, the DoD Manual would have offered an ideal opportunity to state and support that perspective. More likely, the US position is that many activities in this arena fall under the broad rubric of "espionage," activities at which the US excels and does not wish to limit through the international legal structure.[17] Even stating that clearly would have been helpful to the practitioners who will rely on the Manual to form legal opinions in support of cyber operations.

Another weakness with the examples the Manual uses is that they are far too facile. A legal advisor with no previous experience in cyber operations could surely have determined that activities causing dams to fail and planes to crash would be international acts of aggression. These obvious examples provide little guidance to practitioners who must advise on where the line is drawn between cyberattacks and lesser cyber-insults. A single example, also from the 1999 paper, may provide more information about where the line between peace and war is drawn, but it is unclear exactly how it fits with the message of the chapter. "[C]yber operations that cripple a military's logistics systems, and thus its ability to conduct and sustain military operations, might also be considered a use of force under *jus ad bellum*."[18] Compared to a nuclear meltdown and plane crashes, this type of operation seems almost benign.

Although it is not clear what "crippling" a military logistics system means, the type of disruptive cyber-action that could be taken against an unclassified logistics system seems similar to the events in Estonia in 2007. In that case, government and economic websites, as well as internet infrastructure sites, were targeted with denial of service attacks that significantly impaired their functioning for three weeks.[19] The events in Estonia were not considered sufficient to support a claim of international self-defense.[20] This interpretation also seems to be a departure from US practice as stated in the Manual. In addition to the failure to react publicly to operations carried out against public utilities and financial systems, the US characterized the 2014 Sony hack, which stole massive amounts of data and was designed to corrupt or destroy more, as "cyber-vandalism," explicitly characterizing it as an activity

[17] K. Zetter, "NSA Hacker Chief Explains How to Keep Him Out of Your System," *Wired* (Jan. 28, 2016), www.wired.com/2016/01/nsa-hacker-chief-explains-how-to-keep-him-out-of-your-system/.

[18] DoD Law of War Manual, ¶ 16.3.1.

[19] E. Tikk, K. Kaska, and L. Vihul, "Estonia 2007," in *International Cyber Incidents* (Tallinn: CCD COE, 2010), 33.

[20] "[I]t was clear to the Estonian authorities that the cyber attacks could – and should – be treated as cyber crime . . . The question of invoking article 5 of the Washington Treaty [which requires NATO members to consider an armed attack against any member State to be an attack against all member States] was never seriously considered." *Ibid.*, 25–26.

calling for a law enforcement rather than a military response.[21] It is simply unclear where the military logistics system example is meant to fit in the scheme set out with the other examples, and in the context of US (and international) practice to date.

Even if a cyber-activity is determined not to cross the armed attack/use of force threshold, victims are not without military recourse. The notion of cyber-countermeasures to respond to aggressive but sub-use of force cyber-actions has received significant attention in the international legal community, although it rates little more than a footnote in the chapter.[22] Other than in the cyber chapter, the Manual refers to countermeasures as reprisals, which it defines as "acts taken against a party: (1) that would otherwise be unlawful; (2) in order to persuade that party to cease violating the law."[23] In other words, if undertaken as a countermeasure, unlawful responsive cyber-measures are rendered legal if they remain below the level of a use of force, and are conducted for the purpose of ending the original unlawful activity.

Paragraph 16.3.3.3 of the Manual discusses countermeasures and retorsion together, emphasizing the availability of retorsive responses to cyber-insults, such as diplomatic measures.[24] Both are important concepts for cyber operations, but they are distinct. Retorsion in general is defined in paragraph 18.17 of the DoD Manual: "unfriendly conduct, (1) which is not inconsistent with any international obligation of the State engaging in it, and (2) which is done in response to an internationally wrongful act." An understanding of both in the cyber context is especially critical because it is not always clear when an action in cyberspace is unlawful. When the law on the original action is unclear, responses may be phrased as equivalent; that is, if the initial action was lawful,

---

[21] K. Zetter, "Sony Got Hacked Hard: What We Know and Don't Know So Far," *Wired* (Dec. 3, 2014), www.wired.com/2014/12/sony-hack-what-we-know/; B. Fung, "Obama Called the Sony Hack an Act of 'Cyber Vandalism.' He's Right," *Washington Post* (Dec. 14, 2014), www.wash ingtonpost.com/news/the-switch/wp/2014/12/22/obama-called-the-sony-hack-an-act-of-cyber-va ndalism-hes-right/?utm_term=.695b58b3bc1a.

[22] DoD Law of War Manual, ¶ 16.3.3.3 fn. 33. See M. N. Schmitt, "'Below the Threshold' Cyber Operations: The Countermeasures Response Option and International Law" (2014) 54 *Virginia Journal of International Law*; and O. A. Hathaway and R. Crootof, "The Law of Cyber-Attack," Faculty Scholarship Series, Paper 3852 (Jan. 2012), 857–59, http://digitalcom mons.law.yale.edu/fss_papers/3852.

[23] DoD Law of War Manual, ¶ 18.18.1.

[24] An example is when the Obama Administration, partly in response to allegations the Russian Government had hacked into Democratic National Committee servers, stolen information, and then released it in an attempt to influence the 2016 presidential election, expelled thirty-five suspected Russian intelligence operatives and closed two Russian facilities in the US. D. E. Sanger, "Obama Strikes Back at Russia for Election Hacking," *New York Times* (Dec. 29, 2016), www.nytimes.com/2016/12/29/us/politics/russia-election-hacking-sanctions.html?_r=0.

then the same thing done in return would be retorsion.[25] If the triggering action was unlawful, then the response would be a countermeasure, rendered lawful by its status.[26]

2.2 What Is Cyber-Spying?

Determining whether cyber-activities would cross the line from operations to espionage remains a difficult issue for cyber legal advisors. Espionage is generally unregulated under international law but, unlike in the physical world, espionage in cyberspace can be quite difficult to distinguish from the preparation for and conduct of more aggressive military operations.[27] The Manual notes that to the extent "cyber operations resemble traditional intelligence and counterintelligence activities, such as unauthorized intrusions into computer networks solely to acquire information, then such cyber operations would likely be treated similarly under international law."[28] This would be more helpful if there were an easy way to ascertain the nature of the cyber-activity in the first place.

Whether a cyber operation is undertaken for the purpose of espionage or military operations, it normally will require some penetration of the targeted system to gain access. Once access to the system is established, the aggressor might engage in espionage or attack. Even if the mission is espionage, the operator might leave behind malware to facilitate future access to the system, and that future event might be either an attack or spying. How should system penetrations be treated under the law when the actor's intent is unknown? How should pre-implanted capabilities be treated when they are discovered, especially on critical infrastructure or sensitive national security systems? If an espionage event goes wrong and results in accidental damage to a system, does it become an attack at that point? There may be no way for the victim of the event to determine the actor's intent, especially in a timely fashion.

[25] For a discussion on the level of attribution required, see section 3.1 of this chapter.

[26] Not discussed in the Manual is the plea of necessity, which term "is used to denote those exceptional cases where the only way a State can safeguard an essential interest threatened by a grave and imminent peril is, for the time being, not to perform some other international obligation of lesser weight or urgency." Draft Articles on State Responsibility, Art. 25, http:// legal.un.org/ilc/texts/instruments/english/commentaries/9_6_2001.pdf.

[27] "[T]he international legal system generally imposes no sanctions upon nations for acts of espionage except for the political costs of public denunciation." DoD Law of War Manual, ¶ 18.21.2 fn. 305. See also G. D. Brown, "Spying and Fighting in Cyberspace," *Journal of Law and National Security Policy* (Mar. 29, 2016), http://jnslp.com/2016/03/29/spying-fighting-cyberspace/.

[28] DoD Law of War Manual, ¶ 16.3.2.

The Manual provides no satisfactory answers to these questions. The Manual suggests that the intent of the actor controls, which is perhaps the worst model to choose, because intent is notoriously difficult to discover. The natural anonymity of the internet and the nature of cyber operations makes intent that much more difficult to ascertain. A better reflection of international law is to characterize operations by their effects. For example, espionage is not prohibited by international law, but activities enabling or supporting it may be, depending on their effects. Effects are relatively clear, but misapprehending intent is common and could completely alter the legal range of options available in response.

2.3 What Is a Cyberattack?

Although it is not immediately apparent, the issue of what cyber-activity constitutes an attack in the context of armed conflict is a critical one. US military legal advisors take for granted that the principles of the law of war – distinction, proportionality, humanity, and military necessity – all apply during armed conflict.[29] With regard to kinetic attacks, of course, these principles do apply. The challenge with wartime cyber operations is that they can be quite disruptive without being destructive. Legal advisors must be able to distinguish operations that must refrain from targeting civilian objects, for example, and those that fall below the attack threshold.

The cyber operations chapter takes note of the issue in a general way, pointing to paragraph 5.4 for details on how attacks are covered by the law of armed conflict (LOAC). That paragraph iterates that attacks must be carried out in compliance with the principles of distinction, proportionality, and precautions, but paragraph 16.5.2 notes with some circularity that "[a] cyber operation that does not constitute an attack is not restricted by the rules that apply to attacks." It goes on to give examples of operations that would not constitute attacks: defacing government web pages; briefly disrupting internet service in a minor way; briefly disrupting, disabling, or interfering with communications; or disseminating propaganda. Unfortunately, these examples do little to draw the line between aggressive, non-attack cyber-activity and activity that would qualify as an attack. For example, do the qualifications in the examples mean that DoD would label a brief disruption of internet service in

---

[29] See Ray Murphy's contribution to this book in Chapter 7. Chapter II of the DoD Manual lists the principles of the law of war as military necessity, humanity, proportionality, distinction, and honor. The principle of honor seems particularly attenuated from cyberwarfare; it is not discussed in the Manual with reference to cyberwarfare, and will be omitted here, as well.

a major way an attack? Further, it is unclear that the principles of LOAC apply to any cyber-activity that stops short of causing damage, destruction, or injury. This gap in the law has led some experts to suggest that LOAC ought to apply to cyber operations that affect the functionality of computer systems without actually damaging them.[30]

The Manual states "[i]f a cyber operation constitutes an attack, then the law of war rules on conducting attacks must be applied to those cyber operations."[31] Of course, this invites the question of what constitutes an attack. Operational legal advisors who consult the manual for guidance on this question will learn that wartime operations that destroy computers are attacks.[32] While this is true, it is also the simplest case – kinetic effects directly caused by cyber operations clearly are attacks. On the more difficult questions of whether loss of functionality of a computer system, without damage to it, is an attack, or whether harm significantly attenuated from the original event, would similarly constitute an attack, the Manual is silent.[33]

After identifying the way cyberwarfare techniques might not be governed by the principles of the law of war, the Manual suggests that the case is not closed. "[E]ven if a cyber operation is not an 'attack' or does not cause any injury or damage that would need to be considered under the proportionality rule, that cyber operation still should not be conducted in a way that unnecessarily causes inconvenience to civilians or neutral persons."[34] This seems to contradict an earlier statement in the Manual, and may be read as *lex ferenda* rather than an articulation of the law.[35] Legal advisors who rely on the Manual for guidance would be better served if the Manual made clear this is a US policy rather than the law. The United States might well put such policy restrictions in its own rules of engagement, but if it is meant to be read as a restriction grounded in law, the Manual should have provided some affirmative authority for this belief.

In a legal advisor's analysis of whether a cyber-activity constitutes an attack, the Manual notes the importance of considering whether the effects created

---

[30] See M. N. Schmitt, "Rewired Warfare: Rethinking the Law of Cyber Attack" (2014) 96(893) *International Review of the Red Cross* 189, www.icrc.org/en/international-review/article/rewired-warfare-rethinking-law-cyber-attack; and C. Droege, "Get Off My Cloud: Cyber Warfare, International Humanitarian Law, and the Protection of Civilians" (2012) 94(886) *International Review of the Red Cross* 533.

[31] DoD Law of War Manual, ¶ 16.5.1.   [32] *Ibid.*

[33] On the issue of attenuation, see M. Roscini, *Cyber Operations and the Use of Force in International Law* (Oxford University Press, 2014), 221. "[T]he crux of the matter is whether the effect is a reasonably likely or foreseeable consequence of the operation on the basis of the information available at the time of the attack."

[34] DoD Law of War Manual, ¶ 16.5.2.   [35] *Ibid.,* ¶ 5.12.1.2.

are temporary or reversible, but it is unclear why this would be important under the law. Neither is that distinction explained in the text. The terms are not relevant with reference to kinetic methods of warfare and, as there are no cyber-specific agreements governing cyberwarfare, there should be no additional restrictions on operations in the law – though the United States is free to limit its own operations by policy. One problem with this particular provision is that there is no agreed concept of "reversible" effects, and even "temporary" has no set meaning in this context. Presumably, temporary means something other than merely non-permanent, or else it would be synonymous with reversible. Reversible is similarly ambiguous, as a reversible cyber-effect could either prohibit the deletion of data or permit the deletion of data if a backup exists that could be used to return the targeted system to its original state. Without more detail, it is not clear that these terms add much meaning to the section.

In this section of the chapter, DoD reveals a deep unease with the use of cyber-capabilities in war. The cautious approach regarding cyber-capabilities is perhaps not what one would expect when cyberwarfare seems less likely than kinetic means to cause civilian casualties and damage. Nevertheless, when the Manual assesses the application of the principle of proportionality to kinetic attacks, it specifically excludes any inconvenience to civilians from consideration, noting that such ancillary aspects of a military attack "need not be considered."[36] In contrast, the Manual mandates consideration of "civilian inconvenience" even in cyber operations that are too minor to be considered attacks under the law of war. It is logically inconsistent – and not a reflection of international law – to require no consideration of inconvenience before conducting a lethal attack, but to require that higher standard before a non-lethal cyber-action aiming to achieve the same result, such as disrupting military communications over a dual-use network node.[37] If this is US policy, it ought to be set out as policy, and could be reflected in rules of engagement, but it is potentially confusing to cyber operators who refer to the Manual as a source of law.

Although not listed as one of the distinctive principles of the law of war in the Manual, the cyber operations chapter discusses the obligation of precautions. There are two precautions-related requirements under generalized LOAC. The first is precautions in the attack, which requires States, when engaging in an attack, to take all feasible steps to minimize harm to the civilian

---

[36] *Ibid.*, ¶ 5.12.1.2.

[37] "[E]ven if a cyber operation is not an 'attack,' or does not cause any injury or damage that would need to be considered under the proportionality rule, that cyber operation still should not be conducted in a way that unnecessarily causes inconvenience to civilians or neutral persons." *Ibid.*, ¶ 16.5.2.

population.[38] The second is precautions against the effects of attacks, which requires States to "take other necessary precautions to protect the civilian population, individual civilians and civilian objects under their control against the dangers resulting from military operations."[39] This second might be thought of as an obligation of defenders to ensure that military and strategic objects are not commingled with civilian objects in a way that would make it impossible for attackers to distinguish between the two.

For the reasons discussed above, precautions in the attack is not a particularly intriguing topic in a cyber-specific context. Cyber-events not qualifying as attacks are not covered by this provision of law, and those that are attacks present the same issues as traditional kinetic warfare. While it is true that destructive cyberattacks could result in the loss of civilian access to internet-based services, for example, so might kinetic attacks. Bombing or destroying bridges and electrical power infrastructure, often part of traditional military campaigns, also frequently results in loss of connectivity due to broken communications lines and lack of power. The consideration of these ancillary civilian effects is the same whether the instrumentality is cyber or kinetic.

By contrast, cyberspace operations present a unique opportunity to apply the principle obligating defenders to avoid commingling civilian and military objects. The cyber-infrastructure States use for military and national security missions is the same as that used for civilian activities from personal communications to providing essential utilities such as electricity and water. It might be argued that in choosing to commingle civilian and military capabilities on a single infrastructure, States all violated the defensive application of precautions, leaving the internet more susceptible to attack as a dual-use target.

In the cyber context, Manual paragraph 16.5.3 proclaims that "[p]arties to a conflict must take feasible precautions to reduce the risk of incidental harm to the civilian population and other protected persons and objects." It is unclear why the two aspects of precautions would be conflated in the cyber chapter. For clarity, the cyber-precautions provisions should track the language in AP I and in the other provisions of the Manual.

---

[38] Protocol Additional to the Geneva Conventions of Aug. 12, 1949, and Relating to the Protection of Victims of International Armed Conflicts, June 8, 1977, 1125 UNTS 3 (AP I), Art. 57. "Combatants must take feasible precautions in planning and conducting attacks to reduce the risk of harm to civilians and other persons and objects protected from being made the object of attack." DoD Law of War Manual, ¶ 5.11.

[39] AP I, Art. 58.

2.4 *What Is the Definition of a Cyberweapon?*

Both international and US law require that weapons be reviewed for legal compliance before they may be acquired or used. AP I codifies the requirement to conduct legal reviews of weapons.[40] The United States is not a party to AP I, but its practice of conducting legal reviews of weapons is consistent with the requirement, and predated AP I.[41] DoD requires that weapons reviews determine whether a proposed weapon's intended use is calculated to cause superfluous injury, whether it is inherently indiscriminate, and whether it is specifically prohibited, for example by treaty.[42]

Cyberspace operations have introduced new challenges in complying with what is ordinarily a straightforward provision of law. Recognizing that cyberweapons must be subjected to a legal review before acquisition or use does not answer the question of what, exactly, a cyberweapon is. In the case of more traditional weapons, it is generally straightforward to recognize that something is a weapon. Defining "cyberweapon," on the other hand, can be quite tricky. It is difficult to know how to define cyberweapons, as the Manual recognizes: "Not all cyber capabilities ... constitute a weapon or weapons system."[43] Nearly every function of a modern military is at least supported by cyber capabilities. Logistics, medical processes, communications, etc. are all highly dependent on computers and networks, yet those particular capabilities would not be classified as weapons. In the case of offensive capabilities, computers, networks, and servers might all be considered part of a cyberweapons system, and legal reviews of the hardware would be straightforward (and pointless, because the same equipment can be used to support civilian and defensive functions). The heart of a cyber-capability is the code on which it is based, and the Manual offers little practical guidance on the proper classification of malware or other commonly encountered cyber techniques.

Rather than take on the difficult task of providing a basis for determining whether a cyber-capability is a weapon, the Manual punts, noting that the military services address which cyber-capabilities require legal reviews. This would be more helpful if the services actually did address the issue. The pertinent Army regulation is dated 1979, and the Navy's 2011 regulation lacks cyber-specific language. Only the Air Force has addressed the issues

---

[40] AP I, Art. 36.
[41] The Defense Acquisition System, DoD Directive 5000.1, ¶ E1.1.15 (certified current Nov. 20, 2007); DoD Manual, ¶ 6.2.3.
[42] DoD Law of War Manual, ¶ 6.2.2. [43] *Ibid.,* ¶ 16.6.

surrounding cyberweapons specifically, so its instruction provides the DoD guidance by default.[44]

The Air Force defines "weapons" as "devices designed to kill, injure, disable or temporarily incapacitate people, or destroy, damage or temporarily incapacitate property or materiel."[45] The Air Force instruction also defines a "cyber capability" as "any device or software payload intended to disrupt, deny, degrade, negate, impair or destroy adversarial computer systems, data, activities or capabilities," but excludes "a device or software that is solely intended to provide access to an adversarial computer system for data exploitation."[46]

The Air Force directs that "all cyber capabilities being developed, bought, built, modified or otherwise acquired by the Air Force ... are reviewed for legality under LOAC, domestic law and international law prior to their acquisition for use in a conflict or other military operation."[47] Unlike kinetic means of warfare, cyber means largely consist of intellectual property in the form of computer code. Physical weapons must be designed and manufactured, so changes tend to be infrequent. In contrast, computer code may be changed instantly and easily. It is often altered multiple times in the course of an operation.[48] The practical problem created is that it appears dozens or hundreds of legal reviews might be required for a single cyber capability.

An alternate view of the problem is provided in the Tallinn Manual, which addresses the question of what constitutes a cyberweapon in rule 103. "[C]yber weapons are 'cyber means of warfare' that are used, designed, or intended to be used to cause injury to, or death of, persons or damage to, or destruction of, objects, that is, that result in the consequences required for qualification of a cyber operation as an attack."[49] In the Tallinn Manual cyberattack is defined as "a cyber operation, whether offensive or defensive, that is reasonably expected to cause injury or death to persons or damage or destruction to objects."[50] DoD could consider adopting a modified version of this definition, making a simple change: "design, use, or intended use *reasonably* capable of causing." This change would exclude imaginable but remote possibilities of harm that exist with every computer program, but would continue to create

---

[44]   Whether weapons reviews are controlled by international law or by US policy, it would be preferable to have a single interpretation from DoD, rather than potentially conflicting interpretations provided by individual services.

[45]   AFI 51-402, Legal Reviews of Weapons and Cyber Capabilities (July 27, 2011), 6.

[46]   *Ibid.*, 5.   [47]   *Ibid.*, para 1.1.2.

[48]   See discussion in G. D. Brown and A. O. Metcalf, "Easier Said Than Done: Legal Reviews of Cyber Weapons" (2014) 7(1) *Cybersecurity* 128, 133, http://jnslp.com/2014/02/12/easier-said-than-done-legal-reviews-of-cyber-weapons/. Modifying any weapon without authorization runs afoul of DoD guidance. DoD Law of War Manual, ¶ 6.3.2.

[49]   Tallinn Manual, rule 103(2).   [50]   *Ibid.*, rule 92.

a mostly objective category of cyberweapons not dependent on the intent of any involved party, which is frequently difficult to ascertain. However, the Air Force definition described above may provide an indication that leaving aside the subjective element of intent might be unacceptable to the United States because the definition would then capture cyber-espionage tools under the definition of weapon.[51]

Even a workable definition of cyberweapons does not answer all the challenges. The Manual provides no guidance to help determine what "inherently indiscriminate" means with regard to a cyber-capability. Malware is often spread indiscriminately but may by design have no significant negative effect on untargeted computer systems. Malware may use untargeted systems as vectors to reach its intended target, where it might have great effect. This was the case, for example, in the Stuxnet incident, where malware was spread to over 100,000 computers, but had no significant effects until it reached the computer system at the Natanz nuclear enrichment facility, where it destroyed over 1,000 nuclear centrifuges.[52] The Manual takes no position on whether inert code copied indiscriminately and without permission to the hard drives of thousands of computers makes use of that malware unlawful. Based on the extant State practice to date, the answer is probably "no," but the Manual would be a good vehicle for putting the issue to rest.

Cyber "weaponry" is a controversial issue in the larger national security community, as well. The tools and vulnerabilities necessary to conduct computer- and network-based operations for national security missions can also be used against civilian systems in support of intelligence and criminal activity. The US Government has a process to determine whether cyber-vulnerabilities should be disclosed in order to protect the public or held as part of the cyber-arsenal to be used in support of national security.[53] Some citizen groups argue that States have an obligation to disclose cyber-vulnerabilities they discover so the public can protect themselves from exploitation.[54] States have been less keen to recognize that there is such an obligation, as it would essentially

---

[51] One way to handle the espionage/operations overlap on this issue is to simply exclude espionage tools by intent. Another way would be to accept that weapons can be used in espionage in ways that are not attacks, such as using a machete to cut through vegetation on a fence line. The operation should be analyzed by its effects rather than by its means.

[52] K. Zetter, *Countdown to Zero Day* (New York: Broadway Books, 2014), 96, 175.

[53] A. Schwartz and R. Knake, "Government's Role in Vulnerability Disclosure," The Cyber Security Project, Discussion Paper 2016-04 (June 2016), http://belfercenter.ksg.harvard.edu/files/Vulnerability%20Disclosure%20Web-Final4.pdf.

[54] D. E. Sanger, "Obama Lets N.S.A. Exploit Some Internet Flaws, Officials Say," *New York Times* (Apr. 12, 2014), www.nytimes.com/2014/04/13/us/politics/obama-lets-nsa-exploit-some-internet-flaws-officials-say.html?_r=1; R. Gallagher, "Cyberwar's Gray Market," *Slate* (Jan. 6,

require them to render obsolete many of the cyber-capabilities they acquire or develop.

An inability to define what computer code constitutes a weapon also affects arms trade agreements. For example, the Wassenaar Arrangement, developed to control the transfer of arms and dual-use technologies, was amended in 2013 to include some cyber-capabilities.[55] One of the new prohibited categories is intrusion software, which is software "specially designed or modified to avoid detection by 'monitoring tools', or to defeat 'protective countermeasures', of a computer or network capable device, and performing [data extraction, data modification, or installation of malware]." The intent of the language was to keep powerful computer tools out of the hands of repressive regimes, but the additions also prevented university researchers and law-abiding cyber-intrusion specialists from properly conducting research, because they were unable to share code across national borders.[56]

Given the range of complex issues surrounding cyberweapons, some indication of the appropriate direction here would have been useful not just to US practitioners, but also to other States that look to the United States for leadership in international law, and particularly value the DoD role in clarifying LOAC. DoD has more experience than any organization in the world at assessing weapons for compliance with international law. It may be as befuddled as everyone about how to define and assess cyber weapons, but setting a single DoD policy, even an imperfect one, would have been a superior course than leaving the issue to be determined by individuals across the US services and the international community, perhaps in very different ways.

3 OTHER ISSUES

The major issues cyber operations law advisors must be equipped to field are discussed above. The other commonly recurring issues are attribution, neutrality, perfidy, and the role of civilians. All of these are noted in the Manual and are discussed below.

2013), www.slate.com/articles/technology/future_tense/2013/01/zero_day_exploits_should_the_hacker_gray_market_be_regulated.html.

55   C. Anderson, "Considerations on Wassenaar Arrangement Control List Additions for Surveillance Technologies," https://cda.io/r/ConsiderationsonWassenaarArrangementProposalsforSurveillanceTechnologies.pdf.

56   *Ibid.*; T. Herr and P. Rosenzweig, "Cyber Weapons and Export Control: Incorporating Dual Use with the PrEP Model" (2016) 8 *Journal of Law and National Security Policy* 301–9, http://jnslp.com/wp-content/uploads/2016/04/Cyber-Weapons-and-Export-Control_2.pdf.

3.1 *Attribution and Standards of Proof*

Attribution is one of the most commonly discussed aspects of cyber operations. Because of the internet's architecture and operation, concealing the identity and location of actors is relatively simple, while discovering the same can be an expensive and time-consuming process that often fails to deliver a certain answer.[57] The Manual says but little about attribution, merely noting that it is difficult. If the goal of the Manual is to be useful to practitioners, this is a section that could be more complete. For example, there is no indication of what level of proof should be required for various responses.

The Tallinn Manual offers the guidance that, while pinpointing the origin of an attack does not mean the State owner of the infrastructure is responsible for the attack, it does provide a sort of rebuttable presumption that the host State is responsible.[58] And, although there is no set standard of proof necessary to engage in countermeasures, the Commentary to the Articles on State Responsibility notes that the standard for attribution in such cases is "reasonable certainty."[59] Legal advisors are not starting from scratch when determining the appropriate standard to apply; international law does provide guidance that is helpful, even in the new area of cyber operations. It would be useful for this standard, at least, to be referenced in the Manual.

3.2 *Neutrality*

Neutrality plays a limited role in the cyberspace context. Neutrality under the law of war only applies during international armed conflict and conflicts between States have become very much the exception. Non-international armed conflict (NIAC) is common, however, and aggressive cyber-activities in support of NIAC, and in support of sub-armed conflict State activity, is common.[60] The Manual's discussion of when neutrality principles apply is

---

[57] Even in two high-profile instances where the US Government asserted attribution was certain, controversy about the identity of the culprits continued for months. Cybersecurity experts seem to have as many different opinions as lawyers. "FBI Still Believes North Korea Is Responsible for Sony Hack," *CBS News* (Dec. 30, 2014), www.cbsnews.com/news/fbi-still-believes-north-korea-is-responsible-for-sony-hack/; S. Biddle, "Here's the Public Evidence Russia Hacked the DNC – It's Not Enough," *Intercept* (Dec. 14, 2016), https://theintercept.com/2016/12/14/heres-the-public-evidence-russia-hacked-the-dnc-its-not-enough/.

[58] Tallinn Manual, rule 6(39).

[59] Responsibility of States for Internationally Wrongful Acts, Art. 1, GA Res. 56/83, Annex, UN Doc. A/RES/56/83 (Jan. 28, 2002), citing *Yeager v. Iran*, 17 Iran-US Cl. Trib. Rep. 92, 101–02 (1987).

[60] NWP 1-14M, The Commander's Handbook on the Law of Naval Operations (July 2007), para. 7.1; Tallinn Manual, p. 248.

based on both the 1907 Hague Convention and on the opinion of international legal experts.[61] Of particular note, the chapter in the Manual addressing the law of neutrality is silent with respect to cyber operations. In DoD's interpretation, some principles of neutrality apply in NIACs, although beyond respecting sovereignty, which is a principle of international law independent of neutrality, it is unclear which specific principles apply to belligerents in such conflicts.[62]

With regard to non-participating States in NIACs, the Manual cites the UN General Assembly: "Every State has the duty to refrain from organizing, instigating, assisting or participating in acts of civil strife or terrorist acts in another State or acquiescing in organized activities within its territory directed towards the commission of such acts, when the acts referred to in the present paragraph involve a threat or use of force."[63] At some point, such activities would result in the offending State becoming a party to the conflict, converting it to an international armed conflict (IAC), so the Manual is apparently citing the language to capture relatively low-level, indirect assistance.[64] In any event, the Manual suggests that nonbelligerent States in NIACs should refrain from "acquiescing in organized activities" within their territories when the activities are directed to acts of civil strife or terrorism.

The Manual suggests a contrasting approach in the cyber context, asserting that a State's neutrality (a term that appears to be used in this chapter to refer to both neutral States and, unconventionally, to nonparticipating States in NIACs) is not dependent on whether it polices its cyber-infrastructure, as long as it does not take steps to discriminate among users of its infrastructure. The Manual explicitly notes that even if data could be characterized as a cyber weapon or otherwise could cause destructive effects in a belligerent State, relaying it would not impact a State's status as a neutral.

The disconnect here is probably more about trying to govern cyberspace with a treaty over a hundred years old than it is about neutrality. The Manual fails to take into account that aggressive computer code, in the form of data packets transmitted over the internet, can be the actual means of waging war, not merely communications about waging war, which is what Hague V was meant to address. There is little logical distinction between allowing the transmission of a virtual attack across neutral infrastructure and allowing the

---

[61]   DoD Law of War Manual, ¶ 15.2.1 and Chapter XVII fn. 211.   [62]   *Ibid.,* ¶ 15.2.1.3.

[63]   Declaration on Principles of International Law concerning Friendly Relations and Co-operation among States in accordance with the Charter of the United Nations, annex to UN General Assembly Resolution 2625 (XXV), UN Doc. A/RES/2625(XXV) (1970), cited at DoD Manual, Chapter XVII fn. 210.

[64]   See *Nicaragua v. U.S.* (ICJ, 1986).

launching of an attack through neutral territory – if one of these violates neutrality, both should.

The Tallinn Manual takes a different approach to cyber-neutrality, with most of the experts opining that a State would violate its status as a neutral if it knowingly allowed the transmission of a cyberweapon across infrastructure it controlled.[65]

The application of neutrality in cyberspace as set out in the DoD Manual is problematic because the United States appears to support the assertion of the *rights* of national sovereignty by States hosting internet infrastructure, but not the normal *responsibilities* of a sovereign. If States do have sovereign rights over code passing through internet infrastructure located in their territory, they ought to have the responsibility to ensure the code they host is doing no harm. Otherwise, the host State is essentially protecting cyber-aggressors from effective action by victim States, which is inconsistent with the application of neutrality in the physical world.[66] The ultimate conclusion may be left to whether States decide packets of information making up cyber-means of warfare are more akin to communications or to weapons.[67]

3.3 *Perfidy and Protective Emblems*

The issue of perfidy has limited practical application in cyberwarfare, but it frequently comes up in conversations with cyber operators. The issue is briefly discussed in the Manual under "Improper Use of Signs."[68] International law prohibits using perfidy to kill, injure, or capture an adversary.[69] Perfidy is widely understood as "[a]cts inviting the confidence of an adversary to lead him to believe that he is entitled to receive, or is obliged to accord, protection under the rules of international law applicable in armed conflict, with the

---

[65] Tallinn Manual, rule 152.

[66] "These sources make clear that neutrality law permits a belligerent to use force on a neutral state's territory if the neutral state is unable or unwilling to prevent violations of its neutrality by another belligerent." A. S. Deeks, "'Unwilling or Unable': Toward a Normative Framework for Extraterritorial Self-Defense'" (2012) 52(3) *Virginia Journal of International Law* 499, www.vjil.org%2Fassets%2Fpdfs%2Fvol52%2Fissue3%2FDeeks_Post_Production.pdf.

[67] On the other hand, States could also have determined that military aircraft crossing neutral territory are permitted, as long as they are only delivering messages. Instead, the mission of the aircraft appears to be irrelevant.

[68] DoD Law of War Manual, ¶ 5.24. Misuse of protective emblems, treachery, and perfidy are often discussed together, and often (if inaccurately) grouped together as perfidy. As perfidy is the most common of the terms in the operations community, it is used as the section title here.

[69] AP I, Art. 37(1). The United States asserts that customary international law prohibits only killing or injuring by means of perfidy, a position shared by the Tallinn experts. DoD Manual, para. 5.22; Tallinn Manual, rule 60(2).

intent to betray that confidence."[70] To be perfidious, a cyber operation would have to both rely on feigning legal protection and proximately result in death or injury (or capture under the international formulation).[71] For example, an email falsely claiming to be from the International Committee of the Red Cross that successfully lured enemy troops to an armed ambush that resulted in their deaths would constitute perfidy.[72] One might also imagine a similar false email that escaped electronic scrutiny because of its purported protected sender that, when opened, introduced malware into the adversary network. If that malware directly led to death or injury – by causing a catastrophic failure of a military installation's power plant, for example – it would be an example of perfidy. If death or injury did not result, it would still be an example of a misuse of a protective emblem.

The Manual also states it would be inappropriate to use "communications that initiate non-hostile relations, such as prisoner exchanges or ceasefires" to gain entry into an enemy's computer network.[73] The Manual's support for this proposition is limited to cross-referencing other provisions in the Manual. While the United States may determine this is a good practice, such ruses are not prohibited under LOAC.[74]

Similarly, the DoD Manual asserts "it would be prohibited to fabricate messages from an enemy's Head of State falsely informing that State's forces that an armistice or cease-fire had been signed."[75] This, like the prior paragraph's suggestion that perfidy prohibits false communications that initiate non-hostile relations, is inconsistent with established international law. Such practices may not be good policy, but they are not illegal. According to the 1977 International Red Cross (ICRC) Commentary on Additional Protocol I "the central element of the definition of perfidy is the deliberate claim to legal protection for hostile purposes," which these lack.[76] There are arguments to the contrary but, as unchivalrous as these situations may be, they do not meet the definition of perfidy.[77]

Cyber operations can be the most effective method of disseminating and obtaining information, so the portions of LOAC related to information are

---

[70]   AP I, Art. 37(1).   [71]   Tallinn Manual, rule 122(3).
[72]   This is an adaptation of an example from the Tallinn Manual, rule 122(5).
[73]   DoD Law of War Manual, ¶ 16.5.4.   [74]   *Ibid.*, ¶¶ 12.2, 5.21.   [75]   *Ibid.*, ¶ 16.5.4.
[76]   ICRC, *Commentary on the Additional Protocols of 8 June 1977 to the Geneva Conventions of 12 August 1949* (7), 429, www.loc.gov/rr/frd/Military_Law/RC_commentary-1977.html.
[77]   See S. Watts, "Law of War Perfidy" (2014) 219 *Military Law Review* 172, www.jagcnet.army.mil /DOCLIBS/MILITARYLAWREVIEW.NSF/0/02eb1ceb45ec8dd285257cf9004f63cf/$FILE/ By%20Sean%20Watts.pdf; and M. J. Greer, "Redefining Perfidy" (2015) 47 *Georgetown Journal of International Law* 260, www.law.georgetown.edu/academics/law-journals/gjil/rece nt/upload/Greer.pdf.

important. Protective emblems, such as the Red Cross (and other protected emblems), enemy prisoners of war (EPW) protections, and the blue shield that protects cultural property publicly note that certain facilities or individuals are protected from direct attack. Determining how best to translate the requirement of and respect for physical signage to virtual demarcation is still underway.

An area that is insufficiently addressed in the law is medical information. AP I requires that medical units and transports be marked as such.[78] The Tallinn Manual opined that the marking and protection obligations extend to "[c]omputers, computer networks, and data that form an integral part of the operations or administration of medical units and transports."[79] The DoD Manual is silent on the issue, but it is one that merits consideration and decision so that it can be uniformly implemented. This would help ensure the protection of medical data and protect against accidental misuse of the protective emblem.

3.4 Civilians as Combatants

The DoD Manual succinctly summarizes the law on civilian employees' involvement in cyberwarfare. Civilian employees are permitted to directly participate in hostilities (DPH), but they forfeit any protection they would receive as civilians during the participation. There may be political or other policy rationales for preventing civilians from acting as cyber "trigger-pullers," but it is permissible under LOAC. One reason DoD is comfortable with this broad reading of appropriate civilian conduct may be that cyberwarfare tends to be conducted from a distance, so there is less concern about increasing the chance that other, non-participating civilians could be mistaken for lawful targets.

4 CONCLUSION

This chapter of the Commentary has focused more on developments of the law and shortcomings in the Manual than some other chapters. That is because, despite the lessons learned over many years of armed conflict about how the law of war should apply to best protect civilians and prevent unnecessary suffering, there are gaps in its practical application to cyberwarfare. As noted above, many questions remain about exactly how the law should apply to operations in cyberspace, yet the disruptive and destructive

---

[78] AP I, Art. 18.   [79] Tallinn Manual, rule 132.

capabilities and vulnerabilities available to cyber-actors are increasingly being acknowledged. State custom, practice, and norms are being created rapidly, as well, more through inaction than action. The cyber operations chapter in the Manual offered an opportunity for the United States to guide both the present and the future of cyber operations law, but DoD chose not to grasp it.

Although DoD minimizes the role of military manuals in the development of international law, noting specifically in the DoD Manual that the views "do not necessarily reflect the views of [other federal agencies] or the US Government as a whole," any information the United States provides will carry great weight.[80] States are hungry for guidance on how the law of war applies to cyberwarfare, and the US owns the most important voice in the field. This may be why DoD was reluctant to take a bolder stand on the key issues that matter to coalition partners and experts in the field, but it also carries the risk that others, who may not share the interests of the United States with respect to ensuring freedoms of expression and association, may succeed in filling in the gaps.[81] In the absence of official guidance, academic works carry more than their usual weight, as well, and the musings of academics are less likely to be constrained by practicality. It would be in DoD's selfish interest to encourage a practical body of law that supports military operations, rather than an idealistic set of pronouncements that will be ignored.

The most critical failing of the cyber operations chapter is that it offers no useful ideas on how to apply international law, or even US policy, to the most likely cyber-scenarios. Although military cyberspace operations are in their infancy, useful examples could have been drawn from a short list of real-world events. Cyber-incidents in Estonia (2007), the Republic of Georgia (2008), Iran (2009), and Saudi Arabia (2012) are just a few examples that might have been used to walk through various issues in a way relevant for operations lawyers.[82] More recently, Russia's alleged use of cyber-methods to disseminate

---

[80]   DoD Law of War Manual, iv. The US has generally not encouraged relying on military manuals as reflections of *opinio juris*. "Although [military manuals and other guidelines published by States] may provide important indications of State behavior and *opinio juris*, they cannot be a replacement for a meaningful assessment of operational State practice in connection with actual military operations." Initial Response of US to ICRC Study on Customary International Humanitarian Law with Illustrative Comments (Nov. 3, 2006), www.state.gov/s/l/2006/98860.htm.

[81]   E.g., China, Kazakhstan, Kyrgyzstan, Russia, Tajikistan, and Uzbekistan jointly sponsored the International Code of Conduct for Information Security (Jan. 9, 2015) at the UN, https://ccd coe.org/sites/default/files/documents/UN-150113-CodeOfConduct.pdf.

[82]   C. A. Theohary and J. W. Rollins, "Cyberwarfare and Cyberterrorism: In Brief," Congressional Research Service (Mar. 27, 2015), https://fas.org/sgp/crs/natsec/R43955.pdf; Tikk et al. (above note 19), 25–32, 79–84.

information in an attempt to influence the 2016 Presidential election, and to bolster its influence in Ukraine offer rich examples of real-world events to which DoD must be prepared to respond.[83] Even without using real-world events, the examples would have been more useful had they involved more nuanced cases, rather than using as examples cyber-events with serious physical results that are clearly hostile attacks.

There remain many unanswered questions regarding the law governing cyberwarfare. The brevity and lack of specificity in the chapter may be an indication that DoD believes the law is insufficiently developed for it to provide guidance. Unfortunately, discomfort with the state of the law does not remove the responsibility of government legal advisors, who are the target audience of the Manual and must provide advice on cyber operations with or without legal direction from the manual. Even if the area is changing rapidly, it would be useful for DoD to provide more complete guidance to the field that would also suggest a framework for the international community. Even providing complete footnotes (as opposed to mostly internal references) would be a great help to practitioners; it would give them a jumping-off point for filling in the substantive gaps left by the Manual.

DoD seems to be committed to making online changes to the Manual, and has demonstrated some alacrity in doing so. The cyber operations chapter is a likely candidate for significant development in the near future, and we can hope that future revisions will provide more specific guidance on how the law applies, or does not apply, to the emerging area of cyberwarfare.

---

[83] "Russian Hacking and Influence in the U.S. Election," *New York Times* (through Nov. 4, 2017), www.nytimes.com/news-event/russian-election-hacking.

16

The DoD Law of War Manual as Applied to Coalition Command and Control

Michael A. Newton[*]

1 INTRODUCTION

This chapter considers the provisions of the Department of Defense (DoD) Law of War Manual (the Manual) in light of its larger implications for effective operational command and control relationships within military coalitions. The Manual serves a vital need in consolidating American military perspectives on the law of war. As even a cursory review of the forest of footnotes indicates, the Manual's articulations of US legal and policy positions derive from a cacophony of contexts to present an integrated whole. The Manual's complexity and ambitious scope undermines its usefulness as a ready reference for US tactical warfighters through the failure to explicitly address core dilemmas that are the *sine quibus non* of modern armed conflicts.[1] The paradox of the Manual is that this myopic approach to articulating US interests, of course appropriate for a document of its nature, also risks relations with military partners and allies through the selfsame failure to provide concrete guidance needed by coalition commanders. From a slightly different perspective, this chapter considers the areas where the Manual's fixation on articulating US policy prerogatives and legal positions may affirmatively damage the larger goal of preserving cohesive coalitions with other nations that help advance American interests.

The Foreword to the Manual quotes an American general for the proposition that "the laws of war have a peculiarly American cast."[2] However, the fundamental imperatives of the law of war cut across cultures and contexts. Commanders throughout history have recognized that the humanizing influence of the norms for conducting conflict is a vital dimension of a combat-effective unit that cannot be ignored or devalued. The Roman philosopher

---

[*] Errors and oversights are my sole responsibility.   [1] See above Chapters 1, 3, 4, and 6.
[2] DoD Law of War Manual, ii.

Seneca called for significant restraint especially during times of armed conflict in his essays "On Anger" and "On Mercy."[3] The Manual's Foreword, over the signature of the General Counsel of the Department of Defense acknowledges the truism:

> that the laws of war have shaped the U.S. Armed Forces as much as they have shaped any other armed force in the world. The law of war is a part of our military heritage, and obeying it is the right thing to do. But we also know that the law of war poses no obstacle to fighting well and prevailing. Nations have developed the law of war to be fundamentally consistent with the military doctrines that are the basis for effective combat operations. For example, the self-control needed to refrain from violations of the law of war under the stresses of combat is the same good order and discipline necessary to operate cohesively and victoriously in battle.[4]

The law of armed conflict[5] developed as a restraining and humanizing necessity to facilitate commanders' ability to accomplish the military mission even in the midst of fear, fatigue, factual uncertainty, moral ambiguity, and horrific violence conducted under the dual impulses of surging adrenaline and inculcated training.[6] The historical grounding of the laws and customs of war as deriving from the unyielding demand of military discipline under the authority of the commander (or in historical practice the sovereign power) explains why the status of lawful combatant was reserved for the armed forces fighting on behalf of a State or to paramilitary forces incorporated into those armed forces.[7] Writing in 1625, Hugo Grotius documented the Roman practice that "it is not right for one who is not a soldier to fight with an enemy" because "one who had fought an enemy outside the ranks: and without the

---

3   Seneca, "On Anger," in *Seneca: Moral and Political Essays*, ed. J. M. Cooper and J. F. Procopé (Cambridge University Press, 1995), 97–98; and "On Mercy," 132–34; J. D. Reynolds, "Collateral Damage on the 21st Century Battlefield: Enemy Exploitation of the Law of Armed Conflict, and the Struggle for a Moral High Ground" (2005) 56(8) *Air Force Law Review* 1.

4   DoD Law of War Manual, ii.

5   The phrase "law of armed conflict" serves a sort of straddling function between "the laws of war" and "international humanitarian law." Many North Atlantic Treaty Organization (NATO) militaries and other experts prefer usage of "the law of armed conflict" as shorthand for the larger field of the laws and customs of warfare, and manuals of, *inter alia*, Australia, Canada, UK, and Germany employ that term in addition to many US policy documents.

6   D. Schindler and J. Toman (eds.), *The Laws of Armed Conflicts: A Collection of Conventions, Resolutions, and Other Documents* (Leiden: Nijhoff, 1988), vii.

7   C. Garraway, "Combatants: Substance or Semantics?," in M. Schmitt and J. Pejic (eds.), *International Law and Armed Conflict: Exploring the Faultlines, Essays in Honour of Yoram Dinstein* (Leiden: Martinus Nijhoff, 2007), 317.

command of the general was understood to have disobeyed orders," an offense that "should be punished with death."[8]

The values articulated by the Manual are therefore the common property of all professionalized military forces. By extension, professionalized military forces that operate in good faith to implement the law and customs of warfare do so on behalf of the civilized societies that foot their cost and fill their ranks. Compliance with the law of war is thus a primary focus of the forces in the field as well as the nations whose interests they serve. In its entire 1,193 pages, there is only one instance where the Manual expresses that reality:

> implementation and enforcement of the law of war are also supported by the fact that violations of the law of war are counterproductive to the political goals sought to be achieved by military operations. For example, violations of the law of war in counter-insurgency operations may diminish the support of the local population. *Violations of the law of war may also diminish the support of the populace in democratic States, including the United States and other States that would otherwise support or participate in coalition operations.*[9]

President Obama's Executive Order prescribing policies related to civilian casualties in US operations is cited in one footnote that obliquely echoes the same concerns:[10]

> The protection of civilians is fundamentally consistent with the effective, efficient, and decisive use of force in pursuit of U.S. national interests. Minimizing civilian casualties can further mission objectives; *help maintain the support of partner governments and vulnerable populations, especially in the conduct of counterterrorism and counterinsurgency operations; and enhance the legitimacy and sustainability of U.S. operations critical to our national security.* As a matter of policy, the United States therefore routinely imposes certain heightened policy standards that are more protective than the requirements of the law of armed conflict that relate to the protection of civilians.

The point is that the Manual does little to emphasize the import of its provisions as they relate to the larger cohesion and legitimacy of coalition

---

[8] H. Grotius, *De Jure Belli ac Pacis* (1625), III, Chapter 18. Grotius explained the necessity for such rigid discipline as follows: "The reason is that, if such disobedience were rashly permitted, either the outposts might be abandoned or, with increase of lawlessness, the army or a part of it might even become involved in ill-considered battles, a condition which ought absolutely to be avoided." www.lonang.com/exlibris/grotius/gro-318.htm.

[9] DoD Law of War Manual, ¶ 18.2.3 (emphasis added).

[10] DoD Law of War Manual, ¶ 5.1.2.1 (emphasis added) (citing Executive Order 13732, "United States Policy on Pre- and Post-Strike Measures to Address Civilian Casualties in U.S. Operations Involving the Use of Force," 81 Federal Register 44485, § 1 (July 1, 2016)).

operations. The text seems to have tunnel vision. The forceful (and often entirely correct) articulations of fundamental American perspectives on the law of war demonstrate inadequate appreciation of their implications for US allies. This is a thematic flaw throughout the Manual's structure. Therefore, section 2 of this chapter will consider the Manual's formulations as they relate to commanders' responsibilities during operations alongside other national forces. Section 3 summarizes the Manual's interrelationship to the emerging practice of the International Criminal Court (ICC), while section 4 focuses on the modern parameters of the duty to investigate allegations of war crimes. American leaders and lawyers need to be vigilant in implementing the Manual's "guidance" in ways that reinforce relationships with other professionalized military forces and international institutions, thereby advancing US interests while simultaneously strengthening *jus in bello* norms.

2 THE COMMANDER'S ROLES AND RESPONSIBILITIES

The military commander is responsible both for decision-making needed to employ a disciplined force and the sustained combat readiness and training of those whom he or she is privileged to lead. The Israeli Supreme Court summarized this notion by noting that the authority of commanders "must be properly balanced against the rights, needs, and interests of the local population: the law of war usually creates a delicate balance between two poles: military necessity on one hand, and humanitarian considerations on the other."[11] An effective commander issues plans and guidance prior to the onset of operations, and sets a command climate of professionalism in which he or she empowers subordinates as the conflict unfolds.[12] General David Petraeus accordingly wrote[13] to "Soldiers, Sailors, Airmen, Marines, and Coast Guardsmen serving in Multi-National Force-Iraq":

---

[11] *Beit Sourak Village Council v. The Government of Israel* [2004] HCJ 2056/04, ¶ 34, http:elyoni. court.gov.il/files_eng/04/560/020/A28/04020560.a28.htm (quoting Y. Dinstein, "Legislative Authority in the Administered Territories" (1973) 2 *Iyunei Mishpat* 505, 509).

[12] ICRC, *Commentary on the Additional Protocols of 8 June 1977 to the Geneva Conventions of 12 August 1949* (Geneva: ICRC, Martinus Nijhoff, 1987), Article 87, ¶ 3550, www.icrc.org/ihl .nsf/COM/470-750001?OpenDocument ("Undoubtedly the development of a battle may not permit a commander to exercise control over his troops all the time; but in this case he must impose discipline to a sufficient degree, to enforce compliance with the rules of the Conventions and the Protocol, even when he may momentarily lose sight of his troops").

[13] See, e.g., Letter from General David H. Petraeus, Commanding Officer of Multi-National Force-Iraq, to Multi-National Force-Iraq (May 10, 2007) (copy on file with author).

Our values and the laws governing warfare teach us to respect human dignity, maintain our integrity, and do what is right. Adherence to our values distinguishes us from our enemy. This fight depends on securing the population, which must understand that we – not our enemies – occupy the moral high ground. This strategy has shown results in recent months. Al Qa'ida's indiscriminate attacks, for example, have finally started to turn a substantial proportion of the Iraqi population against it.

To accomplish the larger strategic mission, which necessarily includes sustaining a strong sense of legitimacy within the civilian population of coalition States as well as within the zone of conflict, a commander could decide to impose greater restrictions on attacks in areas where civilians are known to be present. The Manual describes such rules of engagement by affirming that commanders may impose constraints "even beyond the requirements of the law of war."[14]

Michael Waltzer is entirely correct in the conclusion that belligerent armies are "not entitled to do anything that is or seems to them necessary to win wars. They are subject to a set of restrictions that rest in part on the agreements of States but that also have an independent foundation in moral principle."[15] The Manual provides the example of guidance given to the International Security and Assistance Force in Afghanistan that required coalition forces to:

> continue – indeed, redouble – our efforts to reduce the loss of innocent civilian life to an absolute minimum. Every Afghan civilian death diminishes our cause. If we use excessive force or operate contrary to our counterinsurgency principles, tactical victories may prove to be strategic setbacks. We must never forget that the center of gravity in this struggle is the Afghan people; it is they who will ultimately determine the future of Afghanistan ... Prior to the use of fires, the commander approving the strike must determine that no civilians are present.[16]

Compliance with the legal and moral imperatives for waging war determines the dividing line between pride in one's service and shame that cannot be discarded like a dirty uniform. It is also the glue that holds viable military coalitions together. Commanders must be keen to ascertain the precise line between legal obligation and discretionary policy.

---

[14] DoD Law of War Manual, ¶¶ 5.11.2 and 17.5.1.3 (citing General Petraeus, Unclassified Excerpts from Tactical Directive, Aug. 1, 2010).
[15] M. Walzer, *Just and Unjust Wars* (New York: Basic Books, 1977), 131.
[16] DoD Law of War Manual, ¶ 17.5.1.3 fn. 95.

By extension, US commanders striving to implement the Manual's prescriptions in good faith must be sensitive to varying national perspectives. For many nations, such "higher thresholds" may well represent legal mandates rather than policy-based pragmatism. In this vein, NATO Allies would have benefited from one clear consolidated chart listing the provisions of Additional Protocols I and II to the Geneva Conventions (AP I and AP II) that the United States accepts as binding customary international law. It is true that the text accepts some provisions as binding the United States, despite the failure to ratify the relevant treaty. Drafters largely neglected to address key details that would have helped commanders charged with leading coalition operations. For example, the principle of precautions requires that parties to a conflict take certain precautionary measures to protect civilians. AP I states: "[i]n the conduct of military operations, constant care shall be taken to spare the civilian population, civilians and civilian objects."[17] As an additive duty, parties must take all feasible precautions in launching attacks that may affect the civilian population. This includes taking all feasible measures to ensure that targets are military objectives,[18] as well as selecting the means and method of attack expected to provide the greatest protection against loss of civilian life and damage to civilian property.[19] The Manual provides a representative sampling of such precautions as follows:

> Feasible precautions are those that are practicable or practically possible, taking into account all circumstances ruling at the time, including humanitarian and military considerations. These circumstances may include:[20]
> - the effect of taking the precaution on mission accomplishment;
> - whether taking the precaution poses a risk to one's own forces or presents other security risks;
> - the likelihood and degree of humanitarian benefit from taking the precaution;
> - the cost of taking the precaution, in terms of time, money, or other resources; or
> - whether taking the precaution forecloses alternative courses of action.

---

[17] AP I, Art. 57(1).   [18] DoD Law of War Manual, ¶ 5.2.3.2.

[19] E.g., one common method of taking precautions is to launch attacks on particular targets at night when the civilian population is not on the streets or at work, thus minimizing potential casualties. The NATO attacks on the Radio Televizije Srbije building in the territory of the Federal Republic of Yugoslavia took place at a time when civilian employees were not expected to be present. Decision as to the admissibility of Application No. 52207/99 of 12 December 2001 (Grand Chamber) in the case *Bankovic and others v. Belgium and 16 Other Contracting States*, App. No. 52207/99, [2001] ECHR 890, 123 International Law Reporter 94.

[20] DoD Law of War Manual, ¶ 5.2.3.2.

For example, a commander may determine that a precaution would not be feasible because it would result in increased operational risk (*i.e.*, a risk of failing to accomplish the mission) or an increased risk of harm to his or her forces.

The Manual's text in this, as in so many other areas, provides scant assistance to commanders implementing its guidance across national boundaries. In fact, the statement that the "standard for what precautions must be taken is one of due regard or diligence, not an absolute requirement to do everything possible. A wanton disregard for civilian casualties or harm to other protected persons and objects is clearly prohibited" provides the lowest common denominator that is uncontroversial but also unhelpful in actual operational practice.[21]

As a variation on this theme, the Manual describes the requirement to seek affirmative personal identification (termed "PID" and defined as "reasonable certainty that the proposed target is a legitimate military target")[22] as an example of the commander's authority to "impose greater restrictions than the requirements of the law of war" by "applying heightened standards of identification."[23] The text describes the PID Rule of Engagement as "a policy choice to reduce the risk of incidental harm in conducting an attack."[24] In reality, experience in Iraq and Afghanistan has repeatedly shown that PID is an essential safeguard for lawful operations. Consider the case of the US Marines that killed twenty-four unarmed Iraqi civilians in the village of Haditha by entering their homes following the death of one Marine from an improvised explosive device. What should have been a swift arc of investigative efficiency became bogged down with rationalizations and red tape that shifted only after the shock of public revelation and recrimination. The official investigation documented a command culture that devalued the lives of Iraqi civilians, which contributed to the incident and made follow-up a low priority. In the official terminology of the investigation conducted by Major General Bargewell: "All levels of command tended to view civilian casualties, even in significant numbers, as routine and as a natural and intended result of insurgent tactics."[25] The pervasive attitude that all Iraqis were either the enemy or supporters of the enemy removed the incentive for individual

[21] *Ibid.* [22] *Ibid.*, ¶ 5.4.3.1 fn. 87. [23] *Ibid.*, ¶ 5.4.3.1. [24] *Ibid.*
[25] US Dep't of the Army, Major General Eldon A. Bargewell, Investigation, *"Simple Failures" and "Disastrous Results"*, 18 (June 15, 2006). The first investigation under US Army Major General Eldon Bargewell was notable for the simple reason that a well-regarded US Army General was tasked to investigate allegations of Marine misconduct. The official investigation resulted in the removal of Lieutenant Colonel Jeffrey Chessani, the commanding officer, and the company commander, Captain Luke McConnell along with another commander,

Marines to follow applicable rules of engagement that mandate ceaseless efforts to distinguish between combatants and noncombatants. One US Marine, SSgt Frank Wuterich (who entered a plea of guilty at his court-martial) remarked that "As for the PID (Positive Identification of civilians versus combatants as required in the Rules of Engagement), we didn't want my Marines to check if they had weapons first. We told them to shoot first and deal with it later."[26] His conviction resulted from the issuance of the unlawful order, which violated the rules of engagement and in legal terms violated the principle of distinction.

In practice, the *lex lata* applicable to armed conflict embeds principles of military necessity, discretion, and concepts of reasonableness at the precise points of friction within the law where they are relevant to the actual conduct of military operations. Thus, perpetrators cannot subjectively inject those concepts at their own convenience because they are baked into the extant structure of the laws and customs where relevant. This is particularly important in combined forces operating under uniform rules of engagement and with consolidated reporting mechanisms. Actions that may be discretionary policy to some forces may well be viewed as legally obligatory by others within a multinational coalition. Hence, US commanders need to be sensitive and vigilant in assessing the concretized application of the Manual's principles across national command structures.

3 THE MANUAL'S APPROACH TO THE INTERNATIONAL CRIMINAL COURT (ICC)

Similarly, the US position *vis-à-vis* the ICC is plainly, but superficially, stated in the Manual. The text observes with some understatement that the "United States has objected to certain aspects of the jurisdiction of the International Criminal Court, and there are certain restrictions in U.S. domestic law on support to the International Criminal Court."[27] In a separate instance, it notes without explanation that the United States is "not a State Party to the Rome

---

Captain James Kimber, from their duties, along with subsequent courts-martial for key Marines. Major General Bargewell concluded that: "Statements made by the chain of command during interviews for this investigation, taken as a whole, suggest that Iraqi civilian lives are not as important as U.S. lives, their deaths are just the cost of doing business, and that the Marines need to get 'the job done' no matter what it takes. These comments had the potential to desensitize the Marines to concern for the Iraqi populace and portray them all as the enemy even if they are noncombatants." This excerpt is from Army Major General Eldon A. Bargewell's report, *Washington Post*, Apr. 21, 2007.

[26] Sworn Statement of SSgt Frank D. Wuterich (taken Feb. 21, 2001).

[27] DoD Law of War Manual, ¶ 18.12.4.

Statute,"[28] which is the constitutive treaty for the ICC.[29] In fact, on December 31, 2000, which was the last permissible day,[30] Ambassador David Scheffer signed the Rome Statute at the direction of President Clinton, who was then serving the last days of his second term. The White House statement clarified that President Clinton ordered the signature because the United States sought to "remain engaged in making the ICC an instrument of impartial and effective justice in the years to come," and reaffirmed America's "strong support for international accountability."[31] President Clinton's statement nonetheless made clear that he would "not recommend that my successor submit the treaty to the Senate for ratification until our fundamental concerns are satisfied."[32] In its operative paragraph, President Clinton, wrote that:

> In signing, however, we are not abandoning our concerns about significant flaws in the Treaty. In particular, we are concerned that when the Court comes in existence, it will not only exercise authority over personnel of States that have ratified the treaty, but also claim jurisdiction over personnel of States that have not. With signature, however, we will be in a position to influence the evolution of the Court. Without signature, we will not. Signature will enhance our ability to further protect U.S. officials from unfounded charges and to achieve the human rights and accountability objectives of the ICC. In fact, in negotiations following the Rome Conference, we have worked effectively to develop procedures that limit the likelihood of politicized prosecutions. For example, U.S. civilian and military negotiators helped to ensure greater precision in the definitions of crimes within the Court's jurisdiction.

The Manual notes that the United States "has a longstanding and continuing objection to any assertion of jurisdiction by the ICC with respect to nationals of States not Party to the Rome Statute in the absence of consent from such States or a referral by the Security Council."[33] This formulation does a disservice to the larger linkages between its *jus in bello* formulations and

---

[28]   Rome Statute of the International Criminal Court, UN Doc. A/CONF.183/9, 2187 UNTS 90 (July 17, 1998), entered into force July 1, 2002, reprinted in 37 ILM 999 (hereinafter Rome Statute), Art. 8.

[29]   DoD Law of War Manual, ¶ 18.20.3.

[30]   Rome Statute (above note 28), Art. 125(1) (stipulating that States may accede to the Statute at a later time, but that signature was permissible only until Dec. 31, 2000).

[31]   "Statement on the Rome Treaty on the International Criminal Court (Dec. 31, 2000)," 37 Weekly Comp. Pres. Doc. 4 (Jan. 8, 2001), repr. in Sally J. Cummins and David P. Stewart (eds.), *Digest of United States Practice in International Law* (2000), 272, www.state.gov/docu ments/organization/139599.pdf.

[32]   *Ibid.*   [33]   DoD Law of War Manual, ¶ 18.20.3.1.

the reality of the modern ICC. This conceptual gap in the Manual is important because the ICC is a maturing institution intended to be a permanent fixture on the international institutional landscape and because key US allies, to include all other NATO members, have ratified the Rome Statute. Framing the US relationship to the ICC in a purely oppositional posture ignores the commonalities shared between US forces and many other allies who will deploy alongside them. As the following sections demonstrate, framing the US relationship to the Court as simply one of abstention fails to provide a complete picture of the powerful synergies between the Manual's formulations and established ICC practice.

3.1 *The Essence of Article 8*

Modern international criminal law is an integrated discipline that is far more than the "codeless myriad of precedent" that Lord Tennyson famously described as a "wilderness of single instances."[34] The Rome Statute was designed to largely align criminal norms with actual State practice based in the realities of warfare. The text of Article 8 is neither a rejection of prior practice nor an evisceration of the core precepts that were widely accepted prior to the treaty's completion in 1998. The range of war crimes embodied by Article 8 reflects the paradox that its operative provisions are revolutionary yet broadly reflective of the actual practice of warfare. The text of Article 8 baked in a complex commingling of *lex lata* hard law and established State practice, as informed by the much more diffuse expectations and assessments of expert practitioners.

Article 8 of the Rome Statute articulates an array of offenses that combine to replicate the Grave Breach provisions of the Geneva Conventions (Article 8(2)(a)), clarify the normative content of many offenses applicable to international armed conflicts (Article 8(2)(b)), criminalize the conduct proscribed by Common Article 3 of the 1949 Geneva Conventions (Article 8(2)(c)), and specifically incorporate a series of offenses applicable to armed conflicts not of an international character (Article 8(2)(e)). Even as Article 8 embodied notable new refinements, the Rome Statute made such sweeping legal advances against a backdrop of pragmatic military practice. The intentional integration of hard and soft law within the structure of Article 8 is ubiquitous in its fabric. There are dozens of instances whereby Article 8 incorporates terminology drawn from the larger framework of established *jus in bello* without

---

[34] Alfred, Lord Tennyson, "Aylmer's Field" (1793), www.everypoet.com/archive/poetry/Tennys on/tennyson_contents_aylmers_field.htm.

amplification; commonly encountered law of war terms such as, *inter alia,* "military necessity," "direct participation in hostilities," "combatant," "civilian," and "military objective" appear throughout Article 8.

Given that the war crimes enunciated in Article 8 largely represent an outgrowth from the preexisting body of humanitarian law, they are riddled with references to that body of law. In some areas, the relationship is simply that the offenses from previous treaty law are included whole cloth (i.e., directly replicated) as noted above. Article 8(2)(a) consolidates the Grave Breaches drawn from the respective 1949 Geneva Conventions. The text is logically consistent in that it embeds the established legal principles drawn from the Conventions (and the Manual) into the structure of the crimes and elements. For example, victims of any offense under Article 8(2)(a) must be "protected persons" within the meaning of one or more of the Geneva Conventions, though that legal term of art is nowhere explained in the Rome Statute.[35] Article 8(2)(b)(xxii) correspondingly prohibits the use of "protected persons as human shields" to "favour [sic] or impede military operations."[36] Similarly, the Grave Breach of "Extensive destruction and appropriation of property not justified by military necessity and carried out wantonly and unlawfully" (Article 8(2)(a)(iv)) may only be committed against property protected under one or more of the Geneva Conventions. As noted above, the text of Article 8(2)(c) reproduces the language of Article 3 that is replicated in each of the four Geneva Conventions of 1949. All of these criminal provisions draw their lifeblood from the practice of States and the accumulated understandings from established understandings of the 1949 Geneva Conventions, to include the specific understandings of Common Article 3. The Manual's definitions are obviously most helpful in aligning the established expectations of States to the normative content of these ICC crimes.

In a slightly more tangential reference to underlying *jus in bello* precepts, the fabric of Article 8 offenses contains an abundance of obvious references to the underlying body of humanitarian law. Apart from the textual reference to military necessity in the Grave Breach provision of Article 8(2)(a)(iv), the concept is repeatedly referenced in elements for other offenses committed during both international and non-international armed conflicts (IACs and NIACs). Military necessity, for example, is specifically included in the textual requirements for proving the war crime in Article 8(2)(b)(viii) of displacing the civilian population because the elements require that the perpetrator's order "was not justified by the security of the civilians involved or by military necessity." Similarly, the Article 8(2)(b)(v) war crime of attacking undefended

---

[35]   DoD Law of War Manual, ¶¶ 5.14, 5.11, 10.5, 10.29, 11.20.   [36]   *Ibid.,* ¶ 5.16.

places cannot be established in the absence of evidence that the "towns, villages, dwellings, or buildings did not constitute military objectives." The legally defined term of art "military objective" is also included in the elements of the war crime of attacking civilian objects in both IACs (Article 8(2)(b)(ii) and (ix)) and NIACs (Article 8(2)(e)(iv)).[37] Finally, the concept of *"hors de combat"* is embedded in all of the offenses under Article 8(2)(c) without any additional clarification or explanation. These allusions to established precepts defined under preexisting *jus in bello* require reference to that body of law as articulated in the Manual as an essential predicate to authoritative interpretive decisions regarding those offenses either in charging or judicial decision-making in the Court.

Even extensive reliance on legally specific terminology defined outside the boundaries of the Rome Statute does not exhaust the textual basis for reference by jurists and counsel to the underlying body of law explicated in the US Manual. In addition to the express and obvious references, there is a third layer of Article 8 provisions with oblique reliance on preexisting legal precepts. Article 51(3) of AP I, for example, provides that civilians "shall enjoy the protection afforded by this Section, unless and for such time as they take a direct part in hostilities." The concept of civilians under *jus in bello* stands in contradistinction to the rights and duties that inhere to lawful combatants under customary international law. The war crime of "making improper use of a flag of truce, of the flag or of the military insignia and uniform of the enemy or of the United Nations, as well as the distinctive emblems of the Red Cross, resulting in death or serious personal injury" (Article 8(2)(b)(vii)) requires proof that the perpetrator "made such use for combatant purposes in a manner prohibited under the international law of armed conflict." The elements make clear that the perpetrator "knew or should have known of the prohibited nature of such use" at the time of the *actus reus*. These offenses are not replicated in the Article 8(2)(e) language applicable to NIACs because the concept of combatancy is an oxymoron during armed conflicts of a non-international nature.

By contrast, the war crimes provisions of the Rome Statute extended the Article 51, AP I, baseline protections to criminalize "intentionally directing attacks against the civilian population as such or against individual civilians not taking a direct part in hostilities" in the context of all armed conflicts, both international (Article 8(2)(b)(i)) and non-international (Article 8(2)(e)(i)). References to "direct participation" import a great deal of controversy and international debate directly into the fabric of the Rome Statute. The term

[37]   *Ibid.,* ¶ 5.6.

stands alongside other oblique references such as Article 8(2)(b)(vi) which rely upon the concept of combatancy and its limitations without explanation or specific reference to a particular provision of law. Similarly, the war crime of treacherously wounding or killing (Article (8)(2)(b)(xi)) relies upon the premise that the perpetrator "invited the confidence or belief of one or more persons that they were entitled to or were obliged to accord, protection under rules of international law applicable in armed conflict." The war crimes of destroying or seizing the enemy's property (Articles 8(2)(b)(xiii) and 8(2)(e)(xiii)) require proof that "the property was protected from that destruction or seizure under the international law of armed conflict." ICC practitioners must realize that for all its sophistication and noble intentions, the Rome Statute cannot be implemented as a self-standing island of international law principles isolated from the larger definitional underpinnings of *jus in bello*; hence the Manual represents a highly influential resource to guide ICC experts and judges.

As a final example of this phenomenon, lethal force in armed conflicts is permissible whenever reasonably necessary to achieve a military objective absent evidence of some prohibited purpose or unlawful tactic.[38] As early as 1863, this permissiveness was expressed in Article 14 of the Lieber Code as follows: "Military necessity, as understood by modern civilized nations, consists of the necessity of those measures which are indispensable for securing the ends of the war, and which are lawful according to the modern law and usages of war."[39] The human rights regime requires a statement of affirmative authority while *jus in bello* operates on a permissive basis subject to express limitations. As an additive requirement, lethal force under the human rights paradigm must be proportionate to the immediate context, meaning that the force used is directly proportionate to the risk posed by the individual at the moment force is employed. In the express language of Article 8(b)(2)(b)(iv), *jus in bello* proportionality by definition and accepted State practice will very likely depend upon the broader contextual set of aggregate circumstances, which in turn inform the commander's assessment of the "overall military advantage anticipated." This Rome Statute formulation accords perfectly with the Manual's framing of the same concepts.

---

[38] N. Meltzer, "Targeted Killing or Less Harmful Means? – Israel's High Court Judgment on Targeted Killing and the Restrictive Function of Military Necessity" (2006) 9 *Yearbook of International Humanitarian Law* 109.

[39] General Order No. 100, Instructions for the Government of Armies of the United States in the Field (Apr. 24, 1863), reprinted in *The War of the Rebellion: A Compilation of the Official Records of the Union and Confederate Armies*, Series III, Vol. 3 (GPO 1899) (the Lieber Code), www.loc.gov/rr/frd/Military_Law/Lieber_Collection/pdf/Instructions-gov-armies.pdf, Art. 14.

Finally, Article 22(2) of the Rome Statute makes the Manual an essential resource for ICC practitioners by mandating the principle of strict construction for the substantive offenses of Article 8. The text reads as follows: "The definition of a crime shall be strictly construed and shall not be extended by analogy. In case of ambiguity, the definition shall be interpreted in favour [sic] of the person being investigated, prosecuted or convicted." This subparagraph is a notable innovation over preexisting tribunal models. The canon of strict construction operates to the benefit of an accused insofar as ambiguity is to be resolved in such a manner as to prevent the imposition of criminal liability where there is doubt about the appropriate meaning of a particular provision of Article 8. The principle of *in dubio pro reo* protects fundamental due process on its face.[40] The Article 22 text is important because it implicitly draws upon and implements the broader framework of treaty law and State practice with respect to the conduct of hostilities. In fact, the strict constructionist principle of Article 22(2) could be read as one of the most express limitations on the overarching authority of the Court because the body of war crimes law is widely developed both in theory and practice. This requirement is the only concrete attempt in the Statute to limit the Court's interpretive authority, and therefore it implicitly incorporates the authoritative backdrop of the agreed-upon principles of the laws and customs of warfare.

The Manual serves a vital purpose in putting the ICC on notice regarding the acceptable framing of the myriad of war crimes found in the text of Article 8. The Court is not free to disregard existing interpretations or understandings of the body of law that developed in the implementation of the law of war. To be more precise, the Court *could* embark on an exercise of judicial creativity, but that is vastly a different proposition than arguing that it should engage in an ambitious teleology on its own authority. Such efforts, whether centered among jurists or counsel, would depart from the clearly permissible limits of the Rome Statute and its accompanying Elements of Crimes. Overt teleological experimentation would contravene the mandate of Article 21, which states that the Court "shall" rely upon the text of the Statute, the constituent Elements as modified "where appropriate" by "applicable treaties and the principles and rules of international law, including the established principles of the international law of armed conflict." Simply put, the Court cannot create norms in its unfettered discretion nor should it disregard *lex lata* at its convenience. The Manual is an indisputably authoritative source to guide that effort.

[40] W. A. Schabas, *The International Criminal Court: A Commentary on the Rome Statute* (Oxford University Press, 2010), 410.

3.2 *Conformity to the Elements*

As noted above, the structure of Article 8 and its accompanying Elements of Crimes was intentionally designed to comport with the historical understandings embedded in established *jus in bello*. President Clinton's signing statement references the US role in negotiating the Elements of Crimes, which for the first time in world history specify the *actus reus, mens rea,* and circumstantial elements for every offense in the Rome Statute. Delegations negotiating the Elements of Crimes expressly sought to preserve the interpretive force of accepted *jus in bello* norms. The US delegation originally proposed the concept of Elements of Crimes due to concerns that the principle of legality required international agreement over the scope of the substantive crimes described in the Rome Statute. Delegations in Rome initially opposed the proposal on the basis that agreements would be difficult to develop between common and civil law understandings of the relevant international law, but also on the basis that the effort to achieve such agreement might well entail delay for the Rome Statute's entry into force.

However, on June 30, 2000, all nations reached consensus on the authoritative elements for every specific crime listed in Articles 6, 7, and 8. The consensus adoption of the Elements included delegations from major non-States Party to include the United States, China, and Russia. The Elements also provide a vitally important template in the official languages of the United Nations that can be exported for adoption and emulation in the domestic systems of any nation. The world may yet see Arabic judges importing the Arabic text of the ICC Elements into a *sui generis* tribunal created to adjudicate the egregious crimes committed in the Syrian civil war, for example. Though the ICC Elements accord with US practice, the Manual fails to note that the United States joined consensus on their normative content. There are, however, dozens of instances whereby US practice as articulated in the Manual aligns with the ICC Elements of Crimes.

For example, Article 23 of the 1899 Hague II Convention stated that it was forbidden "[t]o destroy or seize the enemy's property, unless such destruction or seizure be imperatively demanded by the necessities of war."[41] The Rome Statute copied that same language in Articles 8(2)(b)(xiii) and 8(2)(e)(xii) (respectively applicable during IACs and NIACs). Based on their belief that the concept of military necessity ought to be an unacceptable component of military decision-making, some civilian delegates sought to introduce a higher

---

[41] DoD Law of War Manual, ¶¶ 2.2.2.2 and 5.17.2. M. A. Newton, "Modern Military Necessity: The Role & Relevance of Military Lawyers" (2007) 12 *Roger Williams University Law Review* 877, 896.

subjective threshold by which to second-guess military operations.[42] Some delegations proposed a verbal formula for the Elements of Crimes that any seizure of civilian property would be valid only if based on "imperative military necessity."[43] There is no evidence in the *travaux préparatoires* of the Rome Statute that its drafters intended to alter the preexisting fabric of the laws and customs of war in such a manner.[44] Introducing a tiered gradation of military necessity as proposed would have built a doubly high legal test with predictably paralyzing effects on military operations. A double threshold for the established concept of military necessity would have clouded the decision-making of commanders and soldiers who must always balance the legitimate need to accomplish the mission against the mandates of the law.

From the military practitioners' perspective, requiring "imperative military necessity" as a necessary condition for otherwise permissible actions would have introduced a wholly subjective and unworkable formulation that would foreseeably have exposed military commanders to *post hoc* personal criminal liability for their good faith judgments. The ultimate formulation in the Elements of Crimes translated the poetic but impractical 1899 phrase into the simple modern formulation "military necessity" that every commander and military attorney understands. The important point for our purposes is that the twin concepts of military necessity and feasibility preserve *jus in bello* as a practicable body of law that balances humanitarian and military considerations, at least when applied by reasonable, well-intentioned, and well-trained forces.[45] In sum, the delegates leveraged established practice and common military understanding as the cornerstone of diplomatic consensus.

The Manual's definitions and articulations largely comport with the established framework of the ICC Elements, and therefore seldom represent outliers from the usages and interpretations accepted by nations around the world. The synergy between Manual formulations and established ICC

---

[42] M. A. Newton, "Humanitarian Protection in Future Wars" (2004) 8 *International Peacekeeping: The Yearbook of International Peace Operations* (ed. H. Langholtz et al.) 349, 358.

[43] K. Dörmann, *Elements of War Crimes Under the Rome Statute of the International Criminal Court* (Cambridge University Press, 2003), 249.

[44] W. A. Schabas, *The International Criminal Court: A Commentary on the Rome Statute* (Oxford University Press, 2010), 240–41 (noting that the provisions of the Rome Statute referencing military necessity were "quickly agreed to at the Rome Conference" and that the concept may be invoked only when the laws of armed conflict provide so and only to the extent provided by that body of law).

[45] See M. A. Newton, "The International Criminal Court Preparatory Commission: The Way It Is & The Way Ahead" (2000) 41 *Virginia Journal of International Law* 204, 211–12.

templates for imposing criminal liability for war crimes remains unacknowledged in the Manual text.

3.3 The Concept of "Ordinary Crimes"

It is appropriate to close this subsection by noting yet another area in which US practice as articulated in the Manual accords precisely with established ICC standards. The Manual recites US treaty-based duties to punish Grave Breaches of the Geneva Conventions[46] as well as "all acts contrary" to the Geneva Conventions.[47] In detailing the mechanisms for implementing these obligations, it recognizes that:[48]

> In some cases, prosecutions in national courts for conduct constituting violations of the law of war are carried out by charging violations of ordinary domestic law or military law, and in other cases, such prosecutions are carried out by charging violations of international law. For example, the murder of a POW may be prosecuted under the ordinary criminal statutes prohibiting murder. On the other hand, the same conduct may be prosecuted under special criminal statutes that are framed in terms of "war crimes." *The United States has no international law obligation to prosecute an offense as a "war crime" as opposed to an ordinary criminal offense.* Prosecutions in national courts remain domestic prosecutions for violations of domestic statutes, even when those domestic statutes were enacted pursuant to treaty obligations or are framed in terms of violations of international law (*e.g.*, war crimes).

These tenets align with well-established US practice, though some provisions of US criminal law do refer explicitly to terminology drawn from the laws of war.[49] Pursuant to these authorities, US prosecutors have convicted many perpetrators for acts that violate established *jus in bello* in both military and civilian courts.[50] The vast majority of convictions under US law have resulted

---

[46] DoD Law of War Manual, ¶ 18.9.3.   [47] *Ibid.*, ¶ 18.9.3.3.
[48] *Ibid.*, ¶ 18.19.2 (emphasis added).
[49] *Ibid.*, ¶¶ 18.19.3.3–18.19.3.8 (noting a range of offenses proscribed under US federal criminal law deriving from the laws of war or other relevant international treaties).
[50] See, e.g., *U.S. v. Bram*, No. Army 20111032, 2014 WL 7236126 (Army Ct. Crim. App., Nov. 20, 2014) (convicting appellant of solicitation to commit murder in Afghanistan, sentencing appellant to a dishonorable discharge, confinement for five years, and reduction from the grade of E-5 to the grade of E-1, and subsequently denying appeal because there was no doubt that "this was anything but a criminal venture well outside the bounds of the rules of engagement or law of armed conflict"); *U.S. v. Morlock*, No. Army 20110230, 2014 WL 7227382 (Army Ct. Crim. App., Apr. 30, 2014) (upholding conviction of attempted murder for an agreement between appellant and other soldiers from his unit, while deployed to

from charges reciting the terminology of ordinary criminality rather than the express language of the laws of war.

Though unacknowledged in the Manual, this approach perfectly comports with ICC practice to date. ICC judges have definitively settled the question whether domestic charges must conform to the phrasing and elements set forth in international practice. In the *Senussi* case, the holdings are clear that the admissibility requirements of Article 17 preclude the ICC from exercising its jurisdiction based solely on the form of domestic charges. Assessment of domestic proceedings by ICC judges must focus on the charged conduct rather than its legal characterization. This conclusion is consistent with the *travaux préparatoires* and the expressed intent of the drafters to exclude the ordinary crimes exception provided in the ad hoc international tribunals of prior years. In other words, as established by the ICC Appeals Chamber, domestic investigation or prosecutions that address "substantially the same conduct" as envisioned in the ICC investigation serve to preclude ICC authority because the sovereign State has taken "concrete and progressive" steps towards authentic accountability.[51]

As one noted commentator observed, the ICC "has been viewed as a legitimate substitute of domestic jurisdiction (i.e. *Katanga, Gbabo*). In other cases, it has been perceived as a competing forum (Libya), or even

---

Afghanistan, to murder non-hostile Afghan males through the use of grenades and automatic weapons and then claim their victims had either committed a hostile act or exhibited hostile intent); *United States v. Behenna*, 71 MJ 228, 229 (CAAF, 2012) (resulting in a sentence of dismissal from the service, twenty-five years confinement, forfeiture of all pay and allowances on charges of unpremeditated murder and assault); *United States v. Girouard*, 70 MJ 5, 7 (CAAF, 2011); *United States v. Maynulet*, 68 MJ 374, 377 (CAAF, 2011); *United States v. Clagett*, No. Army 20070082, 2009 WL 6843560, at *1 (Army Ct. Crim. App. 2009); *United States v. Green*, 654 F.3d 637, 646–47 (6th Cir. 2011), cert. denied 132 S. Ct. 1056 (2012) (Green was convicted and sentenced to life in prison for participating in a sexual assault and multiple murders while stationed in Iraq as an infantryman in the United States Army. Green was discharged due to a personality disorder before senior Army officials became aware that he and three fellow soldiers were involved in these crimes. He was convicted in federal court and the three coconspirators were tried by courts-martial and each sentenced to between 90 and 110 years imprisonment); K. Vaughan, "Soldier Pleads Guilty to Killing Jailed Taliban Commander," *Denver Post* (May 26, 2011), https://perma.cc/EA2A-79GZ (archived Mar. 1, 2016) (chronicling the story of a soldier sentenced to life in prison, which limited to a term of no more than twelve and a half years through an agreement between the Army and the soldier's lawyers, and who was dishonorably discharged, and had rank reduced to E-1 after soldier pleaded guilty to premeditated murder of a detainee committed during deployment in Afghanistan).

51 *The Prosecutor v. Saif Al-Islam Gaddafi and Abdullah Al-Senussi*, Case No. ICC-01/11-01/11-565, Judgment on the appeal of Mr. Abdullah Al-Senussi against the decision of Pre-Trial Chamber I of 11 October 2013 entitled "Decision on the admissibility of the case against Abdullah Al-Senussi" (July 24, 2014), para. 87. www.icc-cpi.int/Pages/record.aspx?docNo=ICC-01/11-01/11-565&ln=en.

as an obstacle to domestic justice efforts (Kenya)."[52] The drafters intended the Rome Statute to help prevent systematized impunity. That is why the preamble recalls that "it is the duty of every State to exercise its criminal jurisdiction over those responsible for international crimes." The Manual documents US policy to comply with those legal obligations, and future ICC efforts to dismiss US investigations or prosecutions based on the form of the charges would represent a departure from its own legal obligations. Conversely, US prosecutors should be confident that the ICC is compelled to respect good faith investigation or prosecution of war crimes as described in the Manual.

4 DEFINING THE MODERN DUTY TO INVESTIGATE

The Manual correctly notes that military commanders "have a duty to investigate reports of alleged law of war violations committed by persons under their command or against persons to whom they have a legal duty to protect."[53] Recognition of this overarching duty is reinforced by the reminder that "duties to implement and enforce the law of war also imply duties to investigate reports of alleged violations of the law of war. In addition to taking measures to meet the requirements of DoD policy, commanders may also take other measures they deem appropriate to ensure appropriate investigation and reporting of alleged violations of the law of war within their command."[54] As in so many other places in the Manual, these wholly correct mandates remain divorced from their broader context in modern coalition operations. In particular, the Manual fails to address the important ramifications of the growing interface between the law of war and human rights law. To be more precise, it offers no guidance regarding the contours of what it terms "appropriate" investigations into war crimes. The Manual's omission of any discussion regarding the scope and substance of modern law of war investigations does a distinct disservice to commanders charged with overseeing complex coalition operations.

In Chapter 18 of this Commentary, Aurel Sari comments on the reality that the "law of war and international human rights law occupy the same

[52] C. Stahn, "Admissibility Challenges before the ICC: From Quasi-Primacy to Qualified Deference?," in C. Stahn (ed.), *The Law and Practice of the International Criminal Court* (Oxford University Press, 2015), 28. See also M. A. Newton, "The Quest for Constructive Complementarity," in C. Stahn and M. El Zeidy (eds.), *The ICC and Complementarity: From Theory to Practice* (Cambridge University Press, 2011), 304 (making the argument that the intent of the statute is emphatically not to substitute the discretion of the ICC Prosecutor for that of domestic officials acting in good faith to uphold the law).
[53] DoD Law of War Manual, ¶ 18.4.3.   [54] *Ibid.*, ¶¶ 18.13.

normative space, are deeply intertwined and appear to be locked into a process of gradual convergence."[55] The Manual avoids analysis of this interrelationship by noting the US "view that the International Covenant on Civil and Political Rights (ICCPR) does not create obligations for an Occupying Power with respect to occupied territory because a contracting State's obligations under the ICCPR only extend to persons within its territory and subject to its jurisdiction."[56] Though the text admits "some coalition partners, may interpret their human rights treaty obligations to create obligations for their military operations outside their home territory in the context of belligerent occupation,"[57] there is no acknowledgment that the US perspective is an increasingly minority view. The literature on the relationship between human rights norms and the broader field of international humanitarian law is vast; but the forces of many allied nations deployed alongside US forces and under the overall command of US leaders will export their own treaty-based human rights obligations over any area or persons where they exercise "effective control."[58]

The Manual's failure to describe the contours of coalition investigations arises in part from its inadequate analysis of the *lex specialis* concept as applied. It notes with an unwarranted tone of finality that because the law of war constitutes the *lex specialis*, it serves as the "controlling body of law" during all armed conflicts.[59] In addressing the wrinkles inherent during armed conflicts not of an international character, the Manual appears to distinguish between "an internal non-international armed conflict" during which states "continue to be bound by applicable human rights treaty obligations" and other NIAC contexts in which:

> applicability of human rights treaty obligations during non-international armed conflict may depend on a variety of factors. Such applicability depends on the terms of the particular treaty in question, and whether the State has exercised an authorized derogation from its provisions due to an emergency situation. The applicability of a human rights treaty obligation with respect to an individual, such as an obligation under the International Covenant on

---

[55] R. Provost, *International Human Rights and Humanitarian Law* (Cambridge University Press, 2002); R. Kolb and G. Gaggioli (eds.), *Research Handbook on Human Rights and Humanitarian Law* (Cheltenham: Edward Elgar, 2013); and G. Oberleitner, *Human Rights in Armed Conflict: Law, Practice, Policy* (Cambridge University Press, 2015).

[56] DoD Law of War Manual, ¶¶ 11.1.2.6.   [57] *Ibid.*

[58] R. Wilde, "Triggering State Obligations Extraterritorially: The Spatial Test in Certain Human Rights Treaties," in R. Arnold and N. N. R. Quénivet (eds.), *International Humanitarian Law and Human Rights Law: Towards a New Merger in International Law* (Leiden: Martinus Nijhoff, 2008), 133.

[59] DoD Law of War Manual, ¶¶ 11.3.2.

Civil and Political Rights, for example, may depend on whether the person is located outside the territory of the State Party. In addition, law of war rules constitute the *lex specialis* during situations of armed conflict, and as such, serve as the controlling body of law with regard to the conduct of hostilities and the protection of war victims.[60]

With respect to "appropriate" investigations, the conjunction of human rights law and law of armed conflict in the same operational time and space requires careful consideration when it comes to operationalizing "appropriate investigations" in particular. The Manual's formulation that *lex specialis* law of war requires other bodies of law either to remain subordinated to *jus in bello* norms or be interpreted in such a manner as to remain consistent with accepted law of war principles does not fully accord with accepted international law. Applying the *lex specialis* doctrine, both human rights law and the law of war require investigations into alleged improprieties, hence the duty is not contradictory. At best, the duty to investigate might represent what scholars term "an opposing norm" in the sense that there is no conflict as both legal regimes include the duty to investigate but depending on the context would "require actions that cannot be fulfilled at the same time."[61]

The sweeping conclusion that *lex specialis* law of war duties serve to displace the human rights standards with respect to investigations obviously offers little aid to coalition commanders in this context. There are at present competing models for the form and function of field investigations, such as the Fact Finding Assessments used by Israeli forces, the Joint Investigative Assessment Teams used by the International Security Armed Force (ISAF) in Afghanistan, modern American administrative inquiries such as the Taguba Report into the crimes committed at Abu Ghraib or the published CENCTOM report analyzing the Kunduz bombing.[62] The Manual offers commanders little comfort in selecting between these variants in order to comply with the overarching duty to investigate alleged war crimes. The investigative environment between armed conflicts and normal peacetime investigations envisioned by the human rights regime are vast, yet application of the norms might not be automatically incompatible.

Absolute uniformity of investigative standards across all contexts is impossible, but commanders should know that the human rights articulation

---

60   *Ibid.*, ¶¶ 17.2.1.3.

61   D. Marianna Banaszewska, "Lex Specialis," in F. Lachenmann and R. Wolfrum (eds.), *The Law of Armed Conflict and The Use of Force, The Max Planck Encyclopedia of Public International Law* (Oxford University Press, 2017), 659, 660.

62   http://fpp.cc/wp-content/uploads/01.-AR-15-6-Inv-Rpt-Doctors-Without-Borders-3-Oct-15_CLEAR.pdf.

provides the standard of minimum protections that should be unassailable in any human rights-based forum, domestic or international. The line of European Court of Human Rights (ECtHR) cases that culminated in the *Jaloud* case in November 2014 illustrate the litmus test for an "effective investigation" in human rights terms.[63] To be sure, there are questionable aspects of the ECtHR analysis in *Jaloud* as applied to the actions of a Dutch officer whose troops were taking fire at a roadblock during operations in Iraq, but the discussion of what constitutes an effective investigation for the purposes of European human rights law is illustrative to coalition commanders in NATO operations:

> For an investigation into alleged unlawful killing by State agents to be effective, it is necessary for the persons responsible for and carrying out the investigation to be independent from those implicated in the events. This means not only a lack of hierarchical or institutional connection but also a practical independence (see, for example, *Shanaghan*, cited above, § 104). A requirement of promptness and reasonable expedition is implicit in this context. While there may be obstacles or difficulties which prevent progress in an investigation in a particular situation, a prompt response by the authorities in investigating a use of lethal force may generally be regarded as essential in maintaining public confidence in their adherence to the rule of law and in preventing any appearance of collusion in or tolerance of unlawful acts. For the same reasons, there must be a sufficient element of public scrutiny of the investigation or its results to secure accountability in practice as well as in theory. The degree of public scrutiny required may well vary from case to case. In all cases, however, the victim's next-of-kin must be involved in the procedure to the extent necessary to safeguard his or her legitimate interests (see *Ahmet Özkan and others*, cited above, §§ 311–314; *Isayeva*, cited above, §§ 211–214 and the cases cited therein).[64]

As *Jaloud* stressed, the duty to conduct an effective investigation is "not an obligation of result, but of means."[65] For coalition commanders, the hallmarks of investigative independence paired with a fully informed and neutral prosecutorial determination mark the pathway to satisfying the duty to investigate under both human rights law and the law of armed conflict. The goal is to ensure that any investigation includes appropriate follow-up and authoritative oversight. Processes for securing key evidence and the potential sharing of that evidence with either a criminal investigation or an international tribunal remain necessary cornerstones. *Jaloud* provides an overall template of

[63] *Jaloud v. The Netherlands*, App. No. 47708/08, Nov. 20, 2014, Judgment.
[64] *Ibid.*, para. 167. [65] *Ibid.*, para. 166.

considerations, though a full autopsy of every civilian death is obviously impossible under all circumstances. In the middle of ongoing conflicts, procedural differences between normal domestic criminal investigations and those conducted in a combat zone may well be overcome by the commander's clear explication of the investigation's legal sufficiency in a particular context. This is far from a simple cookie-cutter invocation of *lex specialis*, as the Manual implies. In any event, careful explication of the contextual goal of an "appropriate investigation" may well allow harmonization of the law of war within a specific human rights analysis.[66]

5 CONCLUSION

The Manual seeks to "address the law of war that is applicable to the United States, including treaties to which the United States is a Party, and applicable customary international law. It provides legal rules, principles, and discussion, particularly with respect to DoD practice."[67] DoD accordingly admits that the Manual does not seek to "describe the views of other States, which may differ from views expressed in this manual."[68]

In contrast, coalition commanders add the imperative that they must manage competing national visions and priorities as a necessary precondition for victory. Commanders "consider the broader imperatives of winning the war as quickly and efficiently as possible," which inevitably requires consideration of many competing factors because "*military necessity* justifies those measures necessary to achieve the object of war, and the object of war is not simply to prevail, but to prevail as quickly and efficiently as possible."[69] In its efforts to articulate the nuances of the law of war, the Manual underserves the larger need to emphasize the import of its provisions *vis-à-vis* the cohesion and legitimacy of coalition operations. Sadly, this represents a significant missed opportunity. DoD may well have overlooked Shakespeare's admonition in King Lear that "Striving to better, oft we mar what's well."[70]

---

[66] *Hassan v. United Kingdom*, App. No. 29750/09, Judgment, Sept. 16, 2014, para. 104 ("accommodating," as far as possible, the power to detain in international armed conflict with the right to liberty, but expressly declining to extend that right broadly into all armed conflict scenarios).

[67] DoD Law of War Manual, ¶ 1.1.2.   [68] *Ibid.*   [69] *Ibid.*, ¶ 2.2.3.1.

[70] William Shakespeare, *King Lear*, act.1, sc. 4.

Armed Groups and the DoD Manual: Shining a Light on Overlooked Issues

Katharine Fortin

1 INTRODUCTION

The purpose of this chapter is to examine how the Department of Defense (DoD) Law of War Manual (the Manual) addresses certain issues specific to armed groups operating in non-international armed conflicts (NIACs). The decision to include a chapter focusing specifically on armed groups stems from an apprehension that nowadays the majority of armed conflicts are between States and armed groups, rather than between States. This changed conflict landscape creates an imperative to give more attention to how armed groups fit within the legal framework applying in times of NIAC.[1] Indeed, in a system where it is largely accepted that States are the primary makers of the law applying in times of NIAC, it might seem all too tempting to ignore armed groups in the development of policy and practice regarding military operations to be carried out by States. However, it is noteworthy that although the purpose of the Manual is to address the law of war that is applicable to the United States,[2] the principle of equality suggests that the Manual is also implicitly setting out the law that is applicable to non-State armed groups.[3] This observation explains why it is imperative to examine DoD's assessment of the law of war in respect to NIAC not only in respect of the rules it sets out for State armed forces, but to also examine how the Manual sets out rules relating to armed groups and their members.

---

[1] Notable recent studies focusing on the legal framework applying in NIAC and the obligations of non-State armed groups include S. Sivakumaran, *The Law of Non-International Armed Conflict* (Oxford University Press, 2012); K. Fortin, *The Accountability of Armed Groups under Human Rights Law* (Oxford University Press, 2017); D. Murray, *Human Rights Obligations of Non-State Armed Groups* (Oxford and Portland OR: Bloomsbury, 2016).
[2] See DoD Law of War Manual, ¶ 1.1.2.   [3] See *ibid., inter alia* ¶ 17.2.4.

In assessing how the Manual addresses issues relevant to armed groups, this chapter examines only a select number of issues. In order to avoid overlap with other chapters, it does not focus in detail on how the Manual handles the threshold of NIAC or the classification of armed conflicts. It also does not examine how the Manual addresses detention by armed groups or the detention of armed group members, as this issue is addressed in another chapter. Instead, this chapter examines four issues which have not been addressed elsewhere in this volume, which are specifically relevant to armed groups and/ or their members and which have hitherto slipped under the radar in existing analysis of the Manual. Section 2 of the chapter examines how the Manual understands armed groups to be addressees of international humanitarian law. In other words, it analyses how the Manual understands armed groups to be bound by different sources of law (e.g., treaty law, custom), and considers how the Manual explains these sources to be binding upon them. Connectedly, section 3 examines how the Manual addresses the principles of international humanitarian law, looking in particular at the Manual's reliance on the concept of honor in NIAC. Section 4 assesses the approach that the Manual takes to the targetability of members of armed groups. Section 5 examines the assertion that members of insurgent groups can be compelled to fight on behalf of a State.

2 HOW ARE ARMED GROUPS BOUND BY THE LAWS OF WAR?

Although it is generally accepted that armed groups are bound by the law of war, the question of *how* armed groups are bound has puzzled and divided academics ever since Common Article 3 was drafted.[4] The legal question is as follows: How can States bind non-State actors to international norms without their consent? As NIACs have become the more dominant paradigm in recent decades, increased academic attention has been given to this question.[5] The existence of this debate makes it interesting to examine how the

---

[4]	F. Siordet, "Les Conventions de Genève et la guerre civile" (1950) 81 *Bulletin International des Sociétés de la Croix-Rouge* 104–22, 105; Y. Dinstein, "The International Law of Civil Wars and Human Rights" (1976) 6 *Israel Yearbook on Human Rights* 62–80, 68; R. Baxter, *"Jus in Bello Interno*: The Present and Future Law," in J. Moore (ed.), *Law and Civil War in the Modern World* (Baltimore: John Hopkins, 1974), 527; A. Cassese, "The Status of Rebels under the 1977 Geneva Protocol on Non-International Armed Conflicts" (1981) 30 *International and Comparative Law Quarterly*, 416; T. Fleiner-Gerster and M. Meyer, "New Developments in Humanitarian Law: A Challenge to the Concept of Sovereignty" (1985) 34 *International and Comparative Law Quarterly* 267, 272.

[5]	L. Moir, *The Law of Non International Armed Conflict* (Cambridge University Press, 2002), 52; J. Kleffner, "The Applicability of International Humanitarian Law to Organised Armed

Manual approaches this matter, as it is rare to see a State's view on the issue. Perhaps most importantly, the Manual strongly affirms that armed groups *are* largely bound by international humanitarian law, to the same extent as States in a NIAC.[6] The fact that the United States is not a party to either Additional Protocol I (AP I) or Additional Protocol II (AP II) of the 1949 Geneva Conventions adds a number of qualifications to this position. First, the Manual makes clear that the United States does not accept that national liberation movements are bound by the rules of IAC.[7] Second, on the basis that the United States is not a party to AP II, the Manual recognizes only one threshold of NIAC, namely the threshold of Common Article 3. As such, the Manual does not distinguish between armed groups which control territory and armed groups which do not control any territory.

Strangely, in certain places, the Manual seems to indicate that only some armed groups will be bound by international humanitarian law. For example, Chapter III implicitly indicates that *only* armed groups "with the intention of conducting hostilities" will be bound by the law of war.[8] Similarly, in the section entitled "Binding Force of the Law of War on Insurgents and Other Non-State Armed Groups" in Chapter XVII, the text asserts that customary law of war rules are binding on "those parties to the armed conflict that intend to make war and to claim the rights of a belligerent, even if they are not States."[9] These two passages indicate that the "intention" of the armed group is a determinative factor in assessing whether an armed group is bound by the law of war. The second passage also seems to indicate that only armed groups with belligerent status are bound by customary international law. If this was indeed the US position, it would constitute an unusual stance, as it is widely accepted elsewhere in doctrine that the question of whether an armed group is bound by the law of war, or can enjoy belligerent status, is not dependent upon subjective factors – that is, its own beliefs, intentions, or claims.[10] Yet in other

---

Groups" (2011) 882 *International Review of the Red Cross* 443–61; S. Sivakumaran, "Binding Armed Opposition Groups" (2006) 5 *International and Comparative Law Quarterly* 369–94; D. Murray, "How International Humanitarian Law Treaties Bind Non-State Armed Groups" (2014) 20(1) *Journal of Conflict and Security Law* 101–31; Fortin (above note 1), Chapter 7.

6   See DoD Law of War Manual, ¶ 3.4.1.2, and ¶ 17.2.4.

7   *Ibid.*, ¶ 3.3.4 (on the basis of strong US objections "to this provision as making the applicability of the rules of international armed conflict turn on subjective and politicized criteria that would eliminate the distinction between international and non-international conflicts.").

8   *Ibid.*, ¶ 3.4.1.2 compared to ¶ 3.4.2.2 and in particular fnn. 75 and 76.

9   *Ibid.*, ¶ 17.2.4. This text may have originated from the 1956 Manual which states "The customary law of war becomes applicable to civil war upon recognition of the rebels as belligerents."

10   Sivakumaran (above note 1), 10–11 on the belligerency framework. At times, the language that the State authority has used to describe or address the violence has been noted in decisions

sections of the Manual, more mainstream positions come to the fore. For example, when setting out the threshold of NIAC in Chapter III, the Manual does not indicate a need to assess whether an armed group has the "intention to conduct hostilities."[11] This constitutes an implicit recognition that armed groups acting in circumstances where this threshold has been met will be bound by the law of war, irrespective of whether they manifest an intention to conduct hostilities.

The Manual sensibly chooses to refrain from getting heavily involved in the legal debate about how armed groups are bound by treaty law.[12] However, the Manual does provide a view that treaty provisions in NIAC bind not only the State, but each party to the conflict. It goes on to explain that as a "practical matter" non-State armed groups would "often be bound by their State's treaty obligations due to the very fact that the leaders of those non-State armed groups would claim to be the State's legitimate representatives."[13] The Manual's adoption of this line of reasoning raises the interesting question whether the US would also accept that armed groups who claim to be a State's legitimate representatives will be bound by human rights treaty law, as well as treaties containing the law of war. For while the Manual does not address this point, it is noteworthy that the growing practice of holding armed groups bound by human rights law is often justified on similar lines, albeit without reference to the armed groups' subjective views.[14] The Manual also notes that special agreements are another important means by which the parties to a non-international armed conflict can bring the law of war rules into force. It highlights that Article 3 of the Geneva Conventions and Article 19(2) of the Hague Cultural Property Convention urges the parties to endeavor to bring about a fuller application of the law pertaining to IACs to NIACs.[15]

3 ARMED GROUPS AND HONOR

When examining the sources that the Manual draws upon in relation to armed groups, another important point to note is the way the Manual asserts and relies on the principle of honor. Chapter II of the Manual identifies three

---

determining the application of international humanitarian law, but no consideration is given to the views of the armed group on the matter. See *Prosecutor v. Boškoski and Tarčulovski*, Case No. IT-04-82-T, Trial Judgment, ¶ 800 (ICTY, July 10, 2008; *Prosecutor v. Milutinović et al.*, Case No. IT-05-87-T, Trial Judgment, ¶¶ 238, 245–47 (ICTY, Feb. 26, 2009).

[11]　DoD Law of War Manual, ¶ 3.4.2.2.　　[12]　See above note 5 for literature on this debate.

[13]　DoD Law of War Manual, ¶ 17.2.4.

[14]　For a discussion of these arguments see Fortin (above note 1), 19–20, 155–57, 240–84, and 375–78.

[15]　DoD Law of War Manual, ¶ 17.3.

interdependent core principles – military necessity, humanity, and honor – underlying the law of war and indicates that these principles "provide the foundation" for other law of war principles, such as proportionality and distinction, and most of the treaty and customary rules of the law of war.[16] The Manual then enters into a detailed discussion of how the three main principles are defined, how they manifest themselves in the legal framework, and how they are applied in practice. In Chapter XVII, addressing NIAC, the Manual asserts that the foundational principles are common to both IAC and NIAC.[17]

Indeed, Chapter XVII asserts that the principles will likely be "most useful" when assessing the rules applicable during NIAC, presumably due to their gap-filling function in an area where treaty law is scarce.[18] For according to the Manual, the principles have two core functions. First, they "provide the foundation for the rules applicable during non-international armed conflict" and, second, they provide a "general guide for conduct," when no specific rule applies.[19] Since the Manual's publication, a number of commentators have remarked that the Manual's emphasis on the principles of the law of war constitutes a "significant recalibration" of the 1956 Manual.[20] While a debate can be had about the advantages and disadvantages of this recalibration in more general sense, the following paragraphs demonstrate how this recalibration poses particular challenges with respect to the principle of honor and armed groups.

It seems fair to assume that the principle of honor in the Manual is the successor to the principle of "chivalry" which was one of the three principles identified by the 1956 DoD Manual on the Law of War, alongside the principles of humanity and military necessity.[21] Chapter II stipulates that the terms "honor" and "chivalry" are largely synonymous; the main difference being that the term "honor" draws from warrior codes beyond those that emerged in Europe during the Middle Ages.[22] The Manual clarifies that honor demands a certain amount of fairness in offense and defense and an acceptance that belligerent rights are not limited, forbidding the resort to means, expedients, or conduct that constitute a "breach of trust" with the enemy.[23] It finds the principle to underlie rules requiring that enemies deal with one another in "good faith" in their non-hostile relations. It also finds that

---

[16] *Ibid.*, ¶ 2.1.2.   [17] *Ibid.*, ¶ 17.1.2.2.   [18] *Ibid.*   [19] *Ibid.*, ¶ 17.2.2.1.

[20] S. Watts, "The DoD Law of War Manual's Return to Principles," *Just Security Blog*, June 30, 2017, www.justsecurity.org/24270/DoD-law-war-Manuals-return-principles.

[21] Field Manual 27-10, The Law of Land Warfare (Washington: US Dep't. of Army, July 18, 1956) (FM 27-10), ¶ 3.

[22] DoD Law of War Manual, ¶ 2.6.1.   [23] *Ibid.*, ¶ 2.6.2.2.

the concept of "good faith" (and therefore honor) underlies the prohibition of perfidy, the misuse of certain signs, fighting in the enemy's uniform, feigning non-hostile relations in order to seek a military advantage, and compelling nationals of a hostile party to take part in the operations of war directed against their own country.[24] According to the Manual, the principle of honor – in addition to being a tenet of personal conduct – is based on, and demands, a certain mutual respect between opposing military forces. The Manual states that "opposing military forces should respect one another outside of the fighting because they share a profession and they fight one another on behalf of their respective States and not out of personal hostility."[25] Later, the Manual states that the principle of honor reflects the premise that military forces are a common class of professionals who have undertaken to comport themselves honorably.[26] As a result, it demands a "certain mutual respect between opposing military forces."[27]

Rachel van Landingham has noted that the Manual's reliance on the principle of 'honor' will be objectionable to many, as it draws on traditions that are "outdated, chauvinistic, and frankly distasteful."[28] She points out that its invocation connotes "elitism and the inhumanity of the Crusades," and argues that it harks back to the "assumed, white, Christian superiority of the day."[29] In making this critique, van Landingham questions whether it is necessary for the US Manual to resort to the principle of honor, when it could have relied upon the term humanity for many of the same provisions.[30] However, it is no coincidence that all the law of war rules which the Manual finds to be based on the principle of "honor" protect enemy fighters, rather than civilians or fighters *hors de combat*. For although some of these provisions can indeed be deemed to be rooted equally in the principle of humanity (e.g., perfidy) many, such as the prohibition of fighting in the enemy's uniform, cannot, as their violation brings no consequences for protected persons.[31] This observation sheds light on the fact that the inclusion of the principle of honor recognizes that there are other restrictive principles at

---

[24] *Ibid.*　　[25] *Ibid.*, ¶ 2.6.3.　　[26] *Ibid.*, ¶ 2.6.3.2.　　[27] *Ibid.*, ¶ 2.6.

[28] R. van Landingham, "The Law of War Is Not about 'Chivalry'," *Just Security Blog*, July 20, 2017, www.justsecurity.org/24773/laws-war-chivalry/.

[29] *Ibid.* See also L. Doswald-Beck and S. Vité, "International Humanitarian Law and Human Rights Law" (1993) 33 (293) *International Review of the Red Cross* 94–119, who state "The last criterion [chivalry] seems out of place in the modern world."

[30] For a similar questioning see R. Liivoja, "Chivalry without a Horse: Military Honor and the Modern Law of Armed Conflict" (2012) 15 *ENDC Proceedings* 75–100, 77.

[31] For analysis of the crime of perfidy in NIAC rooting it in the principle of distinction see R. Jackson, "Perfidy in Non-International Armed Conflicts" (2012) 88 *International Law Studies* 237–62. See also Sivakumaran (above note 1), 418 who points out that the reasoning

play in the legal framework, in addition to military necessity and humanity.[32] Rather than aiming to protect persons or restrict and protect military operations, the principle of honor or chivalry has been invoked primarily to remind parties of the need to respect a moral sensibility and prevent battlefield practices from descending into wanton destruction.[33]

While recognizing that it may be necessary to rely on a force beyond military necessity and humanity, it remains important to question what kind of role the concepts of honor or chivalry should play in a modern military manual espousing the law of war, if any. Indeed, the need to question this issue arises not only because of the chauvinism and elitism that the terms evoke but also because modern historical scholarship increasingly advises against viewing chivalry or honor in a rose-tinted manner. Indeed, modern scholars of chivalry have commented that the greatest honor in medieval times, was to "win."[34] They have equally pointed out that romantic tales placing chivalric exploits of knightly courage in the foreground, often admit a "mind-numbingly constant" ravaging, looting, raping, burning, destruction, and arson in the background.[35] They also stress the specific historical context of the concept, emphasizing that individuals adopting chivalric codes in a military sense would be equally familiar with the idea of honor in a social sense.[36] For these reasons, literature on honor and chivalry warns against modern attempts to "return to Camelot," questioning whether honor or chivalry ever existed as something to realistically be emulated as a best practice and highlighting the impossibility of transposing such principles out of the specific social context in which they emerged.[37]

At a baseline, these critiques reinforce the need for the drafters of the Manual to have given serious consideration to whether the notions of honor

---

behind the prohibition of certain perfidious conduct is that committing the prohibited acts will decrease respect for the law of armed conflict.

[32] Liivoja (above note 30), 93.

[33] T. Gill, "Chivalry: A Principle of the Law of Armed Conflict?," in M. Matthee, B. Toebes, and M. Brus (eds.), *Armed Conflict and International Law: In Search of the Human Face* (The Hague: TMC Asser Press, 2013), 33–51, 35. Jean Pictet noted that the principle of chivalry "brought with it the recognition that in war as in during a game of chess there should be rules and that one does not win by overturning the board." J. Pictet, *Development and Principles of International Humanitarian Law* (Dordrecht: Martinus Nijhoff, 1985), 15.

[34] R. Kaeuper, *Medieval Chivalry* (Cambridge University Press, 2016), 165, 169, 183–84. See also Gill (above note 3), 169.

[35] Kaeuper (above note 34), 165, 169, 183–84. See also Gill (above note 3), 47.

[36] C. Taylor, *Chivalry and the Ideals of Knighthood in France during the Hundred Years War* (Cambridge University Press, 2013), 55; and Kaeuper (above note 34), 8 and 22.

[37] For analysis of historical instances of romantic revival termed "return to Camelot" and their distortions, see Kaeuper (above note 34), 16–20.

is a concept that is sufficiently alive in modern culture to be drawn upon as an effective source of norms today. Indeed, on the basis that the Manual is aimed at DoD personnel it is most pressing to consider whether the concept is alive in US culture. Yet on the basis that it is also intended to be a "description of the law" more generally, binding upon States and non-State groups, it is also important to look beyond US shores.[38] During the course of this review, it is also relevant to consider the extent to which the notion of honor that is articulated in the Manual is referring back to the reciprocal codes of warrior brethren, or a value of personal conduct. For, in its latter incarnation, one can see that such a concept may have significant value with a State's armed forces and be particularly useful in NIAC. Indeed, it is often said that in insurgency – an environment characterized by "violence, immorality, distrust and deceit" – even greater steps need to be taken to safeguard the "ethical climate" of the organization and the "values" of soldiers and marines.[39] It is also noted that "honor" is one of the seven US Army values, alongside loyalty, duty, respect, selfless service, integrity, and personal courage. Significantly, new recruits are encouraged to "exhibit a higher sense of honor than that to which they are exposed in popular culture."[40] Equally, it would be misguided to conceive of members of armed groups as strangers to conceptions of honor, bravery, courage, and principled fighting.[41] While adherence to them may be poor, many armed groups have internal rules which reiterate values such as honor, morality, and discipline.

Yet as a source of rules, the notion of honor in the US Manual is articulated mainly as a shared code between "enemies," rather than as a personal value. In this embodiment, the principle is based upon professional solidarity between soldiers on opposing sides. In this incarnation, the principle of honor relies upon reciprocity in the sense that it arises out of a mutual respect between the fighting parties. Herein lies the problem in NIAC. For while it is widely accepted that the notion of good faith between sides remains important in NIAC (e.g., in the context of negotiating special

---

[38] DoD Law of War Manual, p. 1 and p. 2.
[39] Brigadier General H. R. McMaster, "Remaining True to Our Values – Reflecting on Military Ethics in Trying Times" (2010) 9(3) *Journal of Military Ethics* 183–94, 188.
[40] *Ibid.*, 189.
[41] O. Bangerter, "Reasons Why Armed Groups Choose to Respect International Humanitarian Law or Not" (2011) 93(882) *International Review of the Red Cross* 353–84, 358 fn. 22. O. Bangerter, *Internal Control: Codes of Conduct within Insurgent Armed Groups*, Occasional Paper 31 (Geneva: Small Arms Survey, 2012), 15–16 and 90 for an example of a code of conduct emphasizing honor.

agreements and peace agreements),[42] it is often severely strained. Indeed, from a State perspective, combatants might question why they should "fight in accordance with notions of chivalry and honor, or even in accordance with the laws of war against a foe which has no regard for them and routinely violates the law of war."[43] From an armed group's perspective, a fighter might question why they should fight in accordance with the laws of war, if they are already condemned to criminal prosecution when they first resort to arms. Crucially, the Manual's recourse to this kind of reciprocal honor would not be so important if it was not given such a strong normative role in the Manual. The 1956 Manual, for example, identifies chivalry as one of the principles of the law of war at the beginning but never mentions the principle again with the result that its inclusion, though open to critique, is not of substantial normative consequence.

Yet the 2016 Manual not only clearly states that the principle of honor articulated in Chapter II is relevant in NIAC, it also identifies it as a core concept upon which other concrete rules that many States accept apply in NIACs are based, such as perfidy.[44] Perhaps of even more concern, the Manual finds the principle of honor to "support the entire system" of the law of war and give parties confidence in it.[45] On the basis that the concepts of chivalry and honor translate uncomfortably into relations *between* State forces and armed groups and relations *between* armed groups and armed groups, the Manual's strong reliance upon the concepts of honor and chivalry in NIAC is troubling. Indeed, it is helpful to remember that studies into the forces that motivate parties to violate or comply with the law of war show that while reliance on principles can be effective in encouraging compliance with the law, rules are also essential.[46] Moreover, while the paragraphs above have shown that humanity and military necessity cannot be used to explain all rules of the law of war, equally there is no need for the Manual to rely as heavily on the principle of honor in NIACs as it does. It would have also been possible for

---

[42] See, e.g., rule 66 of the ICRC's Study on Customary International Law which holds that the principle of good faith applies by definition in both international and non-international armed conflicts. J.-M. Henckaerts and L. Doswald-Beck (eds.), *Customary International Humanitarian Law*, I: *Rules* (Cambridge University Press, 2005), 228.

[43] Gill (above note 33), 48.

[44] It is unclear whether the Manual finds the prohibition of perfidy to apply in NIACs, as, despite Chapter XVII referring back to Chapter II, Chapter II does not show any awareness of Chapter XVII or any mention of NIACs.

[45] DoD Law of War Manual, ¶ 2.1.2.3.

[46] ICRC, "The Roots of Behaviour in War: Understanding and Preventing IHL Violations" (2004), 15; ICRC, "The Roots of Restraint in War" (2018), 32.

the Manual to have relied upon personal (rather than reciprocal) honor, treaty law, historical precedent, and (sometimes) humanity to provide a justification for many of the rules mentioned in Chapter II.

4 MEMBERSHIP AND TARGETING

The third issue which this chapter examines is the issue of how the Manual treats armed groups and their members for the purposes of targeting. These rules are found in Chapter V of the Manual on "The Conduct of Hostilities." Reciting the full history of the Manual's provisions on membership would take readers deep into the history of the "direct participation in hostilities" debates that took place in the context of the International Committee of the Red Cross's proceedings between 2003 and 2008.[47] While it is not possible to do justice to these debates here, it remains important to note that this is a key section of the Manual where there are problems with the Manual's intention to provide guidance to US troops on the one hand and be a more general statement of the law on the other. For the Manual takes a position (quite likely driven by litigation interests and ongoing political debates) relative to "membership," that differs from the approach taken by the International Committee of the Red Cross (ICRC) and States who have ratified AP I.[48] DoD asserts that like members of enemy forces, individuals who are formally or functionally part of a non-State armed group that is engaged with hostilities may be made the object of attack because they share their group's hostile intent.[49] According to the Manual, formal membership can be demonstrated by formal or informal information: for example, the use of a rank, title, or style of communication; the taking of an oath of loyalty to the group of the group's leader; wearing of uniform or other clothing, adornments, or body markers; carrying of documents issued or belonging to the group that identify the individual as a member, for example membership lists, identity cards, or membership applications.[50]

According to the Manual, formal membership may also be denoted by an individual's behaviour. Examples of behaviour denoting formal membership include acting at the direction of the group or within its command structure; performing a function for the group that is analogous to a function usually performed by a member of a State's armed forces; taking direct part in

---

[47] See ICRC Clarification Process on the Notion of Direct Participation in Hostilities (Proceedings), www.icrc.org/eng/resources/documents/article/other/direct-participation-article-020709.htm.

[48] See DoD Law of War Manual, ¶ 5.8.2.1 where this is emphasized.   [49] *Ibid.*, ¶ 5.7.3.

[50] *Ibid.*, ¶ 5.7.3.1.

hostilities (taking into account frequency, intensity and duration of those hostilities); accessing facilities exclusive to the armed group, such as safehouses or training camps, travelling along clandestine routes used by those groups, or travelling with members of the groups in remote locations.[51] The Manual goes on to note that not all groups are organized in a formal command structure. In recognition of this, the Manual sets out how a group's *functional* members can be identified and distinguished from individuals merely sympathetic to the group. According to the Manual, it is relevant to find evidence that an individual is integrated into a group, such that its hostile intent may be imputed to him or her. Evidence that an individual is integrated into a group in this manner may be found in the fact that an individual follows the directions of the group or its leaders; takes part in hostilities on behalf of the group on a sufficiently frequent or intensive basis; or performs tasks for the group similar to those provided in combat, combat support, or combat service support roles.[52]

While setting out these concepts of membership, DoD recognizes that it takes a different position to other States that, for example, treat individuals associated with armed groups as "civilians," who cannot be attacked unless and until they participate directly in hostilities.[53] It clarifies that it does not recognize a "revolving door" protection, where a civilian repeatedly regains and loses his or her protection.[54] It explains that such an approach would place civilians who directly participate in hostilities on a better footing than members of the US armed forces, who can be targeted even when not taking part in hostilities.[55] The Manual also confirms that although AP I recognizes a presumption in favor of civilian status when conducting attacks, the United States does not consider this provision to be part of customary international law. In a similar vein, it refutes the contention that there is a rule preventing military commanders from acting upon information available to him, in doubtful cases.[56]

The Manual explains its position on these points by arguing that a legal presumption of civilian status "would not account for the realities of war."[57] It also indicates a view that opposing sides might exploit the existence of such a presumption, by blurring their status and thereby escaping lawful targeting.[58] It thus explains that the US non-recognition of a lack of civilian presumption is intended to avoid an increase of harm to the civilian population, and decreased respect for the law of war.[59] This provision is particularly important when reading the rules on membership of armed groups, because – when

---

[51] *Ibid.*, ¶ 5.7.3.1.   [52] *Ibid.*, ¶ 5.7.3.2.   [53] *Ibid.*, ¶ 5.8.2.1.   [54] *Ibid.*, ¶ 5.8.4.2.
[55] *Ibid.*, ¶ 5.4.3.2.   [56] *Ibid.*   [57] *Ibid.*   [58] *Ibid.*   [59] *Ibid.*

combined with the Manual's approach on membership – it constitutes a double permissibility. A soldier can draw inferences from the persons with whom an individual associates or by his location, and, any doubts she or he has regarding the accuracy of his or her assessment do not constitute a prohibition to targeting that individual.

The approach espoused by the Manual to the targetability of so-called members of armed groups is not only far-reaching but also significantly idiosyncratic. Notably while the ICRC, the formal guardian of the law of war, has recently also espoused the notion of membership when considering the targetability of individuals associated with armed groups, it takes a much more restrictive and cautious approach to its definition. Indeed, like the United States, the ICRC's starting point is that membership can be difficult to discern because members of armed groups rarely express or declare their membership in ways analogous to members of State forces.[60] Yet rather than reacting to this difficulty by casting the net of membership widely, the ICRC explicitly rejects adopting membership criteria based on abstract affiliation.[61] Instead, the ICRC defines "members" as individuals whose continuous function involves the preparation, execution, or command of acts or operations amounting to direct participation of hostilities.[62] Unlike the United States, the ICRC does not include individuals accompanying the armed group, with a supporting role or those who assume political, administrative, or other noncombat roles.[63] It also does not include individuals whose location (e.g., in a particular guesthouse) or behavior (e.g., travelling along a particular path) suggests that they have an affiliation with the armed group. Additionally, the ICRC underlines that the evaluation of whether an individual has a continuous function directly participating in hostilities should be subject to all feasible precautions and to the presumption of protection in the case of doubt.[64]

While a full comparison of the different approaches of the United States and ICRC on this issue is beyond the scope of this chapter, a few important points are noted below. The first is that the US position towards membership seems to come close to drawing a geographical perimeter around the leadership of an armed group and identifying all individuals that come within that physical space as members of the armed group. The Manual indicates that an individual's location in a safehouse, training camp, or base is enough of an

---

[60] N. Melzer, *Interpretative Guidance on the Notion of Direct Participation in Hostilities under International Humanitarian Law* (Geneva: ICRC, 2009), 32–33.
[61] *Ibid.*, 33. [62] *Ibid.*, 34. [63] *Ibid.*, 34.
[64] *Ibid.*, 35. This presumption is contained in Art. 50(1) of AP I which states "in cases of doubt whether a person is a civilian, that person shall be considered to be a civilian."

indicator for membership. It is argued that such an approach ignores the variation of operation and organization between armed groups and new research emerging on rebel governance.[65] Specifically, it remains unclear how such criteria can effectively be applied in areas under the control of armed groups, without scooping up large proportions of the civilian population. It also remains unclear how the criteria can take account of the reality that civilians are often forced to cooperate with armed groups, on matters of governance for their survival.[66] The criteria also leaves little scope for distinguishing between individuals with a fighting function and individuals working in an armed group's civilian infrastructure, such as police force, judges, and government workers. Unless this distinction is respected, it seems little use for the international community to continue to exhort armed groups such as the Taliban to cease targeting Afghan judges and government workers, on the basis that it is unlawful under international humanitarian law.[67] Perhaps most worryingly, there is a risk that the Manual's broad-brush approach to membership will end up as a self-fulfilling prophecy. Multiple studies have shown that the loss of a family member is a key motivating factor for individuals to join armed groups.[68] This observation highlights the important final fact that while the Manual justifies its approach to membership in strategic terms, there is actually a strong strategic argument for approaching conceptions of membership narrowly.

There are also concerns about the appropriateness of the Manual adopting a subjective criteria for membership, such as the one it mentions, requiring that individuals share the hostile intent of the armed group. The inclusion of this criterion is presented as the basis upon which the Manual rationalizes the fact that an individual can be targeted, at times when he or she is not conducting

[65] The notion of rebel governance is an expanding topic in social science disciplines. See, e.g., A. Arjona, N. Kasfir, and Z. Mampilly (eds.), *Rebel Governance in Civil War* (Cambridge University Press, 2015).

[66] *Ibid.* See, e.g., E. Wisam and S. al-Hawat, "Civilian Interaction with Armed Groups in the Syrian Conflict," Conciliation Resources, Insight 2 (2015), www.c-r.org/accord/engag ing-armed-groups-insight/syria-civilian-interaction-armed-groups-syrian-conflict. See also K. Stathis, *The Logic of Violence in Civil War* (Cambridge University Press, 2006), 91–110.

[67] This has been a key issue for the United Nations Assistance Mission in Afghanistan. See, e.g., United Nations Assistance Mission in Afghanistan (UNAMA) and the Office of the United Nations High Commissioner for Human Rights (OHCHR), Afghanistan Annual Report 2015, "Protection of Civilians in Armed Conflict," 45–46.

[68] See, e.g., P. K. Davis and K. Cragin (eds.), *Social Science for Counterterrorism: Putting the Pieces Together* (Santa Monica: RAND, 2009), 86–90; International Alert, "Why Young Syrians Choose to Fight" (2016), 10–14; Y. Guichaoua, *Understanding Collective Political Violence* (Basingstoke: Palgrave Macmillian, 2011), 158; R. Haer, *Armed Group Structure and Violence in Civil Wars: The Organisational Dynamics of Civilian Killing* (Oxford: Routledge, 2015), Table 7.2.

hostilities.[69] However, it is questionable how this criterion can be reliably tested, during the conduct of military operations. Indeed, ironically, while the critique of the Manual's criteria for membership has been criticized above for being too far-reaching, it is argued here that the requirement of "intention" is too restrictive. For while a finding of an individual's "hostile intent" is often one of the requirements mentioned by rules of engagement (ROE) to determine situations where a solder can use deadly force, it has little discernible foundation or relevance in international law.[70] Recourse to such a subjective criterion also fails to take account of the myriad of other considerations that may motivate individuals to join an armed group, alongside hostility towards the opposing party. Indeed, it is well-known that children are often coerced into joining armed groups, and while their forcible recruitment may be a mitigating factor in their sentencing, it is not a mitigating factor in either their ability to violate the law of war or their ability to be targeted by State forces.[71] Indeed, the Manual's reference to individuals' hostile intent sits uneasily with the traditional separation between *jus ad bellum* and *jus in bello* according to which the law of armed conflict is traditionally agnostic to the motivations of either individual fighters or parties.

5 USE OF FORMER INSURGENTS IN COUNTERINSURGENCY

The final issue that this chapter examines is the assertion by the Manual that State forces may use captured or enemy personnel in operations against enemy non-State armed groups. While some readers may be surprised to learn that the US army would want to use captured personnel in their military operations, in fact the use of so-called "turned" insurgents has a long history in counterinsurgency operations. Former insurgents can often provide unique access to the group's location and workings, which States often struggle to obtain in an insurgency.[72] Indeed, although the footnotes to the Manual supporting this provision describe such former insurgents as "pseudoforces," when looking at the examples given a distinction can better be made between pseudoforces and "counter gangs." Although both may include former insurgents, their modus operandi is different.[73] While counter gangs are typically

---

[69]   DoD Law of War Manual, ¶ 5.7.1.

[70]   See, e.g., ROE for US. Military Forces in Operation Restore Hope, Somalia 1992-1993, www.globalsecurity.org/military/library/policy/army/fm/100-23/fm100_10.htm.

[71]   See, e.g., *Prosecutor v. Dominic Ongwen*, Case No. ICC-02/04-01/15, Confirmation of Charges Decision, ¶¶ 151-54 (Mar. 23, 2016).

[72]   Bangerter (above note 41), 37.

[73]   G. Hughes, "Intelligence-Gathering, Special Operations and Air Strikes in Modern Counter-Insurgency," in P. Rich and I. Duyvesteyn (eds.), *The Routledge Handbook of Insurgency and Counterinsurgency* (London & New York: Routledge, 2012), 109-18, 111-12.

groups of fighters with an intelligence-gathering role, who may also take part in military operations, psuedoforces pose as insurgents on a longer-term basis, in order to secure intelligence, capture weapons and fighters, and conduct surprise attacks on their so-called comrades.[74] Examples of pseudoforces include Force X in the Philippines insurgency and the Selous Scouts in Kenya, both of which included turned insurgents.[75] The use of counter forces and pseudoforces in operations against armed groups raises a number of questions of international law that have been given little attention so far in reviews of the Manual or academic literature more generally.

The first question relates to the legality of compelling a member of an armed group to fight against his or her former comrades. The need to analyze the legality of this practice stems from the recollection that it is strictly unlawful in IAC to compel nationals of a hostile party to take part in the operations of war directed against their own country.[76] Acts violating these prohibitions were the subject of numerous prosecutions after World War II.[77] While recognizing these prohibitions in IAC, the Manual asserts that the situation is different in a NIAC, justifying its position on two main grounds.[78] First the Manual recalls that the prohibitions in IAC are based on the notion that it is unconscionable to force an individual to commit treason, which is not the case when you force an individual to fight on behalf of his or her own State.[79] Second, the Manual recalls that a State can often compel its citizens to fight on its behalf in a NIAC, via draft, meaning that

---

[74] G. Hughes and C. Tripodi, "Anatomy of a Surrogate: Historical Precedents and Implications for Contemporary Counter-insurgency and Counter-Terrorism" (2009) 20(1) *Small Wars & Insurgencies* 1–35, 16–17.

[75] Major L. M. Greenberg, *The Hukbalahap Insurrection: A Case Study of a Successful Anti-Insurgency Operation in the Philippines: 1946–1955* (Washington, DC: US Army Centre of Military History, 2005); and Lieutenant Colonel R. Reid-Daly, *Selous Scouts: Top Secret War* (London & Johannesburg: Galago Publishing, 1982).

[76] See Art. 130 of Geneva Convention Relative to the Treatment of Prisoners of War of August 12, 1949 which makes it a Grave Breach to compel a prisoner of war to serve in the forces of the hostile power and Art. 147 of Geneva Convention Relative to the Protection of Civilian Persons in Time of War of August 12, 1949 which makes it a Grave Breach to compel a protected person to serve in the forces of a hostile power. See also Arts. 6 and 52 of Hague Regulations respecting the Laws and Customs of War on Land, Annex to Convention (IV) respecting the Laws and Customs of War on Land. See DoD Law of War Manual, ¶¶ 5.27.2 and 17.12.1.

[77] See, *inter alia, The Milch Case, No. 2, United States v. Milch,* Judgment, Green Series, Vol. II, 773 (Mil. Trib. No. 12947-04-15).

[78] DoD Law of War Manual, ¶¶ 5.27.2 and 17.12.1.

[79] *Ibid.,* ¶ 5.27 which states that the prohibition in IAC is based on the principle that States must not compel foreign nations to commit treason or to otherwise violate their allegiance to their country.

former insurgents should be equally compellable.[80] It will be shown below
that it remains doubtful whether these arguments are sufficient to prove the
legality of this practice, when comparing it to modern interpretations of
common Article 3 and human rights norms on torture and inhuman and
degrading treatment.

When analyzing this provision, it is relevant to note that the Manual
indicates that a mixture of strategies will be employed to get insurgents to
fight on the side of the State, ranging from threats and inducements.[81] From
a legal perspective, it is clearly unproblematic for a State to recruit former
insurgents when they are willing to cooperate with the State. Indeed, there are
many historical examples of captured insurgents being persuaded to fight on
behalf of the State through gentle treatment, promises of financial remunera-
tion, or amnesties.[82] However, there are also many historical examples of
former insurgents being persuaded by means of harsh treatment in the form
of the threat of severe penalties (e.g., long prison sentences or the death
penalty)[83] or physical punishment sometimes amounting to torture.[84] While
the Manual recognizes the need to be careful in this respect – stating that
inhumane treatment or other illegal methods cannot be used – it specifically
indicates a view that insurgents can be "compelled" to take part in military
operations against their former comrades through threats of criminal
punishment.[85] It is asserted that the employment of coercion in these circumstances gives cause for concern when compared against modern war crimes
jurisprudence. While the historical prohibition on forcing detainees to do
work of a military nature in IACs was based on the idea that it would be
unconscionable to force an individual to commit treason, in modern case law
the prohibition has also been based on notions of inhumane, degrading, or
cruel treatment.

---

[80] *Ibid.*, ¶¶ 17.12.1 and 4.5.2.4.   [81]   *Ibid.*, ¶ 17.12.2.

[82] D. French, "Nasty Not Nice: British Counter-Insurgency Doctrine and Practice: 1945–1967"
(2012) 23(4–5) *Small Wars & Insurgencies* 744–61, 755; T. Gatchel, "Pseudo-Operations –
A Double-Edged Sword of Counterinsurgency," in J. Norwitz (ed.), *Armed Groups: Studies in
National Security, Counterterrorism and Counterinsurgency* (Newport, RI: US Naval War
College, 2008), 61–72; L. Cline, *Pseudo Operations and Counterinsurgency: Lessons from
Other Countries* (Pennsylvania: Strategic Studies Institute, 2005), 12–14.

[83] Gatchel (above note 82), 65.

[84] See also Cline (above note 82), 22 on the use of torture against Algerian National Liberation
Front activists. It is also noteworthy that Frank Kitson an oft-quoted and influential proponent
of the use of former insurgents recommended that the first stage of "taming" insurgents should
involve "harsh treatment of the prisoner, including chaining him and only feeding him the
most basic food." See Gatchel (above note 82), 64.

[85] See DoD Law of War Manual, ¶ 17.12.2.

Most relevantly, while the Appeals Chamber of the International Criminal Tribunal for Yugoslavia (ICTY) recognized that the use of forced labor is not always unlawful, it found that the use of persons taking no active part in hostilities to prepare military fortifications for use in operations and "against the forces with whom those persons identify or sympathise" is a serious attack on human dignity and causes serious mental (and, depending on the circumstances, physical) suffering or injury.[86] It likewise found that any order to compel "protected persons" to dig trenches or prepare other forms of military installations, in particular when such persons are ordered to do so against their own forces in an armed conflict, constitutes "cruel treatment."[87] On the basis of this analysis, the ICTY Appeals Chamber found such actions to be a violation of common Article 3(1)(a) of the Geneva Conventions, indicating that the practice of coercing captured detainees to take part in military operations against their former comrades is by modern standards prohibited in both IACs and NIACs.[88] It is hard to predict where a criminal tribunal would find the line between coercion and persuasion to fall, but it seems likely that forcing an individual to choose between military service and the death penalty as a possibility subsequent to criminal conviction would be deemed to amount to coercion.[89] Notably, such practices may equally be held to violate human rights standards such as the prohibition of cruel, inhuman, and degrading treatment.

Although the footnotes of the Manual assert that pseudoforces can be of "immense importance," their use raises several important legal questions which suggest that their use should not be eagerly embraced. First, it is important to consider whether it is lawful for pseudoforces to conduct hostilities against members of an armed group while disguised as members of that armed group. Indeed, while it is widely accepted that it is unlawful to take part in hostilities while wearing the uniform of the opposing side in an IAC, the legality of the equivalent practice in NIAC remains a "matter of debate."[90] Notably, the ICRC has argued that the equivalent rule "should" apply in instances where armed groups wear uniforms.[91] Yet if one assumes that such a prohibition does not yet exist, it is important to be aware that the use of subterfuge is more problematic for State forces than for armed groups.

---

[86] *Prosecutor v. Blaškić*, Case No. IT-95-14-A, Appeals Chamber Judgment, ¶ 597 (ICTY, July 29, 2004).

[87] *Ibid.*   [88] *Ibid.*

[89] This conclusion can even be reached by an analysis of the definition of the word "compel" given at ¶ 5.27.1 of the DoD Law of War Manual.

[90] Sivakumaran (above note 1), 417.

[91] Henckaerts and Doswald-Beck (above note 42), rule 62, 214.

The fact that many armed groups do not wear uniform, means that State forces conducting hostilities while disguised as members of a non-uniform-wearing armed group need to be constantly careful not to violate the principle of distinction and the prohibition of perfidy, which although not explicitly recognized by the Manual, is widely seen to be a war crime in NIACs.[92] While in practice the risk may often be small, due to the fact that individuals employed as pseudoforces generally take steps to look "the part" by bearing weapons or adopting dress that clearly identify them as members of that group, it remains an important consideration to bear in mind.[93]

Equally, although the Manual refers to pseudoforces as being of "immense importance," it does not sufficiently note the ethical and legal dilemmas that accompany their use. Indeed, from an operational and command perspective, many authors warn that careful thought needs to be given to "how far" pseudoforces should be allowed to go to attain their goals of gaining acceptance as insurgents or discrediting the armed group among the civilian population.[94] For example, literature on the topic offers up disturbing examples of pseudoforces targeting civilian infrastructure in order to validate themselves as insurgents, in clear violation of international humanitarian law.[95] Equally, pseudoforces have been used to implicate innocent villagers in acts of betrayal, leading sometimes to their execution.[96] Likewise, pseudoforces sometimes deliberately committed atrocities or indiscretions against civilians, in order to turn populations against the "real" armed group.[97] These historical examples demonstrate the challenge of ensuring that pseudo-operations remain lawful, in environments where violations of the law may be strategically advantageous and eminently deniable.[98] For, most dangerously, pseudoforces operate entirely outside the scrutiny of the international community and national oversight mechanisms, making it difficult to attribute

---

[92]   See Art. 8(2)(e)(ix) of the Rome Statute.
[93]   See W. Hays Parks, "Special Forces' Wear of Non-Standard Uniforms" (2003) 4 *Chicago Journal of International Law* 493–560, 517. See Human Rights Watch, *Between a Rock and a Hard Place*, Human Rights Watch Report Vol. 16 (No. 12C) (October 2004), www.hrw.org /sites/default/files/reports/nepal1004.pdf, where it is recounted (at p. 27) that police disguised themselves as Maoists by dressing in Maoist-style clothing with red bandanas and giving Maoist greetings.
[94]   Cline (above note 82), 16.
[95]   J. Cilliers, *Counter-Insurgency in Rhodesia* (London, Sydney, Dover, New Hampshire: Croom Helm, 1985), 127–28.
[96]   *Ibid.*, 128; Reid-Daly (above note 75), 128.
[97]   Cilliers (above note 95), 119 and 128; Hughes and Tripodi (above note 74), 6 and 21.
[98]   Hughes and Tripodi (above note 74), 6.

responsibility for unlawful killings.[99] Indeed, it is for these reasons that it would be appropriate for the Manual to emphasize the dangers of their employment.[100]

6 CONCLUSION

When reviewing the Manual for issues pertaining to armed groups, there are a multitude of issues that come to the fore. Indeed, in the preceding analysis, it has been shown that the need to take account of armed groups when clarifying the legal framework that applies in times of armed conflict requires more than an "add armed groups and stir" approach. This is particularly true in relation to issues relating to sources of law, where there is an intense need to be consistent about the indicators that are necessary for armed groups to be bound by the law of war. Likewise, there is a need for serious consideration to be given to whether the principles that are considered to function as the bedrock of the legal framework can be easily transposed to NIAC, without careful consideration of whether they are also meaningful in that context. On this point, the chapter has suggested that while there may be reasons to emphasize notions of "personal honor" in the Manual, it makes less sense for the Manual to assert a heavy reliance on reciprocal honor between fighting parties, as the principles upon which it is based are often under severe strain in fighting between armed groups and States. Equally, studies indicate that compliance with the legal framework is best achieved by emphasizing concrete legal rules, rather than the principles or ethics that underpin them.

In the second half of the chapter, attention has been given to the approach taken by the Manual to the issue of targeting. Here, it has been pointed out that the Manual's associative approach risks drawing too many people into the net of membership. The problems with such an approach are myriad, and do not take into account the wealth of new knowledge on armed groups and governance. This literature not only points out that armed groups increasingly carry out governance activities in areas under their control, but also demonstrates that armed groups often have intricate relationships with civilian populations under their control that require a significant degree of interaction between armed groups and civilians. As it is currently formulated, the US approach to membership and targeting not only risks putting such civilians

---

[99] *Ibid.*, 6 and Reid-Daly (above note 75), 133; Human Rights Watch (above note 93), 55, for evidence of this difficulty in practice.

[100] Cline (above note 82), 16; Hughes and Tripodi (above note 74), 22; Reid-Daly (above note 75), 110; Cilliers (above note 95), 132–33.

at risk, but also risks becoming a self-fulfilling prophecy, by attracting more individuals into the ranks of armed groups. Finally, the chapter explores the legality and associated risks of using former insurgents in military operations against their comrades. This is an aspect of the Manual which has been almost entirely unexplored in legal literature, but which deserves careful attention. In particular, the chapter demonstrates that the use of pseudoforces raises serious legal and ethical issues that pose a severe risk to the legal framework.

18

Hybrid Law, Complex Battlespaces: What's the Use of a Law of War Manual?

Aurel Sari[*]

1 INTRODUCTION

For an undertaking of its scale, the Department of Defense (DoD) Law of War Manual (the Manual) is rather tightlipped about the reasons for its own existence. The Manual's purpose, we are told, is "to provide information on the law of war to [DoD] personnel responsible for implementing the law of war and executing military operations."[1] It seems self-evident that civilian and military personnel responsible for implementing the law of war should be informed about the applicable rules. Manuals are a tried and tested method for transmitting this information. Indeed, the present Manual is merely the last installment in a venerable line of texts stretching back more than one and a half centuries.[2] The first among these, the Lieber Code, was promulgated by the Secretary of War in 1863 "for the information of all concerned."[3] Against this background, it seems superfluous, if not pedantic, to expect the Manual to justify its existence and purpose at length. Even wars have rules, those rules must be disseminated and this is what the Manual is for.

On closer inspection, matters are not quite so straightforward. There is a degree of tension in the Manual's mission statement, which speaks

---

[*] All views are expressed in a personal capacity.   [1] DoD Law of War Manual, ¶ 1.1.1.

[2] On the evolution of these texts, see D. A. Wells, *The Laws of Land Warfare: A Guide to the U.S. Army Manuals* (Westport: Greenwood Press, 1992).

[3] War Department, *Instructions for the Government of Armies in the Field* (Washington: US Government Printing Office, 1863), 1. The Lieber Code is widely regarded as the first modern law of war manual. See R. R. Baxter, "The First Modern Codification of the Law of War: Francis Lieber and General Orders No. 100" (1963) 3 *International Review of the Red Cross* 171–89, 234–50; S. Vöneky, "Der Lieber's Code und die Wurzeln des modernen Kriegsvölkerrechts" (2002) 62 *Zeitschrift für ausländisches öffentliches Recht und Völkerrecht* 423–60, 424.

about providing information to those responsible for implementing the law of war and those engaged in the execution of military operations. These two activities do not always coincide. Not every mission is subject to the law of armed conflict.[4] While the DoD requires its components to comply with the law of war even where the latter is not formally applicable,[5] in such circumstances any rules of international law that apply as a matter of law necessarily take precedence over principles that apply as a matter of mere policy. Yet even where the law of armed conflict is formally applicable, it does not stand in isolation, but operates in conjunction with other branches of international law.[6] There is no escaping the fact that military deployments are governed by a multitude of legal regimes over and beyond the law of war, even during times of armed conflict.[7] However, if the law of armed conflict constitutes merely one aspect of the legal framework of warfare and military operations, does a manual dedicated to the law of war offer the right kind of information to personnel tasked with implementing its rules and with executing military operations?[8] In other words, in an era of increasing

[4] On the difficulties of determining the applicable legal framework, see G. S. Corn, "Legal Classification of Military Operations," in G. S. Corn, R. E. van Landingham, and S. R. Reeves (eds.), *U.S. Military Operations: Law, Policy, and Practice* (Oxford University Press, 2016), 67–90.

[5] DoD Directive 2311.01E, DoD Law of War Program, ¶ 4.1 (May 9, 2006, Certified Current as of Feb. 22, 2011); Chairman of the Joint Chiefs of Staff, Standing Rules of Engagement for US Forces, CJCSI 3121.01B, June 13, 2005, Enclosure A, ¶ 1(d). See also Corn (above note 4), 81–84.

[6] Chairman of the Joint Chiefs of Staff, Legal Support to Military Operations, Joint Publication 1-04, Aug. 2, 2016, speaks about "the myriad of regulations, laws, policies, treaties, and agreements that apply to joint military operations" (at II-1) and identifies a range of relevant legal regimes (at I-14). See also Ministry of Defence, *Legal Support to Joint Operations*, JDP 3-46 (2010).

[7] See M. Odello and R. W. Piotrowicz, "Legal Regimes Governing International Military Missions," in M. Odello and R. W. Piotrowicz (eds.), *International Military Missions and International Law* (Leiden: Martinus Nijhoff, 2011), 25–44; D. Fleck, "Development of New Rules or Application of More than One Legal Regime?," in C. Harvey, J. Summers, and N. D. White (eds.), *Contemporary Challenges to the Laws of War: Essays in Honour of Professor Peter Rowe* (Cambridge University Press, 2014), 51–70; and more generally, D. Fleck and T. D. Gill (eds.), *The Handbook of the International Law of Military Operations*, 2nd ed. (Oxford University Press, 2015).

[8] Pursuant to Protocol Additional to the Geneva Conventions of Aug. 12, 1949, and Relating to the Protection of Victims of International Armed Conflicts, 1977, 1125 UNTS 3 (AP I), Art. 82, it is mandatory to make legal advisors available to commanders at the appropriate level to offer advice on the law of armed conflict. Some commentators suggest that the duty to offer legal advice now extends to other branches of international law as well. See M. Kuhn and A. C. Berger, "Legal Advisers in the Armed Forces," in A. Zidar and J.-P. Gauci (eds.), *The Role of Legal Advisers in International Law* (Leiden: Brill, 2016), 337–51, 340.

operational and legal complexity, has the law of war manual as a *genre* had its day?⁹

We might dispose of these questions in short order. It is true that contemporary missions take place in a complex environment and are subject to a multitude of legal regimes in addition to the law of war. Those responsible for planning and executing military deployments must be aware of these regimes. But, surely, this does not diminish the need to be familiar with the law of war itself! In fact, numerous treaties require their signatories to promote the study of the law of war[10] and to instruct members of their armed forces in its implementation.[11] National manuals are one way of complying with these obligations.[12] Nor should we overlook the fact that, from a purely practical perspective, a considered treatment of the law of war leaves little room for much else. It takes the Manual more than 1,200 pages, weighing in at a mighty 4.6 pounds, to address the subject. One shudders to envisage the Manual's sheer bulk had its authors decided to include other branches of international law within its scope. A text of such proportions might be informative, but practical it certainly would not be.[13]

Whilst these are compelling points, they do not put to rest all doubts about the utility of the Manual. They merely prove that law of war manuals remain a valid undertaking to the extent that studying the law of war as a distinct subject remains appropriate and useful. However, it is precisely this latter

---

9   By comparison, see Judge Advocate General's School, United States Air Force, "Air Force Operations and the Law" (2014); The Judge Advocate General's Center and School, US Army, "Operational Law Handbook" (2015). *Cf.* A. P. V. Rogers, "The United Kingdom Manual of the Law of Armed Conflict," in N. Hayashi (ed.), *National Military Manuals on the Law of Armed Conflict*, 2nd ed. (Oslo: Torkel Opsahl, 2010), 89–96, 94 (noting a trend towards more operational level manuals).

10 E.g. Convention for the Amelioration of the Condition of the Wounded and Sick in Armed Forces in the Field (GC I), 1949, 75 UNTS 31, Art. 47. Although this provision does not require the contracting parties to issue implementing instructions, the Manual states that such a duty "may be understood as part of the general obligation of Parties to undertake to respect and to ensure respect for the Conventions." DoD Law of War Manual, ¶ 18.7.1.2.

11 E.g. Convention (IV) Respecting the Laws and Customs of War on Land and its Annex: Regulations concerning the Laws and Customs of War on Land (Hague Regulations), Oct. 18, 1907, 205 CTS 277, Art. 1; Protocol on Explosive Remnants of War to the Convention on Prohibitions or Restrictions on the Use of Certain Conventional Weapons which may be deemed to be Excessively Injurious or to have Indiscriminate Effects (Protocol V), Nov. 28, 2003, 2399 UNTS 100, Art. 11.

12 H.-P. Gasser, "Military Manuals, Legal Advisors and the First Additional Protocol of 1977," in N. Hayashi (ed.), *National Military Manuals on the Law of Armed Conflict*, 2nd ed. (Oslo: Torkel Opsahl, 2010), 61–62.

13 For a superb account of the practicalities of writing and using military manuals, see M. Meyer and H. McCoubrey (eds.), *Reflections on Law and Armed Conflicts: Selected Works on the Laws of War by the late Professor Colonel G.I.A.D. Draper* (The Hague: Kluwer, 1998), 115–20.

point which is increasingly open to question.[14] Over the course of the last century, the law of war has lost its status as the exclusive regulatory framework of warfare. In some cases, its rules now operate in parallel with other applicable legal regimes, without intersecting much. For example, the law governing the use of force complements the law of war in certain respects,[15] but does not encroach upon its distinct regulatory function.[16] The same cannot be said for international human rights law. The law of war and international human rights law occupy the same normative space, are deeply intertwined and appear to be locked into a process of gradual convergence.[17] One of the pressing legal questions of our age is how this trend is going to evolve: will the law of war gradually become a hybrid creature or will it retain its distinct normative pedigree?[18] The answer will have a significant impact on the continued utility of law of war manuals. In turn, law of war manuals may have an impact on the outcome to this question too.

With this in mind, the purpose of the present chapter is to assess how the Manual approaches the relationship between the law of war and international human rights law, as seen against the broader context of the changing legal framework of warfare and military operations. National military manuals are widely understood to serve two main functions.[19] They are an instrument for

---

[14] In favor of a more holistic approach, see K. Watkin, *Fighting at the Legal Boundaries: Controlling the Use of Force in Contemporary Conflict* (Oxford University Press, 2016), 604–10.

[15] E.g., M. N. Schmitt, "Charting the Legal Geography of Non-International Armed Conflict" (2013) 52 *Military Law and Law of War Review* 93–112, 108–9. See also C. Greenwood, "Self-Defence and the Conduct of International Armed Conflict," in Y. Dinstein and M. Tabory (eds.), *International Law at a Time of Perplexity: Essays in Honour of Shabtai Rosenne* (Dordrecht: Nijhoff, 1988), 273–88.

[16] *Cf.* G. S. Corn, "Self-Defense Targeting: Blurring the Line between the *Jus ad Bellum* and the *Jus in Bello*" (2012) 88 *International Law Studies* 57–92, 64–75.

[17] The literature on the relationship between the law of armed conflict and international human rights law is vast. E.g., see R. Provost, *International Human Rights and Humanitarian Law* (Cambridge University Press, 2002); R. Arnold and N. N. R. Quénivet (eds.), *International Humanitarian Law and Human Rights Law: Towards a New Merger in International Law* (Leiden: Martinus Nijhoff, 2008); O. Ben-Naftali (ed.), *International Humanitarian Law and International Human Rights Law* (Oxford University Press, 2011); R. Kolb and G. Gaggioli (eds.), *Research Handbook on Human Rights and Humanitarian Law* (Cheltenham: Edward Elgar, 2013); and G. Oberleitner, *Human Rights in Armed Conflict: Law, Practice, Policy* (Cambridge University Press, 2015).

[18] See Y. Dinstein, "Concluding Remarks: LOAC and Attempts to Abuse or Subvert It" (2011) 87 *International Law Studies* 483–94, 488–91.

[19] See W. M. Reisman and W. K. Leitzau, "Moving International Law from Theory to Practice: The Role of Military Manuals in Effectuating the Law of Armed Conflict" (1991) 64 *International Law Studies* 1–18; C. Garraway, "The Use and Abuse of Military Manuals" (2004) 7 *Yearbook of International Humanitarian Law* 425–40.

disseminating the law of war and for expressing a nation's understanding of its own legal obligations. The first function is essentially passive. Manuals convey the rules to their readers, even if this means translating the black letter of the law into a different format.[20] The second function is dynamic. As Professor Garraway notes, the aim of national manuals "is not to reach a consensus agreement, but to reflect the position adopted by the State concerned."[21] In doing so, national manuals shape the law by applying, reaffirming, and developing it.[22] These two functions pull the Manual in different directions. Promoting a better understanding of the challenges posed by international human rights law requires a nuanced approach that acknowledges the multi-faceted relationship between the law of war and human rights. However, such subtlety is difficult to reconcile with the certainty that the application of the law on the battlefield and the effective promotion of the United States' national position on these matters demands. In its response to the changing legal framework of warfare, the Manual is thus torn between enlightenment and advocacy.

I will develop these arguments in three steps. The first section of the chapter will trace the evolving character of the legal framework of warfare, including the impact of international human rights law. The second section will explore the Manual's response to these developments. The third section will assess the Manual's approach against the two traditional functions of military manuals, the law-disseminating and the law-shaping function.

2 THE LEGAL FRAMEWORK OF WAR: A FAREWELL TO CERTAINTY

For lawyers, war used to be a simpler business. Until the middle of the twentieth century, war in a formal sense was a relationship between sovereign nation States.[23] Since war belonged to the sphere of inter-State relations, the rules governing the conduct of warfare fell within the scope of international law. By contrast, acts of violence emanating from non-State

---

[20]   *Cf.* DoD Law of War Manual, ¶ 18.7.2.1.   [21]   Garraway (above note 19), 431.

[22]   Reisman and Leitzau refer to military manuals as "part of the process of making international law" (above note 19), 7. See also M. H. Hoffman, "Can Military Manuals Improve the Law of War? The San Remo Manual on the Law of Non-International Armed Conflict Considered in Relation to Historical and Contemporary Trends" (2007) 37 *Israel Yearbook on Human Rights* 241–58, 242–50.

[23]   E. D. Vattel, *The Law of Nations or the Principles of Natural Law: Applied to the Conduct and to the Affairs of Nations and of Sovereigns* (Washington: Carnegie, 1916), 235 ("It is the sovereign power alone . . . which has the right to make war.").

actors remained subject to the rules of ordinary domestic law,[24] unless the law of war was extended to such disturbances through the recognition of belligerency.[25] By distinguishing war in a material sense from war in a legal sense,[26] international law during the nineteenth and early twentieth century imposed a binary legal framework on warfare, based on a strict separation between war and peace, international and internal, State and non-State, regular and irregular.[27]

This is not to say that these distinctions reflected the actual practice of warfare. Far from it. Throughout this period, States and their adversaries used force across the entire spectrum of conflict, relying on a mix of symmetric and asymmetric methods.[28] What we now call "hybrid warfare" is not a novel phenomenon.[29] However, international law for the most part remained blind to this more complex reality,[30] as States refused to extend the applicability of the law of war to irregular adversaries not acting on behalf of a recognized belligerent.[31] During the course of the twentieth century, the binary distinctions on which the traditional legal framework of warfare rested began to decay. The certainty that character-ized the law gave way to uncertainty, leaving the law of war in its current state of flux.

---

[24] H. W. Halleck, *International Law or Rules Regulating the Intercourse of States in Peace and War* (New York: Van Nostrand, 1861), 386 ("the hostile acts of individuals, or of bands of men, without the authority or sanction of their own government, are not legitimate acts of war, and, therefore, are punishable according to the nature or character of the offense committed").

[25] L. Moir, "The Historical Development of the Application of Humanitarian Law in Non-International Armed Conflicts to 1949" (1998) 47 *International and Comparative Law Quarterly* 337–61.

[26] L. Oppenheim, *International Law: A Treatise*, II: *War and Neutrality*, 1st ed. (London: Longmans Green and Co., 1906), §§ 54–58 and 93.

[27] See G. Schwarzenberger, "Jus Pacis ac Belli?: Prolegomena to a Sociology of International Law" (1943) 37 *American Journal of International Law* 460–79, 460.

[28] This is reflected in such concepts as "small wars" and "imperial policing." See C. E. Callwell, *Small Wars: Their Principles and Practice*, 3d ed. (London: HMSO, 1906); and C. W. Gwynn, *Imperial Policing*, 2nd ed. (London: Macmillan, 1939).

[29] See W. Murray and P. R. Mansoor (eds.), *Hybrid Warfare: Fighting Complex Opponents from the Ancient World to the Present* (New York: Cambridge University Press, 2012). However, this is not to deny the novelty of the legal challenges that hybrid warfare presents. See A. Sari, "Hybrid Warfare, Law and the Fulda Gap," in M. N. Schmitt et al. (eds.), *Complex Battle Spaces* (Oxford University Press, 2017), https://ssrn.com/abstract=2927773.

[30] For an illustration of the simplicity of this legal landscape, see War Office, *Manual of Military Law*, 4th ed. (London: HMSO, 1899), 2–3.

[31] This reluctance is reflected in the debates surrounding the permissibility of irregular resistance to enemy forces in the context of regular war, as recounted by J. M. Spaight, *War Rights on Land* (London: Macmillan, 1911), 47–56.

2.1 The Changing Character of Warfare

The adoption of Common Article 3 of the Geneva Conventions of 1949 extended the law of war beyond the realm of inter-State relations.[32] As some delegates present at the diplomatic conference in Geneva feared,[33] this move precipitated the erosion of the traditional legal boundaries of war. The majority of the negotiating States agreed that Common Article 3 should not apply to acts of banditry and rioting,[34] but only to "proper armed conflicts" involving a "certain degree of organization" on the part of the rebels.[35] Yet these vague notions provide no firm guidance as to where the dividing line between mere disturbances of the peace and "proper" non-international armed conflicts (NIACs) lies.[36] While international tribunals have developed more detailed criteria to assist in this matter,[37] their application remains fraught with difficulty.[38]

The emergence of the law of NIAC thus has blurred the line between war and peace. At the same time, it has also eliminated the notion of war as a matter belonging exclusively to the international sphere. States have only partially extended the applicability of the law of war to non-State actors. In particular, they have declined to confer combatant status on individuals fighting on behalf of non-State adversaries,[39] but have retained the freedom to subject such individuals to the full force of their penal laws.[40] Accordingly,

---

[32] For an overview of the negotiation of Common Art. 3, see G. Best, *War and Law Since 1945* (Oxford: Clarendon Press, 1994), 168–79.

[33] Eighteenth Plenary Meeting, July 28, 1949, Federal Political Department, *Final Record of the Diplomatic Conference of Geneva of 1949* (Bern: Federal Political Department, 1949), II, Sec. B, 327–30 (Burma).

[34] *Ibid.*, Nineteenth Plenary Meeting, July 29, 1949, *ibid.*, 333 (Venezuela).

[35] *Ibid.*, 335 (Switzerland).

[36] Additional Protocol II (AP II), Art. 1(2), distinguishes NIACs from "internal disturbances and tensions, such as riots, isolated and sporadic acts of violence and other acts of a similar nature," but this does not offer much more clarity.

[37] *Prosecutor v. Boškoski and Johan Tarčulovski*, Case No. IT-04-82-T, Trial Judgment, ¶¶ 175–205 (ICTY, July 10, 2008). See A. Cullen, *The Concept of Non-International Armed Conflict in International Humanitarian Law* (Cambridge University Press, 2010), 117–58; and S. Sivakumaran, *The Law of Non-International Armed Conflict* (Oxford University Press, 2012), 156–82.

[38] Generally, see M. Marko and H.-V. Vidan, "A Taxonomy of Armed Conflict," in N. White and C. Henderson (eds.), *Research Handbook on International Conflict and Security Law: Jus ad Bellum, Jus in Bello and Jus post Bellum* (Cheltenham: Edward Elgar, 2013), 256–314.

[39] *Military Prosecutor v. Omar Mahmud Kassem and others*, Apr. 13, 1969 (Israel, Military Court sitting in Ramallah), (1971) 42 International Law Reports 470, 483; Revisión Constitucional de los artículos 135, 156 y 157 del codigo penal y 174, 175, 178 y 179 del codigo penal militar, Judgment, Apr. 25, 2007 (Constitutional Court of Colombia), sec. 3.3.1.

[40] This principle is confirmed in express terms by AP II, Art. 3(1). Among other examples, see also Second Protocol to The Hague Convention of 1954 for the Protection of Cultural Property in the Event of Armed Conflict, Mar. 26, 1999, 2253 UNTS 212, Art. 22(3).

since NIACs never cease to be a problem of internal public order, the line between warfighting and law enforcement in such conflicts has become uncertain.

The changing parameters of warfare have further hastened the erosion of the traditional legal framework. Technology and global interconnectedness have rendered non-State adversaries more lethal and more mobile. Confronted with this new reality on September 11, 2001, the Bush Administration denied that Common Article 3 applied to the fight against Al-Qaeda due to the transnational, rather than non-international, character of the "war on terror."[41] In essence, the Administration embraced a pre-1949 legal position which rejected the law of war as irrelevant to hostilities waged against irregular adversaries abroad.[42] In *Hamdan*, the Supreme Court rebuffed this approach and confirmed that the law of war does apply to transnational conflicts.[43] Yet this merely exposed the shortcomings of the legal regime created by Common Article 3 and AP II. The conventional rules of the law of NIAC have little to say about the legal authority to detain adversaries, the principles governing targeting or the geographical scope of hostilities in the context of multiple transnational armed conflicts.[44] The international community responded to this lacuna by extending the applicability of the key rules governing the conduct of hostilities in international armed conflict (IAC) to NIAC, as reflected in State practice,[45]

---

[41] See President George W. Bush, Memorandum to the Vice President, Secretary of State, Secretary of Defense et. al., "Humane Treatment of al Qaeda and Taliban Detainees," Feb. 7, 2002, 134–35, repr. in K. J. Greenberg and J. L. Dratel (eds.), *The Torture Papers: The Road to Abu Ghraib* (Cambridge University Press, 2005), 134. For the underpinning legal argument, see Jay Bybee, Assistant Attorney General, US Department of Justice, Memorandum for Alberto R. Gonzales, Counsel to the President, and William J. Haynes II, General Counsel of the Department of Defense, "Application of Treaties and Laws to Al Qaeda and Taliban Detainees," Jan. 22, 2002, 85–89 repr. *ibid.*, 81.

[42] *Cf.* War Office, *Manual of Military Law*, 6th ed. (London: HMSO, 1914), 235 ("It must be emphasized that the rules of International Law apply only to warfare between civilized nations, where both parties understand them and are prepared to carry them out. They do not apply in wars with uncivilized States and tribes, where their place is taken by the discretion of the commander and such rules of justice and humanity as recommend themselves in the particular circumstances of the case."). See also C. Elbridge, "How to Fight Savage Tribes" (1927) 21 *American Journal of International Law* 279–88.

[43] *Hamdan v. Rumsfeld*, 126 S. Ct. 2749 (2006), 2795–97.

[44] *Cf.* N. K. Modirzadeh, "Folk International Law: 9/11 Lawyering and the Transformation of the Law of Armed Conflict to Human Rights Policy and Human Rights Law to War" (2014) 5 *Harvard National Security Journal* 225–304.

[45] E.g., United States Central Command, Investigation Report on the Airstrike on the Médecins Sans Frontières / Doctors without Borders Trauma Center in Kunduz, Afghanistan on October 3, 2015, Nov. 21, 2015, 90–95 (applying the concepts of lawful target, combatant, military objective, precautions and proportionality in attack in the context of a NIAC);

international agreements,[46] the jurisprudence of international courts,[47] and authoritative clarifications of the law.[48] This development has resolved some of the doubts surrounding the targeting of non-State adversaries.[49] However, it has also set the law of war on a collision course with international human rights law.[50]

2.2 The Advent of Human Rights Law

The principle is well-established that human rights treaties remain applicable during times of armed conflict. As the International Court of Justice put it, "the protection offered by human rights conventions does not cease in case of armed conflict."[51] Indeed, this is evident from the very terms of the relevant treaties. For example, Article 2(2) of the Convention against Torture provides that "[n]o exceptional circumstances whatsoever, whether a state of war or a threat of war . . . may be invoked as a justification of torture."[52] Article 4 of the International Covenant on Civil and Political Rights (ICCPR) entitles its

---

Kunduz Case, Judgment, Oct. 6, 2016 (Federal Court of Justice, Germany), paras. 46–55 (applying Arts. 50, 51, 52, and 57 of AP I in the context of a NIAC).

[46] E.g., Rome Statute of the International Criminal Court, July 17, 1998, 2187 UNTS 90, Art. 8(2)(e), as amended by Amendment to Art. 8 of the Rome Statute of the International Criminal Court, June 10, 2010, 2868 UNTS 195.

[47] *Prosecutor v. Tadić*, Case No. IT-94-1-A, Decision on the Defense Motion for Interlocutory Appeal on Jurisdiction, ¶ 127 (ICTY, Appeal Chamber, Oct. 2, 1995) (indiscriminate attacks, protection of civilian objects, certain means and methods of warfare); *Prosecutor v. Stanislav Galić*, Case No. IT-98-29-T, Judgment, ¶¶ 57–58 (ICTY, Appeal Chamber, Dec. 5, 2003) (indiscriminate attacks, proportionality, precautions).

[48] J.-M. Henckaerts and L. Doswald-Beck (eds.), *Customary International Humanitarian Law*, I: *Rules* (Cambridge University Press, 2005), xxix; International Institute of Humanitarian Law, *The Manual on the Law of Non-International Armed Conflict with Commentary* (San Remo: IIHL, 2006); N. Melzer, *Interpretive Guidance on the Notion of Direct Participation in Hostilities under International Humanitarian Law* (Geneva: ICRC, 2008).

[49] See W. H. Boothby, *The Law of Targeting* (Oxford University Press, 2012), 429–54; Y. Dinstein, *Non-International Armed Conflicts in International Law* (Cambridge University Press, 2014), 211–23; S. Sivakumaran, *The Law of Non-International Armed Conflict* (Oxford University Press, 2012), 336–429.

[50] See C. Garraway, "The Law Applies, But Which Law? A Consumer Guide to the Law of War," in M. Evangelista and H. Shue (eds.), *The American Way of Bombing: Changing Ethical and Legal Norms, From Flying Fortresses to Drones* (Ithaca: Cornell University Press, 2014), 87–105, 100.

[51] *Legal Consequences of the Construction of a Wall in the Occupied Palestinian Territory* (Advisory Opinion) (2004) ICJ Rep. 136, para. 106. See also *Armed Activities on the Territory of the Congo (Democratic Republic of the Congo v. Uganda)* (Judgment) (2005) ICJ Rep. 168, para. 216.

[52] Convention against Torture and Other Cruel, Inhuman or Degrading Treatment or Punishment, Dec. 10, 1984, 1465 UNTS 112.

State parties to derogate from its provisions in time of "public emergency which threatens the life of the nation."[53] Although this phrase does not refer to war in express terms, it was specifically understood by its drafters to include war.[54] Both the Convention against Torture and the ICCPR thus presume that their substantive provisions apply during war.

The concurrent applicability of international human rights law and the law of war is shifting the traditional balance between military necessity and humanitarian considerations in favor of the latter.[55] For example, the fact that combat operations and law enforcement are not mutually exclusive activities in NIAC means that the very same act may conceivably be characterized as falling within the regulatory framework of the law of war and that of international human rights law. In the *Isayeva* case, the European Court of Human Rights thus assessed Russian combat operations carried out during the Second Chechen War against "the normal legal background" that governs the activities of law enforcement bodies.[56] Although the Court invoked the concept of "precautions in attack" in its judgment, it did not identify and apply it as a law of war rule.[57] Instead, it relied on the concept in support of the human rights duty to "minimize, to the greatest extent possible, recourse to lethal force."[58]

This use of the notion of precautions does not reflect, and in fact risks misrepresenting, the standards of the law of war. Other examples for the progressive humanization of the law of war through the medium of international human rights law abound. They include granting prisoners of war access to an independent court to determine their legal status,[59] carrying out a human rights-compliant investigation into the killing of civilians during armed conflict,[60] and the application of procedural safeguards drawn from human rights to detention by non-State armed groups.[61]

---

53 International Covenant on Civil and Political Rights, Dec. 16, 1966, 999 UNTS 171.
54 General Assembly, Draft International Covenants on Human Rights, Report of the Third Committee, A/5655, Dec. 10, 1963, para. 53; Commission on Human Rights, Draft International Covenants on Human Rights and Measures of Implementation, Summary Record of the 330th Meeting, July 1, 1952, E/CN.4/SR.330, 4.
55 See M. N. Schmitt, "Military Necessity and Humanity in International Humanitarian Law: Preserving the Delicate Balance" (2010) 50 *Virginia Journal of International Law* 795–839.
56 *Isayeva v. Russia*, App. No. 57950/00, Judgment (2005) 41 EHRR 38, 191.   57 AP I, Art. 57.
58 *Isayeva* (above note 56), paras. 175–76.
59 Working Group on Arbitrary Detention, United Nations Basic Principles and Guidelines on the Right of Anyone Deprived of their Liberty to bring Proceedings before a Court, WGAD/CRP.1/2015 (2015), May 4, 2015, ¶¶ 10 and 95.
60 *Al-Saadoon and others v. Secretary of State for Defence* [2016] EWHC 773 (Admin) (High Court), para. 94.
61 A. Clapham, "Detention by Armed Groups under International Law" (2017) 93 *International Law Studies* 1–44.

To the extent that they apply in times of armed conflict, human rights norms may come into conflict with the permissive, combat-enabling[62] aspects of the rules governing the conduct of hostilities. However, even where human rights norms are not formally applicable, the uncertainty surrounding the relevant legal standards and the risk of litigation may compel States to adopt a more cautious approach and forego otherwise available law of war authorities at the expense of operational effectiveness.[63] More generally, human rights norms amplify arguments for the further humanization of the law of war by serving as a conduit for the reinterpretation of its key principles.[64]

The extraterritorial applicability of human rights treaties also presents considerable challenges. Outside their national territory, States may lack both the legal authority and the capacity to comply with their obligations under international human rights law in full.[65] While international courts have shown themselves to be aware of this difficulty,[66] it is open to debate whether they have drawn an appropriate balance between the scope of a State's human rights obligations and its capacity to implement those obligations in the context of overseas military deployments.[67] Overall, international

---

[62] Cf. N. Berman, "Privileging Combat: Contemporary Conflict and the Legal Construction of War" (2004–5) 43 *Columbia Journal of Transnational Law* 1–72.

[63] One example of how legal uncertainty and complexity leads to such outcomes is the 96-hour detention rule applied by International Security Assistance Force in Afghanistan. See P. Rowe, *Legal Accountability and Britain's Wars 2000-2015* (Abingdon: Routledge, 2016), 224–27; Written evidence from Professor Michael Clarke, Royal United Services Institute (RUSI), in House of Commons Defence Committee, UK Armed Forces Personnel and the Legal Framework for Future Operations, Twelfth Report of Session 2013–14, Mar. 26, 2013, HC 931, Ev 100, Ev 103.

[64] E.g., Oberleitner (above note 17), 136–41.

[65] E.g., *R. (Al-Skeini and others) v. Secretary of State for Defence* [2005] EWCA Civ 1609 (CA), paras. 113–28 (finding that the United Kingdom was not in effective control of Basrah City for the purposes of the ECHR). See also the weight given to *de facto* control and other practical considerations in *Boumediene v. Bush*, 553 US 723 (2008); and *Maqaleh v. Hagel*, 605 F.3d 84 (DC Cir. 2010), 94–99 (holding that issuing a writ of habeas corpus would be impractical in the context of an active theater of war).

[66] E.g., *Jaloud v. The Netherlands*, App. No. 47708/08, Judgment (2015) 60 EHRR 29, para. 226 ("The Court is prepared to make reasonable allowances for the relatively difficult conditions under which the Netherlands military and investigators had to work."). But see *Al-Saadoon and Mufdhi v. United Kingdom*, App. No. 61498/08 (2010) 51 EHRR 9, paras. 138–43 (the lack of a legal basis under international law to detain foreign nationals abroad against the wishes of the local government cannot justify their transfer into local custody in contravention of the European Convention).

[67] Joint Concurring Opinion of Judges Casadevalli, Berro-Lefevre, Šikuta, Hirvelä, López Guerra, Sajó and Silvis, *Jaloud* (above note 66), ¶¶ 6–8 ("we respectfully regret that the Grand Chamber also found it appropriate to scrutinise the investigations in Iraq in such a painstaking way that eyebrows may be raised about the role and competence of our Court"). See A. Sari, "Untangling Extra-Territorial Jurisdiction from International Responsibility in

human rights law and discourse presents significant challenges, both direct and indirect, to the law of war and the conduct of military operations.

3 PARADISE LOST: TIME FOR REARGUARD TACTICS

While the normative foundations of the law of war are shifting, it would be a mistake to blame this development solely on the advent of international human rights law. As we have seen, the extension of the law of war into the sphere of NIACs and the changing character of warfare are key drivers of this transformation. Nonetheless, international human rights law complements and augments these trends in a way that has increased the complexity of the legal operating environment, accelerated the erosion of the traditional legal boundaries of warfare, and created new areas of legal uncertainty. How does the Manual respond to this development?

In essence, the Manual mounts a rearguard action. When examined in its totality, the Manual's clarification of this normative morass is minimal. International human rights law features on its pages in two principal forms. On a handful of occasions, the Manual refers to human rights materials to support or illustrate its interpretation of the law of war. It cites the *Abella* case decided by the Inter-American Commission on Human Rights regarding the threshold of NIACs[68] and the *Konovov* case before the European Court of Human Rights concerning the customary status of the rules codified in the Lieber Code.[69] It also cites the first report prepared by the United Nations Secretary General on respect for human rights in armed conflict in relation to prisoners of war[70] and a report by the UN Commission on Human Rights in connection with special agreements between warring parties.[71]

In addition to these scattered references to human rights materials, the Manual offers only a general theory of the relationship between the law of war and other branches of international law, including international human

Jaloud v. The Netherlands: Old Problem, New Solutions?" (2014) 53 *Military Law and the Law of War Review* 287–318, 312–13.

[68] *Juan Carlos Abella v. Argentina*, Case No. 11.137, Report No. 55/97, Nov. 18, 1997 (Inter-American Court of Human Rights). See DoD Law of War Manual, ¶ 3.4.2.2 fnn. 74 and 77.

[69] *Kononov v. Latvia*, App. No. 36376/04, Judgment, (2010) 52 EHRR 21. See DoD Law of War Manual, ¶ 19.3 fn. 60.

[70] General Assembly, Respect for Human Rights in Armed Conflicts: Report of the Secretary-General, A/7720, Nov. 20, 1969. See DoD Law of War Manual, ¶ 9.3.4 fn. 65.

[71] Commission on Human Rights, Report on the Situation of Human Rights in Afghanistan Prepared by the Special Rapporteur, Felix Ermacora, in accordance with Commission on Human Rights Resolution 1984/55, E/CN.4/1985/21, Feb. 19, 1985. See DoD Law of War Manual, ¶ 17.3 fn. 68.

rights treaties. According to the Manual, the law of war may relate to other bodies of law in four ways.[72] Law of war rules may supersede rules forming part of other legal regimes, inform the interpretation of such rules with the aim of avoiding norm conflicts, determine the content of more general legal standards, and, finally, incorporate concepts originally drawn from other bodies of law. Having set out this general scheme, the Manual hastens to add the following caveat:

> In some cases, it may be difficult to distinguish between these approaches, and different entities may apply different approaches to achieve the same result. Although there are different approaches and although the ultimate resolution may depend on the specific rules and context, the law of war, as the *lex specialis* of armed conflict, is the controlling body of law with regard to the conduct of hostilities and the protection of war victims.[73]

This passage is instructive, for it sets out the Manual's core thesis and betrays its priorities. Despite acknowledging the multifaceted nature of the relationship between the law of war and other branches of international law, the bottom line, according to the Manual, is that the law of war constitutes the controlling body of law with regard to the conduct of hostilities and the protection of war victims.[74] Although it does not define the term, the Manual equates "controlling" with the concept of *lex specialis*, which it defines as the maxim whereby "[a]s a rule the special rule overrides the general law."[75] Consequently, the law of war is understood to be "controlling" in the sense that its rules override conflicting rules of international law with respect to armed conflict. It is worth noting that this understanding of the term corresponds with its use by the US Supreme Court in *The Paquete Habana* (though the application of *lex specialis* to modern conflicts is far more complex than in 1900).[76]

The Manual describes the relationship between the law of war and human rights treaties along the same lines. Having noted that in some circumstances the two bodies of rules "may appear to conflict," it suggests that such apparent

---

[72] DoD Law of War Manual, ¶ 1.2.2.   [73]   *Ibid.* (footnotes omitted).

[74]   The Manual cites the Observations of the United States of America on the Human Rights Committee's Draft General Comment 35: Art. 9, June 10, 2014, para. 20, www.state.gov/docu ments/organization/244445.pdf, as the origin of this formula.

[75]   DoD Law of War Manual, ¶ 1.3.2.1, quoting *Colleanu v. German State*, Jan. 12, 1929 (Germano-Rumanian Mixed Arbitral Tribunal), (1929) 5 International Law Reports 438, 440.

[76]   *The Paquete Habana*, 175 US 677 (1900), 700 ("International law is part of our law . . . where there is no treaty and no controlling executive or legislative act or judicial decision, resort must be had to the customs and usages of civilized nations."). *Cf.* L. Henkin, "The President and International Law" (1986) 80 *American Journal of International Law* 930–37.

norm conflicts may be resolved with recourse to the principle that the law of war is the controlling body of law during situations of armed conflict.[77] In support of this position, the Manual recalls that some international courts and treaty bodies have "interpreted the rights conveyed by human rights treaties in light of the rules of the law of war, as the applicable *lex specialis*, when assessing situations in armed conflict."[78] This passage suggests that *lex specialis* is an interpretive principle whereby apparent contradictions between two rules may be resolved by way of harmonious interpretation.[79] Remarkably, this understanding differs from the Manual's preferred version of *lex specialis* as a principle for resolving normative conflicts in a hierarchical manner. Leaving this inconsistency aside, the critical point is that the Manual embraces a stronger, hierarchical version of *lex specialis* for resolving conflicts between the law of war and human rights law. To round off its discussion of human rights treaties, the Manual briefly notes that some States may take different perspectives on the applicability of human rights treaties[80] and recalls the US position on the extraterritorial applicability of the ICCPR and the Convention against Torture.[81]

Overall, international human rights law is marked more by its absence and exclusion than by its presence in the Manual. This should not come as a surprise. The United States has long taken the position that its responsibilities under international human rights agreements are curtailed by two factors. First, successive administrations have argued that the law of war is the governing body of law in times of armed conflict. Past formulations of this position seemed to imply that the law of war completely displaces international human rights law.[82] By contrast, in recent years, the United States has adopted a more

---

[77] DoD Law of War Manual, ¶ 1.6.3.1.

[78] The Manual cites three cases: *Coard et al. v. United States*, Case 10.951, Report No. 109/99, Sept. 29, 1999 (Inter-American Commission on Human Rights), para. 42; *Abella* (above note 68), ¶ 166; *Legality of the Threat or Use of Nuclear Weapons* (Advisory Opinion) (1996) ICJ Rep. 226, para. 25.

[79] See International Law Commission, Report of the Study Group on the Fragmentation of International Law, Finalized by Martti Koskenniemi, A/CN.4/L.682, Apr. 13, 2006, paras. 88–107. On the difference between genuine and apparent norm conflicts, see M. Milanović, "Norm Conflict in International Law: Whither Human Rights?" (2009) 20 *Duke Journal of Comparative and International Law* 69–131, 72–73.

[80] DoD Law of War Manual, ¶ 1.6.3.2.   [81] *Ibid.*, ¶¶ 1.6.3.3 and 1.6.3.4.

[82] E.g., *Coard* (above note 78), ¶ 35 (the United States "maintained that the matter was wholly and exclusively governed by the law of international armed conflict"). See also "Response of the United States to Request for Precautionary Measures: Detainees in Guananamo Bay, Cuba" (2002) 41 *International Legal Materials* 1015–27, 1020; J. B. Bellinger, III, Legal Advisor, US Department of State, Opening Remarks, US Meeting with UN Committee Against Torture, May 5, 2006, www.state.gov/j/drl/rls/68557.htm; Reply of the Government of the United States of America to the Report of the Five UNCHR Special Rapporteurs on Detainees

conciliatory approach in recognizing that the law of war does not displace international human rights norms completely.[83] Second, successive administrations have also taken the view that the ICCPR does not apply in an extraterritorial manner.[84] Despite the Human Rights Committee[85] and the International Court of Justice[86] taking the opposite view, the United States has stuck to this position, including in its most recent periodic report under the ICCPR.[87] In the past, the United States has also adopted a restrictive reading of the extraterritorial reach of the Convention against Torture.[88] More recently, it has accepted that the relevant obligations apply to "all places that the State Party controls as a governmental authority."[89] For the most part, the Manual simply replicates these preexisting national positions without making efforts to engage opposing perspectives.

4 DISSEMINATION AND LAW-SHAPING: ENLIGHTENMENT OR ADVOCACY?

As noted earlier, military manuals are widely understood to serve two functions: they are instruments for disseminating and for expressing national

in Guantánamo Bay, Cuba, Mar. 10, 2006, 22–24, www.state.gov/documents/organization/98 969.pdf.

[83] E.g., Human Rights Council, Report of the Working Group on the Universal Periodic Review – United States of America, A/HRC/16/11, Jan. 4, 2011, para. 53; Human Rights Committee, Fourth Periodic Report, United States of America, CCPR/C/USA/4, May 22, 2012, para. 507.

[84] Human Rights Committee, Consideration of Reports Submitted by States Party under Article 40 of the Covenant, Summary Record of the 1405th Meeting, CCPR/C/SR.1405, Apr. 24, 1995, para. 21. The argument is set out in more detail in Annex I to Human Rights Committee, Third Periodic Reports of States Party due in 2003, United States of America, CCPR/C/USA/ 3, Nov. 28 2005. See also Reply to the Report of the Five UNCHR Special Rapporteurs (above note 82), 25–30.

[85] Human Rights Committee, General Comment No. 31, The Nature of the General Legal Obligation Imposed on States Party to the Covenant, CCPR/C/21/Rev.1/Add. 13, May 26, 2004, para. 10.

[86] *Legal Consequences of the Construction of a Wall* (above note 51), ¶¶ 107–11.

[87] Fourth Periodic Report (above note 83), paras. 504–05.

[88] John B. Bellinger, III, United States' Response to the Questions Asked by the Committee Against Torture, May 5, 2006, www.state.gov/j/drl/rls/68561.htm ("The United States does not accept the concept that 'de facto control' equates to territory under its jurisdiction"); Observations by the United States of America on Committee Against Torture General Comment No. 2: Implementation of Article 2 by States Party, Nov. 3, 2008, www.state.gov/ documents/organization/138853.pdf, paras. 26–29.

[89] Mary E. McLeod, Acting Legal Advisor, US Department of State, Opening Statement, Committee Against Torture, Nov. 12, 2014, https://geneva.usmission.gov/2014/11/12/acting-legal-adviser-mcleod-u-s-affirms-torture-is-prohibited-at-all-times-in-all-places/.

positions on the law. Dissemination is the more static function of the two, in as much as its aim is to convey the law to an audience rather than to affect the law itself. However, this is not to suggest that military manuals merely reproduce the letter of the law in a mechanical fashion. On the contrary, national manuals typically present the relevant rules in a systematic and more agreeable manner, elucidate their meaning, and place them within their broader context. The aim of dissemination is not simply to increase knowledge, but also to enhance understanding.[90] It follows that one of the criteria for evaluating how effectively a manual performs its dissemination function is the extent to which it is capable of enhancing its audience's understanding of the applicable law.[91] As regards their second function, it is clear that military manuals are not themselves a source of international law. However, they may reveal how a nation understands and implements its own legal obligations. In other words, military manuals may have some "evidentiary value"[92] as to a nation's State practice and *opinio juris*.[93] Whether this is the case depends on the terms of a manual itself. Where a manual does express a national position on the law, its effectiveness should be judged against how compelling a justification it offers for that position. Judged against these criteria, the Manual's treatment of the relationship between the law of war and international human rights law is something of a mixed success.

4.1 Promoting Understanding

It is important to underline that the Manual does not claim that law of war displaces international human rights law in its entirety.[94] Rather, it suggests that specific rules of the law of war override specific rules of human rights treaties in the event of a conflict. This is a critical concession, for it implies that

---

90   House of Commons Defence Committee (above note 63), para. 120. See also N. Hayashi, "Introduction," in N. Hayashi (ed.), *National Military Manuals on the Law of Armed Conflict*, 2nd ed. (Oslo: Torkel Opsahl, 2010), 1–34, 9.

91   For a full set of criteria, see Reisman and Leitzau (above note 19), 5–7.

92   Cf. *Trial of Wilhelm List and others (Hostages Trial)* (1946) Law Reports of Trials of War Criminals, Vol. VIII, 34 (United States Military Tribunal), 51. See also Field Manual 27-10, The Law of Land Warfare (Washington: US Dep't. of Army, July 18, 1956) (FM 27-10), ¶ 3.

93   See also F. Kalshoven, "The Respective Roles of Custom and Principle in the International Law of Armed Conflict and the Law of Armed Conflict" (2006) 2 *Acta Societatis Martensis* 48–68, 59.

94   This approach is widely discredited in the literature and enjoys limited support in practice. E.g., *Georgia v. Russia*, App. No. 38263/08, Judgment, Dec. 13, 2011, para. 69 (according to Russia, "the [ECHR] did not apply to a situation of international armed conflict where a State Party's forces were engaged in national defence . . . In such circumstances the conduct of the State Party's forces was governed exclusively by international humanitarian law.").

in times of armed conflict human rights norms remain applicable where they do not conflict with the rules of the law of war. The Manual acknowledges as much when it declares that human rights treaties are controlling "with respect to matters that are within their scope of application and that are not addressed by the law of war."[95] Nevertheless, this language of controlling bodies of law obscures the more intricate dynamics between the law of war and human rights treaties.

It is certainly correct to suggest that some matters are governed by the law of war, others by human rights law, and that still other matters fall within the ambit of both regimes.[96] What the Manual fails to acknowledge, however, is that the range of questions subject to both bodies of rules is vast and often on the margins of each area of controlling law. This is a critical point. For example, it is difficult to see how the matters regulated under the Third Geneva Convention (GC III)[97] could not, in principle, be framed to engage every single one of the substantive rights set out in Part III of the ICCPR, from the right to liberty and freedom of movement to the freedom of expression and the right to form and join trade unions. The simple fact is that the treatment of individuals as prisoners of war under GC III does not, *prima facie*, preclude their treatment as human beings from falling within the scope of the ICCPR. In many cases, this regulatory overlap poses no difficulties, either because the relevant rules are compatible or can be interpreted and applied in a compatible manner, even without recourse to the principle of *lex specialis*.[98]

The Manual is mostly silent on these compatibilities and other complementary aspects of the two legal regimes. For instance, the Manual acknowledges that Common Article 3 reflects minimum humane treatment standards for detainees in any military operation, including in operations "not addressed by the law of war."[99] This suggests that the standards embodied in Common Article 3 cannot be matters exclusively of the law of war, otherwise it is difficult to see how they could bind US forces outside times of armed conflict when the

---

[95] DoD Law of War Manual, ¶ 1.6.3.1.
[96] *Cf. Legal Consequences of the Construction of a Wall* (above note 51), para. 106.
[97] Convention Relative to the Treatment of Prisoners of War (GC III), Aug. 12, 1949, 75 UNTS 135.
[98] E.g., the fact that prisoners of war may be compelled to perform certain types of work pursuant to Arts. 49 and 50 GC III seems to contradict the prohibition of "forced or compulsory labour" under Art. 8(3)(a) of the ICCPR. However, such work could be interpreted to constitute "service of a military character" under Art. 8(3)(c)(ii), due to the work being performed whilst in military captivity, and thus be exempted from the prohibition. But see P. Rowe, *The Impact of Human Rights Law on Armed Forces* (Cambridge University Press, 2006), 14–16.
[99] DoD Law of War Manual, ¶ 3.1.1.2.

law of war is not formally applicable. Yet if these minimum standards do not belong within the exclusive province of the law of war, how can Common Article 3 constitute the controlling set of rules in relation to the corresponding rules of human rights law?

Similar questions arise in relation to Article 75 of AP I. The Manual recalls that the US Government has chosen "out of a sense of legal obligation to treat the principles set forth in Article 75 as applicable to any individual it detains in an international armed conflict."[100] Bearing in mind that Article 75 was intended to close certain gaps in the Geneva Conventions of 1949,[101] and that it did so with reference to the standards of the ICCPR,[102] one wonders whether this "sense of legal obligation" derives from the preexisting rules of the ICCPR, to which the United States is a party, or from the text of AP I, to which it is not.

In other areas, the Manual's silence has potentially more far-reaching consequences. Common Article 3 and Article 75 of AP I both prohibit torture.[103] However, neither of these provisions or other rules of the law of war actually define torture. International criminal tribunals have therefore turned to international human rights law, including the Convention against Torture, to determine the meaning of the term for the purposes of the law of war and international criminal law.[104] The Manual fails to acknowledge this vital link. Instead, it declares that the "Convention against Torture was not intended to supersede the prohibitions against torture already contained in customary international law and the 1949 Geneva Conventions or its Additional Protocols" and repeats its core thesis that the law of war is the controlling body of law with respect to the conduct of hostilities and the protection of war victims.[105] Regrettably, this mantra leaves the concept of

---

[100] *Ibid.*, ¶ 8.1.4.2.

[101] Summary Record of the Forty-Third Meeting, Apr. 30, 1976, para. 2 (International Committee of the Red Cross), in Federal Political Department, *Official Records of the Diplomatic Conference on the Reaffirmation and Development of International Humanitarian Law Applicable in Armed Conflicts* (Bern: Federal Political Department, 1978), 25; and Summary Record of the Forty-Fourth Meeting, May 3, 1976, para. 28 (Byelorussian Soviet Socialist Republic) and para. 38 (Greece), *ibid.*, 45.

[102] *Ibid.*, Summary Record of the Forty-Third Meeting, para. 8 (International Committee of the Red Cross).

[103] Common Art. 3(1)(a); AP I, Art. 75(2)(a)(ii).

[104] *Prosecutor v. Akayesu*, Case No. ICTR-96-4, Judgment, ¶ 593 (ICTR Trial Chamber, Sept. 2, 1998) (ICTR Trial Chamber); *Prosecutor v. Furundžija*, Case No. IT-95-17/1-T, Judgment, ¶¶ 159–64 (ICTY, Dec. 10, 1998); *Prosecutor v. Delalić*, Case No. IT-96-21-T, Judgment, ¶¶ 446–97 (ICTY, Nov. 16, 1998); *Prosecutor v. Kunarac, Kovač, and Vuković*, Case No. IT-96-23 & 23/1, Judgment, ¶¶ 465–97 (ICTY, Feb. 22, 2001).

[105] DoD Law of War Manual, ¶ 1.6.3.4.

torture undefined.[106] Given recent memories of prisoner abuse,[107] this is unhelpful at best.[108]

Overall, the Manual paints a rather one-dimensional portrait of the relationship between the law of war and international human rights treaties. The obvious attraction of such an approach is that it offers clarity and certainty, which are among the most highly prized qualities of any military manual.[109] Indeed, few will object to the idea that the Manual should assist its readers in navigating an increasingly complex legal environment and offer "guidelines that can be translated into an effective operational framework for warfighters."[110] Rather, the question is how much detail and complexity the Manual should sacrifice in the interests of clarity and certainty? Other official pronouncements made on behalf of the US Government on the subject of human rights law offer a useful comparison in this respect. The latest US periodic report under the ICCPR is far more forthcoming than the Manual in acknowledging that the law of war and international human rights law are complementary and mutually reinforcing.[111]

Most importantly from a practical perspective, the report recognizes that "[d]etermining the international law rule that applies to a particular action taken by a government in the context of an armed conflict is a fact-specific determination, which cannot be easily generalized, and raises especially complex issues in the context of non-international armed conflicts occurring within a State's own territory."[112] The Manual could have adopted this more subtle approach without foregoing clarity and certainty. In particular, it could have determined the circumstances, if only in general terms as it has done in other difficult areas,[113] where human rights norms may be more relevant,[114]

---

[106] Despite invoking the prohibition of torture in numerous contexts (e.g. ¶¶ 5.26.2; 7.5; 8.2.1; 8.4.1; 9.28.7.5; 11.7.1.1; 18.9.3.1), the Manual offers a definition of the term only once, drawn from 18 USC § 2340, in a footnote and in the context of defining threats to commit inhuman treatment. This is singularly unhelpful.

[107] See AR 15-6 Investigation of the 800th Military Police Brigade (Taguba Report), Oct. 19, 2004, www.thetorturedatabase.org/files/foia_subsite/pdfs/DODDOA000248.pdf.

[108] It also sits uneasily with the position articulated by the United States in other fora: see McLeod (above note 89).

[109] *Cf.* House of Commons Defence Committee (above note 63), para. 120. See also N. Hayashi, "Introduction," in N. Hayashi (ed.), *National Military Manuals on the Law of Armed Conflict*, 2nd ed. (Oslo: Torkel Opsahl, 2010), 1–34, 9.

[110] G. S. Corn, "Mixing Apples and Hand Grenades: The Logical Limit of Applying Human Rights Norms to Armed Conflict" (2010) 1 *International Humanitarian Legal Studies* 52–94.

[111] Fourth Periodic Report (above note 83), para. 507.   [112] *Ibid.*

[113] E.g., see the "rule of the thumb" in DoD Law of War Manual, ¶ 3.4.2.2.

[114] E.g., C. Garraway, "War and Peace: Where Is the Divide?" (2012) 88 *International Law Studies* 93–115 (distinguishing between different levels of violence); Corn (above note 110), 67–74 (distinguishing between pre- and post-submission of the enemy).

drawn certain red lines where human rights law should give way to the law of war pursuant to the principle of *lex specialis*,[115] and identified certain human rights norms, including the prohibition of torture and inhuman or degrading treatment or punishment, which are relevant in most if not all circumstances. Addressing the subject at this greater level of granularity would have enabled the Manual to do justice to the complexity of the legal environment whilst still providing clear guidance.

In the absence of greater granularity, the Manual risks luring its readers into a false sense of complacency. This creates unnecessary legal risks. The United States accepts that certain human rights norms are complementary to the law of war.[116] Overlooking their applicability could expose US military operations to international censure that may otherwise be avoided. In this respect, it is important to recall that the Manual only addresses the relationship between the law of war and human rights treaties, but does not deal with the applicability and potential impact of customary international human rights law.[117] It is also worth remembering that neither human rights law nor the US position on the extraterritorial applicability of its human rights obligations is permanently fixed. Accordingly, the legal costs of complacency may manifest themselves only in the future.

A more nuanced understanding of international human rights law is also essential from an interoperability perspective.[118] In multinational operations, the human rights obligations of foreign partners are among the key drivers of national caveats. To address the challenges that such caveats present to mission accomplishment, US commanders must fully understand the legal position and sensitivities of coalition partners.[119] In the context of consensual deployments, the human rights obligations of the territorial State may also be relevant to US forces in a more direct manner. There is at least one example where a domestic court has accepted that a sending State must respect the international human rights obligations of a receiving State as a consequence of private international law.[120] A corresponding responsibility to respect the

---

[115] E.g. Corn (above note 110), 74–84; S. Aughey and A. Sari, "Targeting and Detention in Non-International Armed Conflict: Serdar Mohammed and the Limits of Human Rights Convergence" (2015) 91 *International Law Studies*, 60–118, 97–108.

[116] McLeod (above note 89).   [117] DoD Law of War Manual, ¶ 1.6.3 fn. 83.

[118] The Manual makes precisely this point in ¶ 1.6.3.2, but fails to offer much detail and seems to imply, wrongly, that military occupation triggers the applicability of the European Convention on Human Rights pursuant to *Al-Skeini and others v. United Kingdom*, App. No. 55721/07, Judgment (2011) 53 EHRR 18. But see *Jaloud* (above note 66), para. 142.

[119] Cf. D. Stephens, "Coalition Warfare: Challenges and Opportunities" (2006) 36 *Israel Yearbook on Human Rights* 17–27.

[120] *Nuhanović v. The Netherlands*, Judgment, 200.020.174/01, July 5, 2011 (Court of Appeal in The Hague), paras. 6.3, 6.4, and 6.8.

international human rights obligations of the receiving State may also be derived from the sending State's duty to respect the local law in force in the territory of the receiving State. In practice, the impact of this duty will be limited as long as the sending State benefits from wide-ranging jurisdictional immunities.[121] However, in the territory of other North Atlantic Treaty Organization (NATO) Allies, US forces do not normally benefit from such extensive immunities.[122] In fact, US forces should expect any exemptions they may claim from locally applicable human rights norms to be greeted with more robust scrutiny than in the case of operations taking place outside the North Atlantic area.[123] Finally, it is worth recalling some of the in-built limitations of the law of armed conflict. For example, the bulk of the protections afforded to civilians under the Fourth Geneva Convention (GC IV) do not apply to nationals of a co-belligerent State.[124] Consequently, the provisions of GC IV at best can serve only as a partial legal basis and regulatory framework for the detention of co-belligerent nationals in situations where US forces engage in hostilities in the territory of an ally. The Manual's monochrome portrayal of the relationship between the law of war and human rights law fails to capture the true impact of human rights norms and as such does not adequately support commanders and their legal advisors in accurately assessing their legal operating environment.

4.2 *Promoting* Lex Specialis

The fact that the humanitarian standards of the law of war and international human rights law are compatible does not mean, however, that it is immaterial whether these standards apply under the former legal regime or the latter.[125] The supervisory mechanisms of the two bodies of rules are different. Law of war treaties typically do not contain mechanisms for periodic oversight and

---

[121] E.g., Military Technical Agreement between the International Security Assistance Force (ISAF) and the Interim Administration of Afghanistan (Interim Administration), Jan. 4 2002, (2002) 41 ILM 1032, Annex A, sec. 1.

[122] See Agreement between the Parties to the North Atlantic Treaty Regarding the Status of Their Forces, June 19, 1951, 199 UNTS 68, Arts. VII and VIII.

[123] Cf. *McElhinney v. Ireland*, App. No. 31253/96, Judgment (2002) 34 EHRR 322, paras. 37–38.

[124] Convention Relative to the Protection of Civilian Persons in Time of War (GC IV), 1949, 75 UNTS 287, Art. 4.

[125] Cf. J. B. Bellinger III, "The Convention against Torture: Extraterritorial Application and Application to Military Operations," *Lawfare* (Oct. 26, 2014), www.lawfareblog.com/convention-against-torture-extraterritorial-application-and-application-military-operations ("both [international humanitarian law] and [human rights law] prohibit torture … the issue is not whether the substantive law is different, but which body of law governs").

individual petition,[126] whereas human rights treaties do.[127] Yet here too the Manual's preoccupation with the idea of controlling bodies of law obscures the intricacies of the subject. As we saw earlier, the Manual declares that human rights treaties must be considered controlling with respect to matters that are not addressed by the law of war.[128] This statement is overly broad and contradicts the more carefully crafted phrase, used elsewhere in the Manual, whereby the law of war is said to constitute the controlling body of law "with regard to the conduct of hostilities and the protection of war victims."[129] By designating the law of war as the controlling body with regard to the protection of war victims, this formula pre-empts arguments that the protections offered by the law of war and human rights law are accumulative, in the sense that a higher standard of protection under one regime automatically surpasses a lower or lacking standard of protection under the other. Such an accumulation of standards would impose far more stringent demands on belligerents than is currently the case. For example, it would no longer suffice to determine the status of prisoners of war before a "competent tribunal" in accordance with the law of war,[130] but individuals whose status is in doubt would have to be granted the right to initiate proceedings before an independent court without delay to challenge the arbitrariness and lawfulness of their detention and to receive appropriate and accessible remedies, in line with the requirements of human rights law.[131]

The reason why the law of war at times adopts a lower standard of protection is not necessarily because it is less sophisticated than human rights law, but because it balances humanitarian considerations against military necessity. For example, as the Manual confirms, the law of war does not recognize an individual right to compensation for violations of its rules.[132] Differing (and often lower) standards in the law of war are not necessarily an oversight that

---

[126] But see, e.g., the Committee for the Protection of Cultural Property in the Event of Armed Conflict established under the Second Protocol to Convention for the Protection of Cultural Property (above note 40), Art. 24.

[127] ICCPR, Art. 40; Convention against Torture, Art. 19. The United States has not recognized the competence of the Human Rights Committee or the Committee against Torture to receive and consider communications by individuals claiming to be the victims of a violation of their rights by the United States.

[128] DoD Law of War Manual, ¶ 1.6.3.1.   [129] *Ibid.*, ¶ 1.3.2.   [130] GC III, Art. 5.

[131] Basic Principles and Guidelines on the Right of Anyone Deprived of their Liberty to bring Proceedings before a Court (above note 59), paras. 30 and 95. See Reply to the Report of the Five UNCHR Special Rapporteurs (above note 82) ("This result is directly at odds with well-settled law of war that would throw the centuries-old, unchallenged practice of detaining enemy combatants into complete disarray.").

[132] DoD Law of War Manual, ¶ 18.16. See *Kunduz Case* (above note 45), paras. 16–17 (confirming the absence of such a right, notwithstanding human rights norms).

must be remedied by human rights law, but may reflect a deliberate normative choice made by States.[133] This point is often overlooked. There is little
doubt, for instance, that the procedural rules governing the interment of
members of organized armed groups by a State in the context of a NIAC
would benefit from further development and codification.[134] While human
rights standards may play a role in this context, their uncritical[135] extension to
govern the detention of members of organized armed groups could fundamentally alter the balance between humanity and military necessity.[136]
Well-intentioned attempts to reconcile the differences between the law of
war and human rights law often lead to the same outcome. It has been
suggested, for example, that human rights norms could help to recast the
law of war principle of proportionality so that it would permit an attacking
party to cause incidental civilian harm not exceeding the military advantage
anticipated from the attack *only if* the military objective to be attacked poses
an immediate threat.[137] Leaving aside that such a rule would be difficult, if
not impossible, to apply where the military objective to be attacked is an
object,[138] as far as persons are concerned, a rule to this effect would essentially render offensive operations unlawful in a broad range of circumstances. In fact, such a rule would actively encourage adversaries to co-
locate civilians among military objectives in order to shield them from

[133]   *Cf.* Observations of the United States of America on Preliminary Draft Principles and
      Guidelines on Remedies and Procedures on the Right of Anyone Deprived of his or her
      Liberty to Bring Proceedings before Court, Nov. 10, 2014, 3, www.state.gov/documents/orga
      nization/244516.pdf.
[134]   E.g., L. Hill-Cawthorne, *Detention in Non-International Armed Conflict* (Oxford University
      Press, 2016), 98.
[135]   *Cf. Kunarac* (above note 104), para. 470 (in relying on human rights norms "to define an
      offence under international humanitarian law, the Trial Chamber must be mindful of the
      specificity of this body of law"). However, as this case illustrates, a law of war prohibition may
      well be stricter than the corresponding human rights prohibition.
[136]   E.g., the Basic Principles and Guidelines on the Right of Anyone Deprived of their Liberty to
      bring Proceedings before a Court (above note 59), para. 96 suggest that "[a]dministrative
      detention or internment may only be permitted in the exceptional circumstance where
      a public emergency is invoked to justify such detention" and where the detaining State has
      shown that "[t]he emergency has risen to a level justifying derogation". If status-based
      detention in an IAC is not arbitrary for the purposes of the ICCPR (see Human Rights
      Committee, General Comment No. 35, Art. 9 (Liberty and security of person), CCPR/C/
      GC/35, Dec. 16, 2014, para. 64), it is unclear why it should be arbitrary in NIAC. *Cf. Aughey
      and Sari* (above note 115), 97–108.
[137]   Oberleitner (above note 17), 138. For a sophisticated argument in favor of a threat-based
      paradigm of targeting outside zones of active hostility, see J. C. Daskal, "The Geography of
      the Battlefield: A Framework for Detention and Targeting outside the Hot Conflict Zone"
      (2013) 161 *University of Pennsylvania Law Review*, 1165–234, 1214–17.
[138]   *Cf.* AP I, Art. 52(2). Inanimate objects do not display hostile intent.

attack. To borrow the words of the Prosecution in the *Galić* case, "lawful combat would, in effect, become impossible."[139]

These considerations throw a different light on the Manual's insistence that the law of war is the controlling body of rules with regard to the conduct of hostilities and the protection of war victims. The normative integrity of the law of war is under sustained pressure and must be safeguarded if the law of war is to serve as an effective and distinctive component of the overall legal framework of warfare. There is ample evidence that States did not intend to undermine the core principles of the law of war through the adoption of human rights treaties.[140] The continued development and implementation of the law of war in international practice further demonstrates that States have no intention of abandoning it as a distinct branch of international law.[141] Preserving the integrity of the law of war against humanitarian overreach thus reflects State intentions. However, it also better serves the humanitarian imperatives of the law. Humanizing the law of war beyond its pragmatic foundations risks creating battlefield expectations that are unrealistic, which in turn risks undermining compliance with the law itself.[142]

The promise of *lex specialis* is that it addresses these matters at the level of principle. Compared to other solutions, such as United Nations Security Council resolutions[143] or derogations made pursuant to the applicable human rights instruments,[144] *lex specialis* has the potential to regulate the interaction between the law of war and human rights norms with general effect, irrespective of the forum and without the need for additional affirmative action. However, the general character of the doctrine of *lex specialis* is

---

[139] Galić (above note 47), para. 144.

[140] E.g., Commission on Human Rights, Draft International Covenant on Human Rights, Summary Record of the Ninety-Seventh Meeting, E/CN.4/SR.97, June 3, 1949, 8 (Philippines: "[t]he Commission, however, could not, either directly or indirectly, alter the laws of war in any way whatsoever"); *ibid.*, 6–7 (UK); Commission on Human Rights, Draft International Covenant on Human Rights, Summary Record of the 194th Meeting, E/CN.4/SR.194, May 25, 1950, para. 34 (France: the "purpose was to ensure protection of human rights, but not to endeavour to change or amend international law as it was practiced"); Commission on Human Rights, Summary Record of the 330th Meeting (above note 54), 7 (Belgium: suggesting that the ICCPR would be suspended between belligerents).

[141] Above notes 41–50. *Cf.* D. Schindler, "The International Committee of the Red Cross and Human Rights" (1979) 19 *International Review of the Red Cross* 3–14, 14.

[142] Generally, see N. K. Modirzadeh, "The Dark Sides of Convergence: A Pro-Civilian Critique of the Extraterritorial Application of Human Rights Law in Armed Conflict" (2010) 86 *International Law Studies* 349–410.

[143] *Cf. Abd Ali Hameed Al-Waheed v. Ministry of Defence; Serdar Mohammed v. Ministry of Defence* [2017] Judgment, UKSC 2 (UK Supreme Court), paras. 18–30.

[144] *Cf.* Observations of the United States of America (above note 133), 3–4.

also one of its weaknesses.[145] The principle carries different meanings and cannot be relied upon mechanically to provide clear guidance on how to resolve norm conflicts in specific cases, as commentators have repeatedly pointed out.[146] Nevertheless, it is wrong to dismiss the notion that the law of war is the controlling body of law in times of armed conflict as "patently false."[147] The principle of *lex specialis*, and its application to the law of war more specifically, benefits from widespread support in international practice, ranging from national governments and courts[148] to international organs and judicial authorities,[149] including human rights bodies.[150] The principle therefore has a legitimate and useful role to play, both as a guide to interpretation and as a means for prioritizing conflicting norms, in preserving the normative foundations and distinct regulatory function of the law of war.

While the Manual falls short, by some margin, of articulating a comprehensive theory of *lex specialis*, it deserves attention and credit as one of the most detailed official endorsements of the principle.[151] Regrettably,

[145]   O. A. Hathaway et al., "Which Law Governs During Armed Conflict? The Relationship Between International Humanitarian Law and Human Rights Law" (2011–12) 96 *Minnesota Law Review* 1883–943.

[146]   E.g., A. Lindroos, "Addressing Norm Conflicts in a Fragmented Legal System: The Doctrine of *Lex Specialis*" (2005) 74 *Nordic Journal of International Law* 27–66; N. Prud'homme, "Lex Specialis: Oversimplifying a More Complex and Multifaceted Relationship" (2007) 40 *Israel Law Review* 357–95; A. Orakhelashvili, "The Interaction between Human Rights and Humanitarian Law: Fragmentation, Conflict, Parallelism, or Convergence?" (2008) 19 *European Journal of International Law* 161–82; M. Milanovic, "The Lost Origins of Lex Specialis: Rethinking the Relationship between Human Rights and International Humanitarian Law," in J. D. Ohlin (ed.), *Theoretical Boundaries of Armed Conflict and Human Rights* (Cambridge University Press, 2016), 78–117.

[147]   J. J. Paust, "Errors and Misconceptions in the 2015 DOD Law of War Manual" (2017) 26 *Minnesota Journal of International Law* 303–44, https://ssrn.com/abstract=2712004.

[148]   E.g., Commission on Human Rights, Report of the Working Group on Arbitrary Detention, E/CN.4/2005/6, Dec. 1, 2006, para. 6; *Public Committee against Torture in Israel et al. v. Government of Israel et al.*, HCJ 769/02, Dec. 13, 2006 (Supreme Court of Israel sitting as the High Court of Justice), para. 18; Human Rights Committee, Replies to the List of Issues to be taken up in Connection with the Consideration of the Fifth Periodic Report of the Government of Australia, CCPR/C/AUS/Q/5/Add.1, Feb. 5, 2009, para. 19.

[149]   E.g., International Law Commission, "Conclusions of the Work of the Study Group on the Fragmentation of International Law" (2006) II (Pt II) *Yearbook of the International Law Commission* 177, 178–79, as noted by the United Nations General Assembly in Resolution A/RES/61/34, Dec. 4, 2006, para. 4; *Nuclear Weapons* (above note 78), para. 25.

[150]   E.g., Commission on Human Rights, Situation of detainees at Guantánamo Bay, E. CN.4.2006.120, Feb. 27, 2006, para. 24 (accepting the principle of *lex specialis*, but denying its applicability in the circumstances concerned); *Hassan v. United Kingdom*, App. No. 29750/09, Judgment, Sept. 16, 2014, para. 104 ("accommodating," as far as possible, the power to detain in IAC with the right to liberty).

[151]   By comparison, the phrase is not mentioned at all in Ministry of Defence, *Manual of the Law of Armed Conflict*, JSP 383 (2004).

the legal value of this endorsement is overshadowed by the Manual's own disclaimer clause. According to the Manual, its pronouncements represent the legal views of DoD, but they neither preclude the Department from subsequently changing its interpretation of the law nor do they necessarily reflect the views of other departments or the US Government as a whole.[152] Such caution seems prudent. The US Government has long protested against the reliance on military manuals for the purposes of identifying rules of customary international law in lieu of assessing the actual operational practice of States on the battlefield.[153] As the Manual itself explains, "a State's military manual often recites requirements applicable to that State under treaties to which it is a Party, or provides guidance to its military forces for reasons of national policy."[154]

Adding a disclaimer clause should dampen the zeal of commentators wrongly believing the DoD Manual to be a manifestation of *opinio juris* from cover to cover. It should also save the United States from sharing the fate of the British Government, which some time ago saw its own manual being invoked against its position in litigation, at considerable cost to the taxpayer.[155] The disclaimer nevertheless deflates the Manual's momentum. It has been suggested that the Manual "cannot be assumed to reflect U.S. *opinio juris* or to generate customary international law" at all.[156] This goes too far. Evidently, certain passages of the Manual do express the *opinio juris* of the US Government, such as its continued rejection of the competence of the Inter-American Commission of Human Rights to apply the law of war.[157] Whether or not a particular passage reflects *opinio juris* must therefore be assessed on a case-by-case basis. Where does this leave the idea that the law of war constitutes the controlling body of law with regard to the conduct of hostilities and the protection of war victims? Bearing in mind that the Manual describes *lex specialis* as a general principle of law, and that the

---

[152] DoD Law of War Manual, vi and ¶ 1.1.1.

[153] J. B. Bellinger III and W. J. Haynes II, "A US Government Response to the International Committee of the Red Cross Study Customary International Humanitarian Law" (2007) 89 *International Review of the Red Cross* 443–71, 445, 446–47. See also DoD Law of War Manual, ¶ 1.8.2.2. But see Y. Dinstein, "The ICRC Customary International Humanitarian Law Study" (2006) 36 *Israel Yearbook on Human Rights* 1–15, 6.

[154] DoD Law of War Manual, ¶ 1.8.3.1.

[155] See *N. V. de Bataafsche Petroleum Maatschappij and others v. The War Damage Commission*, Apr. 13, 1956 (Singapore, Court of Appeal), (1956) 23 *International Law Reports* 810, 822 (holding that the respondents are bound to accept the British Manual of Military Law's definition of "munitions-de-guerre").

[156] See above Chapter 11; A. A. Haque, "Off Target: Selection, Precaution, and Proportionality in the DoD Manual" (2016) 92 *International Law Studies* 31–84, 83.

[157] DoD Law of War Manual, ¶ 1.2.2.1.

US Government has designated the law of war as the controlling legal regime in other fora,[158] the Manual's pronouncements on the relationship between the law of war and human rights treaties should be understood as evidence of State practice and *opinio juris*.

5 CONCLUSION

The law of war is in a state of flux. Though it is not the only factor at play, international human rights law is one of the forces driving this transformation. During the Cold War period, human rights norms and discourse have exerted a mostly benign and complementary impact on the law of war, in particular by influencing the evolution of its conventional rules.[159] However, developments in more recent decades, including the prevalence of transnational armed conflicts fought against non-State actors, the progressive expansion of the extraterritorial reach of human rights treaties and the rise in human rights litigation and scrutiny, have exposed the fundamentally different normative assumptions that underlie the law of war and human rights law.[160] In certain fields, above all in the area of status-based targeting, the longstanding convergence between the law of war and human rights law is now approaching a crunch point: further significant humanization of the law of war is not possible without radically altering the balance between humanity and military necessity. Such a development would transform the normative character of the law of war and call into question its continued ability to serve as a distinct and effective regulatory framework for the conduct of hostilities.

Whether by accident or design, the Manual takes the lead among military manuals in resisting this human rights overreach. By describing the law of war as the controlling body of law with regard to the conduct of hostilities and the protection of war victims, the Manual offers one of the most detailed and

---

[158] E.g., Submission of the Government of the United States to the Inter-American Commission on Human Rights with respect to the Draft Report on the Closure of Guantánamo, OEA/Ser. L/V/II, Doc. 30 January 2015, Mar. 30, 2015, 2, www.state.gov/documents/organization/258201 .pdf; Permanent Representative of the United States of America to the Organization of American States, Moath Al Alwi, Petition No. P-98-15, Mustafa Al Hawsawi, Petition No. P-1385-14, Joint Response to Petitions, Oct. 6, 2015, www.state.gov/documents/organization/ 258407.pdf; Observations of the United States of America on the Committee Against Torture's Draft General Comment No. 1 (2017) on Implementation of Article 3 in the Context of Article 22, Apr. 5, 2017, 2 fn. 4, www.ohchr.org/Documents/HRBodies/CAT/GC Article3/US.docx.

[159] Oberleitner (above note 17), 52–76.

[160] *Cf.* D. Luban, "Human Rights Thinking and the Laws of War," in J. D. Ohlin (ed.), *Theoretical Boundaries of Armed Conflict and Human Rights* (Cambridge University Press, 2016), 45–77.

potent official endorsements of the *lex specialis* principle. Few partner nations have so far embraced the concept in their military manuals, despite the fact that it offers the best prospect for preserving the normative integrity of the law of war in a principled, rather than ad hoc, manner. Notwithstanding the Manual's disclaimer clauses, its designation of the law of war as the controlling body of law should thus be read as evidencing *opinio juris*.

At the same time, we should not overlook the fact that *lex specialis* is not capable of mechanical application. Nor does the language of controlling bodies of law capture the multifaceted interplay between the law of war and human rights law, the true complexities of the contemporary legal operating environment, and the direct as well as indirect impact that human rights norms and expectations may have on US forces. The Manual should have acknowledged these challenges. Without such caveats, describing the law of war as the controlling body of law can all too easily turn into a convenient mantra that masks the underlying uncertainties. This could generate friction between commanders and their legal advisors, drive a wedge between the United States and its allies and create unnecessary legal risks for the force. Moreover, in the long run, there is little hope for arriving at a lasting division of labor between the law of war and international human rights law in the context of military operations unless we are prepared to ensure that the core principles of both legal regimes are preserved or at least accommodated. Simple recitation of the *lex specialis* principle cannot be the final word in this process.

A more nuanced understanding of the impact of human rights law is therefore essential. Short of converting it into a textbook on operational law, the present Manual may not be the most appropriate medium for exploring the relationship between the law of war and human rights law in all its intricate detail. After all, there is plenty of ground to cover already. However, commanders and their legal advisors must benefit from an authoritative, but more subtle, assessment of human rights law if they are to play an effective role in preserving the law of war as a viable legal framework for the conduct of warfare in the future.

Selected Literature and Original Sources

TREATIES FREQUENTLY CITED

1899 Hague Regulations: Regulations Respecting the Laws and Customs of War on Land, annexed to Convention with Respect to the Laws and Customs of War on Land, Jul. 29, 1899, 32 Stat. 1803, 1 Bevans 247

1925 Geneva Protocol: Protocol for the Prohibition of the Use in War of Asphyxiating, Poisonous, or Other Gases, and of Bacteriological Methods of Warfare, Jun. 17, 1925, 94 LNTS 65

1929 GPW: Geneva Convention Relative to the Treatment of Prisoners of War, Jul. 27, 1929, 47 Stat. 2021

AP I: Protocol (I) Additional to the Geneva Conventions of 12 August 1949, and Relating to the Protection of Victims of International Armed Conflicts, Jun. 8, 1977, 1125 UNTS 3

AP II: Protocol (II) Additional to the Geneva Conventions of 12 August 1949, and Relating to the Protection of Victims of Non-International Armed Conflicts, Jun. 8, 1977, 1125 UNTS 609

AP III: Protocol (III) Additional to the Geneva Conventions of 12 August 1949, and Relating to the Adoption of an Additional Distinctive Emblem, Dec. 8, 2005, 2404 UNTS 1

CCW: Convention on Prohibitions or Restrictions on the Use of Certain Conventional Weapons Which May be Deemed to be Excessively Injurious or to Have Indiscriminate Effects, Oct. 10, 1980, 1342 UNTS 137

CCW Protocol I: Protocol (I) on Non-Detectable Fragments, Annexed to the Convention on Prohibitions or Restrictions on the Use of Certain Conventional Weapons Which May be Deemed to be Excessively Injurious or to Have Indiscriminate Effects, Oct. 10, 1980, 1342 UNTS 137

CCW Protocol II: Protocol (II) on Prohibitions or Restrictions on the Use of Mines, Booby-Traps and Other Devices, as Amended on May 3, 1996, Annexed to the Convention on Prohibitions or Restrictions on the Use of Certain Conventional Weapons Which May be Deemed to be Excessively Injurious or to Have Indiscriminate Effects, May 3, 1996, 2048 UNTS 93

CCW Protocol III: Protocol (III) on Prohibitions or Restrictions on the Use of Incendiary Weapons, Annexed to the Convention on Prohibitions or Restrictions on the Use of Certain Conventional Weapons Which May be Deemed to be Excessively Injurious or to Have Indiscriminate Effects, Oct. 10, 1980, 1342 UNTS 137

CCW Protocol IV: Protocol (IV) on Blinding Laser Weapons, Annexed to the Convention on Prohibitions or Restrictions on the Use of Certain Conventional Weapons Which May be Deemed to be Excessively Injurious or to Have Indiscriminate Effects, Oct. 13, 1995, 1380 UNTS 163

Cultural Property Convention: Convention for the Protection of Cultural Property in the Event of Armed Conflict, 249 UNTS 240 1955

ENMOD: Convention on the Prohibition of Military or Any Other Hostile Use of Environmental Modification Techniques, Dec. 10, 1976, 1108 UNTS 151

GWS or First Geneva Convention: Geneva Convention for the Amelioration of the Condition of the Wounded and Sick in Armed Forces in the Field, Aug. 12, 1949, 6 UST 3114, 75 UNTS 31

GWS-Sea or Second Geneva Convention: Geneva Convention for the Amelioration of the Condition of the Wounded, Sick and Shipwrecked Members of Armed Forces at Sea, Aug. 12, 1949, 6 UST 3217, 75 UNTS 85

GPW or Third Geneva Convention: Geneva Convention Relative to the Treatment of Prisoners of War, Aug. 12, 1949, UST 3316, 75 UNTS 135

GC III or Fourth Geneva Convention: Geneva Convention Relative to the Protection of Civilian Persons in Time of War, Aug. 12, 1949, 6 UST 3516, 75 UNTS 287

Hague IV or Hague Regulations: Convention (IV) Respecting the Laws and Customs of War on Land, Oct. 18, 1907, 36 Stat. 2277 Hague IV Reg. Regulations Respecting the Laws and Customs of War on Land, Annex to Convention (IV) Respecting the Laws and Customs of War on Land, Oct. 18, 1907, 36 Stat. 2295

ICCPR: International Covenant on Civil and Political Rights, Dec. 16, 1966, 999 UNTS

Rome Statute or ICC Statute: Rome Statute of the International Criminal Court, UN Doc. A/CONF.183/9, 2187 UNTS 90 (July 17, 1998), *entered into force* July 1, 2002, *reprinted in* 37 ILM 999

Torture Convention: Convention against Torture and Other Cruel, Inhuman or Degrading Treatment or Punishment, 1465 UNTS, *entered into force* 26 June 1987)

VCLT: Vienna Convention on the Law of Treaties, May 23, 1969, 1155 UNTS 331

LITERATURE AND OTHER SOURCES

Abbott, K., "A Brief Overview of Legal Interoperability Challenges for NATO Arising from the Interrelationship between IHL and IHRL in Light of the European Convention on Human Rights" (2014) 96 *International Review of the Red Cross* 107.

Abella v. Argentina, Case 11.137, Inter-Am. Comm'n HR, Report No. 55/97,OEA/Ser.L/ V/II.98.

Adjutant General's Office, Instructions for the Government of Armies of the United States in the Field: Originally Issued as General Orders No. 100, 1863 (1898) (Lieber Code).

Al Bahlul v. United States, Case No. 11–1324, Brief for the United States on Petition for Review from the US Court of Military Commission Review, July 10, 2013.

Al Maqaleh v. Hagel, DC Circuit Court of Appeals, 738 F3d 312 (2013).

Aldrich, George, "The Taliban, Al Qaeda and the Determination of Illegal Combatants" (2002) 96 *American Journal of International Law*.

Al-Saadoon and Mufdhi v. United Kingdom, App. No. 61498/08 (2010) 51 EHRR 9.

Al-Saadoon and Others v. Secretary of State for Defence [2016] EWHC 773 (Admin) (High Court).

Al-Skeini and Others v. United Kingdom, App. No. 55721/07, Judgment (2011).

American Bar Association Standing Committee on Law and National Security, DoD Law of War Manual Workshop (Jan. 9, 2017).

Anonymous v. State of Israel, CrimA (TA) 6659/06 (2008).

Arai-Takahashi, Y., *The Law of Occupation: Continuity and Change of International Humanitarian Law, and Its Interaction with International Human Rights Law* (Leiden: Brill, 2009).

"Preoccupied with Occupation: Critical Examinations of the Historical Development of the Law of Occupation" (2012) 94 *International Review of the Red Cross*.

Arjona, A., N. Kasfir, and Z. Mampilly (eds.), *Rebel Governance in Civil War* (Cambridge University Press, 2015).

Armed Activities on the Territory of the Congo (Democratic Republic of the Congo v. Uganda), Judgment, International Court of Justice [2005].

Arnold, R. and N. N. R. Quénivet (eds.), *International Humanitarian Law and Human Rights Law: Towards a New Merger in International Law* (Leiden: Martinus Nijhoff, 2008).

Aughey, S. and A. Sari, "Targeting and Detention in Non-International Armed Conflict: Serdar Mohammed and the Limits of Human Rights Convergence" (2015) 91 *International Law Studies*, 60–118.

Azarova, V. and I. Blum, "Belligerency," *Max Planck Encyclopedia of International Law* 249 (Sept. 2015).

Banaszewska, D. M., "Lex Specialis," in F. Lachenmann and R. Wolfrum (eds.), *The Law of Armed Conflict and The Use of Force, The Max Planck Encyclopedia of Public International Law* (Oxford University Press, 2017).

Bangerter, O., "Reasons Why Armed Groups Choose to Respect International Humanitarian Law or Not" (2011) 93(882) *International Review of the Red Cross*.

Barone, M., "The Overlawyered War," American Enterprise Institute, Sept. 17, 2007.

Barr, W. P., Assistant Attorney General, US Department of Justice, Office of Legal Counsel, "Authority of the Federal Bureau of Investigation to Override International Law in Extraterritorial Law Enforcement Activities," Memorandum Opinion for the Attorney General, June 21, 1989.

Bartels, R., "Dealing with the Principle of Proportionality in Armed Conflict in Retrospect: The Application of the Principle in International Criminal Trials" (2013) 46 *Israel Law Review.*

Baxter, R., "Jus in Bello Interno: The Present and Future Law," in J. Moore (ed.), *Law and Civil War in the Modern World* (Baltimore: John Hopkins, 1974).

"So-called 'Unprivileged Belligerency,' Spies, Guerrillas, and Saboteurs" (1951) 28 *British Yearbook of International Law.*

"The First Modern Codification of the Law of War: Francis Lieber and General Orders No. 100" (1963) 3 *International Review of the Red Cross.*

Beit Sourak Village Council v. The Government of Israel [2004] HCJ 2056/04.

Bellal, A. (ed.), *The War Report: Armed Conflict in 2014* (Oxford University Press, 2015).

Bellinger III, J. B., "The Convention Against Torture: Extraterritorial Application and Application to Military Operations," *Lawfare* (Oct. 26, 2014).

"Obama's Announcements on International Law," *Lawfare* (Mar. 8, 2011).

Bellinger III, J. and W. J. Haynes, Letter to Dr. Jakob Kellenberger, President, International Committee of the Red Cross, Regarding Customary International Law Study (Nov. 3, 2006).

"A US Government Response to the International Committee of the Red Cross Study Customary International Humanitarian Law" (2007) 89 *International Review of the Red Cross.*

Ben-Naftali, O. (ed.), *International Humanitarian Law and International Human Rights Law* (Oxford University Press, 2011).

Benvenisti, Eyal, *The International Law of Occupation*, 2nd ed. (Oxford University Press, 2012).

"The Origins of the Concept of Belligerent Occupation" (2008) 26 *Law and History Review.*

"Water Conflicts during the Occupation of Iraq" (2003) 97 *American Journal of International Law.*

Berman, N., "Privileging Combat: Contemporary Conflict and the Legal Construction of War" (2004–5) 43 *Columbia Journal of Transnational Law.*

Best, G., *War and Law Since 1945* (Oxford: Clarendon Press, 1994).

Blank, L. R., "Extending Positive Identification from Persons to Places: Terrorism, Armed Conflict, and the Identification of Military Objectives" (2013) *Utah Law Review.*

Bolgiano, D. G. and J. Taylor, *"Can't Kill Enough to Win? Think Again"* (Dec. 2017) 144 *Proceedings.*

Boon, K., "Obligations of the New Occupier: The Contours of *Jus Post Bellum*" (2008) 31 *Loyola LA International and Comparative Law Review.*

Boothby, W. H., *The Law of Targeting* (Oxford University Press, 2012).

Bothe, M., K. J. Partsch, and W. Solf, *New Rules for Victims of Armed Conflicts: Commentary on the Two Protocols Additional to the Geneva Conventions of 1949* (Leiden/Boston: Martinus Nijhoff, 1982).

Boumediene v. Bush, 553 US 723 (2008).

Brown, G. D., "Spying and Fighting in Cyberspace," *Journal of Law and National Security Policy* (Mar. 29, 2016).

Brown, G. D. and A. O. Metcalf, "Easier Said than Done: Legal Reviews of Cyber Weapons," *Journal of National Security Law and Policy* (Feb. 12, 2014).

Callwell, C. E., *Small Wars: Their Principles and Practice*, 3rd ed. (London: HMSO, 1906).

Cameron, L., et al., "Common Article 3: Conflicts not of an International Character," in ICRC, Commentary on the First Geneva Convention (I) for the Amelioration of the Condition of the Wounded and Sick in Armed Forces in the Field, 2nd ed. (Cambridge University Press, 2016).

"The Updated Commentary on the First Geneva Convention: A New Tool for Generating Respect for International Humanitarian Law" (2015) 97 *International Review of the Red Cross*.

Canestaro, N. A. "Legal and Policy Constraints on the Conduct of Aerial Precision Warfare" (2004) 37 *Vanderbilt Journal of Transnational Law*.

Cassesse, A., "The Status of Rebels under the 1977 Geneva Protocol on Non-International Armed Conflicts" (1981) 30 *International and Comparative Law Quarterly*.

Center for Law & Military Operations, The Judge Advocate General's Legal Center & School, US Army, "Legal Lessons Learned from Afghanistan and Iraq, Vol. I Major Combat Operations 11 Sept. 2001–1 May 2003" (Aug. 1, 2004), 54.

Center for Naval Warfare Studies, Oceans Law and Policy Department, *Annotated Supplement to the Commander's Handbook on the Law of Naval Operations* (Newport: US Naval War College, 1997).

Chang, K., "Remarks on U.S. and International Perspectives on the New U.S. Department of Defense Law of War Manual" (2016) 110 *Proceedings of the American Society of International Law Annual Meeting* 115.

Chesney, R., "Hays Parks on the Demise of the DOD Law of War Manual," *Lawfare* (Dec. 8, 2012).

Cilliers, J., *Counter-Insurgency in Rhodesia* (London, Sydney, Dover, New Hampshire: Croom Helm, 1985).

Clapham, A., "Detention by Armed Groups under International Law" (2017) 93 *International Law Studies*.

Clapham, A., P. Gaeta, and M. Sassòli (eds.), *The 1949 Geneva Conventions: A Commentary* (Oxford University Press, 2015).

Clausewitz, C. von, *On War*, ed. and trans. M. Howard and P. Paret (Princeton University Press, 1976), I.

Cline, L., *Pseudo Operations and Counterinsurgency: Lessons from Other Countries* (Pennsylvania: Strategic Studies Institute, 2005).

Coalition Provisional Authority Regulation No. 1, §1(1) (May 16, 2003).

Coard et al. v. United States, Case 10.951, Report No. 109/99, Sept. 29, 1999.

Colby, E., "Occupation *under the Laws of War*" (1925) 25 *Columbia Law Review*.

Coleman v. Tennessee, 97 US 509, 517 (1878).

Colleanu v. German State, Jan. 12, 1929 (Germano-Rumanian Mixed Arbitral Tribunal) (1929) 5 International Law Reports.

Cooper, J. M. and J. F. Procope (eds.), *Seneca: Moral and Political Essays* (Cambridge University Press, 1995).

Corn, G. P., "Should the Best Offense Ever Be a Good Defense? The Public Authority to Use Force in Military Operations: Recalibrating the Use of Force Rules in the Standing Rules of Engagement" (2016) 49 *Vanderbilt Journal of Transnational Law*.

Corn, G. S., "Belligerent Targeting and the Invalidity of a Least Harmful Means Rule" (2013) 89 International Legal Studies.

"Hamdan, Lebanon, and the Regulation of Armed Conflict: The Need to Recognize a Hybrid Category of Armed Conflict" (2007) 40 Vanderbilt Journal of Transnational Law.

"Legal Classification of Military Operations," in G. S. Corn, R. E. van Landingham, and S. R. Reeves (eds.), U.S. Military Operations: Law, Policy, and Practice (Oxford University Press, 2016).

"Mixing Apples and Hand Grenades: The Logical Limit of Applying Human Rights Norms to Armed Conflict" (2010) 1 International Humanitarian Legal Studies.

"Self-Defense Targeting: Blurring the Line between the Jus ad Bellum and the Jus in Bello" (2012) 88 International Law Studies.

"War, Law, and the Oft Overlooked Value of Process as a Precautionary Measure" (2015) 42 Pepperdine Law Review.

Corn, G. S., and J. A. Schoettler, Jr., "Targeting and Civilian Risk Mitigation: The Essential Role of Precautionary Measures" (2015) 223 Military Law Review.

Corn, G. S., R. E. van Landingham and S. R. Reeves (eds.), U.S. Military Operations: Law, Policy, and Practice (Oxford University Press, 2015).

Corn, G. S., J. A. Schoettler, D. Brenner-Beck, V. M. Hansen, R. Jackson, E. T. Jensen, and M. W. Lewis, The War on Terror and the Laws of War: A Military Perspective, 2nd edn (New York: Oxford University Press, 2015).

Crawford, E., "The Principle of Distinction and Remote Warfare," in J. D. Ohlin (ed.), Research Handbook on Remote Warfare (Cheltenham: Edward Elgar, 2017).

Clausewitz, C. von, On War, ed. and trans. M. Howard and P. Paret (Princeton University Press, 1976), I.

Cullen, A., The Concept of Non-International Armed Conflict in International Humanitarian Law (Cambridge University Press, 2010).

Cummins, S. J. and D. P. Stewart (eds.), Digest of United States Practice in International Law 2000.

Danish Ministry of Defence, "Militærmanual om Folkeret for Danske Væbnede Styrker i Internationale Militære Operationer" (2016).

Daskal, J. C., "The Geography of the Battlefield: A Framework for Detention and Targeting outside the Hot Conflict Zone" (2013) 161 University of Pennsylvania Law Review.

Davis, G. B., "Doctor Francis Lieber's Instructions for the Government of Armies in the Field" (1907) 1 American Journal of International Law.

Davis, P. K. and K. Cragin (eds.), Social Science for Counterterrorism: Putting the Pieces Together (Santa Monica: RAND, 2009).

Debuf, E., Captured in War: Lawful Internment in Armed Conflict (Paris: Pedone, 2013).

Deeks, A. S., "'Unwilling or Unable': Toward a Normative Framework for Extraterritorial Self-Defense" (2012) 52 Virginia Journal of International Law.

Democratic Republic of the Congo v. Uganda, Armed Activities on the Territory of the Congo (Judgment) (2005).

Department of the Air Force, AFP 110–31, "International Law— The Conduct of Armed Conflict and Air Operations" (1976).

Department of the Army Field Manual 27–10, Rules of Land Warfare (Oct. 1, 1940).

Department of the Army Field Manual 27–10, *The Law of Land Warfare* (Jul. 18, 1956 with *Change* 1, Jul. 15, 1976).

Department of Defense, Directive 2311.01E, DoD Law of War Program (2006).

Department of Defense, Directive 5100.77, DoD Law of War Program (1998).

Department of Defense, Military Commission Instruction No. 2 (Apr. 30, 2003).

Department of Defense, Office of the General Counsel, "An Assessment of International Legal Issues in Information Operations," 2nd ed. (Nov. 1999).

Dill, J., "The 21st-Century Belligerent's Trilemma" (2015) 26 *European Journal of International Law.*

Dinstein, Y., "Concluding Remarks on Non-International Armed Conflicts," in K. Watkin and A. J. Norris (eds.), *Non-International Conflict in the Twenty-First Century,* International Law Studies 88 (Newport: US Naval War College, 2012).

"Discussion: Reasonable Military Commanders and Reasonable Civilians," in Andru E. Wall (ed.), *Legal and Ethical Lessons of NATO's Kosovo Campaign,* International Law Studies 78 (Newport, RI: Naval War College, 2002).

Non-International Armed Conflicts in International Law (Cambridge University Press, 2014).

The Conduct of Hostilities under the Law of International Armed Conflict 2nd ed. (Cambridge University Press, 2010).

"The ICRC Customary International Humanitarian Law Study" (2006) *Israel Yearbook on Human Rights.*

The International Law of Belligerent Occupation (Cambridge University Press, 2009).

Dobbins, J., et. al., "Occupying Iraq: A History of the Coalition Provisional Authority," www.rand.org/content/dam/rand/pubs/monographs/2009/RAND_MG847.pdf.

Dörmann, K., *Elements of War Crimes Under the Rome Statute of the International Criminal Court* (Cambridge University Press, 2003).

"The Legal Situation of 'Unlawful/Unprivileged Combatants'" (2003) 85 *International Review of the Red Cross.*

Doswald-Beck, L. and S. Vité, "International Humanitarian Law and Human Rights Law" (1993) 293 *International Review of the Red Cross.*

Doty, G. R., "The United States and the Development of the Laws of Land Warfare" (1998) 156 *Military Law Review.*

Droege, C., "Get Off My Cloud: Cyber Warfare, International Humanitarian Law, and the Protection of Civilians" (2012) 94 *International Review of the Red Cross.*

Dunlap, C. J., "Getting the Law Right on Carpet Bombing and Civilian Casualties," *War on the Rocks* (Mar. 16, 2016).

"How the New York Times Misconstrues the Law on Civilian Casualties," *Lawfire* (Oct. 13, 2017).

"Lawfare 101: A Primer," *Military Review* (May–June 2017).

"The Moral Hazard of Inaction in War," *War on the Rocks* (Aug. 19, 2016).

"Understanding War-Sustaining Targeting: A Rejoinder to Iulia Padeanu," *Yale Journal of International Law* (Apr. 6, 2017).

Elbridge, C., "How to Fight Savage Tribes" (1927) 21 *American Journal of International Law.*

Estreicher, S., "Privileging Asymmetric Warfare? Defender Duties under International Humanitarian Law" (2011) 11 *Chicago Journal of International Law*.

Ex parte Quirin, 317 US 1, 27–46 (1942).

Farrell, B. R., *Habeas Corpus in International Law* (Cambridge University Press, 2017).

Ferraro, T., "Determining the Beginning and End of an Occupation under International Humanitarian Law" (2012) 94 *International Review of the Red Cross*.

Fleck, D., "Development of New Rules or Application of More than One Legal Regime?," in C. Harvey et al. (eds.), *Contemporary Challenges to the Laws of War: Essays in Honour of Professor Peter Rowe* (Cambridge University Press, 2014).

Fleck, D. and T. D. Gill (eds.), *The Handbook of the International Law of Military Operations*, 2nd ed. (Oxford University Press, 2015).

Fleiner-Gerster, T. and M. Meyer, "New Developments in Humanitarian Law: A Challenge to the Concept of Sovereignty" (1985) 34 *International and Comparative Law Quarterly*.

Fortin, K., *The Accountability of Armed Groups under Human Rights Law* (Oxford University Press, 2017).

"Forum on 'Direct Participation in Hostilities'" (Spring 2010) 42 *New York University Journal of International Law and Politics*.

Fox, G. H., "The Occupation of Iraq" (2004) 36 *Georgetown Journal of International Law*.

"Transformative Occupation and the Unilateralist Impulse – ICRC" (2012) 94 *International Review of the Red Cross*.

France et. al. v. Goering et. al., 22 IMT 411, 466 (IMT, 1946).

French, D., "Nasty Not Nice: British Counter-Insurgency Doctrine and Practice: 1945–1967" (2012) 23(4–5) *Small Wars & Insurgencies*.

French Ministry of Defence, "Manuel de Droit des Conflits Armés – Edition 2012" (2012).

Gallis, P. E., "Kosovo: Lessons Learned from Operation *Allied Force*," Congressional Research Services Report for US Congress (Nov. 19, 1999).

Gardam, J. G., "Proportionality and Force in International Law" (1993) 87 *American Journal of International Law*.

Garraway, C., "Combatants: Substance or Semantics?," in M. Schmitt and J. Pejic (eds.), *International Law and Armed Conflict: Exploring the Faultlines, Essays in Honour of Yoram Dinstein* (Leiden: Martinus Nijhoff, 2007).

"The Law Applies, But Which Law? A Consumer Guide to the Law of War," in M. Evangelista and H. Shue (eds.), *The American Way of Bombing: Changing Ethical and Legal Norms, From Flying Fortresses to Drones* (Ithaca: Cornell University Press, 2014).

"The Use and Abuse of Military Manuals" (2004) 7 *Yearbook of International Humanitarian Law*.

"War and Peace: Where Is the Divide?" (2012) 88 *International Law Studies*.

Gatchel, T., "Pseudo-Operations – A Double-Edged Sword of Counterinsurgency," in J. Norwitz (ed.), *Armed Groups: Studies in National Security, Counterterrorism and Counterinsurgency* (Newport: US Naval War College, 2008).

General Order No. 100, Instructions for the Government of Armies of the United States in the Field (Apr. 24, 1863), *reprinted in The War of the Rebellion: A Compilation of the Official Records of the Union and Confederate Armies* (Lieber Code), Series III, vol. 3 (GPO, 1899).

Georgia v. Russia, App. No. 38263/08, Judgment, Dec. 13, 2011.

German Federal Ministry of Defence, "Law of Armed Conflict – Manual" (2013).

Giladi, R., "A Different Sense of Humanity: Occupation in Francis Lieber's Code" (2012) 94 *International Review of the Red Cross*.

Gill, T., "Chivalry: A Principle of the Law of Armed Conflict?," in M. Matthee, B. Toebes, and M. Brus (eds.), *Armed Conflict and International Law: In Search of the Human Face* (The Hague: TMC Asser Press, 2013).

Glahn, G. von, *The Occupation of Enemy Territory: A Commentary on the Law and Practice of Belligerent Occupation* (University of Minnesota Press, 1957).

Glazier, D., "A Critical Assessment of the New Department of Defense Law of War Manual" (2017) 42 *Yale Journal of International Law*.

Goodman, R., "Authorization versus Regulation of Detention in Non-International Armed Conflicts" (2015) 91 *International Law Studies*.

"Targeting 'War-Sustaining' Objects in Non-International Armed Conflicts" (2016) 110 *American Journal of International Law*.

Grant, J. P. and J. C. Barker, "Co-belligerent(s)," in *Parry and Grant Encyclopaedic Dictionary of International Law* (Oxford University Press, 2009).

Greenberg, K. J. and J. L. Dratel (eds.), *The Torture Papers: The Road to Abu Ghraib* (Cambridge University Press, 2005).

Greenberg, L. M., *The Hukbalahap Insurrection: A Case Study of a Successful Anti-Insurgency Operation in the Philippines: 1946–1955* (Washington, DC: US. Army Centre of Military History, 2005).

Greenwood, C., "Self-Defence and the Conduct of International Armed Conflict," in Y. Dinstein and M. Tabory (eds.), *International Law at a Time of Perplexity: Essays in Honour of Shabtai Rosenne* (Dordrecht: Nijhoff, 1988).

Greer, M. J., "Redefining Perfidy" (2015) 47 *Georgetown Journal of International Law*.

Grotius, H., *De Jure Belli ac Pacis* (1625), III.

Guichaoua, Y., *Understanding Collective Political Violence* (Basingstoke: Palgrave Macmillan, 2011).

Gurulé, J. and G. S. Corn, *Principles of Counter-Terrorism Law* (St. Paul: West Academic Publishing, 2011).

Gwynn, C. W., *Imperial Policing*, 2nd ed. (London: Macmillan, 1939).

Haer, R., *Armed Group Structure and Violence in Civil Wars: The Organisational Dynamics of Civilian Killing* (Oxford: Routledge, 2015).

Haque, A. A., *Law and Morality at War* (Oxford University Press, 2017).

"Off Target: Selection, Precaution, and Proportionality in the DoD Manual" (2016) 92 *International Law Studies*.

Halleck, H. W., *International Law or Rules Regulating the Intercourse of States in Peace and War* (New York: Van Nostrand, 1861).

Hamdan v. Rumsfeld, 126 S. Ct. 2749 (2006).

Hamdi v. Rumsfeld, 542 US 507 (2004).

Hannaman, F., Chief Legal Advice Division, Memorandum to Office of Economic Affairs – Finance Division on Revenues from Laender-Owned Property (Mar. 30, 1951), repr. in XX Selected Opinions January 1, 1951–April 30, 1951 of Office of the United States High Commissioner for Germany, Office of General Counsel, Frankfurt, Germany.

Harvard Law School Program on International Law and Armed Conflict, and Stockton Center for the Study of International Law at US Naval War College, "The Future of U.S. Detention under International Law: Workshop Report" (2017) 93 *International Law Studies.*

Hassan v. United Kingdom, App. No. 29750/09, Judgment, Sept. 16, 2014.

Hathaway, O. A., et al., "Which Law Governs during Armed Conflict? The Relationship Between International Humanitarian Law and Human Rights Law" (2011–2012) 96 *Minnesota Law Review.*

Hayashi, N., "Introduction," in N. Hayashi (ed.), *National Military Manuals on the Law of Armed Conflict*, 2nd ed. (Oslo: Torkel Opsahl, 2010).

"Requirements of Military Necessity in International Humanitarian Law and International Criminal Law" (2010) 28 *Boston University International Law Journal.*

Head Money Cases, 112 US 580, 598 (1884).

Henckaerts, J.-M. and L. Doswald-Beck (eds.), *Customary International Humanitarian Law*, 2 vols. (Cambridge University Press, 2005).

Henkin, L., "The President and International Law" (1986) *American Journal of International Law.*

Herr, T. and P. Rosenzweig, "Cyber Weapons and Export Control: Incorporating Dual Use with the PrEP Model," *Journal of Law and National Security Policy* (2016).

Hill, S., "The Role of NATO's Legal Adviser," in A. Zidar and J. P. Gauci (eds.), *The Role of Legal Advisers in International Law* (Leiden: Brill; Boston: Nijhoff, 2016).

Hill-Cawthorne, L., *Detention in Non-International Armed Conflict* (Oxford University Press, 2016).

Hodgkinson, S. L., "Detention Operations: A Strategic View," in G. Corn, R. E. van Landingham, and S. R. Reeves (eds.), *U.S. Military Operations: Law, Policy & Practice* (Oxford University Press, 2015).

Hoffman, M. H., "Can Military Manuals Improve the Law of War? The San Remo Manual on the Law of Non-International Armed Conflict Considered in Relation to Historical and Contemporary Trends" (2007) 37 *Israel Yearbook on Human Rights.*

HPCR Manual on the International Law Applicable to Air and Missile Warfare, 2010.

Hughes, G., "Intelligence-Gathering, Special Operations and Air Strikes in Modern Counter-Insurgency," in P. Rich and I. Duyvesteyn (eds.), *The Routledge Handbook of Insurgency and Counterinsurgency* (London & New York: Routledge, 2012).

Hughes G. and T. Christian, "Anatomy of a Surrogate: Historical Precedents and Implications for Contemporary Counter-Insurgency and Counter-Terrorism" (2009) 20(1) *Small Wars & Insurgencies.*

Human Rights Watch, *Needless Deaths in the Gulf War: Civilian Casualties during the Air Campaign and Violations of the Laws of War* (New York: HRW, 1991).

Hutchinson, D. J., "'The Achilles Heel' of the Constitution: Justice Jackson and the Japanese Exclusion Cases" (2002) *Supreme Court Review.*

International Code of Conduct for Information Security (Jan. 9, 2015).

International Committee of the Red Cross (ICRC), "A Study on the Roots of Restraint in War" (2017).

Commentary on the Additional Protocols of 8 June 1977 to the Geneva Conventions of 12 August 1949 (Geneva: ICRC, Martinus Nijhoff, 1987).

Commentary on the Geneva Convention (I) on Wounded and Sick in Armed Forces in the Field (Cambridge University Press, 2016).

Customary International Humanitarian Law Study (Oct. 29, 2010).

"Interpretive Guidance on the Notion of Direct Participation in Hostilities under International Humanitarian Law" (2009) 90 *International Review of the Red Cross.*

International Criminal Tribunal for the former Yugoslavia, "Final Report to the Prosecutor by the Committee Established to Review the NATO Bombing Campaign Against the Federal Republic of Yugoslavia" (1999).

International Institute of Humanitarian Law, *The Manual on the Law of Non-International Armed Conflict with Commentary* (San Remo: IIHL, 2006).

International Law Commission, "Conclusions of the Work of the Study Group on the Fragmentation of International Law" (2006) II (Pt II) Yearbook of the International Law Commission.

Irons, P., *Justice at War* (New York: Oxford University Press, 1983).

Isayeva v. Russia, App. No. 57950/00, Judgment (2005) 41 EHRR 38.

Jackson, R., "Perfidy in Non-International Armed Conflicts" (2012) 88 *International Law Studies.*

Jackson, R. H., "Wartime Security and Liberty Under Law" (1951) 1 *Buffalo Law Review* 103, 116.

Jaloud v. The Netherlands, App. No. 47708/08, Judgment, 20 November 2014.

Jensen, E. T., "Precautions against the Effects of Attacks in Urban Areas" (2016) 98(1) *International Review of the Red Cross.*

"The Future of the Law of Armed Conflict: Ostriches, Butterflies, and Nanobots" (2015) 35 *Michigan Journal of International Law.*

Johnson v. Eisentrager, 339 US 763, 789 n. 14 (1950).

Joint Chiefs of Staff, Joint Pub. 1–04, *Legal Support to Military Operations* (Aug. 2, 2016).

Joint Pub. 3–0, *Joint Operations* (Aug. 11, 2011).

Juan Carlos Abella v. Argentina, Case No. 11.137, Report No. 55/97, Nov. 18, 1997.

Kaeuper, R., *Medieval Chivalry* (Cambridge University Press, 2016).

Kahneman, D., *Thinking, Fast and Slow* (New York: Farrar, Straus, and Giroux, 2011).

Kaikobad, K. H., "Problems of Belligerent Occupation: The Scope of Powers Exercised by the Coalition Provisional Authority in Iraq, April/May 2003–June 2004 Current Developments: Public International Law: Part I" (2005) 54 *International & Comparative Law Quarterly.*

Kalshoven, F., "The Respective Roles of Custom and Principle in the International Law of Armed Conflict and the Law of Armed Conflict" (2006) 2 *Acta Societatis Martensis.*

Kittrie, O. F., *Lawfare: Law as a Weapon of War* 1 (New York: Oxford University Press, 2016).

Kleffner, J., "The Applicability of International Humanitarian Law to Organised Armed Groups" (2011) 882 *International Review of the Red Cross.*

Kolb, R., "Etude sur l'occupation et sur l'Article 47 de la IVème Convention de Genève du 12 Août 1949 relative à la protection des personnes civiles en temps de guerre: le degree d'intangibilité des droits en territoire occupé" (2002) 10 *African Yearbook of International Law*.

Kolb, R. and G. Gaggioli (eds.), *Research Handbook on Human Rights and Humanitarian Law* (Cheltenham: Edward Elgar, 2013).

Kolb, R. and S. Vité, *Le Droit de l'occupation militaire: perspectives historiques et enjeux juridiques actuels* (Brussels: Bruylant, 2009).

Kononov v. Latvia, App. No. 36376/04, Judgment (2010).

Korematsu v. United States, 584 F. Supp. 1406, 1416–19 (ND Ca. 1984).

Kretzmer, D., "The Law of Belligerent Occupation in the Supreme Court of Israel" (2012) 94 *International Review of the Red Cross*.

Krofan v. Public Prosecutor (1966) (Sing.), reprinted in 1 *Malayan Law Journal* 133 (1967); 52 ILR 497 (1979).

Kuhn, M. and A. C. Berger, "Legal Advisers in the Armed Forces," in A. Zidar and J.P. Gauci (eds.), *The Role of Legal Advisers in International Law* (Leiden: Brill, 2016).

Kunduz Case, Judgment, Oct. 6, 2016 (Federal Court of Justice, Germany).

Landais, C. and L. Bass, "Reconciling the Rules of International Humanitarian Law with the Rules of European Human Rights Law " (2015) 97 *International Review of the Red Cross*.

Lauterpacht, H., *The Function of Law in the International Community* (Oxford: Clarendon Press, 1933).

  Recognition in International Law (Cambridge University Press, 1947).

Legal Consequences of the Construction of a Wall in the Occupied Palestinian Territory, *Advisory Opinion*, International Court of Justice [2004].

Legality of the Threat or Use of Nuclear Weapons, *Advisory Opinion*, International Court of Justice, 1996 ICJ 226.

Lewis, M. W., "The Law of Aerial Bombardment in the 1991 Gulf War" (2003) 97 *American Journal of International Law*.

Lietzau, W. K., "U.S. Detention of Terrorists in the 21st Century," in G. Rose and B. Oswald (eds.), *Detention of Non-State Actors Engaged in Hostilities* (Leiden: Brill, 2016).

Liivoja, R., "Chivalry without a Horse: Military Honor and the Modern Law of Armed Conflict" (2012) 15 *ENDC Proceedings*.

Lilienfeld, S. O., R. Ammirati, and K. Landfield, "Giving Debiasing Away: Can Psychological Research on Correcting Cognitive Errors Promote Human Welfare?" (2009) 4 *Perspectives on Psychological Science*.

Lin, P., "Could Human Enhancement Turn Soldiers into Weapons that Violate International Law? Yes," *The Atlantic* (Jan. 4, 2013).

Lindroos, A., "Addressing Norm Conflicts in a Fragmented Legal System: The Doctrine of *Lex Specialis*" (2005) 74 *Nordic Journal of International Law*.

Lippold, M., "Between Humanization and Humanitarization? Detention in Armed Conflicts and the European Convention on Human Rights" (2016) 76 *Heidelberg Journal of International Law*.

Luban, D., "Human Rights Thinking and the Laws of War," in J. D. Ohlin (ed.), *Theoretical Boundaries of Armed Conflict and Human Rights* (Cambridge University Press, 2016).

McChrystal, S., COMISAF Tactical Directive, July 6, 2009.

McElhinney v. Ireland, App. No. 31253/96, Judgment (2002).

MacLeod v. United States, 229 US 416, 425 (1913).

McMaster, Brigadier General H. R., "Remaining True to Our Values – Reflecting on Military Ethics in Trying Times" (2010) 9(3) *Journal of Military Ethics*.

McNair, A. D., "Municipal *Effects of Belligerent Occupation*" (1941) 57 *Law Quarterly Review*.

McNeal, G. S., "Targeted Killing and Accountability" (2014) 102 *Georgetown Law Journal*.

Madsen v. Kinsella, 343 US 341 (1952).

Maqaleh v. Hagel, 605 F.3d 84 (DC Cir. 2010).

Margulies, P., "Making Autonomous Weapons Accountable: Command Responsibility for Computer-Guided Lethal Force in Armed Conflicts," in J. D. Ohlin (ed.), *Handbook on Remote Warfare* (Northampton: Edward Elgar, 2017).

Marko, M. and H. V. Vidan, "A Taxonomy of Armed Conflict," in N. White and C. Henderson (eds.), *Research Handbook on International Conflict and Security Law: Jus ad Bellum, Jus in Bello and Jus post Bellum* (Cheltenham: Edward Elgar, 2013).

Martin, C., "The Means–Methods Paradox and the Legality of Drone Strikes in Armed Conflict" (2015) 19 *International Journal of Human Rights*.

Martinovic, M. A., *The Challenges of Asymmetric Warfare. Enhancing Compliance with International Humanitarian Law by Organized Armed Groups* (Hamburg: Anchor Academic Publishing, 2016).

Matheson, M. J., "The United States position on the Relation of Customary International Law to the 1977 Protocols Additional to the 1949 Geneva Conventions" (1987) 2 *American University Journal of International Law and Public Policy*.

Melander, E., "Organized Violence in the World 2015: An Assessment by the Uppsala Conflict Data Program," UCDP Paper 9 (2015).

Melzer, N., *International Humanitarian Law: A Comprehensive Introduction* (Geneva: ICRC, 2016).

Interpretative Guidance on the Notion of Direct Participation in Hostilities under International Humanitarian Law (Geneva: ICRC, 2009).

Targeted Killing in International Law (London: Oxford University Press, 2008).

"Targeted Killing or Less Harmful Means? – Israel's High Court Judgment on Targeted Killing and the Restricive Function of Military Necessity" (2006) 9 *Yearbook of International Humanitarian Law*.

Meron, T., *Bloody Constraint: War and Chivalry in Shakespeare* (New York: Oxford University Press, 1998).

Merriam, J. J., "Affirmative Target Identification: Operationalizing the Principle of Distinction for U.S. Warfighters" (2016) 56 *Virginia Journal of International Law*.

Meyer, J. M., "Tearing Down the Facade: A Critical Look at the Current Law on Targeting the Will of the Enemy and Air Force Doctrine" (2001) 51 *The Air Force Law Review*.

Meyer, M. and H. McCoubrey (eds.), *Reflections on Law and Armed Conflicts: Selected Works on the Laws of War by the late Professor Colonel G. I. A. D. Draper* (The Hague: Kluwer, 1998).

Milanovic, M., "The Lost Origins of *Lex Specialis*: Rethinking the Relationship between Human Rights and International Humanitarian Law," in J. D. Ohlin (ed.) *Theoretical Boundaries of Armed Conflict and Human Rights* (Cambridge University Press, 2016).

"Norm Conflict in International Law: Whither Human Rights?" (2009) *Duke Journal of Comparative and International Law*.

Military Prosecutor v. Omar Mahmud Kassem and Others, Apr. 13, 1969 (Israel, Military Court sitting in Ramallah) (1971).

Modirzadeh, N. K., "Folk International Law: 9/11 Lawyering and the Transformation of the Law of Armed Conflict to Human Rights Policy and Human Rights Law to War" (2014) 5 *Harvard National Security Journal*.

Moir, L., "The Historical Development of the Application of Humanitarian Law in Non-International Armed Conflicts to 1949" (1998) 47 *International and Comparative Law Quarterly*.

The Law of Internal Armed Conflict (Cambridge University Press, 2002).

Moore, J. N., *Law and Civil War in the Modern World* (Baltimore: Johns Hopkins University Press, 1974).

Munaf v. Geren, 553 US 674 (2008).

Murray, D., "How International Humanitarian Law Treaties Bind Non-State Armed Groups" (2014) 20(1) *Journal of Conflict and Security Law*.

Human Rights Obligations of Non-State Armed Groups (Oxford and Portland, OR: Bloomsbury, 2016).

Murray, W. and P. R. Mansoor (eds.), *Hybrid Warfare: Fighting Complex Opponents from the Ancient World to the Present* (New York: Cambridge University Press, 2012).

Newton, Michael A., "Contorting Common Article 3: Reflections on the Revised ICRC Commentary" (2018) 45 *Georgia Journal of International and Comparative Law*.

"Exceptional Engagement: Protocol I and a World United Against Terror" (2009) 4 *Texas International Law Journal*.

"How the International Criminal Court Threatens Treaty Norms" (2016) 49 *Vanderbilt Journal of Transnational Law*.

"Humanitarian Protection in Future Wars" (2004) 8 *International Peacekeeping: The Yearbook of International Peace Operations*.

"Modern Military Necessity: The Role & Relevance of Military Lawyers" (2007) 12 *Roger Williams University Law Review*.

"The International Criminal Court Preparatory Commission: The Way It Is & the Way Ahead" (2000) 41 *Virginia Journal of International Law*.

"The Iraqi High Criminal Court: Controversy and Contributions" (2006) 88 *International Review of the Red Cross*.

"The Quest for Constructive Complementarity," in C. Stahn and M. El Zeidy (eds.), *The ICC and Complementarity: From Theory to Practice* (Cambridge University Press, 2011).

Newton, M. A. and L. May, *Proportionality in International Law* (Oxford University Press, 2014).

Nissenbaum, D., "In Former Taliban Sanctuary, an Eerie Silence Takes Over," *Wall Street Journal* (Jan. 26–27, 2013).

Nuhanović v. The Netherlands, Judgment, 200.020.174/01, July 5, 2011 (Court of Appeal in The Hague).

N.V. de Bataafsche Petroleum Maatschappij and Others v. The War Damage Commission, Apr. 13, 1956 (Singapore, Court of Appeal) (1956) 23 International Law Reports.

Oberleitner, G., *Human Rights in Armed Conflict: Law, Practice, Policy* (Cambridge University Press, 2015).

Odello, M. and R. W. Piotrowicz, "Legal Regimes Governing International Military Missions," in M. Odello and R. W. Piotrowicz (eds.), *International Military Missions and International Law* (Leiden: Martinus Nijhoff, 2011).

Office of General Counsel, US Department of Defense, Department of Defense Law of War Manual, 1st ed. (June 12, 2015).

Office of General Counsel, US Department of Defense, Department of Defense Law of War Manual, 2nd ed. (May 31, 2016).

Office of General Counsel, US Department of Defense, Department of Defense Law of War Manual, 3rd ed. (Dec. 13, 2016).

O'Keefe, R., "Response: '*Quid*,' Not '*Quantum*': A Comment on 'How the International Court Threatens Treaty Norms'" (2016) 49 *Vanderbilt Journal of Transnational Law*.

Olson, L. M. "Practical Challenges of Implementing the Complementarity between International Humanitarian and Human Rights Law – Demonstrated by the Procedural Regulation of Internment in Non-International Armed Conflict" (2009) 40 *Case Western Reserve Journal of International Law*.

Operation Inherent Resolve, Remarks by General Townsend in a media availability in Baghdad, Iraq (July 11, 2017).

Oppenheim, L., *International Law: A Treatise*, II: *War and Neutrality*, 1st ed. (London: Longmans Green and Co., 1906).

Orakhelashvili, A., "The Interaction between Human Rights and Humanitarian Law: Fragmentation, Conflict, Parallelism, or Convergence?" (2008) 19 *European Journal of International Law*.

Oswald, B. and T. Winkler, "Guidelines on the Handling of Detainees in International Military Operations," *American Society of International Law Insights* (Dec. 26, 2012).

Paquete Habana, The, 175 US 677 (1900).

Parks, W. Hays, "Air *War and the Law of War*" (1990) 32 *Air Force Law Review*.

  "Asymmetries and the Identification of Legitimate Military Objectives," in W. Heintschel von Heinegg and V. Epping (eds.), *International Humanitarian Law Facing New Challenges* (New York: Springer, 2007).

  "National Security Law in Practice: The Department of Defense Law of War Manual," Remarks delivered to the American Bar Association's Standing Committee on Law and National Security (Nov. 18, 2010).

  "Special Forces' Wear of Non-Standard Uniforms" (2003) 4 *Chicago Journal of International Law*.

  "Update on the DOD Law of War Manual," Remarks delivered to the American Bar Association's Standing Committee on Law and National Security (Dec. 2012).

Parks, W. Hays and E. Williamson, "Some Questions for State and DoD Legal Adviser Nominees," *Weekly Standard* (Jul. 22, 2013).

Partington, E. A. "Manuals on the Law of Armed Conflict," in F. Lachenmann and R. Wolfrum (eds.), *The Law of Armed Conflict and the Use of Force, The Max Planck Encyclopedia of Public International Law* (Oxford University Press, 2017).

Paulsen, M. S., "The Constitutional Power to Interpret International Law" (2009) 118 *Yale Law Journal* 1762.

Paulus, A. and M. Vashakmadze, "Asymmetric War and the Notion of Armed Conflict – A Tentative Conceptualization" (Mar. 2009) 91 *International Review of the Red Cross*.

Paust, J. J., "Errors and Misconceptions in the 2015 DOD Law of War Manual" (2017) 26 *Minnesota Journal of International Law* 303.

Peers, Lt. Gen. W. R., *The My Lai Inquiry* (New York: Norton, 1979).

Pictet, J. S., *Commentary IV Geneva Convention Relative to the Protection of Civilian Persons in Time of War* (Geneva: ICRC, 1958).

Development and Principles of International Humanitarian Law (Dordrecht: Martinus Nijhoff, 1985).

The Geneva Conventions of 1949: Commentary, 4 vols. (Geneva: ICRC, 1952).

Prize Cases, 67 US 635, 671 (1862).

Provost, R., *International Human Rights and Humanitarian Law* (Cambridge University Press, 2002).

Prosecutor v. Akayesu, Case No. ICTR-96–4, Judgment, ¶ 593 (ICTR Trial Chamber, Sept. 2, 1998).

Prosecutor v. Ahmad Al Faqi Al Mahdi, Case No. ICC-01/12–01/15, Judgment and Sentence (Sept. 27, 2016).

Prosecutor v. Blagojević and Jokic, Case No. IT-02–60-T, Trial Judgment (ICTY, Jan. 17, 2005).

Prosecutor v. Blaškić, Case No. IT-95–14-A, Appeal Judgment (ICTY, July 29, 2004).

Prosecutor v Boškoski and Tarčulovski, Case No. IT-04–82-T, Trial Judgment (ICTY, July 10, 2008).

Prosecutor v. Delalić, Case No. IT-96–21-T, Trial Judgment (ICTY, Nov. 16, 1998).

Prosecutor v Dominic Ongwen, Case No. ICC-02/04–01/15, Confirmation of Charges Decision (Mar. 23, 2016).

Prosecutor v. Furundžija, Case No. IT-95–17/1-T, Judgment (ICTY, Dec. 10, 1998).

Prosecutor v. Galić, Case No. IT-98–29-T, Trial Judgment (ICTY, Dec. 5, 2003).

Prosecutor v. Galić, Judgment, IT-98–29-A, Appeals Chamber (ICTY, Nov. 30, 2006).

Prosecutor v. Gotovina, Markač, and Čermak, Case No. IT-060–90-T, Trial Chamber Judgment (ICTY, Apr. 15, 2011).

Prosecutor v. Jean-Pierre Bemba Gombo, Case No. ICC-01/05–01/08, Judgment pursuant to Article 74 of the Statute (Mar. 21, 2016).

Prosecutor v. Katanga and Mathieu Chui, Case No. ICC-01/04–01/07, Pre-Trial Chamber I, Decision on the Confirmation of Charges (Sept. 30, 2008).

Prosecutor v. Kordić and Cerkez, Case No. IT-95–14/2, Appeal Judgment (ICTY, Dec. 17, 2004).

Prosecutor v. Kunarac, Kovač, and Vuković, Case Nos. IT-96–23, IT-96–23/1-A, Appeals Judgment (ICTY, June 12, 2002).

Prosecutor v. Kupreškić, Case No. IT-95–16-T, Trial Judgment (ICTY, Jan. 14, 2000).

Prosecutor v. Martić, Case No. IT-95–11, Trial Judgment (ICTY, June 12, 2007).

Prosecutor v. Milutinović et al., Case No. IT-05–87-T, Trial Judgment (ICTY, Feb. 26, 2009).

Prosecutor v. Naletilić and Martinović, Case No IT-98–34-T, Judgment (ICTY, Mar. 31, 2003).

Prosecutor v. Orić, Case No. IT-03–68-T, Trial Judgment (ICTY, June 30, 2006).

Prosecutor v. Rutaganda (Judgment) ICTR- 96–3- T (Dec. 6, 1999).

Prosecutor v. Saif Al-Islam Gaddafi and Abdullah Al-Senussi, Case No. ICC-01/11–01/ 11–565, Judgment on the appeal of Mr. Abdullah Al-Senussi against the decision of Pre-Trial Chamber I of Oct. 11, 2013 entitled "Decision on the admissibility of the case against Abdullah Al- Senussi" (July 24, 2014).

Prosecutor v. Strugar, Case No. IT-01–42-T, Trial Chamber Judgement (ICTY, Jan. 31, 2005).

Prosecutor v. Tadić, Case No. IT-94-1-A, Decision on the Defense Motion for Interlocutory Appeal on Jurisdiction, Appeals Chamber (ICTY, Oct. 2, 1995).

Provost, R., *International Human Rights and Humanitarian Law* (Cambridge University Press, 2002).

Prud'homme, N., "Lex Specialis: Oversimplifying a More Complex and Multifaceted Relationship" (2007) 40 *Israel Law Review*.

Public Committee against Torture in Israel et al. v. Government of Israel et al., HCJ 769/ 02, Israel Supreme Court Sitting as the High Court of Justice (Dec. 11, 2005).

Queguiner, J.-F., "Precautions under the Law Governing the Conduct of Hostilities" (2006) 88 *International Review of the Red Cross*.

R. *(Al-Skeini and Others) v. Secretary of State for Defence* [2005] EWCA Civ 1609 (CA).

R. *v. Jogee* [2016] UKSC 8.

Rabin, M., "Psychology and Economics" (1008) 36 *Journal of Economic Literature*.

Rabkin, J. and J. Yoo, *Striking Power: How Cyber, Robots, and Space Weapons Change the Rules for War* 125 (New York: Encounter Books, 2017).

Reid-Daly, Lt. Col. R. *Selous Scouts: Top Secret War* (London & Johannesburg: Galago Publishing, 1982).

Reisman, M. and W. Lietzau, "Moving International Law from Theory to Practice: The Role of Military Manuals in Effectuating the Law of Armed Conflict" (1991) 64 *International Law Studies*.

Responsibility of States for Internationally Wrongful Acts, Art. 1, GA Res. 56/83, Annex, UN Doc. A/RES/56/83 (Jan. 28, 2002).

Reynolds, J. D., "Collateral Damage on the 21st Century Battlefield: Enemy Exploitation of the Law of Armed Conflict, and the Struggle for a Moral High Ground" (2005) 56 *Air Force Law Review*.

Roberts, A., "Transformative Military Occupation: Applying the Laws of War and Human Rights" (2006) 100 *American Journal of International Law*.

"What Is a Military Occupation?" (1984) 55 *British Yearbook of International Law*.

Rogers, A. P. V., "The United Kingdom Manual of the Law of Armed Conflict," in N. Hayashi (ed.), *National Military Manuals on the Law of Armed Conflict*, 2nd ed. (Oslo: Torkel Opsahl, 2010).

Rona, G., "Is There a Way Out of the Non-International Armed Conflict Detention Dilemma?" (2015) 91 *International Law Studies*.

Roscini, M., *Cyber Operations and the Use of Force in International Law* (Oxford University Press, 2014).

Rose, G. and B. Oswald (eds.), *Detention of Non-State Actors Engaged in Hostilities*, (Leiden: Brill, 2016).

Rowe, P., *The Impact of Human Rights Law on Armed Forces* (Cambridge University Press, 2006).

Legal Accountability and Britain's Wars 2000–2015 (Abingdon: Routledge, 2016).

Ruddock v. The Queen [2016] UKPC 7.

San Remo Manual on International Law Applicable to Armed Conflicts at Sea 1994.

Sandoz, Y., "The Dynamic but Complex Relationship between International Penal Law and International Humanitarian Law," in J. Doria, H.-P. Gasser, and M. C. Bassiouni (eds.), *The Legal Regime of the ICC: Essay in Honour of Professor Igor Pavlovich Blishchenko* (Leiden: Martinus Nijhoff, 2009).

Sari, A., "Hybrid Warfare, Law and the Fulda Gap," in M. N. Schmitt et al. (eds.), *Complex Battle Spaces* (Oxford University Press, 2017).

"Untangling Extra-Territorial Jurisdiction from International Responsibility in *Jaloud v.Netherlands*: Old Problem, New Solutions?" (2014) 53 *Military Law and the Law of War Review*.

Sassòli, M., "Targeting: The Scope and Utility of the Concept of Military Objectives for the Protection of Civilians in Contemporary Armed Conflict," in D. Wippman and M. Evangelista (eds.), *New Wars, New Laws? Applying the Laws of War in 21st Century Conflicts* (New York: Transnational Publishers, 2005).

Sassòli, M., A. Bouvier, and A. Quentin (eds.), *How Does Law Protect in War*, 3 vols. (Geneva: ICRC, 2011).

Savage, C., *Power Wars* (New York: Little, Brown and Co., 2015).

Sawin, C. E., "Laws of War: The Legality of Creating an Army of Super Soldiers," *Journal of High Technology Law* (Nov. 3, 2015).

Schabas, W., *The International Criminal Court, A Commentary on the Rome Statute*, (Oxford University Press, 2010).

Scheffer, D. J., "Beyond Occupation Law" (2003) 97 *American Journal of International Law*.

Schindler, D., "The International Committee of the Red Cross and Human Rights" (1979) 19 *International Review of the Red Cross*.

Schindler, D. and J. Toman (eds.), *The Laws of Armed Conflicts: A Collection of Conventions, Resolutions, and Other Documents* (1988).

Schmitt, M. N., "'Below the Threshold' Cyber Operations: The Countermeasures Response Option and International Law" (2014) 54 *Virginia Journal of International Law*.

"Charting the Legal Geography of Non-International Armed Conflict" (2013) 52 *Military Law and Law of War Review*.

"Fault Lines in the Law of Attack," in S. Breau and A. Jachec-Neale (eds.), *Testing the Boundaries of International Humanitarian Law* (London: British Institute of International and Comparative Law, 2006).

"Human Shields in International Humanitarian Law" (2008) 38 *Israel Yearbook on Human Rights*.

"Investigating Violations of International Law in Armed Conflict" (2011) 2 *Harvard National Security Journal*.

"Military Necessity and Humanity in International Humanitarian Law: Preserving the Delicate Balance" (2010) 50 *Virginia Journal of International Law*.

"Precision Attack and International Humanitarian Law" (2005) 87 *International Review of the Red Cross*.

"Rewired Warfare: Rethinking the Law of Cyber Attack" (2014) 96 *International Review of the Red Cross*.

"The Interpretative Guidance on the Notion of Direct Participation in Hostilities: A Critical Analysis" (2009) 1 *Harvard National Security Journal*.

Schmitt, M. N., C. Garraway, and Y. Dinstein, *The Manual on the Law of Non-International Armed Conflict* (Leiden/Boston: Martinus Nijhoff, 2006).

Schmitt, M. N. and J. J. Merriam, "The Tyranny of Context: Israeli Targeting Practices in Legal Perspective" (2015) 37 *University of Pennsylvania Journal of International Law*.

Schmitt, M. N. and J. Pecjic (eds.), *International Law and Armed Conflicts: Exploring the Faultlines* (Leiden: Martinus Nijhoff, 2007).

Schmitt, M. N. and L. Vihul (eds.) *Tallinn Manual 2.0 on the International Law Applicable to Cyber Operations* (Cambridge University Press, 2017).

Schwarzenberger, G., "Jus Pacis Ac Belli?: Prolegomena to a Sociology of International Law" (1943) 37 *American Journal of International Law*.

Serdar Mohammed v. Secretary of State for Defence [2015] EWCA (Civ) 843 (Eng.).

Shanker, M. G., "The Law of Belligerent Occupation in the American Courts" (1952) 50 *Michigan Law Review*.

Shany, Y., "A Human Rights Perspective to Global Battlefield Detention: Time to Reconsider Indefinite Detention" (2017) 93 *International Law Studies*.

Siordet, F., "Les Conventions de Genève et la guerre civile" (1950) 81 *Bulletin International des Sociétés de la Croix-Rouge*.

Sivakumaran, S., "Binding Armed Opposition Groups" (2006) 5 *International and Comparative Law Quarterly*.

The Law of Non-International Conflict (Oxford University Press, 2012).

Solis, G., *The Law of Armed Conflict*, 2nd ed. (Cambridge University Press, 2016).

Spaight, J. M., *War Rights on Land* (London: Macmillan, 1911).

Stahn, C., "Admissibility Challenges before the ICC: From Quasi-Primacy to Qualified Deference?," in C. Stahn (ed.), *The Law and Practice of the International Criminal Court* (Oxford University Press, 2015).

"Response: The ICC, Pre-Existing Jurisdictional Treaty Regimes, and the Limits of the *Nemo Dat Quod Non Habet* Doctrine – A Reply to Michael Newton" (2016) 49 *Vanderbilt Journal of Transnational Law*.

Stathis, K., *The Logic of Violence in Civil War* (Cambrdige University Press, 2006),

Statute of the International Criminal Tribunal for the former Yugoslavia, UN Doc. S/RES/827 (1993).

Stephens, D., "Coalition Warfare: Challenges and Opportunities" (2006) 36 *Israel Yearbook on Human Rights*.

Stirk, P., *The Politics of Military Occupation* (Edinburgh University Press, 2009).

Stone, J., *Legal Controls of International Conflict* (Sydney: Maitland Publications, 1954; reprinted with supplement 1959).

Swiss Military Manual on Behaviour during Deployment, Rechtliche Grundlagen für das Verhalten inm Einsatz, Reglement 51.007/IV.

Talmon, S., *The Occupation of Iraq*, II: *The Official Documents of the Coalition Provisional Authority and the Iraqi Governing Council* (Oxford: Hart Publishing, 2013).

Recognition of Governments in International Law (Oxford: Clarendon Press, 1998).

Taylor, C., *Chivalry and the Ideals of Knighthood in France during the Hundred Years War* (Cambridge University Press, 2013).

Tennyson, Lord Alfred, "Aylmer's Field" (1793).

Theohary, C. A., and J. W. Rollins, "Cyberwarfare and Cyberterrorism: In Brief," Congressional Research Service (Mar. 27, 2015).

Thirty Hogsheads of Sugar v. Boyle (1815) 13 US 191, 195 (US Supreme Court).

Thorington v. Smith, 75 US 1 (1868).

Townsend, S. J., "Reports of Civilian Casualties in the War Against ISIS Are Vastly Inflated," *Foreign Policy* (Sept. 15, 2017).

Trial of Wilhelm List and Others (Hostages Trial) (1946) Law Reports of Trials of War Criminals, Vol. VIII, 34 (United States Military Tribunal).

Turkel Commission, Second Report, The Public Commission to Examine the Maritime Incident of 31 May 2010, "Israel's Mechanisms for Examining and Investigating Complaints and Claims of Violations of the Laws of Armed Conflict According to International Law" (Feb. 2013).

United Kingdom, Ministry of Defence, JSP 383, The Joint Service Manual of the Law of Armed Conflict (2004).

United Kingdom, Ministry of Defence, "The Joint Service Manual of the Law of Armed Conflict" (2013).

United States v. Altstoetter et al., Trials of War Criminals Before the NMT III.

United States v. Behenna, 71 MJ 228, 229 (CAAF, 2012).

United States v. Bram, No. ARMY 20111032, 2014 WL 7236126 (Army Ct. Crim. App., Nov. 20, 2014).

United States v. Clagett, No. ARMY20070082, 2009 WL 6843560, at *1 (Army Ct. Crim. App., 2009).

United States v. Curtiss-Wright Export Corp., 299 US 304, 318 (1936).

United States ex rel. DR, Inc. v. Custer Battles, LLC, 376 F. Supp. 2d 617 (ED Va. 2005).

United States v. Girouard, 70 MJ 5, 7 (CAAF, 2011).

United States v. Green, 654 F.3d 637, 646–47 (6th Cir. 2011), cert. denied 132 S. Ct. 1056 (2012).

United States v. List (Wilhelm) and others, Trial Judgment, Case No. 7 (1948).

United States v. Maynulet, 68 MJ 374, 377 (CAAF, 2011).

United States v Milch, Judgment, Green Series, Vol. II at 773 (Mil. Trib. No. 12947-04-15).

United States v. Morlock, No. ARMY 20110230, 2014 WL 7227382 (Army Ct. Crim. App., Apr. 30, 2014).

United States v. Rice, 17 US 246 (1819).

United States v. von Leeb et al. ("The High Command Trial") (1948) 11 LRTWC 1, 9 TWC 462 (United States Military Tribunal).

US Army, Center for Law and Military Operations, The Judge Advocate General's Legal Center and School, "Legal Lessons Learned from Afghanistan and Iraq, I: Major Combat Operations 11 Sept. 2001–1 May 2003" (Aug. 1, 2004).

US Army, International and Operational Law Department, "Law of War Deskbook" (2000).

US Army, International and Operational Law Department, JA 422, "Operational Law Handbook" (2017).

US Central Command, Investigation Report on the Airstrike on the Médecins Sans Frontières/Doctors without Borders Trauma Center in Kunduz, Afghanistan on Oct. 3, 2015, Nov. 21, 2015.

US Department of the Army, Major General Eldon A. Bargewell, Investigation, "'Simple Failures' and 'Disastrous Results'" (June 15, 2006).

Vattel, E. D., *The Law of Nations or the Principles of Natural Law: Applied to the Conduct and to the Affairs of Nations and of Sovereigns* (Washington: Carnegie, 1916).

Vöneky, S., "Der Lieber's Code und die Wurzeln des modernen Kriegsvölkerrechts" (2002) 62 *Zeitschrift für ausländisches öffentliches Recht und Völkerrecht.*

Walzer, M., *Just and Unjust Wars* (New York: Basic Books, 1977).

Watkin, K., *Fighting at the Legal Boundaries Controlling the Use of Force in Contemporary Conflict* (Oxford University Press, 2016).

"Warriors Without Rights? Combatants, Unprivileged Belligerents, and the Struggle Over Legitimacy," Program on Humanitarian Policy and Conflict Research, Occasional Paper Series, Winter 2005.

Watts, S., "Law of War Perfidy" (2014) 219 *Military Law Review.*

"Regulation-Tolerant Weapons, Regulation-Resistant Weapons and the Law of War" (2015) 91 *International Law Studies.*

Waxman, M. C., "Detention as Targeting: Standards of Certainty and Detention of Suspected Terrorists" (2008) 108 *Columbia Law Review.*

Wells, D. A., *The Laws of Land Warfare: A Guide to the U.S. Army Manuals* (Westport: Greenwood Press, 1992).

Wet, E. de and J. Kleffner (eds.), *Convergence and Conflicts of Human Rights and International Humanitarian Law in Military Operations* (Pretoria: PULP, 2014).

Whittemore, L. A., "Proportionality Decision Making in Targeting: Heuristics, Cognitive Biases, and the Law" (2016) 7 *Harvard National Security Journal.*

Wilde, R., "Triggering State Obligations Extraterritorially: The Spatial Test in Certain Human Rights Treaties," in R. Arnold and N. N. R. Quénivet (eds.), *International Humanitarian Law and Human Rights Law: Towards a New Merger in International Law* (Leiden: Martinus Nijhoff, 2008).

Winthrop, W., *Military Law and Precedents*, 2nd ed. (Washington: Gov't Printing Office, 1920).

Wisam, E. and S. al-Hawat, "Civilian Interaction with Armed Groups in the Syrian Conflict," Conciliation Resources, Insight 2 (2015).

Witt, J. F., *Lincoln's Code: The Laws of War in American History* (New York: Free Press, 2012).

Wittes, B., "Where Is the Law of War Manual? Here!," *Lawfare* (Jul. 26, 2013).

Yeager v. Iran, 17 Iran-US Cl. Trib. Rep. 92, 101–02 (1987).

Yoo, J., "Iraqi Reconstruction and the Law of Occupation" (2004) 11 *UC Davis Journal of International Law and Policy.*

Zetter, K., *Countdown to Zero Day* (New York: Broadway Books, 2014).

Zwanenburg, M., "International Humanitarian Law Interoperability in Multinational Operations" (2013) 95 *International Review of the Red Cross.*

Index

Cassese, Antonio, 247
central principles governing targeting and the
    use of force, 264
Certain Conventional Weapons Convention
    (CCW), xv, 11
Chairman of the Joint Chiefs of Staff, Standing
    Rules of Engagement for US Forces,
    CJCSI 3121.01B, 404
Chamberlain, Neville, UK Prime Minister, 164
changing character of war. *See* cyberwar
Changing Character of War Centre, 5
chaos of war, 261
Charter of the United Nations
    Article 51, 84
Chatham House, 56
checkpoint attacks, 252
children engaged in hostilities, 117
chivalry, only mentioned in FM 27–10, 391
Civil War era
    need for new legal code, 9
Civil War, Lincoln's blockade order, 34
civilian internment
    limited to absolute necessity, 221
civilian population
    morale as an unlawful military
        objective, 136
civilian workers who place themselves in or on
    the military objective, 191
civilians as human shields, 257
Clapham, Andrew, 289
clarity of the legal principles, 268
Clausewitz, 137
Clinton, President
    signing statement on the Rome Statute of
        the International Criminal Court,
        368, 374